EXPLORATIONS IN THE ETHNOGRAPHY OF SPEAKING

SECOND EDITION

Studies in the Social and Cultural Foundations of Language

The aim of this series is to develop theoretical perspectives on the essential social and cultural character of language by methodological and empirical emphasis on the occurrence of language in its communicative and interactional settings, on the socioculturally grounded "meanings" and "functions" of linguistic forms, and on the social scientific study of language use across cultures. It will thus explicate the essentially ethnographic nature of linguistic data, whether spontaneously occurring or experimentally induced, whether normative or variational, whether synchronic or diachronic. Works appearing in the series will make substantive and theoretical contributions to the debate over the sociocultural-function and structural-formal nature of language, and will represent the concerns of scholars in the sociology and anthropology of language, anthropological linguistics, sociolinguistics, and socioculturally informed psycholinguistics.

Editorial Board

EXPLORATIONS IN THE ETHNOGRAPHY OF SPEAKING

SECOND EDITION

EDITED BY

RICHARD BAUMAN
Folklore Institute, Indiana University

AND

JOEL SHERZER
Department of Anthropology
University of Texas at Austin

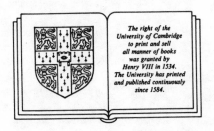

The right of the
University of Cambridge
to print and sell
all manner of books
was granted by
Henry VIII in 1534.
The University has printed
and published continuously
since 1584.

CAMBRIDGE UNIVERSITY PRESS

Cambridge

New York   Port Chester   Melbourne   Sydney

Published by the Press Syndicate of the University of Cambridge
The Pitt Building, Trumpington Street, Cambridge CB2 1RP
40 West 20th Street, New York, NY 10011–4211, USA
10 Stamford Road, Oakleigh, Melbourne 3166, Australia

© Cambridge University Press 1974, 1989

First published 1974
Second edition 1989
Reprinted 1991

Printed in Great Britain at the University Press, Cambridge.

British Library cataloguing in publication data

Explorations in the ethnography of speaking. –
2nd ed. – (Studies in the social and
cultural foundations of language).
1. Speech. Ethnic aspects.
I. Bauman, Richard, 1940– . II. Sherzer, Joel.
306'.4

Library of Congress cataloguing in publication data

Explorations in the ethnography of speaking / edited by
Richard Bauman and Joel Sherzer. – 2nd ed.
p.   cm. – (Studies in the social and cultural
foundations of language; 8)
ISBN 0 521 37063 9. ISBN 0 521 37933 4 (pbk)
1. Language and culture. 2. Language and languages – Variation.
I. Bauman, Richard. II. Sherzer, Joel. III. Series: Studies in the social and
cultural foundations of language; no. 8.
P35.E95 1989
408.9 – dc19   88–29427   CIP

ISBN 0 521 37063 9 hard covers
ISBN 0 521 37933 4 paperback

CONTENTS

IV. SPEECH ACTS, EVENTS, AND SITUATIONS

V. THE SHAPING OF ARTISTIC STRUCTURES IN PERFORMANCE

VI. TOWARD AN ETHNOLOGY OF SPEAKING

Contents

INTRODUCTION TO THE
SECOND EDITION

When we published *Explorations in the Ethnography of Speaking* back in 1974, we framed the work as ushering in a new phase of research in the ethnography of speaking. The first phase, beginning with the publication of Dell Hymes's foundational essay, 'The Ethnography of Speaking,' in 1962 and proceeding through the early 1970s, was preliminary and programmatic, marked by a series of articles and edited collections that sought to define this new subfield of linguistic anthropology and to suggest what kinds of research might be carried out under its aegis (see Preface; Bauman and Sherzer 1975). Much of this work was seen to be converging and contributing toward the ethnography of speaking, but not yet exemplifying it, insofar as little research published in that first period was expressly and primarily undertaken for a purpose that might appropriately be called the ethnography of speaking, that is, carrying out the program outlined by Hymes and Gumperz. By the early 1970s, however, the ethnography of speaking had finally developed to a point where a number of scholars had taken up the repeated calls for fieldwork issued in the first decade and carried out original research guided by its principles. *Explorations in the Ethnography of Speaking* grew out of our mutual concern to present the first fruits of that research and to attempt to synthesize its results – however exploratory that synthesis might be – in a way that might help to shape the subsequent development of the field. We are gratified that the book has in fact fulfilled that goal and that it has remained useful to scholars in a number of disciplines who have been persuaded of the productiveness of the ethnography of speaking as a vantage point on social life as communicatively constituted and on language as socially constituted.

The years since *Explorations in the Ethnography of Speaking* was published have certainly proven the program and its perspective to be a significant stimulus to primary research. Among the prospects for the development of the ethnography of speaking in its subsequent phase that we anticipated in our original Introduction to the volume were the publication of more extended and complete ethnographies of speaking and a general increase in the number of available case studies of speaking in particular societies. We noted, in fact, that many of the contributions to the book were segments of more comprehensive works in progress, and indeed, six of the chapters are linked to subsequent full-length books or monographs, to which the original essays remain useful introductions or complements. Susan U. Philips' chapter on Warm Springs 'Indian Time' is summarized in her monograph, *The Invisible Culture: Communication in Classroom and Community on the Warm Springs Reservation* (1983); Anne Salmond's essay on the Maori *hui* became *Hui: A Study of Maori Ceremonial Gatherings* (1975); Joel Sherzer's survey of three types of Kuna speech event establishes one of the principal organizing dimensions of his *Kuna Ways of Speaking: An Ethnographic Perspective* (1983); Michael Foster's analysis of three Iroquois longhouse speech events is extended and amplified in his *From the Earth to Beyond the Sky: An Ethnographic Approach to Four Longhouse Iroquois Speech Events* (1974); Gary Gossen's exploration of the metaphor of heat in Chamula speaking is continued and elaborated in *Chamulas in the World of the Sun: Time and Space in a Maya Oral Tradition* (1974); and Richard Bauman's treatment of the role conflict of the seventeenth-century Quaker minister introduces some of the major themes of his *Let Your words Be Few: Symbolism of Speaking and Silence among Seventeenth-Century Quakers* (1983). The last work, we might note, is historical in subject and scope, demonstrating some of the advantages and disadvantages that attend the extension of the perspectives of the ethnography of speaking to historical cases.[1] A recent bibliographical survey of fieldwork in the ethnography of speaking by Philipsen and Carbaugh (1986) lists more than 200 items, among which the work of contributors to *Explorations in the Ethnography of Speaking* has a prominent place, though they represent but a fraction of the more than 150 authors whose work is listed. The compilers of the survey acknowledge that their bibliographical inventory is not exhaustive, and a complete listing would be significantly longer. This is a lot of work. What has it yielded? How might the directions and achievements of the ethnography of speaking since 1974 be characterized?

In *Explorations in the Ethnography of Speaking* and the review article we wrote for the *Annual Review of Anthropology* the following year (1975), we set out a number of needs and anticipated directions for the further development of the new field in the phase that we hoped would be ushered in by the work. In addition, several reviewers of the book (especially Bloch 1976; Borker 1976; Leach 1976) took the opportunity to proclaim what the field – and our book – had not yet achieved, thus suggesting still further directions for the next phase. And, not content to leave the criticism to

---

[1] In addition, Bricker's essay in this volume is a useful complement to her full-length study of *Ritual Humor in Highland Chiapas* (1973), published earlier.

others, Sherzer himself published a firm critique of work in the field – including prominently our own – pointing out the gaps to be filled and the lines to be explored (1977).

One question brought to the fore quite early by the publication of *Explorations in the Ethnography of Speaking* has to do with the problem orientation of the ethnography of speaking. Here are eighteen substantive essays, dealing with societies from all over the globe – what is the point of all this ethnographic particularism? Where are the 'generalizing propositions,' the 'common problems' to be solved? This is a complex issue, one that implicates the basic goals and purposes of the entire enterprise represented by the ethnography of speaking. Our primary motivation in producing the book was to establish the viability and productiveness of the ethnography of speaking program, that is, to elucidate the patterns and functions of speaking as a cultural system or as part of cultural systems organized in other terms. It is important to remember that this was a concern that up to that point had fallen through the cracks between grammars and ethnographies, taken separately or analytically combined. With a small handful of exceptions, there were no accounts in the anthropological literature of speaking as a cultural system, cross-culturally variable in organization, before ours. Therefore, we took it as our task to show that there is pattern, there is systemic coherence, and there is difference in the ways that speaking is organized from one society to another, and that this pattern, this coherence, this difference are to be discovered ethnographically. They needed – and they still need – to be *demonstrated* in all their culture specific particularity, not taken for granted or assumed a priori. At the most basic level, then, *that* is the central problem, or proposition, of the book.

There are, however, different analytical and presentational vantage points represented in the collection. Some of the contributors take speaking itself in a particular society as the point of departure, and attempt to elucidate the principles by which it is organized and by which it ramifies throughout social life. Others begin with a particular social or linguistic problem – phonological variation, marriage, role conflict, gender, etc. – and demonstrate how it can be illuminated in speaking-centered terms. Either way, however, the unifying principle is that society and culture are communicatively constituted, and that *no* sphere of social or cultural life is fully comprehensible apart from speaking as an instrument of its constitution. We felt it necessary, then, to be extensive rather than intensive, to let speaking lead us where it might rather than circumscribing the scope of the book by imposing a set of shared problem orientations. The book was intended as an adumbration of broad possibilities, not as a work in the service of this or that limited linguistic or social problem, even at the risk of offering a collection that might appear diffuse to readers with more specific research agendas or theoretical concerns.

From the beginning, though, we saw the accumulation of case studies as providing the basis for generalization, for a meaningful ethnology of speaking that would in turn inform the ethnographic enterprise by focusing the problem orientation of the field; the Introduction, the final section of the book, and several of the papers, most notably Grimshaw's, call for such generalization, as do subsequent papers of our own (Bauman and Sherzer 1975; Sherzer 1977).[2] And indeed, an effort at generalizing comparisons, drawing on the growing base of available case studies, has proceeded apace, and the number of clearly problem-focused works has burgeoned.

For example, one of the most fully and richly developed lines of comparative inquiry generated by the ethnography of speaking concerns the nature, forms, functions, and situational contexts of use of political language. This growing literature, linked with classic concerns in political anthropology and in social theory more generally (e.g., the domain of politics in small-scale societies, the foundations of social authority), is founded more immediately in the recognition of forms of talk as constitutive of political action (Bloch 1975:4) and in the service of exercising power and reproducing the mechanisms that make power possible (Brenneis and Myers 1984:4). This work, then, provides a valuable critical complement to the predominantly social structural tradition in political anthropology, demonstrating that the political process as *enacted* turns fundamentally on the control and use of expressive means, whatever might be the structure of power and authority in a given society. In the writings of participants in this unfolding discussion (including Arno 1985; Bloch 1975; Brenneis and Myers 1984; Howe 1986; Irvine 1979; Paine 1981; Parkin 1984; Watson-Gegeo 1986; Werbner 1977), the core concepts of the ethnography of speaking figure centrally and prominently: the work is fundamentally about patterns and functions of speaking in the conduct of social life, framed in terms of genres, speech styles, speaking roles, the multi-functionality of speaking, form-function interrelationships, and speech events. In addition, this work develops an impressive range of generalizing comparisons, illustrating well the scope of comparative investigation in the field. Some scholars, for example, have essayed broadly cross-cultural generalizations, drawing their data from ethnographic case studies the world over, including both complex Western societies and relatively more

[2] We also note (p. 454, note 10) that this collection itself provides the basis for areal study of speaking in native Mesoamerica in the papers of Bricker, Gossen, and Stross, and the literature on this area has grown to impressive proportions in the years since this volume was published. See for example Bricker (1973), Burns (1983), Gossen (1974), Hanks (1986, 1987), Haviland (1977), Hill and Hill (1986), Tedlock (1983, 1985, 1987)

small-scale and traditional ones. Others, by contrast, have operated with a more limited areal focus, with Polynesia and Melanesia figuring especially prominently, and both together providing the basis for Pacific-wide comparison. Typology has also figured prominently in the development of an ethnology of political language, some of it socially based, as in Brenneis and Myers' contrast between egalitarian and hierarchical societies (1984), some founded on speech function, such as Arno's distinction between impressive and persuasive speech (1985), still others centering on varieties of speech styles and events, as in Irvine's examination of formality versus informality in communicative events (1979). This last essay, an incisive and widely cited critique of concepts too often loosely and uncritically employed, is an excellent example as well of the way in which comparative study in the ethnography of speaking serves to refine the core concepts of the field itself (for other critical reviews of concepts, see Bauman 1987; Gumperz 1984; Irvine 1987; Philips 1987).

While the comparative study of political language is perhaps the most extensively developed line of generalizing inquiry founded in the ethnography of speaking, and thus can stand as a useful index of the larger enterprise, comparative work of great richness and variety has been undertaken at an accelerating rate over the past decade. To cite only a few illustrative studies that might serve to indicate the scope and diversity of the field, we might mention Fox's consolidative work on canonical parallelism (1977), Brown and Levinson's influential exploration of politeness phenomena (1978), Ochs and Schieffelin's richly textured essay on language acquisition and socialization (Ochs and Schieffelin 1982; see also Schieffelin and Ochs 1986), Urban's rigorous areal investigation of ceremonial dialogues and ritual wailing in South America (Urban 1986, 1988), Sherzer's typologically suggestive examination of speech and gender (Sherzer 1987a), and Katriel's and Brenneis's examinations of direct and indirect speech, respectively (Katriel 1986; Brenneis 1986). None of this work, it is safe to say, would have been possible without the proliferation of case studies in the ethnography of speaking, guided by the principles first set out by Gumperz and Hymes and furthered – we are immodest enough to believe – by *Explorations in the Ethnography of Speaking*. We must recognize, though, that comparative and generalizing work in the ethnography of speaking is still in its nascent stages; Philipsen and Carbaugh's (1986) bibliography should be invaluable in advancing the enterprise in its next phase.

Analogous in certain ways to cross-cultural comparative work in the ethnography of speaking is a line of study devoted to the patterns and functions of speaking in cross-cultural encounters and multilingual speech communities, where culturally different ways of speaking are brought together (Tannen 1985). To comprehend such contact situations requires the comparative understanding of speaking in the respective groups from which participants in the contact situation are drawn and of the emergent system that organizes speaking in the contact situation itself. As the ethnography of speaking extends the study of language beyond lexicon and grammar, so these studies extend the study of language contact beyond traditional investigations that focus on language differences alone. In fact, some of the most illuminating studies of speaking in interethnic encounters are those that focus on situations in which all participants speak mutually intelligible varieties of English, but have culturally different ways of speaking; it is not language in the narrow sense where interference resides, but rather the ways in which it is used. Gumperz has been especially influential in investigating interethnic communication in terms of conversational inference based on culturally organized systems of discourse cues (1982), while Kochman has analyzed black and white communication in conflict in terms of significant differences in expressive style (1981). While Gumperz and Kochman focus on the interethnic encounters themselves, Basso (1979) offers a penetrating analysis of joking routines that are expressive take-offs of white ways of speaking by Western Apaches, pointed, tendentious, and delicate representations that comment trenchantly on the differences between them. Interestingly, in the light of our anticipation in *Explorations in the Ethnography of Speaking* that the ensuing period would see the development of historical studies in the ethnography of speaking, a number of the most innovative and illuminating studies of speaking in situations of culture contact are historical in orientation, such as Foster's study of speaking precedence in eighteenth-century Iroquois-white councils (1984), Abrahams's establishment of the creole genesis of Afro-American traditions of eloquence (1983), and Hanks's rigorous and detailed tracing of the emergence of new discourse forms out of the interaction of Maya and Spanish systems of communication in colonial Yucatan (1986, 1987). Gal's methodologically sophisticated study of social determinants of language shift over time in a Hungarian–German bilingual community in Austria (1979) and Scollon and Scollon's meticulous tracing of linguistic convergence at Fort Chipewyan, Alberta (1979), illustrate especially clearly the productiveness of the ethnography of speaking in the diachronic study of language contact and multilingualism.

One species of cross-cultural or interethnic encounter of special significance for anthropologists is the ethnographic encounter itself, the speech events in which the field researcher interacts verbally with a native consultant for the purpose of eliciting ethnographic data. These encounters, no less than those involving lay people of different cultures, are susceptible to misunderstanding rooted in different ways of speaking, not just differences in language. Thus, it behooves *every* ethnographer who gathers data in verbal encounters of any kind to understand *first* how the getting and giving of information is patterned in the native culture and his or her own, that is to be a comparative ethnographer of speaking. This reflexive vantage point on ethnographic practice, founded in the ethnography of speaking, is the focus of a small but vitally important line of exploration, pursued by Paredes in a telling critique of ethnographers of Mexican and Mexican-American culture who are led to embarrassing errors by their inability to understand when they are being performed to, played with, or outright lied to by their informants (1977; cf. Howe and Sherzer 1986), and by Briggs in a meticulous appraisal of the role of the interview in social science research, including detailed formal and functional analysis of interview transcripts, that must be required reading for all would-be ethnographers, regardless of the problems they wish to investigate (1986). Let us make the point explicit: these works demonstrate beyond question that the ethnography of speaking can no longer be viewed simply as one line of special investigation within linguistic anthropology, but must be a critical and reflexive part of any ethnographic investigation that involves the gathering of data by verbal means.

As Paredes and Briggs both focus on Anglo fieldworkers' encounters with members of Hispanic groups in the United States, their work is also relevant to a further trend that we foresaw in *Explorations in the Ethnography of Speaking* and elsewhere, namely, the extension of the ethnography of speaking into studies of contemporary North American society and the application of these research findings to the solution of practical social problems. To be sure, the problematics of interethnic communication figure significantly in ethnographic studies of speaking in the United States, focusing on the ways in which members of minority cultures are placed at a disadvantage by having their ways of speaking ignored, disvalued, or misunderstood by the agents and institutions of mainstream culture – in schools, courts of law, medical institutions, job seeking, and so on and on. Here, though, by contrast with the former trends in the field that we have discussed, developments subsequent to 1974 are more difficult to assess in clearly ethnography of speaking terms. The problem, essentially, is that while linguistic anthropologists tend to have the field largely to themselves in the study of language in the more exotic parts of the world, and this work is relatively easy to identify in terms of its disciplinary orientation and the influence of the ethnography of speaking upon it, the study of language in complex Western societies is conducted by scholars from a host of disciplinary vantage points, including many that share a concern with aspects of language in use: sociolinguistics, discourse analysis, conversational analysis, folklore, psycholinguistics, linguistic pragmatics, and more. Moreover, there has been an energizing and productive methodological and conceptual eclecticism among practitioners of these various lines of investigation. Consequently, while one can identify certain studies of language use in medicine, education, law, minority groups, traditional communities, and so on, explicitly identified with the ethnography of speaking, the lines become blurred before very long and it gains us little to try to draw them apart. Eclecticism notwithstanding, however, surveys of language use in American life do clearly and explicitly acknowledge the significant contribution of the ethnography of speaking to the larger enterprise (e.g., Ferguson and Heath 1981; Heath 1984; Mehan 1985; O'Barr 1982; Shuy 1984), and Dell Hymes, the founder of the field, has devoted significant effort to the application of the ethnography of speaking in educational contexts (Hymes 1980).

Especially interesting in this regard is Shuy's recent survey of linguistics in medicine, education, and law (1984). At the conclusion of his review (1984:440), Shuy outlines nine common threads that unite the recent work of linguists (he uses the term broadly here, to include the ethnography of speaking as well as all other language disciplines) in the study of the professions:

1 Reliance on direct *observation* of the communicative event rather than quantified, symbolized, or interpreted representations.
2 Analysis of the human *interactions* themselves rather than of artifacts or interpretations of these communicative events.
3 Discovery of the *structure* of these communicative events in order to obtain a holistic, contextualized perspective of these communicative events.
4 Permitting the language *data* to suggest the units of analysis rather than beginning with a unit of analysis and then searching for it in the language data.
5 Reliance on *performance* data rather than on represented, or pre-interpreted, or self-report data.
6 Taking the *perspective* of the patient, defendant, plaintiff, and learner in addition to the perspective of the physician, lawyer, educator.
7 The use of recent *technology* (audio and video taping and photocopying in particular) to capture and freeze the event being studied for multiple examinations.
8 The *expansion of the previously perceived domain* of linguistic study to the everyday, dynamic language events of the real world.
9 Meaning, referential and inferential, is *constructed* by the interaction of participants in a conversation.

What we find noteworthy about these points is that they accord extremely closely with the program of the ethnography of speaking, whatever other lines of inquiry they may characterize. Perhaps the essential point, then, is to acknowledge a broad community of interest drawing together scholars with a range of disciplinary or subdisciplinary affiliations around the study of language use in modern society, with the ethnography of speaking standing as a full partner in the enterprise. And however the scholars engaged in this work may wish to identify themselves, our ethnographic understanding of language and medicine (e.g., doctor–patient communication, therapy talk, hospital admission interviews), language and law (e.g., lawyer–client communication, language in the courtroom), language and education (e.g., teacher–parent communication, language in the classroom, the social acquisition and uses of literacy, educational testing), the social implications of bi- and multi-lingualism and social dialects, and related problems are all significantly richer, deeper, and more nuanced than when *Explorations in the Ethnography of Speaking* first appeared.

One area that deserves special mention in this regard is the relationship between spoken and written discourse, which has figured prominently in research on language in education. The extension of the perspective of the ethnography of speaking to writing is explored in this volume by Keith Basso, in what has since become a foundational essay (pp. 425–32). The intervening years have seen a great burgeoning of interest in many disciplines in orality and literacy, much of it, as in the work of Ong (1982) and Goody (1977, 1987), a revival in language-centered terms of the nineteenth-century typological and evolutionary tradition devoted to differentiating 'primitive' from 'civilized' society. As with all such gross social typologies, the oral-literate contrast is susceptible to grand a priori generalizations, and here the ethnography of speaking/writing has had an especially vital role to play in providing ethnographic correctives to such speculations. The literature in the field is far too extensive to review here, but we might mention the work of Finnegan (1977), Basso (1980), Chafe and Tannen (1987, especially useful as a review of the literature) as effective critiques of the 'Great Divide' theorists as against careful empirical investigations of the patterns and functions of speaking and writing in specific societies, and Frake (1983) as a clear statement of the political implications of this problem. The productiveness of the perspectives offered by the ethnography of speaking to the study of the interrelationship between spoken and written discourse in American (including Canadian) educational contexts is demonstrated with rigor and elegance in Shirley Brice Heath's *Ways with Words* (1983), Ron and Suzanne Scollon's *Narrative, Literacy and Face in Interethnic Communication* (1981), and Amy Shuman's *Storytelling Rights* (1986).

When it comes to the application of this research in all its dimensions, it is clear that students of language use in American society at least have been centrally concerned with the relevance of their work to the politics of culture and to practical problem solving, including conspicuously the training of educational, legal, and medical practitioners. O'Barr, for example, devotes an entire section of his survey of the language of law in American society to the implications of research in this field for the training of lawyers (1981:404-6), noting that, based on the language-centered work he reviews, 'there are serious discrepancies between what a lawyer is taught to do and what he is actually required to do in the practice of law' (1981:404). Ethnographers of speaking have been most actively engaged in incorporating its perspectives and findings into the training of educators: Dell Hymes, Courtney Cazden, Shirley Brice Heath, and a growing number of others have worked energetically in the training of school teachers and educational administrators. It is also worth mentioning that the *Working Papers in Sociolinguistics*, an important outlet for case studies in the ethnography of speaking (Bauman and Sherzer 1980, 1982), were published for a time under the auspices of the Southwest Educational Development Laboratory, a research and development laboratory in education, and with the sponsorship of the National Institute of Education. Still, one must acknowledge that the impact of this work still remains to be felt in any significant way: Heath (1981:84), O'Barr (1981:404-6), and Shuy (1984:425-6) all say as much, though their commitment and that of many of their colleagues remains undiminished.

One of the points on Shuy's outline warrants somewhat more attention with regard to the concerns and contributions of *Explorations in the Ethnography of Speaking*, namely, 'Reliance on *performance* data' (1984:440). The notion of performance is the most central organizing concept in our volume. As stated in the Introduction (p. 7):

The task of the ethnographer of speaking . . . is to identify and analyze the dynamic interrelationships among the elements which go to make up performance, toward the construction of a descriptive theory of speaking as a cultural system in a particular society.

There are, in fact, two basic senses of performance that have assumed a place near the center of the ethnography of speaking (Bauman 1987). The first of these we might call performance as speaking praxis, the situated use of language in the conduct and constitution of social life (Duranti 1988). Performance here is seen as a creative and emergent accomplishment, a form of social production and reproduction. Speech performance in this sense is a part of the basic charter of the ethnography of speaking; there can be no true ethnography of speaking without it.

It is worth remarking that the performance-centered approach to language presented in *Explorations in the Ethnography of Speaking* has been identified by Ortner (1984) as one of the early lines of that agent-centered, practice-oriented perspective on society and culture that she advances as anthropological theory for the 1980s. While it is gratifying to know that we as ethnographers of speaking got there early, we should be reminded that agent- and practice-centered perspectives are currently being developed as counterbalances to traditional structural, systemic, collective, normative conceptions of society and culture, and this takes us to the heart of the deepest problem in the social disciplines: the dynamic interplay between the social, conventional, ready-made in social life and the individual, creative, and emergent qualities of human existence. In the ethnography of speaking, no less than in other sectors of anthropology, the illumination and comprehension of that key problem demand a great deal more work.

In addition to speaking praxis, the second, more marked sense of performance that has figured prominently in the ethnography of speaking centers on performance as artful, the poetics of performance (see Section V). Performance as practice illuminates spoken art as productively as it does any other mode of speaking, but offers no special insight into artistic verbal performance. Accordingly, there have been a number of efforts to construct a framework for the study of the poetics of performance, including such definitional efforts as those of Hymes (1975) and Bauman (1977a, 1987, 1988–9) and the translational and analytical enterprise of ethnopoetics in its various guises (Hymes 1981; Sherzer and Woodbury 1987; Tedlock 1983). Performance in its artful sense may be seen as a specially marked way of speaking, one that sets up or represents a special interpretive frame within which the act of speaking is to be understood. In this sense of performance, the act of speaking is put on display, objectified, lifted out to a degree from its contextual surroundings, and opened up to scrutiny by an audience. Performance makes one communicatively accountable; it assigns to an audience the responsibility of evaluating the relative skill and effectiveness of the performer's accomplishment. To the extent that the skill and effectiveness of expression may become the focus of attention in any act of communication, the potential for performance is always present. In these terms, then, performance is a variable quality, relatively more or less dominant among the multiple functions served by a communicative act. It may range along a continuum from sustained, full performance to a fleeting breakthrough into performance.

This approach to performance has proven useful in a number of lines of investigation, helping to distinguish between renditions of verbal forms framed as performance as against other modes of presentation (report, play, etc.). It has directed attention to the social patterns and functions of artistic verbal performance in many dimensions of social life, from politics and diplomacy (Beeman 1982; Duranti 1981) to curing (Hanks 1984; Sherzer 1986), from sociable encounters (Bauman 1986a, Bell 1983) to the acquisition of communicative competence (McDowell 1978; Sanches and Kirshenblatt-Gimblett 1976; Trosset 1986), from the symbolic construction of the moral landscape (Basso 1984, 1988; Fernandez 1988; Kuipers 1984) to the management of gossip disputes (Goodwin 1982) – the ways in which artistic verbal performance may work in the ultimate service of persuasion, power, pleasure, and the general intensification of social experience. And in its convergence with ethnopoetics, it has directed close attention to the formal devices and patterns of spoken art and the formal means of keying the performance frame. Indeed, it is in the examination of verbal art as performance that the ethnography of speaking has been most formal in its analysis, moving ever more steadily into the close analysis of artistic texts in terms of linguistic patterning principles from phonology and intonation to syntax to generic structures to conversational structures (Bauman 1977b; Mannheim 1986).

While it is firmly rooted in the ethnography of speaking, this approach to performance has been a ground on which the perspectives of the ethnography of speaking have gained currency in adjacent disciplines. Scholars in other fields with an interest in the poetics of performance, such as folklore (e.g., Limón and Young 1986), speech communication (e.g., Fine 1984; Fine and Speer 1977), literary criticism (e.g., Wiget 1985), and semiotics (e.g., McDowell 1985; Proschan 1983; Stoeltje and Bauman 1988), have taken up and explored the notion of verbal art as performance from the scholarship in the ethnography of speaking. Moreover, this same performance orientation has been taken up as well in at least one field of study that does not center on language, namely, ethnomusicology, where it has been found useful in the conceptualization and analysis of musical performance (Basso 1985; Béhague 1984; Brenneis 1987; Feld 1982; McLeod and Herndon 1980; Stone 1982), thus carrying us from the ethnography of speaking to a more general ethnography of communication. Such extension may also be seen to be operating from within anthropology as well, as scholars begin to draw ideas of artistic performance beyond the verbal channel into other realms of behavior (e.g., Bauman 1986b; Herzfeld 1985).

Connections of these kinds that link the ethnography of speaking to various disciplines in terms of performance or other concepts were of special concern to us in framing and organizing *Explorations in the Ethnography of Speaking*. The contributions to the conceptual framework of the ethnography of speaking of Kenneth Burke's literary theory, Bronislaw Malinowski's social anthropology, and Edward Sapir's and Roman Jakobson's linguistics were acknowledged from the very first (Hymes

1962), and the incorporative vision of Gumperz and Hymes ensured that the foundation they laid down would cut across disciplinary boundaries. In the publication of *Explorations in the Ethnography of Speaking*, the multi-disciplinary relevance of the ethnography of speaking was maintained by the inclusion in the collection of contributors from anthropology, linguistics, folklore, and sociology; thus the effort in the general Introduction to the volume and the separate section introductions to make explicit the significance of the ethnography of speaking to those disciplines, suggesting that as the ethnography of speaking had drawn from or shared concepts, orientations, methods from those various fields, so might it in turn have something to offer back to them.

In the years since then, clearly, that offer has been taken up in those four disciplines and others with an interest in the sociocultural dimensions of discourse.[3] Not only is 'anthropology ... currently sensitive to the "ethnography of speaking" ' (Turner 1986:21), but the ethnography of speaking has found a place – sometimes a prominent place, sometimes just a corner as yet – in linguistics, primarily in those lines of linguistic inquiry that attach central importance to language in use, such as pragmatics (e.g., International Pragmatics Association 1987; Levinson 1983) or functional grammar (e.g., Nichols 1984; Nichols and Woodbury 1985; Silverstein 1976, 1978, 1985); in folklore, most centrally in relation to problems of genre, performance, oral poetics, and oral narrative (e.g., Bauman 1977a, 1986b; Ben-Amos 1976; Ben-Amos and Goldstein 1975; Limón and Young 1986); in sociology, in studies of conversation and other aspects of the interaction order (e.g., Goffman 1983; Goodwin 1980; Grimshaw 1988); in history (e.g., Bauman 1983; Burke 1981; Burke and Porter 1987; St George 1984); in literary studies, particularly in explorations of the relationship between oral and written literature and literature as socially and culturally grounded discursive practice (e.g., Ormsby-Lennon 1977; D. Sherzer 1986; Stewart 1978); and so on. But it is precisely the extent to which the ethnography of speaking has infiltrated these various disciplines that makes it far more difficult now than it was in 1974 to view the ethnography of speaking itself in disciplinary or subdisciplinary terms. Perhaps in some general institutional sense the center of gravity of the enterprise still lies within lingustic anthropology, if one were to count, say, the number of its practitioners who gather under the aegis of the Society for Linguistic Anthropology or are affiliated with anthropology departments as against other scholarly societies or departments. Such institutional considerations aside, however, we would suggest that in broader intellectual terms, the ethnography of speaking is currently in

[3] On the ethnography of speaking and the study of discourse, see Duranti (1985) and Sherzer (1987b, 1988–9).

transition from subdisciplinary to transdisciplinary status, as part of that
refiguration of social thought heralded by Clifford Geertz (1980). That is to
say, we envisage the enthnography of speaking in the next phase of its
development as assuming a place ever more clearly as an integrative,
discourse-centered perspective on language, literature, society, culture,
and history that transcends disciplinary divisions of intellectual labor. The
pages that follow represent part of the foundation of that transdisciplinary
perspective on which the ethnography of speaking can continue to build.

REFERENCES

Abrahams, R. (1983). *The Man-of-Words in the West Indies: Performance and the
    Emergence of Creole Culture.* Baltimore. 21–39.
Arno, A. (1985). Impressive Speeches and Persuasive Talk: Traditional Patterns of
    Political Communication in Fiji's Lau Group from the Perspective of Pacific
    Ideal Types. *Oceania* 56:124–37.
Basso, E. (1985). *A Musical View of the Universe: Kalapalo Myth and Ritual
    Performances.* Philadelphia.
Basso, K. (1979). *Portraits of the Whiteman.* Cambridge.
    (1980). Review of *The Domestication of the Savage Mind* by J. Goody. *Language in
    Society* 9:72–80.
    (1984). "Stalking With Stories": Names, Places, and Moral Narratives Among
    the Western Apache. In E. Bruner (ed.), *Text, Play, and Story: The Construc-
    tion and Reconstruction of Self and Society.* Washington, D.C. 19–55.
    (1988). "Speaking With Names": Language and Landscape Among the Western
    Apache. *Cultural Anthropology* 3:99–130.
Bauman, R. (1977a). *Verbal Art as Performance.* Prospect Heights. IL.
    (1977b). Linguistics, Anthropology, and Verbal Art: Toward a United Perspec-
    tive, with a Special Discussion of Children's Folklore. In M. Saville-Troike
    (ed.), *Linguistics and Anthropology.* Washington, D.C. 13–36.
    (1982). Conceptions of Folklore in the Development of Literary Semiotics.
    Semiotica 39:1–20.
    (1983). *Let Your Words Be Few: Symbolism of Speaking and Silence Among
    Seventeenth-Century Quakers.* Cambridge.
    (1986a). *Story, Performance, and Event: Contextual Studies of Oral Narrative.*
    Cambridge.
    (1986b). Performance and Honor in 13th-Century Iceland. *Journal of American
    Folklore* 99:131–150.
    (1987). The Role of Performance in the Ethnography of Speaking. *Working
    Papers and Proceedings of the Center for Psychosocial Studies* no. 11:3–12.
    (1988–9). Performance. In E. Barnouw (ed.), *International Encyclopedia of Com-
    munications.* Oxford.
Bauman, R. and Sherzer, J. (1975). The Ethnography of Speaking. In B. J. Siegel
    (ed.), *Annual Review of Anthropology,* vol. 4. Palo Alto. 95–119.
    (eds.) (1980). *Language and Speech in American Society.* Austin.
    (eds.) (1982). *Case Studies in the Ethnography of Speaking.* Austin.
Beeman, W. (1982). *Culture, Performance and Communication in Iran.* Tokyo.
Bell, M. (1983). *The World From Brown's Lounge.* Urbana.
Ben-Amos, D. (ed.) (1976). *Folklore Genres.* Austin.

Ben-Amos, D., and Goldstein, K. (eds.) (1975). *Folklore: Performance and Communication*. The Hague.

Béhague, G. (1984). *Performance Practice*. Westport, CT.

Bloch, M. (1975). *Political Language and Oratory in Traditional Societies*. London.

(1976). Review of *Explorations in the Ethnography of Speaking*, R. Bauman and J. Sherzer (eds.). *Language in Society* 5:229–34.

Borker, R. (1976). Performing with Words. *Reviews in Anthropology* 3:152–9.

Brenneis, D. (1986). Shared Territory: Audience, Indirection, and Meaning. *Text* 6:339–47.

(1987). Performing Passions: Aesthetics and Politics in an Occasionally Egalitarian Community. *American Ethnologist* 14:236–50.

Brenneis, D., and Myers, F. (eds.) (1984). *Dangerous Words: Language and Politics in the Pacific*. New York.

Bricker, V. R. (1973). *Ritual Humor in Highland Chiapas*. Austin.

Briggs, C. (1986). *Learning How to Ask: A Sociolinguistic Appraisal of the Role of the Interview in Social Science Research*. Cambridge.

Brown, P., and Levinson, S. (1978). Universals in Language Usage: Politeness Phenomena. In E. Goody (ed.), *Questions and Politeness*. Cambridge. 56–289.

Burke, P. (1981). Languages and Anti-Languages in Early Modern Italy. *History Workshop* 11:24–32.

Burke, P., and Porter, R. (1987). *The Social History of Language*. Cambridge.

Burns, A. (1983). *An Epoch of Miracles: Oral Literature of the Yucatec Maya*. Austin.

Chafe, W., and Tannen, D. (1987). The Relation Between Written and Spoken Language. In B. J. Siegel (ed.), *Annual Review of Anthropology*, vol. 16. Palo Alto. 383–407.

Duranti, A. (1981). *The Samoan Fono: A Sociolinguistic Study*. Canberra.

(1985). Sociocultural Dimensions of Discourse. In T. van Dijk (ed.), *Handbook of Discourse Analysis*, vol. 1. London.

(1988). Ethnography of Speaking: Toward a Linguistics of the Praxis. In F. J. Newmeyer (ed.), *Language: The Socio-Cultural Context*. Cambridge.

Feld, S. (1982). *Sound and Sentiment: Birds, Weeping, Poetics, and Song in Kaluli Expression*. Philadelphia.

Ferguson, C., and Heath, S. B. (eds.) (1981). *Language in the USA*. Cambridge.

Fernandez, J. (1988). Andalusia On Our Minds: Two Contrasting Places in Spain As Seen in a Vernacular Poetic Duel of the Late 19th Century. *Cultural Anthropology* 3:21–35.

Fine, E. (1984). *The Folklore Text: From Performance to Print*. Bloomington.

Fine, E. and Speer, J. (1977). A New Look at Performance. *Communication Monographs* 44:374–389.

Finnegan, R. (1977). *Oral Poetry*. Cambridge.

Foster, M. (1974). *From the Earth to Beyond the Sky: An Ethnographic Approach to Four Longhouse Iroquois Speech Events*. Ottawa.

(1984). On Who Spoke First at Iroquois–White Councils: An Exercise in the Method of Upstreaming. In M. Foster, J. Campisi, and M. Mithun (eds.), *Extending the Rafters: Interdisciplinary Approaches to Iroquoian Studies*. Albany. 183–207.

Fox, J. (1977). Roman Jakobson and the Comparative Study of Parallelism. In J. D. Armstrong and C. H. van Schooneveld (eds.), *Roman Jakobson: Echoes of His Scholarship*. Lisse. 59–90.

Frake, C. (1983). Review of *The Psychology of Literacy*, by S. Scribner and M. Cole. *American Ethnologist* 10:368–71.

Gal, S. (1979). *Language Shift: Social Determinants of Linguistic Change in Bilingual Austria*. New York.

Geertz, C. (1980). Blurred Genres: The Refiguration of Social Thought. *The American Scholar* 42:165–79.

Goffman, E. (1983). The Interaction Order. *American Sociological Review* 48:1–17.

Goodwin, M. H. (1980). He-Said-She-Said: Formal Cultural Procedures For the Construction of a Gossip Dispute Activity. *American Ethnologist* 7:674–95.

(1982). 'Instigating': Storytelling as Social Process. *American Ethnologist* 9: 799–819.

Goody, J. (1977). *The Domestication of the Savage Mind*. Cambridge.

(1987). *The Interface Between the Written and the Oral*. Cambridge.

Gossen, G. (1974). *Chamulas in the World of the Sun: Time and Space in a Maya Oral Tradition*. Cambridge, MA.

Grimshaw, A. (ed.) (1988). *Conflict Talk: Sociolinguistic Investigations of Arguments in Conversation*. Cambridge.

Gumperz, J. (1982). *Discourse Strategies*. Cambridge.

(1984). Communicative Competence Revisited. In D.Schiffrin (ed.), *Meaning, Form, and Use in Context: Linguistic Applications*. Washington, D.C. 278–89.

Hanks, W. (1984). Sanctification, Structure, and Experience in a Yucatec Ritual Event. *Journal of American Folklore* 97:131–66.

(1986). Authenticity and Ambivalence in the Text: A Colonial Maya Case. *American Ethnologist* 13:721–44.

(1987). Discourse Genres in a Theory of Practice. *American Ethnologist* 14:668–92.

Haviland, J. (1977). *Gossip, Reputation and Knowledge in Zinacantan*. Chicago.

Heath, S. B. (1983). *Ways With Words*. Cambridge.

(1984). Linguistics and Education. In B. J. Siegel (ed.), *Annual Review of Anthropology*, vol. 13. Palo Alto. 251–74.

Herzfeld, M. (1985). *The Poetics of Manhood: Contest and Identity in a Cretan Mountain Village*. Princeton.

Hill, J., and Hill, K. (1986). *Speaking Mexicano: Dynamics of Syncretic Language in Central Mexico*. Tucson.

Howe, J. (1986). *The Kuna Gathering: Contemporary Village Politics in Panama*. Austin.

Howe, J. and Sherzer, J. (1986). Friend Hairyfish and Friend Rattlesnake or Keeping Anthropologists in Their Place. *Man* 21:680–96.

Hymes, D. (1962). The Ethnography of Speaking. In T. Gladwin and W. C. Sturtevant (eds.), *Anthropology and Human Behavior*. Washington, D.C. 13–53.

(1975). Breakthrough into Performance. In D. Ben-Amos and K. S. Goldstein (eds.), *Folklore: Performance and Communication*. The Hague. 11–74.

(1980). *Language and Education: Ethnolinguistic Essays*. Washington, D.C.

(1981). *In Vain I Tried to Tell You: Essays in Native American Ethnopoetics*. Philadelphia.

International Pragmatics Association (1987). Constitution of the International Pragmatics Association. *IPrA Bulletin* 3:15–17.

Irvine, J. T. (1979). Formality and Informality in Communicative Events. *American Anthropologist* 81:773–90.

(1987). Domains of Description in the Ethnography of Speaking: A Retrospective on the 'Speech Community.' *Working Papers and Proceedings of the Center for Psychosocial Studies* no. 11:13–24.

Katriel, T. (1986). *Talking Straight: Dugri Speech in Israeli Sabra Culture.* Cambridge.

Kochman, T. (1981). *Black and White Styles in Conflict.* Chicago.

Kuipers, J. (1984). Place, Names, and Authority in Weyéwa Ritual Speech. *Language in Society* 13:455–66.

Leach, E. (1976). Social Geography and Linguistic Performance. *Semiotica* 16:87–97.

Levinson, S. (1983). *Pragmatics.* Cambridge.

Limón, J. and Young, M. J. (1986). Frontiers, Settlements, and Development in Folklore Studies, 1972–1985. In B. J. Siegel (ed.), *Annual Review of Anthropology,* vol. 15. Palo Alto. 437–60.

Mannheim, B. (1986). Popular Song and Popular Grammar, Poetry and Metalanguage. *Word* 37:45–75.

McDowell, J. (1979). *Children's Riddling.* Bloomington.

(1985). Folkloristics. In T. A. Sebeok (ed.), *Encyclopedic Dictionary of Semiotics.* Berlin, 260–6.

McLeod, N. and Herndon, M. (eds.) (1980). *The Ethnography of Musical Performance.* Norwood, PA.

Mehan, H. (1985). The Structure of Classroom Discourse. In T. van Dijk (ed.), *Handbook of Discourse Analysis,* vol. 3. London. 120–31.

Nichols, J. (1984). Functional Theories of Grammar. In B. J. Siegel (ed.), *Annual Review of Anthropology,* vol. 13. Palo Alto. 97–117.

Nichols, J. and Woodbury, A. (eds.) (1985). *Grammar Inside and Outside the Clause: Some Views of Theory From the Field.* Cambridge.

O'Barr, W. M. (1981). The Language of the Law. In C. Ferguson and S. B. Heath (eds.), *Language in the USA.* Cambridge. 386–406.

Ochs, E. and Schieffelin, B. (1982). Language Acquisition and Socialization: Three Developmental Stories and their Implications. In R. Bauman and J. Sherzer (eds.), *Case Studies in the Ethnography of Speaking.* Austin. 327–408.

Ong, W. (1982). *Orality and Literacy.* London and New York.

Ormsby-Lennon, H. (1977). 'The Dialect of Those Fanatick Times': Language Communities and English Poetry From 1580 to 1660. Ph.D. dissertation in English Literature, University of Pennsylvania.

Ortner, S. (1984). Theory in Anthropology Since the Sixties. *Comparative Studies in Society and History* 26:126–66.

Paine, R. (ed.) (1981). *Politically Speaking: Cross-Cultural Studies of Rhetoric.* Philadelphia.

Paredes, A. (1977). On Ethnographic Work Among Minority Groups: A Folklorist's Perspective. *New Scholar* 7:1–32.

Parkin, D. (1984). Political Language. In B. J. Siegel (ed.), *Annual Review of Anthropology,* vol. 13. Palo Alto. 345–65.

Philips, S. U. (1983). *The Invisible Culture: Communication in Classroom and Community on the Warm Springs Indian Reservation.* New York.

(1987). The Concept of Speech Genre in the Study of Language and Culture. *Working Papers and Proceedings of the Center for Psychosocial Studies* no. 11:25–34.

Philipsen, G., and Carbaugh, D. (1986). A Bibliography of Fieldwork in the Ethnography of Speaking. *Language in Society* 15:387–97.

Proschan, F. (1983). The Semiotic Study of Puppets, Masks, and Performing Objects. *Semiotica* 47:3–44.

St George, R. (1984). "Heated" Speech and Literacy in Seventeenth-Century New England. In D. Hall and D. G. Allen (eds.), *Seventeenth-Century New England*. Boston. 275–322.

Salmond, A. (1975). *Hui: A Study of Maori Ceremonial Gatherings*. Wellington.

Sanches, M., and Kirshenblatt-Gimblett, B. (1976). Children's Traditional Speech Play and Child Language. In B. Kirshenblatt-Gimblett (ed.), *Speech Play*. Philadelphia. 65–110.

Schieffelin, B. and Ochs, E. (1986). Language Socialization. In B. J. Siegel (ed.), *Annual Review of Anthropology*, vol. 15. Palo Alto. 163–91.

Scollon, R., and Scollon, S. (1979). *Linguistic Convergence: An Ethnography of Speaking at Fort Chipewyan, Alberta*. New York.

(1981). *Narrative, Literacy and Face in Interethnic Communication*. Norwood, NJ.

Sherzer, D. (1986). *Representation in Contemporary French Fiction*. Lincoln.

Sherzer, J. (1977). The Ethnography of Speaking: A Critical Appraisal. In M. Saville-Troike (ed.), *Linguistics and Anthropology* (GURT 1977). Washington, D.C. 43–57

(1983). *Kuna Ways of Speaking: An Ethnographic Perspective*. Austin.

(1986). The Report of a Kuna Curing Specialist: The Poetics and Rhetoric of an Oral Performance. In J. Sherzer and G. Urban (eds.), *Native South American Discourse*. Berlin. 169–212.

(1987a). A Diversity of Voices: Men's and Women's Speech in Ethnographic Perspective. In S. U. Philips, S. Steele, and C. Tanz (eds.), *Language, Gender and Sex in Comparative Perspective*. Cambridge. 95–120.

(1987b). A Discourse-Centered Approach to Language and Culture. *American Anthropologist* 89:295–309.

(1988–9). The Ethnography of Speaking. In E. Barnouw (ed.), *International Encyclopedia of Communications*. Oxford.

Sherzer, J., and Woodbury, A. (eds.) (1987). *Native American Discourse: Poetics and Rhetoric*. Cambridge.

Shuman, A. (1986). *Storytelling Rights: The Uses of Oral and Written Texts By Urban Adolescents*. Cambridge.

Shuy, R. (1984). Linguistics in Other Professions. In B. J. Siegel (ed.), *Annual Review of Anthropology*, vol. 13. Palo Alto. 419–45.

Silverstein, M. (1976). Shifters, Linguistic Categories, and Cultural Description. In K. Basso and H. Selby (eds.), *Meaning in Anthropology*. Albuquerque. 11–56.

(1978). The Three Faces of "Function": Preliminaries to a Psychology of Language. In M. Hickman (ed.), *Proceedings of a Working Conference on The Social Foundations of Language and Thought*. Chicago. 1–12.

(1985). The Functional Stratification of Language and Ontogenesis. In J. Wertsch (ed.), *Culture, Communication, and Cognition: Vygotskian Perspectives*. Cambridge. 205–35.

Stewart, S. (1978). *Nonsense: Aspects of Intertextuality in Folklore and Literature*. Baltimore.

Stoeltje, B. J. and Bauman, R. (1988). The Semiotics of Folkloric Performance. In

J. Umiker-Sebeok and T. A. Sebeok (eds.), *The Semiotic Web 1987*. Berlin: de Gruyter. 585–99.

Stone, R. (1982). *Let the Inside Be Sweet: The Interpretation of Music Event Among the Kpelle of Liberia*. Bloomington.

Tannen, D. (1985). Cross-Cultural Communication. in T. van Dijk (ed.), *Handbook of Discourse Analysis*, vol. 4. London. 203–15.

Tedlock, D. (1983). *The Spoken Word and the Work of Interpretation*. Philadelphia.

(1985). *Popul Vuh*. New York.

(1987). Hearing a Voice in an Ancient Text: Quiché Maya Poetics in Performance. In J. Sherzer and A. Woodbury (eds.), *Native American Discourse: Poetics and Rhetoric*. Cambridge.

Trosset, C. (1986). The Social Identity of Welsh Learners. *Language in Society* 15:165–91.

Turner, V. (1986). *The Anthropology of Performance*. New York.

Urban, G. (1986). Ceremonial Dialogues in South America. *American Anthropologist* 88:371–86.

(1988). Ritual Wailing in Amerindian Brazil. *American Anthropologist* 90:385–400.

Watson-Gegeo, K. A. (1986). The Study of Language Use in Oceania. In B. J. Siegel (ed.), *Annual Review of Anthropology*, vol. 15. Palo Alto. 149–62.

Werbner, R. P. (1977). The Argument in and About Oratory. *African Studies* 36:141–4.

Wiget, A. (1985). *Native American Literature*. Boston.

I

PREFACE AND INTRODUCTION

PREFACE

This volume is rooted in the conviction that something has been missing from our understanding of language, and that established lines of linguistic research will not – even cannot – fill the gap. Whether one's concern is with the analysis of language as a purely scientific subject, or with the role of language in practical affairs, questions arise that are quite outside the declared scope of the conventional disciplines which claim an interest in language. Patterns and functions of speech are recognized that are not taken into account in grammars, ethnographies, and other kinds of research. Differences in the purposes to which speech is put and the ways it is organized for these purposes are observed, whereas the scholarly literature seems to consider only the ways that languages and their uses are fundamentally the same. In recent years, work to remedy this situation has come to be known as the ethnography of speaking.

The ethnography of speaking has had a relatively short history as a named field of inquiry. It was called into being by Dell Hymes' seminal essay of 1962,[1] which drew together themes and perspectives from a range of anthropological, literary, and linguistic scholarship, and brought them to bear on *speaking* as a theoretically and practically crucial aspect of human social life, missing from both linguistic descriptions and ethnographies, and on *ethnography* as the means of elucidating the patterns and functions of speaking in societies.[2]

The 1962 essay was programmatic, intended as a stimulus and guide to ethnographic research. Much the same was the purpose of *The Ethnography of Communication*, published two years later under the editorship of John Gumperz and Dell Hymes (1964). Here, a further development by Hymes of the framework for the ethnography of speaking was accompanied by a series of exemplary essays, mostly substantive treatments of phenomena relevant to the ethnography of speaking, though not undertaken under its charter, but converging and contributing toward the establishment of the field (Gumperz & Hymes 1972:vi; 1964:9).

The decade which followed the definition of the ethnography of speaking as an area of anthropological research produced further efforts to develop

3

the conceptual and methodological framework of the field (e.g., Ervin-
Tripp 1969; Gumperz 1962, 1964; Hymes 1964b, 1967, 1971, 1972;
Sherzer & Darnell 1972; Slobin 1967), and a suggestive corpus of substantive studies undertaken under the stimulus of the ethnography of speaking
or convergent with it in some way (e.g., Bright 1966; Gumperz & Hymes
1972). By 1972, the field had developed to the point where a significant
number of scholars had undertaken research directly on the ethnography
of speaking and were ready to report on their findings. On the premise
that the field would be materially advanced by bringing these researchers
together in a forum which would allow them to present and discuss their
findings toward some kind of synthesis, however exploratory, the Conference on the Ethnography of Speaking was held in Austin, 20–23 April
1972.

The present volume is in large part an outgrowth of that conference.
To the core of papers derived from the conference, others have been added;
all have been revised, or, in some cases, written or rewritten, for this volume
in the light of discussions at and subsequent to the conference. The result,
we think, is a more unified work on the ethnography of speaking than any
of its predecessors. Little credit can be claimed by the editors for this
unity of scope; it is rather a sign that earlier works provided a firm and
productive basis for a significant line of research. The organization of the
papers into sections is meant to facilitate the presentation of what seem
to us to be significant themes emerging from the ethnography of speaking
in this second exploratory stage of its development, but readers will, we
hope, be aware of the many common threads which run through the entire
volume and contribute to its overall unity; we have tried to indicate some of
these in the general introduction which follows, and in the introductions to
the several sections. Sections II–V are made up of detailed substantive
studies of various aspects of the patterning of speaking in particular
societies, including cases from North America, South America, Europe,
Africa, Asia, and the Pacific. Section VI brings together a range of papers
which summarize the present state of the ethnography of speaking and
recommend extensions of its focus or scope, or both, toward a more general
theory of the social use of language.

The preparation for and of this volume involved several years and
many people, without whom it would not have been conceivable, much
less possible. Our oldest and greatest debt is to Dell Hymes, mentor,
sponsor, and friend. It will be obvious what we owe to his scholarship,
but we must also acknowledge with gratitude his extensive aid and encouragement in the planning of the conference and the shaping of this
book. As Chairman of the Social Science Research Council Committee
on Sociolinguistics, he was instrumental in securing the support of

the Social Science Research Council for the Conference on the Ethnography of Speaking under a grant from the National Science Foundation; we would also like to express our thanks to the other members of the committee at that time, Charles Ferguson, Allen Grimshaw, John Gumperz, and William Labov, and to David Jenness of the SSRC, for their aid and counsel. We are grateful also to Gordon Whaley, then Dean of the Graduate School, and Winfred P. Lehmann, then Chairman of the Department of Linguistics, for their aid in securing for us the support of the Graduate School of the University of Texas.

All of the contributors, as well as the editors, owe much to the following individuals, for their participation at the Conference on the Ethnography of Speaking: Dan Ben-Amos, Ben Blount, David DeCamp, Dale Fitzgerald, Nicholas Hopkins, Rolf Kjolseth, Edgar Polomé, Michelle Rosaldo, David Roth, Mary Sanches, Henry Selby, Roger Shuy, John Szwed, and Rudolph Troike.

Special thanks and credit must be given to Nancy Hewett, for her very perceptive, intelligent, and careful editorial assistance in the preparation of this volume. The contributors may not be aware how much they owe to her, but the editors certainly are. Frances Terry has been involved with us on the project from the writing of the first exploratory letters to the proofreading of the manuscript and preparation of the index, invaluable, as ever, at every step of the way.

Finally, more than thanks are due to Louise and Dina, for their capacity to bear with us through all those hours of talk about talk about talk ...

October 1973

Richard Bauman
Joel Sherzer

INTRODUCTION

Since at least the time of Descartes and Leibniz, there has been current in western thought a conception of language which holds that insofar as language is governed by laws, they are 'the specifically linguistic laws of connection between linguistic signs, within a given, closed linguistic system ... Individual acts of speaking are, from the viewpoint of language, merely fortuitous refractions and variations or plain and simple distortions of normatively identical forms' (Vološinov 1973:57; see also Hymes 1970a). The prominence, or predominance, of this view in our own century and our own time, makes it especially important to state at the outset of this book our commitment to a contrary view. This work is built on, and intended as a contribution to, a conception which holds that the patterning of language goes far beyond laws of grammar to comprehend the use of language in social life, that such organization inescapably involves the radical linking of the verbal and the sociocultural in the conduct of speaking. The field of inquiry devoted to the discovery of this organization is the ethnography of speaking.

Consistent with current views of the nature and purpose of ethnography, the ethnography of speaking may be conceived of as research directed toward the formulation of descriptive theories of speaking as a cultural system or as part of cultural systems. In order to construct such theories, we need to formulate, heuristically for the present, theoretically later, the range of things that might enable us to comprehend the organization of speaking in social life, the relevant aspects of speaking as a cultural system.[1]

The point of departure in such a formulation is the speech community, defined in terms of the shared or mutually complementary knowledge and ability (competence) of its members for the production and interpretation of socially appropriate speech.[2] Such a community is an organization of diversity,[3] insofar as this knowledge and ability (i.e., access to and command of resources for speaking) are differentially distributed among its members; the production and interpretation of speech are thus variable and complementary, rather than homogeneous and constant throughout the community.

6

Within the overall context of the speech community, the ethnographer of speaking seeks to determine, among other factors, the means of speaking available to its members.[4] The means include, first of all, the linguistic varieties and other codes and subcodes, the use of which counts as speech within the community, and the distribution of which constitutes the linguistic repertoires of its members (Gumperz 1964). Also constituting means of speaking are the conventional speech acts and genres available to the members for the conduct of speaking.

An additional aspect of the system is the set of community norms, operating principles, strategies, and values which guide the production and interpretation of speech, the community ground rules for speaking. The interest here, for example, is in the nature and distribution of norms of interaction to be found within the community, insofar as these organize spoken interaction. To the extent that these norms of interaction are goal-directed, they may be viewed as strategies, to be studied with reference to the goals of the participants. Goals, in turn, are closely related to values, hierarchies of preference for the judgment and evaluation of speaking. Finally, there are norms of interpretation, conventional understandings brought to bear on the interpretation of speech by the receivers of spoken communication.

All of the foregoing may be seen as resources available to the members of a speech community for the conduct of speaking. This speaking is situated within and seen as meaningful in terms of native contexts of speech activity, i.e., culture-specific settings, scenes, and institutions in which speaking is done. Moreover, this speaking is carried on by the members of the community as incumbents of speaking (and listening) roles, socially defined and situated in relevant contexts.

The nexus of all the factors we have outlined is performance. We conceive of performance in terms of the interplay between resources and individual competence, within the context of particular situations. Performances thus have an emergent quality, structured by the situated and creative exercise of competence.[5]

The task of the ethnographer of speaking, then, is to identify and analyze the dynamic interrelationships among the elements which go to make up performance, toward the construction of a descriptive theory of speaking as a cultural system in a particular society. The studies in this volume represent just such analyses, in the form of case studies. None of the contributions purports to be a complete ethnography of speaking; each is, rather, an exploration in the ethnography of speaking, focusing on particular and salient aspects of individual cultural systems. Not all the aspects of the framework we have outlined have received equal attention, but all are at least touched upon in the papers that follow. The sections of the book are consistent with the framework and reflect the major concerns of the ethnography of speaking at this stage of its development.

Although the ethnography of speaking was first proposed as 'a special opportunity, and responsibility, of anthropology' (Hymes 1962), it has become increasingly clear in the intervening years that its commitments are substantially shared by a number of disciplines concerned with speaking as an instrument of social life. The ethnography of speaking offers a perspective which cuts across these various disciplines, drawing theoretical and methodological insights from all of them, and contributing in its own right to the development of each. Most centrally involved in this common venture are anthropology, linguistics, sociology, and folklore, all of which are represented in this volume through the identifications and interests of the contributors.

From anthropology, besides the ethnographic method and the traditional anthropological commitment to the importance of language, the ethnography of speaking draws the basic relativism of its perspective (Hymes 1961, 1966), the understanding that speaking, like other systems of behavior – religious, economic, political, etc. – is organized in each society in culture-specific ways, which are to be discovered. This is not to deny the existence of universals, but to assert that they, like other generalizations, must emerge through comparison of individual systems, investigated first in their own terms.

In its turn, the ethnography of speaking fills the gap in the anthropological record created by the neglect by anthropological linguists of the social use of language and by the lack of interest of ethnographers in patterns and functions of speaking. The importance of the ethnography of speaking to anthropology cuts far deeper than this, however, for a careful focus on speaking as an instrument for the conduct of social life brings to the fore the emergent nature of social structures, not rigidly determined by the institutional structure of the society, but rather largely created in performance by the strategic and goal-directed manipulation of resources for speaking. It is for this reason that we have stressed the theme of performance in the organization of this volume.

While it is clearly possible – at times even necessary – to account for certain aspects of the patterns and functions of speaking in a community without immediate reference to linguistic detail, a complete ethnography of speaking must incorporate the linguistic means available to the members of the community. To be consistent with the ethnographic perspective, however, those modes of linguistic description based upon a 'linguistic theory ... concerned primarily with an ideal speaker–listener, in a completely homogeneous speech community, who knows its language perfectly and is unaffected by such grammatically irrelevant conditions as memory limitations, distractions, shifts of attention and interest, and errors (random or characteristic) in applying his knowledge of the language in actual performance' (Chomsky 1965:3) are patently inadequate. Recently, however, an increasing number of linguists have begun to argue for an expansion of linguistic theory, recognizing that it is impossible to describe language adequately without taking into consideration aspects of language use that have previously been considered extraneous to linguistic theory such as speech acts, presuppositions, politeness, and conversational rules.[6] It is important to stress the strong philosophical bent of much of this research, however, and the fact that it represents a gradual development out of generative-transformational linguistics.[7]

The papers in this volume approach language from a wider ethnographic and social perspective. In this sense, they contribute toward what Hymes has called a socially constituted linguistics, concerned fundamentally with socially based modes of organization of linguistic means rather than the abstract grammar of a single language (Hymes 1973:316). The locus of description is not limited to single individuals, but includes social networks, groups, or communities. The speech community is viewed as inherently heterogeneous; the structure of the heterogeneity must be described. Language use does not occur in isolated sentences, but in natural units of speaking; stated abstractly: speech acts, events, and situations; stated more concretely: greetings, leave-takings, narratives, conversations, jokes, curing chants, or periods of silence. It should be noted that certain concepts and techniques of formal description provided by linguistics, i.e., phrase-structure and transformational rules, have proven useful for the formalization of the structure of such units.

Linguistic anthropologists and folklorists have long come together on the common ground provided by their shared interest in folklore texts, though each discipline has pursued its own particular lines of analysis in the study of these texts, once collected. With the development of the ethnography of speaking, however, paralleled by the development of interest among folklorists in the socially situated performance of folklore, the community of interest has shifted and developed beyond simply the exploitation of common materials, to the pursuit of certain shared analytical goals.[8] To the ethnography of speaking, folklorists bring a particular sensitivity to genre as an organizing factor of verbal performance, which goes beyond the sentence and directs attention to matters of form, content, performance role, performance situation, and function. By studying the most highly marked, artistic verbal genres in these terms, folklorists contribute not only toward the filling in of the ethnographic record, but also give prominence to a notion of performance as creative in a sense which goes beyond simply novelty to encompass transcendent artistic achievement.

Awareness of the broader goals of the ethnography of speaking can allow folklorists to view the performance of artistic verbal forms in terms of the overall structure of verbal performance as a whole, establishing both the continuities and discontinuities between verbal art and other modes of speaking within a single unified system. The perspectives and methods of the ethnography of speaking are also indispensable in the determination of native categories of genres and scenes, as well as the elucidation of culture-specific esthetics of spoken language and functions of verbal art forms. All of these represent a crucial counter to the *a priori* taxonomies, esthetic principles, and functionalist assumptions with which folklorists have operated since the emergence of the discipline.

Within the discipline of sociology, there has been a convergence with the ethnography of speaking on the part of a group of scholars who have arrived at an interest in the socially situated use of language through a concern with the commonsense understandings that enable participants to enter into and sustain social interaction. Since speech is the principal instrument of social interaction, this effort has led to investigations of the situated meanings carried by verbal messages in the conduct of an interaction.[9] These microfunctional analyses of the implicit intentions and understandings which attend participation in conversation carry the analysis of the social use of speech to a finer level than anthropologists have reached, but in terms quite consistent with the conceptual framework of the ethnography of speaking, in its concern with native understandings and rules for the production and interpretation of speech. A closer convergence between the two approaches sees ethnographers looking more closely at the structure of conversation in interaction, while the sociologists enlarge their scope to include other cultures and the organization of contexts of speaking beyond the conversation, as well as careful attention to the features of language itself as integrated with its use.

We have attempted thus far to locate the ethnography of speaking in terms of the disciplinary and interdisciplinary relations among its practitioners, theoretical commitments, and substantive foci of interest. Allowing this general introduction and the essays and introductions which follow to stand as a composite indication of the present state of the ethnography of speaking, what might be suggested concerning the future? How might the field advance during the next decade?

The development which seems to be most immediately in prospect is the publication of more complete ethnographies of speaking, devoted to particular societies. Many of the contributions to this volume, in fact, are segments of more comprehensive works in progress. These works, when available, will constitute the first full-scale analyses of the patterns and functions of speaking as they ramify throughout the sociocultural life of whole communities, standing as, or approaching, the comprehensive theories of speaking as a cultural system which represent the first major goal of the ethnography of speaking.

A further prospect, as the ethnography of speaking exploits the momentum it has gained during the past decade, is an increase in the number of available case studies of speaking in particular societies. Although the areal coverage of this volume, for example, spans many of the major culture areas of the world, the studies reported on are in many instances the first and only direct explorations in the ethnography of speaking for those areas. Moreover, in this early stage of the development of the field, the tendency has been for ethnographers to study societies or activities in which speaking is a cultural focus and a positively valued activity. Consequently, a reliable base for comparative generalization is yet to be developed since societies differ as to the importance of speaking, both absolutely and relative to particular contexts. As the record expands, however, a more confident ethnology of speaking will be possible. And, as more research is done within geographical areas already represented in the literature, areal patterns and influences will become amenable to investigation.[10]

Areal studies, in turn, introduce the dimension of historical process and change. There have as yet been few attempts to utilize perspectives from the ethnography of speaking in elucidating areal distributions and linguistic change (e.g., Gumperz 1967; Weinreich, Labov & Herzog 1968; Sherzer & Bauman 1972), but it is only in the study of pidgins and creoles that such perspectives can be said to be at all prominent, largely through the contribution of the recent *Pidginization and Creolization of Languages* (Hymes 1971b). The full potential of an ethnographic framework for the analysis of linguistic change remains to be reached.

Far less developed, even, than an ethnographic view of linguistic change, is a historical view of patterns and functions of speaking. Like most ethnography, the ethnography of speaking has been synchronic in scope, and studies of change in patterns and functions of speaking within particular communities are conspicuously lacking in the literature (for exceptions cf. Abrahams 1967; Bauman 1974; Rosaldo 1973). We expect that this situation will change as ethnographic base lines are established from which processes of change may be analyzed either forward or backward in time, and as ethnographers of speaking turn more to the investigation of historical cases through the use of historical materials.

Many more prospects for the ethnography of speaking might be suggested, but perhaps the most important lies in its potential for the clarification and solution of practical social problems. Through awareness of and sensitivity to the socioexpressive dimension of speaking, and to intergroup differences in ways of speaking within heterogeneous communities, ethnographic investigators are particularly well equipped to clarify those problem situations which stem from covert conflicts between different ways of speaking, conflicts which may be obscured to others by a failure to see beyond the referential functions of speaking and abstract grammatical patterns. Understanding of such problem situations is a major step toward their solution, laying the groundwork for planning and change. Some work in this branch of applied sociolinguistics has already been proposed and carried out (e.g., Abrahams 1972; Bauman 1971; Cazden, John & Hymes 1972; Gumperz & Herasimchuk 1973; Kochman 1969; Philips 1970; Shuy MS.); and we are convinced that the next decade will see more and more ethnographic studies of speaking in schools, hospitals, and other institutions of contemporary culture in heterogeneous societies, toward the solution of practical social problems. If our work leads us to understand speaking in social life as adaptive and creative practice, and as a means for the creation of emergent structures, it is only appropriate that we endow the ethnography of speaking with a similar role.

II
COMMUNITIES AND RESOURCES
FOR PERFORMANCE

INTRODUCTION

A basic element of an ethnography of speaking is the description of the speech community and its linguistic resources. Investigators are continually struck by the diversity of linguistic means in use in communities and the concomitant ability of members of the communities to communicate with one another nevertheless.

Every society makes available to its members a repertoire of linguistic alternatives or resources which they draw on (in an ecological sense) for both referential and stylistic purposes (see paper by Hymes in section VI). The nature of the communicatively meaningful contrasts within the 'sociolinguistic' repertoire varies dramatically from society to society. It might involve slight differences in the pronunciation of single sounds that must be described in terms of statistical tendencies. Thus Labov (1966) studies the social implications of the variable pronunciations of the sounds /th/, /dh/, and /r/, among others, in New York City. Gillian Sankoff here discusses the pronunication of the variable /l/ in Montreal French; speakers have available to them the choice of pronouncing this variable as either [l] or ∅. This choice depends on both linguistic and social contexts of usage.

A society's linguistic resources might, on the other hand, consist of a complex of related dialects. Thus, James Fox shows that on the island of Roti, individuals speak the particular dialect of their *nusak* 'native domain' in everyday, colloquial speech, but draw on other Rotinese dialects for the formation of formal, ritual speech.

Or a society's linguistic resources might include wholly different and perhaps even unrelated languages. One cannot but be impressed by the linguistic ability of the Indians of the Vaupés area of Colombia (as described by Jean Jackson), who are fluent in at least three and often four or five languages and who sometimes understand as many as ten.

What characterizes a speech community is a heterogeneity of linguistic means organized by rules of speaking and interpretation shared by members of the community. By sharing we do not mean a monolithic 'replication of uniformity,' but mutually compatible ways of participating in speech activities (see Wallace 1970). Just as the typological nature of the linguistic resources varies from society to society, the nature and functions of the rules can be quite diverse. Thus the variable pronunciation of /l/ as [l] or ∅ in certain contexts in Montreal French reflects an individual's sex as well as membership in the professional or working class. A single linguistic variable is mapped onto several important social dimensions.

The many languages in the Vaupés linguistic repertoire function primarily as badges of membership in particular social groups. These social groups have no geographic boundaries and practically no overt markers other than the linguistic badge associated with them. The social groups and the languages which are associated with them function in the regulation of marriage partners in that the groups are exogamous – no one is permitted to marry someone who wears an identical linguistic badge. It is interesting that there is no hierarchical ranking of Vaupés languages in terms of prestige and no mapping of linguistic choices onto a scheme of social stratification. The native Vaupés attitude toward language relationships, language learning, and language use fits well with the notion of language as a badge. Vaupés Indians stress the mutual unintelligibility of Vaupés languages. Furthermore individuals will not speak a language until they know it quite well and will not 'mix' languages while speaking.

Rotinese dialect differences are not ordinarily exploited by speakers in colloquial discourse; nor do they map onto or relate in any way to Rotinese social stratification. Rather they are drawn on as the primary resource in the construction of parallelistic structures characteristic of ritual speech. (For discussion of parallelism see section V.) Thus the Rotinese seem to orient themselves to their own *nusak* 'domain' for the purposes of everyday interaction, while they orient themselves to the entire island of Roti, with its dialect complexity, for the purpose of formal, ritual speech.

The Rotinese situation is a good example of the fact that individuals are typically oriented to participation in several and overlapping speech communities. Thus a New Yorker is usually a participating member of the New York City speech community as well as the United States speech community. He may also be a member of the New York City Italian speech community or the Brooklyn Jewish speech community. Roger Abrahams' paper (in section IV) might be read as evidence for a single Black speech community within the United States as a whole. Of course, the individual members of this community might also be members of the New York City speech community, the Oakland speech community, etc. What is important is that each of these communities can be defined in terms of shared linguistic repertoires and rules for speaking. Which one or ones an individual orients himself to at any given moment is part of the strategy of speaking.

The two speech communities focused on by Sankoff are relatively delimitable in geographic space. They are:

1. the native French speakers of Montreal, Canada, and
2. the Neo-Melanesian speakers of Lae, New Guinea.

Given these speech communities, the analyst's task is to describe the sociolinguistic rules which organize them. Here, methods become crucial. Adequate representation of different social groups within the community and of different contexts of language use are essential. The results are impressive. A careful investigation of the patterning of a single linguistic variable, for example /l/ in Montreal French, reveals much more about the social organization of the community than would an impressionistic approach to many linguistic variables.

Speech communities in the Colombian Vaupés are not so easily delimited. In fact, their nature and limits form the focus of Jackson's entire paper. Given the patterns of marriage-partner selection in the context of Vaupés multilingualism, it is impossible to identify single languages with single communities. Jackson argues that each multifamily longhouse in the Vaupés constitutes a single speech community, in that it has its own set of rules for speaking which organize a unique set of languages. But the Vaupés as a whole, and perhaps the entire Northwest Amazon, can also be defined in terms of shared rules for speaking, organizing an incredible diversity of linguistic means and making possible communication among various groups of people. Jackson treats this larger area – the Vaupés or even the Northwest Amazon as a whole – as a speech area. It is often problematic, as Jackson is well aware, to determine the boundaries of speech communities and speech areas. In any case, it is crucial to recognize that the concepts speech community and speech area are sociolinguistic concepts – they cannot be dealt with in purely social or purely linguistic terms.

The focus on speech communities and the linguistic resources associated with them has certain implications for linguistic theory. An adequate grammar of a language must distinguish what is categorical in that language from what is variable. This distinction is clearly part of native speakers' linguistic competencies, and as such must be represented in grammars. Thus Sankoff's variable rule format is a contribution to our understanding of the notion 'rule of grammar.' There are areas of grammar which are intimately intertwined with social and cultural domains, so much so that the former cannot be described without reference to the latter. Thus Sankoff's variable rules include social as well as linguistic contexts. The theory of grammar-writing is even more complicated in situations such as that described by Jackson, where native speaker competence is not limited to a single language, but involves equivalent ability in several. For such situations, linguists may well have to write 'multilingual grammars.' Finally, it should be clear that linguistic descriptions must achieve both psychological and sociological validity. They must reflect the perspective not only of single individuals but also of social groups, networks, or communities.

A QUANTITATIVE PARADIGM FOR THE STUDY OF COMMUNICATIVE COMPETENCE

GILLIAN SANKOFF

The past decade has seen a great increase in scholarly efforts directed to exploring the systematicity of the relationships between sociocultural organization and language use. A basic assumption behind this search has been that speakers functioning as members of a particular society in terms of a particular culture have internalized not only rules of grammar, but also rules of appropriate speech usage which are broadly shared by other members of their society, and which they apply in their speech behaviour. Thus *competence* has been extended from the notion of the mastery of a set of grammatical rules to the mastery of a set of cultural rules which include the appropriate ways to apply grammatical rules in all speech situations possible for that society (Hymes 1972b). The notion of context has been extended to apply not only to linguistic context or environment, but to the social-situational circumstances of the speech event, even to the intent or ends of the speaker.

Many important concepts were developed during the 1960s for dealing with systematic sociolinguistic variability, as it came to be generally recognized that no community or individual is limited to a single variety of code (Hymes 1967). Such concepts include the idea of a *linguistic repertoire* (Gumperz 1964, 1965, 1968) of a community or of an individual, the *code matrix* of a community, consisting of all of its codes and subcodes, including languages, dialects, styles (Gumperz 1962), or registers (Halliday 1964) in their functional relationships; the idea that speech events can be characterized in terms of a set of *components*, such as channel, setting, participants, etc. (see Ervin-Tripp 1972; Hymes 1967, 1972a), each of which may be factored into a number of relevant *features*. 'Relevant' is used here in a functional sense, i.e., the components interact with each other in terms of co-variation of features. A related idea was that variation in language use could be dealt with in terms of the variable *functions* of speech (see Jacobson 1960; Hymes 1962, 1969), the basic notion here being that what might be referentially 'synonymous' could at the same time be a socially meaningful distinction.

Within this broad framework, there is a general recognition both of the heterogeneity of all known speech communities, and of the extent to which variation in use carries sociostylistic meaning, i.e., of the *structure* of linguistic variation within speech communities. Given this general agreement, however, there are several possible approaches to the study of speech use within its sociocultural context, approaches which are not, in my view, mutually incompatible. Most of the contributors to this volume have taken as a starting point the examination of the sociocultural matrix of language use, whether in terms of interpersonal interaction or in terms of culturally defined situations of speech use, and have proceeded to investigate in some detail their linguistic concomitants. Most of the research reported in this paper starts from the other side of the same coin, trying to demonstrate that the distribution of linguistic features cannot be understood solely in terms of their internal relationships within grammar, but must be seen as part of the broader sociocultural context in which they occur. Despite this apparent difference, however, I will argue that the theoretical and methodological issues I raise are of direct relevance for both approaches.

At the most general level, the basic problem is that of the accountability of a description of any behaviour to some data base, a problem which can also be seen as the quite straightforward matter of how to generalize from a set of observations. In any analysis, one searches for structure, pattern, and relationships; I contend that in speech behaviour as in many other kinds of behaviour there is a great deal of statistical variability. This does not imply that such variability is unstructured, nor does it imply that there do not exist categorical (non-variable) rules and relationships in language and in language use. However in attempting to find patterns which are expressible other than as categorical rules, it may be possible to pioneer techniques which will prove useful to sociolinguists of various persuasions. Many sociolinguists are now working with situations in which rules appear to be more categorical than variable, situations of highly marked speech use including rituals, greetings, games, insults, and the like. In dealing with such cases, it appears convenient and indeed logical to borrow models and formalisms from linguistics, and to attempt to formulate the types of rules suggested in Ervin-Tripp (1972). But most models originating from modern linguistics have no way of treating variability, and tend to carry with them idealistic postulates of homogeneity and determinacy which I believe will prove unsuitable for sociolinguistics in the long run, as they have proven unsuitable in the field of ethnosemantics (see G. Sankoff 1971, 1972a), and as scholars working on purely grammatical problems are beginning to find in this area as well (Elliot, Legum & Thompson 1969; Ross 1972, 1973; Sag 1973).

The variability of speech as people actually use it has been only too painfully obvious to anyone attempting to work with large bodies of recorded speech of any sort. It is my contention in this paper that quantitative techniques can be fruitfully used in demonstrating not only the general patterns existing within a speech community, but also the subtle distinctions internalized by individuals which are based on the human ability to deal with differences of degree, both in producing speech and in interpreting the speech of others. A meaningful and realistic framework need not imply that if only the analyst could exercise enough ingenuity, all variation could be accounted for, deterministically, by specifying long enough lists of constraints.

One might well ask why it is necessary at all to talk about behaviour when dealing with questions of internalized ability to use speech grammatically and appropriately, i.e., with questions of competence. Whether we assume such competence to be a property of the individual or of the community (in the sense of shared rule systems), and whether we understand it to mean linguistic or sociolinguistic competence, we are faced with the problem of what kind of evidence we can use as a basis for our analysis. Since all evidence (with the possible exception of introspection by the analyst himself but including elicited grammaticality judgments) consists of behaviour, and generally verbal behaviour (performance) of some sort, it is virtually impossible to escape the problem of making inferences from behaviour. (On the perils of introspection, see DeCamp 1973; Labov 1970.) It is my view that performance consists essentially of *samples* of competence (see also Cedergren & D. Sankoff 1974), and that in dealing with it, it is important to recognize the problems that the statistical fluctuation inherent in all probabilistically generated behaviour leads to, in any attempt to abstract from it the kinds of patterns we would expect in competence. Most of the issues here hinge on the nature of similarity and difference. What degree or extent of difference in performance would lead us to infer difference in competence?

The analytic goals which different sociolinguists set for themselves are many and varied. In the work I describe here, the goal is not to start afresh and write whole grammars; I think it is essential to build on the work of scholars concerned with narrowly linguistic rather than sociolinguistic competence. But a clearer understanding of those particular areas of grammar which are intimately intertwined with social and cultural domains, and of the detailed nature of these interconnections, is one of the most clearly definable and attainable goals of sociolinguists.

The nature of the quantitative paradigm

A number of proposals have been made by linguists and sociolinguists in the past few years for dealing with some of the aspects of linguistic variation discussed in the previous section. The quantitative approach advocated here implies a number of procedures for data collection and analysis which are shared to some extent with other approaches, but which are nevertheless worthwhile discussing, as together they form a unique and coherent system. Not only are such procedures necessary for the adequate formulation of variable rules; they also provide crucial data for verifying categorical rules of grammar or of speech use.

Many of the properties of the approach I am proposing are shared by what C.-J. N. Bailey (1970) has referred to as the 'dynamic paradigm.' The notion of structured variability can, however, usefully be applied not only to dynamic studies, but also to the understanding of various kinds of linguistic subcodes, systems, or varieties, whether these be defined in terms of particular sociolinguistic events (genres, routines, etc.) or of subcategories of speech community members.

Quantitative studies of speech behaviour within a speech community perspective depend on good data. This means that it is essential to have sufficient types and amounts of clearly recorded speech data on individuals or communities whose social properties are taken into account. Accordingly, the following sections deal with the nature of the data base, and particularly with the question of the representativity of recorded speech data; subsequent steps in data processing and analysis; and how such data can be used in the writing of variable rules.

THE DATA BASE

Grounded in the notion of a speech community, the paradigm involves the collection and analysis of a corpus which adequately represents the speech performance of members of that community. A systematic set of recordings must be made which will represent the various dimensions of variability existing within the community. Thus sampling is important, as is the problem of how to control for the presence of the observer in altering 'normal' performance. Both of these problems are common to other behavioural investigations, and here the sociolinguist has much to learn from other social sciences, though the fact that speech behaviour is the object of study causes special problems.

In sampling, there are three types of decision which must be made.

(a) The first is to delineate, at least roughly, the geographic, social, etc., boundaries of the speech community or subcommunity of interest, i.e., to define the sampling universe.

(b) The second is to assess the possibly relevant geographic, social, and sociolinguistic dimensions of variation within the community, i.e., to construct a stratification for the sample. As the goal of sampling is to tap the existing linguistic variation in a community, it is important for the investigator to consider carefully all types of variation which exist. Are there ethnic groups which display different speech variants? Might age, sex, class make a difference? Do immigrants represent regional dialects? Do individuals speak differently in different social circumstances? Sampling should take account of at least these dimensions, as well as any others which might be relevant to a particular situation.

(c) The third type of decision is to settle on the number of informants and the amount of material to be collected from each, i.e., to fix the sample size.

A speech community sample need not include the large number of individuals usually required for other kinds of behavioural surveys. If people within a speech community indeed understand each other with a high degree of efficiency, this tends to place a limit on the extent of possible variation, and imposes a regularity (necessary for effective communication) not found to the same extent in other kinds of social behaviour. The literature as well as our own experience would suggest that, even for quite complex speech communities, samples of more than about 150 individuals tend to be redundant, bringing increasing data handling problems with diminishing analytical returns. (Cf. Labov 1973 on the homogeneity of peer group speech behaviour.) It is crucial, however, that the sample be well chosen, and representative of all social subsegments about which one wishes to generalize.

Once these decisions are made, sampling can proceed, either by formally random methods, or through personal contact channels. In the latter approach, one must rely on the stratification scheme, and on deliberate attempts to diversify, in order to ensure a degree of representativity of the sample and to avoid sampling just a small circle of personal friends.

The nature of these procedures can be best understood through examples. For our study of Montreal French, we defined our universe as consisting of all native French speakers resident in predominantly French areas of Montreal since early childhood. We stratified according to age, sex, socioeconomic level of residence area, and geographic area. The sample of 120 was picked using formal methods involving random choices in a street directory, and a strict protocol for selecting informants. (For further methodological details on this study, see D. Sankoff & G. Sankoff 1973.)

In Labov's study of Black English (Labov *et al.* 1968) he concentrated on the male adolescent subculture in Harlem, and stratified mainly by age, choosing to focus on peer groups at each of several age levels. His work on the Lower East Side is based on a more formally produced sample of 122 speakers which he culled according to linguistic and residential criteria from a survey carried out by sociologists.

For her investigation of Spanish in Panama, Cedergren (1972) chose 79 native Spanish-speaking informants stratified according to age, sex, socio-economic level, and age on arrival in the city.

In our work on Neo-Melanesian (New Guinea Tok Pisin), Laberge and I searched for some subsection of the New Guinea urban community in which there would be a concentration of first-language speakers. We found such a situation in the town of Lae, in neighbourhoods where there were numerous interlanguage marriages. We were then able to construct a carefully matched sample of about 25 adolescents and children, all of whom spoke Neo-Melanesian as a first language, and an equal number of their parents, who spoke it as a second language.

Ma and Herasimchuk (1968:666) describe the selection of 45 informants chosen for a study of Spanish–English bilingualism in Jersey City, on the basis of residence within the two-block predominantly Puerto Rican area being studied, sex, and occupational and educational characteristics.

Shuy *et al.* (1968) based their Detroit sample on families having children in elementary school, in ten geographical areas of the city. Though a total of 702 interviews from over 250 families were completed, only 48 of these were actually used in analysis in the most detailed study of the Detroit material to appear (Wolfram 1969).

There is often a conflict between the goals of representing in a systematic series of recordings both interindividual and intraindividual variation. That is, in systematically sampling for different types of individuals, it is impossible not to deal with strangers, but the very fact of not knowing people makes it difficult to record them in more than one kind of situation, usually that of an interview, in which they exhibit only a particular segment of their linguistic repertoire. The resulting data may be limited grammatically as well as stylistically. For example, people being interviewed are not likely to use many interrogatives. It also often happens that the more informal (natural) the situation, the more difficult it is to record, as background noise seems to increase exponentially with informality. The closer the microphone is to the mouth of the speaker, the better quality recording is made (technically) and the more likely it is to intimidate the speaker into a more formal style; the farther away from the speaker, the greater the informality and the lower the technical quality. Hidden microphones tend to be inefficacious as well as unethical.

In our Montreal French study, we decided to approach some of these problems by working with two different samples of people. The 120 carefully sampled subjects were interviewed as a 'one-shot' study, by individual interviewers, who tried to encourage informal speech by various means: urging other members of the subjects' families to remain in the room during the interview and participate in the conversation; using Lavaliere microphones which are less obtrusive than a visible microphone held or on a stand in front of the speaker; discovering through a pretest the topics on which Montrealers appeared to enjoy talking freely, etc. Interviewers also attempted to tap more formal styles toward the end of the interview, where we thought the topic of language attitudes would encourage greater self-monitoring and editing. Last, subjects were asked to read a short text both to elicit careful style and to guarantee comparability through the use of the same measuring instrument for all subjects. Particularly important for phonology, the text included minimal pairs on which we wanted data. Tape recorders were left running throughout the interviewers' visits, including before and after the interview proper and during interruptions of various sorts.

Despite all of these measures, we could not hope in the space of an hour or so to tap the whole range of subjects' linguistic repertoires, especially those specific to situations and activities other than those typically occurring within the home. Thus in a second part of the Montreal study, we made a series of recordings of individuals and groups over a wide range of interaction situations. This, of course, involves the cooperation of the people chosen, as well as a period of becoming accustomed to the presence of the field worker and recording instruments. Studies in which similar procedures have been carried out, in addition to our own work in New Guinea (G. Sankoff 1968, 1972b; Sankoff & Laberge 1973), include Brunel (1970), Lefebvre (1971), Mitchell-Kernan (1971), Gumperz (1964), Labov *et al.* (1968), Saint-Pierre (1969).

It should be remembered that we are primarily interested in describing 'everyday' speech, that is, the kind of speech which is, from the participants' point of view, *least* marked for special features, whether linguistic or social, and which differs in some respects from the highly marked genres of ritual speech, linguistic games, oral literature, and so on. Our approach can, however, be extended for describing the specific linguistic nature of many other kinds of speech which are of social significance in the communities being studied, whether these differences involve 'marking' by one or more categorical features, or whether the differences can be described in terms of proportions.

THE HANDLING OF DATA AND THE CHOICE OF VARIABLES

Methods developed for dealing with variability stem from an appreciation of the fact that a particular underlying element in language may have two or more surface realizations which are not completely determined by environmental constraints. A first step involves the extraction of all (or a systematic sample judged to be sufficiently large) examples of the variants of one or other of the variables in the corpus. This implies that recordings be in accessible form, at least as well documented tapes, and at best accompanied by complete transcriptions in a detailed and specific orthography.

Usually some compromise is made between these two extremes. In order to automate some parts of the analysis, we have developed and are using procedures for putting our Montreal corpus on computer cards and tapes.

It is rare that one knows in advance of the analysis exactly which variables are to be studied. This means that many 'passes' have to be made over the complete corpus. This is not inefficient, however, since it is confusing to try to extract several unrelated variables during the same pass; more important, each search inevitably leads to a better 'feeling' for the material, to unsuspected discoveries of patterns and of further variables to investigate.

The basic principle in extracting information on variation is that of noting not only each instance of a particular variant, but also the number of instances in which it could have occurred, but did not. As Labov says, 'any variable form [a member of a set of alternative ways of 'saying the same thing'] should be reported with the proportion of cases in which the form did occur in the relevant environment, compared to the total number of cases in which it might have occurred' (1969:738). Other types of statistics may also be interesting, but if the ultimate goal is an assessment of competence in terms of grammatical rules, then proportions, or relative frequencies, are essential.

ANALYSIS: HOW TO EXPAND ENVIRONMENTS

In analyzing variable linguistic data according to the quantitative paradigm being proposed in this paper, extralinguistic as well as linguistic constraints are examined. That is, the notion of environment is expanded both to include different kinds of constraints and to deal with questions of proportion or degree.

An example from our study of Montreal French will illustrate both points. Underlying /l/[1] in the pronoun *il* in Montreal French exhibits a variable surface realization, being uttered as either [l] or ø. Thus we have the following forms.

(1) *il fait* [i fɛ] 'he does'
(2) *il est* [y e] 'he is'

We also, however, find the forms (3) and (4).

(3) *il fait* [il fɛ] 'he does'
(4) *il est* [il e] 'he is'

According to any kind of conventional linguistic analysis, therefore, we have not discovered a rule which handles the alternate realizations of /l/ as [l] on the one hand, and as ø on the other. We have to treat it as an unconstrained optional rule or as 'free variation,' unless we can find some other constraint which will categorically handle the alternate realizations.

In looking at a large number of cases of *il* in the speech of six Montrealers, however, we found that the distribution of the various alternate realizations of /l/ is phonologically conditioned, and that the succeeding phonological environment has a very definite effect on the deletion of /l/. Where it is followed by a consonant or glide [− syll]² it is much more likely to be realized as ∅ (93.7% of 648 cases) than when it is followed by a vowel [+ syll] (57.1% of 196 cases). In addition, the phonological realization of /l/ is conditioned by the grammatical function of the pronoun in which it occurs. As we see in Table 1 (from Sankoff & Cedergren 1971:74), where *il* is impersonal, as in *il pleut* 'it is raining,' or *il y a* 'there is/are,' /l/ is realized as ∅ almost 100% of the time in a [−syll] environment; the personal pronoun is realized as ∅ only 80% of the time in the same environment. The distinction is maintained before vowels, the personal pronoun undergoing less frequent /l/-deletion.

TABLE 1.   *Deletion of /l/ in 'il' for 6 Montrealers according to grammatical category and succeeding phonological environment*

Forms	Environment	
	/___ [−syll]	/___ [+ syll]
il impersonal	97.2% (516)	69.9% (13)
il personal	80.6% (139)	56.3% (183)

Thus though all of these speakers demonstrated variability in their realization of /l/, their behaviour was nonetheless constrained by phonological and grammatical factors. It could be argued that if we were clever enough to think of a few other factors it might be possible to explain away the remaining variation. I would counter that in this case and in many others like it, variability is inherent, and speakers alternate in their use of the two or several alternate forms.

Understanding that, on the one hand, such variability may be maintained even in the most closely and carefully specified phonological and syntactic environments, and that, on the other, it is to some extent constrained by these environments, as shown in the percentages, is central to an understanding of how the 'quantitative paradigm' can be used in the more difficult (when attempted deterministically) case involving non-linguistic environments. Thus though such variability, for some particular linguistic variable, may be characteristic of even a single speaker in a stable situation, within a small segment of connected discourse, it is in fact the case that variation is constrained, again to varying degrees, by social and stylistic factors. With an 'all-or-nothing' mental set, the linguist can be caught in a never-ending search for an ever-vanishing determinacy. The realization that 'languages' are not homogeneous led to an unsuccessful search for homogeneity at the 'dialect,' then the 'idiolect' level (see Bloch 1948, and discussion in Weinreich, Labov & Herzog 1968). If, however, we accept a quantitative analytical method for its demonstrated ability to locate systematicity in terms of purely linguistic environments, its extension to non-linguistic environments becomes a powerful tool for sociolinguistic analysis.

The 'proof' that variable use of a given feature carries social or stylistic meaning need not be in terms of all-or-nothing rules. In fact, since Fischer's (1958) early study showing quantitative variation in the use of *-in* versus *-ing* in the English present participle by a group of New England school children, it has been clear that by aggregating performance data in various ways, regularities and relationships can be determined which are surely part of the competence of normal native speakers, though they are not categorical.

TABLE 2. *Deletion of /l/ by occupation and sex, for 16 individuals (4 per subgroup) and for 8 forms. In general, percentages increase from left to right and from bottom to top*

	Professional		Working class	
Form	Women	Men	Women	Men
il (impersonal)	94.7% (249)	98.5% (340)	100.0% (351)	99.4% (314)
ils	67.7% (242)	88.4% (139)	100.0% (358)	100.0% (330)
il (personal)	54.0% (187)	90.0% (180)	100.0% (353)	100.0% (397)
elle	29.8% (77)	29.7% (47)	74.6% (225)	96.4% (114)
les (pronoun)	16.0% (50)	25.0% (28)	50.0% (46)	78.1% (32)
la (article)	3.8% (314)	15.7% (414)	44.7% (440)	49.2% (378)
la (pronoun)	0.0% (8)	28.5% (7)	33.3% (24)	50.0% (8)
les (article)	5.4% (315)	13.1% (297)	21.7% (326)	34.6% (254)

A further example from our data on /l/-deletion by Montrealers indicates how non-linguistic features can be treated as part of the environment within a quantitative paradigm. Table 2 (from G. Sankoff & Cedergren 1971:82) shows that people differ in systematic ways with respect to their surface deletion of underlying /l/. /l/ deleted in initial position produces examples like these.

(5) [dæ̃: rü] 'dans la rue' (in the street)
(6) [ʃe: sœr] 'chez les soeurs' (at the nuns' place)

The table contains a total of 6844 cases for sixteen speakers subdivided into four groups. For each form *il*, ... , *les*, we find that /l/-deletion follows the order: women professionals < men professionals < women workers < men workers, with only one exception to this for the eight forms considered, women workers > men workers for *il* (impersonal). Again, reading vertically, we see that each subgroup of four individuals maintains a regular order in terms of deletion rates for individual forms. Thus *il* (impersonal) > ... > *les* (article), with only five figures 'out of order.' In fact, this is the same order we obtain from aggregating and averaging the deletion percentages for all sixteen individuals.

This is not to imply, however, that we presume to be discussing four 'dialects,' or that because individuals can be subdivided into groups showing different mean scores for particular speech behaviour, their speech constitutes linguistically valid subgroupings of any sort (see G. Sankoff & Cedergren 1971: section 4.2). What Table 2 shows is that higher rates of /l/-deletion are a tendency characteristic of men and of working class people.

VARIABLE RULES

While tabular displays such as Tables 1 and 2 are illuminating and useful, a true integration of information into competence models has only been achieved through Labov's development of variable rules. Ordinary generative grammars, where deep structure strings and phrase markers are successively transformed by a series of rules into a surface string, allow for some rules to be optional. If a string satisfies the structural conditions of an optional rule, then both application and non-application of the rule are permitted at this stage in the generation of the sentence.

Labov noted that, in a large corpus, the frequency of application of a given optional rule might depend strongly on details of the linguistic context. Thus, of two contexts, both of which satisfy the structural description of an optional rule, one might favour application 80% of the time and the other only 10% of the time, and he proposed that such tendencies be incorporated into the formal statement of the rule. Thus for any optional rule in the grammar for which this information is available, there should be associated with each linguistic context satisfying the structural description of the rule, a number between zero and one, specifying the probability that the rule will apply in this context.

Because of the potentially enormous number of different contexts which might satisfy a given structural description, associating a probability with each one could well be unfeasible. Labov suggested that it suffices to examine a limited number of components of each linguistic context, and calculate a probability based on the independent contributions from each of these components. This would greatly simplify the notation, and if it predicted behaviour well, then it would tell us something about the interaction of syntactic, phonological, etc., contexts, in influencing rule probabilities. Labov proposed one way of doing this, and applied it to his rules for contraction and deletion of the copula and other phonological rules in

TABLE 3. *Frequency of non-contracted copula by preceding and following environment, abstracted from Labov (1969) by Cedergren and D. Sankoff (1974)*

Preceding environment	Succeeding environment			
	__NP	__PA-Loc	__Vb	__gn
Pro__ [−cons]	2/32	1/65	1/34	0/23
Other NP __ [+cons]	22/35	24/32	5/14	1/9
[−cons]	13/64	7/23	2/14	0/6

Black English. The details of his method have been improved by Cedergren and D. Sankoff (1974), and I will briefly sketch their procedure.

The variable rule is written:

$$
\begin{bmatrix} +\text{voc} \\ -\text{str} \\ +\text{cen} \end{bmatrix} \rightarrow \langle \emptyset \rangle \Big/ \genfrac{}{}{0pt}{}{\langle \text{Pro} \rangle}{\langle -\text{cons} \rangle} \quad \#\# \underset{[+T]}{\underline{\quad}} C_0^1 \#\# \left\langle \begin{matrix} \text{Vb} \\ \text{gn} \\ \text{NP} \\ \text{PA-Loc} \end{matrix} \right\rangle .
$$

This means, roughly, that an underlying unstressed central vowel will variably have a zero surface representation, depending on:

(a) whether the preceding noun phrase consists of a pronoun or not;

(b) whether the preceding phonological segment is a consonant or not;

(c) whether the copula is followed by a verb, 'gonna,' a predicate adjective or locative, or a noun phrase.

More precisely, the probability of contraction in an environment $A \#\# \underset{[+T]}{\underline{\quad}} C_0^1 \#\# B$ is given by the formula $1 - (1 - p_0)(1 - \alpha(A))$ $(1 - \beta(A))(1 - \gamma(B))$ where p_0 is an 'input probability' common to all environments, α depends on whether A is a pronoun or not, β depends on whether the final segment in A is $[-\text{cons}]$ or not, and γ depends on the grammatical nature of the constituent B.

The statistical method of maximum likelihood produces the following estimates.

$p_0 = 0.25$
$\alpha(\text{Pro}) = 0.86; \alpha(-\text{Pro}) = 0$
$\beta(+\text{cons}) = 0; \beta(-\text{cons}) = 0.65$
$\gamma(\_\_\text{NP}) = 0.16; \gamma(\_\_\text{PA-Loc}) = 0; \gamma(\_\_\text{Vb}) = 0.49; \gamma(\_\_\text{gn}) = 0.89$

These estimates predict, instead of the figures in Table 3, performance as presented in Table 4.

TABLE 4. *Predictions of non-contracted copula according to estimates of* p_0, α, β, *and* γ

Preceding environment	Succeeding environment			
	__NP	__PA-Loc	__Vb	__gn
Pro__ [−cons]	1/32	2.3/65	0.6/34	0.1/23
Other NP__ [+cons]	21.9/35	24/32	5.3/14	0.8/9
[−cons]	14/64	6/23	1.9/14	0.2/6

The correspondence between Tables 3 and 4 is extremely good, by visual inspection and when measured by chi-square. In this small example, Cedergren and D. Sankoff estimated six parameters (the three zero parameters do not count, since the method always requires one feature in each position to have a zero parameter) instead of twelve separate parameters for twelve contexts. This is not much of a saving, but for more complicated conditioning, the economy of this procedure increases geometrically. In addition, the multiplicative formula which in general is

$$1 - (1\text{-}p_0)\,(1\text{-}\alpha(A))\,(1\text{-}\beta(B)) \ldots (1\text{-}\omega(Z))$$

where A, B, ..., Z are the relevant features present in an environment, implies that these features act independently on the rule probability (see Cedergren & D. Sankoff 1974 for further details). Finally, this procedure extends without any amendment to incorporate features in the non-linguistic environment.

DIFFERENCES FROM THE STANDARD GENERATIVE PARADIGM

Though the ultimate product of the quantitative paradigm is similar to that of generative grammar, i.e., a set of grammatical rules describing competence, the similarity does not go much farther. The quantitative paradigm requires a radically different type of data, involving a deliberate selection of various kinds of informants speaking in a variety of social contexts. There is much less reliance on the major tools of much linguistic analysis, such as introspection and judgments of grammaticality and paraphrase. Labov (1970) and particularly C.-J. N. Bailey (1971) discuss a number of ways in which an approach to linguistic analysis based on the regular structures of variation imbedded in speech communities differs from standard linguistic analysis; for further details see also G. Sankoff (1973).

The scope of the paradigm

Several characteristics of the paradigm need clarification, especially in the light of some recent discussion by scholars who recognize the importance and extent of variability, but who have not incorporated all of the implications of variability into their analyses. One important point has to do with the existence of different *kinds* of linguistic variables. These variables are articulated in different ways with the social structure and the sociolinguistic system of language use of the community, and with the complex processes of linguistic change. A further important issue has to do with the psychological and social reality of variable rules.

TYPES OF LINGUISTIC VARIABLES

In his early studies of a number of different phonological variables both in Martha's Vineyard and in New York City, Labov (1965, 1966) pointed out that the variables in question exhibited very different behaviour with respect to their distribution both socially (among different groups of people) and stylistically (on the intraindividual level). He distinguished between *stereotypes, markers,* and *indicators.* On a synchronic level, these distinctions have to do mainly with the categorical vs. variable nature of the social and stylistic marking involved. Both markers and indicators are variables which seem to be largely out of conscious awareness, but whereas indicators are categorical for a particular group of speakers and do not show stylistic variation, markers are involved in stylistic variables which can 'become the overt topic of social comment, and ... eventually disappear' (ibid.:112). Differential awareness of linguistic variables in Montreal French was found by Laberge and Chiasson-Lavoie (1971).

STRUCTURE OF VARIATION WITHIN A SPEECH COMMUNITY

Some linguistic variables appear to be maintained over long periods of time as a stable system of alternates which may, at one extreme, not be 'noticed' by the community at all (i.e., do not serve any purpose of social or stylistic differentiation), or which may, at the other extreme, serve to categorically mark social or stylistic difference. Between these extremes there is, of course, a range of possibilities, and though some of the particular structures we find may be related to change processes (see the section below on variability and linguistic change), synchronic data can tell us much about the nature of the linguistic marking of social and stylistic differences within a community.

A particular rule may be categorical for one person, optional for another. If we are prepared to admit that the *nature* of distributions is important, we will see that for some variables, speakers are clustered around a relatively small range of values, whereas for others, the distribution is much more spread. This may also be the case with respect to particular environments for a single rule. In one environment, speakers may be clustered about a relatively small range of values (not necessarily 0 or 1, for a variable with two alternatives); in another environment, they may display a much greater range of values.

Further data from our work on /l/-deletion in Montreal will illustrate the point that real, socially meaningful differences between individuals or groups of individuals are very often differences of degree, rather than categorical differences. In this regard, let us examine individually the speech of the 16 Montrealers of Table 2 with respect to their deletion of /l/ in the personal pronouns *il* and *elle* and in the articles *la* and *les*. (The masculine singular article *le* does not undergo /l/-deletion; it is the schwa which is lost in rapid speech [Picard 1972]). Fig. 1 shows that 10 of the 16 individuals had a categorical deletion rule for *il* (these were the people not included in Table 1), that two people had a categorical rule for *elle*, showing 100% deletion, and that one had a categorical rule for *les*, showing no deletion. Everyone exhibited variable /l/-deletion for *la*, as did most people for *elle* and *les*. It is abundantly clear, however, that despite the relative lack of all-or-nothing behaviour, people do differ in systematic ways with respect to their *proportion* of deletion. Working class people show generally higher deletion proportions for each form, yet there appears no clear break between them and the professionals; it is clear that there are not two (or sixteen!) 'dialects' with respect to this variable. For all forms except *il*, people are distributed very evenly along the continuum, and most individuals tend to follow the order *il* > *elle* > *la* > *les* in terms of their relative proportions of deletion. Though the few people at the top and at the bottom of the continuum for each form tend to be the same ones (linked by straight lines in Fig. 1), some crossing over is already evident (e.g., number 16 exhibits the lowest deletion for *il*, *elle*, and *la*, but is only the third lowest for *les*), and more crossing over would be shown were all individuals indicated.

/l/-deletion is a complex phenomenon and we are unable to say for sure at present what is happening with respect to change, though analysis of our full sample, with careful age distributions of speakers, will probably clarify this. There has been a tendency historically in French toward loss of /l/ in a number of environments, with deletion of final /l/ in *il* documented several centuries ago, and in *elle* indicated for the early twentieth century in France. It appears possible that the rule has gone to completion for *il* in Montreal, and that the minority of speakers who do not delete 100% result from a long-standing hypercorrective tendency. It also appears that the rule has been extended to apply to *elle*, categorically for some speakers, and to initial

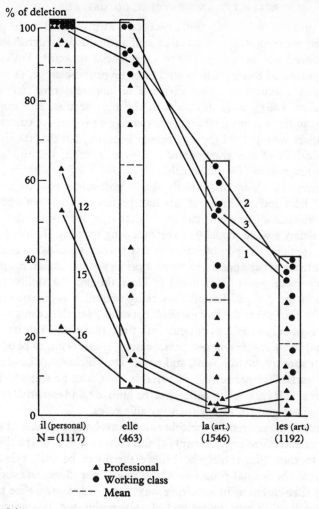

Fig. 1. /l/-deletion percentages for 16 subjects on 4 forms. Percentages for subjects 1, 2, 3, 12, 15, 16 on each form are linked by straight lines. Other subjects are not joined because crossing of lines obscures the patterns for each form.

environments for *la* and *les*. Though the fate of this change is presently unclear, it is obvious that varying /l/-deletion rates are of current social significance in differentiating speakers. The regularity in the relative frequencies for each form, as well as the ordering of individuals, indicates that relative proportions can be structured in an orderly way, imbedded in the social structure of the community.

VARIABILITY AND PSYCHOLOGICAL REALITY

Relative proportions of rule application can, as illustrated in the previous section, be incorporated into social as well as linguistic structure, and distinctions need not be categorical to carry social meaning. Powerful use has been made of this notion in studies of linguistic change, especially in interpreting a synchronic slice in terms of 'apparent time' (cf. Hockett 1950; Labov 1965), as is discussed in the next section. It is important, therefore, to show that variability is not *merely* a property of communities, or an important aspect of the way change operates, but that it exists as an ordinary aspect of the grammar of single individuals, i.e., to clarify the psychological reality of variable rules.

Bickerton (1971), in his analysis of the 'post-creole continuum' in the speech of East Indian Guyanese, has interpreted variability in a particular rule as evidence of ongoing change in that rule over time, according to C.-J. N. Bailey's wave model (see the following section). He has, however, taken the option left open by Bailey in any particular analysis, and set out to demonstrate what appears to be an a priori assumption on his part that variability is in general infelicitous. Thus though variability must be admitted in the data, Bickerton, in seeking to limit it as much as possible, attempts to prove that for any particular speaker, variability in a particular rule can exist only in one environment at a time, that after a rule has become categorical for a speaker in one environment, it can begin to be optionally applied in another environment, and so on. Thus Bickerton's basic mistrust is not of variability per se, but of variable *rules*, and he states in the first part of his article (p. 460) his belief that the human mind essentially operates in terms of cat_gorical, rather than variable rules.

Bickerton characterizes a variable rule as involving a statement such as: 'When you recognize environment X, use feature Y Z% of the time,' and goes on to state that those who believe there can be such rules should demonstrate the mental processes which must exist to mediate such rules. He notes that children, in acquiring language, tend to generalize rules for things like English past tenses and plurals, noting the 'exceptions' later. In fact it may well be that part of becoming a normal native speaker, rather than continuing to sound like a child or a foreigner, consists of learning how to use variable rules, thereby replacing some of an earlier set of categorical rules by the more usual and normal variable rules. Slobin, for example, has noted (personal communication) that children tend to use full forms much more frequently than do adults in utterances which can be realized as either full or contracted forms. The argument really depends on whether or not one believes that degrees of variability can be processed by the human brain, and in the absence of evidence that it can only work in all-or-nothing terms, I do not see why we would want to assume that this is the case. In the light of abundant evidence given in Labov (1965, 1966) about the different kinds of variables that can exist, in terms of their perception by hearers as well as their production by speakers, it appears that human beings can indeed process and deal with this kind of variation.

Bickerton interestingly and convincingly analyzes change in the 'preinfinitival complementizers *fu* (or *fi*) and *tu*' in the 'creole speech continuum of Guyana' (p. 462). Rather than halting the search for relevant environments on the phonological or lexical-morphological levels, he finds that a semantic–syntactic distinction provides an important environment for constraining the choice of F (*fu* or *fi*) or T (*tu*) by the speakers he studied. Thus he establishes three categories: I. inceptives; II. desideratives and other 'psychological' verbs; III. non-inceptives/non-desideratives. His analysis that replacement of T by F proceeds from environment III, through II, to I for any speaker, is convincing. But to insist that variation can only occur for a particular speaker in one environment at a time seems unnecessary, and unwarranted by his data, especially if the implication is that this result casts serious doubt on variable rules as a principle.[3]

To argue that the normal, natural use of human language involves inherent variability, and that the human mind is perfectly capable of handling this, does not mean that the linguist should abandon his search to locate relevant environments which will further clarify the way a rule operates, but this is as applicable to a variable rule model as to any other model. Indeed, within the framework proposed by Cedergren and D. Sankoff (1974) for dealing with variable rules, not only is it possible to further specify environments without altering the fundamental nature of a particular rule, but the predictions may provide a check on whether relevant environments have been excluded (Cedergren 1973).

A complementizer example from Montreal French demonstrates that while variability can indeed occur in more than one environment (even for one speaker), this does not necessarily detract from the systematicity of the processes involved. It will be apparent that a further objection of Bickerton, which I will call the 'grouping problem' (see the section of that title below), can be dealt with appropriately in terms of the kind of variable rule model I have adopted.

The case in point has to do with the deletion of complementizer *que* by the same sixteen speakers who were discussed with respect to /l/-deletion (G. Sankoff, Sarrasin & Cedergren 1971). Here again, it is the phonological environment which is important, and the dominant process seems to be one of consonant cluster simplification. (Grammatical and phonological features interact in the deletion of *que* as a relative marker; cf. Sankoff 1973). Two examples of complementizer *que* present and deleted, taken from our taped interviews, are as follows:

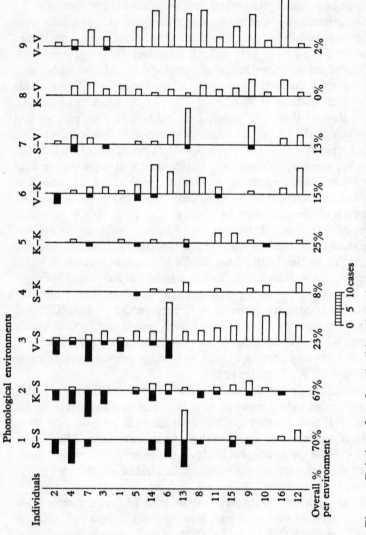

Fig. 2. Deletion of *que* for 16 subjects in 9 phonological environments. Black bars on the left represent *que* absent; white bars on the right represent *que* present.

$$S = \begin{bmatrix} +sib \\ -sib \end{bmatrix}; K = \begin{bmatrix} +cons \\ -sib \end{bmatrix}; V = [-cons].$$

(7) A l'école on nous enseignait *que* les protestants c'est des pas bons. 'At school they taught us that the Protestants are no good.' (Subject no. 12)

(8) Le séparatisme. Au début je pense ⊘ ça a été plutôt un snobisme. 'Separatism. At the beginning I think it was more a kind of snobbery.' (Subject no. 14)

A series of phonological environments relevant to the deletion of *que* are displayed as Fig. 2. It is clear that though more than half of the individuals display variability in more than one environment, deletion decreases fairly regularly for all the individuals from environments 1 through 9, with only one person exhibiting no deletion in any environment. Of the nine people who exhibit variability in more than one environment, virtually all show greater proportions of deletion in the environments closer to the left side of the figure. Deletion proportions tend to follow the order of environments such that $1 > 2 > \ldots > 9$. Environments scale in more or less the same order when we average all 16 individuals' deletion proportions

TABLE 5. *Percentage of deleted 'que' in 3 environments for 16 individuals*

	Environment				
Individual	I (1, 2 of Fig. 2) %	II (3–6 of Fig. 2) %	III (7–9 of Fig. 2) %	Overall deletion %	N
2	100	87.5	0	82.4	17
4	91.7	25.0	27.5	55.5	27
7	100	66.7	0	53.1	32
3	100	16.7	28.5	41.2	17
1	–	50.0	0	33.3	9
5	50.0	40.0	0	23.3	21
14	75.0	12.5	0	21.6	37
6	75.0	25.0	0	21.0	53
13	44.4	8.3	4.4	18.9	53
8	100	0	0	12.0	25
11	50.0	9.1	0	11.1	18
15	40.0	0	0	9.5	21
9	40.0	0	4.6	7.7	39
10	0	9.1	0	6.7	15
16	50.0	0	0	2.9	35
12	0	0	0	0	25
Overall deletion	68.5%	19.2%	4.0%	23.0%	
N	89	177	178		444

for each environment (except for fluctuation due to low numbers in environments 4 and 8). Individuals are ordered in Fig. 2 according to their overall deletion frequencies, which range from 0 to 82.4%.

Table 5 regroups the data of Fig. 2 in terms of proportions. In all cases where individuals had variable *que* in environments I and II, their proportion of deletion was much higher in environment I than in environment II. There were only four individuals who had any deletion at all in environment III (three cases for no. 4; two cases for no. 3; and one case each for nos. 9 and 13), and though three of them had slightly higher percentages in environment III than in environment II, this can be seen in terms of statistical fluctuation in a variable rule model.

The fact that more than half of the speakers in our sample exhibited variable *que* deletion in more than one of the nine closely distinguished environments of Fig. 2, and that these environments can be ordered in terms of *proportions* of deletion – proportions which hold up remarkably well for individual speakers as well as on the average – would appear to indicate that these speakers have no trouble in consistently producing regularly variable behaviour in specific environments. In the absence of any sound psychological evidence as to why people should *not* be able to produce such behaviour, I suggest that it be accepted as it stands.

VARIABILITY AND LINGUISTIC CHANGE

Since most of our data on communities so far studied in great detail (i.e., taking account of the structure of linguistic variability within the social and cultural structure of the community) is synchronic rather than diachronic (a few exceptions are noted in Weinreich, Labov & Herzog 1968), inferences with respect to change must generally be based on the distribution of the value of particular variables within the population sampled at one particular point in time. In the simplest case, the proportion of occurrence of some variant of a particular variable is correlated with age. More often the age distribution is complicated by the fact that changes follow more complex sorts of social boundaries within a community or society. A change may originate in a particular class, or ethnic or occupational group, and spread from there to other groups in one subgroup of a population, whereas it has barely begun in another segment. In most communities it appears that almost any division existing within the population which has any kind of social significance is somehow reflected in the linguistic behaviour of that community, and changes in progress do not operate without regard for these existing differences.

Cedergren (1972) has quantitatively documented in detail a number of phonological changes in the Spanish of Panama City, changes originating in various subsegments of the population and being differentially involved with, and at present at different stages of, the change process. Labov's work in both Martha's Vineyard and New York also contains several examples of the complex quantitative interrelationships between social groups and subgroups and phonological changes in progress. Labov (1965) and Weinreich, Labov & Herzog (1968) set forth a series of possible stages for the interrelationships of ongoing changes to social groups and processes.

C.-J.N. Bailey (1969–70; 1970) has produced a dynamic, or wave, model for linguistic change (diffusion) which incorporates a number of the kinds of variation mentioned above. Of particular importance in his work is the idea that a rule, which may change 'from variable to categorical or from one environment to the next . . . initially operates variably . . . in each successive environment or situation in which it operates' (1970:178). There are, however, two possibilities in the further changes to the rule, according to Bailey. Either 'variability ceases in one environment before going on to another' or the rule is variable in more than one environment at a time, with the proportion of application of the rule in the two or more environments in question indicating the progression of the rule.

An example which demonstrates the significance of proportions in the analysis of linguistic change in progress is drawn from data on New Guinea Tok Pisin collected by Suzanne Laberge and myself during June–August 1971. A guiding hypothesis of this study was that native speakers (most of whom are under twenty) would show different competence in the language than even fluent non-native speakers. We made a number of tape recordings of families who use Tok Pisin in everyday communication, but for whom Tok Pisin is the native language of the children only. The decade of the 1960s was probably the first to see significant numbers of native speakers, though Tok Pisin has existed for a hundred years or so as a second-language lingua franca in New Guinea.

In a study of some of the speakers in this corpus (G. Sankoff & Laberge 1973), we found evidence to support the hypothesis that the adverb *baimbai* has been reduced to *bai*, and that it is being increasingly treated like an obligatory future tense marker rather than an optional adverbial indicator of future time. Of a total of 395 cases for eighteen speakers (nine children between the ages of five and seventeen; nine adults, parents of seven of the children, between the ages of approximately twenty-five and forty-five, all of whom use Tok Pisin as the normal medium of communication in the family), there are only five instances of *baimbai*, pronounced [bə'mbai] or [bə'bai]. *Baimbai* occurred in the speech of three of the nine adults in our sample; there were no instances in the speech of any of the nine children.

Table 6 shows the results of tabulating the stress level for all cases of *baimbai* and *bai* in our sample. *(Bai)mbai* never receives primary stress in a

TABLE 6.   *Differential stress of 'bai' for 9 children (native speakers) and 9 adults (non-native speakers)*

Stress level	Children %	Adults %
2	29.1	51.7
3	60.4	47.3
4	10.4	1.0
N	(192)	(203)

sentence, but it frequently receives secondary stress (analogous to stressed syllables in nouns or pronouns), and tertiary stress, equivalent to 'unstressed' syllables in nouns or adjectives, or to most prepositions. The fourth stress level involves a reduction of the vowel nucleus to [ə], or even its disappearance, so that *bai* is barely, if at all, distinguishable as a syllable, the only audible indication of its presence being [b]. Examples of each of these levels are as follows:

$$\overset{3}{Em}\ \overset{2}{bai}\ \overset{2}{yu}\ \overset{1}{kam,}\ \overset{2}{bai}\ \overset{2}{yu}\ \overset{1}{dai.}$$
(9) Em bai yu kam, bai yu dai. 'You come; you'll die.' (Mrs T.)

(10) Ating bai klostu belo. 'It must be nearly noon.' (Mrs D.)

(11) Suga bilong mi klostu bai [bə] finis nau. 'My sugar cane is nearly finished now.' (C.W.)

The cases of stress level 4, though not exhibited by every speaker, are interesting in that stress level 4 was found for six of the nine children, but for only two of the nine adults. In addition, Fig. 3 shows that the differences between children and adults are not mere artifacts of aggregating cases; when we calculate the percentage of level 2 stress for each speaker, we find that there is minimal overlap between children's and adults' ranges. Thus four of the nine children and two of the nine adults have between 35% and 43% of *bai* in their speech receiving secondary stress. The five other children fall below 35%; the seven other adults above 43%. Fig. 3 also indicates some correlation of the percentage of secondary stress with age for these speakers, and it is probable that native speakers are simply carrying further a trend in the reduction of *(bai)mbai*. Although all speakers vary the stress they give to *bai*, it is clear that for the children in the sample, there is a tendency to place a lesser stress on *bai*. As we have argued, this is partial evidence for a change from adverb to tense marker for *baimbai*.

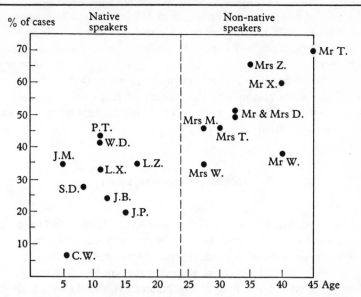

Fig. 3. Percentage of cases of *bai* showing secondary stress for 9 children and 9 adults. Last initials identify members of the same families.

Though not many languages are presently undergoing a change toward being, for the first time, native languages, the kinds of intergenerational differences observable among these speakers can be seen in other speech communities, and differences among groups need not be categorical to be significant. Even in this case, where change would be expected to be more rapid and dramatic than in most situations, change occurs by degrees, and intelligibility is preserved among the different groups of speakers. Native speakers of Tok Pisin exhibit more morphophonological reduction than non-native speakers, yet this does not mean that the two groups cannot understand one another.

It is probably completely out of the awareness of members of the Tok Pisin speech community today that its younger members exhibit less stress in their pronunciation of *bai*, and that they no longer seem to use *baimbai* at all. Yet adults do say that children speak the language very fluently and rapidly. They also freely admit that there are differences in competence among speakers of Tok Pisin, that rural people who have not been exposed to Tok Pisin at home, and who have recently arrived in town, do not speak as fluently as the urbanites. Town dwellers said that for their children Tok Pisin was a native language. They do not need to be aware of, and able to state, precise features which vary, to be able to observe that there are differences between the way they and their children speak, or between the way they and the newly arrived speak. Nor do people need to be assumed to have some kind of mechanical device clicking away in their heads keeping track of percentages in order to exhibit regularly variable behaviour. It appears (see, for example, Labov 1966 Part III) that people may often perceive behaviour in ways that are more categorical than the behaviour itself. This is one reason why the validity of linguists' judgments of unrecorded speech behaviour, as well as the unsystematic citing of examples, is so open to question.

Approaches to heterogeneity

SCALING

Since the insightful paper of Elliot, Legum & Thompson (1969), it has become fashionable to describe variability in terms of Guttman scales. Not only grammars of individual community members, but also styles, regional dialects, and historical stages of the same dialect can be scaled. DeCamp, as one of the first to experiment extensively with scaling, has pointed out their theoretical power in dealing with problems of rule ordering (1971).

There is no doubt that such scales, where they exist, are interesting and useful (see, Bickerton 1971; Day 1971; Labov 1971; C.-J.N. Bailey 1972; Ross, 1972, 1973 in addition to DeCamp 1971). It is, however, important to notice that in its strong form, scaling can be used as a last-ditch, wheels-within-wheels attempt to account for variation without changing the deterministic assumptions of the traditional generative paradigm. The underlying hypothesis here is that the heterogeneity in a community is due to the fact that it comprises a whole range of individual grammars which can be linearly arranged so that each one differs slightly, but categorically, from its neighbours on either side.

My critique of an over-reliance on scaling as the main way of 'explaining' (away) variability is both theoretical and methodological. On the theoretical level, there is no reason for whole individual grammars to be scalable except for special cases where political, geographical, and social factors all affect language in a coincidental way over time. This would be confined to certain highly polarized social systems, perhaps including the post-creole continuum, or to a chain of dialects along a river valley or some other linear configuration, or to a pattern of change emanating for a long historical period from a single metropolitan focus, each change affecting distant points in order of their proximity to the centre.

This type of special configuration is only *necessary* for scaling; it is not sufficient. Other conditions are also required, such as that all changes, innovations, pressures, etc., must emanate from one or other end of the linear configuration. When a non-end point becomes the focus of a change, this tends to destroy scaling. In general, as in Bailey's wave model, where the geography offers more than one dimension of change and influence, where the social stratification is not necessarily correlated with geography, where historical change may be reversible, there is no reason to expect one-dimensional scaling. Well known phenomena such as middle-class hypercorrection of conscious variables, multiple geographic foci of innovations, and age group specific usages are all incompatible with simple scaling.

Cedergren's (1972) analysis of the complex of linguistic constraints and social factors affecting a series of phonological variables in Panamanian Spanish is instructive here. Different phonological variables are differently affected by the factors of age, sex, class, and rural vs. urban origin, as well as being differently involved in stylistic marking. For example, a rule involving velarization of /n/ is favoured by younger speakers in formal styles within Panama City, but appears to have originated with non-city-born speakers. A lenition rule for /č/ also favoured by younger speakers in formal styles, is especially characteristic of women, and originated with city-born speakers. It is clear that though speakers may be scalable in one way for a particular variable, scaling on another variable will not always result in the same ordering of speakers.

On the methodological side, as mentioned in the section on varability and psychological reality above, the strong categorical view of scaling almost inevitably produces some amount of 'error' which it seems preferable to regard as normal statistical fluctuation. The more data are added, the more likely one is to run into 'exceptions' to categorical scale types. On the other hand, a somewhat weaker view of scaling such as that proposed by DeCamp (1973) may be able to nicely incorporate 'more or less' notions to replace 'all or nothing' postulates, with consequent benefit to the analysis. Otherwise we may be lost in a never-ending cycle of finding variability in previously categorical environments, and of searching for categorical environments to explain away variability.

THE GROUPING PROBLEM

Once we have accepted that people's speech differs both from the speech of others and from their own speech at other times, and that the ways in which they differ may be more a question of relative presence of some feature, rather than its total presence or absence, we must face the grouping problem. That is, how we decide on the status of variants, whether social (groups of people; 'styles') or linguistic (groups of speech variables).

For grouping to be other than arbitrary, especially in a situation of extreme variability, it is essential to attempt to follow procedures of description and analysis which will clearly indicate the kinds of systems which obtain. There are basically two ways of doing this: first, one can define a grid of some sort beforehand, whether in terms of groups of people defined on the basis of social characteristics, or of particular occasions on which people would generally be likely to exhibit more or less formal behaviour, or even in terms of categorical grammars of two or three speech varieties, gradations between which will be seen as some sort of mixture. Second, an alternate method is to examine the linguistic variation as the main object of study and try to use its internal structure as discovered, to map or group the non-linguistic variables. There are some obvious advantages and disadvantages to both methods, and in dealing with each of these in turn, I will attempt to clarify these are precisely as possible. Essentially, the difference is between trying to fit linguistic data to non-linguistic data, or vice versa.

The methods developed by Labov to deal with variability grew out of a realization that at no level, whether that of the language, the dialect, the idiolect, the style or register, or whatever, could homogeneity be found in speech. Most of his published work demonstrates a particular way of dealing with this problem, involving the selection of a number of non-linguistic variables which can be shown to influence speech, the segmentation of each variable (or sometimes an index derived from combining variables), and the demonstration that grouping non-linguistic variables according to this segmentation results in different configurations of speech (usually means or averages) for each defined segment.

Examples of this technique can be found in the New York City study (1966) where a combination of socioeconomic variables was used in the construction of a nine-segment index for 'class,' and individuals grouped according to it could be shown to display different speech behaviour; if performance was averaged for a particular variable, the different subgroups of people showed different behaviour which was, nevertheless, regular. Groups tended to show progressively higher or lower scores on a particular variable according to a well defined pattern, deviant groups (the hypercorrecting lower middle class) could be defined, etc. Similarly for five (mainly) non-linguistically defined points on a stylistic continuum of 'formality,' Labov was able to show systematic differences in behaviour. In other cases, he has used more 'emically' valid grouping procedures, and given mean scores for actually existing groups on particular variables, for example, in the studies of various peer groups in Harlem (Labov *et al.* 1968; Labov 1973).

In choosing to work within this framework, Labov has made the same choice as a number of other sociolinguists, that of using socially or culturally valid units as a basic framework for analysis, and attempting to investigate the way the linguistic behaviour patterns itself according to such categories. In somewhat the same vein, Gumperz chooses to work within the general framework of the 'speech community' rather than the 'language' (the former presumably has some social validity whereas with the latter one is faced with most difficult problems of definition), partly because local varieties and 'dialects' can often be linguistically quite far from 'standards' (see also Hymes 1968; G. Sankoff 1969 on boundaries). Many other scholars have attempted to define the kinds of linguistic behaviour appropriate to (or usually observed in) named (by the community in question) linguistic varieties or speech events (see. B. L. Bailey 1971).

There remains the objection that groupings of linguistic behaviour based on non-linguistic criteria will be in some sense arbitrary. DeCamp for example states (1971:355) that

A linguistic geographer would be properly horrified at the following suggestion: Let us use state boundaries as preconceived pigeonholes for sorting the data from an American linguistic atlas, and then merely indicate the percentage of New York State informants who say *pail* as opposed to *bucket*, the equivalent percentage for Pennsylvanians, for Virginians, etc. ... Why, then, have sociolinguists so often correlated their linguistic data to preconceived categories of age, income, education, etc., instead of correlating these non-linguistic variables *to* the linguistic data?

The reason, I think, lies on the one hand in the desire of sociolinguists for their results to have some sociocultural validity, and to attempt to define categories which are socially meaningful to the people whose linguistic behaviour is being investigated, and on the other from the realization that variation will not be eliminated completely, no matter what categories are defined. In other words, sociolinguists who start by defining categories based on social or cultural criteria are not doing so to be arbitrary, but so that their results will correspond to socially or culturally meaningful categories. There are, of course, two principal ways one can do this: proceding by either 'etic' or 'emic' categories. With the variable 'age,' for example, one could in adopting the view that age might be important as a variable differentiating speech, proceed by cutting the sample into regular age categories: 0–9, 10–19, . . . , 90–99 ('etic' procedure); or one could find out how the people themselves define various age groups; e.g., 'infants' might be from 0 to 2, 'children' from 3 to 11, 'adolescents' from 12 to 17, 'young adults' from 18 to 30, and so on. Similarly one could group people according to years of formal education, or according to labelled categories with presumably some cultural meaning (e.g., one can be a 'high school dropout' having completed anywhere from seven to twelve years of schooling). Another example involving grouping kinds of behaviour rather than people would involve the difference between the analyst creating an index of formality using a number of criteria defined by him, vs. examining the differences between behaviours according to labelled speech events, e.g., 'rap session,' 'seminar,' 'lecture.' The difference between using one or the other kind of non-linguistic category can be debated; it is often necessary to use both kinds.

I submit, however, that the dialect geographer would not be horrified, properly or otherwise, at the suggestion that one use the political boundary between Italy and France as a convenient location for the dialect atlas of Italy to stop and that of France to begin, nor at the suggestion that one can find speech patterns specific to 'estate labourers' by investigating the population of Jamaicans who work as employees of sugar estates, as opposed, for example, to 'peasant farmers' (DeCamp 1971). The fact that ten-year-olds may share a feature or rule with fifty-year-olds (or shopkeepers with estate labourers, or high school dropouts with lawyers, or the 'rap session' situation with the 'formal lecture' situation) does not necessarily invalidate using such criteria to investigate speech differences. If it is the case that a particular non-linguistic variable has no relevance, no effect, in defining the distribution of a linguistic variable, then one of course discards it. Certainly anyone would object to the use of arbitrary criteria (as well as to gross or infelicitous ones), especially when it can be shown that there are much better ones available (a mountain range may be a more effective boundary than a state boundary, except for cases like the Berlin wall), and anyone trying to use extralinguistic criteria must display intelligence, sensitivity, and intuition in experimenting with such criteria, as well as an awareness of the importance of linguistic criteria.

One further basically cultural category is that of labelled languages or language varieties. What the community refers to as different speech varieties (particularly in the case of non-standard varieties) may show some rules in common with each other, some rules categorically different, some rules variably different, and so on.

The second major kind of approach one can use is to try to match the non-linguistic behaviour to the linguistic behaviour. For example, in the case of a variable discussed earlier, rather than trying to see how /l/ behaves according to various sociocultural categories, we might take all the realizations as /l/ and observe where they occur; similarly with all the realizations as ∅. But unless we are prepared to look at proportions, we will find no constraints for forms like *elle* and *la*. If we examine all the cases where /l/ appears as [1], we will find that higher proportions of them occur after consonants, before vowels, and out of the mouths of women and professionals.

It appears that with either approach, one is involved methodologically in a process of testing, of going back and forth between linguistic and non-linguistic features, retaining in one's analysis those which best account for the linguistic data under consideration.

In a new mathematical framework for dealing with variable rules, Cedergren and D. Sankoff have made a number of proposals which make it possible to eliminate some of the problems associated with grouping and with the choice of constraints. Rather than seeing non-linguistic variables as necessarily defining different discrete groupings, it is possible to see them as environments which define continua, which make it possible to deal separately with individuals if it seems advisable to do so, and to follow the kinds of groupings which come most naturally out of the linguistic data. The variable parameters attached to rules can apply to communities or to individuals, and can also take account of situational variability.

Discussion

The object of this paper has been to describe and illustrate a theoretical standpoint and a set of procedures for the study of communicative competence within a speech community perspective, and as part of a quantitative paradigm. A central motivation has been the attempt to systematically and rigorously relate linguistic performance to competence. Performance data consist, in the studies considered here, of large bodies of recorded speech of samples of the members of particular communities in a variety of speech situations. The problem is to infer the competence of these people, given the fact that, like any other behavioural data, speech performance data will contain statistical fluctuation. My position has been that statistically fluctuating performance data need not be interpreted as reflecting underlying competence which is categorical in nature, and that a paradigm which represents competence as containing some probabilistic and non-deterministic components is a better approximation to linguistic reality than one which insists on categoriality and determinacy. Note that this does *not* imply the non-existence of categorical rules, but simply the existence as well of probabilistic rules.

Such an assumption does not counter the principle that (socio)linguistic competence is what exists in people's heads; rather, it takes the position that people can internalize rules which are not categorical.

The first kind of situation in which this principle can be seen to operate is the case of purely linguistic constraints on the operation of a rule for a particular speaker. Thus we saw in Fig. 2 that subject no. 6 deletes *que* categorically in environment S–S, deletes approximately 50% in environment K–S, approximately 30% in environment V–S, and o in all other environments. This statistically variable performance we interpret as reflecting an underlying different *probability* of deletion for the various environments for this particular speaker which ranges from 100% in one environment to 0 in another set of environments, and which differs *in terms of degree* in intervening environments. Speaker no. 6 may have a probability of, say 0.4 or 0.6 in environment K–S which was realized in behaviour in the cases we observed as 0.5; similarly, in environment V–S her probability may be 0.25 or 0.36. The important point is that when we observe a sufficient number of cases for a particular speaker, we can assume that relative differences count for something, that competence need not fall into only three boxes: '0,' 'variable,' and '1.'

I have tried to refute a frequent criticism of the early work on variable rules: that statistical tendencies on the level of the community reflect only a mixture of different categorical grammars for different speakers. Our *que* example, the /l/ example, the *bai* example, and a number of examples studied by Cedergren (1972) show that statistical tendencies on the community level are reflections of statistical tendencies at the level of each individual.

If we accept that there can be significant differences of degree in particular linguistic environments, we can extend this principle in two important ways: (1) to apply to extralinguistic environments, including things like degrees of formality, particular speech situations or topics, or emotive or expressive marking (few examples of this have been cited in this paper as we have not yet completed the analysis of any such cases in our own data; however examples can be found in Labov 1966, 1969; Brunel 1970); and (2) to say something about the differences between speakers or groups of speakers. Whereas the first aspect of difference (non-linguistic constraints on a rule) can be built into a rule as part of the conditioning on that rule (see Cedergren & D. Sankoff 1974), the second (difference between speakers) is of course *not* part of a speaker's competence, though it can still be incorporated into a variable rule model in terms of different *input probabilities* for different kinds of speakers. Several examples have been cited from our own work in New Guinea and Montreal of how differences between individuals or groups of speakers can be significant in terms of proportions of occurrences of particular rules (e.g., applying less than secondary stress to *bai* in New Guinea Tok Pisin), rather than total presence or absence of a particular rule.

If we look at sociolinguistics from the broad perspective sketched by Hymes in 1962, where the linguistic resources of a community were viewed as means, articulated within its total communicative structure, the work outlined in this paper can be seen as an attempt to investigate the nature and distribution of these means within particular communities. Indeed, as soon as we stop talking about 'a language' in an abstract and ill defined way and begin looking at what actually goes on in the speech community, we find that the distribution of these means, of features and rules, across situations and across individuals, is structured in non-trivial and investigable ways.[4]

APPENDIX

Phonetic symbols
 phonetic brackets [ ]
 phonetic symbols ɛ æ ü œ ʃ

Feature notation
 [-syll]   consonant or glide
 [+syll]   vowel
 [cons]   consonantal
 [voc]   vocalic
 [str]   stressed
 [cen]   central
 [+T]   type or tense marker

Other symbols used in variable rules
 NP   noun phrase
 PA-Loc   predicate adjective or locative
 Vb   verb
 #gn   'gonna'
 Pro   pronoun (note that subject pronouns always end in a vowel
        segment)
 ⟨ ⟩   elements within angle brackets are variably present
 $p, \alpha, \beta, \gamma, \omega$ probabilities affecting the variable rule
 C_0^1 zero or one consonant segment
 ##   word boundary

LANGUAGE IDENTITY OF THE
COLOMBIAN VAUPÉS INDIANS

JEAN JACKSON

In the Vaupés territory of southeastern Colombia[1] are over twenty exogamous patrilineal descent units, each of which is identified with a distinct language. In the literature on the Vaupés, these units have always been called 'tribes.' Although no single generally accepted definition of tribe exists,[2] those most frequently offered in the literature are concerned with the presence of factors such as (1) tribal territory; (2) political, ceremonial, or warrior roles as tribesmen; (3) more intra-tribal as opposed to intertribal interaction; (4) some proportion of marriages occurring within the tribal unit; and (5) some cultural differences between neighboring tribes. None of the definitions utilizing these factors permits calling the Vaupés units tribes; at present these units mainly function as marriage classes, even though they are each identified with different languages. Hence, thinking of them as tribes is misleading and in this paper they are called 'language-aggregates.'

This paper is concerned with the role language plays in the Vaupés as a symbol of membership in a language-aggregate, and with the relationship between language and Vaupés social structure. The first section gives a brief ethnographic introduction and description of Vaupés multilingualism. The second section analyzes Vaupés languages as emblems of the language-aggregates and as badges of identity for individual Indians. Finally, some ways in which the Vaupés data apply to some of the current issues on sociolinguistics and the ethnography of speaking are suggested.

Vaupés multilingualism: ethnographic background

The Vaupés is in tropical rainforest and is known for its treacherous, rapids-filled rivers. Travel and transportation are by dugout canoe or jungle trail. All Indian settlements are on or near rivers, and all Indians except the nomadic Makú (who are not considered in this paper) are excellent rivermen. Indians are semi-sedentary swidden horticulturalists, the women growing bitter manioc and other crops, and the men hunting and fishing. Multifamily longhouses are the traditional units of settle-

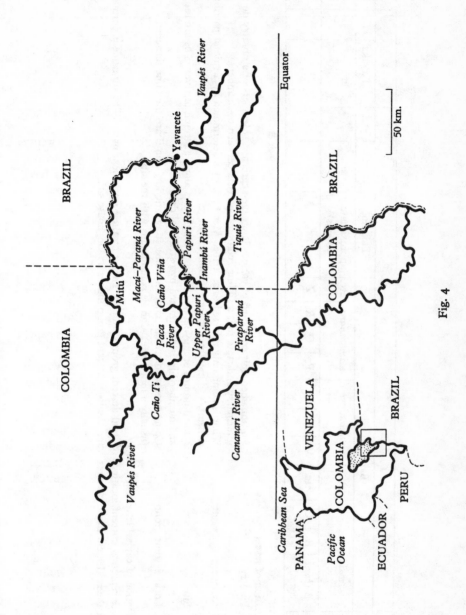

Fig. 4

	I								2		3
			Bará								
								Tukano	Yurutí,	etc.	Tuyuka	etc.	etc.
I											
II		*vaí maha*		*vaiñakörou*		*wamutañara*	etc.	(approximately 30 sibs)	etc.	etc.	etc.
III											
IV	A *(bará yóara)*	B	C	etc.	M	N	O	P	Q	R	Z

Explanation of levels

I. Phratry — An unnamed unit composed of various language-aggregates. Members of a phratry do not intermarry and state that a sibling relationship exists between co-members.

II. Language-aggregate — What is commonly referred to as 'tribe.' Membership is determined by a rule of patrilineal descent, and members share a 'father-language.'

III. Sib — Named groups occupying one or more longhouses along a stretch of river. Sibs are ranked, and membership is determined by patrilineal descent.

IV. Local descent group — Co-agnates who are one another's closest agnatic kin who share the same settlement (usually a longhouse). Can be coterminous with the sib.

Explanation of capital letters in level IV

These represent current locations of local descent groups who are known by their settlement name. The sib name is permanent, but the settlement name changes when the local descent group moves its longhouse site.

Fig. 5

ment, and are from two hours to a day's travel apart. Residence is patrilocal, with from four to eight nuclear families inhabiting a long-house.[3]

Vaupés social structure is segmentary, and follows a rule of patrilineal descent (see Fig. 5). Its units, in ascending order of inclusion, are the local descent group, the sib, the language-aggregate, and the phratry. The unit we are concerned with, the language-aggregate, is a named patrilineal descent unit identified with a specific language (henceforth its 'father-language'), the members of which: (1) observe a rule of exogamy, (2) terminologically distinguish agnates from other kinsmen, and (3) identify with co-members as 'brother-people.' Membership is permanent and public; the one fact which will be known about an Indian before anything else will be his language-aggregate membership. If he marries a woman from far away, this is often the only information some of his relatives will have about her.

It should be stressed that Vaupés language-aggregates do not occupy discrete territories (see Fig. 6). Nor are language-aggregates corporate groups in any sense. The vast majority of interaction situations occur between Indians of more than one language-aggregate. Furthermore, all Vaupés Indians, regardless of their language-aggregate membership, share a strikingly homogeneous culture. The few differences which coincide with language-aggregate boundaries besides the possession of a distinct name and language are separate semi-mythical founding ancestors and rights to manufacture certain ceremonial objects and use certain intangible property, such as chants and names.

Indigenous languages spoken in the Vaupés include those of the Eastern Tukanoan, Arawak, and Carib families (Greenberg 1960; Sorensen 1967). Information on Vaupés languages is sparse. Some publications by early travellers and missionaries are available (Koch-Grünberg 1909–10; Brüzzi 1962; Giacone 1965; Kök 1921–2) which consist of word lists and Tukano grammars. Linguists of the Summer Institute of Linguistics, which has for some time maintained a group of fieldworkers in the Vaupés region, consider all languages of the Vaupés to be mutually unintelligible (personal communication from Betty West). The only other linguist who has published his results, as well as the only one to carry out systematic comparative research, is Sorensen (1967, 1969, 1970), who also affirms the mutual unintelligibility of Vaupés languages. The most closely related pair is 'considerably more distant . . . than Jutish is from Standard Danish' (1967:674). He states that Tukanoan languages seem to be less closely related than Central Algonquian or Romance languages. Areas of differentiation include grammar and lexicon and, to a lesser extent, phonology. However, Sorensen did not construct formal tests to explore degrees of mutual intelligibility,

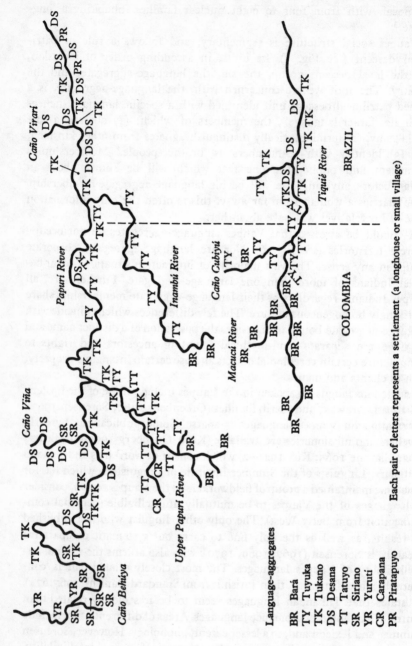

Language-aggregates

BR Bará
TY Tuyuka
TK Tukano
DS Desana
TT Tatuyo
SR Siriano
YR Yurutí
CR Carapana
PR Pir'tapuyo

Each pair of letters represents a settlement (a longhouse or small village)

Fig. 6

relying on direct interrogation of informants with respect to mutual unintelligibility and on listening for comments from Indians when they weren't understanding a language being spoken. The problem of intelligibility is further complicated by the presence of multilingualism in all Indians. With the exception of some Cubeo (many Cubeo are bilingual or multilingual according to Goldman 1963), all semi-sedentary Indians in the Vaupés are multilingual. All speak fluently at least three languages, many speak four or five, and some understand as many as ten.

Since there is much communication between Indians with different father-languages, a question arises with regard to defining and delimiting Vaupés speech communities. According to Gumperz, a speech community is '. . . any human aggregate characterized by regular and frequent interaction by means of a shared body of verbal signs and set off from similar aggregates by significant differences in language usage' (1968, quoted from 1971:126). It should be stressed that a speech community is a socially derived concept and is not defined by the characteristics of the referential structure of the particular linguistic code or codes used in communication. Hymes (1962) also points out that the homogeneity or boundaries of a linguistic code do not necessarily delimit a speech community. Overall frequency of interaction is not the only defining feature of a speech community; since all of the speech varieties employed within the community are related to a shared set of social norms, they necessarily compose a system of verbal behavior (see Gumperz 1968).

Using this definition, the entire central Northwest Amazon, including Brazilian territory, can be thought of as a multilingual speech community. The specific verbal repertoires of Indians and the code matrices of the settlements are results of the operation of cultural rules and patterns which are shared by all Indians, regardless of the languages involved. The most important of these relate to marriage exchange, rubber camp experiences, personal friendships, and trade relationships. For example, some marriages occur between individuals whose natal settlements are ninety linear miles apart. Thus the Vaupés can be seen as a single network of intervisiting and intermarrying settlements (see Goodenough, 1971:1).

Another way to describe the Vaupés is to consider the territory characterized by lanuage exogamy as a speech *area* (Hymes 1967:18 and Sorensen 1967:677, following Neustupny's *sprechbund*). All Indians share rules for speech, even though some Indians' verbal repertoires do not overlap (lack of overlap is rare, however, because of the use of Tukano as a lingua franca). If the Vaupés, or the entire central Northwest Amazon, is a speech area, then the individual settlements — longhouses or villages — are its speech communities (see Sorensen 1967:682). Although longhouses can have as few as two nuclear families, they are nonetheless multilingual speech communities.

The Indians who reside there are always affiliated to more than one father-language, and more than one language is used in many speech acts. Further-more, no rules create rigid boundaries, geographical or otherwise, which result in predictable combinations of languages; hypothetically, all com-binations are possible in either the repertoires of individual Indians or longhouses. This is almost the case if the possible combinations of father-languages represented by the inhabitants are being considered. Because of the operation of patrilocal residence rules and phratric principles, some languages will not co-occur as father-languages at the same settlement. For example, Bará Indians cannot marry Tukanos and thus no longhouses can be found where both Bará and Tukano are present as father-languages. Because of demographic factors and marriage patterns, there is an effective limit of five father-languages represented at a single longhouse at present. Unless the rule of patrilocal residence has been broken, this means that as many as four different father-languages can be represented by the in-married women at the longhouse.

Vaupés multilingualism contrasts in several ways with multilingual situations thus far reported. However, it should be noted that much more research is needed, particularly in areas where total bilingualism or multi-lingualism is the rule rather than the exception. Therefore, it is difficult to speculate on how atypical the Vaupés situation will seem after more knowl-edge about multilingual communities has been acquired and general-izations have emerged. While we know of situations where the majority of people are bilingual, such as South India (Gumperz 1964; Gumperz & Wilson 1971), Norway (Blom & Gumperz 1972), and Paraguay (Rubin 1968), and about style-switching within a single language, such as New York English (Labov 1966), much more research should be carried out in regions similar to the Vaupés such as interior South America, Australia, and New Guinea,[4] where the linguistic situation might resemble the Vaupés more than can be ascertained from the literature available. For example, no longer can we conclude that multilingualism is lacking in tribal societies unless they maintain trade relationships with outsiders or have specialized languages for ritual (Gumperz 1962). However, whether or not the Vaupés is unique in all, some, or none of the atypical characteristics exhibited by its multilingualism cannot be concluded at present.

To begin with, the degree of multilingualism in the Vaupés, in terms of number of languages, verbal repertoires, and speech itself, is unusually extensive. Estimates of population are approximate, ranging from 5280 for the Colombian Vaupés (Rodríguez 1962) to 10 000 for the entire central Northwest Amazon (Sorensen 1967:670). That within this number of people are more than twenty language-aggregates, each representing a language, is without doubt quite unusual, especially considering the dispersed settlement pattern and the low population density, which is estimated at 0.2 inhabitant per square kilometer, including non-Indians (*Atlas de Colombia*, p. xiii). It is apparently unnecessary to have either a high population density or a large number of speakers per language as preconditions for multilingual speech communities.

Even considering only the father-languages of Vaupés settlements, both the Vaupés as a whole and any region within it (regardless of how internal boundaries are drawn) are multilingual. All settlements are multilingual, as well as all semi-sedentary Indians (with the exception of some Cubeo). Fig. 6 illustrates the father-language affiliation of settlements in a region of the Vaupés. A map showing language distribution which illustrated the father-languages of all inhabitants of each settlement would be far more complicated, and still more complicated would be a map of language distribution which considered the total code matrix of each settlement.

Another point is that in the Vaupés, language is by far the most important marker distinguishing the language-aggregates and their members. It is primarily the Bará language which all Bará Indians share and which separates them as a category from Indians affiliated to other languages. In most other multilingual situations which have been reported on, language is but one of several such markers, others such as physical characteristics, dress, differences in technology, eating patterns, etc., being of equal or greater importance, at least in the eyes of the natives. As stated above, formal language affiliation in the Vaupés is determined by membership in a named patrilineal descent group, which also confers the right to manufacture certain ceremonial artifacts (this is limited to adult men) and to use various chants and names associated with the language in its role of father-language. No other differences exist which coincide with language-aggregate membership, regardless of whether one is looking for markers used by the Indians themselves to classify one another or looking for more subtle differences the Indians may not be aware of or choose not to acknowledge. For instance, ranking, whether of an overt or partially concealed nature, of the social groups which are associated with distinct codes is common (see Ferguson 1959; Lambert 1967; Labov 1966), but is lacking in the Vaupés. Ranked social groups do occur in the Vaupés, but stratification is not a component of the language-aggregate system. Indians not only deny, but are antagonistic to suggestions that language-aggregates are differentially valued or that members of a given language-aggregate are superior or inferior in any way by virtue of their membership. (For a discussion of the mild prestige claimed by Tukano Indians, as well as evidence of ranking within exogamous phratries, see Jackson 1972). As would be expected in such a situation, Vaupés languages are not differentially esteemed or stigmatized, and there is resistance on the part of Indians to suggestions that such invidious comparisons might be made. The Vaupés supports Gumperz' assertion that 'The common view that multilingualism ... also reflects deep social cleavages is clearly in need of revision' (1969:447). Given that the language-aggregates are the exchange units in a prescriptive bilateral marriage system, a lack of hierarchical differentiation is to be expected.

Another way in which the Vaupés differs from many multilingual situations that have been reported on is in the nature of the sociolinguistic rules prescribing selection of language in speech. In many other multilingual situations a single code is used for encounters between people who are identified with more than one language or dialect, regardless of whichever others they may have in common. Sometimes the language (or dialect) used is the first language of neither and yet one of the speakers understands the first language of the other. In situations involving dialect differences, speakers of separate dialects will use a more standard form with each other yet slip back into regional or class dialects with members of their own group. In situations involving languages, French or Mandarin Chinese, for example, will be used in situations where both speakers want validation of their membership in the educated elite, even though one of the speakers understands the first language of the other. In other cases, situational constraints rather than speaker identity determine the choice of code. These are such factors as setting, activity, topic, or role of participant (see Ervin-Tripp 1972). An example is the use of Latin or Hebrew in religious ceremonies. In the Vaupés, the rules which determine the selection of language do take into consideration situational constraints such as location, etc., but these rules always operate in conjunction with the particular father-language identities of the participants (as well as, of course, with other components of their individual identities, such as sex and age). Intelligibility for all participants is not always the paramount consideration; thus situations arise where the father-language of the host longhouse is used even though it isn't understood by all those present. For example, the rule governing which language to use to a shaman would be stated, 'Use a shaman's father-language, when known, out of deference to him' and not something like, 'Use Siriano when conversing with shamans' (implying that Siriano is the language of shamans or something to this effect). The one exception to the generalization that Vaupés languages lack role specificity is that Tukano is a lingua franca; all Indians will use Tukano in certain types of situations, regardless of their own father-languages or whichever languages besides Tukano the participants in a given speech event share. However, when Tukano is not being used as a lingua franca but as the father-language of some of the participants, it too lacks role specificity.

Code-switching in Vaupés speech is undoubtedly meaningful – the switch itself conveying information – just as is initial selection of code. However, to determine the meaning intended by switching we must know the rules governing such switches, how flexible their implementation is, and the language identity of the participants. I have been with women who said, 'Let's speak Tukano' and did so for a period of time, even though none of them had Tukano as a father-language and all spoke both Bará and Tuyuka as well as Tukano. In order to know the meaning behind such a switch, we must know that no woman present was Tukano as well as knowing the rules governing such conscious and arbitrary (and playful) switches to other languages. Depending on the identities of the participants, such a switch may be made out of politeness in one instance and in another out of a wish to vary the conversation through code-switching.

In conclusion, the aspects of Vaupés multilingualism most germane to the topic of this paper are the following: (1) the extent of multi-lingualism – in individuals, in speech situations, and in almost all social groups or categories (e.g., the longhouse, a group of neighboring or inter-visiting longhouses, a region in the Vaupés); (2) the problem of defining and delimiting the units of communication – what is the nature of the speech community in the Vaupés? – since to a certain extent the entire central Northwest Amazon is a single network of interacting individuals and groups; (3) the absence of specific roles and differential native eval-uations of the various Vaupés languages; and (4) the lack of correlation between linguistic diversity and non-linguistic cultural diversity.

Language as a badge of identity in the Vaupés

BADGES AND EMBLEMS

Barth (1964, 1969) discusses badges of identity, which he refers to as 'diacritica.' In a system characterized by a high degree of interaction among different categories of people, the differences between the inter-acting social units are standardized, and, consequently, highly stereotyped. The more such units interact and the longer the period of interaction, the more these units become structurally similar and differentiated only by a few clear diacritica. The total inventory of cultural differences is reduced, but the differences which remain, because of their new role as badges or emblems of identification with distinct social groups, become more impor-tant. Badges and emblems of identity can be seen as a kind of message, the successful transmission, reception, and decoding of which is necessary to the interaction taking place. The particular differences which are assigned the role of information-bearing message often change in directions which increase their visibility, unambiguity, and discreteness – the characteristics that can be seen to facilitate the successful transmission of the message that badges and emblems are intended to send. Another obvious requirement for successful communication of information is that the sender and receiver of a message see it as important enough to warrant their time and energy. When specific cultural differences assume the role of badges, their form and content become quite significant to the people using them to classify themselves and others around them yet frequently are judged by outsiders as trivial, superficial, and overemphasized. The *features* which render each badge distinct from others in the set can become highly charged with meaning, both for the individuals who belong to the category the badge represents and for members of other categories. Such meaning may have a negative or positive value. Similarly, the *dimension* within which all of these distinctive features are contained can also become highly significant; it is this significance which often appears exaggerated to the outsider. In the Vaupés, the dimension is the one of language or linguistics, and the features are those linguistic elements which are seen by the Indians as making Vaupés languages mutually unintelligible. Vaupés Indians assign great importance to all aspects of language and see much of their social structure as modelled after and explicable by the linguistic varieties present in the Vaupés and the criteria used to distinguish them.

Much of the sociolinguistic literature deals with the ways in which individuals send and receive information about social identity through the use of language. Most of this work is concerned with speech behavior itself; some studies have concentrated on the way in which speakers themselves are aware that speech can indicate social status (Labov 1966). Many anthropologists have noted in passing that speech provides clues to distinct social and ethnic identities,[4] and Blom notes that

differences in speech between various kinds of groups that are in frequent contact are not in themselves responsible for the establishment and maintenance of social boundaries. These differences rather *reflect* features of social organization through a process of social codification (1969:83).

Multilingualism studies have pointed out two ways in which social identity is signalled by the use of distinct languages, both of which are important to understanding the Vaupés case. First, an individual's speech can be an indicator of social class, ethnic or regional background, economic mobility, etc. Much of the literature on this topic is concerned with how the speaker will consciously or unconsciously send signals about his social identity, and how the receiver, also consciously or unconciously, will interpret these signals. Second, an individual's formal affiliation to a language is a component of his social identity. To the degree to which this is public knowledge, it will be a factor in his interactions with others, regardless of the way he speaks. Obviously this second way in which a language signals social identity requires that the interacting parties be aware of the language each formally represents. However, how one individual evaluates his own linguistic affiliation may differ from how others evaluate it: most Germans probably differ from most Frenchmen regarding the privilege of identifying with German as opposed to French as one's mother-tongue.

VAUPÉS LANGUAGES AS BADGES OR EMBLEMS

Any anthropological research carried out in the Vaupés must eventually concern itself with questions such as the following: Why are over twenty languages spoken, given (1) the small numbers of Indians identified with each language, (2) the low population density, (3) the homogeneous culture throughout the region, (4) the lack of stratification along language boundaries, and (5) the lack of role specificity for the various languages? Why do Indians learn at least three languages, and some as many as ten, when they could all communicate in Tukano? Why do some places have separate names in all the languages? Why do Indians so strongly emphasize the mutual unintelligibility of the languages? It is very unlikely that such questions can be answered without postulating that Vaupés languages are emblems of the language-aggregates and badges of membership in them for individual Indians. The possession of a distinctive father-language is important because the language-aggregates function as discrete units in the distribution of women.

In some situations in the Vaupés, the public display of language-aggregate identity through actual speech occurs. Sorensen gives an example: 'Each individual initially speaks in his own father-language during such a conversation in order to assert his tribal affiliation and identification.' (1967:678). An Indian who is publicly acknowledging his language-aggregate membership is reaffirming this aspect of his social identity the vast majority of the time, rather than announcing a hitherto unknown fact about himself. Indians normally interact with other Indians whom they have known for a long time, and language-aggregate membership is permanent and unambiguous (i.e., there are no 'marginal members,' boundary crossings, or dual memberships). Furthermore, this membership is the one fact which will be known about an Indian before any other, and therefore the speech behavior exemplified in the above speech act rarely informs other Indians of something they don't already know. Thus, the fact that very few speech events allow an Indian to signal his language-aggregate identity in the manner of the above example does not indicate that language-aggregate identity is not an extremely important aspect of Vaupés life. There is no need to continually remind one another of this particular aspect of social identity, and thus in most situations and in all informal speech events various other sociolinguistic rules determine which languages are to be used.

Linguistic data show the close association between statements about language and statements about language-aggregate membership, which is evidence that languages serve as badges of such membership. For example, the question *ñe wadegú niti mü*, which glosses roughly as 'What (male) language-speaker are you?' invariably elicits a response about the interlocutor's language-aggregate membership. There is no ambiguity about the intention of the question as it stands in Bará. A Bará male will answer: *yü ni baráyü* 'I am Bará,' or (*yü-*)*ye waderá ni bará* 'My father-language is Bará.' These inquiries about language-aggregate membership are grammatically quite distinct from inquiries and response about speech itself, such as *ñe wadegáti mü* 'What do you say?' or *nohkõro waderá mahiti mü*? 'How many languages do you know (how to speak)?'

Verbal evidence from informants indicates that Indians are aware of the emblematic nature of Vaupés languages with respect to language-aggregate identity. An example of this is from a conversation which I had with a Bará Indian about the relationship between sibling terminology and marriage rules. I was hoping to get an explicit genealogical explanation of the rule of exogamy as it applies to all Bará Indians, such as 'We are all brothers because we descended from a common ancestor and therefore don't marry our sisters.' However, after preliminary comments relating marriage rules and kin terms (such as 'We don't marry our sisters'), the fact of language affiliation immediately entered the picture. What emerged was something like: 'My brothers are those who share a language with me. Those who speak other languages are not my brothers, and I can marry their sisters.' Another time, when I directly asked an Indian why they spoke so many languages rather than relying on Tukano exclusively, he answered, 'If we all were Tukano speakers, where would we get our women?'

That Indians consciously try to maintain linguistic boundaries when speaking is further indication that language is the main badge of language-aggregate membership. Sorensen states that languages appear to be kept fastidiously apart, and that when two languages are closely related an Indian will 'carefully and even consciously keep them apart' (1967:675). Sorensen also states that an Indian will not attempt to speak a language he is learning until he feels quite competent to speak it correctly. This suggests that interference in speech from a father-language or another language in an individual's repertoire is socially disapproved of. I observed instances where women were scolded for allowing words from other languages to creep into conversations which were being held in Bará. Other Indians would comment that such women were not setting a good example for their children, who should learn to speak their father's and mother's languages correctly. Occasionally such language mixing would be overtly criticized because of my presence, with remarks to the effect that I would shame the longhouse if I learned to speak Bará with Tuyuka words. I did not collect data which measured the amount of interference taking place and the frequency with which interference was criticized by other Indians. It seemed clear that when a word from another language entered a person's speech and was seen by those present as a mistake, i.e., was defined by the Indians as interference, such speech was not approved of. It was my impression that it would be hard to obtain objective measures of what Indians considered to be mistakes, however. I was surprised several times to find that a word which was frequently used in Bará was considered by the Indians to be a Tuyuka word, and definitely not Bará. When asked, Indians would always know the Bará word, and they would have a reason for preferring the Tuyuka word. More importantly, I would be reassured that 'everyone *knows* it's a Tuyuka word.' This suggests that Indians are aware of intrusive words in their language's lexicon, but that this is accepted as long as the co-occurrence rules which separate one language from another are not seen as breaking down. Undoubtedly the emphasis on speaking a language 'purely' varies with the situation; it is my impression that women can get away with more unintentional switching in relaxed discourses than is allowed in settings which involve men and are more formal.

It is probably the case that while the lexicons of languages in the Vaupés are changing because of contact with other languages, there are nevertheless strict co-occurrence rules which are operating at any given time which maintain the languages as separate categories in a specific individual's or group's repertoire. The presence of these rules is evidence for the emblematic nature of Vaupés languages. That Indians are aware of speech 'mistakes,' that they place a high value on correct speech, and that they see Vaupés languages as mutually unintelligible also support this hypothesis.

The Vaupés suggests some possibilities for rethinking in the following areas: (1) the criteria used to determine whether two or more varieties are languages or dialects; (2) linguistic change and the study of linguistic convergence, particularly with respect to the effects of speaker attitudes about linguistic variation on language change; (3) the assumption that linguistic diversity is invariably related to barriers in communication and hence, to some degree, cultural diversity; and (4) the generalizations concerning multilingualism as a general phenomenon which can be made from studying bilinguals in predominantly monolingual communities. The Vaupés also contributes to studies concerned with the ways in which languages can serve purposes other than communicating referential information. Labov and others have pointed out that language can communicate social information about the speaker. This can be done through speech itself or by common knowledge of individual identification with distinct codes and a certain amount of agreement regarding the implications of such identification. In this manner language can become a codification of many aspects of an individual's social identity, serving as a badge or emblem of that identity. Furthermore, language and linguistic varieties can serve as native models which are seen as explaining and justifying other areas of the social order. It is interesting to note that in the Vaupés the native view of genetic linguistic history meshes nicely with the function of language in the region – as an emblem of the language-aggregate and in the regulation of marriage.

The relationship between grammar and individual linguistic competence raises some interesting questions in the Vaupés, for if a grammar is supposed to reflect in some way native speaker linguistic competence, grammars of individual Vaupés languages will not be adequate. Any 'ideally fluent speaker – hearer' or even the most 'homogeneous speech community' in the sense of Chomsky (1965:3) will be multilingual (see Sorensen 1967:682). Moreover, the multilingualism involves over twenty languages and the rules which give rise to individual repertoires do not result in a small number of predictable combinations of languages. The rules concerning correct usage are not specific to particular languages (with the exception of Tukano as a lingua franca), and cannot be stated by expressions such as 'Use X language in contexts A and B' (as are, for example, rules governing switching in South India). The rules for usage in the Vaupés are always dependent on the father-language identity of at least some of the participants and whether or not the language to be used is in the speaker's and at least some of the hearers' repertoires.[5]

3

'OUR ANCESTORS SPOKE IN PAIRS': ROTINESE VIEWS OF LANGUAGE, DIALECT, AND CODE

JAMES J. FOX

For a Rotinese, the pleasure of life is talk – not simply an idle chatter that passes time, but the more formal taking of sides in endless dispute, argument, and repartee or the rivaling of one another in eloquent and balanced phrases on ceremonial occasions. Speeches, sermons, and rhetorical statements are a delight. But in this class society, with hierarchies of order, there are notable constraints on speech. In gatherings, nobles speak more than commoners, men more than women, elders more than juniors; yet commoners, women, and youth, when given the opportunity as they invariably are, display the same prodigious verbal prowess. Lack of talk is an indication of distress. Rotinese repeatedly explain that if their 'hearts' are confused or dejected, they keep silent. Contrarily, to be involved with someone requires active verbal encounter and this often leads to a form of litigation that is conducted more, it would seem, for the sake of argument than for any possible gain.

Three hundred years of Dutch records for the island provide an apt chronicle of this attitude toward speaking. The Dutch East India Company annual reports for Timor in the eighteenth century are crammed with accounts of the shifting squabbles of related Rotinese rulers. By the twentieth century, the colonial service had informally established Roti as a testing ground. If a young administrator could weather the storms of the litigious Rotinese, he was due for promotion. The Rotinese, in turn, obliged the Dutch by reviving all old litigation to welcome each incoming administrator. Even occasional visitors to the island were struck by these Rotinese qualities. In 1891, the naturalist Herman ten Kate, on a tour of the islands of eastern Indonesia, briefly visited Roti and observed: 'Nearly everywhere we went on Roti, there was a dispute over this or that. The native, to wit the Rotinese, can ramble on over trivia like an old Dutch granny. I believe that his loquaciousness is partially to blame for this, for each dispute naturally provides abundant material for talk' (1894:221). As an ethnographer, I was fortunate to arrive on Roti late at night and therefore did not become involved in dispute until early the next morning.

An ethnography of speaking on an island where speech takes so many complex forms is a daunting undertaking. Here my concern is to discuss certain views Rotinese hold of themselves, of their language, and of their dialects. My object, however, is to focus these conceptions in the examination of a single, islandwide form of speaking, a code used mainly in situations of formal interaction. This ritual language is an oral poetry based on a binate semantics that requires the coupling of fixed elements in the production of phrase and verse. It is a particular instance of the phenomenon of canonical parallelism whose extensive distribution among the oral traditions of the world has only begun to be surveyed (Bricker, this volume; Gossen, this volume; Jakobson 1966; Edmonson 1970; Fox 1971a; Kramer 1970; Sherzer & Sherzer 1972). That this phenomenon should occur in the traditions of such diverse languages as Cuna, Finnish, Hebrew, Mongolian, Quiche, Rotinese, and Toda and can be found among the languages of the Ural–Altaic area, in Dravidian areas of India, through most of southeast Asia, in Austronesian languages from Madagascar to Hawaii, and in Mayan languages compels critical attention. The first task, in comprehending the role of this ritual language, is to sketch the general language situation and to examine the various forms of speaking that obtain on the island.

Rotinese: The general language situation

The island of Roti lies off the southwestern tip of the island of Timor in eastern Indonesia. It is a small island, the southernmost of the Indonesian archipelago. In length, it measures 80 kilometers and at its widest point is no more than 25 kilometers across.

The Rotinese made early adaptations to the arrival of the Portuguese and Dutch in eastern Indonesia: their rulers accepted alliances, contracts of trade, and Christianity. By the middle of the eighteenth century, they were already supporting their own local schools. By deft token compliance with the Dutch they avoided major interference in their island affairs and by comparison with other peoples of eastern Indonesia, they seem to have taken maximum advantage of the colonial situation. Roti was an area of indirect rule; but with a subsistence economy dependent on the tapping of lontar palms, the island was never drawn into the colonial cultivation system. In a region of increasing aridity, this palm-centered economy affords the Rotinese distinct economic advantages over neighboring peoples whose swidden agriculture has reached its limits. There are over 100 000 Rotinese: approximately 70 000 on Roti itself and more than 30 000 on Timor and other islands of eastern Indonesia. Migration from Roti, begun and fostered during the colonial period, continues to the present. The Rotinese are a proud, assertive, and energetic people. They neither model themselves on, nor are they assimilating to, any other local group in the area.

Apart from language, dress is a distinctive mark of Rotinese identity. Their attire is unique in Indonesia. Everyday dress – particularly of Rotinese men – is strikingly unlike that of any other people in eastern Indonesia. Instead of a headcloth, men wear a broad sombrero-like palm hat, originally modeled on that of the seventeenth-century Portuguese. Their traditional tie-and-dye cloths combine native design motifs with *patola* patterns taken from Gujarati cloths imported, as elite trade goods, by the Dutch East India Company in the eighteenth century. Except when working, a Rotinese man wears one of these cloths folded and draped over his shoulder. Together, cloths and hats are ideal visible badges and are worn as a conscious mark of differentiation. To the outsider, these are a badge of identity.

Language is another marker of identity. *Dedeäk*, the Rotinese word for 'language' or 'speech', has multiple levels of specification. It may refer to 'Rotinese' (*Dedeä Rote* or *Dedeä Lote*) or to any dialect of Rotinese: *dedeä Pada* 'dialect of Pada' or *dedeä Oepao* 'dialect of Oepao.' Without a qualifying term, *dedeäk* may refer to any organized coherent speech: 'a court case,' 'a dispute,' 'some specific news' or 'piece of recent information.' At this level, *dedeäk* emphasizes what is current, is still in process, and is personal. It is closely related to *kokolak* 'talk' or 'conversation' but distinguished from other forms of organized speaking such as *tutuik* 'tales'; *tutui-teteëk* 'true tales or history'; *neneuk* 'riddles'; *namahehelek ma babalak* 'beliefs and consequences'; *lakandandak meis* 'dream interpretations';[1] *aäli-oölek*, a highly standardized form of 'mockery'; or *bini*, the designation for all compositions in parallel verse, since all of these relate to some past event or follow a fixed 'ancestral' pattern. At one level, *dedeäk* comprises all forms of speaking; at another, it contrasts ordinary speech with other forms of more formal speaking. (The distinction resembles that between English 'speech' and 'a speech.') The use of *dedeäk*, or any other form of speaking, is not simply situation-specific but situation-creative. Litigants in a court case are involved in *dedeäk*; lords and elders, in comment and in rendering judgment, invoke *bini*. Bridewealth negotiations require *bini*; if these overtures are successful, details in the negotiation can be worked out in *dedeäk*. A change in speaking can indicate a subtle change of phase in a continuous speech event.

Dedeä Lote is the language of Roti. It is identified with Roti and is said to be spoken by all Rotinese throughout the island. Interestingly, it is not credited with qualities that make its speakers uniquely 'human.' *Dedeä Lote* is contrasted with other known languages of the area: *Dedeä Ndao* 'Ndaonese', *Dedeä Helok* 'Helong', or *Dedeä Malai* 'Malay or Indonesian'. To its speakers, even those who have migrated to other islands, it is a distinct and delimitable language. The situation is, however, more complex. To the west of Roti is the tiny island of Ndao; to the east the slightly larger, small island of Semau. On both of these islands live separate ethnic groups of 2000 or less persons conscious of their gradual linguistic, cultural, and economic assimilation by the Rotinese. For the Ndaonese, the situation is of long standing (Fox 1972a). Since the 1720s, Ndao has been treated as one of the semi-autonomous political domains of Roti. The Ndaonese economy, like that of Roti, is dependent on palm utilization. But the Ndaonese have the special distinction that all men of the island are gold-smiths and silversmiths who, during each dry season, leave their island to fashion jewelry for the people of the Timor area. Ndaonese have migrated to Roti for centuries. In every domain of Roti, there is one clan said to be of 'Ndaonese origin' and to this clan, new immigrants can readily assimilate. Recently – in the last two generations – Ndaonese have adopted Rotinese hats and the design motifs of west Rotinese cloths. Women have begun to leave the island in large numbers to sell finished cloths or to take orders for the weaving of new cloths. Ndaonese is of the Bima–Sumba subfamily of languages; Rotinese of the Timor–Ambon grouping of languages. Most Ndaonese are polyglots, having spent long periods on neighboring islands; virtually all Ndaonese men are, at least, bilingual in Rotinese and Ndaonese and an increasing number of women are becoming similarly bilingual. The assimilation is gradual, increasing but also selective. Rotinese parallel songs, for which there are said to be no Ndaonese equivalents, seem to have already been completely adopted. There are, thus, fluent Rotinese speakers who dress much like Rotinese but who retain their own language and separate homeland. Many of these speakers, when they cease their special occupation, abandon their language entirely and become full Rotinese.

For Helong speakers of Semau and of a single remaining coastal village near Kupang on Timor, the situation is somewhat different (Fox 1972b). Helong is a language closely related to Rotinese, but recent contact between speakers of these languages has only occurred in the past hundred years. The Helong, under pressure from the Timorese, accompanied their ruler to Semau some time prior to 1815, the time of the first wave of Rotinese migration to Timor. From Timor, Rotinese later began to settle on Semau. The result is that the Helong, with a precarious swidden economy, have been swamped by Rotinese. Lacking a viable and separate means of live-lihood and in the midst of Rotinese, the remnant Helong seem to be rapidly adopting Potinese ways.

The other language with which Rotinese speakers have long been in contact is Malay. Unlike Ndaonese or Helong, Malay, in some form, is understood by a large majority of Rotinese. Not long after 1660, Rotinese rulers began an annual exchange of letters with the Dutch East India Company's governor general in Batavia. This correspondence and other dealings with the company's representatives were carried out through

Malay-speaking scribes and interpreters located in Kupang on Timor. In 1679, the Dutch General Missives report that one young Rotinese ruler was actually transported to Kupang for the express purpose of learning Malay (Coolhaas 1971:338). By 1710, the first company interpreter was stationed on Roti; by 1735, the first Malay-speaking schoolmaster from Ambon arrived on the island. Within a generation (1753), there were six local schools, maintained by Rotinese rulers, and Rotinese had begun themselves to replace company-appointed teachers from other islands. From the beginning, Malay was a 'literary language' linked with Christianity. Knowledge of Malay was necessary to read the Bible and to carry on official correspondence with the Dutch.

Malay also became the language of the heterogeneous settlement of peoples that grouped around the company's fort, Concordia, at Kupang. Eventually, Rotinese predominated in this settlement and in the surrounding area. Over a period of three hundred years, this language of Kupang, known as *basa Kupang* [*bahasa Kupang*] became a distinct dialect of colloquial Malay with unmistakable Rotinese influences. Many Rotinese who live on Timor regard it as their own peculiar and special form of speaking. It is never the language of official business nor the language of home or village but, like other local variants of Malay, it is a language of the 'marketplace,' spoken in town when dealing with friends and acquaintances. Later with the increasing use of Malay in the colonial administration, with its adoption as the official language of the nation, and with its use in all the schools, Rotinese were introduced to a new standard form of Malay, the official language of national unity and identity – modern Indonesian.

These three varieties of Malay ('Biblical' Malay, *basa Kupang*, and Indonesian) are sufficiently different from one another to be segregated and confined to regularized situations. A Christian Rotinese, with some education, will deal with government officials (even fellow Rotinese) in Indonesian, will attend church services conducted in Biblical Malay, and will rely on *basa Kupang* when visiting friends or relatives on Timor. In a sense, the Rotinese have added these new forms of speaking (or writing) to their other conventional forms of speech. But, as with other forms of speaking, there is a strong tendency not 'to mix speech' inappropriately.[2]

These three varieties of Malay are, however, sufficiently similar that the furtherance of one has consequences for the others. On conclusion of the national literacy campaign in the late 1950s, when the island was certified as literate in Indonesian, there was mass conversion to Christianity. Malay had served as a check on conversion and when, by decree, all Rotinese became Malay speakers this obstacle was removed. Significantly Biblical Malay is itself seen as a formal ritual language indispensable for Christian rituals. The parallelism that pervades the Old Testament accords well with

Rotinese ideas of a ritual language. A church service consists of readings from the Bible with translations in Rotinese, Malay songs, and long sermons, often in Malay, with long paraphrases in Rotinese, or interspersed Malay and Rotinese, or even a cacophony of two simultaneous sermons, with one preacher speaking Malay, the other translating in Rotinese.

The dialect community of Roti

Rotinese is the language of a small, hilly island with no natural barriers to communication. Any village area is within a day's walk or horse ride of any other. Politically, however, the island is divided among eighteen native states or domains (*nusak*). Each domain is ruled by its own lord who, together with the representative lords of the various clans of that domain, presides at a court and makes decisions based on the customary law of the domain. Although borders have always been disputed, the separate existence of these states can be traced, through continuous archival records, over three hundred years, to the mid-seventeenth century when their rulers were first recognized by contracts of trade with the East India Company. By preventing the expansion of any one state, hampering the fluctuations of men and territory, and by actually dismembering the largest of these states, the Dutch fostered conditions that maintained separate entities. They froze, in effect, what was a more fluid and flexible situation and created a 'new' tradition of rule. Later they attempted to counter the effects of their previous policies, but all of these twentieth-century schemes for the amalgamation of states have failed. As a consequence, there exist, at present, virtually the same local political domains as existed in 1656 (Fox 1971c). These domains are afforded administrative existence within the bureaucratic structure of the Republic of Indonesia, their lords are acknowledged as administrative officials, and their courts retain jurisdiction over most civil disputes.

With its political divisions, local classes, unique clan privileges and subtle social discriminations, its styles of dress and fluctuation of fashion, its variations in the performace of rituals, and its differences in customary law, Rotinese culture forms a complex structure by which men are distinguished. Among themselves, Rotinese emphasize their minor social peculiarities rather than overall similarities. In particular, they invest the slight shades of difference between domains with a high degree of significance to denote their separateness from one another. The result is a family of resemblances, traceable throughout the island – a continuous variation along a multitude of inequivalent scales. Dress – to the outsider, the mark of Rotinese identity – is internally a heraldic display that identifies a person's domain, class, status, and, in some instance, court office. Language is the other prime mark of identity. Where no natural, visible barriers occur,

Fig. 7. The island of Roti

the Rotinese have erected political barriers fostered by indirect colonial rule. On the island, there is a proliferation of dialects.

By native account, Rotinese, *Dedeä* Lote, consists of eighteen domain dialects, *dedeä nusak*. The statement is as much political as it is linguistic. The assertion is that every state has its own language. *Nusak*, like *dedeäk*, has multiple levels of meaning. It may refer to the 'domain,' the 'resident village' of the lord (*nusak lain* 'high *nusak*'), or the 'court' of the domain. The claim to separate *dedeä nusak* implies not only a unique dialect but unique law and court procedure for dealing with litigation and other 'affairs' of state.

When qualifications are made to statements about the separateness of domain dialects, the qualifications are also political. The small domains of Keka and Talae achieved Dutch recognition of their independence from their neighboring state, Termanu, in 1772. By arguments based on a kind of folk etymology in which Rotinese find a particular delight, the people of Talae are said to have 'fled' (*ita lai* 'we flee') from Termanu. When, in Termanu, it is claimed that Termanu, Keka, and Talae have a common dialect, this is both a recognition of a close linguistic relationship and a tactic assertion of past political claims. It is sometimes said that the small domain of Bokai has 'no language of its own.' Again this is not a linguistic statement so much as a reference to a well known myth that relates the curse of the Lord of the Sea on the original inhabitants of this domain. The curse limits the number of these original inhabitants to thirty persons and so the domain is said to be composed mainly of outsiders who speak other dialects. The far western domain of Delha, mentioned early in company records, was the last domain to achieve Dutch recognition of its separation from Oenale whose dialect it shares. Political factors, especially its long 'non-recognition,' have contributed to make Delha a hotbed of resistance to all forms of rule. To other Rotinese, Delha is the backwater area of their island. (People there, it is said, are not Christians, speak no Malay, and, prior to 1965, were 'communist' to a man.) When the lord of Korbaffo, a domain of east Roti, was appointed a government administrative coordinator for the island, he would – as he proudly explains – speak regularly in Oenale but use an interpreter when touring Delha. All Rotinese statements about dialect intelligibility have an important political component.

A subject Rotinese never seem to tire of discussing is domain and dialect differences. The point of reference is the local dialect and comparison is always pairwise with some other dialect. Evidence is specific, selective, and piecemeal. Domains are self-centered to the point that there are relatively few persons with a thorough knowledge of another dialect. Except for the high nobility, marriage occurs within the domain. One effect of Dutch rule was to impede the former migration of persons among states. Contact with other dialect speakers is frequent but usually temporary. And thus the curious situation exists that a large number of Rotinese have visited Kupang on Timor while a far smaller number have spent a single night in a domain one removed from their own. What passes therefore as information on dialect difference, although rarely incorrect, is highly standardized. These selective features are taken up, occasionally in folk tales involving strangers, in pseudo-imitation of actual differences.

In 1884, D. P. Manafe, a Rotinese school teacher from Baä, wrote the first account of the Rotinese language. Through the auspices of the Dutch linguist Kern, this article in Malay, *Akan Bahasa Rotti*, was published in a Dutch journal (Manafe 1889: 633–48). The article consists almost entirely of a listing of words in the dialects of the island and various verb paradigms in the dialect of Baä. Although more extensive and systematic than Rotinese conversational models, the article is itself an excellent native model. After dividing the island into its two divisions, east and west, Manafe presents his own grouping of dialects according to their 'sound.' Although the dialects have different sounds, anyone in the east, he writes, can, without too much trouble, understand anyone in the west. His list of dialects is as follows:

1. Oepao, Ringgou, and Landu	6. Baä and Loleh
2. Bilba, Diu, and Lelenuk	7. Dengka and Lelain
3. Korbaffo	8. Thie
4. Termanu, Keka, and Talae	9. Oenale and Delha
5. Bokai	

This list joins several dialects of contiguous domains; the precise criteria for this grouping are not, however, specified and the paradigms that follow illustrate differences in 'sounds' in dialects that are grouped together. The list, however, conforms to Rotinese standards that all valid groupings consist of nine elements, the number of totality. But by no means is the list misleading. Intuitively, taking into account language, politics, and local geography, it is an accurate representation of perceived domain differences. As a description of dialects, it formed the basis for the dialect study of the Dutch linguist J. C. G. Jonker (1913:531–622).

In discussing dialects, certain sound shifts are particularly noted. Dialects are divided into those that use /l/ and /r/ and those that use /l/ exclusively; those that replace /p/ with /mb/ or those that use /n/ in medial position instead of /nd/. The shift from /ngg/ to /ng/ to /k/ in medial position and the presence or absence of initial /h/ or /k/ are other often-cited distinguishing features. Since a few words, with several of these sound shifts, may be given as evidence of dialect difference, all domains can be shown to have 'a separate language.' Thus while they are concerned with linguistic discriminations, Rotinese are not interested in systematic dialectology.

The semantic diversity of dialects is of more significance, to Rotinese, than any phonological differences. The sound patterns of Rotinese form a continuum, but the occurrence of different words for the same object introduces radical disjunction. Such disjunction can be used to justify social and political separation. In describing themselves, Rotinese readily point out, for example, that the word for 'man' or 'person' through most of Roti is *hataholi* (or its cognate *hatahori, atahori*), while in Bilba and Ringgou, it is *dae-hena* (or *dahenda*); that the word for a man's 'hat' is *tii-langa* in most eastern areas of Roti, but *soi-langga* (or *so-langga*) in Baä and Thie; or that the word for the annual post-harvest ritual is *hus* in Termanu and east Roti but *limba* (or *limpa*) in Thie, Baä, and west Roti.

This semantic diversity is a resource for ritual language. Some native awareness of this diversity is essential to the continuance of ritual language as an islandwide code. Reflexively, this ritual language provides Rotinese with yet another view of their language and dialect.

Ritual language: A formal speech code [3]

Ritual language is a formal speech code. It consists of speaking in pairs. The semantic elements that form these pairs or dyadic sets are highly determined. Sets are structured in formulaic phrases and their presentation generally consists in compositions of parallel verse. A *bini* may vary in length from two lines to several hundred lines. It includes the genre of 'proverbs' (*bini kekeuk* 'short *bini*'), 'songs' (*soda bini* 'to sing *bini*'), and 'chants' (*helo bini* 'to chant *bini*'). Rotinese can qualify the category *bini* in innumerable ways. A taxonomy of these forms would vary on, at the least, two dimensions: one, an enumeration of the various methods of producing *bini*: 'singing,' 'saying,' 'chanting,' 'wailing,' ...; the other, a listing of the myriad situations for which *bini* are appropriate: greetings, farewells, petitions, courtship, negotiations, and all the ceremonies of Rotinese life. *Bini mamates* 'funeral *bini*,' for example, are further subdivided in a host of *bini* appropriate to categories of deceased persons: for a young child, an elder child, a virgin girl, a young noble, a rich man, a widow, etc. The common feature to all uses of these *bini* is their occurrence in circumstances of formal social interaction. [4] All *bini* are based on the same repertoire of dyadic sets. The same dyadic sets may, therefore, occur in any particular form of *bini* whether proverb, song, or funeral chant. Many forms are equally applicable to a variety of situations. The three *bini* that I quote here may fit any 'situation of succession': the installation of a new lord to continue a line of rule, or the replacement of father by his son or of a lineage member by another lineage member. The imagery is of regeneration and renewal.

VARIATION (1)

1.	Oe No Dain biïn	The goat of Oe No from Dai
2.	Na biï ma-pau henuk	The goat has a yellow-necklaced beard
3.	Ma Kedi Poi Selan manun	And the cock of Kedi Poi from Sela
4.	Na manun ma-koa lilok.	The cock has gold-stranded tailfeathers.
5.	De ke heni pau biïn	Cut away the goat's beard
6.	Te hu ela lesu biïn	Leaving but the goat's throat
7.	De se lesun na pau seluk	That throat will beard again
8.	Fo na pau henu seluk;	And the beard will be a yellow necklace again;
9.	Ma feä heni koa manun	And pluck out the cock's tailfeathers
10.	Te sadi ela nggoti manun	Leaving only the cock's rear
11.	Fo nggotin na koa seluk	That rear will feather again
12.	Fo na koa lilo seluk.	And the tailfeathers will be gold strands again.
13.	Fo bei teman leo makahulun	Still perfect as before
14.	Ma tetu leo sososan.	And ordered as at first.

COMMENTARY (1)

This short *bini* is composed of seven dyadic sets (*biï*//*manu* 'goat' // 'cock,' *koa*//*pau* 'tailfeathers'//'beard,' *henu*//*lilo* 'yellow-bead'//'gold(-strand),' *feä*//*ke* 'pluck'//'cut,' . . .), one redoubled personal name (*Oe No*//*Kedi Poi*), one dyadic place name (*Dai*//*Sela*), and a number of invariable connective elements (*ma, fo, ela, de, seluk,* . . .). *Te hu* (line 6) is generally invariable, but in this composition, the chanter has attempted to cast it in dyadic form: *te hu* is intended to form a couple with *te sadi* (line 10). This is not a required set in ritual language but is the embellishment of a particularly capable chanter. As is evident, parallel lines need not be consecutive or alternating. Sequencing is complex and variable. The parallel lines of this *bini* are: 1/3, 2/4, 5/9, 6/10, 7/11, 8/12, 13/14. Knowledge of dyadic sets indicates which lines are parallel. Composition is based on these sets, not on whole parallel lines.

VARIATION (2)

The second variation on the theme of succession uses many of the same sets. It is slightly longer and its imagery more dense. Full explication of its significance would require a diverting discussion of Rotinese cosmological ideas. It is only appropriate to the succession of a high noble or lord and implies his influence over the sea. Like the first, this variation can only be used in situations of male succession. In ritual language, the complex (cross-over) formula for a male child is *popi koa*//*lanu manu* 'a rooster's tailfeathers'//'a cock's plume.'

1. Benga la-fafada	Word is continually told
2. Ma dasi laka-tutuda:	And voice continually let fall:
3. Manu ma-koa lilok	A cock with gold-stranded tail-feathers
4. Do bïi ma-pau henuk.	Or a goat with yellow-necklaced beard.
5. Lae: koa lilon loloso	They say: The tailfeathers' gold strands flutter
6. Na loloso neu liun	They flutter toward the ocean
7. Fo liun dale laka-tema	The ocean depth˄ are calmed
8. Ma pau henun ngganggape	And the beard's yellow necklace waves
9. Na ngganggape neu sain	It waves toward the sea
10. Fo sain dale la-tetu.	The sea depths are ordered.
11. De besak ia koa lilon na kono	Now the tailfeathers' gold strands drop
12. Ma pau bïin na monu	And the beard's yellow necklace falls
13. Te hu bei ela nggoti manun	Still leaving but the cock's rear
14. Na dei nggotin na koa bai	But that rear feathers once more
15. Fo na koa lilo seluk	And the feathers are gold strands again

16. Ma bei ela lesu biïn	And still leaving the goat's throat
17. Na dei lesun na pau seluk	That throat beards again
18. Fo na pau henu seluk.	And the beard is a yellow necklace again.
19. Fo leo faik ia	Just like this day
20. Ma deta ledok ia	And as at this time [sun]
21. Boe nggati koa manakonok	A change of tailfeathers that were dropped
22. Ma pau manatudak ndia.	And this beard that had fallen.

COMMENTARY (2)

This *bini* introduces eight new sets (*benga//dasi* 'word'//'voice,' *-fada//-tuda* 'to tell'//'to fall,' *loso//nggape* 'to flutter'//'to wave,' *fai//ledo* 'day'//'sun,' ...) and omits only two sets of the previous *bini* (*feä//ke*, (*h*)*ulu//sosa*). Parallel lines are: 1/2, 3/4, 5/8, 6/9, 7/10, 11/12, 13/16, 14/17, 15/18, 19/20, 21/22. A feature of most invariable elements is that they may be omitted in the second of two parallel lines. Thus *te hu* (line 13) neither recurs nor is paired with *te sadi* in its corresponding line (line 16). The connective *ma* 'and' is used instead. An interesting embellishment in this composition is the attempt to create a pairing of the morphological elements *la-//laka-* (lines 1/2, 7/10). This *bini* also illustrates one of the most crucial features of ritual language semantics. An element or word may form a pair with more than one other element. Most elements are not confined to a single fixed dyadic set but rather have a variable range of other elements with which they form acceptable sets. In this composition, the element *-tuda* 'to fall' forms a set with *-fada* 'to speak, to tell'; *kono* 'to drop, to tumble down' forms a set with *monu* 'to fall off, to fall from', but in the final lines, *kono* forms another set with *tuda*. New pairings 'highlight' different aspects of the same semantic element. The linking of elements creates a means of formal inquiry on the semantics of this language.

VARIATION (3)

This third variation is the shortest of the three. Its format closely resembles that of the first *bini*. The imagery of succession has been changed by the use of different sets. Instead of 'goat's beard' and 'cock's tailfeathers,' renewal is phrased in terms of 'sugar cane sheaths' and 'banana blossoms.' Both sugar cane and bananas are, in Rotinese, botanic icons for male persons.

1. Lole faik ia dalen	On this good day
2. Ma lada ledok ia tein na	And at this fine time [sun]
3. Lae: tefu ma-nggona lilok	They say: The sugar cane has sheaths of gold

4. Ma huni ma-lapa losik.	And the banana has blossoms of copper.
5. Tefu olu heni nggonan	The sugar cane sheds its sheath
6. Ma huni kono heni lapan,	And the banana drops its blossom,
7. Te hu bei ela tefu okan	Still leaving but the sugar cane's root
8. Ma huni hun bai.	And the banana's trunk too.
9. De dei tefu na nggona seluk	But the sugar cane sheaths again
10. Fo na nggona lilo seluk	The sheaths are gold again
11. Ma dei huni na lapa seluk	And the banana blossoms again
12. Fo na lapa losi seluk.	The blossoms are copper again.

COMMENTARY (3)

This *bini* is based on eight sets. The set *fai*//*ledo* is the only set retained of the previous variations. *Lilo* 'gold' forms a new set with *losi* 'copper' while *kono* forms yet another set with *olu* 'to shed'. The linkage that occurs in these short *bini* (*fada*//*tuda*::*tuda*//*kono*::*kono*//*monu*, *kono*//*olu*) gives an indication of the combinatorial possibilities of elements in ritual language. Underlying all expressions in this language is a stable network of semantic elements whose interrelations can be formally represented in complex graphs.

The network of some of the words for 'speaking' provides a simple example of this kind of graph. The slight differences among the various terms for speaking, questioning, requesting, or promising are often difficult to gloss or indicate in translation. These uses are nonetheless crucial and strictly defined. *Fada*, the general verb 'to speak, to say, to tell,' is a critical *point of articulation* (in terms of graph theory), since it may pair with a number of other elements. It forms dyadic sets with *hala* which occurs as a noun for 'voice' or as a verb 'to voice'; with *nae*, an inflected verbal element for indicating direct quotation; with *noli*, the verb 'to teach, to instruct'; with *nosi*, an element that occurs only in ritual language and is therefore interpreted with the same sense as its permitted co-occurrent elements; with *tuda*, the verb 'to fall, to let fall'; and with *tudu* 'to show, to point out.' In turn, most of these elements form sets with other elements. *Hala* forms a set with *dasi* 'the voice or song (of a bird), to sing (of birds), to say something in a pleasing voice.' *Dasi* forms another set with *benga* 'to inform, to explain, to speak when introducing something.' *Nosi* links with various different verbs: 'to question, to ask, to request, to demand.' These include the verbal dyadic set, *dokodoe*//*taiboni* which is used almost exclusively for that special 'gentle demanding' that is supposed to characterize bridewealth requests. *Tuda* is another articulation point for a series of verbs of falling, with glosses 'to fall off, to tumble, to crumble, to shed, to peel.' The most interesting of these is the verb *olu* 'to shed, to peel,' since it forms a seemingly curious set with *tui*. According to native exegesis, this verb *tui* is identified as the same element as the verb 'to tell a story,' as in the partially reduplicated noun *tutuik* 'tale.' In Rotinese, it may be literally said, of trees, that they 'peel bark and tell leaves.' This idiom seems less peculiar when seen in light of those connections in the semantic field of which it forms a part. *(N)ae* pairs with two verbs that occur in the most common formulaic prelude, *lole hala//selu dasi*, for introducing direct speech. *Selu* is the verb 'to reply, to alternate, to exchange' and thus also pairs with *tuka* 'to change, to exchange, to barter.' *Selu* is one of the elements that link this network to a larger network of relations. That some of the main verbs for 'speaking' should belong so intimately to the same semantic field as the verbs for 'falling' and also the verbs for 'exchanging' is one of the more interesting discoveries of this form of analysis.

The formal interrelations of all these elements are as follows [→ = 'forms a set with']:

1.	fada	→	hala, nae/ae, noli, nosi, tuda, tudu
2.	hala	→	fada, dasi
3.	nae/ae	→	fada, helu, lole, selu
4.	noli	→	fada
5.	nosi	→	fada, tane
6.	tuda	→	fada, kona, kono, monu, sasi
7.	tudu	→	fada
8.	dasi	→	benga
9.	benga	→	dasi
10.	helu	→	ae
11.	lole	→	ae, selu
12.	selu	→	ae, lole, tuka
13.	tuka	→	selu
14.	tane	→	tata, teni
15.	tata	→	tane, teni
16.	teni	→	tata, dokodoe
17.	dokodoe	→	teni, taiboni
18.	taiboni	→	dokodoe
19.	kona	→	tuda
20.	kono	→	tuda, monu, ngga, olu
21.	monu	→	tuda, kono
22.	sasi	→	tuda
23.	ngga	→	kono
24.	olu	→	kono, tui
25.	tui	→	olu

These formal associations account for all uses of these elements in approximately 5000 lines of parallel verse.

A graphic representation of these interrelations can also be made. It is of interest to note that more general semantic elements are points of articulation while those elements that are idiomatic or have restricted contextual uses are found on the extreme edges of the graph's branching structure. At this stage in the development of a dictionary on ritual language, networks comprising several hundred interrelated elements can be constructed from a core lexicon of a thousand dyadic sets (Fox MS.)

While these short *bini* provide some idea of the structure of Rotinese composition, they give no idea of its poetic complexity. Further variations, using similar sets, are unlimited. By describing, for example, only the loss of the 'sugar cane sheath' and 'banana blossom' and by interweaving this with other plant imagery, this *bini* of succession can be transformed to a funeral chant (cf. Fox 1971b:242–4). Most chants continue for hundreds of lines. With elaborations and repetitions, their performance may occupy several hours of an evening. At present estimate, an individual must have knowledge of approximately 1000–1500 dyadic sets to achieve a minimal fluency and become socially recognized as a promising chanter. My specific object in this paper is to examine the relationship of Rotinese language and dialects to this rich repertoire of poetic words.

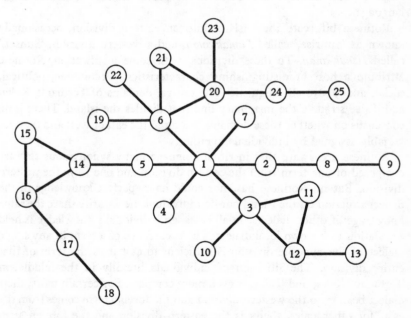

Fig. 8.   Formal associations on the verb *fada* 'to speak'

Ritual language and dialect semantics

One direction of some previous studies on parallelism, those that have followed leads outlined by Lowth (1753, 1779), has been to distinguish three sorts of parallels: (1) synonymous parallels, (2) antithetic parallels, and (3) synthetic parallels. As a general typology, this approach is somewhat useful, but in any precise analysis of a large lexicon of dyadic sets, it has only limited value. The criteria for synonymy or antithesis are difficult to make precise and the more precise these criteria are made, the more the residual class of synthetic parallels tends to increase. Furthermore, the approach limits analysis to the single relation between elements of a pair and takes no account of an element's range of associations or its location as a node in a network of semantic interrelations.

Using, however, a loose notion of synonymy, it is apparent that many pairs have 'similar' meaning. Were these the only class of pairs in ritual language, there would be some justification for reducing parallelism to a mere ritual redundancy. But near synonyms account for only a portion of the lexicon in traditions of pervasive parallelism, and even between paired elements, differences between these elements cannot be discounted. The general effect is always that of carefully calibrated stereoscopy, a fusion of separate images.[5] A loose notion of synonymy can nonetheless serve as a starting point in the examination of the use of dialect variants in ritual language.

Rotinese bifurcate their island into an eastern division, occasionally known as 'Sunrise,' called *Lamak-anan*, and a western division, 'Sunset,' called *Henak-anan*. To these divisions, with some justification, Rotinese attribute a host of distinguishing characteristics – economic, political, social, and, above all, linguistic. The central domains of Termanu, Keka, and Talae straddle the imaginary line that divides the island. There is no consensus on whether these domains belong to the east or west and they are variably assigned by individuals to either.

Rotinese are aware that in ritual language many synonymous sets are composed of one term from the eastern division and one from the western division. But no Rotinese has, nor could have, perfect knowledge of the dialect situation on the island nor do individuals necessarily share the same knowledge of other dialects. In all cases, an individual's knowledge is held in relation to his own local dialect. The occurrence of a term in any single dialect of the opposite division is sufficient to cast it as the term of that entire division. The situation of individuals literally in the middle, in Termanu, Keka, and Talae, is even more complex. For certain pairs, their dialect belongs to the western division and the foreign term comes from the east; for other pairs, theirs is the eastern division and the foreign term comes from the west. Like all native models, the Rotinese view of division dialects is a partial, specific, though not inaccurate, perception that closely partakes of the phenomenon it is intended to describe. Imperfect knowledge is essential to the maintenance of the model.[6]

The simplest illustration of the use of dialect semantics, one that would confirm the native view, is the following list of dvadic sets:

	Eastern Roti		Western Roti	Gloss
1.	daehena	[Bilba]	hataholi	[Termanu]	'man, human person'
2.	luak	[Korbaffo]	leak	[Termanu]	'cave, grotto'
3.	nafa	[Ringgou]	li	[Termanu]	'waves, breakers'
4.	pela	[Bilba]	longe	[Termanu]	'to dance in a specific way'
5.	lain	[Termanu]	ata	[Dengka, Oenale]	'heaven, sky; above'
6.	ka	[Termanu]	kiki	[Thie, Dengka]	'to bite'
7.	sele	[Termanu]	tane	[Loleh]	'to plant'
8.	paik	[Termanu]	sola	[Oenale]	'corner of leaf bucket'
9.	-lo	[Termanu]	-nggou	[Thie, Baä]	'to call loudly, to invite'

Examples 4 and 5 illustrate the aspects of borrowing. *Longe* (from *ronggeng*) and *ata* (from *atas*) are probably Malay borrowings. Evidence from Borneo (Hardeland 1858:4–5; Evans 1953:495–6) suggests that the direct borrowing of one term from Malay and the coupling of this term with a term from the native language is a possible, and undoubtedly widespread, means of creating synonymous dyadic sets (cf. use of Spanish loanwords in the construction of Zinacanteco couplets, as reported by Bricker, this volume). Interestingly, given Rotinese use of Malay, recognizable Malay words in ritual language are surprisingly few. Direct borrowing does not seem to occur. The few Malay words in ritual language are dialect words adopted from Malay in some – but not necessarily all – dialects on the island. Ritual language remains remarkably impermeable to Malay. The same is true of the few Dutch and Portuguese words in ritual language. Instead of being strange foreign words, they are current words in ordinary speech. Two dyadic sets happen, in fact, to combine one Dutch- and one Portuguese-derived term. *Kana(k)* 'small table' from Dutch *knaap* forms a set with *kadela* 'chair, stool' from the Portuguese *kadera*; *kuei* 'socks, slippers,' a word compounded of Dutch *kous* and Rotinese *ei(k)* 'foot,' forms a set with *sapeo* 'non-Rotinese hat' from the Portuguese *chapeo*.

10.	henu	[Termanu]	sofe	[Thie]	'full, sufficient'

Example 10 illustrates a further important effect of the use of dialect words. It would be almost impossible to expect dialect terms to be so conveniently segregated in eastern and western areas. The set *henu//sofe* is one of the standard sets cited as an example of division dialect segregation. But the fact is that *sofe* (or more often *sofe-sofe*) occurs in Termanu dialect. Its sense is altered slightly. Instead of meaning 'full, sufficient,' it occurs adverbially to indicate something that is 'too much, overflowing, brimming.' In native exegesis, *sofe*, by its concurrence with *henu*, is taken to have the 'same' meaning and this meaning of *sofe* is, correctly, identified as a dialect usage in Thie. Other examples can be shown:

11. pada   [Termanu]   bata   [Loleh]   'to forbid'

Probably these words are ancient cognates, although /b/ → /p/ and /d/ → /t/ do not presently operate as dialect sound shifts. *Bata* means 'to forbid' in Loleh, but it also occurs in Termanu with the related sense 'to hinder, to hamper.'

12. tenga   [Termanu]   nggama   [Baä]   'to take up, to grasp'

Tenga is 'to grasp' something in the hand; it forms a set with *nggama*, a verb which in Baä has the similar meaning 'to take up' or 'to pick up' something. This verb, when it occurs in Termanu, has quite a different sense: 'to undertake something, to be on the point of doing something.'

13. bali   [Termanu]   seö   [Baä]   'to mix, to blend'

This set illustrates a minor but common use of dialect words. Seö is recognizably *sedo* in Termanu. Both words have much the same meaning, 'to mix non-liquids,' but it is Baä's dialect form, not Termanu's ordinary form, that occurs in the ritual language of Termanu. In the third *bini* variation quoted earlier in this paper (lines 4 and 12), the words *losi(k)* 'copper' occurs with *lilo* 'gold.' The dialect, or other origin, of *losi(k)* is uncertain. The chanter who provided the *bini* noted that *losi(k)* = *liti(k)* 'copper' in Termanu dialect. The sets of ritual language are formulaically fixed. Whether a knowledgeable chanter might legitimately substitute *sedo* for *seö* or *liti* for *losi(k)* is a question I cannot yet determine.

14. ndano   [Loleh]   toko   [Thie]   'to catch//to throw
                                                           away'

The use of dialect words is not confined to synonymous sets nor are these paired elements always from eastern and western divisions. This is an antithetic set made up of words from two domains of the western division. *Ndano* is equated with *ndaso* in Termanu since both verbs have a similar sense;

toko in Termanu has the meaning 'to beat, to knock' rather than 'to throw away.'

15. lima   [Termanu]   kala   [Bilba, Thie]   'hand//chest'

Lima, the word for 'hand,' is used throughout Roti; one element in its range of pairs is *kala* 'chest.' This is equated with Termanu dialect term *fanak*. *Kala* (or *kara*) however occurs both in eastern dialects and in western dialects but not in Termanu. In areas where *kala* is used, this is not a dialect set. In Termanu, it is; but its distribution does not fit the native dialect model.

16. pu   [Termanu]   oku   [Keka]   'to scream, to flush
                                                    animals with noise'

Pu is found generally through all the dialects; *oku* is apparently specific to Keka. Therefore for individuals in Termanu (but not Baä) this set is also at variance with the native model. Dialect use pervades ritual language as a fundamental process in the creation of an elaborate tradition of parallelism. No simple model would be sufficient to explain all its aspects.

Conclusions

The impression of ritual language on its hearers is one of some strangeness. The use of dialect variants contributes to this strangeness. Words are used in a variety of ways that make them slightly discrepant from their ordinary usage; but the concurrence of each of these words with another that signals its sense creates a kind of resonant intelligibility, an intelligibility that varies from individual to individual. This ritual code, in its entirety, is probably beyond the comprehension of any of its individual participants. To these participants, it is an ancestral language which they continue. It is a language into which individuals 'grow' as their age and acquaintance increase. This process should last a lifetime and tales are told of former elders, who – as they approached extreme old age – ceased to speak ordinary language and uttered only ritual statements.

As a linguistic proposition, I would suggest that all elaborate forms of parallelism possess dialect variants in their repertoire of poetic words. Language diversification is a process that parallelism exploits. The Hebrew poetry of the Old Testament shares sets, in a common tradition, with the ancient Canaanite epics. Similarly, the related ritual languages of Borneo utilize dialect diversity. And there is good indication that this may hold as well for various Mayan languages. More comparative research is necessary.

In a speculative vein, I would point to the recent neurophysiological research of Pollen, Lee & Taylor (1971) that suggests, rather strongly, that the brain's processing of visual information is of the same form as its processing of auditory information. The analogy of linguistic parallelism with visual stereoscopy, a fusion of separate images, is by no means strained. Nor is parallelism a limited and trivial phenomenon. Systems of pervasive canonical parallelism are extreme (and relatively transparent) elaborations on a principle that appears to underlie much linguistic expression and, as Jakobson has repeatedly argued, most poetry. It is further remarkable that canonical parallelism, in its distribution in the world's oral traditions, is reserved for special situations: scriptures, the utterance of sacred words, ritual relations, curing, and the communication with spirits. In future studies of semantics, the formal structural systems on which traditions of canonical parallelism are based may provide cases for special study. From these it may appear that what we refer to as meaning is neither the listing of components nor the accumulation of features but the interval of a function.

Finally I would call attention to the special role of the chanters (*manahelo*) in the maintenance of ritual language as an intelligible code. At the present time, on Roti, those designated as chanters are a few male elders recognized by a loose popular consensus in each domain. But in an earlier account of Rotinese life, Heijmering (1843–4:356–7) describes chanters as an elite profession of wandering poets who would journey from domain to domain performing ritual services, particularly at funeral ceremonies. Chanters have now become, or are in competition with, Christian preachers. Almost without exception, the chanters from whom I gathered texts were men of wide experience and capable in their other activities. Those who could provide exegesis on chants had spent some time in one or another domain. My own teacher in ritual language, S. Adulanu, was Head of the Earth (*Dae Langak*) in clan Meno of Termanu; he had lived for a period of his youth in Diu. An old man of near seventy, he was still improving his chant knowledge. In addition to myself, there was another man in his late forties who spent time learning from the old man. After what consisted of more than a year's apprenticeship, I began gathering texts from chanters in other domains. Old Meno was always anxious that I read to him what I had gathered. Those chants that pleased him, he would have me repeat several times until he could render them as his own. When I questioned him on how he had learned all that he knew, he would tell me the same brief story that as a child, he would lie beside his father, at night, on a sleeping platform and his father would instruct him. Old Meno is dead now but his line continues.

It is a Rotinese practice, as the final act of the funeral ceremonies a year or more after burial, to erect a raised ring of smooth stones around the base of a large tree to honor a dead man. In alluding to this custom, Meno gave me this further variation on the theme of succession.

VARIATION (4)

1. Nggongo Ingu Lai lalo	Nggongo of the Highland dies
2. Ma Lima Le Dale sapu.	And Lima of the Riverbed perishes.
3. De lalo ela Latu Nggongo	He dies leaving Latu Nggongo
4. Ma sapu ela Enga Lima.	And perishes leaving Enga Lima.
5. Boe te ela batu nangatun	But he leaves a stone to sit on
6. Ma lea ai nasalain.	And leaves a tree to lean on.
7. De koluk Nggongo Ingu Lai	Plucked is Nggongo from the Highland
8. Te Latu Nggongo nangatu	But now Latu Nggongo sits
9. Ma haik Lima Le Dale	And scooped is Lima from the Riverbed
10. Te Enga Lima nasalai.	But now Enga Lima leans.
11. Fo lae Nggongo tutuü batun	They say: Nggongo's sitting stone
12. Na tao ela Latu Nggongo	Was made for Latu Nggongo
13. Ma Lima lalai ain	And Lima's leaning tree
14. Na peda ela Enga Lima.	Was placed for Enga Lima.[7]

III
COMMUNITY GROUND RULES
FOR PERFORMANCE

INTRODUCTION

A community's system of speech situations and events constitutes the structural matrix within which speaking occurs in that community. Giving shape to these scenes as they are enacted, and underlying the dynamics of communicative activity within them, are sets of general cultural themes and social-interactional organizing principles, which may be seen from the point of view of the ethnography of speaking as the implicit or explicit community ground rules for performance. Such ground rules are only analytically separable from the speech activities themselves, and most of the papers in this volume contain information about organizing principles of this kind. The papers in this section, however, are distinguished by their principal focus on this aspect of the speech economy of particular communities (for speech economy, see Hymes, section VI).

The analysis of community ground rules for performance may serve a particularly important function for the ethnography of speaking in that such ground rules, by the generalness of their scope, often represent the means for establishing the continuity between speaking and other forms of expressive behavior. Speech activity does not necessarily constitute a discrete domain within cultures, and the analysis of general social and cultural principles governing speaking may show these to cut across a range of activities and govern other kinds of behavior besides speaking, in a way that the study of specifically speech acts, situations, and events cannot. The paper by Susan Philips, for example, demonstrates that there is a unified set of rules which regulate participation in a range of scenes on the Warm Springs Reservation, including traditional religious events (such as wakes, memorial dinners, and religious feasts), war dancing, and general councils. Only the last of these should properly be considered a speech event per se, in which speech activity is the dominant feature of the event; moreover the range and importance of speaking vary considerably across the three kinds of activities. Nevertheless, these scenes are most appropriately considered together because they all run on 'Indian time,' which is the way both Indians and non-Indians designate the fact that participation in all is governed by a distinctively Indian way of proceeding, baffling and frustrating to outsiders who do not have the cultural knowledge necessary to make sense of activity organized in terms of deep-seated Indian patterns. Non-Indians, for example, who bring to a ritual event the expectation that the full cast of active participants will be assembled before the event commences and that they will sustain their participant roles throughout the event, have great difficulty understanding an event on Indian time in which activity may commence before all the participants have arrived and in which individual participants may move in and out of role throughout the course of the event. It is the elucidation of precisely such cross-cultural differences affecting ways of speaking that is at the heart of the ethnography of speaking.

Equally striking and disturbing to the outsider is the 'noise' of Antiguan conversation, described by Karl Reisman. A general American ground rule for participation in conversation is that it shall consist of 'turns,' with one voice holding the floor and speaking at a time (see Sacks, section V), on a subject relevant to the topic addressed by the participants whose turns preceded one's own. Among Antiguan peasants, this ground rule does not obtain. Rather, in a range of situations, one is likely to hear an entire group maintaining what Reisman terms a contrapuntal conversation, with all voices participating simultaneously, each aggressively carrying its own burden. Reisman suggests that such conversations are only the most striking and ultimate consequence of the fundamental thrust among Antiguans toward individual, self-assertive, and competitive expression in interaction, and the concomitant impulse to make counter-noise in the face of noise — spoken or otherwise — which impinges upon oneself. These are, in other words, implicit cultural ground rules which shape a wide range of communicative interactions in Antigua. In a similar vein, Philips interprets the rules for participation in events on Indian time, which determine what activities occur within particular events, when they begin, and how long they take, as themselves the behavioral and interactional manifestation of an even more general theme at Warm Springs, the maximization of the possibility that everyone who wants to participate is given the chance, when he or she chooses and in the way he or she chooses, consistent with the Indian ideals of individuality and self-determination. Though the structure of particular events is basic to both Philips' and Reisman's analyses, what is more important is the interplay between event structure and ground rules for participation in the events, which provides a broader and more flexible structural framework within which to analyze the events as performed, and to comprehend both the unity and variability of these events, within the speech economy of a particular group.

The ground rules elucidated by Philips and Reisman operate at the level of implicit participational organizing principles, largely unarticulated at the conscious level. The ethnographer, however, will frequently find a set of explicit principles, consciously referred to by members of the community in guiding and evaluating their own and others' speech behavior. These may take the form of normative moral principles defining valued or 'proper' kinds of speech behavior, as against improper or disvalued ways of speaking, as in the Malagasy distinction between *kabary* and *resaka* discussed by Elinor Keenan (cf. Bricker, section V). Here *kabary* and *resaka* are symbolic classifiers which operate at the most cultural level to divide the domain of speaking in Malagasy society into two principal segments, one considered elegant, artful, and good, the other crude and inferior. Anthropologists, or course, are trained to look beyond such ideal norms to patterns of actual behavior and the cultural assumptions that accompany them, for failure to live up to ideal norms is just as much a fact of social life as the ideal norms themselves, and no society is without institutionalized means of understanding and coping with this fact. Thus, an interest in ideal norms must be accompanied by a quest for the sociological norms which obtain within specific domains of behavior. Keenan, for instance shows how the distinction between *kabary* and *resaka* constitutes an important dimension of sex-role definition among the Malagasy of the Vakinankaratra, for *kabary* is conceived of by both sexes as the province of men, and *resaka* of women; women are thus by cultural definition inferior speakers, and are, in fact, characterized by *resaka*, thus living up to cultural expectations by adhering, in effect, to the cultural ground rule for performance defined by this mode of speaking. Pursuing the matter still further, though, Keenan discovers that there is a significant level on which this 'inferior' speech of women is in fact valued and used as a strategic social resource, for it affords women a distinct advantage in certain kinds of situations, including economic ones, in which bluntness and directness are more efficient means of getting things done than the indirect and allusive *kabary* standard to which the men feel they must adhere. The interplay between ideal and actual norms is thus seen as an interplay between ideal and actual cultural ground rules for performance.

While the contrast between valued and disvalued or good and bad speech has been found by ethnographers of speaking to be present in a wide range of societies, other cases have been described in which the most powerful moral distinction contrasts speaking as a whole with another mode of behavior, frequently refraining from speaking, or silence. In such cases, speaking itself may be disvalued, and silence considered morally preferable, as among the seventeenth-century Quakers, for whom silence carried an especially high degree of moral and symbolic significance, as described by Richard Bauman. Since no natural society has found it possible to refrain from speaking altogether, the disvaluation of speaking carries with it a potential for conflict, which centers in the unattainability of absolute silence in social life. Among the most telling points at which this conflict impinged upon the Quakers was the role of the minister, who was, because of his role and sphere of activity, subject to all but mutually incompatible demands with regard to speaking. We are not accustomed to looking for the roots of role conflict in a society's ground rules for speaking, but this is the very point of doing ethnographies of speaking, to uncover the variety of distinctive ways in which speaking ramifies through social and cultural life, without taking any aspect of the domain for granted.

4

WARM SPRINGS 'INDIAN TIME': HOW THE REGULATION OF PARTICIPATION AFFECTS THE PROGRESSION OF EVENTS

SUSAN U. PHILIPS

That people of different cultures have different concepts of time is a fairly popular notion, and one which many people find appealing in an exotic sort of way. Most often this realm of cultural diversity is dealt with in rather grand and mysterious terms that compare 'our' western European – derived concepts of time with those of 'other' cultures. Thus while we may conceive of time in primarily 'linear' terms, others will have an essentially 'cyclical' orientation; while our activity is regulated by clock and calendar units, that of others is governed by the seasonal shifts in nature.

Among the peoples of the world whose activities have been drawn on for illustration of cultural variation in concepts of time, North American Indians can only be matched in popularity by Latin Americans, as evidenced by the Indians' repeated appearances as bearers of a distinctive temporal orientation in works as diverse in approach as A. I. Hallowell's 'Temporal Orientation in Western Civilization and a Preliterate Society' (1937), Benjamin L. Whorf's 'An American Indian Model of the Universe' (1950), Edward Hall's *The Silent Language* (1959), and Stan Steiner's *The New Indians* (1968).

It is Hall's orientation toward time as a dimension of activity which in itself conveys information and is systematically organized that perhaps comes closest to the present-day orientation of the ethnography of communication, especially when he is informally discussing the meaningfulness of 'when' an event happens:

Whenever they want to make an important announcement they will ask: 'When shall we let them know?' In the social world a girl feels insulted when she is asked for a date at the last minute by someone whom she doesn't know very well, and the person who extends an invitation to a dinner party with only three or four days' notice has to apologize (1959:17)

or when he discusses the importance of 'ordering' of events in determining the meaningfulness of any single event:

92

The week is the week not only because it has seven days but because they are in a fixed *order*. Ordering as a formal isolate would seem to be an expression of *order* as in the laws of order, selection, and congruence ... We keep constant track of all sorts of things which are otherwise identical and *only distinguish between them because of their order* ... The seventh day is different from the first day; the middle of the week is different from the end, and so on. (1959:132)

Although Hall never really deals in detail with the relevance of sequencing as it affects not only our assignment of meaning to any communicative act, but also our notions of what restrictions prevail in determining 'what can happen next,' the concern is still very much with us. In the ethnography of speaking, the interest in sequencing and temporal process arises out of the need to consider the social contexts in which speech occurs, in accounting for the diversity in styles of speaking within a given speech community, and in detailing what one must know to speak in a socially appropriate, as well as grammatical and meaningful fashion – i.e., to enjoy 'communicative competence' (Hymes 1971). A speaker must have some notion of temporal ordering, or sequencing, in whatever he is doing, if he is to speak appropriately. And it is with this recognition that we arrive at a concern with process.

There are already descriptions of activities or events involving speech that deal with temporal process by dividing the activity into units or segments and ordering those units in a sequence (e.g., Frake 1964; Schegloff 1972), with the implication that the speaker must be familiar with the sequence, and with the restrictions and possible variations allowed him within it. This segmenting approach has been further encouraged by recommendations that linguistic conceptualizations, involving attention to the 'syntagmatic axis' and to 'co-occurrence rules,' be applied in sociolinguistic analysis (e.g., Ervin-Tripp 1972). And such recommendations have been implemented in the phrase structure grammar models used by Salmond (this volume) and Irvine (this volume).

But there is much involved in temporal process that cannot be captured through an analysis that proceeds through segmentation and sequencing. In this paper I will deal with aspects of process that can neither be easily segmented nor incorporated into a linguistics-derived model, but must nevertheless be considered if we are to understand what must be known for a person to do and say the right thing at the right time.

At the same time, I will try to show some of the ways in which the processual structure of events on the Warm Springs Indian Reservation is sufficiently distinct from that of their non-Indian neighbors to contribute to the perpetuation of the special notion of 'Indian time.' And I would express the hope that such an analysis will further non-Indian acceptance of and participation in the Indian way of doing things.

The Warm Springs Reservation is located in central Oregon and is populated by approximately 1500 descendents of Warm Springs Sahaptin, Wasco Chinook, and Paiute Indians. The Indians of Warm Springs now refer to themselves collectively as 'the tribe,' and constitute a single closely integrated community with a substantially shared culture, developed in the course of more than a hundred years of living together on the reservation.

Events on Indian time

When, for whatever reason, non-Indians take it upon themselves to attend or participate in an event being held on the Warm Springs Reservation, they often experience one or several of the following: (1) They try to learn from Indians at what time the event will begin. Often the person questioned will say he doesn't know, but if pressed, he may give a specific time – e.g., 8 PM, or 'some time after 9.' The non-Indians will arrive at that time, only to find that 'nothing is happening' yet, and no one seems to know when something will happen. They may wait anywhere from twenty minutes to several hours before the event 'begins.' (2) They have come to see something in particular, perhaps 'war dancing' or 'the Root Feast,' but while they see a great deal of activity going on, with people milling about, they cannot tell when something has 'begun.' They would like to ask, as children sometimes do, 'Has it started yet?' But they usually don't ask. (3) They may find that although they stay the whole time, what they came to see never happens, although a white friend later assures them it has happened every time *he's* gone, and they wonder how they could have missed it. And finally, (4) they come with the feeling that they should be there from the beginning until the end. But they can't tell how much longer the event will last, and the activities began so long after they arrived that they feel they really must leave. Is it 'all right' to leave? *When* is it all right to leave? They don't know.

Many Indians are aware that non-Indians are confused and sometimes disturbed by these experiences, and it is in such contexts that the explanation 'We're on Indian time' comes up most frequently in response to white expressions of frustration or uncertainty – as if to make it clear to them that these experiences are the result of neither mismanagement nor misrepresentation of the situation by Indians, but rather a matter of a known, accepted, and deliberately different way of dealing with time.

From the Indians' point of view, there are some activities on the reservation that run on Indian time, and other activities that run – or are supposed to run – on white time (for which there is no analogous term of reference, 'Indian time' being the marked category). At present, events on 'Indian time' take place for the most part on the weekends and in the evenings, for during the eight-to-five workday, the children are in schools run on white time, and the adults are at jobs run on white time. Some aspects of Indian time do tend to carry over into the eight-to-five workday activities, so that both children and adults are more often 'late' or 'miss' school and work than would be the case in a non-Indian community. In addition, there are some activities that are in so many respects a combination of Indian and non-Indian ways of doing things, that people within the Warm Springs community differ and vary in their expectations about whether an event is being run or should be being run on Indian or white time. Nevertheless, there are at each end of the Indian–non-Indian continuum certain activities that clearly run on one kind of time or the other. And in attempting to pin down what it is about events on Indian time that accounts for the experiences which whites have, we will focus attention on some of the events that most clearly run on 'Indian time.'

The events with which we will be dealing most explicitly can be identified as Indian rather than non-Indian in the following ways. First, they are sponsored and carried out by tribal members, rather than by non-Indian Bureau of Indian Affairs administrators or other whites who have various links and involvements with the Warm Springs Indians (e.g., school personnel, businessmen in the area).

In addition, information about these events – when they will be held, where they will be held, what or who they will involve – is communicated primarily through word of mouth from one person to another, rather than being disseminated through some form of written communication. Those who are thought to be appropriate persons to pass this information on to will vary, depending on the event. If it is a large celebration, then word will be passed not only to Warm Springs residents, but to Indians from other reservations, and to non-Indian friends as well. If it is a general council, word will usually go around the whole Warm Springs community, but not outside it, unless to specially invited guests. If it is an event of relevance to only a specific sector of the community, like the members of a particular neighborhood or kin group, then it is these people that others will make a point of telling. Notices of events that are open to at least the whole reservation are sometimes posted in the local store and tribal office. Yet even with these notices, the news is spread primarily by one person telling another. In addition, it is usually not required of people that they say whether or not they will come at the time that they learn of the event. The number of persons who may come to an event is always limited by the number of face-to-face encounters through which information is transmitted within the period of time between when people decide to do something and when it takes place. Yet at the same time, the number is usually open-ended, or uncertain, because people do not have to commit themselves.

While there are many events that have all or some of the features being discussed, attention will be focused, for the purposes of this paper, on only those events that are open to at least the whole Warm Springs community and are attended by non-Indians at least occasionally as well – events of which it is said 'everyone is welcome.' There are several reasons for this focus. First of all, these large-scale events are the ones in regard to which the issue of 'Indian time' comes up quite frequently, probably because the Indians' awareness of the contrast in timing of events is heightened by the presence or expected presence of non-Indians. These are occasions when it is most relevant to mention that a time estimate of how long something will take is in terms of 'Indian time.' Second, these events are those which involve the largest numbers of people and the greatest diversity of activities. They thus provide the opportunity to observe a wider range of ways in which the timing of events is being affected.

These large social events include:

(1) *Traditional religious events*: funeral wakes that go on all night before the deceased is buried; community-wide memorial dinners which open the way for the family of recently deceased persons to once again take part in social activities; the annual Root Feast and Huckleberry Feast, which provide the blessing of first roots and berries, and insure their yield will be bountiful. All of these activities are today incorporated into what Warm Springs Indians refer to as 'the longhouse religion,' 'the old people's way of worshipping,' or 'worship dance.' Anthropologists have called this religious activity the Prophet cult, and it was believed by Leslie Spier to date back before the coming of white people into this part of the country (Spier 1935), although it has also been perceived as a crisis reaction to the advent of non-Indians into the area, and as a precursor to the Ghost Dance of the Plains.

(2) *War dancing*, which occurs at the time of a variety of social celebrations. While war dancing actually includes other kinds of Indian social dancing besides the War Dance, such as the Round Dance and the Owl Dance (differing from one another in dance step, sociospatial formation, and in the songs and drum beats that accompany them), the events are known by their most prominent form of dancing, the War Dance. War dancing usually takes place in the evenings at times when other activities are going on as well. It often occurs at the time of the Root and Huckleberry feasts, and on holidays, such as July 4th, New Year's Eve, and Labor Day, and at pow-wows, or any other time when many Indians have come together to spend at least some time enjoying themselves socially.

Non-Indians sometimes confuse or group together the sacred or religious worship dance and the non-religious or secular war dancing, because both sometimes take place on the same day, as at the time of the Root Feast, and because the ways in which they differ do not involve culturally familiar ways of distinguishing the secular and the sacred. However, the two are kept conceptually separate by the Indians themselves, have different historical developments, and are marked by different regalia, different songs and dances, and to some extent, different leadership, participation in organization, and active involvement.

(3) *General councils.* These meetings, open to the whole community, are usually called by the tribal council, although they can be called by others as well, to inform the Warm Springs people of issues before the council, to get feedback from tribal members regarding these issues, to make councilmen available for questioning, and to provide the opportunity to bring issues people feel are of community-wide interest before the council in an open and public way.

Thus far, the events to be considered have been characterized by their sponsorship (Indian), their invitation by word of mouth, their lack of a requirement for advance commitment to be present or absent, and their openness to all. Another characteristic that these events share is the use of, or organization within, the context of basically the same sociospatial arrangement. Whether in the gym or social hall of the community center, or one of the three longhouses on the reservation, the center of activity is usually an enclosed rectangular space. Seating is along the two long sides and one short side of this space, while the second short side and the center of the space are reserved for the activities that are the foci of attention during the event. Traditionally men sat along the left side of the space, and women along the right side, if one is facing the front, or short side that is an activity focus. Today this sexual division is no longer clear but one often sees more women on the right. The location of the entrance into the area varies, depending on the building, but nowadays is from the center of the back or one side.

This, then, is the primary area in which the events under consideration are said to take place. There is however, always a peripheral area outside this enclosed space which is of relevance to these events. It includes, minimally, a kitchen, usually adjacent and accessible through a doorway between it and the area just described.

The kitchen area is important, because a final characteristic of all of these events is that at least one meal is served to everyone present at some point during the event. The amount and kind of food varies, as does the elaborateness of the setting-up, but the meals have this in common: the food is for everyone who is present when it is served, and is provided by those who sponsor the event at no cost to the individual guests; and the meal is usually set up and served to those seated in the primary area, after having been prepared in the kitchen. The sharing (and serving to guests) of food is an important way of maintaining relationships and expressing good will and hospitality to visitors.

These features, then, characterize all of these events, and in combination mark them as deriving from an Indian rather than a non-Indian cultural tradition.

How the regulation of participation affects the progression of events

In turning now to an elucidation of features of event organization that contribute to the sense of 'Indian time,' attention will focus on the ways in which participation in such events is regulated, or what conditions how people move in and out of activities, because of the importance of these factors in determining what activities occur, when they begin, and how long they take.

In recalling what non-Indians experience when they attend Indian events, it is useful to make a distinction between their inability to recognize relevant signals in participants' behavior (signals that communicate and define the progression of activity which is meaningful in the context of the event, rather than incidental to it, or even in violation of it) on the one hand, and the inability to predict exactly when something will happen on the other. Indians have the relevant information to recognize the signals, and can judge approximately but not exactly when they will occur. Non-Indians can neither recognize the relevant signals, nor predict when they will occur. They tend to confuse the one issue with the other, thinking that if they could recognize signals, they could make temporal predictions. The two are not completely separable, but here the primary concern will be with accounting for what is involved in both Indian and non-Indian nonspecificity in predicting when something will start and how long it will take.

All of the events under consideration involve a meaningful sequence of activities, in that there are certain things that must happen, and must happen in a certain order, in order for it to be said that the event has in fact taken place. These will be referred to as 'obligatory' activities, to distinguish them from 'optional' activities, certain of which can occur, but do not have to occur, at particular junctures in the obligatory sequence for any given event.

For any given activity that must get done, there are varying ways in which persons present at an event may participate. They may sit and watch what goes on in the primary rectangular sociospace; they may take part in the activities that others are watching; and they may take part in activities that are preparatory to that which is deemed relevant to be watched or witnessed. For some activities there are no people simply watching, but it is always possible to distinguish those participants whose actions are relevant to the actual getting done of obligatory activities. For example, when a meal or feast takes place, everyone who is present in the primary sociospace eats. But only some people prepare food, serve it, and then clean up, and in the case of a ritual feast, only a small number would be involved in the necessary sacred blessing of the ritual Indian foods.

That which most strikingly characterizes the conditions for participation in obligatory activities, and has the greatest significance for the progression of an event, is the extent to which these conditions parallel those for the minimal participants who witness the event. Earlier it was stated that anyone can come to these events, and that one need not make a commitment in advance as to whether he will come or not, and implicitly, as to *when* he will come, if he is coming. While all of the obligatory activities involve *some* precommitted personnel to carry out necessary actions, and all involve some criteria limiting or defining who can take part, *no* obligatory activity is carried out solely by precommitted persons. And no activity is limited by any social criteria to a finite number of specific individuals who must show up; there is always more than one person who qualifies to do what must be done.

In part this is made possible by the kind of criteria that define who can do what. The two most important are sex and age-linked ability. Thus there are many things that only men do, or only women do, and many that mainly younger people do (partly because of the stamina required) or mainly older people do (because of the number of years it takes to become skillfull or knowledgeable). There are other more specific criteria that are involved in specific activities. For example, in the Root Feast, it is desirable that those women who are ritual servers be, among other things, women who participated in the actual digging of the new roots several days beforehand. However, this particular criterion is one of several; which of these are ultimately adhered to will depend on who comes forward. There are, then, always more women who qualify than there are slots open in this activity. Who actually serves will then vary from one feast to another, yet always within a framework of a certain set of criteria.

The effect that this dependence on voluntary labor has on the progression of an event should be apparent. An activity cannot begin until people come forward to carry out certain necessary actions. Who will come forward and when they will come forward is indeterminate, until they actually do come forward, since they are not precommitted. When an event begins is affected by these factors of participation because they hold true for whatever the first activity is, and how long an event takes is likewise affected because they hold true for later activities as well. The extent to which the initiation of any given activity is affected by these factors will depend on other ways that participation is regulated, and these will now be considered.

First, there is variation in how the necessary participants are required to coordinate their actions in relation to one another, or, in other words, in the extent to which their actions are interdependent. Depending on the activity, their actions may be totally interdependent, so that everyone participating must begin at the same time; or their actions may be relatively independent in that one person can begin alone, with others joining in at various times, with some restrictions on how they must then coordinate with others already engaged in the activity. The range of combinations of interdependent and independent actions is considerable, and how it works affects the 'timing' of activities. For example, in the ritual serving and blessing of Indian foods at a feast, all of the servers must be assembled to begin the serving at the same time. When the activity of worship dancing takes place, however, the interdependence of participants is more complex. There are essentially two kinds of participants here: drummer–singers, and dancers who dance to their songs. While there are seven slots open to drummers (i.e., usually seven drummers stand up at the front), the singing is sometimes started with less than seven, with others coming up to join in the singing any time after they arrive. The dancers cannot begin to dance however, until the drummers have begun. But any time after that, any number of persons can join in the dancing at the beginning of a song. In this activity one drummer is enough to start, but even if there were fifty dancers ready they couldn't begin without the drummers, whereas the reverse does not hold true. In a third kind of necessary activity, that of preparing (rather than serving) food, one person can begin, and others can join in as they arrive, coordinating their actions with others.

At a general council meeting, it is not necessary that persons to talk on all the topics to be covered be present for the meeting to begin. It is only necessary that some *one* from among those qualified by knowledge and/or experience on one of the topics to be discussed be present to speak on that topic. However, it is also necessary for there to be more than a few people present to *listen* to what he says. This presents a contrast with many activities in which speaking does not occur (e.g., dancing, singing, feasting), for at these an audience or non-participating witness is not required to be present for the activity to begin.

From these brief examples, it should be possible to see that the way participants' actions are coordinated with one another for any given activity varies, and in combination with the voluntary nature of participation, enters into the determination of when something will begin.

A second dimension of regulation of participation that, in conjunction with the above, affects the progression of an event is the *number* of people required to initiate an activity. Here it is helpful to distinguish between the *possible* number and the *necessary* number. The number of either possible or necessary participants for an activity may be *finite*, or always a specific number; it may be *open-ended*, so that one is sufficient, with any number acceptable up to limits based on physical space; or it may be finite and specific, yet varying from one occasioning of the same activity to another, depending on aspects of the situation that are peculiar to the specific occasion.

The ritual serving at feasts would be an example of this last kind of variation. The number of servers at a feast will vary, yet always be a multiple of the number of ritual foods served, so that if there are seven foods, there could be seven or fourteen servers. If there are five foods, there could be twenty servers. The number of foods may be affected by how many have contributed what foods to the feast. And the number of multiplications of servers for each food is affected by the number of women who meet the criteria for servers and come forward, and by the number of people to be served.

When an activity does not require that the *possible* number (whether it is finite or situation-determined) be the *necessary* number, things can get started sooner than they otherwise would. The indeterminacy of when an activity begins, then, is conditioned by the number who must be present to begin, and would increase as the number required increases.

In activities where the possible number of participants at any given time is specific and finite, there are often ways in which it is organizationally made possible for more than that number to participate. Thus, for example, when there are more than seven drummers present for worship dancing, they will often trade off, moving in the out of the drumming activity as it is going on. Women setting up a meal will sometimes replace one another. If, during war dancing, there are enough drummers for more than one large drum around which they sit to drum, another drum will be set up, and the two groups will alternate drumming, and move off and on the drum as well. Even longhouse leaders presiding over an event, or those who speak for others at a memorial dinner, will sometimes replace one another. And at a general council, those who sit up front because they are presiding or there to make a report will sometimes leave their position of audience focus and sit on the sides, while others, who emerge during the meeting as having a great deal of information to contribute on a subject that comes up, may take their place.

There is, then, a very widespread moving in and out of an activity while the activity itself continues. Because of this, those who wish to participate in any given activity know they have considerable temporal leeway in terms of when they arrive. Even when the number of possible participants is finite, they do not need to worry about all the slots filling up in a way that will bar their participation. There is rarely such a thing as 'first come, first served' with its implied 'last come, excluded' that non-Indian events often involve. Because individual potential participants do not feel the pressure to get there first, the indeterminacy of when something will begin is increased.

In activities where the number of persons who can participate is variable, how many actually come forward sometimes (but not always) affects how long the activity takes as well as when it begins. Whether it does have an effect depends again on a number of features of activity organization. Here the dimensions involved become rather complex, but it is possible to sort out at least a few of those that affect the progression of events, by beginning with two contrasting examples:

(A) In worship dancing, songs are sung in sets of seven. Each drummer takes a turn 'starting' a song, and is then joined by the other drummers. Each song is repeated twice. All of the songs are about the same length. If there are fewer than seven drummers, then some drummers will take more than one turn starting a song. The number of drummers does not then affect how long a set of songs takes. Since the number of dancers is open-ended, and their dance pattern is geared to the songs, the number of dancers also does not affect how long a set of songs takes.

(B) If, however, we look at the activity of distributing goods, which occurs after a funeral and during memorial dinners, as well as at other times, a different picture emerges. In this activity, the family of the deceased brings a number of goods onto the floor in the front-center of the longhouse. Women sort through the bundles, and individually take up as many scarves, blankets, pieces of material, and other appropriate items as they can comfortably carry. Going counter-clockwise around the longhouse, they pass these out to people (anyone and everyone) seated around the sides. When they run out of goods, they return to the bundles and repeat their actions until all the goods have been given out. How many times each woman goes around and how long the whole thing takes depends in part on how many women are doing it. But it also depends on how many goods have been brought out. The number of goods will in turn depend on how many people gave how much time and money to collecting them before the funeral or dinner.

Using these contrasting examples, it is possible to say this much:

(1) The effect of the number of people involved on the amount of time an activity takes is related in part to what it is possible to label as 'repeated' actions, and to what determines the number of times an action is repeated. Above it was stated that each song is sung three times, that there are seven songs in a set, that the women go around the room an indefinite number of times. Here actions have implicitly been identified as being in some meaningful sense the 'same thing' and as being repeated. In worship dancing, then, the number of repetitions (of songs) is preset, whereas in the distribu-

tion of goods, the number of repetitions (or women going around the longhouse) is determined in part by the number of material goods and in part by the number of women distributing them. Hypothetically the number of goods distributed could be limited by a set number of repetitions and a set number of women, as is the case with the songs. But it isn't.

(2) In activities where the number of repetitions is not preset, but instead defined by the amount of work to be done (goods to be distributed, tables to be laid, food to be served, benches to be set up), the number can make a difference, then, in how long something takes. But whether or not it does depends on whether participants are duplicating one another's actions at the same time, or one after another (*synchronically* vs. *diachronically*). If they can duplicate one another's actions at the same time (synchronically) and the number who come forward varies, then the amount of time the activity takes will vary from one occasion to another. If they must take turns, one after another (diachronically), then the number involved will not affect how long the activity takes.

Thus far, consideration has been given to obligatory activities only. Before turning to a consideration of the additional complexities of the regulation of participation in optional activities, and their affect on the progression of events, it may be useful to summarize what has been discussed.

In order to account for the variability in the temporal progression of Indian events, one must recognize the following distinctions:

1. Advance individual commitment to participate in a necessary activity may be present or absent; and advance commitment to participate at a particular *time*, either in clock terms or point-in-the-sequence terms, may also be present or absent.

2. The actions of a participant will require varying degrees and kinds of mutual monitoring or interdependence with other participants.

3. The number of persons involved in an activity will also affect when it begins and how long it takes. Here it is useful to distinguish between the number that is necessary for something and the number that is possible. Either can be finite (specific) or open-ended (non-specific).

4. The number of times an action may be repeated may be preset (finite and specific) or not preset (open-ended). And the repetitions may be done by more than one person at the same time (synchronically) or sequentially, by one person after another (diachronically), or both.

Given the above, what one would want to say about the obligatory Indian activities in the events under consideration is that the indeterminacy of progression of activity is the result of the combined effect of:

1. absence of precommitment to participate;

2. presence of considerable interdependence of participants' actions;

3. the *number* of persons *possible* for an activity being *open-ended*;

4. many *repetitions* of actions being *not preset*, but rather determined by the amount of work to be done, and by an open-ended number of people repeating their actions *synchronically*.

All of the activities do not have all of these features. It is enough that *some* of the activities have *some* of them for temporal progression of events to vary considerably. And previous discussion should have made it clear that what is being suggested is that there is *more* of this variability based on these features in *Indian* events than there is in non-Indian events that both Indians and non-Indians see as analogous (e.g., church services, meetings). And this difference contributes to the perpetuation of the notion that there is a distinctly 'Indian' time.

In turning our attention now from obligatory activities to optional activities, it will become clear that in these, the same dimensions of the regulation of participation operate in a somewhat different way, but with the similar effect of indeterminacy of timing in the progression of an event.

Earlier, in making the distinction between obligatory and optional activities, the former were defined as those which must take place in order for the event to be said to have occurred. In addition to these obligatory activities, however, all of the events with which we are concerned here have certain optional activities that will not take place at all, unless people who want to engage in them come forward indicating that they wish to carry them out.

These optional activities have some of the same key features that hold true for those which are obligatory: (1) if they are going to take place, they must take place at a certain point in the temporal sequence of the event, although there is often more than one point in the sequence open for a given optional activity; (2) 'anyone' who wants to can come forward, and is not obliged to make or keep an advance commitment to do so, although people sometimes do; (3) who 'anyone' is is in fact limited by certain criteria, although these differ in some cases from the kinds that are most relevant for obligatory activities, as should become clear further on.

An example of an optional activity is 'testifying.' In worship dancing, at the end of the final repetition of a song, one or several persons can come to the front-center of the dance area and testify, although only one will speak. At a funeral wake, testimony would involve expression of respect toward and sense of loss of the deceased, whereas at a feast, it could involve welcoming of people to the event, expression of pleasure that the old ways are being maintained, and other similar feelings. There would be this opportunity to testify at the end of each song, but the opportunity need not be taken advantage of. There are, in addition, other times during an event when anyone can get up and 'say a few words.'

These are fairly simple examples. There are, however, other optional activities that are more complex. Those that occur most often could be characterized as subevents that accomplish changes in an individual's or a family's social status within the community. These would include: the giving of an Indian name, which can occur at a memorial dinner, and 'brings out' a family name, creating the potential for or validation of the recipient having the same personal qualities as the long-deceased person who formerly bore the name; the 'joining' of a child to the war dancing; and the activities at memorial dinners that enable the members of the family of a recently deceased person to once again participate in social events.

These are activities that can occur during certain of the larger communitywide events initially listed. They are open to any and all of the families for whom they have become relevant. However, they do not have to occur at any particular event for any particular family. The family can choose to do them at any event to which they are appropriate, any time after they have become relevant – e.g., a joining would be relevant only after the children in a family were old enough to dance. And, nowadays at least, the family doesn't ever *have* to do them. When a family feels ready may depend on a number of things.[1]

In some instances, practically everything that happens at a large communitywide event could be called 'optional' as it has been defined here. Thus while the memorial dinners held before the feasts are in a sense for the entire community, and make it possible for everyone to bear witness to what goes on, most of what goes on consists of specific families opening the way for their families to join in social events like rodeos and pow-wows, ending the time of non-participation following a death.

Similarly, while a general council is usually called for a specific purpose and has an agenda, it is often the case that people are more concerned to deal with issues *not* on the agenda. What occurs at a general council depends on who comes and what issues they want to raise at such an open meeting. Quite often the issues that get raised have been widely discussed among people within the community for some time before they are raised here. A person will come to a meeting and speak on an issue when he is 'ready,' and that often means when it is clear that the issue is important to many people and it is time for something to be done about it. Who and how many later come forward to speak in support of what has been said can have considerable effect on what is done about it. Non-Indians who have been invited to a meeting to speak may be startled to find that an agenda is set aside, or that what they have said is not necessarily followed by anything they can recognize as relating to what they said. But this simply means that people feel other things are more important at this time. It is the Indian way.

In these optional activities, the number of times something occurs or is repeated is determined by the number who come forward. The repetitions are always through time, or diachronic, with one person or family following another until everyone who wants to has had a chance. This presents a structural contrast with the obligatory activities (although one can perceive obligatory activities within optional activities, once the option has been taken) in which the number of repetitions is *sometimes* finite and determined by a combination of the amount of work to be done, and the number who can repeat the same action synchronically.

These, then are some of the ways in which the regulation of participation affects the progression of events.

Interpretations

If the non-Indian visitor's perceptions are reexamined in light of the preceding discussion, the sources of confusion can to some extent be explained. It should be evident why there is so much variation in when an event begins and in how long it takes. And because of the number of optional activities, it is possible to see how an expected activity could fail to take place. These are part of the objective variation in event progression that both Indians and non-Indians perceive in events on 'Indian time.'

It is perhaps less obvious what in the above discussion helps account for the non-Indian's inability to recognize the culturally relevant signals indicating when something has begun, is continuing, or has ended.

Of the various aspects of participant regulation that have been discussed, there are two that seem helpful here. The first is the frequency of occurrence of activities in which only one person is necessary to begin an activity, with others joining in as they arrive. The second is the frequency of movement in and out of activities by people, as the activities themselves continue.

Particularly in regard to ritual activities, non-Indians tend to have a perceptual set that leads to the expectations that the 'full cast' will be assembled when an event begins, and that the cast members will sustain the roles in which they began the activity as long as they are visible. Given such expectations, Indian ritual activity seems to have few sharp boundaries. In worship dancing, one often will not see the full and ideal form of seven drummers taking turns starting the seven songs, accompanied by one row of female dancers and one row of male dancers until well after the first few drummers have begun, if ever. And when a drummer leaves his position to trade off, to bring in more benches for people to sit on, or to rest, only to return to his drumming, the non-Indian does not know whether to interpret these actions as prescribed, and marking a meaningful shift in activity, or as incidental.

Nor is he in a position to determine with ease whether or not the same kinds of movements in and out of activity are relevant to or apply to himself. Indians are well aware of the many temporal options open for coming into and going out of the primary sociospace, and will not feel personally restricted by the indeterminacy of the progression of an event. But non-Indians are not clear on when they can come and go, and accordingly feel less comfortable with the unpredictable flow of activity.

A question which arises in relation to both the indeterminacy of timing of Indian events and the difference in culturally relevant signals marking progression and movement in and out of activity is: In what, if any, sense are the features that have been elicited here as contributing to the phenomenon of 'Indian time' distinctive to events that go on at Warm Springs?

First of all, it is important to make it clear that 'Indian time' is not *just* what has been considered here. The notion of 'Indian time' is widespread among North American Indians. It usually seems to have a boundary-maintenance function in that it is always something viewed as peculiarly Indian and *not* non-Indian. However, actual use of the phrase conveys a range of nuances in meaning, depending on who is using the phrase for what purpose, and what positive or negative moral value is assigned to it.

Here an effort has been made to describe some features of the progression of Indian events that contribute to the continued viability of the notion on the Warm Springs Reservation, with the suggestion that there is, minimally, a real difference between Indians at Warm Springs and non-Indians they have contact with in the ways in which participation at large-scale events is regulated, a suggestion that will now be elaborated upon.

There is a wide variety of ways in which the factors involved in participant regulation can be combined. An activity can involve participants who are committed or not committed in advance, or both. Whom the activity is open to can be defined in terms of a wide range of social criteria. The number of possible and/or necessary participants can be finite, or situation-determined. For any bounded activity, participants may be obliged to sustain their engagement in that activity, or they may be replaced by others at certain points. Warm Springs Indian activities involve the actualization of certain specific combinations of these dimensions from among the probably infinite possible combinations, and it is the range and frequency of what the Indians perceive as possible and desirable combinations that distinguishes them from other groups of people.

If it is possible to speak in terms of choices having been made without the implication of an active collective conscious making the choices, then it would be appropriate to suggest, as I have already in greater detail elsewhere (Philips 1972), that the Warm Springs Indians have repeatedly made organizational choices that maximize the possibility that everyone who wants to participate is given the chance when he or she chooses to and in the way he or she chooses to.

In 'Cultural Segments and Variation in Contemporary Social Ceremonialism on the Warm Springs Reservation, Oregon,' Katherine French has suggested that 'In social ceremonial life, the observed tolerance of alternatives seems to be in fairly close accord with ideals of individuality and self-determination' (1955:160). And she offers as evidence for this, from non-ceremonial contexts, the avoidance of the imposition of one person's will upon another. People do not argue or cajole, in the way that non-Indians do, to get their way (p. 159). In the same vein, I would suggest that the value emphasis on treating everyone as equal, and the avoidance of putting oneself above another are also reflected in the ways in which activities are organized. Not only is everyone given a chance to participate, but in addition, the various ways in which they participate are notably lacking in assignment of status or rank value to the order or sequence of participant appearance in both synchronic and diachronic sequences – e.g., who is first in a line of dancers, first to start a song, or first to give a speech is not relevant, although the potential for assignment of import to such series is patently there, just as it is in Hall's earlier-mentioned days of the week.

This emphasis on egalitarianism can also be seen in everyday interactions, as much in the restraint used in telling others what to do, which French has linked to the appreciation of individuality and self-determinism, as in other respects. The authority of the old over the young, especially within a family, is clear-cut and respected. There are not often other bases, however, for acceptance of one person's giving orders to another, although this is changing with increasing Indian involvement in non-Indian hierarchically organized bureaucracies. The management of one person's getting another to do what he wants is usually handled rather delicately, and questions, invitations, and requests presented in such a way that the person addressed often has considerable leeway in what kind of a response he can make, ranging from immediate commitment, to response at a later time, to ignoring the issue.

It is possible, then, to suggest interpretive links between event organization, cultural values, and everyday modes of interaction. And it seems plausible to raise the possibility that in other societies one will encounter different ranges of actualized combinations of the dimensions elicited here (as well as other dimensions not mentioned here) from among those that are possible, which in turn can similarly be related to other aspects of social interaction.

I turn finally to the concern with process, sequencing, and the importance of temporal context in our efforts to make explicit what is involved in communicative competence. For this purpose, consideration of the ways in which the regulation of participation affects the progression of events must be related to the individual participant.

Here, the application of conceptual distinctions developed by Goffman in his analyses of face-to-face interaction (1963) may be useful. The events considered in this paper can be viewed as a set of 'social occasions,' sharing the features outlined early in the paper. What I have referred to as the activities through which a social occasion is realized cannot be called 'gatherings' in the sense that Goffman uses the term, but activities share with Goffman's gatherings the signalling through various means by the participants that there is mutual involvement and monitoring in the regulation of participation which is special among them and is not extended to everyone who has access to that involvement or who is present in the social occasion. One can, then, be either 'in' or 'out' of the activities.

In addition, while the activities have beginnings, middles, and ends, an individual's participation is not *necessarily* of the same duration as the activity itself. Thus when a person enters the bounded sociospace of a social occasion, he must make immediate assessments regarding the nature of ongoing activities and determine where he can 'fit in' — not only 'now,' but also ten minutes from now, and an hour from now. The conditions for participation in activities — e.g., whether the number who can participate is finite or open-ended, whether one must be there at the 'beginning' of a particular activity to participate, whether groups or individuals can sustain a particular activity at the same time as other groups or individuals, or must wait for a 'turn' — change continuously through time in a given social occasion. Such changes are part of what creates the sense that there *is* a progression.

If the individual is to become an actual participant, and is to sustain his participation, he must at all times be able to recognize and identify the nature of the regulation of participation, know how it will alter, and recognize in what direction it is altering, as it is altering. Otherwise, he will be like the soldier who turns south while the rest of the platoon marches north.

This knowledge is knowledge of 'social context' or 'situation'; and it is knowledge which the individual must have merely to sustain his co-presence with other participants in ongoing activity, and thus be in a *position* to speak, let alone speak in a socially appropriate fashion. It is in this respect that an understanding of the regulation of participation can be seen as a necessary aspect of the ethnography of speaking.

5

CONTRAPUNTAL CONVERSATIONS IN AN ANTIGUAN VILLAGE

KARL REISMAN

The conventions which order speech interaction are meaningful not only in that they order and mediate verbal expression, but in that they participate in and express larger meanings in the society which uses them. This paper attempts a look at a particular structure of conventions and associated meanings in Antigua, West Indies.

George Lamming, the West Indian writer, opens his book *The Pleasures of Exile* with a quotation from Shakespeare's *The Tempest* – a play which he discusses at length in the book as a symbol of the cultural relations of the metropolitan countries with their Caribbean colonies:

> Be not afeard; the isle is full of noises,
> Sounds and sweet airs, that give delight and
> hurt not.

The word 'noise' has unfamiliar meanings here – and the ambiguities that result may serve us, as I feel they often do West Indians, to characterize and to symbolize both the structure and the ambivalent value of certain central patterns of West Indian speech.

Lamming himself is aware of these ambiguities. Of a West Indian politician in England he remarks, 'He would shout his replies when the devil's disciples came to heckle. And that is as it should be; for there is no voice which can make more noise in argument than the West Indian voice' (1960:91). And of himself, 'So I made a heaven of a noise which is characteristic of my voice and an ingredient of West Indian behaviour' (1960:62).

The Elizabethans, too, were ambivalent about the word – as evidenced by the present meaning it has for us. In one sense a 'noise' was a band of musicians; in another it was 'an agreeable or melodious sound' – each instrument made its noise – and yet in a third sense a 'noise' was a 'quarrel.' (It is not completely irrelevant that, as with personal names, Elizabethan and seventeenth-century senses of words play a significant role in English-based creoles.)

On the island of Antigua there are a variety of ways of speaking that

Antiguans sometimes call 'making noise.' It is the significance of these which I wish to examine. 'To make noise' may refer to the assertion of oneself by the sound of one's voice, as in the quotations from Lamming. Such 'noise' is involved in a set of conventions which pattern what, following Hymes (1967), we may call channel functioning: who speaks when to whom, who is heard when by whom, etc. The phrase also refers to three genres: boasting, cursing, and argument, whose form and uses are distinctive. And finally these conventions and genres collectively act to create certain speech events of a striking kind that, following the musical analogy inherent in the word 'noise,' I want to call contrapuntal – in the sense that, as we shall see, each voice has a 'tune' and maintains it and that the voices often sing independently at the same time.

There are problems involved in the structural notions required to deal with shared meanings at such different levels of patterning. What Hymes has called 'linguistic routines': 'sequential organizations beyond the sentence, either as activities of one person, or as the interaction of two or more' (MS.), are fairly broadly, but also loosely, conceived. How formally structured must speech be to qualify as a routine? Some parts of conversations, particularly openings and closings, may be quite strictly structured, while other parts may be more open. There are routines, such as sermons, quite sharply defined by the institutional framework in which they normally occur: changes in sermon style in the seventeenth century – and now too – being a source or at least a concomitant of considerable institutional turmoil. Other kinds of routines, particularly those involving more than one speaker, seem to emerge out of the hubbub of ordinary speech by principles that are not too clear. Some good work is now being done starting from the vocabulary of routines and occasions, and relating behavior to the classifications of this vocabulary. But some societies are more explicit in their use of terminology than others. For a number of reasons the West Indies is exceptionally difficult in this regard, both in a desire to avoid explicitness, and to keep from explicit awareness patterns that may deviate from accepted European usage.

Speech routines are forms of *expression*, having living ties with the people who use them. Descriptions of such routines in terms of explicit formal models, whether of sequential organization or variations of transformational models, while worthwhile, often seem to take us further away from rather than closer to revelations of their functions and meaning. Such descriptions have been less effective than similar abstractions of linguistic competence, for it is harder to separate the formal structure of symbols more closely involved with expression from the variety of broader factors (including performance factors) which may contribute to meaning.[1]

The main body of everyday speech is an area often felt to be structurally open. In fact how 'creative' (in this sense) the genres of everyday speaking are may vary and/or be a matter of debate (as to some extent the degree and kind of 'newness' of sentences is, or should be, in linguistics). But between the formulas of prayers and greetings and such totally innovative use of language as may exist there is the large range of speech patterned to communicate meanings: about feelings, status, cultural identity, personality, skills, etc.; about the significance of different types of communicative acts; and about the meanings of expression and communication themselves. In these areas creative choices of means of expression must be made by speakers.

Consider for example the relations between speech and silence. Many Americans (and many English people) have a rule that in social conversation silences must be filled. A silence maintained too long is a sign of some kind of failure of rapport (unless it is defined as somehow seeking the solution to a problem, etc.). In Denmark by contrast there is a tendency, particularly in small informal groups, to treat silences as valuable signs – perhaps of the well-being of those present, at least a kind of affirmation that people speak only when moved to do so, that their feelings are genuine, etc. Some Danes appear to 'nourish' a silence as one might appreciate a cozy fire. These norms can be quite strong. I used to have some Danish in-laws and once while we were visiting them an American friend announced that he was arriving for a visit. We welcomed him, but as we knew he was particularly prone to filling gaps in conversations we suggested quite strongly and explicitly that he let silences sit for awhile before talking. Although the rule is quite simple, it is usually quite difficult for people to change their cues, habits, or what have you in these matters. My in-laws had been quite glad to see him. No disagreements of any kind arose between them, yet by the end of the first evening these kindly Danes could stand his presence no longer – simply because an evening without silence was emotionally intolerable.

There are other kinds of silences. Keith Basso has recently been exploring in depth the silences of some American Indians (Basso 1970). The extreme of silence in my own experience was with some Lapps in northern Sweden (not in Norway) in an area once converted to Laestadian Christianity. We spent some days in a borrowed sod house in the village of Rensjoen (about 30 km west of Kiruna).[2] Our neighbors would drop in on us every morning just to check that things were all right. We would offer coffee. After several minutes of silence the offer would be accepted. We would tentatively ask a question. More silence, than a 'yes' or a 'no.' Then a long wait. After five or ten minutes we would ask another. Same pause, same 'yes' or 'no.' Another ten minutes, etc. Each visit lasted approximately an hour – all of us sitting formally. During that time there would be six or seven exchanges. Then our guests would leave to repeat the performance the next day. While I don't know any of what these silences represented I will hazard a partial guess. As one goes north in the Scandinavian peninsula, particularly in Sweden, what is called 'the difficulty in expressing one's feelings' and the need for honesty and sincerity increase, while the amount of speech per hour decreases. Our neighbors felt they ought to visit, but perhaps one part of their silence was simply that they didn't have anything to say.

The conventions of speech transition are also interesting, and as we shall see later, relevant. In our society there are some interesting disagreements about the norms and meanings of interruption, for example. Some of these are ethnic, some appear now to be generational. A number of factors are involved, but one meaning that seems to be attached to interruption in some minds is 'sincerity,' another 'intolerance' – not to mention more specifically normative reactions of rudeness and selfishness.[3] A full discussion would take us too far afield. But we might notice Paul Goodman's remarks in *Making Do* (1963:35) about his behavior at a conference: 'I refused to be moved, but suddenly cut in, as I do – parenthetically, so to speak – to make a point that, in my opinion, needed saying at once, if we were going to make sense and not waste one another's time.' I suspect that there will be varieties of feeling, opinion, and interpretation of Goodman's practice of excusable interruptions.

We have looked at some conventions about silence and transitions. By contrast Antiguan conventions appear, on the surface, almost anarchic. Fundamentally there is no regular requirement for two or more voices not to be going at the same time. The start of a new voice is not in itself a signal for the voice speaking either to stop or to institute a process which will decide who is to have the floor.

When someone enters a casual group, for example, no opening is necessarily made for him; nor is there any pause or other formal signal that he is being included. No one appears to pay any attention. When he feels ready he will simply begin speaking. He may be heard, he may not. That is, the other voices may eventually stop and listen, or some of them may; eyes may or may not turn to him. If he is not heard the first time he will try again, and yet again (often with the same remark). Eventually he will be heard or give up.

In such a system it is also true that there is no particular reason to find out what is going on or who is talking before one starts oneself. There is little pressure to relate one's subject to any state of the group. Therefore it is also quite reasonable to arrive talking, so to speak, and the louder one does so the greater the chances that one is heard.

There is no general norm against interruption, although as I've said one may not be heard. But the fact that one is not heard does not mean one has to stop. One can go right on with perhaps one listener, or perhaps none. On some occasions, perhaps more serious, or particularly in more formal settings as part of an almost ritualized debate between sets of conventions, someone will be told to 'have some behavior' or 'let the man speak.' In many conversations, however, several participants already involved may feel that the point they are making is not receiving sufficient attention and will each of them continue speaking, repeating the point they are making – so that several people are speaking at once.

A number of norms and conventions insure that the stream of speech will be broken. While I have said that someone entering a group will not be given a place, he will be greeted. This greeting will be an aside. It will not let him in, or stop the main flow; but it will break it. It is not an invitation to join the conversation. There is a strong rule that all people with whom one has acquaintance or wishes to maintain any relations at all must be greeted. (Walking lost in thought is not recommended in the West Indies if one wants to keep one's friends. The amount of constant scanning and attention to others that most West Indians practice makes them all the rivals of some of our best politicians). In a village if a group is sitting within sight of the road or standing on it then the people that must be greeted include everybody who comes up the road. Greetings will be exchanged in this way even with people who are inside their houses and who never look out. These greetings may just be a call or a name, but they may well include questions and answers, the making of future appointments, etc., all totally separate from the main stream of conversation which will continue just where it left off, which may well be and usually is the middle of a sentence.

But one does not need the excuse of having to greet someone. It is quite normal to interrupt oneself, perhaps to comment on something one sees out the window, and then perhaps a few minutes later continue one's sentence. It is also permissible among friends or with guests to fall asleep while talking, again perhaps waking up in a couple of minutes and continuing. In a brief conversation with me, about three minutes, a girl called to someone on the street, made a remark to a small boy, sang a little, told a child to go to school, sang some more, told a child to go buy bread, etc., all the while continuing the thread of her conversation about her sister.

There are of course in these settings no apologies for interruption, nor any set of signals (such as exceptionally quiet behavior on coming late to a lecture, etc.) that would mark or apologize for interrupting behavior. On the contrary there is a pervasive pattern of making what we can call *counternoise*. If there is music on the radio in the living room someone in the kitchen may start talking loudly to himself, or hum, or bang the pots extra-loud. As someone told me, if one member of his household makes a noise the other always want to outdo him. (That this is also relevant to speech, if not already clear, will become so when we look at the structure of argument). Can we now begin to ask the significance of these patterns? What, if anything, is expressed by them? First, one very general thing we can say is that if there is no sense of interruption, or need to fit carefully into an ongoing pattern of conversation, or need to stop if somebody else speaks, then the impulse to speak is not cued by the external situation but comes from within the speaker. These conventions treat the act of speaking, I would say, as primarily the expression, assertion, or proclamation of the speaker and/or his feelings – or his interests.

Thus to enter a conversation one must assert one's presence rather than participate in something formalized as an exchange. Similarly at restaurant counters or in stores there is the same failure to signal readiness for communication. One says aloud what one wants, nobody asks you. Neither is any sign given that your request has been heard. If you feel your request is not getting attention you may repeat it (how often depending on your character, how big a noise you like to make generally). But one must not assume in the remarks one makes that one has *not* been heard the first time or one will be rebuked. One is listened to. Assertion is also involved in patterns of counter-noise and argumentative reactions.

On the one hand speech is organized as a form of assertion. It is also closely tied to spontaneous expression of feelings. Questions on why people can fall asleep or shift subject in the middle of a sentence are usually answered in terms of the person's feelings – 'That's what he feels to do' – and the strong value put on not constraining one's feelings by artificial structures. A very beautiful and subtle attention to the feelings of others is a marked feature of West Indian tact.

Seeing the impulses to speech treated as coming from within, and closely tied to genuine expression of feeling, may help account for the fact that loud talking to oneself in the home or on the street or elsewhere is much more common in Antigua than in America. This is both expression of feeling and dramatization of oneself to others.

A most dramatic case of solitary, though public, expression of feeling occurred in Trinidad. A Barbadian woman who had lived twelve years in a north coast Trinidad village, was reported by a neighbor for building a house on government land at the back of the beach. The government came and took away the house – i.e., the woman's wordly possessions. As night came she collected all the scrap wood that was left from the demolition and started a fire, and all through the night she walked back and forth in front of the fire – cursing the village, proclaiming her ancestry, etc.

As opposed to their meaning as internal expression, assertion, proclamation, and dramatization – everyone playing his own tune in one Elizabethan sense of noise – these conventions have a set of meanings which they got when contrasted with the more formal conventions associated with English culture: meanings of rudeness; stubbornness; 'ignorance' in the sense of unruly behavior, stupidity; 'noise' in the sense of disorder.

Some background is necessary. These patterns are primarily speech patterns of village life, although they pervade speech throughout much of the society on appropriate (informal), and on inappropriate, occasions. This is on an island of 108 square miles, which throughout almost all of its colonial history has been English. Since the latter part of the seventeenth century it has been primarily devoted to sugar plantations, these having been merged for most of the twentieth century into one large syndicate (which was recently liquidated). The flatness of the island, the absence of large refuge areas, has meant that the stratification system, and many of the customs, of plantation society have persisted until very recently. At emancipation the slaves had no place to go. Their dependence on the plantations was complete. There was no need to import laborers from India or elsewhere. The primary group in the population are thus descendants of African and New World–born slaves. A color class system (Smith 1956) of fairly typical form exists, with a few whites at its head. A number of other significant groups or subgroups exist, and there have been recent changes and divisions in the power structure, but these do not yet – or are only beginning to – affect the pattern I am discussing here. About three-quarters of this population (this figure changes rapidly) live in villages. Although various kinds of people live in the villages, they are primarily associated with 'lower class' residents. The significance of villages as social units, and some of the principles which organize social relations in them, have been discussed by R. T. Smith (1956:4–5, 148–9, 203–17) and recently by Peter Wilson (1969).[4] Even where cultural traditions of villagers and the metropole, England, are most merged, it is clear that the idea of cultural division is present; alternate moral values exist and can be elicited, but they are normally communicated in indirect ways. An English-based creole language coexists and merges with local standard English. The speech conventions I am talking about in this paper coexist with more formal English patterns used on formal occasions. As I have said elsewhere (1970), Antiguans tend to maximize ambiguities of cultural reference and of expressive and moral meaning and then play with them to hide and manipulate the contradictions in their cultural patterns of value and expression. There is a duality of cultural patterning, both of creole vs. English speech and of 'African' vs. English culture. But this underlying duality is denied and covered by what is both a historical process and an ongoing symbolic technique of 'taking on' dominant cultural forms and 'remodelling' them so that the two cultural strands are woven into a complex garment of cultural and linguistic expression. We shall return to the ways these relations organize alternate meanings of conventions and genres toward the end of the paper.

Some of the same meanings that we have seen at work in fundamental *conventions* organizing relations of speakers in space and time also attach to those *genres* of speaking which can be referred to as 'making noise.'

A principal form of proclamation of self is 'boasting.' It is a routine which shows up in a number of different conversational genres. Cross-culturally boasting varies greatly in its meanings, from our own concerns with 'reticence' and 'blowing your own horn' to the heroic boasting of Beowulf and the old Scandinavians. Antiguan boasting runs a fine line between being an intrinsic source of humor and an eloquent, even preening, appreciation of one's own fine qualities. (One thinks a little of the twinkle in Douglas Fairbanks' eye as he performed some marvelous stunt).

A number of good examples show up in Trinidadian calypsoes by the Mighty Sparrow, such as:

> We young and strong
> We ain't fraid of soul in town
> Who think they're bad
> To meet them we're more than glad
>
> I've got my gun
> And Pardner I ain't making fun
> If you're smart, clear the way
> And if you think you bad
> Make your play.

The boast is bravado plus challenge. Another calypso goes:

> Is me the village ram
> I don't give a damn
> If any woman say that I
> Leave she dissatisfy
> She lie, she lie, she lie.

In Antigua these boasts have a special place as speakers announce themselves in speech competitions called singing meetings. One such speaker went by the title The Champion of Champions, and part of his march to the podium included such quatrains as:

> I am the champion of champions
> From my head to my toes
> I must remain a champion
> Wherever I goes.

Such assertions are always followed by loud noise and cheering, banging on tables, etc.

Similar rhymes may be found in a village context, such as:

> mi no ke wa mi du
> kaz mi big, mi bad an mi buos
> an mi jain di polis fuos.

Boast, in this usage, means 'being assertive,' and returns us to the problem of the fine line between the serious and humorous.

'He just feels he's set' or 'He just feels he's good' are approving remarks for preening behavior when the person is felt to be able to live up to the image he's creating. At the same time it is still felt as amusing, as joke. Boasting, as I have said, is a basic form of humor. If a boast is made with nothing at all to back up the claim, then it is still funny – but at the expense of the person who makes it.

It is the lack of this tension between claim and reality, of the element of self-awareness and mockery which makes the claim made by East Indians in Trinidad – that their political leader, Dr Capildeo, is the world's greatest mathematician – belong to another world of discourse.

It is our lack of understanding of the convention that made so many Americans originally take Cassius Clay's boasting dead seriously, and consider him narcissistically sick. Eventually he educated many of us, yet the present negative feelings of some Americans toward him may in fact be determined not only by his later political positions, but by a lingering suspicion attached to his boasting behavior.

Indeed the line is a fine one, and some West Indians working within the convention may yet be expressing a very genuine narcissism.

Boasting is an essential form of defense against all forms of attack or criticism. Thus, when one woman challenged another for hogging the fruit, 'You eat off all the mango, man,' she was answered, 'No bother me, man, me nyam as me like,' 'I eat as I like,' i.e., I do what I want, I'm powerful. Most such criticism is often called 'teasing' – a term that covers things from mild banter or challenge to public statement of previously private truths (or supposed truths), to outright defamation and insult. There is in village conversation a constant pressing of the other party. This teasing is used, among other things, to maintain a valued quality of 'hardness' in people, a positive acceptance of conditions in which they find themselves. Small children who fall and hurt themselves are bounced up and down as long as necessary until they laugh. A particularly strong form of teasing is likely to appear if one shows signs of weakness. To give one example: a strong man in his twenties was sitting on a back step bent over with stomach

pains; a girl came up to him and asked with no sympathy at all, 'You sick?'
I asked her if she didn't have any sympathy with his pain, to which she
answered 'mi want im fu ded,' 'I want him to die.' This gentle teasing is a
steady part of village life. Emotional consolation is hard to come by. If you
show you need it you will be teased, until you come back strong. This
drives people in varying degrees inside themselves.

The appropriate response to a tease or challenge is thus a boast, a show
of strength. To reply with insults in kind is felt to be unpolitic and is thus
taken as a sign of weakness, i.e., an indication that the other person's attack
is hitting home. Such teasing may be related to patterns of Relajo in Puerto
Rico (Lauria 1964) and perhaps distantly to the dozens (Abrahams 1962).

Cursing (Jamaican *kas-kas*, related by Cassidy and LePage [1967] to
Twi *kasa-kasa*; they give a Jamaican definition: 'to throw words') is a
highly stylized conversational genre, marked off by stylization from other
patterns of speaking, although it shares expressive features and meanings
with more private patterns of 'getting vex,' Cassidy and LePage include
in kaskas a 'row' which is public enough to become a 'scandal' – what
Antiguans call 'meli' as in the phrase 'meli high,' which refers in part to the
verbal noise people make when a dispute breaks into the open. 'Anancy
never like fe se' two people live neutral, so him start fe carry lie and story
between dem, and start big kaskas' (1967:265). Cassidy and LePage report
a clear separation between curse and the use of curses: to curse vs. to curse
bad words. But in Antigua at least the ambiguities are maintained between
'cursing' (which is legally actionable)[5] and using indecent language (not
directed at anybody). The same ambiguity is maintained between the term
for creole, 'talk bad,' and the use of indecent language.

A cursing is a verbal dispute. It requires a public setting – an audience –
and one of the participants is thus usually on the road, directing abuse at
someone in or by a house. The main content of cursing turns out to be
interchanges of 'teasing' and 'boasting.' The aim is to shame the person
publicly (even though the cursing is officially a personal interchange) by
unveiling some private behavior he wished kept hidden or that is talked
about but never to his face. Sometimes between younger women things
will turn into a fight, in which case the aim is still to shame by unveiling –
tearing off clothes – thus giving entertainment to the men.

As with boasting, cursing exhibits a nice combination of the expressive and the rhetorical. In general one is felt to resort to cursing when
carried away by strong feelings so that one can't help it. (In general it is
women's behavior, as 'argument' is men's.) One 'breaks away' into it. That
it is in fact deeply imbedded can be seen in the fact that some middle-class
town women will subject themselves to public ridicule for engaging in this

lower-class behavior when the provocation is great enough. The mother of a runner-up in the Antigua Carnival Queen beauty contest was so disappointed at her daughter's failure to win the title that she paraded for three days, several hours each day, before the house of the winner's mother, cursing the mother and impugning her relationship with the judges.

On the other hand all cursings are fundamentally theatrical and public events, and as such they are highly stylized. One person usually stands on the road (a man might prefer to be on a donkey – to maintain some dignity) and starts cursing, 'heating up' the other woman until usually she will come out and return the fire. Particularly if she feels the 'audience' is moving against her she will feel compelled to come out, unless she feels in a position to assert superior 'class' status, or reputation for conduct. One form of cursing is considered strictly rhetorical (although it does not differ noticeably in style) and is called 'showing off.' In one case I observed, a woman stood before the house of two of her brother's twenty-year-old daughters, cursing them for about two hours for taking food from her, and cursing her own daughter for bringing it to them. In spite of the violence of her harangue I was assured that she was just using the occasion to let the village know that she was feeding the two girls and their small children. In another case a respected man passed down the road cursing a cow he was driving before him, and it was explained to me that 'It's pride makes him do it,' i.e., he was showing off his cow.

The public theatrical quality of cursing is supported by the fact that it is a learned behavior in which one may take pride. Once when I expressed an interest in cursing, a twelve-year-old girl was called over, and her exceptional cursing ability was shown off to me. (Since cursing has been and sometimes still is actionable, most cursing is hard to record – neither notebook nor tape recorder are appreciated.) The performance is featured by a characteristic intonation, an extension of pitch range, emphatic high pitches and rising glides, with a tendency to rhythmic even stress on each syllable. There are often pauses between sentences, accompanied by a spinning motion, turning away, arms akimbo, leaning from the waist, head stuck forward – reconstituting one's forces and then spinning back to the attack.

Common attacks are for a woman to reveal that another woman is sleeping with her husband. She might begin, 'Why don't you find your own man and leave other people's men alone?' To which a response is a boast in three parts: 1. If your man didn't want me, he wouldn't come by me. 2. I never called him. 3. If he likes me better than you, I'm not responsible. In one case the wife then took off on the other woman's thinness and character, combining into her attack a threat and boast of her own. The gist of her argument was:

You don't have any flesh!
I'm going to work obeah (witchcraft) on you!
And this here (clutching her genitals) is going to pay for it!
And you won't be able to do the same back,
Because you're too thin!
You're too thin!

After which she turned to finish off the woman's character by asserting:

Father, Son, and Holy Ghost,
You have them all!

In neither cursing nor argument does anyone stoop to answer directly the other's accusation or position. But if insult and boast at least form complementary patterns of utterance and response in cursing, the essential feature of argument is the *non-complementarity of repetition*. Each person takes a point or position and repeats it endlessly, either one after the other, or both at once, or several at once depending on the number of people participating. Points of view are rarely developed, merely reasserted. The pure type is the argument after a cricket game, or other sport. The young men converge on the field and proceed to take a position on who was the best player, who should have won, etc. Each keeps yelling his point full voice until, usually, certain voices seem to prevail and the others fade. This type of 'discussion' may last for an hour or two.

We have said that everyone is pushing his own point implying, perhaps, except for our restaurant counter example, that they were not listening at all. But this is not true. There is a kind of scanning process at work which listens with multiple attention and which ultimately determines which voices will prevail. The constant repetition of the same point is of relevance here. One 'tends to hear' what is being said and if you miss it the first time it will probably be repeated.

Repetition is not only acceptable speech behavior in Antigua, it appears to have positive value attached. Things, including humor, improve and enrich with repetition. As opposed to traditions which seek to make sharp or subtle confrontations of meaning by the context in which words are placed, West Indian humor seems to leave the word free to pick up what meanings the audience rather than the speaker can provide. He extends the invitation. This may be done by stressing a word, by repetition, or more particularly by using a word which everybody knows is funny this season. The kinds of relationships that are discovered are not unsubtle; it is just that the subtlety may as well rest with the group as with the speaker. Repetition then has the effect of intrinsically making something funny, and the word which is the center of concern is somehow valuable in its own right, as a vehicle of interpersonal activity. One device of this kind is illustrated by a man who went into an ice cream store and ordered 'a double.' 'Double what?' asked the girl behind the counter. 'Double, now' answered the man, meaning 'I said a double,' or 'Come, now, a double,' (*now* in this use has rising intonation). In other words he gives a challenge to make what you can of the word. The pattern is very common.

Just as a song, by repetition, becomes part of the very fabric of life on the island before it slowly fades away, so words are similarly taken up, elaborated, put through all their paces, and then replaced by new ones. Such a word was 'knuckle,' introduced from Trinidad. 'Knuckle' in its simplest use meant that a girl was unfaithful to you, with some of the same overtones and direct humorous reaction as cuckold's horns had in Europe and England at one time. It was put in the context of the words *get* and *give*. One started by getting knuckle. Then one gave it. Soon the girls were taking up the word as a claim, partly humorous, to equal sexual rights or to the fidelity of their men. They were saying that they didn't keep knuckle. That they could give as well as get, and do it just as well. The word began appearing everywhere. Contexts were no longer necessary at all. Hardly a conversation for several weeks occurred without 'knuckle' appearing. A hotel owner shot at his wife's boyfriend at a swimming pool party. Soon the phrase all over the island was 'nəkl a di kapitl a antiiga' 'Knuckle is the capital of Antigua.' And then the word died. The whole thing lasted about four months.

To have something to say that is worth hearing and also repeatable implies that it is fairly short, and as a result, there is a process of condensation and allusion at work all the time. One is expected in many contexts to 'catch' the meaning. And conversely there is a feeling that undue explicitness implies a dull person.

Repetition is essential, then, to the structure of argument. In developed form argument is primarily men's conversation. But it is available as a means of expression in a variety of social contexts – including between daughters of the urban middle class at the kitchen table. It is not, primarily, serious, i.e., expressive of deep emotions (although natural feelings find openings through its forms). And while it may contain boasts ('I am the greatest,' 'No, I am') it avoids teasing.

Many kinds of conversation may turn to argument. Indeed it doesn't need an excuse. If two men are sitting on a back step, one of them may mention a slightly contentious fact just so they may amuse themselves by having an argument over it. 'The paper say he ran the race in fifty minutes,' 'No man, forty!' and off they go. As sound provokes counter-sound, so any claim can provoke an argumentative response; any boast can be challenged within the egalitarian conventions of ordinary village life.

'So I made a heaven of a noise,' says George Lamming, 'which is characteristic of my voice and an ingredient of West Indian behavior.' 'For,' he says again, 'there is no voice which can make more noise in an argument than the West Indian voice.' Perhaps we are in a better position now to understand what is behind these statements. But we still need to know a little more about how or when a noise is a melodious sound and when cacophony.

Cursing and argument share meanings with the more fundamental conventions which enter into their structure, meanings about expression and assertion, about feeling and rhetoric, which are felt as 'natural' ways of expression and communication by their users and in the ordinary social relations of village life. Events containing boasts and loud argument are a source of humor and entertainment; they are called 'sweet,' i.e., pleasurable in a common West Indian usage, in the same sense as sweet airs in *The Tempest*.

But these conventions are also seen in the perspective of dominant 'English' cultural patterns used in formal settings, in public by people of high status, normally in church and school, and as signs of respect when talking to strangers or to people of higher status.

These 'polite' patterns are accepted as 'better' and from this point of view the kinds of speech we have been looking at are seen as unruly, disruptive, stubborn, and disorderly – in a word as 'noise.' So we have an ambiguity and tension between noise as each person's tune, his inner impulse to expression and assertion (which he doesn't question), and noise as the chaotic result when these impulses are applied within formal settings.

Since formal speech is itself a claim to status such settings are natural triggers for counter-noise when the statuses are not sufficiently high, or the 'respect' is not sufficiently great to maintain more formal order. Many village rituals act out this ambivalence by oscillating in their established conventions between 'formality' and 'argument.' Formality is established by having a 'chairman' and by various forms – notably parliamentary procedure. Books of toasts and other oratory circulate around the village. The tradition of formal eloquence is institutionalized in Singing Meeting speech competitions, and includes false Latin; Latin with some very significant deviations in the translations; the declaiming of hymn rhymes from the Sankey hymnal, proverbs, and school-memorized poetry; and a number of tags calling for appropriate behavior such as:

> I ask for your best decorum
> Your strict attention
> and above all your taciturnity

or:

> A is for attention
> B is for behavior
> C is for conduct
> and D is for dignity.

The assertion even of temporary status as 'chairman' and the assertion of these 'higher' cultural patterns, by a fellow villager, will almost immediately provoke an argumentative response, disrupting the very pattern that has been called for. Even in church, on such occasions as Harvest services, when villagers give recitations and sing solos, there will be disruptive response just to the degree that someone seems to be enjoying the role of speaker.[6]

But christening party ritual is perhaps the best example of what I am talking about. While this begins with all the usual formal apparatus, the central ritual is an 'argument.' A table is set up with a cake in the middle and a plate at each end. The master of ceremonies then says, 'I am determined on my determination that this cake mustn't cut,' and puts some money on the plate near him. Someone else answers by saying, 'The cake must be cut,' and money is put on the other plate. This goes on, with interruptions, alternate themes, occasional chaos, and occasional hymns, for about an hour, until such money as is available has been raised.

At the beginning of the event the formal scene predominates. Counternoise begins slowly. For a while one may have only a duet. But eventually things will warm up to a crescendo of 'argument,' which may eventually dissolve into a hymn. The hymn itself may be called for several times, someone may begin to sing the opening line, but often several entries of the hymn – as in entering a conversation – are necessary before the hymn actually begins.

The repetition of theme characteristic of argument, the lack of strong norm against interruption, the acceptance of two or more voices talking at the same time, the pattern of entry into a conversation by knocking several times, and the personal expressive associations of speaking sometimes add up to give to certain conversations a *truly contrapuntal air.*

Such patterns of noise can be seen as, and often are, simple negations of the rational conventions of the society, simple blockheadedness if you will. (One might for example consider the constant advice to Black movements in the United States not to be so 'noisy,' if I may put it that way, not to be so stubborn in their demands, or curse in the courtroom and ignore its form.) I have tried to show how these conventions are tied to underlying notions about expression and about the way people relate or should relate to each other.[7]

6

NORM-MAKERS, NORM-BREAKERS: USES OF SPEECH BY MEN AND WOMEN IN A MALAGASY COMMUNITY

ELINOR KEENAN

The community

Namoizamanga is a hamlet composed of twenty-four households, situated in the southern central plateau of Madagascar. This area is generally referred to as *Vakinankaratra*,[1] meaning 'broken by the Ankaratra.' The Ankaratra Mountains do in fact form a natural boundary in the north. They separate this area somewhat from other parts of the central plateau area. This separation has sociological significance in that the people of this community and communities nearby identify themselves as Vakinankaratra. The present generation recognize an historical link with the dominant plateau group, the Merina, but choose a separate social identity.

A partial explanation for this parochialism lies in the nature of the ties which brought these people formerly in contact. In the late eighteenth century and into the nineteenth century, people of the Vakinankaratra were conquered by the Merina and brought north as slaves. When the French abolished ownership of slaves and the existence of a slave class (*andevo*), many slaves moved back into the traditional homeland of their ancestors. A villager speaks of this time with great difficulty and embarassment. The people know themselves to be former *andevo* and are known by others to be such, but the term itself is almost never used. To address or refer to someone as *andevo* is a grave insult. Genealogical reckoning is shallow, typically going back two to three generations. With some exceptions, local histories begin with the settling of ancestors into these villages in the early part of this century.

Within the village, fixed distinctions in social status are few. All members of a community (who are part of a household) are considered *havana* (kinsmen). Those outside the community are *vahiny* (guests, strangers). Within the *havana* group, those adults who have taken a spouse, especially those with children, are considered to be *ray-aman-dreny* (elders; literally 'father-and mother') of the community. A respected adult without spouse or children can be a *ray-aman-dreny*, but the status typically implies these qualifications.

Decisions which affect a family or the community are usually handled by these *ray-aman-dreny*. Traditionally, village leadership is not fixed with any one particular individual.

Superimposed on this communal framework is a hierarchy of government officials who represent the national political party in power. These officials collect taxes, regulate elections, and act as general liaisons between the government and the people in their sphere of authority. These officials are referred to by French terms: *chef d'hameau* (head of a hamlet), *chef de village* (head of those hamlets which compose an official village), *chef de quartier* (head of those villages which compose a quartier) and so on.

Linguistic repertoire of the community

The language spoken throughout Madagascar, in various dialects, is Malagasy. It is a verb-first, subject-final language belonging to the Western Malayo-Polynesian subfamily of languages. The people of Namoizamanga speak the major dialect of the island, *Merina*. French is taught in local schools but few villagers, and no adults, speak fluently. Nonetheless sets of French terms may be employed to communicate specific information in particular activities. For example, French directional terms are used almost exclusively in giving orders to cows (see Bloch MS.). We will see below that this specific use of French can be understood in terms of the speech norms we shall present.

There are two major modes of speech use distinguished by the villagers. First, there is *resaka*. This term refers to *teny-an-dava'andro* (everyday speaking). *Resaka* is also characterized as *teny tsotra* (simple talk). The specific kinds of speech behavior covered by the term *reseka* are numerous. *Tafatafa* (gossip), *fiarahabana* (greetings), *fangatahana* (requests), *fiantsoana* (calling out), *fierana* (consultations), *dinika* (discussion), *mitapatap'ahitra* (examine closely; literally 'to break grass'), for example, are *resaka*.

Resaka contrasts with *kabary*, which refers both to ceremonial speech situations and to the highly stylized mode of speech which characterizes such situations. *Kabary* speech is governed by a series of well known rules which concern the sequencing and content of particular speeches. *Kabary* is characteristic of formal speech situations. *Fanambadiana* (marriages), *fandevenana* (burials), *famadihana* (ancestral bone-turnings), *famorana* (circumcisions), for example, use a specific *kabary* as part of the ritual. But any situation can become 'ceremonial' if one chooses to use the *kabary* format, as in for example the expression of gratitude by guest to host, or in the expression of sympathy in visiting mourners or the ill.

We consider *resaka* and *kabary* to be contrastive speech uses of the same generality. This consideration is based on comparison of these terms in unsolicited speech of the villagers themselves. In particular, these two modes of speech usage are frequently contrasted with each other by speechmakers. The contrast appears in that part of a *kabary* in which the speechmaker is expected to convey his inability, unworthiness as a speechmaker. He does this frequently by claiming that his words are not *kabary* but *resaka*.

Avoidance of direct affront as a social norm

STATUS AS A NORM

Particular uses of speech by a villager are constrained to some extent by notions of what is expected behavior in particular situations. For example, in the Vakinankaratra, one is expected (in many social situations) to avoid open and direct confrontation with another. One is expected not to affront another, not to put an individual in an uncomfortable or unpleasant situation. It is this sort of expected behavior which I am considering as a behavioral norm, relative to particular situations.

When one conducts oneself in violation of these expectations, as in directly confronting another, the action is censured by other villagers. For example, children who confront strangers (*vahiny*) by making direct demands of them are reprimanded by their mothers or elder siblings. An adult who insults (*manevateva*) another openly is ignored by those sympathetic to the injured party. In one case for example, a family who had offended other members of the village with direct insults was physically cut off from most village social life. The footpath running between their house and the rest of the village was blocked. Sisal shrubs were placed across the passage. No member of the village helped the family with rice-planting, whereas normally groups of men and groups of women from each household cooperatively worked each other's fields.

Another form of public censure is to speak of offensive conduct as causing *henatra* (shame). One who has caused *henatra* is thought to *mangala-baraka* (to steal honor) from one's family or community. One who has caused *henatra* is the center of much gossip (*tafatafa*). One strives not to bring *henatra* upon himself or other individuals, and one way to reduce the risk of *henatra* is to act in ways which support the norm of non-confrontation.

EXPRESSION OF THE NON-CONFRONTATION NORM IN SPEECH INTERACTION

Affront can result from a number of interpersonal actions: catching an individual off-guard, unexpectedly, is an affronting action, for example. Thus, in Namoizamanga, to enter another's house without any warning is always inappropriate. If the callers are *havana* (kinsmen or neighbors),

they shout *haody*, which signals to those inside the house that they are about
to receive visitors. Those inside respond to this signal by saying *mandrosoa*
(enter!). This exchange confirms that those inside the house are, in principle,
ready to receive the callers. Such an exchange allows those inside the house
a moment of preparation to rise from their beds, dress, stop eating, or the
like. On the other hand, if the guests are not *havana*, they may in addition
send a messenger ahead to ascertain whether or not these others can receive
them. It is highly offensive then to catch one unawares, as this may put
him in a disadvantaged position.

Equally inappropriate is an open and direct expression of anger or
disagreement. Physical fighting among adults is almost non-existent. Small
boys have mock fights, but these are always playful, never angry. Typically
anger or disapproval is not directed toward the relevant person or persons.
Rather, each side tells sympathetic associates of their sentiments, and these
sentiments are then made known to the other side by intermediaries.
Disputes then are often resolved by intermediaries, such as local elders
or persons in the area known to be *mpanao fihavanana* (restorers of relationships). These persons are invited by some person associated with both
sides to resolve the dispute.

We should note also that the censuring behavior referred to above
is subject to the norm of non-confrontation. Thus, with one important
exception to be discussed below, censure is not communicated directly
and openly to an adult violator of a norm.

Similarly criticism levelled by speechmakers at each other during *kabary*
performances is also subject to the nonconfrontation norm. Many *kabary*
performances involve at least two speechmakers (*mpikabary*) who engage
in a ritualized dialogue which varies according to the nature of the occasion.
Usually the second speaker or group of speakers represents the listener
group to whom the first speaker addresses himself. The second speaker
normally affirms his (his group's) support for and solidarity with the first
speaker and his group. However, there are occasions when the second
speechmaker wishes to criticize the first one. For example, if the first has
made some error in the sequence of speech acts which constitute the *kabary*
or has given some incorrect information, the second speechmaker will
usually point this out. In so doing he enhances his status as one knowledgeable in matters of the *kabary*. Thus the *kabary* functions on two levels at
once. On one level, it is concerned with the ritual at hand: marriage request,
funeral, circumcision. And on a second level it is a forum displaying the
skill and knowledge of the speakers. An able speechmaker excels by revealing an intimate acquaintance with *kabary* format and with the range of
proverbs (*ohabolana*) and traditional sayings (*hainteny*) associated with
the particular event.

One way of expressing expertise is to dispute some aspect of the *kabary* handled by the other speechmaker. But the expression of disagreement must be done delicately. It must be shown that an error has been made, but it must not be shown too bluntly or explicitly. The second speechmaker must avoid confronting the first with explicit criticism. In fact, if the second speechmaker were to directly confront the first he would bring *henatra* upon himself and his group. On the other hand, the more subtly the criticism is couched, the greater his status as speechmaker becomes. So, rather than making explicit verbal attacks, the speechmaker makes use of a number of stylistic techniques. First, he softens the negative intent of his remarks by prefacing them with compliments. For example:

Thank you very much, sir. The first part of your talk has already been received in peace and happiness. I am in accordance and agreement with you on this, sir. You were given permission to speak and what you said gave me courage and strength. You said things skillfully but not pretentiously. You originate words but also recognize what is traditional. But as for myself I am not an originator of words at all but a borrower. I am more comfortable carrying the spade and basket. You, on the other hand, have smoothed out all faults in the speech; you have woven the holes together. You have shown respect to the elders and respect to the young as well. This is finished. But . . . (Criticism begins.)

Second, criticisms are usually not simply stated but rather alluded to. Proverbs, poetry, traditional expressions are all brought in to reveal bit by bit the direction of the utterance. The same kind of proverbs, poetry, and traditional expressions are used over and over again for these purposes, so that the other speechmaker knows exactly what is being implied by each stylistic device. For example, a criticism might typically begin with the proverb *Atao hady voamangan'Ikirijavola ka potsika amin'ny amboamasony* (Done like Ikirijavola digging sweet potatoes: the digging stick jabbed straight into a potato eye). This proverb refers to a similar behavior performed by the other speaker. It implies that the other speaker has rushed into the *kabary* too swiftly and too abruptly. Like Ikirijavola who has spoiled the sweet potato, the other speaker has mishandled some part of the *kabary*. The proper way of digging sweet potatoes calls for a careful loosening of the earth which surrounds the root. And the proper way of performing a *kabary* calls for a careful treatment of each *kabary* segment. If such a criticism were uttered in all its explicitness the other speechmaker and his group would take offense. They might choose to leave rather than bear this loss of face. In making use of a more allusive frame, the speechmaker not only displays his knowledge and skill, he also allows the *kabary* to continue and maintains the flow of communication between the two groups.

Accusations (*fiampangana*, or more usually *manome tsiny* [give guilt]) are another form of speech behavior subject to this norm in that they are rarely made in an explicit and open manner. Typically suspicions are communicated in conversation and gossip, but explicit accusations are rare. One is not even directly accused when, as they say, one is caught *tratra am-body omby* (caught in the act; LIT 'caught on the back of the cow'). Thus one is rarely held accountable for having done something wrong as others hesitate to confront that person with that information.

The hesitation to commit oneself explicitly to an idea or opinion is itself an important behavioral norm in this community. One is noncommittal for fear that an action openly advocated might have consequences that would have to be borne alone. One avoids accusation because one does not wish to be responsible for providing that information. If the wrongdoer is to be pointed out, the rest of the community must share the responsibility for the act, and they must share any guilt that may result. One speechmaker gave this account of what occurs in such situations:

Even if someone was caught in the act of doing something wrong, then you cannot directly point at this person to dishonor him directly. You must use special expressions or go about it in a roundabout way. But if by chance there are people who demand that this wrongdoer be pointed out directly, then the speaker must say directly in the *kabary* who the person is. But because he must speak directly the speaker must ask the people to lift all guilt from him (*aza tsiny*). If there is someone in the audience who wants to know more, who doesn't understand, then he may respond during a break in the talk, 'It is not clear to us, sir. It is hard to distinguish the domestic cat from the wild cat. They are the same whether calico or yellow or grey. And if it is the wild cat who steals the chicken, we cannot tell him from the others. The wild cat steals the chicken but the domestic cat gets its tail cut off. So point directly to the wild cat.'

In general then one avoids confronting another with negative or unpleasant information. Disputes, criticisms, accusations are typically not straightforward. Disputes are often carried through mediators. Criticisms are veiled in metaphor. Accusations are left imprecise, unless the group is willing to share responsibility for the act of accusation. Direct affront indicates a lowering or absence of respect on the part of the affronter. In public situations, however, show of respect is expected. And, in formal public situations such as the *kabary* performance, it is obligatory. Every speechmaker interviewed stressed the importance of respect:

– In the *kabary*, it is not good to speak directly. If you speak directly the *kabary* is a *kabarin-jaza* (child's *kabary*) and there is no respect and honor.

– Speakers are not afraid to explain to one another, to answer with wisdom. But the censurer must be careful not to dishonor or mock or lower in public that speaker, because this was *fady* (taboo) for our ancestors.

– A *kabary* which blames, disgraces is not a *kabary fankasitrahana* (*kabary* of agreement) but a *kabary fankahalana* (*kabary* of hatred). And the audience leaves. 'This is a *kabary ratsy* (bad *kabary*),' they say.

Direct affront, then, risks censure of others. Directness is associated with the ways of children and with things contrary to tradition. A speech-maker who affronts may be left without an audience. His status as speech-maker is lowered. Direct affront can bring *henatra* and possibly *tsiny* (guilt). These considerations help to explain the general hesitation to openly accuse, criticize, or dispute.

The norm of avoidance of explicit and direct affront underlies other speech acts as well. The speech acts of *fandidiana* (ordering) and *fangatahana* (asking), for example, are affected. These speech acts are particular sorts of interpersonal directives (my terminology): they are used to get someone to do something. The use of an interpersonal directive creates an active confrontation situation. The person directed (ordered, asked) is confronted with having to comply with the directive or with having to reject it. And the director (orderer, asker) is confronted with the possibility that his authority to direct will not be acknowledged. A directive which is too explicit may affront the person directed. An explicit rejection of the directive may affront the director.

We consider *fandidiana* (ordering) and the ways the possibility of affront can be reduced.

First, the order is typically softened by a number of verbal niceties. The order is typically preceded by the word *mba* (please). It is typically followed by the word *kely*, usually translated as 'small' but here just a softening word which reduces the harshness of the speech act. These verbal softeners convey respect to the person ordered. In so doing, they transform the order into a more egalitarian type of encounter where personal affront is less likely.

A more important way in which the orderer shapes the speech act of *fandidiana* is in the handling of imperatives. Orders are frequently formed by imperatives. What is interesting is that the speaker has a choice of three distinct forms of imperative to use: the active imperative, the passive imperative, and the circumstantial imperative.

These imperative forms correspond to the three verb voices in Malagasy. The active and passive voices operate much the same as in Indo-European languages. The passive voice takes some object of the active sentence and makes it a superficial subject. The third verb voice, the circumstantial, operates in much the same way. The circumstantial voice makes a superficial subject out of a constituent which refers to some circumstance – place, time, instrument, etc. – of the action. Thus, the active declarative sentence:

Manasa ny lamba amin'ny savony Rasoa.
'Rasoa is washing the clothes with the soap.'
(LIT washes the clothes with the soap Rasoa.)

becomes in the passive voice:

Sasan-dRasoa amin'ny savony ny lamba.
'The clothes are washed by Rasoa with the soap.'
(LIT washed by Rasoa with the soap the clothes.)

The direct object of the active sentence is moved to subject position (indicated by underlining), and the verb form is modified. In the circumstantial voice, the instrumental constituent of the active is moved to subject position, and its case marker (*amin'ny*) is dropped. Again the verb form is modified:

Anasan-dRasoa ny lamba ny savony.
'The soap is used by Rasoa to wash the clothes.'
(LIT washes Rasoa the clothes the soap.)

The three forms of imperative operate in a similar fashion. In the active imperative:

Manasá ny lamba amin'ny savony.
'Wash the clothes with the soap.'

the person addressed ('you' in this example) is the subject. In the passive imperative:

Sasao ny lamba amin'ny savony.
'Have the clothes washed with the soap.'
(LIT have washed the clothes with the soap.)

it is the object of the active order 'the clothes' which is the subject. Likewise, the circumstantial imperative makes the instrumental complement 'the soap' the subject of the order:

Anasao lamba ny savony.
'The soap is to be used to wash clothes.'
(LIT have-washed-with clothes the soap.)

But although these three forms of imperative are available to the speaker, they are not used with equal ease in ordering. In cases where all three are grammatically possible, the speaker prefers to use the passive or the circumstantial voice. (This preference holds for declaratives as well.) The active imperative differs from both the passive and circumstantial in that the person ordered is the subject of the utterance. In the passive and circumstantial imperative, on the other hand, emphasis is withdrawn from the person ordered by making some other aspect of the order the subject. Thus the passive imperative topicalizes the object of the action – *what* is to be done rather than *who* is to do it. And the circumstantial imperative stresses the instrument or place or person for whom the action is to be accomplished rather than who is to accomplish the action.

To use the active imperative where it is grammatically possible to use the passive or circumstantial causes affront. The active imperative is considered harsh and abrupt, without respect. It is the socially marked form of imperative. The passive and circumstantial forms of imperative convey greater deference and are normally more appropriate in giving orders to persons. They avoid stressing the person ordered and, in so doing, reduce the risk of an unsuccessful, unpleasant social encounter.

A third way of mitigating an order lies in the interesting syntactic possibility Malagasy affords of focusing on some particular part of the action ordered. Syntactically the focus operation relates (1) and (2) below:

(1) *Narian' i John   ny fotsy.*
'The white ones were thrown out by John.'
(LIT: thrown out by John the white.)

(2) *Ny fotsy   no narian' i John.*
'It was the white (ones) that were thrown out by John.'

The semantic effect of moving the constituent *ny fotsy* (the white ones) to the front and inserting the abstract particle *no* is exactly that indicated by its English translation. That is, in the focused sentence, (2), it is the information in the phrase 'the white ones' which is most prominent; it is only that information which can be naturally questioned or denied. That is, the question *Ny fotsy ve no narian'i John?* (Was it the white ones that John threw out?) questions only the identity of the objects thrown out, not whether there were any. Similarly *Tsy ny fotsy no narian 'i John* (It wasn't the white ones that were thrown out by John) still implies that John threw out something – it only denies that the things thrown out were the white ones. Notice however that if we question or deny sentence (1) we are not permitted to infer that John threw out something. For example *Tsy narian'i John ny fotsy* (The white ones were not thrown out by John) leaves open the possibility that John did not throw out anything at all. Thus focusing on a part of a sentence raises that information to the level of explicit assertion and relegates the rest to the level of presupposition, a level which

What is interesting in Malagasy is that this focus operation applies also to imperatives. Thus in addition to the unmarked passive imperative is much less accessible to questioning and denial.

Ario ny fotsy (roughly: have the white ones thrown out) we find *Ny fotsy no ario* (roughly: it's the white ones which are to be thrown out [by you]). The latter order differs in meaning from the former in essentially the same way as the focused declarative (2) differs from the unfocused one (1). Specifically the focused order basically presupposes that something is to be thrown out and asserts that it is the white things.

Thus in focused orders, the speaker focuses on some aspect of the action ordered – such as the object which will be affected by the order or some circumstance of the ordered action – rather than the order itself. The order is taken for granted, that is, presupposed, and the immediate issue in the utterance is the identity of the objects affected by the order. In this way, the speaker can give an order with minimum stress on the fact that it is an order which he is giving. Through the use of the focus operation the speaker is able to shift the attention of the listeners away from the fact that the utterance is an order. This provides the addressee with the option of failing to execute the order by calling into question the identity of the objects rather than by refusing to execute the order. That is, one might naturally respond to *Ny fotsy no ario* (it's the white ones you're to throw out) by questioning *Ny fotsy sa ny mainty?* (The white ones, or the black ones?). Thus, since the identity of the object to be thrown out has been made the issue, it is possible to 'disagree' with an order without actually refusing to execute it – and thus without directly challenging the authority of the orderer or explicitly asserting one's own power.

The risk of affront through direct confrontation is minimized in *fangatahana* (askings) as well. To understand the operation of this norm in this speech act, we must break it down into at least two unnamed modes of use. These two modes are distinguished on the basis of the social category of the asker and the one asked and on the nature of the service or property asked for. One mode of asking applies to situations in which the asker and one asked are *havana* (kinsmen) and in which what is being asked for is some ordinary minor service (expected of *havana*) or some ordinary, not uncommon piece of property, such as tobacco or hair grease. Let us call this category of things asked for category A. A second mode of asking applies to more than one social category and to more than one goods and services category. First of all, it applies to all *fangatahana* in which the asker and asked are *vahiny* (non-kinsmen) regardless of the goods and services asked for. Secondly, it applies to *fangatahana* between *havana* where the good or service asked for is not minor or ordinary or automatically expected of *havana*. Let us call this category of things category B. For example, a *havana* asking to borrow another's plough or wagon would use this mode of *fangatahana*. This second mode of use then applies to *vahiny* for category A or B things and to *havana* for category B things only.

	vahiny	*havana*
Mode 1	—	A
Mode 2	A or B	B

These two modes of use differ in the degree to which the one asked is obligated to comply with the directive. *Havana* asked for category A goods and services are obligated to comply. They must provide these goods and services, provided they are in a position to. This obligation is a basic behavioral expression of the *havana* relationship. Another verbal expression of the *havana* relationship is the greeting which one *havana* gives another when entering his or her house: *Inona no masaka?* (What's cooking?) This expression is taken as a demand for a cooked meal, in particular, for rice. Close *havana* have the right to this food. Many times there is no cooked food in the house, and the visitor does not really expect to eat. He demands just out of form, to emphasize the kind of tie which exists between them. Similarly, a *havana* expects another *havana* to provide him or her with tobacco or sweets or other goods which belong to this category. This kind of obligation is not expected among *vahiny*, however, nor among *havana* for category B goods and services.

Where a strong obligation to comply with the directive does not exist, the person asked is thought to be in a superior position relative to the asker; the one asked has the right to refuse the asker. This difference in status is well understood by speechmakers, who are often put in the position of asking for things in public *kabary*. In every *kabary*, the speechmaker asks for the blessing and support of the audience, permission to speak, guilt to be lifted, and so on. And in these parts of every *kabary*, the speechmaker stresses his inferiority in an elaborate manner.

When I ask for the guilt and blame to be lifted from me (for standing here before you), I am not an originator of words but a preserver only of tradition, a successor to my father by accident. And not only this, I am like a small cricket, not master of the tall plant or able to perch on the tip of the tall plant like the *sopanga* cricket, but my destiny is to stay on the ground because I am the *tsimbotry* cricket, an orphan with no ancestors. I am not the prince of birds, the *railovy*, but the *tsikirity* bird who trails behind in the flock, for I am not an originator of words but a borrower and a preserver of tradition and by accident replace others. So I ask for the guilt and taboo to be lifted, respected gentlemen and all those facing (me) at this moment.

One *kabary* is a *fangatahana* in itself. That is the *kabary vody ondry*, the marriage request. The askers are the boy's family and those asked are the girl's family, and the marriage of the girl to the boy is what is asked for. The *kabary* itself is an elaborate expression of the second mode of *fangatahana*, where the speaker for the boy's family is considered to be much lower than that of the speaker for the girl's family. A speechmaker made these comments to me concerning this relationship:

You should use *teny malemy* (soft words) when you make requests. You shouldn't be like a boaster or person on the same level as the other. It is our *fomba*, custom, to think of requesters, in this case, the boy's family, as lower than the requested, for example, the elders of the girl's family. Even if the girl's speaker is unskilled, you must put yourself in a lower position and appear to lose the *kabary* (that is, to appear less knowledgeable) to give honor to the girl's side of the family.

In the second mode of *fangatahana*, then, the one asked has in principle the option of refusing to comply. In the first mode, the one asked is rather obligated to comply. The risk of affront to the asker is much higher in the second mode than in the first because of this option. That is, a *havana* who asks another *havana* for a category A item is not risking loss of face. He knows the other must comply if possible. On the other hand, where rejection is a possibility as in the second mode of *fangatahana*, affront is also a possibility. Given this, the asker acts in ways which minimize the risk of personal affront. In particular, the asker avoids directly confronting the one asked with having to comply with the directive or having to reject it. He avoids putting the one asked on the spot.

First, direct affront is avoided in this mode of *fangatahana*, which I shall call the request mode, in that the request is often not presented by the actual requester(s) but by a stand-in who represents the actual requester(s). This is formalized in request *kabary* where speechmakers are employed to represent others. This arrangement does not place the actual requester and the one requested in a direct relationship. The actual requester is saved from any possible affront which could result from the request.

Second, the request mode is typically formulated and presented in a veiled manner. The asker does not make it explicit that he is requesting some object or service from the other. Rather, that which is desired is alluded to in the conversational context. Often a request is signaled by an abrupt change in conversational topic. The new topic moves the speaker or speakers to make reference to what is desired from the listener(s). Young boys suddenly speak of a journey to be made that evening and describe the blackness of the night and their lack of candles. Women will chatter about the poor quality of Malagasy soap in relation to European soap in my presence. Men will moan over the shortage of funds for a particular project. The host or listener is expected to pick up these cues and satisfy the request.

A consequence of this format is that neither the requester nor the requestee is committed to a particular action. That is, in alluding to, rather than openly specifying the thing requested, the requester does not commit himself to making the request and is not so open to the rebuff of having the request denied. He may intend the utterance to be taken as a request, but he does not make this explicit.

This lack of commitment, of course, allows the person requested the same option. He is not obligated to recognize the utterance as a request. He may choose just how he wishes to define the activity and need not commit himself to any response at all. Thus the party to whom the request is directed is not forced to deny the request (if that is his intention) and, in so doing, cause great loss of face on both sides. The allusive format, then, enables the one requested to deny the request (by 'misinterpreting' it) without affront.

Where the risk of affront is minimal, as in the first mode of *fangatahana*, these constraints do not exist. The asking is relatively direct and explicit, and there are no stand-in requesters. *Havana* are able to ask for category A items in this manner because compliance, if possible, is assured. The asker is not faced with a possible loss of face or rebuff. The one asked may only grudgingly give up tobacco from the market but he does give in to the *fangatahana*. Where affront is a risk, then, *fangatahana* are inexplicit and indirectly presented (mode 2). Where affront is not a risk or is a minimal risk, *fangatahana* are straightforward.

Women as norm-breakers

According to the norm, one avoids putting another individual in an uncomfortable or unpleasant position, where loss of face could result. One shows respect to the other by avoiding this type of confrontation. Women, however, do not appear to operate according to these community ground rules for speaking. In particular they are associated with the direct and open expression of anger towards others. Their social behavior contrasts sharply with men in this respect. Men tend not to express their sentiments openly. They admire others who use language subtly. They behave in public in such a way as to promote interpersonal ease. In short, they avoid creating unpleasant face-to-face encounters. Women, on the other hand, tend to speak in a more straightforward manner. They express feelings of anger or criticism directly to the relevant party. Both men and women agree that women have *lavalela*, a long tongue.

Men acknowledge this difference in the speechways of men and women. They consider the use of speech by men to be more skillful than that by women. What is not acknowledged is that men often make use of this difference. In other words, men often use women to confront others with some unpleasant information. Women communicate sentiments which men share but dislike expressing. Men are associated with the maintenance of good communication in a relationship, and women are associated with the expression of socially damaging information. In one instance, for example, the young boys of the village played ball against the side of a newly whitewashed house. They chipped off patches of color. The landlord returned, observed this situation but after an entire day in the village, said only, 'If you don't patch that, things might not go well between us.' The next day he returned with his wife. As she approached the village, she accosted the first person she saw (which happened to be the eldest man in the village) with accusations. She told everyone within hearing range of their anger and just what must be done to repair the wall. This outburst caused a great deal of grumbling and unpleasant feelings among the villagers. But the outburst was almost expected. It was not a shocking encounter as it came from the wife and not the landlord himself. Such a display of anger is permissible, perhaps even appropriate, because it is initiated by a woman.

In another instance, the oldest man in the village acquired a wife without consulting other kinsmen in his village. Without a word, the old man conducted the woman into his house. A week went by and no one said anything to him or his woman. Then, as the old man passed in front of a gathering of women one morning, they let loose their criticism of his behavior. He looked down, made excuses, and exhibited signs of discomfort. Then, one of the other village men approached and began to talk of some trivial topic, as if he had been totally unaware of the scene which had just passed. The other man marked his entrance with a change of topic. He refused to be associated with the behavior of the women, even though he agreed with their opinions. Women relieve some social pressure in this way, for after these episodes generally nothing more is said. But women can never be *mpanao fihavanana* (restorers of relationships) because they are thought to lack subtlety and sensitivity and because they are associated with communication of negative information.

In fact, women are associated with direct speech, and they are used by men wherever this manner is useful. A man and woman are walking along the side of a road. It is the woman who waves down our car and asks if they might have a ride. And it is the woman who asks for information such as: Where are you going? Where have you been? How much did that cost? All of these speech acts put the addressee on the spot. All are potentially affronting situations.

It is in part because women are more straightforward that they are the ones who sell village produce in the markets, and the ones who buy the everyday necessities in the markets. Buying and selling is a confrontation situation as bargaining is the norm and as the seller has to declare an initial price. The seller commits himself to wanting to sell by virtue of his position. Women are not afraid to confront the buyer or seller with their opinions as to what the price ought to be. They bargain in an expeditious and straightforward manner. Men bargain as well, but their manner is more subtle and ornate. The encounter is much more elaborate; it can sometimes be a show, where others gather round to watch the proceedings. And, rather than lose face, the buyer will frequently walk away from the last given price and later send a young boy back to buy the item. In this way, both the buyer and seller have avoided an unpleasant confrontation. This kind of bargaining is typical of that between men. But this kind of bargaining does not put as many coins in the pocket as do the more rapid transactions between women. Men sell typically those items which have a more or less fixed price. For example, they sell all the meat in the market. Women tend to sell the more bargainable items such as vegetables and fruit. Sometimes these stalls are manned by a husband and wife. But it is typically the wife who bargains and the man who weighs the items and collects the money. Men pride themselves on their ability to bargain skillfully, but they leave the majority of bargaining encounters to their women.

Women use one kind of power and men another. Women initiate speech encounters which men shy away from. They are the ones who primarily reprimand children. They discuss in detail the shameful behavior of others in daily gossip and speak openly of those who *mangala-baraka*, steal honor away from the family. They are associated with direct criticism and haggling in markets. They are able to put others on the spot, to confront others with possibly offensive information where men cannot or prefer not. Women tend to be direct and open in manner. Men tend to conduct themselves with discretion and subtlety. Women dominate situations where directness is called for. Men, on the other hand, dominate situations where indirectness is desirable.

Indirectness as ideal style

Indirectness is desirable wherever respect is called for, and affront is to be avoided. In particular, it is desirable in all *kabary* (ceremonial speech situations). As mentioned before, the *kabary* performance is a formal dialogue between speechmakers representing different groups, for example, the hosts of a particular ceremony and those who have come to participate, or, as in the marriage request, the family of the girl and the family of the boy. Each speechmaker answers the other. That is, the first speechmaker completes one part of the *kabary* and the second speechmaker responds. The first speechmaker does not proceed without the support of the second speechmaker and the group he represents. Thus, a good deal of the *kabary*

is spent eliciting the approval and support of the other group and affirming this support. For example, in the opening parts of a major *kabary*, the
speechmaker asks for the blessing of the audience and they answer:

*Mahaleova! Mahazaka! Andriamatoa o! Tsy ho solafaka, tsy ho tafintohina fa dia:
mahavita soa aman-tsara.*

Go ahead! Be able! Not to slip, not to bump into things, but to finish good and well.

Furthermore, the speechmaker stresses unity of both groups by making
frequent reference to *isika mianankavy* (we family [inclusive of addressee]).
Often reference to the inclusive *isika* will occur two or three times in one
passage:

*Dia misaotra an'Andriamanitra isika mianankavy, nohon'ny fanomezany tom-
bon'andro antsika rehetra izao, ka tratry izao fotoana anankiray izay nokendrentsika
mianankavy izao.*

Then *we family* thank God for the gift of a tranquil day for *us all* at this time so
one time has arrived now which was envisioned by *us family*.

Support and unity cannot be achieved where respect is not shown by the
speechmaker. And the major way in which respect is expressed is by using
indirect speech. A speechmaker who speaks directly, bluntly, affronts his
audience. This effect is recognized by speechmakers, and they often make
use of traditional sayings relevant to this behavior in the *kabary* itself.
For example:

*Tonga eto aminareo mianankavy izahay. Tsy mirodorodo toa omby manga, fa mitaitsika
toa vorom-potsy, mandeha mora toa akanga diso an'Andringitra, ary mandeha
miandana toy ny akoho hamonjy lapa.*

We come here to you family. Not stampeding like wild bulls but approaching
softly like a white bird and slowly, proceeding carefully like a lost pigeon and
proceeding slowly like a chicken to reach the palace.

   To speak indirectly is to speak with skill. Men and women alike consider
indirect speech to be more difficult to produce than direct speech. Most
villagers can tell you that one who speaks well *manolana teny* (twists words.)
In *kabary*, a good speechmaker *miolaka* (winds in and out). The meaning
of the utterance becomes clear gradually as the speaker alludes to the intent
in a number of ways. This style of speech use is referred to in a number of
proverbs often used by the villagers, for example:

> *Toy ny manoto, ka mamerina in-droa manan'antitra.*
> Like paint, one returns twice and makes it darker.

Each time a speechmaker alludes to the subject matter, the richer the meaning of that subject becomes. A good speechmaker can return to a subject in

many ways. He is able to use proverbs (*ohabolana*), traditional sayings (*hainteny*), and elaborate metaphors to this end. One measures his ability in terms of this kind of richness. Speech which is used in this manner is *tsara lahatra* (well arranged). Speech which is simple and direct is *teny bango tokana* (speech of a single braid), that is, unsophisticated speech.

Men alone are considered to be able speechmakers. Even in everyday *resaka*, they are associated with the style of speaking required for the *kabary*: their requests are typically delayed and inexplicit, accusations imprecise, and criticisms subtle. They conduct themselves so as to minimize loss of face in a social situation. As women are associated with quite the opposite kind of behavior, they are in general considered unsuitable as speechmakers. The one exception to this is the *kabary* given by a woman of a boy's family to women of a girl's family in arranging for a marriage. The *kabary* is short and relatively simple, however, and many times it is replaced by simple *resaka*. Furthermore, it is a *kabary* to be heard by women only: 'When the mother of the boy speaks, it is only the women who listen. It is not right if there are men there,' commented one speechmaker.

Woman are considered able in handling everyday interactions within the village. The people with whom they interact most frequently are other women of the village and children. In fact, women with their young children form a semi-autonomous group within the village. They work together in the fields, and they relax together around the rice-mortars in the village courtyards. They have a more intimate relationship with one another than do men with each other or do men with women. (An exception to this generalization is the intimacy shown in joking relationships such as those which obtain between brothers-in-law, brother- and sister-in-law, and so on (M. Bloch, personal communication)). They use intimate terms of address and talk about intimate subjects: dysentery, intestinal worms, menstruation, malformed babies, sexual relations outside marriage. They are able to invade each other's personal space (Goffman 1971) in a way that would be taboo among most adult men. They dig into each other's hair looking for fleas. They look underneath a pregnant woman's dress to peek at the bands applied by the midwife to her womb. They bathe together in streams. Within this group, intimacy and directness is the norm.

Kabary, on the other hand, typically involve more than one village. They establish settings where people *tsy mifankazatra* (not accustomed to one another) interact – distant *havana* (kinsmen) and *vahiny* (strangers). Within this group, respect and indirectness are the norms.

We have, then, on the one hand, directness associated with women and children, and on the other hand, indirectness associated with men and intervillage situations. But directness and indirectness have further association. Indirectness is considered to be *fomban'ny ntaolo* (the way of one's ancestors). The use of *teny miolaka* (winding speech) represents to the villager a set of social attitudes held in the past, where respect and love for one another were always displayed. It is the traditional Malagasy speechway. The use of direct speech, such as that of women and that of 'askings' between kinsmen, is associated with a loss of tradition, with contemporary mores. It is felt that today people speak directly because they do not value interpersonal relationships:

> The people today speak more directly than the ancestors. The people before took care to preserve relationships. Today people just say directly the faults of others, challenge the other. The ancestors could not answer like that. They made circles around the idea. Today few young people like the *kabary* and proverbs and traditional sayings. They don't like Malagasy language but foreign languages. Children are afraid of being beneath another child in knowledge of French or math. It is like our speechways were lost.... The government should give an examination, make everyone learn these Malagasy ways and the ways of mutual respect (speechmaker at Loharano).

As indicated in this quote, the change in speech use is thought to be due in part to the influence of European languages, in particular of French. Children learn foreign languages in school and they forget traditional speechways – this sentiment is expressed by many elders. The contrast in speech use for Europeans and for Malagasy is evident in urban contexts, where both interact in commercial settings. In these settings, the Malagasy must conform to the more direct, European-style service encounters. For the average villager from the countryside, these encounters are not always successful. For the European or European-trained Malagasy, these encounters are irritating and time-consuming. Some large business firms, in fact, recognize the difference in interactional style to the extent that particular employees are delegated to handle encounters with rural Malagasy. But further, Malagasy are expected to handle service encounters with Europeans in town markets, where *they* are the venders and Europeans form part of the clientele. It is appropriate, then, that women rather than men are recruited from the village to confront the European buyer. Directness and matter-of-factness are characteristic of both.

This final association of directness with the use of European languages helps to explain an important exception in the use of speech by men. There is one consistent situation in which men do not conform to the ideal style of indirect speech. When giving orders to cows, men speak in a terse and abrupt manner (Bloch MS.) But what is interesting is that these orders are couched in French rather than Malagasy. In particular, the French directional terms *à gauche!* and *à droite!* are used. There exists an equivalent set of directional terms in Malagasy. We must ask, then, why French is selected. At least a partial answer can be gained from this analysis, for the contexts in which men address cows necessitate immediate and direct action. For example, many tasks in cultivation are accomplished with cows. And in these contexts allusive speech is not effective. It is consistent with this analysis that men should choose to use French in such moments. Furthermore, animals occupy a low status. They are not approached with respect. The direct use of speech by men expresses this relationship (see also Bloch MS.)

INDIRECTNESS	DIRECTNESS
Men	*Women*
Skilled speech	*Unsophisticated speech*
Traditional speech ways	*Contemporary speech ways*
Malagasy language	*European languages*

We have presented a norm and an ideal speech style. Men tend to conduct themselves in public in accordance with the norm. Women tend to operate outside this norm. Further, the speech of men is thought (by men and women) to come closer to the ideal use of speech than the speech of women. Where subtlety and delicacy are required in social situations, men are recruited – witness the *kabary*. Where directness and explicitness are desirable in social situations, women are recruited.

7
SPEAKING IN THE LIGHT: THE ROLE OF THE QUAKER MINISTER

RICHARD BAUMAN

Like many sectarian religious groups, and in keeping with the fundamentally rhetorical nature of religion (Burke 1961), the Society of Friends (Quakers) was from its very beginning in the mid-seventeenth century highly concerned with and self-conscious about the social and spiritual use of language. In earlier papers, I have discussed some of the guiding principles and characteristics of Quaker sociolinguistic usage in the seventeenth century, including the Quaker notion of Truth, Quaker folk-rhetorical theory, and the rhetorical implications of Quaker plain speech and silence (Bauman 1970, 1972, 1974). The purpose of the present paper is to develop further on the sociolinguistic history of the seventeenth-century Quakers[1] by discussing some of its basic themes from the perspective of a particular communicative role, the *minister*. In a Society which was itself set apart from its wider social environment by distinctive ways of speaking,[2] the minister was further differentiated from his fellow Quakers as the bearer of the only role within the Society of Friends defined in terms of speaking. The role of the minister was the point at which two of the major and opposing themes in Quaker sociolinguistic usage came together, a structural center of the domain of speaking within the Society of Friends.

In addition to contributing to the sociolinguistic history of Quakerism (cf. Samarin 1971), this study is intended as a partial demonstration that the ethnographic perspective on the study of language use need not be restricted to fieldwork in contemporary settings, but may be effectively extended to historical cases as well. The Society of Friends is particularly well suited to an investigation of this kind, because of the high degree of interest Quakers have maintained in language use and the abundance of records which document their sociolinguistic usages through the more than three centuries of the Society's existence.[3]

The Quaker case is also of considerable comparative interest for the ethnography of speaking for two principal reasons, both of which have a bearing on the present paper, as they must on every discussion of Quaker sociolinguistics. First of all, the Quaker case points up extremely well the necessity of taking silence as well as speaking into account in the ethnographic study of language use. In no society do people talk all the time, and no adequate understanding of the communicative economy of any society can therefore be achieved without an understanding of the role of silence as well as speaking in that society (cf. Basso 1970). The second point brought into relief by a study of the Quakers is that there are societies in which speaking may truly be said to constitute a cultural focus, but in which it may nevertheless be negatively valued. The Quakers here stand in contrast to most of the other groups that have drawn the attention of ethnographers of speaking, in which speaking is highly valued and the focus of a great deal of positive affect.

The attitude of the early Quakers toward speech and language was fundamentally ambivalent, coupling a basic distrust of speaking with a recognition that it was essential and desirable for certain purposes which were central to the religious goals of the Society of Friends (Bauman 1970). Part of the key to this ambivalence, and thus to an understanding of the place of speaking in Quakerism, was the Quaker doctrine of direct personal revelation and the Inner Light. One of the basic concerns underlying most of the major historical currents of the period which witnessed the birth of Quakerism was the continuing preoccupation of the Protestant reformation with the nature, source, and transmission of the Word of God. Quakerism developed in reaction against the prevailing Protestant doctrine which held that the Scriptures were *the* Word of God, given once and for all, and to which man's individual spirit was to be subordinated. The essence of Quaker belief, in contradistinction to the above, was that the Scriptures constituted *a* Word of God, one instance (or composite of instances), albeit a most important one, of divine revelation, and that revelation was an ongoing and progressive process, to be realized in every man (D. Barclay 1831:3–67; Braithwaite 1961:17; Brinton 1952:32). The faculty through which this direct personal experience of the Spirit of God within oneself was achieved – and it had to be achieved in order to qualify one for membership in the Society of Friends – was the Inner Light: 'First the Lord brought us by his power and wisdom, and the word by which all things were made, to know and understand, and see perfectly, that God had given to us, every one of us in particular, a light from himself shining in our hearts and consciences; which light, Christ his son, the saviour of the world, had lighted every man withal' (Burrough 1831:12).

By its very nature as the Spirit of God within man, the Inner Light was inaccessible to man's natural and earthly faculties, for '*the natural man discerneth not the things of God, nor can*' (D. Barclay 1831:100, italics his). Thus, a suppression of the earthly self was required of those who were attentive to the Light, and the basic term employed by the Quakers to refer to this state of suppression of self was *silence*: 'Since then we are commanded to *wait upon God diligently*, and in so doing it is promised that our *strength shall be renewed*, this *waiting* cannot be performed but by a *silence* or *cessation* of the natural part on our side, since God manifests himself not to the outward man or senses, so much as to the inward, to wit, to the soul and spirit' (D. Barclay 1831:366, italics his).

Refraining from speech alone did not constitute complete silence, but it was the only outward sign of being in a state of silence, and therefore a highly significant form of behavior. Although silence became the Quaker metaphor for the suppression of every kind of worldly impulse, activity, and inclination, the referent from which it was generalized was speech. The Quakers of the seventeenth century were particularly concerned to do away with the empty formalism in worship into which they considered Christianity had fallen, and since many of the outward forms they rejected were verbal forms,[4] their distrust of speaking and the value they placed upon silence assumed especially high symbolic significance. Speaking was a faculty of the outward man, and was therefore not as valuable as the inward communion with God which could only be achieved through silence. In his curious treatise *A Battle-Door for Teachers & Professors to Learn Singular & Plural*, which was an apology for the distinctive Quaker pronominal usage, George Fox, the principal founder of Quakerism, wrote, 'All Languages are to me no more than dust, who was before Languages were, and am come'd before Languages were, and am redeemed out of Languages into the power where men shall agree ... all Languages upon earth is [sic] but Naturall and makes none divine, but that which was before Languages, and Tongues were' (Fox, Stubbs & Furley 1660:ii).

Nor was ͜peaking as trustworthy a guide to man's spiritual state as his general mode of life, which was not as susceptible to distortion as his words. Fox's caution to Friends was to 'take heed of many words; what reacheth to the life settles in the life' (Fox 1765:268). Or, expressing and emphasizing the primacy of conduct over conversation, 'let your lives speak' (Braithwaite 1961:553). There was, in sum, a strongly negative strain in the attitude of the Friends toward speaking, because they feared it as an expression of the natural rather than the spiritual self: 'fleshly speaking is an unprofitable Action, and is altogether uselesse in point of Salvation and Worship of God' (Farnsworth 1663:14).

But the inward spiritual behavior, which was most important to the Quakers, was simply not open to direct perception and imitation, although the Quaker mission demanded that its message be carried to others. A pure and silent waiting upon God within oneself was not only a radically different mode of religious behavior from those which prevailed at the time, it was also an extraordinarily difficult and painful process for an earthly man to achieve. Both Quakers and non-Quakers required some form of guidance in the attainment of the proper inward experience, and here silence alone would not serve – words were often indispensable. As explained by the apologist Robert Barclay, 'God hath seen meet, so long as his *children* are in this *world*, to make use of the outward senses, not only as a means to convey *spiritual life*, as by *speaking*, *praying*, *praising*, *&c.*, which cannot be done to mutual edification, but when we hear and see one another' (D. Barclay 1831 : 383, italics his; cf. Stafford 1689:20).

In this sphere, then, the dangers inherent in using outward words were offset by their positive potential for bringing people to the desired spiritual state. Words alone could not fill a man with righteousness, but they could be used to help him attain that state, and this was the task of the Quaker minister.

The Quaker ministry began with George Fox's realization that God had sent him 'to turn people from darkness to the light that they might receive Christ Jesus ... to direct people to the Spirit that gave forth the scriptures ... And ... to turn them to the grace of God, and to the Truth in the heart, which came by Jesus ...' (Fox 1765:21).[5] As the Society of Friends grew in numbers, selected individuals, both men and women, felt themselves singled out to continue this mission in the world and to support their fellow Quakers in their spiritual lives (more on this below). The model of the true Christian ministry on which the Quakers drew was that of the primitive Christian church (see, e.g., Farnsworth 1663:8; Parnel 1675:74; Payne 1655:22), and they were emphatic in their condemnation of the institution of a paid, professional clergy, educated for the position and weighted down with earthly forms and the encumbrances of self-will:

The spirit of the world leads you, and you follow in all your works, in your preaching, praying, and in the whole worship, in form and tradition; what you have studied out of books and old authors, you preach to people, and what ye have noted in a book, that you preach by an hour glass, and not as the spirit of God gives you utterance ... For you preach in other men's words, an hour by a glass, leaning upon a soft cushion, and for money and hire preaching to the people, and in this is your manner of practice, and ministry in these nations. But thus did not the apostles, nor Christ's ministers; but the contrary. (Burrough 1831:9)

Quakers thus viewed the ordained clergy of other churches as reliant upon their own doctrinal and clerical reasonings, mechanical in worship, and mercenary in their ministry. Quaker ministers, by contrast, were 'such as the Spirit sets apart for the *ministry*, by its divine power and influence opening their mouths, and giving them to exhort, reprove, and instruct with virtue and power; these are thus ordained of God and admitted to the *ministry* ...' (D. Barclay 1831:320, italics his).[6] They received no outward training for their ministry, nor any pay, and attained to their status as ministers solely through the recognition of their gifts by their fellow members. This being the case, we must consider how the ministerial calling was reached among Friends, and how it was exercised.

In the very earliest years of Quakerism, when the message was being carried solely by Fox and a small handful of others, the ministry involved principally a willingness to preach the Truth of Quakerism to non-Quakers, and so bring them into the fold. The first ministers were recruited chiefly through the efforts of Fox and his immediate followers in public gatherings (more on this below). But once significant numbers of converts began to be won over to the Truth, meetings involving primarily Quakers began to be held, and these then became the forum in which the minister emerged.

Friends began very early in their history to meet together for mutual reinforcement and the comforts which derived from spiritual unity. In fact, the early ministers considered the establishment of meetings among newly convinced Friends to be an essential part of their mission (see Penney 1907). These meetings were held once or twice weekly, and drew together all the Friends in a given locale for common worship. Sensitive to the criticism that their appointment of a time and place for worship was inconsistent with their condemnation of formal, mechanical, by-the-clock worship, the Quaker apologists replied that to meet at set times and places was not in itself a religious act or a part of the worship, but was merely for outward convenience, and constituted only a preparatory accommodation of the outward man to worship. Further, they insisted, 'we set not about the visible acts of *worship* when we meet together, until we be led thereunto by the *Spirit of God*' (D. Barclay 1831:383, italics his).

As for the conduct of the meeting, the following is an early description (1660):

The first that enters into the place of your meeting, be not careless, nor wander up and down either in body or mind, but innocently sit down in some place and turn in thy mind to the light, and wait upon God singly, as if none were present but the Lord, and here thou art strong. Then the next that comes in, let them in simplicity of heart sit down and turn in to the same light, and wait in the Spirit, and so all the rest coming in in the fear of the Lord sit down in pure stillness and silence of all flesh, and wait in the light. A few that are thus gathered by the arm of the Lord into the unity of the Spirit this is a sweet and precious meeting, where all meet with the Lord ... (Braithwaite 1961:509)

This unity of the Spirit was considered a precious and essential aspect of the meeting for worship; it made the difference between a group of people sitting together but engaged in separate, individual acts of worship, and a group of people experiencing real communion (cf. Penington 1863:54). Each member of the meeting followed his own silent way to the attainment of a direct inward experience of the Light, but for all the end was the same. Ideally, in such a situation, there was no need for words, since worship *consisted* in the inward attainment of the Spirit: 'Those who are brought to a pure, still waiting upon God in the Spirit are come nearer to the Lord than words are . . . though not a word be spoken to the hearing of the outward ear . . .' (Braithwaite 1961:509; cf. Penington 1863:56).

Although the silent meeting was the ideal, as described above, there was no 'resolution not to speak' (Penington 1863:54), and few meetings were actually conducted in complete silence. There were, in fact, a number of *openings* in which speech was not only appropriate but necessary. *Opening* was the term used by the Quakers themselves for the points within the meeting at which speaking was appropriate.[7] These openings occurred when a member of the meeting for worship — any adult member, of either sex — became sensible in his attendance on the Inner Light that the Spirit was leading him to a message or an understanding intended for others as well as himself, as a means of helping them to reach inward to the Light, or otherwise enriching the quality of their worship (Banks 1798:47; cf. Burrough 1939:46–7 and Crook 1791:xxiv). The crucial point was that the source of this message had to be spiritual inspiration, not intellect or self-will, and it could not be planned beforehand: 'if any man speak, let him speak as the Oracles of God; if any man minister, let him do it as of the ability which God giveth, that God in all things may be glorified through Jesus Christ' (Farnsworth 1663:9).[8] If, after a period of silent waiting and experiencing of the strength and urgency of his message, the Friend felt certain that his words came from the Light, he was obligated to speak them aloud. To speak thus in a meeting for worship was the *minister* to the meeting.

William Caton, one of the earliest ministers in the Society of Friends, expressed the ministerial experience in illuminating terms:

I am so simple, I am so weak, and I never have anything beforehand, neither do scarce ever known when I go into a meeting of several hundreds, what I shall say, or whether any thing or nothing . . . though I was often that I knew not what I should say, when I went into a meeting; yet even at such a time hath the Lord been pleased to give me his word so plentifully, that through Him I was enabled to speak two, or three, yea sometimes four hours to the congregation, with little or no intermission. And often it hath been with me, that as I knew not *before* the occasion what I should speak in the meeting, neither could I remember *after* the meeting what I had spoken in it; and yet had plenty and fulness, though I was often daily at meetings, and not only so, but in the evenings also: and the Lord gave fresh supply always out of that *good treasury*, which affords *things both new and old*. (J. Barclay 1833:134, italics his; cf. Caton 1689:10)

Caton's account underscores the fact that the minister could not plan beforehand what he would say, nor even know in advance of the meeting that he would be moved to speak at all. This, of course, was the ideal mode of behavior, although it is clear that certain ministers departed from the ideal at times, as discussed at greater length below. The truest ministry, however, was that which relied upon spontaneous inspiration, and there is no doubt that Quaker ministers were moved in their preaching by an inward spiritual impulse.

The rules which governed the speaking of the ministers had interesting implications for the actual style of the ministerial performance. Information concerning this aspect of the ministry is extremely scarce, the fullest account being that of Francis Higginson, a Puritan minister, who was an eyewitness to the preaching of early Friends in the north of England. Despite the obvious bias of his work, *A Brief Relation of the Irreligion of the Northern Quakers*, his description of the ministers rings true and is worth quoting:

For the manner of their Speakings, their Speaker for the most part uses the posture of standing, or sitting with his hat on; his countenance severe, his face downward, his eyes fixed mostly towards the Earth, his hand and fingers expanded, continually striking gently on his breast; his beginning is without a Text, abrupt and sudden to his hearers, his Voice for the most part low, his Sentences incoherent, hanging together like Ropes of Sand, very frequently full of Impiety, and horrid Errours, and sometimes full of sudden pauses; his whole Speech is a mixt bundle of words and heap of Non-sense, his Continuance in speaking is sometimes exceeding short, sometimes very tedious, according to the paucity or plenty of his Revelations: His admiring Auditors that are of his way, stand the while like men astonished, listening to every word, as though every word was oraculous; and so they believe them to be the very words and dictates of Christ speaking in him. (Higginson 1653:12)

The abrupt beginning, the lack of apparent organization, the frequent pauses, and the great variability in the length of the utterances might all be expected as consequences of the requirement of spontaneity in preaching. From a slightly later period, we have evidence that some Quaker ministers resorted to formulaic phrases to fill in the gaps and enhance the fluency of their preaching, but no record of this remains from the period covered by the present paper. [9]

The beliefs concerning the source of the ministerial message were augmented by a body of theory relating to the results of rhetoric, how a religious message was received and *convincement* effected. The foundation of this theory was the Quaker doctrine that the Light of God is present in everyone, though unrealized and unexperienced in some. By virtue of the presence of this Inner Light, every person is potentially responsive to the Truth. If a minister hearkened to the Light within himself and spoke according to its leadings, it followed that his message would arouse the Spirit of God in his auditors, provided they were prepared to receive it, because the Spirit is everywhere unitary and identical.

There were circumstances, to be sure, under which a certain forcefulness was called for on the part of the minister, as when preaching to resistant or hostile gatherings, or in places where conditions particularly abhorrent to Quakers were prevalent, and Quaker ministers were characteristically ready to invoke God's judgment in the strongest of terms at such times. As Fox asserted, 'Christ hath given his Church Power and Authority in his holy Spirit to admonish, exhort, judge, reprove and rebuke in his Power and Spirit' (1684:858). This mode of preaching was sufficiently characteristic of Friends that one of the most prominent themes in the anti-Quaker literature became to berate them for their 'railing' and 'fanatic' spirit (Smith 1873). The point is, though, that the forceful rhetoric of the ministers could not itself effect convincement, by appealing directly to intellect or emotion, because these were faculties of the earthly man, not of the Spirit. A minister's message was validated, its truthfulness made manifest, through the evocation of the Light in others: 'the true Ministers need no Humane Authority, to Authorize their Ministry; for they have a Witness in every man's Conscience' (Aynsloe 1672:6). Those who took offense at the ministers' bluntness and violations of conventional decorum simply revealed themselves unresponsive to the Truth and bogged down in earthly forms.

There were two major forms in which the ministerial message might be expressed, *prayers* and *preaching*. The former were addresses of man to God, and the latter addresses by man to man. In accordance with Quaker belief concerning inward worship through attendance on the Light within, the prayerful expressions of individual Quakers were inward and silent. Thus, when a minister felt an opening to utter a prayer aloud it was not as one expressing his personal relationship to God, but as a voice for the entire meeting as a body in spiritual fellowship that he spoke. The prayers were thus couched in terms of 'we' rather than 'I' (Brinton 1952:89).

In addressing God for the meeting the minister knelt and removed his hat, which signalled the other members to rise and the men among them to uncover their own heads. It will be remembered that the public testimonies of the Society of Friends included a refusal to uncover the head or bow or kneel to other men as a sign of deference, because these were signs of worldly honor and concessions to fleshly pride.[10] They believed that honor was due God alone, and this honor was manifest in the conduct of prayer.

Preaching, however, as an address to other men, did not require the same deferential forms. Here the minister rose, in order to be heard better, while the rest of the meeting remained seated. The minister removed his own hat, because he was speaking in the Spirit and to the Spirit, but the other men kept their own heads covered. Preaching may be further subdivided into *praise* and *exhortation*, the former an expression of praise for God in his love and power and truth, the latter exhorting people to turn inward to the Light.

Both forms of preaching, together with prayer, were ways of *ministering* to others, and, as noted earlier, any member of the meeting could engage in any or all of them. Nevertheless, most people spoke little and seldom – if at all – in the meeting, while a few were moved to speak relatively more frequently, developed an active concern for the ministry, and were especially effective in fostering the spirit of worship. It was these latter individuals who were recognized as ministers. As the Society of Friends grew in size, it came to be the practice for ministers to be certified by their home meetings, but this was a later development, not called for by Fox until 1669 (Walker 1952:121–2).

Once again, the fullest description of the preaching of the early Quaker ministers is to be found in Higginson's anti-Quaker tract. The Friends themselves did not record their preaching, and were opposed even to having their words taken down as they were spoken, for this would have been to place too much emphasis on the words themselves rather than the inspiration which gave them forth at a particular time (Wright 1932:142–6). Higginson's account, however, is quite consistent with all that we know of the themes and concerns of Friends during this period:

The matter of the most serious and ablest of their Speakers, is *quicquid in Buccam venerit*, and for the most part of this Nature. They exhort people to mind the light within, to hearken to the Voice and follow the guide within them, to dwell within, and not to look forth; for that which looketh forth tendeth to darknesse: They tell them that the Lord is now coming to teach his people himselfe alone, that they have an Unction, and need not that any man should teach them; that all their Teachers without, the priests of the world do, decieve [sic] them, away with them; that they speak the Divination of their own brain, and every one seeks for gain from his Quarter, that they take Tithes which are odious in the sight of the Lord. That they teach for Lucre and for the Fleece, and live in Pride, Covetousness, Envie, and in great houses, that they sit in the Seat of the Scribes and Pharisees, go in long Robes, are called of men, Masters; that they scatter people, and delude them with Notions of fleshly Wisdome, and saies of Worship according to their owne wills, and not according to the Mind of the Lord. They call them out of all false waies, and worships, and formes, and false Ordinances (so they call all the Ordinances of God used in our publick Assemblies.) Such stuff as this all their speakings are for most part stuffed with. Something also they speak of Repentance, of living under the Crosse; against Pride in Apparell, and Covetousnesse. But the main Subject and Design of their Speakings, is to invey against Ministers, and

Ordinances, to bring ignorant Country people to hate or forsake them, to mind onely their light within for teaching, which they tell them is sufficient to Salvation. (Higginson 1653:13)

Thus far, we have emphasized the role of the minister in ministering to other Friends, within the context of the meeting for worship. In the early period of Quakerism, however, much of the energy of the developing Society of Friends was turned outward in carrying the Quaker message to the world, and the ministers were the principal agents of this effort. The first Quakers were convinced that their realization of the continual revelation of the divine word in every man, through the Inner Light, constituted a second reformation. God had appointed the Quakers to bear this new doctrine to the world, and, having received it directly from him, they knew it to be the Truth. Thus, the Quaker ministers conducted public gatherings among non-Quakers in order to bring them to the Truth of Quakerism and thereby to the Light: 'The use of words in the work of salvation, is to awaken such who are asleep in sin, and to turn them, as Paul turned the heathens, to an inward guide' (Turford 1807:32–3; cf. Fox 1657a:103). These gatherings, of course, were conducted in public places, chiefly in market places and in the streets, though it was also quite common for Quaker ministers to present themselves at churches, or 'steeple houses,' to confront the clergymen and congregations of the organized churches on their home ground. [11] This too, understandably, was a major target of anti-Quaker diatribes.

In most respects, from the point of view of the minister's activity, the public meetings conducted among non-Friends were similar to the meeting for worship. There was a great deal more preaching than prayer, but the essential goal of bringing people to the Light remained the same. So too did the rhetorical process by which convincement was effected. It must be remembered that Quaker belief was founded on the conviction that the Inner Light was present in every man; the difficulty lay in getting people to attend upon the Light, but whether or not they did so, the faculty was there, and every person was potentially responsive to the Truth: 'now Truth hath an honour in the hearts of people that are not Friends' (Fox 1765:270–1). Edward Burrough, a powerful Quaker minister and apologist of the first generation of Friends, challenged the outside world in these terms: 'and do not they [the Quakers] preach in the power of God, and reach to your consciences, when you hear them? And doth not the light in you answer that they speak the truth?' (Burrough 1831:24). When convincement was effected, it substantiated the fact that the source of the minister's preaching was the divine Spirit, because this was the only way the minister could reach the Spirit of his auditors.

A personal testimony to the effect of a Quaker minister in facilitating convincement is provided in the account of Thomas Symonds, the first adherent to Quakerism in Norwich. Symonds visited Ann Blaykling, one of the earliest women ministers, in prison:

I seeing her sober stayed countenance after some little space began to aske her some questions which she in discreet, and wise manner answered with such tendernesse to me, she seeing in the eternall light of God my condition, spake as she was moved to the witness of God in me, which did soone answer the soundnesse of her words, and I was brought into much tendernesse and many were the teares that then fell from mine eyes, and really such a condition I was then in as I was never made sensible of before, in all the time of my profession, for I was pierced, and wounded, and made sensible to my condition, and exhorted where to wait, which exhortation tooke deepe root in me, not parting from me day nor night, but to the light of Christ in my conscience I was kept which brought me into sobernesse, and stayednesse. (Symonds 1656:5)

Up to this point in our analysis, we have been discussing the role of the Quaker minister from the point of view of what he did for others – essentially convincing non-Quakers of the Truth, and assisting his fellow Quakers in worship. It remains now to consider the implications of the role for the minister himself. What did it mean to be the one who brought outsiders to their first experience of the Inner Light and aided one's fellow Quakers in keeping to the Light? Further, where did these implications place the minister with regard to Quaker attitudes and beliefs concerning language?

At various points in our discussion thus far, we have attempted to account for aspects of the Quaker sociolinguistic system in terms of two opposing principles – the impulse toward silence in its special Quaker sense on the one hand, and the necessity of speaking on the other. If we examine the role of the minister directly, within the field defined by these principles, it is readily apparent that the minister occupied a position within the system which brought the principles together both in personal spiritual and rhetorical terms.

The rhetorical reconciliation of speaking and silence is easier to deal with, because it involves the splitting of the two apparently contradictory principles between two separate individuals, the minister and his auditor. The process we mean to identify is suggested by George Fox's insistence that the activity of a Quaker minister 'is not as a customary preaching; it is to bring people to the end of all outward preaching' (Fox 1765:271; cf. Fox 1657a:103). That is, insofar as a minister's rhetorical task was to turn people inward, and achievement of this required suppression of the outward self – silence – by the worshipper, the minister may be seen as one whose speaking

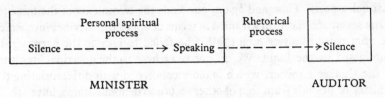

Fig. 9.   The relationship between speaking and silence in the preaching of the minister

was directed at the achievement of silence by his auditors (see Fig. 9). There is an element of paradox here in the use of speech to achieve silence, but the process is readily understandable in terms of Quaker belief and practice.

More complex, however, is the personal spiritual reconciliation of speaking and silence which centers on the role of the minister himself. As we have attempted to establish, it was crucial to the conduct of the ministry that the minister give himself up wholly to divine inspiration from the Light within, serving as God's instrument and not by human impulse. In other words, the minister had to be in a state of spiritual silence in its larger sense when he spoke, for without giving up his earthly nature he would not have been open to the religious inspiration which was required for the ministry. At the same time, however, the conduct of the ministry demanded that he speak, thus departing from absolute silence to the extent of using words, an earthly faculty.

Quaker doctrine could accommodate the paradox by giving primacy to the spiritual state — if the minister attended absolutely to the movings of the Spirit, his outward words would be safe and valuable, because they were given of God — but there was nevertheless an element of extreme tension in the process because speaking is fundamentally a faculty of the earthly man, and there was always therefore the danger that the earthly element would enter in to compromise the religious impurity of the ministry. There was thus a fundamental tension built into the role of the minister which gave the role much of its character, centering on Quaker sociolinguistic usage and principles in their wider implications.

The minister was on the right track if he allowed himself to speak only as divine inspiration provided the impulse, and only far enough for the achievement of spiritual silence on the part of his auditors. He was therefore subject to great psychological and spiritual pressure in walking the fine line between the normally contradictory principles of speaking and silence, and this accounts for the theme of danger and tension which appears so often in the writings of the seventeenth-century Quakers on the ministry, emphasizing the risks of the ministry second only to its positive spiritual aspects. Time and again, one finds the treatments of the minister in the seventeenth century framed in terms of opposing extremes into which the unguarded minister might fall if he failed to keep to the narrow path illuminated by the Light. We do not refer here to the doctrinal literature on the Quaker minister, which is more concerned with differentiating the ministry of Friends from that of other sects and denominations, but to those records which reflect the actual experience and behavior of Quaker ministers, such as personal journals and various kinds of ministerial guides prepared by leaders of the Society of Friends who were themselves in the ministry. Records of this kind provide insights into the ways in which a minister might fail, as well as the course he needed to pursue in order to succeed in his ministry.

The tensions surrounding the Quaker ministry were present from the very point at which a Friend experienced a concern to come forth as minister. This was commonly a stressful and difficult process, which had to be accomplished against the current of the general Quaker distrust of speaking in spiritual affairs. One of the earliest accounts of the spiritual trials experienced by one who felt himself called to the ministry may be found in the journal of William Caton. Writing of the period shortly after his convincement in 1652, Caton recounts that

about that time I begun to know the *motion* of his *power*, and the *Command of his Spirit* by which I came to be moved to go to the places of *Publique Worship*, to declare against the *Deceit of the Priests, and the sins of the People*, and to warn all to repent, for I testified to them that the *Day of the Lord was a coming*. But, Oh the *weakness*, the *fear* and *trembling*, that I went in upon this *Message, Who shall declare it?* And how did I plead with the Lord concerning this matter? For I looked upon my own *weakness* and *insufficiency*, and how unfit I was in my own *apprehension*, for to encounter with Gain sayers, whom I knew would also despite my *Youth*. Howbeit, whatsoever I alledged by way of *Reasoning* against the Lord, concerning this *weighty matter*, I could not be excused, but I must go, and *declare* what he should give me to speak, and his *Promise* was, *He would be with me*.

Wherefore when I saw it must be so, I put on courage in the Name of the *Lord*; and having *Faith* in him which stood in his power, I next gave up to his *Will*, and went in *obedience* to his *Motion*. (Caton 1689:9, italics his)

As Quakerism began to take firmer root, it became the rule that the minister's first call to speak was experienced within the Friends' meeting itself. John Crook, who emerged in the ministry in 1656, may serve as an example:

Out of the mouth of [the] seed of eternal life, would words proceed within me as I sat in meetings with God's people, and at other times, which I was moved to utter with my tongue often times in the cross to my own will, as seeming to my earthly wisdom to be void of wisdom, and most contemptible to my natural understanding, not knowing the end why I should keep such words: yet I was charged with disobedience, and deeply afflicted and troubled in my spirit, when I neglected to speak them forth; and sometimes some others have spoken the same words, while I was doubting in the reasoning about them; and then I was much exercised, that it should be taken from me, and given to another that was faithful.

Crook also feared the prospect that 'I should go and appoint meetings, and gather people together, and should sit as a fool amongst them, having nothing to say unto them.' But he persevered, and 'the Lord made me a minister, and commanded me to publish what I had seen, felt, and handled (and passed through) of the word and work of God; the which, I gave up to do, being thereby fired out of all my reasonings and consultations' (Crook 1791:xxiv-xxvi).[12]

A similar, and equally typical, experience was that of Charles Marshall:

After many years travail of spirit, ... in the year 1670, and the thirty-third year of my age, God Almighty raised me up by his power, which had been working in my heart many years, to preach the everlasting gospel of life and salvation; and then a fresh exercise began: for the enemy tempted me to withstand the Lord, to look to my own weakness of body and spirit, and insufficiency for such a great work ... For when the power of God fell upon me, and a few words were required of me to speak in the assemblies of the Lord's people in Bristol, I reasoned they were a wise people, and how could it be I should add to them; also, that I might hurt myself; that imagination might be the ground of such requirings, and that many wise men therein might look upon me as forward, and so judge me; and I thus reasoned through some meetings until I was in sore distress. When those meetings were over, wherein I had been disobedient, then great was my burden. Oh, then I was ready to engage and covenant with the Lord, that if I felt the requirings of his power again, I would faithfully give up in obedience unto him. Yet when I was tried again, the same rebellious mind would be stirred by the power of the enemy: then hath the Lord withdrawn the motions and the feeling of his power, and all refreshment with it, and hid his face .... And when I began [again] to feel the warming power of God stirring in my inward man, I was glad on one hand, but very sorrowful on the other hand, fearing lest I should be rebellious again: and so hard was it for me to open my mouth in those meetings at Bristol, that had not the Lord caused his power so to be manifest in my heart, as new wine in a vessel that wanted vent, I might have perished. (Marshall 1844:11–12)

Examples might easily be multiplied, each with its own individual nuances, but all basically similar (e.g., Banks 1798:47; Dickinson 1847: 96–7; Gratton 1720:47; Richardson 1867:21–2; Story 1829:26–8). In their accounts of their spiritual travails in coming forth in the ministry, the emergent ministers record a series of doubts which were typical – almost conventional – in the experience of many Quaker ministers. They were beset, first of all, by doubts concerning their physical and spiritual capabilities, and fears of their general insufficiency for the weighty responsibility which the ministry entailed. In addition, they were apprehensive that their callings might have stemmed from their own earthly imaginings rather than from true inspiration, that their messages might be judged foolish or worthless by others wiser than themselves, or that their gifts were transitory and that no words would be vouchsafed to them at critical times, to their embarrassment and dismay. The common element that runs through all these accounts is that the troubled ministers were resisting the call to the ministry out of *selfishness*, relying on *reason*, an earthly faculty, to guide their actions. Their trials grew from the fact that they were more concerned about their personal feelings and welfare than about the spiritual mandate to speak they had received. It was only by giving themselves up to God's will and obeying the call to minister to others that they were able to achieve spiritual peace.

In a sense, however, Caton, Crook, and Marshall and the other Quaker ministers who shared this difficult experience erred on the side of safety, for it would have been equally bad to rush forth into the ministry out of the kind of self-will that Marshall feared might be operating in his own case, for that would have been injurious not only to himself, but to those who were subjected to his unsound ministry. By going through the painful and chastening battle between self-will and spiritual obedience, the minister emerged a better Quaker, as a result of his suffering and eventual submission. Moreover, the struggle might itself then become the subject of his first or later testimony, when victory, through submission, was finally achieved (Dickinson 1847:97; Story 1829:28).

The trials of the minister did not cease when he submitted to the calling to speak the word of God, for he continued to face dangers in the conduct of the ministry of the same kind that beset him in the process of assuming the role. One major tendency that needed to be guarded against was being too *forward* in the ministry, that is, allowing an element of assertiveness to enter into one's preaching, thereby compromising the ministry by an over-hastiness in speaking, without waiting for the proper inspiration: 'for when the seed is up in every particular, there is no danger; but when there is an opening and prophecy, and the power stirs before the seed comes up, there is something that will be apt to run out rashly; there's the danger, and there must be the patience in the fear' (Fox 1765:271). And, having gotten 'above the cross' in beginning his preaching, the forward minister was equally likely to try to stretch an opening beyond its scope, 'speaking beyond [his] line or measure' (Nuttall 1952:90).

More subtle was the danger that the forward minister, eager to speak in order to reassure himself and others of his ministerial gifts, might take a message intended for himself alone and speak it out to the meeting. Thus Margaret Fell warned her brethren not to pursue such worldly credit by 'speaking Words at random, when the Power moves, under pretence of a Burthen, which Burthen is the Earthly Part of yourselves, and the Words that you speak belongs [sic] to your own Particulars' (Fell 1710:55). This same desire to win the credit of others might also lead the minister into the worse trap of telling the people what they desired to hear, or falling into affectations of style – what was often called 'ministering to the itching ear' (Fox 1657b:119; Brinton 1952:85).

The danger of becoming too forward in the ministry was not the only risk to be guarded against, for it was equally possible to err in the opposite extreme, by suppressing one's gift and failing to speak when moved to do so. This impulse was essentially a continuation of the selfish hesitation which often held the new minister back from accepting the ministerial role in the first place. Interesting, for example, is John Stubbs' letter to Margaret Fell, in which he confesses that 'I never fell into more disobedience than the last meeting at thy house, and was warned of it before, for, when the spring and well was set open, then I did not speak, but in the dread I spoke, but the life was shut up, and I felt it to my condemnation' (Nuttall 1952:184). Not only did Stubbs, one of the most faithful of the early Quaker ministers, hold back from speaking when he felt an opening, but he compounded his disobedience by allowing the guilt he felt at his first error to force him to speak up after the opening was shut.

The only solution to such difficulties, as in all things, was a true and faithful attendance upon the Spirit within oneself, 'and all be still, and cool, and quiet, and of a meek spirit, that out of boisterousness and eagerness and feignedness, and self-love you may be preserved in your measures up to God, and if any be moved to speak a few words in your meetings, this we charge you all, that you speak nothing but that which is given in; and in the sense, and in the cross' (Burrough 1672:74).

The reconciliation of the human necessity of speaking with the spiritual need for silence was a problem that every member of the Society of Friends had to contend with throughout his life as a Quaker. In one sense, this was the essence of the Quaker religious experience – reconciling man's natural and earthly life with his eternal and essential spiritual existence. The true Quaker directed his behavior toward making his life maximally expressive of spiritual truth, with the understanding that a silence of the outward man was the best possible way of doing so. Although this was the goal of existence, however, it was also essential that an earthly component be present in one's life, in order to maintain an element of spiritual struggle, for the doctrine of salvation through suffering was also central to Quakerism. The tension between the natural and the spiritual faculties – between speaking and silence – was a necessary component of the Quaker experience.

For the Quaker minister, however, the tension took on an added dimension, because the role demanded that the minister depart from absolute silence by speaking in the very conduct of a fundamentally religious exercise. This was a mixing of speaking and silence within a single behavioral frame in which both components, otherwise contradictory, were indispensable. The ministerial calling was thus set about with a series of complex pitfalls on either side — for the minister who was too hesitant in using words in the work of salvation on the one hand, and the one who was too forward in speaking on the other. That most ministers in the early period of Quakerism avoided the pitfalls to the satisfaction and edification of their brethren is amply attested to in the literature. That some did not succeed is also clear, providing the historian of Quaker sociolinguistics with insights into both norms for speaking in the ministry and failure to live up to the norms in the conduct of an extremely difficult speech role. [13]

IV
SPEECH ACTS, EVENTS, AND SITUATIONS

INTRODUCTION

One of the most central concerns of the ethnography of speaking is the description of speech acts, events, and situations. All of the papers in the book deal with it in some way, but for the papers in this section it is the primary focus of attention. Most formal description within linguistics has been limited to units of sentence length. With this limitation, insights have been achieved in the techniques and theory of linguistic formalization. Yet there is much more to language use than abstract, isolated sentences; and such uses of language as greetings, leave-takings, conversations, speeches, stories, insults, jokes, and puns also have a formal structure. The papers in this section by Judith Irvine and Anne Salmond are examples of the kinds of formal descriptions that can be written for discourse. Irvine provides a grammar of Wolof greetings; Salmond, of an entire Maori speech situation, the ritual of encounter. Rules which formally describe speech acts, events, and situations must include aspects of language and speech which have usually been ignored in traditional grammatical descriptions. Most obvious is perhaps the participants in the event. The grammatical descriptions by Irvine and Salmond are written not from the perspective of a single, isolated, abstract individual, but rather from that of all of the participants in the event. The participants in the Wolof greeting, and especially their social ranking with respect to one another, are incorporated into the greeting rules. The 'appropriate actors' are accounted for within the rules for the Maori ritual of encounter. Similarly, rules for speaking must account for the physical setting of the event, the norms of interaction between participants, purpose of the event, etc.

Formalization for the mere sake of formalization is not a goal of the ethnography of speaking, any more than it is a goal of abstract linguistics. Rather the rules bring out aspects of the relationship of speech to social life that would not otherwise be apparent. It is by means of formal rules, then, that both Irvine and Salmond demonstrate that the speech events they describe involve social interactional strategies in which individual actors maneuver for position. The relative ranking of two Wolof individuals, on which the structure of the greeting partially depends (who initiates and who responds, for example), can be determined according to a number of dimensions – age, sex, nobility, etc. These do not always coincide. The structure of the greeting also depends on the physical distance between two individuals and whether or not they are in a joking relationship to one another. Thus, within the basic structure of an obligatory dyadic greeting exchange, there is room for strategic manipulation in which two individuals can affect their own rank and especially the nature of the interaction subsequent to the greeting. Irvine accounts for this by means of 'phrase structure rules' which represent the invariant, basic greeting exchange and 'transformational rules' which represent the strategic manipulations which can occur. Salmond shows that the social relationships between participants in Maori rituals of encounter cause the rituals to develop into oratorical contests. The three basic strategies available to participants are discussed in terms of phrase structure rules. They are:

1. Manipulate the options provided by the rules.
2. Force the other side to break the rules.
3. Break a rule oneself and get away with it

This last possibility is beautifully exemplified in the anecdote with which Salmond ends her paper.

Roger Abrahams, although he does not write formal rules for Black speech events, also shows the intimate relationship between social interactional strategies and speech usage. The semantic dimensions which underlie his typology of Black speech acts and events are often social interactional in nature.

Barbara Kirshenblatt-Gimblett, while not focusing on the social-interactional details *per se* of storytelling, does make quite clear that the structure of narration in east European Jewish culture cannot be studied independent of the context of its use; the two are intimately bound together. This is especially clear in the case of the parable, which varies in structure from a brief reference to a story listeners know well to a full illustration and explanation. Notice that the short, almost abbreviated version counts as a parable precisely because of its location in context.

It is important to stress that the acts, events, and situations described by Irvine, Salmond, and Abrahams, and some of those described by Kirshenblatt-Gimblett, Stross, and Sherzer, are not absolutely fixed in their structure, but rather develop and emerge through performance. (Cf. section V in which all of the papers are directed primarily to this theme.)

Another way into a society's speech acts and events is through the vocabulary used to describe them. Both Brian Stross and Roger Abrahams exploit this approach, revealing complex subtleties in talking about talk hitherto not described for any group (see also Gossen, section V). One result of looking at the terms used in a society for talking about speech acts and events is the discovery of what dimensions are considered important in the domain of speaking. Thus, for the Tzeltal, among many others, there are personality of speaker and its relation to the strategy of speaking (in that there is a single term for 'speaking reticently,' another for 'speaking self-assertively'), physical arrangement of the group (there is a term for 'talking in a circle arrangement'), gestures accompanying speech ('trembling or shaking while speaking,' 'smiling while speaking'), manner of delivery ('gritting or gnashing teeth accompanying speaking,' 'trilling bursts of air from back of tongue accompanying speech'), and truth value of the message ('invented talk,' 'true speech'). The dimensions underlying the Black terms for speaking, on the other hand, are usually social interactional, strategic, and rhetorical, involving winning others over, putting oneself down, succeeding in verbal competition, etc.

Paying careful attention to terms and to the semantic dimensions which under-lie them is especially meaningful for an understanding of both the Tenejapa Tzeltal and the Black speech communities, precisely because the members of the communities themselves seem to pay attention to them. In both communities, there is much talk about talk. The Tzeltal view speech as a way to read the thoughts and characters of others, as a way to judge personalities. Blacks, too, comment frequently on the speech of others, not so much to judge personalities as to evaluate communicative performance, a crucial aspect of Black culture, as stressed by Abrahams.

The terms for talk, then, are not locked in a dictionary or abstract lexical component of a grammar. They are used in everyday social interaction; and it is from this usage that their meaning derives. Stross points out that the am-biguity inherent in the Tzeltal semantic system is exploited in joking. The terms are also used in mocking another individual and in gossip, an important cul-tural focus in Mesoamerica. The Black terms, like the acts and events they name, are used in the strategies involved in establishing one's reputation, in forging friendship ties, and in courtship.

Both Stross and Abrahams point to ambiguities, fuzziness, and variation that characterize the domain of terms for speaking. Stross notes that in the Tzeltal list, outside of a small core representing three taxonomic levels, there is little consistency between informants, or even a single informant, in assigning the categories to dependency relations with other categories. The resulting ambiguity, as noted above, is exploited in such social interactions as joking. Abrahams, on the other hand, notes a striking consistency through space and time in both Black speech acts and events and the semantic dimensions underlying them. There is tremendous variation, however, in the terms used to label these acts and events. It is the unity in overall semantic structure in the domain of speaking which leads Abrahams to posit a Black speech community through time and space (perhaps even going beyond the boundaries of the United States and including all of Afro-America). In this sense the Black ehtnography of speaking poses fascinating theoret-ical problems for the concept of the speech community in general (see section II).

Finally, attention to speech acts, events, and situations, their names and their structures, can lead to an understanding of the general organizing principles of a society's patterns of speaking. It is by focusing on terms for talking about talk that Stross discovers, among other things, that Tzeltal speakers can be humans of all ages, in all mental and physical conditions, but not supernatural beings, except in myths and folk-tales; and that an audience is not necessary in order for a speech event to occur.

Barbara Kirshenblatt-Gimblett points out that while storytelling does not define roles or even speech events in east European Jewish culture, it is pervasive in many events and situations and is highly valued.

More general patterns can also emerge. It is interesting that two basic and seemingly contradictory principles – importance of exact repetition of verbal forms and creative manipulation of verbal forms – can operate simul-taneously within a single society, or even within a single speech event. Among the Cuna, one type of speech event (the chanting and speaking that occurs in the 'congress house' which constitutes the political and social center of every community) is characterized by adaptive flexibility to current situations. Two other types of speech events (curing rites and girls' puberty festivals) are characterized by exact repetitions of fixed verbal forms. In the Wolof greeting, there is a basic invariant structure within which variations can occur. In certain parts of the Maori ritual of encounter, no variation whatsoever is permitted, whereas in other parts, considerable individual choice is expected and valued.

8

STRATEGIES OF STATUS MANIPULATION
IN THE WOLOF GREETING

JUDITH T. IRVINE

The principle of social inequality is fundamental to the organization of social life among the Wolof. On the broadest level, it is expressed in the division of society into hierarchically ranked status groups, or castes. But it governs more than the arrangement of large groups. It is essential to all social interaction, even the most minute. This paper will examine the principle of inequality at work on the level of greatest interactional detail through analysis of a Wolof linguistic routine, the greeting (*nuyyu* or *dyammantë*). The purpose of such an analysis is first of all to illustrate the importance of status ranking, and to identify the opportunities which individuals have to affect their own rank by manipulating the rules of interaction. A secondary purpose is to describe a familiar, though brief, cultural event in such a way that the impressions of the ethnographer can be related to the 'set of rules for the socially appropriate construction and interpretation of messages' (Frake 1964:132) which enables one to behave appropriately in this situation.

The greeting is of particular interest to a study of the Wolof because it occurs in every interaction. Every social relationship, therefore, must be at least partially statable in terms of the role structure of the greeting. That is, since certain roles are forced onto any interaction by the nature of the greeting exchange, those roles are ingredients in every social situation and basic to all personal alignments. Although the greeting allows for personal strategies and manipulations of its structure, these must be in accord with basic ground rules which in fact limit the kinds of personal motivations that may be culturally appropriate.

I shall first discuss the obligatory occurrence of the greeting, then describe the greeting structure (basic verbal exchange sequences and the speaking roles into which they fall). I shall then consider the strategies a speaker may use to manipulate the role structure of the greeting and to convey his own self-image in relation to those roles. The paper will conclude with a more formal statement of greeting possibilities and their functional interpretations.

The data which I have used come partly from field observation of people greeting each other and partly from informants' statements, both normative (how greeting should be conducted) and interpretive (of participants' motivations in given greeting situations).[1] In addition, the frequency of the greeting situation for the ethnographer, and the necessity for him or her to learn to greet appropriately, enable me to use my own experience of the greeting, and internalization of its rules, as a particularly useful source of data. For example, after I felt I had learned the rules for greeting I tried altering the way I greeted, to see how people would react to and interpret my behavior. In this way I obtained a great deal of information on strategies, demeanor, and the limits of alteration and interruption a greeting can sustain and still maintain intelligibility and identity as a speech event. I have been obliged, however, to use my own internalization of how greeting works rather more than I wished, for two reasons. First, I suspect greetings carried on by others in my presence to have been somewhat skewed toward 'polite' forms and so not to represent a complete range of what I know from my own efforts can be done. It proved difficult to persuade informants to act out hypothetical greeting situations for my benefit, and difficult ever to record greetings on tape (hence the 'typical' greeting I have illustrated on p. 171 is a construct of my own experience rather than a recorded text). Second, I became aware of many aspects of greeting behavior only after I had left the field.

When to greet

Among the Wolof a greeting is a necessary opening to every encounter, and can in fact be used as a definition of when an encounter occurs. I am using 'encounter' here in the sense of 'focused interaction' as defined by Goffman (1961:7); actually, in the rural Wolof village, where each inhabitant knows every other and the number of visiting strangers is small, relatively little 'unfocused interaction,' mere co-presence, or civil inattention occurs at all. Co-presence for the Wolof *requires* talk, a state which must be formally initiated by verbal means.[2] For this reason what is obligatory about the Wolof greeting is not just any behavior which fills a 'greeting' slot but the actual verbal elaboration to be described below. Gestures and eye contact are also necessary to the greeting but are never sufficient.

In principle, a greeting must occur between any two persons who are visible to each other. Out on the road, in the fields, or if someone is entering the compound yard, a greeting must occur even if one party must make a wide detour (perhaps hundreds of yards, outside the village) to accomplish it. In the village center, a large open plaza which usually has many people sitting about, one must greet all those whom one passes within a distance of about a hundred feet. Actually, it would be more accurate to say that the village plaza contains a number of activity zones that determine which persons are to be considered near enough to greet: the main market area; the secondary market area; the well; loading areas outside of shops; the low-caste lounging area; the gathering area for the mosque; the area for secular public meetings (political meetings, public dances, wrestling matches); and three other small shady lounging areas. These zones have boundaries which are very clear even if unmarked, and they do not overlap. As one walks through the plaza one must greet all those persons occupying zones contiguous to one's path. If a zone is empty, one must greet persons in the zone beyond it, and so on to the limits of visibility. But if the nearer zones are occupied, the people in more distant zones need not be greeted. This practical limitation can be called an 'attenuation rule' (following Goffman 1971:84). It also limits the number of people who need be greeted if a zone is occupied by a large crowd: one greets first those nearest one-self, perhaps up to some twenty others in the crowd.[3]

More important than physical distance, however, is the similar attenuation rule which provides for omitting people on grounds of social status. If a person ranks relatively lower than oneself or than some other person present, one may delay greeting him until more important people have been greeted, perhaps even omitting him altogether if there are many higher-ranking persons near. The principal criteria for ranking people in a Wolof community are age, sex, caste, and achieved prestige (which may consist of wealth, or of an exceptional moral character).[4] Because of the rank difference based on age, for instance, one greets adults before greeting children. Relative rank, based on these considerations, also determines which of two persons approaches the other and initiates a greeting. Ideally, one greets 'up': it should be the lower-ranking party who greets the higher. Acceptance or refusal of the role of initiator is of major importance in how one handles the greeting situation. This matter will be discussed at greater length later; the point here is that apart from certain practical limitations, the greeting, which forces the two parties into a decision about their relative ranks, cannot be avoided.

When one person approaches another out in the fields, it is easy to see when the encounter between them begins and ends, and to note that the beginning is marked by a greeting exchange. The onset of a new encounter is less obvious, however, in a group situation such as an evening gathering for conversation in someone's house. Here various people come and go, often more than once, during the course of an evening, so that an individual may reenter the same conversational group several times within a few hours. The first time he or she enters the room he must greet everyone present individually. If he leaves the room briefly he may have to repeat the whole greeting process when he comes in again, if the other participants, or perhaps even the topic of conversation, have changed enough during his absence. Whether the degree of change is significant will usually depend on how long he has been absent (if he has been gone more than about half an hour he will certainly have to repeat the greeting), on how many new persons, who must all be greeted, have entered in the meantime, and on how important a participant he himself is. The entrance (and reentrance) of the village chief, or of a key party in a legal question currently under debate, for instance, in themselves redefine a situation or the topic of discourse. In sum, when the intervening change is great enough, a reentrance defines a new encounter and requires the exchange of greetings. Conversation will be suspended to allow the entrant to greet everyone in turn.

Greeting structure

The foregoing discussion implies that a Wolof greeting is dyadic: one does not greet a group as a whole but each member individually.[5] Although many questions in the greeting exchange can be worded in grammatically plural forms (so that one might ask *na nggëën def?* 'how do you [pl.] do?' for instance), Wolof scarcely ever address a group in such a way. The dyadic nature of the greeting is important in view of the fact that dyadic relations among the Wolof need not be consistent with the relationships of wider groups: e.g., the relationship between a particular noble and a particular griot may be the reverse of the relation between nobles and griots in general.

Table 7 is an illustration of the verbal exchanges which constitute a typical Wolof greeting. For purposes of analysis I have divided them into two groups or stages in the interaction: Sal = Salutation, QP = Questions and Praising God. This division is supported by informants' statements: 'Ordinarily you should not greet with just *salaam alikum* alone. That would be too brusque and rude. You should continue, asking "Do you have peace?" and other questions.' The QP group I have further divided into sets of exchanges which tend to occur together. They are topically distinct:

Q = Questions
Q_1:   Two specific questions concerning the state of the other person. It is obligatory to ask at least one of these.
Q_{2a}:   Questions about the whereabouts of the other person's family and friends [optional].
Q_{2b}:   Questions about the health and state of the other person, his family and friends [optional].
P = Praising God

The questions used in a greeting are stereotypes and are followed by stereotyped responses. If asked about a kinsman's health, the respondent will say he is well even if the kinsman is on his deathbed; the true information about him will only emerge later in the conversation, after the greeting is over. Types of questions not conforming to the topics listed above (e.g., 'Where are you going') do not occur in a greeting but must be postponed to a later point in the conversation. In fact, such questions mark the end of the greeting and the beginning of a new phase of conversation.

In Table 7, an illustration of typical Wolof greeting exchanges, person A has approached person B and extended his hand.[6]

TABLE 7

Sal	1.	A.	*Salaam alikum.*	Peace be with you. [Arabic]
		B.	*Malikum salaam.*	With you be peace. [Arabic]
	2.	(A.	A's name)	[A gives own name]
		(B.	B's name)	[B gives own name]
	3.	A.	B's name	[A gives B's name]
		B.	A's name / *Naam*, A's name	([B gives A's name]) / Yes, A's name

QP				
Q₁	1.	A.	*Na ngga def?*	How do you do?
		B.	*Maanggi fi rek.*	I am here only.
	2.	A.	*Mbaa dyamm ngg' am?*	Don't you have peace?
		B.	*Dyamm rek, naam.*	Peace only, yes.

Q₂(a)	1.	A.	*Ana waa kïr gi?*	Where/How are the people of the household?
		B.	*Nyu-ngga fa.*	They are there.
	2.	A.	*Ana* [name]?	Where/How is X?
		B.	*Mu-ngga fa.*	He/She is there.
(b)	1.	A.	*Mbaa* {*tawaatu* / *feebaru*} *loo?*	Isn't it that you aren't sick?
		B.	*Maanggi sant Yalla.*	I am praising God.
	2.	A.	*Mbaa kenn* {*feebarul?* / *tawaatul?*}	Isn't it that anyone isn't sick?
		B.	*Nyu-nggi sant Yalla.*	They are praising God.

P	1.	A.	*H'mdillay.*	Thanks be to God. [Arabic]
		B.	*H'mdillay.* / *Tubarkalla.*	Thanks be to God. / Blessed be God. } [Arabic]
	2.	A.	*H'mdillay.* / *Tubarkalla.*	Thanks be to God. / Blessed be God.
		B.	*H'mdillay.* / *Tubarkalla.*	Thanks be to God. / Blessed be God.

Step Sal 2, in which the speakers name themselves, occurs only if A and B have not been previously acquainted. Q_2 can be expanded indefinitely since A may inquire about the whereabouts and health of any person he can think of in B's family and acquaintance. Q_2 as a whole is optional, and the order of questions within Q_1, Q_{2a}, and Q_{2b} is flexible.

The constituent structure of the greeting may be formally stated in the rewrite rules below. The initial symbol $G_{A,B}$ means 'a greeting between persons A and B.' For a fuller elaboration of the rules and a statement of notational conventions, see the appendix at the end of the paper.[7]

$$(1)\ G_{A,B} \rightarrow \#\ Sal + QP\ \#$$

$$(2)\ Sal \rightarrow \begin{cases} Sal_{Strangers}\ /A,\ B\ unacquainted \\ Sal_{Normal}\ /Otherwise \end{cases}$$

$$(3)\ QP \rightarrow Q_1 + (Q_2) + (P) + ((Q_1) + (Q_2) + (P) + (\emptyset))^n$$

$$(4)\ Q_2 \rightarrow (Q_{2a}) + (Q_{2b})$$

Each of the above strings consists of one or more Exchanges between the two speakers. For instance,

$$(5)\ Sal_{Strangers} \rightarrow (Exch_{S1}) + Exch_{S2} + Exch_{S3} + (Exch_{S3})^n$$

$$(6)\ Sal_{Normal} \rightarrow (Exch_{S1}) + Exch_{S3} + (Exch_{S3})^n$$

and $(7)\ Q_1 \rightarrow ((Exch_{Q1.1})^n + (Exch_{Q1.2})^n)^n$, and so on.

Each Exchange consists of two Turns, or the utterance of the first speaker (Initiator) and the response of the second speaker (Respondent):

$$Exch \rightarrow Turn^I + Turn^R$$

Most options of elaboration, deletion, or permutation of parts of the greeting concern the strategies of status alignment to be discussed below. In one situation, however, the greeting can be abbreviated to the Salutation only. This form, less frequent than the full greeting, can be called a 'passing greeting.' It occurs if person A is in a hurry for some legitimate reason (i.e., accountable if challenged). Thus I may use this form, for instance, if I am running to catch a bus and the friend I am greeting is not very close to my path, perhaps far enough away so that I must shout to be heard. Or if I have just entered a large group of persons, each of whom must be greeted individually, I can use this quick greeting for the less important persons, reserving my lengthy greetings for the highest-ranking individuals present. If used on other occasions, however (for instance, just strolling through the village) this Salutation-only form will be 'too brusque and rude,' as my informant noted above.

Two kinds of greetings, then, can be distinguished in two contexts (this rule reformulates rule (1)):

(1a) (i) $G_{A,B} \rightarrow$ $\begin{Bmatrix} G_{Passing} \text{ /A in accountable hurry; B is of lower} \\ \text{rank than some other person C} \\ G_{Normal} \text{ /Otherwise} \end{Bmatrix}$

    (ii) $G_{Passing} \rightarrow$ # Sal #

    (iii) $G_{Normal} \rightarrow$ # Sal + QP #

A flow chart (Fig. 10) shows the possible deletions and repetitions in a greeting as well as the ways in which the greeting can lead either into a recycle of the entire sequence or into a Statement which initiates a new topic of conversation.[8] The purpose of the flow chart is to show how A, the Initiator, has control of all options until the very end, B's statements being obligatory responses to the particular salutation or question posed by A. It is not until at least the fourth exchange that B properly has any options, and then only if A has chosen to proceed rapidly to stage P. Moreover, while A has control of the flow of conversation the focus of interest is always B: all remarks after Sal concern the condition and family of B, not of A.

Unlike the American greeting, then, in which the initial statement 'Hello' is to be made by both parties and it is usual for both parties to ask an equal number of questions, the Wolof greeting clearly divides into two dissimilar roles: the Initiator–Questioner and the Respondent. The more active speech role (Initiator–Questioner) coincides with the greater physical activity (person who enters or approaches). These roles correspond to low and high rank respectively, because both physical activity and speech activity are duties which low-status persons perform for persons of higher status. Accordingly, informants state that 'A noble does not go to greet a *nyenyo* (person of low caste) – it is the *nyenyo* who must come to greet him.' The same could be said of older and younger brothers, of men and women, and so on. To visit someone's compound, or to enter his room, is to show him great respect; and it is the person who enters, or who moves toward the other, who must speak first. It is, moreover, out of respect for another that one asks questions about his welfare. A set of associations emerges concerning the two parties to a greeting, associations which recall cultural stereotypes of noble and griot (or noble and low-caste) behavior:

$$\frac{\text{Initiator}}{\text{Respondent}} : \frac{\text{Speaker}}{\text{Non-speaker}} : \frac{\text{Moving}}{\text{Stationary}} : \frac{\text{Low status}}{\text{High status}} : \frac{\text{Griot}}{\text{Noble}} .$$

The Wolof notion that the low-ranking person travels about more and talks more than the high-status person is here replicated in the status-differentiated roles of the greeting.

As a result of the status associations of the greeting, any two persons who engage in an encounter *must* place themselves in an unequal ranking: they must come to some tacit agreement about which party is to take the higher-

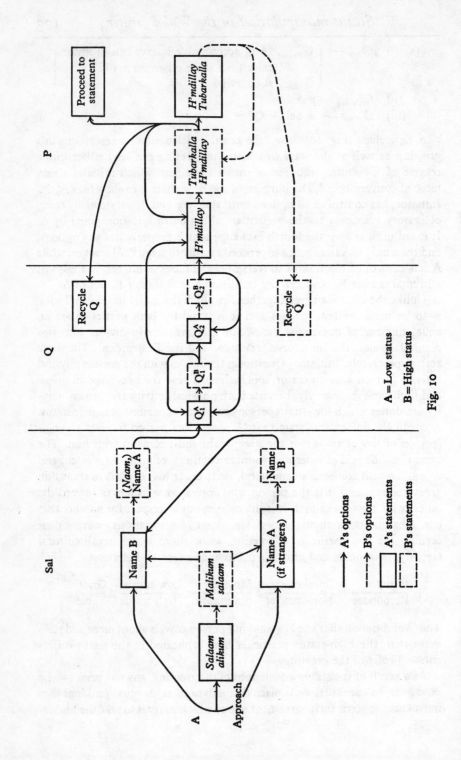

Fig. 10

Sal

Approach

A

Salaam alikum

Malikum salaam

Name B

Name A
(if strangers)

(Naam,)
Name A

Name
B

Q

Q_1^A

Q_1^B

Q_2^A

Q_2^B

Recycle
Q

Recycle
Q

P

H'mdillay

Tubarkalla
H'mdillay

H'mdillay
Tubarkalla

Proceed to
statement

A = Low status
B = High status

→ A's options

⇢ B's options

▢ A's statements

⌐⌐ B's statements

ranking role and which the lower. This ranking is inherent in any greeting no matter how abbreviated, because the mere fact of initiating a greeting is itself a statement of relative status.

A Wolof proverb summarizes the principle of social inequality and the element of competition inherent in the greeting: 'When two persons greet each other, one has shame, the other has glory.' [9]

Status strategies: self-lowering and self-elevating

The flow chart in Fig. 10 is meant to show a 'normal' situation, or one in which there is no conflict or confusion about the assignment of Initiator and Respondent roles. Person A takes the position of relatively lower rank; throughout the greeting sequence, the more he repeats (returns to an earlier step, sometimes even repeating a question he asked before), the more he emphasizes his lowness. B, the person of relatively higher rank, remains passive, giving only the responses specifically required by A's questions. When A cannot think of any more questions, he can proceed to P (the *H'mdillay–Tubarkalla* exchange), these two phrases being repeated several times by A and B, until A perhaps remembers some more members of B's family about whose health he might inquire (Recycle Q). Or, A may proceed directly into the main conversation (Statement).

It is possible, however, that the two parties to a particular encounter do not so readily fall into a tacit agreement on their relative positions. The various criteria of rank may conflict among themselves (e.g., a younger man greeting an old woman) or may not clearly account for the situation. For this reason each party must enter the greeting equipped with some strategy as to which role he will try to take. The two possible strategies of role position, which for convenience I shall call Self-Lowering and Self-Elevating, refer to attempts to take the lower-status or the higher-status role in the greeting (I or R) respectively. These are not the same kinds of behavior as politeness and rudeness, which are larger strategies of demeanor, reaching beyond a person's efforts to take a certain structural role, so as to show his general attitude toward those roles and the status relationship in which he finds himself.

It should not be assumed that a person, whatever his or her caste, will necessarily wish to take the position of higher status. Although high status implies prestige, respect, and political power, it also implies the obligation to contribute to the support of low-status persons. Thus high rank means a financial burden, while low rank has its financial compensations. One may, therefore, wish to be lower than another and dependent on him; and the greeting can be used to help define such a relationship. By taking the lower-status role in the greeting, person A hints that he or she expects sometime to call on the higher-status person B for financial assistance. Even a noble talking to a griot may wish to take the lower-status role to serve some special purpose. The noble may try to take the lower role to prevent the griot from doing so and thus forestall the griot's demands for gifts; or he may do this in order to single the griot out among other griots as a person comparatively worthy of respect and friendship. The noble hints that although no gift is forthcoming on this particular occasion, the special concern implied by this show of deference will be manifested in some appreciable gift later. In my experience a person never asked me for a gift if he or she had not managed to take the lower-status role in greeting me. I soon learned, therefore, to seize the lower role myself sometimes, as a tactful way of forestalling, for the time being, an otherwise overwhelming number of requests.

Self-Lowering in the greeting is, then, the strategy of trying to take the lower-status role of Initiator—Questioner (person A in the example), and it is a strategy which may be used by anyone, no matter what his or her previous standing in terms of categories of caste, age, sex, etc., for purposes which vary according to what that previous standing is. That is, depending on one's status as perceived by oneself and others prior to the beginning of the greeting, a wish to take the lower rank for this particular encounter will be interpreted in different ways. For a slave talking to a noble, or a young man talking to an elder, to take the lower role is to conform with the general duties of one's place in society; for the noble or elder to do so, however, is to relinquish an ascriptive right to the higher role and thereby to mark the occasion as something special.

Practical means by which one may take the lower role are several. The most important is of course initiating the greeting, an act which not only positions the speaker as lower-ranking but guarantees that he will have this lower position for at least four exchanges, during the questioning. If both parties are trying to be the Initiator, it may require some effort for a person to assure himself the role: he must move quickly toward the other, and speak loudly and rapidly, the instant he has caught the other's eye or even before the other has noticed him. Once one has initiated the greeting, he can continue to show deference by making the exchange as long and elaborate as possible. To do this the Initiator will increase the number of different questions (Q_1 and Q_2) and the number of repetitions: any question may be repeated almost indefinitely, or a set of questions recycled, and the same is true for naming. The Initiator should try to postpone step P (*H'mdillay*), certainly avoiding P2, where the other would finally have the option of asking questions in his own right (see first T-rule in the grammar, by which means A and B recycle the questions but with roles reversed, so that B is questioning A). A determined Initiator can keep up the questioning for many minutes, and then after P1 proceed directly to some new topic of conversation, thereby preventing the other from ever reversing the roles and asking his own questions.

The speaker who has failed to obtain the Initiator role can still try to lower himself, however. One way, perhaps the most common, is simply to wait several turns, allowing the Initiator to reach P2 (second round of Praising God); the erstwhile Respondent then starts back to Q himself, instead of allowing the other (original Initiator) to do so (see T-rule 1 in the grammar):

A.	*Ana sa dyabar?*	Where (how) is your wife?
B.	*Mu-ngga fa.*	She is there.
A.	*H'mdillay.*	Thanks be to God.
B.	*Tubarkalla.*	Blessed be God.
A.	*H'mdillay.*	Thanks be to God.
B.	*Mbaa dyamm ngg' am?*	Don't you have peace?

B may even intercept A at P1 (the first round of Praising God), treating it as if it were P2 and jumping right into the questions (see T-rule 2):

A.	*Ana sa dyabar?*	Where (how) is your wife?
B.	*Mu-ngga fa.*	She is there.
A.	*H'mdillay.*	Thanks be to God.
B.	*Mbaa dyamm ngg' am?*	Don't you have peace?

To get the Initiator to the P step sooner, the Respondent may substitute Turn$_{P1}^{I}$ (*H'mdillay*) for his own response to a question (except in response to a question beginning with 'Where'; see T-rule 3). Success is not guaranteed, because A may still keep on questioning, but there will be some constraint on him to repeat *H'mdillay* or respond with *Tubarkalla*, because these, from Turn$_{P1}^{R}$, are normal responses to *H'mdillay* when it is being said by the Questioner. In that case B will be able to recycle the Questioning and assume the initiator role in a new Q:

A.	*Mbaa dyamm ngg' am?*	Don't you have peace?
B.	*H'mdillay.*	Thanks be to God.
A.	*Tubarkalla.*	Blessed be God.
B.	*Na ngga def?*	How do you do?

The other possible Self-Lowering strategy available to B, who has failed to be the Initiator, is to ignore A and try to take over his role. For instance, if A starts with *Salaam alikum*, B ignores him; instead of answering, he jumps into the naming step. When he names A, A must name him back; B starts questioning and has taken over the Initiator role (see T-rule 4):

A. *Salaam alikum.*	Peace be with you. [Arabic]
B. *Ndiaye.* (A's name)	(A's name)
A. *Lo.* (B's name)	(B's name)
B. *Na ngga def?*	How do you do?

A similar strategy can be used if A starts with naming: at Q, B ignores A's question and asks a question himself (see T-rule 5):

A. *Lo.* (B's name)	(B's name)
B. *Ndiaye.* (A's name)	(A's name)
A. *Na ngga def?*	How do you do?
B. *Na ngga def?*	How do you do?
A. *Maanggi fi rek.*	I am here only.

This was a particularly frequent tactic of persons whom I had approached first but who nevertheless wished to ask me for a gift. I also observed it in service encounters, both in the village and in larger towns: e.g., a customer has approached a shopkeeper and greeted him, but the shopkeeper, who hopes to receive a good price and a tip as well, reverses the greeting roles immediately in the manner described above. Thus the shopkeeper becomes the low-status Initiator and the customer the high-status Respondent who will have to give a present to him. Of course, the trouble with any strategy which relies on ignoring A's questions is that A can always do the same. B cannot very well try a second time; a greeting cannot sustain so many disruptions of the flow of conversation. The other speaker, and any on-lookers, will look confused and a little angry (this is how they looked when I tried this; I have never seen a Wolof do so). My informants maintained that persons who disrupt conversation are rude, and rudeness might be the very opposite of the effect B was trying to create.

Self-Elevating in a greeting is the strategy of trying to take the higher-status role of Respondent. The greatest difficulty in this strategy is to avoid initiating the greeting in the first place. This will be awkward if the other is trying to do the same thing, because the greeting *must* take place – it would be unthinkable for two people who know each other at all to come within the greeting range and say nothing. B can try to avoid approaching A, avoid eye contact with him, and wait for him to speak first; but A, after breaking the silence and conducting as brief a greeting as possible, can challenge by asking, 'Why didn't you greet me?' This challenge would be quite proper if B's behavior could have been construed as 'rude' rather than simply 'within his rights' (e.g., B is not sufficiently higher than A for their role assignment to be obvious; or B was already moving and had therefore tacitly assumed the role of Initiator, whereas A was stationary; and so on).

After the greeting has been initiated, a few possible strategies of Self-Elevation remain. A can proceed as quickly as possible through the greeting and introduce some new topic of conversation (Statement). He repeats nothing and asks the minimum number of questions. If he is passing B only at shouting distance and is not trying to show deference, he will not make any detour out of his way to approach B and greet him fully, but will probably give only the Passing Greeting. B's strategy throughout is to remain as passive and taciturn as he can, giving only the brief standard responses to A's questions. When A reaches the stage of Praising God and repeats P several times, B refuses to recycle the questioning or do anything except keep repeating *H'mdillay* or *Tubarkalla*.

It is my impression that a contest of Self-Elevation (that is, a greeting situation in which both parties compete for the higher-status role) does not happen so often as does its inverse, mutual deference. A strategy of Self-Elevation is an ambitious claim; and such a contest can lead, through the challenge, to an open confrontation of motives which is potentially disruptive. A good example of such a confrontation, and one which only narrowly escapes turning into a full-fledged battle, occurs in the following text, a segment of an epic narrative, in which a relationship of political rivalry is enacted in the greeting. In this text, the local chief, Songo Aminata (surname *Ndiaye*) is challenging the power of the king, Lat Dior (surname *Diop*). Lat Dior wishes to confront him, but both are trying to avoid being the lower-status party who must physically approach the other and initiate a greeting. Finally Lat Dior is forced to come all the way to the center of Songo's town to speak with him. Although Songo is then obliged to walk across the central plaza, extend his hand, and name the king, he uses a naming form which is specifically responsive rather than initiating. His 'Yes, Diop?' is a form which would only be used after someone had saluted him first (Turn$^R_{S3}$). Thus he treats Lat Dior's arrival and summons through the messenger as an initial salutation, and assumes the greeting role of Respondent. Lat Dior, however, counters with the same strategy, and the greeting breaks down into challenges:

Lat Dior left Kayor, he went to Saloum. There Maabo Dyoho, his marabout, was to be found. Songo Aminata was here, doing nothing but destroying the towns. All Kayor was angry. From time to time they went over to Saloum to go tell it to Lat Dior. Lat Dior spent three years there. Songo Aminata seized the country, just destroying. When Lat Dior returned, Lat Dior was in Kayor, he sent to Songo Aminata, saying, 'Let him come reply to me.' Songo Aminata said to the envoy, Songo Aminata said to him, 'I am not coming.' Lat Dior saddled up, and went along with his entourage. They came to Baiti Mbaye [neighboring town to Songo's]. He sent to Songo Aminata: 'Tell him, I am here. Let him come to reply.' Songo Aminata said to him [the envoy], 'When you go, tell him, I am not coming; it is the stranger who must go find the town' [i.e., a visiting stranger must come to him, not he to the stranger]. There Songo Aminata did what was like what Matar Mamur [his father] had done here.

Lat Dior saddled up, accompanied by the infants, all of whom he used to go around with, and the guns [i.e., his entire court]. It was at this very hour that they came suddenly to Kïr Matar [Songo's town]. The royal drums arrived in the town square. They formed a barricade with the horses. They sent a messenger; they said, 'When you go, tell Songo Aminata it is Lat Dior who calls him to the town square. It is he who greets him.'

Songo Aminata came out. He wrapped around himself two cloths; he loaded his shoulders with two guns. He went out of the house of the Ndiayes; he came to the town square. He just forded [crossed through] the people [who were like a river]; everyone who was there was laughing, swearing 'Today Lat Dior will kill.' They swore, 'These things which he [Songo Aminata] does in the country will only be complete when Lat Dior kills him. This man, he did not follow after Lat Dior and those whom he causes to accompany him.' And Songo Aminata was not startled. He arrived just crossing through the battlefield. They made way for him that he might pass through the middle of the assembly, just to arrive.

He [Songo Aminata] said, 'My hand, Lat Dior – yes, Diop?' He [Lat Dior] said to him, 'Yes, Ndiaye?' Everyone there was very quiet. Kayor and Baol, the region of the town was chock full. Everyone thus stared at them. Their two foreheads touched; they were speechless – until it was a very long time. Songo Aminata said to him, 'Lat Dior, why did you come here?' He said to him, 'I have spent two months here, between when I came and now.' They were silent. He said to him, 'Songo Aminata, why is it that I had sent to you an envoy who came from Kayor to here, and you did not come to answer me?' He said to him, 'When you came to Baiti Mbaye, heading toward me, Kïr Matar and Baiti Mbaye are one. It is I that you came to. The stranger, it is he who comes to greet the town.' He was silent.[10]

The strategy applied by Songo Aminata can also be stated formally: see T-rule 6 in the grammar.

Joking relationship (kall) *and the joking greeting*

There are certain special cases of greeting which show an alteration both in the form of the greeting and in the social innuendo which the greeting conveys. These cases depend on the particular surnames which are stated by both parties in the naming section of the greeting. Certain pairs of surnames, and the kin groups which bear them, stand in a special relationship to each other, called *kall* 'joking relationship.' The families Diop and Ndiaye, for example, are in joking relationship because, supposedly, 'the Diops are the mothers of the Ndiayes.' In fact the founding ancestor of the village, a man whose surname was Ndiaye, was born of a mother whose surname was Diop. The relationship between the two families echoes the relationship between a mother and her grown son, a relationship which is ambiguous as to precedence and authority. Not all *kall* pairs have a kinship justification – some pairs are 'just friends.' But Wolof informants said that what is 'really' going on in the exchange of insults in a joking relationship is that each person is claiming, *Maa ko moom*, 'It is I who own him'; or 'I am the master and the other is my slave.' This claim must be implicit in the insults, because it is not often actually uttered in the course of the joking repartee.

The greeting forms of the joking relationship are usually initiated by A, the person who initiates the entire greeting, after names have been exchanged (occasionally, if the two parties know each other very well and are on intimate terms, they may skip the naming stage and the regular greeting entirely). The following example illustrates a *kall* greeting:

A.	*Diop!*(B's name)	Diop!
B.	*Ndiaye!* (A's name)	Ndiaye!
A.	*Sant ba neehul!*	That surname is not pleasing!
B.	*Neeh na kaay.*	It is so pleasing.
A.	*Lekk tyeb!*	(The Diops) eat rice! [luxury food; this means they are greedy]
B.	*Ndiaye rek, nyoo ko lekk!*	Only the Ndiayes, it is they who eat it!

This interchange eventually leads into a Statement (of a new topic of post-greeting conversation; see flow chart); or it may be followed by the ɜt of a normal greeting. That is, a joking greeting usually substitutes for the QP of a normal greeting, and in any case takes precedence over it in both sequencing and interest. We have, then, a third basic type of greeting, contextually defined (this rule reformulates rule (1a)):

(1b) (i)
$$G_{A,B} \rightarrow \begin{cases} G_{passing} \text{ / A in accountable hurry;} \\ \quad\quad\quad\quad \text{B is of lower rank than} \\ \quad\quad\quad\quad \text{some other person C} \\ \\ G_{normal} \text{ / Otherwise} \\ \\ G_{joking} \text{ / A, B have certain surnames} \end{cases}$$

(ii) $G_{joking} \rightarrow \#Sal + I + (QP)\#$

where $I \rightarrow Insult_1 + Insult_2 + \dots + Insult_n$

Unlike the joking relationship among the Manding as described by Labouret (1934:102), this mutual insult in the Wolof *kall* relationship is not obligatory, although once it is initiated by one party the other must respond in kind. The general effect of the joking greeting, in contrast to the normal greeting, is one of *equality* between the two speakers, an equality which arises from rivalry (or mock rivalry) rather than from concord. This joking rivalry is not a true contest of insults, because one does not try to win, only to match one's partner equally. Even if one speaker were able (or even tried) to out-insult the other he would not achieve any real victory, because the *kall* is a permanent relationship between groups and transcends the relations of individuals in particular encounters. But because of the equality implied in the joking relationship, a joking greeting will be avoided if the *a priori* status difference between the speakers is too great. It is rare to see a joking greeting between a griot and the Imam of the mosque, for instance, although such a greeting might well occur between a griot and a young or low-ranking noble. Similarly, the non-seriousness of the insults prevents them from being used in serious or somber occasions, in which equality, if appropriate to the occasion at all, must be expressed in some other way. For instance, two chiefs each visiting the village of a third chief for a funeral, may, if they wish to express equality, engage in mutual deference, in which each tries to take the lower-status greeting role in a normal greeting, even though their surnames might happen to be in joking relationship.

Structurally the joking greeting contrasts with the normal greeting in the joking form's symmetry of speaking roles, a symmetry which reflects the overall effect of equality between the two speakers. Although the joking is usually initiated by A after both names have been exchanged, it does not really matter much which party initiates. B can sometimes initiate the joking instead of naming A:

A. *Diop!* (B's name)   Diop! (B's name)
B. *Sa sant Ndiaye neehul!*   Your surname Ndiaye is not pleasing!

After the initiation of the joking greeting, there is no particular division of utterances into insults and responses: each speaker may insult the other without responding specifically to the other's insult of himself. It should also be noted that in the *kall* only stylized insults on conventional topics are permissible. Since the relationship depends on not being specific to individuals, personal insults or 'rudeness' of demeanor (to be described below) would change the interaction into something else that was no longer the *kall* or any other kind of greeting.

The joking relationship provides, however, only a very limited opportunity to express equality. The *kall* involves only certain pairs of surnames, and any one person has only one or two surname groups in which to find joking partners. Some persons may find that their partner surnames are not even represented in the village. An effect of equality is more frequently attained through mutual deference, whereby the normal greeting is recycled many times, the two speakers taking turns at the low-status role. Such an interchange – like the familiar 'after you, Alphonse' – may go on almost indefinitely.

Both the joking greeting and mutual deference thus express equality, but an equality which is effected only through rivalry or competition. Mutual deference is a kind of rivalry for the lower-status role in the greeting, while persons engaging in joking insults vie for the higher-status role (as noted above, such a rivalry for high status is the Wolof's own view of the *kall* insult exchange). Apparently, among the Wolof the expression of equality is only to be attained through some kind of exchange that balances or neutralizes the inequality which is the basic premise of interaction.

Demeanor and speech styles: strategies of style-switching

The strategies discussed so far have all been strategies of role choice: efforts to take particular speaking roles in the greeting and thereby to take the social statuses implied by those roles. Another kind of strategy involves the speaker's persona and demeanor, the way in which he communicates his own self-image and his attitude toward the greeting role he has taken.[11] In particular, he signals whether the status he assumed in the greeting accurately reflects his own estimation of his place in society at large. His demeanor may emphasize the claim to higher or lower status indicated by his greeting role; or he may indicate that, for some reason, he does not really belong in the status in which he finds himself in this particular encounter. Perhaps the role whose lines he is speaking is not the role he intended to take. Or perhaps this encounter is to be understood as a special case, his role in it not being pertinent to his roles elsewhere.

The strategies for communicating one's self-image affect quite different linguistic aspects of the greeting from those involved in choosing a greeting role. Whereas role choice has to do with the selection and ordering of formula sentences, demeanor is particularly manifest in paralinguistic (or non-segmental) phenomena applicable to any of these formula utterances.[12] Three aspects of voice quality are relevant here: *pitch*, *loudness* and *tempo* of speaking. Another aspect of speaking style, *quantity* of speech (verbosity/terseness), is also important. These phenomena combine to give the general cultural stereotypes of speech styles associated with high and low status, as follows:

	STRESS	TEMPO–QUANTITY
Noble	s (− high, − loud)	t (− rapid, − verbose)
Griot	S (+ high, + loud)	T (+ rapid, + verbose)

The high, strident, rapid speech of the griot (as the epitome of the low-caste speaker) contrasts with the low-pitched, quiet, terse speaking style of the high-ranking noble. Since these speech stereotypes will be described more fully in another paper, it will suffice to mention here that a great deal of the actual speech of persons of different castes does in fact correspond to the stereotypes of style, especially when a person is interacting with someone of different caste whose speech style therefore contrasts directly with his own. But although in principle these styles are to be associated with nobles and *nyenyo* (low-caste persons), respectively, in practice they can be drawn upon as indicators of *relatively* high or low status, within a single caste. The availability of these styles to all is what makes them important for personal use in the greeting.

Since the speaking styles do not apply to the same kind of linguistic phenomena as does the assignment of greeting roles, the relevance of these styles for personal use in the greeting lies in the fact that the status implied stylistically by a speaker's intonation need not coincide fully with the status assigned structurally by his greeting role. That is to say, we have here the intersection of an expressive system, based on a patterned usage of intonation and other paralinguistic phenomena, with a referential system, based on a syntactic ordering of utterances in the greeting dialogue. Both systems are concerned with the same social dimension – status ranking – and they complement each other in the total greeting performance and the social meaning which the greeting conveys. Just as a speaker may choose (or be obliged to take) a lower or higher greeting role, Initiator or Respondent, no matter what his or her caste or other *a priori* social status, so he or she may choose a 'griot-like' or 'noble-like' intonation, independently of either *a priori* social status or syntactically defined greeting role. Whether the status implied expressively is the same as that implied referentially, or as that known in advance, will affect others' interpretations of a greeting performance.

In what we might call a normal situation, in which person A is *a priori* of obviously lower status and takes the lower-status role of Initiator– Questioner, and no one is trying to manipulate the situation to imply anything else, the speech styles of A and B will correspond to the 'griot' and 'noble' styles respectively, even if A and B are not members of these castes. But because these speech styles refer to *relatively* higher or lower status and not to membership in specific castes, an individual may switch styles as he interacts with different people. A young man who is a noble but who has not yet amassed wealth or supporters may use the 'low-caste' style (ST) when he is greeting a powerful older noble or the village chief, yet use the 'high-caste' style (st) when talking to a griot. In these two situations he will also normally use different greeting roles, taking the Initiator role when greeting the older noble and taking the Respondent role when greeting the griot. In both instances the speech style he uses and the greeting role he takes fit his true relationship to these persons as he himself and most others would probably define it.

We can say, then, that a person switches *all* features of his speech style in the greeting, and also switches his greeting role, when he feels that in some objective sense he does belong in the new status relative to the new person with whom he is interacting. This is the status to which he has an obvious right, to which others would assign him. By extension, if a person switches all style features when his right to the status he has claimed is *not* obvious, then he is staking a new but permanent claim to that position. For instance, suppose person B claims the higher role though his right to it is doubtful. By using stylistic features st he claims that he truly belongs in a higher rank than person A, that this encounter is a true model of their relationship and not just a special case. In fact, his use of the greeting in this way may be part of his overall effort to climb above A.

Partial switching – that is, switching only some of these aspects of speech style – can also occur, because stress (pitch, volume) and tempo–quantity (rapidity, verbosity) are distinctive features which can vary independently. Partial switching emphasizes a discrepancy between a speaker's true status (in his own estimation) and his greeting role. In these cases the feature of stress (pitch and loudness) indicates the speaker's self-image, his estimation of his proper station with respect to the other. The other feature, tempo–quantity, goes with the greeting role, the 'griot-like' T being associated with the role of Initiator, the 'noble-like' t with the Respondent. Thus a speech style sT (partial switching) will sometimes be used by a noble who has taken the role of Initiator–Questioner in greeting someone whose status is not obviously higher than his own; his performance, or strategy, will be interpreted as 'polite,' because he is showing deference (Initiator role, T) even though he does not have to (s). For example, when my assistant, a noble of high birth but low achievement, greeted nobles other than those of obviously superior status (such as the chief, the Imam, the wealthy shopowners, or his employers), he usually used the Initiator role, with great verbosity but a quiet, low-pitched voice. He explained to me that to be 'polite' one must greet at length, but that he did not speak loudly because he was not a griot and would be ashamed to do so. He was apparently not ashamed, however, to greet me (his employer), or the chief, etc., in a ringing 'griot-like' tone, presumably because he considered himself to have a basically lower rank in relation to these persons, a status which concurred with his lower-status greeting role.

Conversely, the speech style St will occasionally be used by a griot taking the Respondent role when greeting someone of higher rank than himself; his performance will be interpreted as 'rude' or even threatening. The griot is reminding you of his caste (S) but at the same time hinting at his power over you (t); if you do not give him presents and become his patron, he will insult you and spread gossip about you all over town. On some occasions when a griot greeted me in this manner, he made the threat of insult and gossip quite explicit in a later (post-greeting) part of the conversation.

The second feature of speech demeanor, tempo—quantity, appears to correspond with the speaker's particular greeting role, as mentioned above. Rarely does the feature depart from this close association. When I have observed it to differ from what might be expected, given the speaker's greeting role (e.g., when a person takes the lower-status Initiator role but delivers his lines very slowly in a 'noble-like' drawl), the discrepancy has often been corrected by a change of roles (to Respondent) later in the greeting. I conclude that the slow delivery is a matter of reluctance to take the Initiator role and that the Respondent role, to which the speaker switched, was the one he really wanted in the first place. Insofar as this feature varies independently of the greeting role, then, it signals whether the greeting role that the speaker has taken is the role that he really intended to take.

The above discussion applies mainly to the 'normal' greeting; in the joking relationship, vocal features of speech style are not so important because differential ranking is not at issue. Moreover, the blatant statement of a claim to higher rank overshadows any innuendo conveyed by voice tone alone. It may be worth noting, however, that the speech style of both parties in the joking relationship tends to be the griot-like ST. The low-status style, when joined to the stated claim to high rank, results in no claim at all – which is of course the point of the joking greeting.

Summary and formal statement of strategies

We are now in a position to summarize and state formally the kinds of strategies with which a Wolof speaker may approach a greeting and the ways in which he or she may interpret the behavior of others, in reference to these strategies. Both the role in the greeting that a speaker takes and certain paralinguistic aspects of his speaking will have distinctive meaning for his auditors, in terms of the speaker's social rank and his attitude toward the encounter in which he finds himself.

Linguistically, both Self-Lowering and Self-Elevating strategies involve the manipulation of the *sequence* of utterances, each utterance itself being an irreducible unit within the genre/routine. It is possible to construct a generative grammar for the greeting, stating the basic greeting exchange (here defined as the exchange in which the assignment of functional roles inherent in the initiation of the sequence remains the same throughout the greeting) as the phrase structure, and the greeting strategies as transformations (deletions, permutations, etc.). Each strategy, here a transformation, is an operation which reverses the functional roles of the two speakers in the greeting from what they are at the outset of the exchange. These transformations do not affect the meaning of an utterance or sequence of utterances as signals of social rank, but shift the assignment of individual speakers to these ranks. As an appendix to this paper I have drawn up a grammar of the normal greeting (as opposed to the passing greeting or joking greeting): this grammar is a relatively exhaustive set of rules, including those for transforming the greeting sequence in order to apply socially functional strategies. The paralinguistic strategies of demeanor may then be applied to the surface structure of the grammar, its realization in actual utterances.

I have differentiated the paralinguistic aspects of greeting into two distinctive features, stress (S or s) and tempo—quantity (T or t), because these represent the two aspects into which speech styles ('griot-like,' 'noble-like') divide under the conditions of partial switching as outlined above.[13] There are eight possible combinations of the paralinguistic features of performance with the greeting roles to which they may be applied by an individual speaker. The most important of these are the ones which result from combining two kinds of strategies, Self-Lowering/Self-Elevating and Politeness/Rudeness. A third strategy is activated when the speaker relates the feature tempo—quantity to his greeting role: if the speaker varies this feature, he signals that the role he is in is not the one he intended to choose.

These eight combinations correspond to eight possible 'glosses,' distinct greeting 'meanings' or ways of interpreting greetings. Fig. 11 shows, in flow-chart form, the relationship of paralinguistic features of performance to the social features of demeanor which a speaker may intend to convey. The figure also gives, as glosses to the features of performance, the possible ways a hearer may interpret the speaker's greeting demeanor.

By making a formal statement of greeting performances and their glosses in this way, we can see that the social meanings of greeting behavior can be analyzed into features which refer to concrete linguistic phenomena, rule-governed in their turn. We can also see that apart from the joking greeting, which depends on rather special circumstances, these eight performances and their 'meanings' are the *only* ones open to the Wolof speaker at the onset of an encounter. It is structurally impossible, for instance, for a griot talking to a noble to be really polite (as opposed to just not being rude) and still claim dependency. For if he takes option (2) he signals that his self-

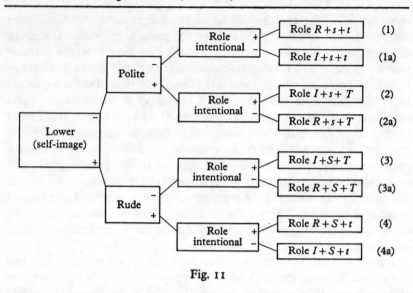

Fig. 11

Glosses
(1) Speaker believes his rank to be fundamentally higher and claims dominance
(1a) Same as (1), but speaker has failed to take the greeting role he wanted
(2) Speaker believes himself higher (or at least, equally high) but wants to be polite; he disclaims any special patronage bond
(2a) Same as (2), but speaker has failed to take the greeting role he wanted
(3) Speaker believes his rank to be fundamentally lower and claims dependency
(3a) Same as (3), but speaker has failed to take the greeting role he wanted
(4) Speaker believes himself lower and wants to be rude, threatening others with the consequences of neglecting him
(4a) Same as (4), but speaker has failed to take the greeting role he wanted

image is not consistent with the expected image of his caste, that he does not consider himself to be in a true griot–noble relationship, and that therefore the noble is not obliged to give him anything. Likewise if a noble talking to a griot chooses options (3) or (4) he will have violated the expectations of demeanor proper to his rank, shown a self-image which is unfitting, and will therefore jeopardize his following (who may suspect that he 'lacks self-control'). The motivations appropriate to a participant in a particular greeting – and therefore to a participant in any Wolof encounter – are limited.

In conclusion, it must be repeated that the Wolof greeting is particularly important because it is obligatory, the considerations and constraints which it presupposes being forced into the structure of every social relationship. The most important such considerations are cultural assumptions of inequality and of the character and motivations of the unequal persons. In addition, analysis of the greeting as a linguistic routine brings out some methodological considerations. It permits a precise statement of social functions of the routine and their linguistic bases, in a generative framework which could perhaps be applied to other such routines and to broader aspects of interaction in this culture. The greeting was chosen among Wolof linguistic routines for its accessibility to the ethnographer. But the precision which is possible in analysis of the greeting encourages extending such analysis of rule-governed behavior beyond the confines of the genre.[14]

APPENDIX: GRAMMAR OF RULES FOR GREETING ('G NORMAL')

Conventions of notation

$\#$ Boundary of greeting routine

$\rightarrow$ Rewrite as (in phrase rules)

$\Rightarrow$ Rewrite as (in transformational rules)

$\neq$ Is not

,   Or

()   Optional (however, if all items in a string are enclosed in parentheses, at least one must be chosen)

{}   Choose any one

/   In the context of

$()^n$ Optional to repeat n times

$\emptyset$ Null symbol

Phrase structure rules

(1) $G_{A,B} \rightarrow \# \text{Sal} + QP \#$

(2) $\text{Sal} \rightarrow \begin{Bmatrix} \text{Sal}_{\text{Strangers}}/\text{A,B unacquainted} \\ \text{Sal}_{\text{Normal}} /\text{Otherwise} \end{Bmatrix}$

(3) $QP \rightarrow Q_1 + (Q_2) + (P) + \left((Q_1) + (Q_2) + (P) + (\emptyset) \right)^n$

(4) $Q_2 \rightarrow (Q_{2a}) + (Q_{2b})$

(5) $\text{Sal}_{\text{Strangers}} \rightarrow (\text{Exch}_{S1}) + \text{Exch}_{S2} + \text{Exch}_{S3} + (\text{Exch}_{S3})^n$

(6) $\text{Sal}_{\text{Normal}} \rightarrow (\text{Exch}_{S1}) + \text{Exch}_{S3} + (\text{Exch}_{S3})^n$

(7) $Q_1 \rightarrow \left((\text{Exch}_{Q1.1})^n + (\text{Exch}_{Q1.2})^n \right)^n$

(8) $Q_{2a} \rightarrow (\text{Exch}_{Q2a})^n$

(9) $Q_{2b} \rightarrow (\text{Exch}_{Q2b})^n$

(10) $P \rightarrow (\text{Exch}_{P1})^n + \begin{Bmatrix} \text{Exch}_{P2} \\ \emptyset \end{Bmatrix}$

Any Exchange is composed of Turns, one for each speaker:

$$\text{Exch} \rightarrow \text{Turn}^I + \text{Turn}^R$$

Thus:

(11) $\text{Exch}_{S1} \rightarrow \text{Turn}^I_{S1} + \text{Turn}^R_{S1}$

(12) $\text{Exch}_{S2} \rightarrow \text{Turn}^I_{S2} + \text{Turn}^R_{S2}$

(13) $\text{Exch}_{S3} \rightarrow \text{Turn}^I_{S3} + \text{Turn}^R_{S3}$

(14) $\text{Exch}_{Q1.1} \rightarrow \text{Turn}^I_{Q1.1} + \text{Turn}^R_{Q1.1}$

(15) $\text{Exch}_{Q1.2} \rightarrow \text{Turn}^I_{Q1.2} + \text{Turn}^R_{Q1.2}$

(16) $\text{Exch}_{Q2a} \rightarrow \text{Turn}^I_{Q2a} + \text{Turn}^R_{Q2a}$

(17) $\text{Exch}_{Q2b} \rightarrow \text{Turn}^I_{Q2b} + \text{Turn}^R_{Q2b}$

(18) $\text{Exch}_{P1} \rightarrow \text{Turn}^I_{P1} + \text{Turn}^R_{P1}$

(19) $\text{Exch}_{P2} \rightarrow \text{Turn}^I_{P2} + \text{Turn}^R_{P2}$

The Turns may be rewritten as the actual sentences of the greeting, or as rules for sentences:

(20) $\text{Turn}^I_{S1} \rightarrow$ *Salaam alikum* 'Peace be with you'

(21) $\text{Turn}^R_{S1} \rightarrow$ *Malikum salaam* 'With you be peace'

(22) $\text{Turn}^I_{S2} \rightarrow$ Name I

(23) $\text{Turn}^R_{S2} \rightarrow$ Name R

(24) $\text{Turn}^I_{S3} \rightarrow$ Name R

(25) $\text{Turn}^R_{S3} \rightarrow$ *(Naam)* Name I. '(Yes) Name I'

(26) $\text{Turn}^I_{Q1.1} \rightarrow$ *Na ngga def?* 'How are you?'

(27) $\text{Turn}^R_{Q1.1} \rightarrow$ *Maanggi fi rek.* 'I am here only.'

(28) $\text{Turn}^I_{Q1.2} \rightarrow$ *Mbaa dyamm ngg' am?* 'Don't you have peace?'

(29) $\text{Turn}^R_{Q1.2} \rightarrow$ *Dyamm rek, naam.* 'Peace only, yes.'

(30) $\text{Turn}^I_{Q2a} \rightarrow$ *Ana NP?* 'Where/how is . . .?'

(31) $\text{Turn}^R_{Q2a} \rightarrow$ *Pron₁ ngga fa.* '. . . is there.'

(32) $\text{Turn}^I_{Q2b} \rightarrow$ *Mbaa VP?* 'Isn't it that . . .?'

(33) $\text{Turn}^R_{Q2b} \rightarrow$ *Pron₂ nggi sant (Yalla).* '. . . is praising (God).'

(34) $\text{Turn}^I_{P1} \rightarrow$ *H'mdillay.* 'Thanks be to God.'

(35) $\text{Turn}^R_{P1} \rightarrow$ { *H'mdillay.* 'Thanks be to God.' }
{ *Tubarkalla.* 'Blessed be God.' }

(36) Turn^I_{P2} { *H'mdillay.* }
{ *Tubarkalla.* }

(37) $\text{Turn}^R_{P2} \rightarrow$ { *H'mdillay.* }
{ *Tubarkalla.* }

(38) NP $\rightarrow$ *waa kïr gi, sa* + Kin Term, Name. 'people of the household, your Kin Term, Name, . . .'

(39) Pron₁ $\rightarrow$ (*Nyu* 'they' / *waa kïr gi* + ___
    plural NP
    Mu 'he, she' / other NP + ___)

(40) VP $\left\{\begin{array}{l}\rightarrow\end{array}\right.$ *tawaatu loo, feebaru loo,*   'you aren't sick, you aren't
feebarul, tawaatul, kenn tawaa- sick, he isn't sick, he isn't
tul, kenn feebarul   sick, no one is sick, no one
is sick'

(41) Pron$_2$ $\left\{\begin{array}{l}\end{array}\right.$ *Maa* 'I' / *tawaatu loo, feebaru loo* + ___
$\rightarrow$ *Mu* 'he, she' / *feebarul, tawatul* + ___
Nyu 'they' / *kenn feebarul, kenn tawaatul* + ___

Transformational rules (strings in which functional roles of speakers are reversed are in italics):

1. T[A,B change roles]:

$$X + \text{Turn}^R_{P2} + Q \Rightarrow X + Q$$

X,Q are strings. Q $\neq$ Sal, P

2. T[A,B change roles; B intercepts P1]:

$$X + \text{Turn}^I_{P1} + \text{Turn}^R_{P1} + (\text{Exch}_{P2})\,(Q) \Rightarrow X + \text{Turn}^I_{P1} + Q$$

X, Q are strings. Q $\neq$ Sal, P

3. T[A,B change roles; B substitutes P1 for his twin (Permutation)]:

$$X + \text{Turn}^I_Q + \text{Turn}^R_Q + Y + \text{Exch}_{P1} + Z \Rightarrow X + \text{Turn}^I_{Q1} + \mathit{Exch}_{P1} + Y + (Z)$$

X, Y, Z are strings. Q $\neq$ Q$_{2a}$

4. T[A,B change roles; B ignores A's '*salaam alikum*,' intercepts with naming]:

$$X + \text{Turn}^R_{S1} + \text{Exch}_{S3} + Y \Rightarrow X + \mathit{Exch}_{S3} + Y$$

X, Y are strings.

5. T[A,B change roles; B substitutes a question for his response]:

$$X + \text{Turn}^R_{Q1} + Y \Rightarrow X + \mathit{Turn}^I_{Q1} + Y$$

X, Y are strings.

6. T[B Self-Elevating]:

$$X + \text{Exch}_{S3} + Y \Rightarrow X + \mathit{Turn}^R_{S3} + Y$$

X is $\emptyset$ or Pause.
Y is a string.

Note: These T-rules are mutually exclusive at whatever stage of the greeting they apply.

9

RITUALS OF ENCOUNTER AMONG THE MAORI: SOCIOLINGUISTIC STUDY OF A SCENE

ANNE SALMOND

Background

The Maori people, New Zealand's Polynesian inhabitants, were first effectively contacted for the European world by Captain James Cook and his party in 1769. They immediately acquired a reputation for belligerence, because whenever the explorers tried to approach a group, 'they rose up and every man produced either a long pike, or a small weapon of polished stone' (Banks 1896:42). In fact it was standard practice for stranger groups to make such ritual displays of strength upon first encounter, but the explorers weren't to know this, and retaliated with musket fire whose effects were anything but ritual. Subsequent arrivals in New Zealand – the missionaries, traders, and whalers – were greeted more tentatively, and as they became better acquainted with Maori custom they learned that challenges, sham fights, and war dances as well as oratory and other verbal arts were an expected part of ceremonial occasions. For their part, the Maori people learned to keep their greeting forms to themselves, and it was only Europeans who had frequent cause to parlay with the chiefs and elders who ever mastered them. As increasing numbers of settlers arrived in New Zealand, the pattern became established. Maori gatherings, or *hui*, once held in the village plaza, were now staged in a *marae* complex, with its carved meeting-house and courtyard for orators fenced off and isolated from other settlement. Europeans were only rarely to be found at a *hui*, and the privacy of the *marae* was jealously preserved.

Until World War II, the Maori were predominantly a rural people, concentrated in parts of the country like the Far North, the Bay of Plenty, and the East Coast. In these areas they farmed remaining Maori lands, built their *marae*, and continued to practise the rituals of encounter on ceremonial occasions. Each *marae* was sponsored by the local core of a descent-group, perhaps 200–500 people; and its meeting-house, with carved slabs about the inner walls each depicting a famous ancestor of the group, was a potent reminder of pre-contact times and a peculiarly Maori past. Although their children attended state schools, increasingly conformed to European behaviour, and forgot to speak Maori, still the elders of each generation continued to hold all life crises and important group events on the *marae*. In doing so, they honoured not only the main figures of the occasion, but also their heritage as Maoris. The *hui* had come to play the role of main repository for Maori culture in a world which was increasingly European, for it was one situation where Maoris were in charge, Maori was the dominant language, Maori food was served, and Maori etiquette prevailed. As an event the *hui* was and still is supremely oriented to the past. Genealogies are recited, traditions re-told, the ancestors are repeatedly invoked, and old oral skills are practised. The main actors themselves are elders, qualified by their age and esoteric knowledge to carry out the sacred forms without mistake, and although the Maori are only a small minority in New Zealand today (8% of the total population), their rituals hark back to the times when they lived in the country undisturbed.

Since World War II, the pattern of rural life has been disrupted by an increasing flow of young people to the cities, and this has had its own special effects on Maori populations. Rural kin-based Maori communities lose their young people, and in many cases the *marae* lies almost idle, with only a few of the older generation to look after it. Urban dwellers often return to the home *marae* for their life crises, but where distances are too great, attention turns to the construction of *marae* in the city. If anything, though, the *hui* and its rituals are now more important than ever as a Maori 'safety valve' from European culture, and *marae* etiquette has become the topic of school and university classes, newspaper articles, and 'grass roots' seminars held by the elders to instruct their younger tribal kinsmen.

Hui then, is the cover term for a whole range of ceremonial gatherings on the *marae*. They last from one to three days, and are sponsored and stage-managed by the *marae*'s owner-group. There are well over a thousand *marae* in New Zealand, and at least two or three *hui* a year will be held on most *marae*, while some are in almost constant use. Each *hui* has its own *take* or cause, and these can range from marriage, death, opening a new meeting-house, or unveiling a gravestone, to celebrations of loyalty to the Maori Queen or welcomes to visiting dignitaries. For each such case, there is a central ceremony, but what really defines the *hui* as a class of occasion are its rituals of encounter.

The rituals of encounter

The Maori people are traditionally divided into non-unilineal descent groups of varying scale. The most inclusive unit in this segmentary system was the tribe, localized in a known area and numbering perhaps a thousand people or more. At present there are forty-two recognized tribes in New Zealand (Metge 1967:125). The next unit was the subtribe, with some hundreds of members each. The subtribe was a closely united group in the past, cooperating in large-scale economic tasks and warfare, and today it is the usual sponsoring group for a *marae*. In traditional times, intertribal and subtribal warfare was endemic, and encounters between groups of this scale were potentially dangerous, as an exchange of insults or some unwitting offense could spark off hostilities on the spot. There was a fierce preoccupation with *mana* or prestige, and even the most peaceful meetings were marked by intergroup rivalry. The rituals of encounter were used on all occasions when different groups met, as a finely balanced mechanism for keeping the peace and allowing competition to proceed without bloodshed. Today there is no fear of warfare, but suspicion and hot pride are still powerful underlying factors in group encounters on the *marae*, and the rituals are played out in a keenly competitive spirit. Actors on both sides exert themselves to give an impressive performance, with the fundamental principle that the more distant and unknown the other part, the more perfect and powerful must be your part in the exchange.

THE SCENE

At this point it seems appropriate to describe one moderately ceremonious ritual of encounter. No matter what the cause of the *hui* might be, visitors attend in groups, recruited by descent and summoned to the *hui* by ties of kinship or friendship with its sponsors. They may have travelled to the *marae* by bus or private car. Upon their arrival, a *marae* policeman directs parking, then the group gradually assembles at the ceremonial entrance to the *marae*. They stand around chatting or tidying up, then move into position – the old women in front, in black dresses, black scarves, and wearing jade ornaments; younger women next; then the men, with the more notable elders at their head. The signal to enter is given by the host group, and the ritual begins. The chief elder of the visiting party calls out a protective incantation (*waerea*)[1] from the gateway of the *marae*, to shield his people from any hostile influences within, and an elderly local woman standing in the porch of the carved meeting-house begins a high wailing call of welcome (*karanga*). 'Enter and bring your dead, we shall weep for them together.' The caller for the visitors replies, and the two old ladies call and answer while all the women present set up a chorus of keening, sobbing, and wailing for the dead. A party of women standing in front of the meeting-house begins the action chant of welcome (*poowhiri*), metaphorically addressing the visiting group as a prized canoe which is being hauled onto the *marae*. The visitors move slowly towards the meeting-house, halting at least twice to drop their tears onto the grass of the courtyard in honour of the dead. The old ladies continue to wail vigorously and wave sprigs of greenery to ward off hostile spirits. If the groups are strangers, the atmosphere is tense and uneasy. It is important to behave correctly, especially if the *marae* belongs to a tribe with a different etiquette; for an invisible horde of the dead hover over each group, and their meeting must be carefully handled. The visitors stop at some distance from the meeting-house, and all displays of grief are redoubled – wailing reaches a crescendo, and handkerchiefs are produced in quantity (*tangi*). This may last from ten to fifteen minutes. The old ladies of the host group are seated in the front porch of the meeting-house, their orators sit silently on a bench to the right of the house, and all other locals are either standing around as spectators or busy in the background cooking, washing dishes, or looking after children.

As the weeping subsides, the visiting men leave their women and sit on the bench for visiting orators which faces the meeting-house, and the women move to join the local ladies on the porch, pressing noses with each one in turn, or go to benches set out behind their menfolk. The space bounded by the meeting-house porch and the two orators' benches is the *marae aatea* or speaking-ground, the true 'stage' in a *hui*. Now the oratory (*whaikoorero*) begins. A local speaker, always an elder, stands with a shout (*whakaaraara*): *Tihei mauri ora!* 'I greet the living!' He walks onto the *marae*, and faces the visitors. He is bare-headed, wears a suit and tie (even if it is pouring, the true orator scorns hat, coat, or umbrella), and carries a carved walking-stick. He stands there and launches into a *tauparapara* or traditional chant, accompanied by vigorous actions and defiant brandishings of his stick. This display gives the orator's credentials and establishes his skill. Then he starts his oration. He strides along in front of the visitors, stops, delivers a few sentences, then turns on his heel and strides back again. His welcome to the dead, to the living, the recitation of genealogy and delivery of humorous asides are all given in these short bursts of speech. As his speech draws to a close, the orator starts up an ancient song (*waiata*), and is joined and supported by members of his group. The song finishes, and he rounds off his performance with a few last words.

In some tribes, all the local orators speak in turn until their side is finished, then all the visitors, a style known as *paaeke*. In other areas, orators of the two sides alternate (*utuutu*). Ritual experts make it their business to be aware of such regional differences, which can be humiliating traps for the unwary. One of the host speakers now calls the visitors over to shake hands. The local people line up in front of the meeting-house, and the visitors move along the line, pressing noses and shaking hands with everyone in turn (*hongi*). In a few areas, the locals do the walking, a custom which is described by other tribes as 'the wharf coming to the steamer.' Now the ritual of encounter for this particular group is complete. The visitors have been given honorary local status by the ceremony, and are no longer threatened by *tapu* qualities on this *marae*. The local people are still busy, however, as the ritual must be repeated in its entirety for each group of visitors; an important *hui* may attract four or five thousand visitors, arriving in groups of ten to several hundred each.

Although the ritual of encounter is repeated for each group, its composition changes by addition or deletion every time in adjustment to the *mana* of the visitors. Groups from distant tribes or those containing important visitors receive the most elaborate ceremonial of all. The arrival of the Queen, the Prime Minister, the Minister of Maori and Island Affairs, or other major officials of state or church is heralded by the ceremonial challenge (*wero*), a part of the ritual which is performed only on these occasions. A warrior wearing a flax kilt runs to the gateway of the *marae* as the official party are about to enter, leaping, grimacing, and whirling his *taiaha* (carved long-staff). This display of intimidation derives from old times, when challengers ran at a visiting party and hurled a spear into their midst, then fled with warriors of the other side hard on their heels. Today the challenger places a carved baton on the ground, which is picked up by one of the visiting party as a sign they come in peace. The challenge is rarely taken up these days, but some years ago New Zealand had a Governor-General who had long been interested in Maori custom. Shortly after he arrived in the country, a great *hui* was staged to welcome him to the Northern area. When he arrived at the *marae* with the official party, he had a young man at his side, stripped for action. The challenger came down the *marae*, all threat and gesticulation, his weapon whirling close to the Governor's face. He knelt down, placed his baton, then started to run back to the meeting-house. About half-way he was felled by a flying tackle from behind – the Governor-General had followed the old custom, and met the challenge with a warrior of his own. The laughter and applause were tremendous, and the Governor's stocks in *mana* went sky-high. On such ceremonious occasions, the full ritual is given, and experts are especially recruited to make certain that everything is carried out correctly.

If a strong delegation of traditional rivals arrives on the *marae*, the ritual is also carried out in full, with both sides competing in the display of traditional skills. Under these circumstances a contest in oratory is likely to develop, and as many as twelve speakers from each side may stand in turn to deliver long, esoteric speeches, until finally one group runs out of qualified men. This sort of contest is most impressive in the alternating style of oratory, where each speaker strives to outdo the one before in grandiloquence and ancient knowledge.

If the visitors are a respected but friendly group, the atmosphere is relaxed, and it would be something of an insult if they delivered a protective incantation on entry to the *marae*. For a small and rather unimportant group, the action chant of welcome will probably be left out altogether, and only a couple of speeches given on each side.

Thus the ritual of encounter is extremely sensitive to social context. In a situation marked formal by the size, status, and kin-distance of the visiting group, all of its elements are triggered in sequence; but in informal situations, certain of the ritual units are optional or even obligatorily deleted.

Towards a formal description

The situational use of language is one of the recognized concerns of the ethnography of speaking. One of the major difficulties, however, is that while linguistic structure has long been studied and formal models proposed for its description, the structure of situations is much less understood. This theoretical inequality can easily produce an imbalance in description, with linguistic patterns the focus of attention, and the social context relegated to the role of background information to which the linguistic patterns respond.

One possible means of redressing this imbalance is to investigate how situations might be made to yield to structural description. Here, the Maori rituals of encounter seem to offer a promising avenue for investigation. Each ritual has a clear-cut beginning and end; and in between, each step of the ritual has a well known Maori label. Just because this particular type of situation is so highly ritualized, there are sets of rules which lay down correct sequences of activity and correct modes of procedure at any given state. The ritual rules in the Maori situation are quite overt. They are consciously formulated, and in most cases people learn only those rules which govern their particular role in the ritual, though they may have a rough idea of others. Ritual, it seems, is a thoroughly self-conscious activity, and this largely explains why the rules are made self-evident. The main roles are carried out by specialists whose esoteric knowledge gives them status, and its structure is only preserved by their expert supervision. Just because the structure of any ritual is artificial, in the sense that it is not inevitably acquired as the child matures, its elements are named for easy reference and their correct relationships are made explicit in verbal principles that can be transmitted to novices.

In Maori rituals of encounter, behaviour is clearly structured into sequential units, each with its own label. These units include not only linguistic behaviour, though this is the most important component, but also clear spatial and kinesic patterns and a structured choice of actors. Some of the units in fact include no speech at all, for example, the ritual challenge, but they are still clearly part of the structure. It would be possible to describe others of the units purely in terms of the linguistic patterns they exhibit, but such a description would be partial and misleading. The exchange of oratory is the natural focus of the ritual, and the only units of the ritual without structured verbal patterns occur at the beginning (ritual challenge or *wero*) and the very end (shaking hands and pressing noses or *hongi*). It seems then, that if one wishes to describe the use of language in a given situation, it is the situation which provides an obvious maximal unit for analysis.

In this paper, I propose to write a situational grammar for the Maori rituals of encounter, which will include, but not exclusively focus on, linguistic patterns. The grammar will use context-sensitive categorial rules of the type familiar in generative linguistic theory, in order to produce a range of rituals appropriate to different situations. The major categories will be identified by their labels in Maori (e.g., *wero*, *hongi*, etc.), and rules for actor selection will accompany them. The grammar should anticipate for any given stage of the ritual its appropriate actors and patterns of verbal behaviour, as well as outlining the structure of the total event. This 'situational' grammar is thus an attempt to apply formal devices developed for the abstract description of language to a description of language in social context.

It should be roughly understood for now that the situational grammar has access to the resources of a linguistic grammar of Maori and a structured universe of actors, and that from these resources it may make principled selections. Its fundamental structure is, however, independent of these resources, and acts as an organizing principle upon them. This point can be illustrated readily by reference to the orations that form the focus of the ritual. Normally these are given in Maori, but a speaker who doesn't know Maori could still maintain the correct internal structure for a formal speech by following the prescribed sequence of topics in English.

The ritual grammar

LINGUISTIC CODES

Virtually every Maori speaker in New Zealand today is bilingual in English, and there are increasing numbers of people in the younger generations, Maori by birth, who speak no Maori at all. Perhaps 10% or less of the Maori population are fluent in their native language, and the process is constantly being accelerated by the influences of urbanization. Maori is now spoken as an everyday language only in some rural areas. For more than a hundred years, English has been the compulsory language of instruction in New Zealand schools, and as recently as twenty-five years ago, children were still being strapped for speaking Maori on school playgrounds. In the last few years, Maori has been offered as a subject in many secondary schools, but this trend is still too recent to show any widespread effects. Given this situation, it is perhaps surprising that Maori continues to be the ritual language of the *marae*, and that ancient chants, proverbs, and songs can still be heard in most parts of the country. On the other hand, the linguistic conservatism of ritual situations is well known, and reverence for the past is a powerful theme in Maori culture. Although to all intents and purposes, Maori is becoming a ceremonial language in New Zealand, within its context it reigns supreme. There is strong feeling against the use of English in *marae* rituals, and those who can't speak Maori, even elders, rarely express themselves on a *marae* unless they have to. At one *hui* I attended, the Minister of Maori and Island Affairs, a European, was the honoured guest. Two old men, both Maori speakers, thought to make things easier for him, and delivered their orations in English. They were cried down and criticized, and soon after left the *marae*. Their use of English was regarded as an insult to the minister at worst, and a foolish mistake at best. This limitation excludes many of the younger generation from active participation in the rituals, but they are effectively excluded anyway as all the main roles are taken by elderly people. It is more serious when people reach middle or old age without learning to speak Maori, and the effects of increasing monolingualism may eventually put an end to *marae* rituals. On the other hand, the *marae* is not only a ceremonial place but also the major Maori political arena, and a surprising number of the younger generation take great pains to learn the chants and old sayings from their elders, sometimes beginning from scratch in middle age to learn the Maori language.

Maori, then, is by far the preferred language in these rituals of encounter, and in most of the ritual categories (incantations, chants and songs, etc.) it is inconceivable that any other language could be used. English or an adapted form of it ('Maori' English) is commonly heard in the background, amongst the cooks, workers, and spectators, but rarely on the speaking ground itself.

ACTORS

Many of the roles in the ritual are played by specialists, and oratory in particular has reached the status of a verbal art among the Maori. The skilled orator is a master of genealogy, ancient chants, local history, and proverbs. Not only is he erudite, but a consummate actor as well. His movements are dramatic and timed to give the greatest possible effect to the statements he is making. The finest orators are well known throughout the country, and when one of their number stands to speak on the *marae*, even the cooks leave what they are doing and come to listen. Oratory is the way for a man to win fame in Maori circles, and these men move about the country to a great many *hui* each year. On each *marae* their words are listened to with respect and their performance watched with interest. The orator is largely self-trained, though he may learn his esoteric knowledge from elders of his own family or tribe, and he acquires his skill by watching others and by experience. In most tribes only male elders can deliver speeches on the *marae*, although on the East Coast, where women have traditionally played an important role in tribal history, the rule is waived for high-born women. If such a woman should stand to speak outside her own tribal area, however, there would be violent protests from the local elders, and it is said that in the old days she would have been killed. Women in general play a supporting role in *marae* rituals. Old women give the call of welcome, wail, and sing the ancient songs. After a man completes his speech, the women stand to sing with him, and this song is said to be the *kiinaki* 'relish' for the oratory. Women also dominate the action chant of welcome, although men join in. Solo opportunities for women are mostly restricted to the *karanga* or call of welcome, and old ladies with clear strong voices and a knack for choosing the right words (sometimes referred to as 'bugles') are widely admired.

The only section of the ritual where a 'young' person (under fifty) is the main actor is the ritual challenge or *wero*. In this case a young warrior represents the strength of the tribe; but otherwise young people mostly act as workers and stagehands for the performance.

Apart from the age and sex dichotomies, the other crucial division among actors is the one between locals and visitors. The ritual is structured as a balanced exchange between local and visiting groups, a pattern which is most obvious in the calls of welcome and exchange of speeches, and this separation cross-cuts the sex and age divisions.

The universe of actors for these rituals of encounter, then, is quite simply structured. It is first divided into locals and visitors; then by age; and finally, by sex:

tangata whenua	[local]
manuhiri	[visitor]
tamaiti	[child]
taane	[mature, male]
wahine	[mature, female]
koroua	[elderly, male]
kuia	[elderly, female]

These features are adequate for the correct selection of categories of actors at different stages of the ritual.

RITUAL CATEGORIES AND RULES

The categories of the ritual of encounter are bounded and ordered in strict sequence. In a given ritual performance the behaviour exemplifying one category often overlaps with others, but the beginning and end of each category is clearly recognized, and when informants discuss the structure of the ritual, they give a common sequential pattern. This pattern is laid out in the first rule of the grammar, with those categories which are optional in certain circumstances specified as such.[2]

RULE I

$$\text{RITUAL}^{Rx} \rightarrow \left(\begin{array}{c}\text{WAEREA} \\ \text{protective} \\ \text{incan-} \\ \text{tation}\end{array}\right) \left(\begin{array}{c}\text{WERO} \\ \text{challenge}\end{array}\right) \text{KARANGA}^{R} \left(\begin{array}{c}\text{POOWHIRI} ^{R} \\ \text{action} \\ \text{chant}\end{array}\right)$$

TANGI	WHAIKOORERO	HONGI
keen-ing	oratory	press-ing noses

where x = number of visiting parties to enter the *marae*. 'Ritual is repeated for each visiting party, and comprises optional WAEREA or protective incantation, optional WERO or challenge, repeated KARANGA or call, optional repeated POOWHIRI or action chant, TANGI or weeping, WHAIKOORERO or oratory, and HONGI or ceremony of pressing noses, in that order.'

The rule specifies the most abstract categories in their correct order, and no information about actors or option choices is included.

The WAEREA or protective incantation is performed when the visiting group is about to enter a strange *marae*. Only a few remaining experts of the Waikato tribes know these chants, and very few are in active use today. The WAEREA is supposed to clear the pathway of hidden obstacles set there by local sorcerers. Its words are archaic, and in most cases they can no longer be understood. For all incantations used in the ritual of encounter, it is important that no mistake should be made in their recitation, or evil will follow. The linguistic choice of the speaker is thus nullified, so that while he can choose between different incantations if he knows more than one, within the text he has no choice at all.

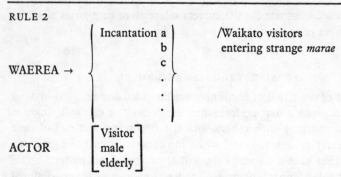

RULE 2

WAEREA →   Incantation a   /Waikato visitors
                        b   entering strange *marae*
                        c
                        .
                        .
                        .

ACTOR   ⎡ Visitor ⎤
         ⎢ male   ⎥
         ⎣ elderly ⎦

'WAEREA chosen in the context: visitors from Waikato tribes entering strange *marae*. One of a set of incantations [later specified in a lexicon of texts] is selected. The actor is an elderly male visitor.'

If the WERO or ritual challenge is performed, as it is when a distinguished visitor or *manuhiri tuaarangi* is entering the *marae*, it precedes all other activity except the incantation. It has already been noted that the challenge includes no structured verbal behaviour, although the warrior may yelp like a dog as he leaps about, to show his warlike intentions. The challenge may be repeated up to three times, depending on the prestige of the visitor, and each of the successive challenges has a special name.

RULE 3

WERO →   RAAKAU   ⎛ RAAKAU   ⎛ RAAKAU   ⎞⎞ /arrival of
          WHAKAARA ⎝ TAKOTO   ⎝ WHAKAWAHA ⎠⎠ VIP

          : number of *raakau* < as *mana* of visitor <

ACTORS   ⎡ local ⎤
          ⎢ male   ⎥ 1–3
          ⎣ mature ⎦

'Category WERO is chosen in the context: arrival of *manuhiri tuaarangi* (VIP). It includes the *raakau whakaara* (warning baton), optional *raakau takoto* (baton laid down), and optional *raakau whakawaha* ('all clear' baton) in that order. If *raakau takoto* is selected, *raakau whakawaha* may follow but not otherwise. The number of challenges increases with the *mana* of the visitors. Actors are 1–3 mature local males.'

The KARANGA, or exchange of calls between old women of the local and visiting parties, presents by far the most difficult problem of description. These high, chanted calls send greetings, invoke the dead, and bring an emotional atmosphere to the *marae*. A good caller, in the words of one of my informants, 'has a voice like a bird – high, light, and airy.' There is no way to transcribe the sound of *karanga* except perhaps musical notation, and the words are almost as difficult. Callers improvise each call to fit the occasion, the *marae* they are on, and their status as local or visitor. One cannot predict the exact structure of any given call, although certain stock phrases recur; the best I have been able to do is to isolate topical features which occur in different types of *karanga*. The following is a fairly typical example of a *karanga* exchange.

local: *karanga* (call)
        haere mai ra e te mana ariki e, mauria mai o
        Welcome, prestige of chiefs, bring our many

        taatou tini aituaa
        dead

        haere mai, haere mai!
        welcome, welcome!

Visitor: *tiiwaha* (Reply)
        Karanga ra te tupuna whare ki te kaahui pani
        Call, ancestral house, to those who mourn

        ki ngaa iwi e, karanga ra!
        call to the tribes!

local: *karanga* (call)
        nau mai ngaa karanga maha o te motu
        draw near from all corners of the island

        mauria mai ngaa mate kua ngaro ki te poo!
        bring the dead who have gone into the night.

Visitor: *tiiwaha* (call)
        hoki wairua mai raa e koro e
        Return in spirit old man

        ki te karanga ki te poowhiri i taa koutou kaahui pani
        To the call and welcome of those who mourn you.

        hoki wairua mai e Paa e!
        Return in spirit, father!

The old women are dressed in black, and as they call, they wave sprigs of greenery and begin to weep. The rules for the KARANGA are as follows.

RULE 4

KARANGA^R →	*Karanga*			*tiiwaha*	
	call			reply	
ACTORS	[local female elderly]	1–3		[Visitor female elderly]	1–3

'The KARANGA category can be repeated, and consists of the *karanga* or call, from 1–3 old ladies, and the *tiiwaha* or reply, from a similar number of visitors.'

RULE 5
karanga →   welcome visitors + welcome their dead
'The *karanga* has as its topics a welcome to the visitors and their dead.'

These topical features are semantic instructions, which indicate the topics to be selected without specifying exactly how they are to be expressed.

RULE 6
tiiwaha →   greet *marae*, locals + greet local dead
'The *tiiwaha* greets the local *marae*, the people, and their dead.'

The POOWHIRI or action chant of welcome is performed by a group of local people, women in front, who stand before their meeting-house. A leader starts up the chant and acts as fugleman, the whole group give the simple rhythmic actions, slapping their thighs and shouting out the chorus. The *poowhiri* is performed for important visitors, and the more important they are, the more people join in, the more chants are given (perhaps two or three in sequence) and the more loudly they are shouted. Sometimes the cycle of chants is repeated, to give the visitors enough time to move into the *marae* in the prescribed stately halting fashion. The chants are taken from old war dances and canoe-hauling choruses, and there are about four or five in popular use. One of the most popular chants is as follows.

Toia mai   (all)   *te waka!*
Haul   the canoe

Ki te urunga te waka!
To the resting place, the canoe

Ki te moenga te waka!
To its bed   the canoe

Ki te takotoranga i takoto ai te waka e!
To its lying place to lie   the canoe!

RULE 7

$$\text{POOWHIRI}^{(R2)} \rightarrow \left\{ \begin{array}{c} \text{chant a} \\ \text{b} \\ \text{c} \\ . \\ . \\ . \end{array} \right\} \quad \begin{array}{l} \text{/visitors have} \\ \textit{mana} \end{array}$$

: choose up to 3 of these in any order; number < as *mana* of visitors <

ACTORS $\begin{bmatrix} \text{local} \\ \text{female} \end{bmatrix}$

'The POOWHIRI cycle may be repeated twice, and consists of up to 3 different chants selected from a repertoire and given in any order. The greater the *mana* of the visitors, the more chants are selected. Local women perform the POOWHIRI for important groups of visitors.'

The TANGI is a high keening wail. When the visitors stop in front of the meeting-house, women of both parties weep for the dead, especially those who have recently died. The wail is a long sustained vowel, breaking off into sobbing.

RULE 8

TANGI   → $\begin{Bmatrix} i-i-i \\ e-e-e \end{Bmatrix}$

ACTORS   [female]

WHAIKOORERO or oratory is the main part of the ritual. Orators are generally male and elderly, although women are permitted to speak in a few tribes, and young men who have achieved high status in the European world may be treated as honorary elders. Sons of a living father and younger brothers are not supposed to speak on the *marae*, but the rule is not strictly followed in many areas. Locals and each group of visitors have their own 'side' of speakers, with the most distinguished orators speaking first and last, and it is not unknown for a group to deliberately stock up on orators before a *hui*, so that they are able to crush all opposition by sheer weight of numbers.

Once an orator is standing on the *marae* he is virtually immune from interruption. Only if the speaker gets impossibly offensive is he stopped, and in an old custom which is still sometimes used, the old women will bend over and flip up their back skirts at him, a great insult in Maori terms.

It has already been mentioned that there are two main regional styles of oratory. In the Northern, East Coast, and Taranaki tribes, local then visiting orators speak *en bloc*; while in other tribes, they alternate. These and other regional variations make people nervous about visiting *marae* in strange areas, in case they should blunder and offend the local people.

Apart from this broad structuring of the oratory, each *whaikoorero* follows a specified internal pattern. The speech begins with a warning shout or WHAKAARAARA which claims the *marae* for the speaker. Once in a while, two speakers give this shout at the same time, and in this case hosts defer to visitors and those of lower status to their superiors. On one occasion the two men were of the same tribe and about equally important. They glared at each other, neither sat down, so they turned their backs and proceeded to deliver simultaneous orations, to the great delight of the crowd. The most common warning shout is *Tihei mauri ora!* 'I sneeze, it is life!'

Following this, the orator gives a TAUPARAPARA, a type of chant which includes a wide range of incantations from earlier days, including chants for tree-felling, carving, adzing, sentry watch, and paddling canoes. Again the chant must be repeated exactly. Many of the words are so archaic as to be incomprehensible, and the chant does not convey specific semantic information so much as establish the orator's claim to esoteric knowledge. There are a great number of *tau* in use.

The orator then greets the ancestors and the dead, perhaps using a genealogy to link his own ancestors with those of the local people. Before he turns to greet the living, he may use a common bridging phrase 'the dead to the dead, we the living to the living.' During a ritual of encounter the speeches are ceremonious, intended to run through the ritual paces rather than to convey information, and if a speaker wishes to discuss some topic (*take*), he doesn't introduce it until all the greetings are complete. Finally he starts up a WAIATA (traditional song) and is joined by others of his group. There are hundreds of *waiata*, and several collections of texts have been published and are in wide circulation.

The structure of Maori oratory then, can be formally presented as follows.

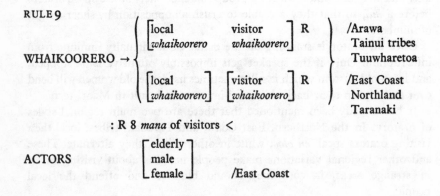

RULE 9

$$
\text{WHAIKOORERO} \rightarrow
\begin{cases}
\begin{bmatrix} \text{local} \\ \textit{whaikoorero} \end{bmatrix} & \begin{bmatrix} \text{visitor} \\ \textit{whaikoorero} \end{bmatrix} R & \left.\begin{array}{l} \text{/Arawa} \\ \text{Tainui tribes} \\ \text{Tuuwharetoa} \end{array}\right\} \\[2em]
\begin{bmatrix} \text{local} \\ \textit{whaikoorero} \end{bmatrix} & \begin{bmatrix} \text{visitor} \\ \textit{whaikoorero} \end{bmatrix} R & \left.\begin{array}{l} \text{/East Coast} \\ \text{Northland} \\ \text{Taranaki} \end{array}\right\}
\end{cases}
$$

: R 8 *mana* of visitors <

ACTORS $\begin{bmatrix} \text{elderly} \\ \text{male} \\ \text{female} \end{bmatrix}$ /East Coast

'WHAIKOORERO or oratory comprises alternating local and visitor speeches in the Arawa, Tuuwharetoa, and Tainui tribal areas; or all local then all visiting speakers, in the East Coast, Northland and Taranaki tribal areas. Speeches are delivered by male elders in general, but female orators are permitted among the East Coast tribes. The greater the *mana* of the visitors, the more speeches are given.'

RULE 10

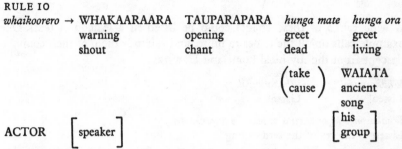

whaikoorero → WHAKAARAARA TAUPARAPARA *hunga mate* *hunga ora*

'A *whaikoorero* comprises a shout of warning, an opening chant, greetings to the dead then to the living, and optional *take* (topic of discussion), given by the speaker, and an ancient song given by his group, in that order.'

Note that while the initial and final categories are selections from a range of texts, the middle categories are topical features, indicating the topics to be selected in their correct order, without specifying how they are to be expressed.

RULE 11

$$\text{WHAKAARAARA} \rightarrow \left\{ \begin{array}{l} \textit{Tihei mauri ora!} \\ \textit{Tihei mauri mate!} \\ \text{short chants a} \\ \qquad\qquad \text{b} \\ \qquad\qquad . \\ \qquad\qquad . \end{array} \right\} \quad \textit{/tangi} \text{ 'funeral'}$$

'The WHAKAARAARA or warning shout gives a choice among two phrases, one for use on general occasions, and one for a funeral on the *marae*, and a series of chants once used by sentries patrolling the terraces of fortified villages.'

An example of such a short chant is:

Kia hiwa raa!	*kia hiwa raa!*	*kia hiwa raa e teenei tuku*
be alert!	be watchful!	be alert on this terrace
Kia hiwa raa e teera tuku!	*kia hiwa raa!*	*kia hiwa raa!*
be alert on that terrace!	be watchful!	be wakeful!

RULE 12

$$\text{TAUPARAPARA} \rightarrow \left\{\begin{array}{l} \text{chants a} \\ \text{b} \\ \text{c} \\ . \\ . \\ . \end{array}\right\}$$

A wide range of these chants could be listed in a lexicon of texts. One example calls on all the tribes to unite, and reminds them of their common descent from the mythical homeland Hawaiki:

Whakarongo!   *Whakarongo!*
Listen!   Listen!

Whakarongo ki te tangi a te manu e karange nei
Listen to the cry of the bird calling

'Tui, tui, tuituiaa!'
Unite, unite, be one!

Tuia i runga, tuia i raro, tuia i roto
Unite above, unite below, unite within,

Tuia i waho, tuia i te here tangata
Unite without, unite together,

Ka rongo te poo, ka rongo te poo
The night hears, the night hears

Tuia i te kaawai tangata i heke mai i Hawaiki nui
Unite the descent lines from Great Hawaiki

I Hawaiki roa, i Hawaiki Paamamao
From long Hawaiki, from Hawaiki far away

I hono ki te wairua, ki te whaiao, ki te ao maarama.
Joined to the spirit, to the daylight, to the world of light.

RULE 13

$$\text{WAIATA} \rightarrow \left\{\begin{array}{l} \text{songs a} \\ \text{b} \\ \text{c} \\ . \\ . \\ . \end{array}\right\}$$

Many of these songs are already in print, e.g., in Sir Apirana Ngata's *Nga Moteatea* (1959), and hundreds could be listed in a lexicon of texts. One example sings of an old woman's loneliness; it begins

Engari te tiitii e tangi haere ana, e
Even the tiitii as it goes, crying

Whai tokorua rawa rau
Travels in a pair

teenaako au nei, e manu e
oh bird! I am like

kei te hua kiwi i mahue i te taawai
The kiwi egg abandoned to the beech tree

ka toro te raakau kai runga e
the roots grow over it

Ka hoki mai ki te pao
When the mother returns for the hatching.

Ka whai uri ki ahau
The offspring are trapped, like me.

Ideally the grammar should include a full lexicon of texts in each category, but this would be impossibly bulky. Instead, one sample text has been given for each type by its appropriate rule in the grammar.

COMMENTS ON THE RULES

One can conclude that it is possible to formalize the patterns to be found in Maori rituals of encounter, and by extension that it should be possible for any type of ritual situation. This is not to deny that the rules have their crudities. The instructions about actor selection are only roughly welded into the grammar, and some more sophisticated formal devices ought to be possible here; also the rules to specify for each type of text its proper mode of presentation, whether sung, chanted, or called. This failure in description stems at least in part from the difficulty of mapping ritual categories into behavioural expression, but it is nonetheless crucial.

A further comment relates to the types of linguistic choice allowed in the grammar. In many parts of the ritual, interestingly enough, no linguistic choice is allowed at all, and mistakes or changes in reciting texts are supernaturally punished. The only choice a speaker has at these points is among texts of a specified category.

At other points in the ritual, however, a different type of linguistic choice is made. In the KARANGA (call) and in speeches, the structure is essentially a specified series of topics. This type of semantic structure is not much discussed, but it may be crucial to the understanding of some types of discourse. In this case at least, an ordered series of topics is dictated to the speaker at given stages in the ritual and it is these instructions, not the smaller linguistic choices, that structure his behaviour.

Much of the verbal behaviour in these rituals is not really aimed at communicating semantic information at all, but rather at fulfilling a required set of ritual paces. It is only when a speaker breaks out of the prescribed pattern of incantations and topics that people sit up and listen, otherwise they mainly watch the way he moves and evaluate his delivery style. The messages being passed are subtle claims to esoteric knowledge and prestige, and the fact that most of the incantations are no longer understood supports this claim.

Playing the rules

This brings us to the point that the most fascinating part of the Maori rituals of encounter, both to the audience and to the ethnographer, are not the rules themselves but the games people play with them. This is the main justification for writing a grammar of such events – that only when the rules are laid down as economically as possible and all the options are made clear can an outsider appreciate the manipulations that people practise. All the considerable drama of these occasions is concentrated at those moments when one side or the other tries to play the rules to its own advantage. The audience watches each ploy intently, enjoying the attacks and counter-attacks, and taking note of gains or losses in prestige. These duels are usually good-humoured, but on rare occasions the game becomes serious as old rivalries are revived or new ones are created. Such moments are the highlight of any gathering, and are talked of for months afterwards.

There are three basic strategies that can be used. The first one is to manipulate options already present in the rules; the second is to force the other side to break a rule; the third and most difficult is to break a rule yourself and get away with it.

In the first strategy, prestige is achieved by a skilful handling of grammatical choices. A large number of the rules of the grammar, for example, require a matching of ritual responses to the relative prestige and social distance of the other group, with the general principle that the greater the prestige-distance of the other side, the more ritual should be given. This applies to the challenge (for VIPs only, and repeated more often as their status rises), the action chant of welcome (given only for important groups, and repeated more often as their status rises), and speeches (more are given as the status of the other side rises). All sorts of subtle claims about *mana* are passed in the way these options are handled. A visiting group might try to elicit a deferential response by arriving at the *marae* in force, with a host of speakers and callers; a local group can show deference and at the same time win prestige by the elaborate excellence of their ritual; or they might choose to insult the visitors by according them only a perfunctory welcome.

This last strategy is dangerous because it invites a direct confrontation and accusations of inhospitality. There is a proverb *ka whakaiti koe i te manuhiri, ka whakaiti koe i a koe* 'in demeaning the visitor, you lower yourself', and local people who follow this strategy could end up with serious losses in prestige. On one occasion when a visiting party was improperly welcomed, the leader of the visitors made no comment, but failed to place his donation on the *marae* at the end of the ceremony. He went off to the bank directly afterwards, and changed his group's fifty pounds into threepences. When he returned to the *marae*, he waited for a suitable moment, then announced that he wished to make his donation. Pulling out a bulging bag from under his coat, he began strewing threepences as far as he could all over the *marae*. The local people were forced to crawl on their hands and knees to collect the money, and the old man had his revenge.

Regional and historical variations in the rules also allow a certain amount of play. The Governor-General who used an ancient form of reply to the ceremonial challenge was manipulating this type of option. Regional variations in turns of talk and permitted categories of speaker give further openings for mistakes and violations. In this case, the local people have the advantage, since it is their etiquette that should properly be followed, and visitors often enter a strange *marae* intimidated in advance by their ignorance of the local ground rules.

In the second strategy, the other side is manipulated into making a mistake. The oratory contests are a clear example of this technique, where one side forces the other to break the proper sequence of speakers by running them out of qualified men. If the visitors come with ten or fifteen speakers, the chances are that the local people will not be able to match this number. In an alternating etiquette, this means that eventually the local people fall out of the sequence, so that one visiting speaker after another stands unanswered on the *marae*. Another trick is to anticipate another speaker's *tau* (opening chant) or *waiata* (song). This puts him off balance, and if he has a very limited repertoire it may force him to deliver an incomplete speech. At one state occasion in Auckland, the Governor-General mentioned earlier and several Maori elders were called upon to deliver speeches. The elders decided that the occasion was not really 'traditional,' so they gave no opening chants. When the Governor stood, however, he delivered a truly magnificent *tau* (an unprecedented performance from such a dignitary) and completely stole their thunder. The elders thought this was a great joke, and took it in good part. At the next *hui* the Governor attended, however, one of their number stood to speak, and with barely suppressed mirth proceeded to 'steal' the Governor's *tau*. No longer equipped for that occasion to astonish the populace, the Governor had to ruefully admit defeat.

If rule-breaking is accidental, people nearly always lose prestige, and other violations may follow to their disadvantage. When a man talks too long on the *marae*, for example, people call out: *kia poto te kakau o too paipa!* 'shorten the stem of your pipe,' a form of interruption not usually permitted. If he keeps on talking, one of his female relatives may stand up, announce: *Anei too wai!* 'here is your song,' and start to sing, effectively cutting him off and short-circuiting the ritual sequence.

Deliberate rule-breaking, however, the last of the three strategies and the most perilous of all, has correspondingly great losses or gains of prestige at stake. An unsuccessful contender with the rules leaves the *marae* in utter humiliation, knowing that people will be talking about his folly for months to come. A successful contender, on the other hand, is greatly honoured, having proved himself above the constraints that bind ordinary people. All the famous orators have at one time or another broken through the rules, while yet making their actions seem morally right and inevitable. These are moments of complete self-assertion, when the individual breaks away from the group, trusting to his charisma to keep him safe. At other times an entire group can seek to assert its ascendancy by violating the rules of another tribe.

I can perhaps end the paper with a story of this sort, where ordinary life passes into legend. About fifty years ago, an old East Coast chieftainess was attending a funeral in the Arawa country. It will be remembered that high-born women are allowed to speak on the East Coast, but definitely not in Te Arawa. The hosts had opened up the oratory, and now it was the guests' turn. The East Coast men were in a dilemma, because the old lady outranked them all, and was properly their first speaker. After a pause, she stood, and launched into a chant. Seconds later the Arawa elders were on their feet yelling in outrage, cursing her and telling her to sit down. The old chieftainess serenely ignored them and continued her speech to the end; then she looked over to the local elders and addressed them with all the pride of her descent: 'You Arawa men! You tell me to sit down because I am a woman, yet none of you would be in this world if it wasn't for your mothers. *This* is where your learning and your grey hairs come from!' and turning her back on them, she bent over and flipped up her skirts in the supreme gesture of contempt. The Arawa men sat speechless, dumbfounded by the grandeur of the insult, and in that silence, the old woman became a legendary figure. She left the *marae* unrebuked, and East Coast people have been telling the story ever since.

SPEAKING OF SPEAKING: TENEJAPA
TZELTAL METALINGUISTICS

BRIAN STROSS

The intent of this paper is to present a picture of the ways that Tzeltal (Maya) speakers themselves categorize their world of verbal communication, the ways that they talk about speech events occurring in their own cultural matrix. Instead of outlining a tightly defined and highly structured cultural domain and analyzing it exhaustively in terms of defining components on each level of contrast, I want to let the native terms and their glosses along with some explanation speak for themselves. There are two reasons for adopting this expository stance.

The first is that the meanings of the native terms as glossed embody the attributes of communicative events that we must assume the Tzeltal speakers single out as relevant and significant in specific situations. Thus, by simple inspection we can see what kinds of events the Tzeltal have chosen to label, what components and functions of speaking are focused on (cf. Hymes 1962), and what attributes of individual speech and speaking style are considered important enough to deserve names. In other words, I have not sought a single grammatical or social frame for generating a universe of discourse and analysis because a priori levels of organization are unnecessary at this point for an understanding of fundamental Tzeltal conceptualizations of verbal interaction.

The second, and more important reason, is that elicitation frames and abstract analysis would be more likely to obscure than to clarify the metalinguistic picture under consideration. The domain of speaking is not for the Tzeltal a well defined and clearly bounded one; it is not as a whole highly structured, although portions of it allow for systematic structural description. The Tzeltal domain of speaking is in fact an open system with fuzzy boundaries, flexible internal structuring of often imprecise units (at times overlapping, at times redundant), and with no cover term. As such it is highly adaptable to change in the social environment and must be seen as constantly evolving. The system's adaptability, allowed for by its openness and imprecision, is the precise explanation for our inability to contain it by means of a formal, exhaustive, and economical ethnographic description (cf. El Guindi 1972).

A substantial portion of the Tzeltal domain of speech events is referred to by labels that have the form *modifier + k'op* (e.g., *yom k'op* 'discussion involving several people who have assembled to decide something'). In fact 416 labels of this form are contained in the appendix, representing a hitherto unsuspected degree of nomenclatural elaboration for Tzeltal ways of speaking. Such elaboration helps to justify the inescapable conclusion that in some sense speech and ways of speaking are a cultural focus for the Tzeltal. In addition to describing the lexicon of *k'op* terms, this analysis of the domain of speaking will take in the following categories: numeral classifiers, affect verbs, other verbs, body parts, and quotatives. Also considered will be speaker evaluation and the range of speech event components revealed by Tenejapa Tzeltal metalinguistics.

The community

Located in the central highlands of Chiapas, Mexico, some twenty miles from San Cristobal de las Casas, Tenejapa is a highland Maya *municipio* of about 9000 Tzeltal speakers. It is one of twelve Tzeltal-speaking municipios among which are distributed seventeen corporate communities, each with its own distinct dialect of the Tzeltal language, and each with its own native civil-religious hierarchy. Tenejapa, as a single corporate entity, consists of twenty-one *parajes*, or hamlets (of from 200 to 900 inhabitants), corresponding to approximately the same number of dispersed patrilineal settlements. These *parajes* are linked together through a ceremonial center, the seat of municipal government, in which reside about 100 Mestizo families and a very small permanent Indian population.

Social interaction outside the household and kinship network centers on weekend activities and a yearly cycle of ceremonial occasions. There are two regional market plazas on Saturdays and one on Sundays. Municipal ceremonies include the change of office for cargo holders, Carnaval, Semana Santa, Todos Santos, Navidad, and the saints' days of San Alonso and San Diego, among others. Earth and crop renewal ceremonies as well as Carnaval also find expression on the local level within the *parajes*. At all ceremonial occasions and frequently in the course of normal weekend activities, such as going to market, running errands, or just social visiting, men lubricate their interaction with alcohol.

The only real barriers to verbal interaction based on age and sex in Tenejapa exist between males of reproductive age and unrelated females (i.e., females with Spanish surnames different from that of the male) of reproductive age. This is doubly true if the female is unmarried and of marriageable age. Any interaction between such pairs that is not purely business is conducted in rather close secrecy, except for courting behavior which traditionally involves the boy's trying to attract the girl's attention semi-covertly by throwing orange peels at her on the trail or by looking at her or playing music for her. The girl's typical response in public to such overtures can range from pelting the boy with stones to smiling (depending upon a number of factors, including how much she likes the boys). Public interaction among males includes greetings, discussions of land, crops, and weather, etc., joking and other forms of verbal play, gossip of several sorts, recounting of folklore (e.g., myths, legends, tales, etc.), quarreling, arguing, fighting, and leave-taking. Public interaction among females and between sexes (except where there are barriers such as those mentioned above) tends to emphasize greetings, gossip, recounting of folklore, and leave-taking, as does private interaction during house visits among kinsmen. Within the household group private interaction most frequently involves gossip, the recounting of folklore, and discussions of land, crops, and weather.

Metalinguistic lexicon

In Tenejapa the spoken word plays a major part in the social life of the inhabitants. Tenejapans not only talk a great deal; they also spend a substantial portion of their time recounting and evaluating the particulars of speech events to which they have access, judging the characters and emotional states of individuals on the basis of their speech, and commenting on or mocking the speech habits of others. As a consequence they have an extensive metalinguistic lexicon and an elaborate system of rules for applying the lexicon to specific situations.

'K'OP'

As in surrounding Tzeltal and Tzoltzil communities, the word *k'op* is a central feature of the Tenejapan metalinguistic lexicon. Alone or augmented, it can be applied to the largest number of speech situations and speech genres. It is at once very general and ambiguous alone and highly productive and specific in combinations.

When combined with other forms, *k'op* can describe a large number of speech situations or aspects thereof. The meanings of some of the combinations can be fairly closely predicted from a knowledge of the meanings of their component forms (e.g., *poko k'op* 'ancient speech' < *poko* 'ancient' + *k'op* 'speech'). The meanings of other combinations are quite difficult or impossible to predict in this way (e.g., *pukuh k'op* 'insults, insulting speech' < *pukuh* 'demon' + *k'op* 'speech'), and are therefore more obviously monolexemic. More than 416 of these *k'op* combinations were elicited from a native speaker of Tzeltal and accepted as correct by two other informants.

The list of 416 terms and their glosses to be found in the appendix represents something quite different from going through a dictionary of

English and listing all the words having to do with speech. The most obvious difference is that all of the terms in this Tzeltal list incorporate the form *k'op*; they all have the sequential structure *modifier + k'op*. An analogous list in English would include 'sweet talk,' 'back talk,' 'baby talk,' 'shop talk,' 'straight talk,' and perhaps a few others. The analogy is a good one in another way. We recognize 'sweet talk' and the others as special terms descriptive of different aspects of speech events. These terms have a 'legitimacy' of their own that is not shared by such *ad hoc* phrases as 'happy talk,' 'Monday talk,' etc. Similarly, all the Tzeltal combinations listed were recognized as 'legitimate' by a Tzeltal speaker in that he had heard them all used, and the list was accepted as correct by two other informants. Many other combinations having the form *modifier + k'op* were suggested during elicitation proceedings, but were judged unacceptable although interpretable by informants. The other important difference between the Tzeltal and English lists is that while the one includes more than 416 terms, the other has probably fewer than ten.

Any form contained in the appendix might be used by any Tzeltal speaker familiar with it, on any occasion appropriate to the meaning of the term, in order to describe some aspect, real or imagined, of a speech situation that has taken place, is happening, or will occur, for any other Tzeltal speaker. The capsule descriptions embodied in these terms may be evaluations, or they may be intended simply to describe more or less objectively.

The various *k'op* combinations focus on a number of different aspects of speech and some of the forms give information about more than one factor simultaneously. Such information may be directly implied by a term, or it may only be alluded to indirectly. Table 8 lists the more salient speech factors encoded in *k'op* combinations. [1]

Although there is probably no single sentence frame into which all of the *k'op* combinations would fit comfortably and meaningfully, a large number of the forms in the appendix could answer the question *bi la ˀaˀpasik* 'what did you do?' For example, a man returns home after having gone out on an errand or house visit, and his wife asks *bi la ˀaˀpasik*ˀ The man might answer *takin k'op naš* 'just talk, no liquor,' or *ˀaltik k'op* 'wasted words (I couldn't sell my bull to him).' Other terms would answer the question *bi ya kaˀy* 'what's that (sound) I hear?' as would, for example, *k'anheš k'op* 'envying talk,' or *ˀamay k'op* 'a flute being played,' or *milmil k'op* '(someone) threatening to kill.'

The word and phrase inventory of *k'op* combinations given in the appendix is not a closed inventory; nor does it include the total list of forms judged acceptable by my primary informant. During this initial elicitation procedure, it became clear that some rules for combining forms with *k'op* are quite productive. They can generate a great number of readily under-

TABLE 8

Speech Event Factor (Focus)	*Examples*
personality of speaker	*t'ut' k'op* (376); *toyem k'op* (368)
physical condition of speaker	*wiʔnal k'op* (397); *ʔalanehem k'op* (18)
mental condition of speaker	*yakubel k'op* (407); *howil k'op* (118)
emotional state of speaker	*ʔak'ol ničim k'op* (14); *šiwel k'op* (341)
postural position of speaker	*hawḍohem k'op* (89); *kotal k'op* (155)
location of speaker	*ʔalan k'op* (17); *bač'en k'op* (34)
social identity of speaker	*winik k'op* (398); *maestro k'op* (220)
voice quality of speaker	*sahsah k'op* (310); *muk'ul k'op* (247)
volubility of speaker	*tutin k'op* (372); *komol k'op (154);* *ʔanimal k'op* (25)
number of participants	*pihtem k'op* (294); *stukel k'op* (326)
arrangement of participants spatially	*hoybil k'op* (119)
social identity of addressee	*tinil mayal k'op* (362) (by implication)
location of speech event	*hobel k'op* (112)
channel sounds accompanying message	*ʔubinahem k'op* (377); *ʔuninahem k'op* (384)
gestures accompanying speech	*nihkel k'op* (262); *šʔumet k'op* (349)
time of speech event	*weweštik k'op* (396); *wohe k'op* (400)
duration of speech event	*minúto k'op* (243); *ʔahk'naš k'op* (3)
message channel	*ʔamay k'op* (22); *k'ayob k'op* (183)
sequencing in the speech event	*lamahem k'op* (210)
truth value of message	*esmahem k'op* (75); *hamal k'op* (83)
reception of message by addressee	*kuybil k'op* (160)
topic	*ʔuʔnil k'op* (383); *p'olmal k'op* (307)
genre	*labanwaneh k'op* (206); *ʔišta k'op* (145)
message form	*kurik k'op* (158); *tohtoh k'op* (365)
code (language)	*yanahem k'op* (409); *č'ol k'op* (65)

stood phrases of the form *modifier* + *k'op*. (1) Given a social context in which someone repeats any word or phrase to the extent that an observer makes note of the repetitions, the observer may verbally characterize the repeated speech (or even the whole speech situation) by appending the word *k'op* to the repeated word or phrase (e.g., *ʔeč' k'op*, no. 69 in the appendix). In such cases, correct interpretation of the resulting phrase is usually dependent upon the context of repeated speech. (2) Any noun that could be considered as standing for a topic of conversation can be combined with *k'op* in the same way, and the resulting phrase could be glossed as 'speech on the topic of X' (e.g., *ʔek' k'op*, no. 71). Again correct interpretation depends upon accurately identifying the context of the original speech event, or at least a knowledge of probable topics relevant to the speech event. (3) The label for any social identity or category, such as man, teacher, baby, curer, etc., can be followed by *k'op* to form a phrase that can be understood to mean either 'the speech of X category' or 'talk on the topic of X category (or an individual pertaining to the category)'[2] (e.g., *winik k'op*, no. 398; *maestro k'op*, no. 220). (4) Any geographical name can precede *k'op* to form a phrase that can be understood as 'speech or conversation occurring at location X' or less commonly as 'talk concerning the topic of location X' (e.g., *hobel k'op*, no. 112). (5) Any named time period, such as Monday, January, yesterday, last year, etc., can be followed by *k'op* to form a phrase that can be glossed 'speech or conversation occurring on specified time period X', or less commonly as 'talk concerning the topic of X' (e.g., *weweštik k'op*, no. 396; *wohe k'op*, no. 400). (6) Any unit of time duration measure, such as a minute, a little while, a day, a month, etc., can be followed by *k'op* to form a phrase that can be glossed 'speech or conversation lasting for specified duration X' or less commonly as 'talk concerning the subject of specified duration X' (e.g., *ʔahk' naš k'op*, no. 3; *minúto k'op*, no. 243).

Given the above six rules for generating meaningful, or at least potentially meaningful, phrases of the form *modifier* + *k'op*, it might appear that the possibilities for expansion of the system are very nearly limitless; and in a sense this is true. The productivity of such combinatory rules allows us to predict with some accuracy the form that phrases not yet used in Tenejapa might take when an appropriate context supplies the meaning for a kind of speech that needs describing or labeling with words. And this is what allows such an open system to accommodate changes in the natural and social environment. On the other hand, the system of naming aspects of speech events in terms of *k'op* is not so limitless as it seems. Not only are some combinations highly unlikely to occur because the situations that they describe are improbable (e.g., *ʔu k'op* 'talk lasting a month' or 'talk about months in general'), but more to the point, informants apparently only recognize as legitimate a rather small segment of the totality of phrases that could be generated by the rules mentioned above, despite their ability to interpret potential meanings of other phrases generated 'if someone were to use the phrase' and given a proper knowledge of the situation to which the phrase applied.

Some of the words and phrases representing combined forms of *k'op* can be given more than one interpretation, depending upon the contexts in which they are used and of course the situations to which they apply. To the extent that the addressee can assume more than one context, they are ambiguous (e.g., *č'ayem k'op*, no. 62; *ʔuȼ k'op*, no. 379). I have argued elsewhere that ambiguity of meaning is a necessary and useful feature of human interaction (Stross 1967). The ambiguity present in some of the elements of the Tzeltal metalinguistic system not only camouflages intent and assists the maintenance of social distance in interaction, it also serves as a base for some humor (cf. Stross 1973). For example, my assistant went off one day to confer with one of the elder men in his hamlet regarding some changing customs about which I wanted information. Although this old man was showing traces of senility, he was likely to know something about the ritual calendar that younger men were less familiar with. When my assistant returned I asked *bi ši²* 'what was said?' or 'what did he say?' My assistant replied *puru rason k'op la ka²y* '(it was) sheer intelligent, sensible, and eloquent speech (that) I heard,' which surprised me; until he added *rason rason ši* 'he said "rason rason,"' suddenly providing the context that forced me to abandon my first and more natural interpretation of *rason k'op* (no. 308). This sudden shift in frame of references was humorous, of course, and my assistant was kidding me by making me think at first that the old man had said some interesting things and then shattering this image by implying that he had provided nothing more interesting than repetitious nonsense. Ambiguity in the system, then, adds flexibility and this contributes to its openness. It also allows a speaker to imply something by the use of a particular form and then to deny the implication by insisting on either a literal or a dominant interpretation – and the two may conflict – in order to safely avoid being held responsible for having said something that might give offense (cf. Bricker 1973).

Earlier I mentioned the presence of overlapping and redundancy in the Tzeltal metalinguistic system. For example *²išta k'op* (no. 145) and *lo²il k'op* (no. 214) exhibit overlapping in that they are used more or less equivalently, although *lo²il k'op* implies a more specific association with the time of year during which Carnaval takes place. On the other hand *²antiwo k'op* (no. 26) and *poko k'op* (no. 297) appear to be completely redundant denotatively and connotatively in almost every possible context: they mean precisely the same thing. Redundancy, or duplication, also occurs on a rather large scale in that a fair number of combinations with *k'op* can substitute *²a²yeh* 'conversation, talk' for *k'op* (e.g., *toyem ²a²yeh = toyem k'op*, no. 368; *kapal ²a²yeh = kapal k'op*, no. 148). The number is so large (i.e., at least a hundred) that at first I thought that *²a²yeh* combinations paralleled *k'op* combinations all along the line. Fuzziness, too, is characteristic of the meanings of some combinations including *k'op*. An especially good example of this is *hurïha k'op* (no. 128) about which informants not only disagree as to meaning; they are unable to attempt definitions for it. An informant who knows the word will invariably refer to some person that he knows who is generally regarded as speaking in a way that can be characterized as *hurïha k'op*, but he will be unable to segregate features of his speaking style that signal the appropriateness of the label.

The form *k'op* also occurs in a different kind of combination with other forms from that already discussed. That is, there are a number of combinations that can be described as *Verb* + *ta* + *k'op* and generally glossed as 'Verb by means of speech' or 'verbal Verbing' or 'Verb verbally.' Some examples are *ʔič'el ta k'op* 'interrogating' (LIT 'getting (information) through speech'), *pukel ta k'op* 'announcing' (LIT 'distributing (information) by means of speech'), *leel ta k'op* 'slander' (LIT 'looking for (crimes) by means of speech'), *tohobtesel ta k'op* 'to correct' (LIT 'to straighten (someone) out verbally'), *sahsunel ta k'op* 'to whisper (words)' (LIT 'to make whispering sounds verbally'), *koltael ta k'op* 'to recommend, stick up for' (LIT 'to help/defend with words'), *ḋalel ta k'op* 'to dispute, argue against' (LIT 'to line up (in opposition) by means of words'), *lihkesel ta k'op* 'to initiate a conversation' (LIT 'to initiate (interaction verbally'), *šwulwun ta k'op* 'the sound of continual incessant talking' (LIT 'verbal roaring'), *suhtawel ta k'op* 'to contradict' (LIT 'returning it verbally'), *halatesel ta k'op* '(to have a) diverting conversation' (LIT 'to be delayed by words'), *makel ta k'op* 'conversational diversion' ('LIT 'to be prevented from passing by means of conversation'), *sepelik ta k'op* 'they (men) are arranged in a circle talking' (LIT 'they are arranged in a circle in speech').

Given the abundance of forms including *k'op* in the Tzeltal speaker's repertoire, I spent a good deal of time trying to ascertain structural relations among categories represented by the labels and also between these and categories of speech labeled by nouns in which *k'op* plays no part. I was looking for a taxonomic structure with which to integrate the categories; in short, a taxonomy of *k'op* (cf. Gossen 1972). The search was something of a disappointment in that outside of a small core representing three taxonomic levels, there was little consistency among informants, and even for a single informant, in assigning the bulk of the categories to dependency relationships with other categories. Informants agreed, however, that all *k'op* 'speech' falls into two directly subsumed categories, *ʔač' k'op* 'recent speech' and *poko k'op* 'ancient speech' or 'traditional speech,' and that all other

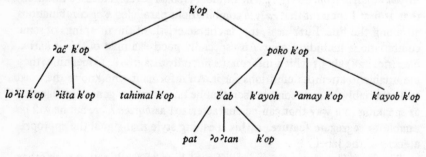

Fig. 12. Taxonomy of *k'op*

kinds of speech can be classed with one or the other of these two and, in some cases, both (e.g., *baḍ'il k'op*, no. 33). Moreover there was complete agreement that *lo³il k'op* 'humorous speech,' *³ištakop* 'word play, humorous speech,' *tahimal k'op* 'verbal games,' and many other kinds of speech are kinds of *³ač' k'op*, whereas *č'ab* 'prayer,' *k'ayoh* 'song,' *³amay k'op* 'flute music,' and *k'ayob k'op* 'drum sounds' are kinds of *poko k'op*. Fig. 12 represents these core taxonomic relationships. Intensive questioning of informants made it clear to me that the Tenejapa Tzeltal speaker tends to think of *poko k'op* as being the way and the words that people spoke in ancient times (elegant, stylized, serious, non-malicious speech, slowly and clearly enunciated) and *³ač' k'op* as being the way and the words that people speak today (with the exception of some *poko k'op* that has been preserved in myths, songs, prayers, and the like). The speaker tends not to conceptualize the domain of *k'op* in taxonomic terms despite his ability to interrelate some of the categories in ways that can be described by us taxonomically.

NUMERAL CLASSIFIERS

The Tzeltal metalinguistic inventory contains two numeral classifiers. These are *hp'al* 'one word' (more precisely 'one lexeme') and *hlam* 'one language.' These combine with numerals in the same way as do other numeral classifiers (cf. Berlin 1968). Thus 'two words' would be *ča³p'al* 'three words,' *³ošp'al*, and so on, while 'two languages' would be *ča³lam*, 'three languages' *³ošlam*, and so on. Clearly these are the two primary units of Tzeltal linguistic analysis, and it may be surprising that there is no classifier referring to the phrase or the sentence. At least it is revealing that these latter two units are relegated to minor status in Tzeltal speech; for indeed they can talk about a unit that encompasses both (i.e, *sp'alap'al ya šk'opoh* glosses 'in phrases (or sentences) he talks') although *sp'alap'al* is not a numeral classifier. There is also a noun that refers to a unit larger than the sentence, and this is *k'op ³a³yeh* which can be variously glossed 'myth,' 'story,' 'legend,' or in some contexts 'conversation.'

AFFECT VERBS

Affect verbs, identifiable by the prefixed *š* or *s*, are occasionally employed to describe disvalued features accompanying or characterizing the speech of individuals, especially in the course of mocking. Such affect verbs include *šwulwun* 'the sound of incessant talking (without content), a rumbling or buzzing in the ears of the listener'); *spa³pun* 'the sound of stuttering accompanying speech'; *š³ep'un* 'the sound of gritting the teeth or gnashing the teeth (accompanying speech)'; *skaḍ'kun* 'the sound of trilling bursts of air from the back of the tongue (accompanying speech).' The suffix $-C_\iota un$

identifies repeated actions of short duration here, and the roots *wul, pa*ˀ, ˀ*ep*, and *kaɬ*ˀ cannot stand alone.

Other affect verbs, suffixed by -*et*, appear to refer to valued (or at least not disvalued) features accompanying or characterizing the speech of individuals. These include *sk'anet* 'talking with a nice, mellow, singing voice'; *sc'ulet* 'falsetto voice, very high voice' (the respect voice of women); *šna*ˀ*et* 'talking very slowly, as if sad'; *štatet* 'talking with a high voice, not quite falsetto, but almost singing' (this is disvalued and is mocked in people); *š*ˀ*awet* 'crying out, yelling.' The -*et* suffix does not accompany the roots *wul, pa*ˀ, ˀ*ep*, or *kaɬ*ˀ, nor does the − *C*₁ *un* suffix accompany the roots *k'an*, *ɬ'ul, na*ˀ, *tat*, or ˀ*aw*.

OTHER VERBS

There are also several other verbs, both transitive and intransitive, which I present in their verbal noun forms and gloss as infinitives, characterizing ways of speaking, many of which have their familiar counterparts in English. These are *ɬiɬel* 'to advise'; *leel mulil* 'to accuse' LIT 'to look for crimes'; *labanel* 'to mock, make fun of'; ˀ*ahtael* 'to count'; *hak'el* 'to answer, reply, respond'; *hohk'oel* 'to ask about'; *nuhp'inel* 'to reply'; *ča*ˀ*alel* 'to repeat'; *tik'beel sk'alel* 'to gossip, tattle'; ˀ*alel* 'to say'; *lotiel* 'to lie'; ˀ*awtael* 'to yell at, shout at'; *k'oponel* 'to talk to'; *k'opohel* 'to talk'; ˀ*ik'el* 'to call, beckon'; ˀ*ok'el* 'to cry, wail'; ˀ*ak'el parte* 'to complain'; ˀ*utel* 'to scold' or 'to respond, reply'; *k'anel* 'to ask for, beg for'; *wokol k'optael* 'to beg, appeal, petition'; ˀ*ahwal k'opohel* 'to beg, appeal, beseech'; *k'ušawanel* 'to praise, commend, talk well of'; *wultael* 'to issue commands of one or two words'; *čitanel* 'to scold by words only and shouting'; *č'abahel* 'to pray'; ˀ*ak'beel skahab* 'to exaggerate, to elaborate in retelling gossip'; *k'anel pawor* 'to ask for a favor'; *k'anel wokol* 'to ask a favor'; *k'anel perton* 'to beg pardon'; *tok'tael* 'to insult, say bad words to someone'; *k'ahinel* 'to sing'; *hešhuntael* 'to envy verbally'; ˀ*a*ˀ*yanel* 'to talk, chat, converse, relate.'

BODY PARTS

Tzeltal has many forms that combine various parts of speech with the names for such body parts as the teeth, lips, mouth, heart, tongue, nose, and throat in the formation of commonly used descriptions of speech defects, voice qualities, speaking abilities, etc. Combinations with *ni*ˀ 'nose' include the following *ma*ˀ*ni*ˀ 'resonantly nasal voice as with big nasal cavity'; *suk ni*ˀ 'breathy nasal voice as with nose partially blocked but with air forced out of it anyway while talking'; *no*ˀ *ni*ˀ 'slightly nasal voice.' Combinations with *ti*ˀ 'lips' include *pa*ˀ *ti*ˀ 'stuttering, stammering'; *hamal ti*ˀ 'speaking well, with confidence, and freely about things'; ˀ*animal ti*ˀ '(breathlessly) relating events right after they happen and relating them rapidly'; *sabal ti*ˀ '(describes someone who is) anxious to talk, interrupting others, and constantly trying to take the floor'; *čul ti²* 'talking with rapid, somewhat incoherent speech patterns, making sequences of unrelated statements'; *tub ti²* '(speaking with) mouth squinched up and lips protruding'; *solel ti²* 'gossiping, but not maliciously.' Combinations with *nuk'* 'throat' include *čehk'el nuk'* 'high scratchy, cracking voice – characteristic of adolescents'; *rondo nuk'* 'low scratchy, cracking voice – characteristic of a sore throat'; *hamal nuk'* 'speaking clearly with good tone and enunciation'; *sah nuk'* 'very weak and slightly scratchy voice – characteristic of very old persons'; *sukul nuk'* 'very weak voice, barely issuing from throat'; *wohč'ol nuk'* 'speaking very softly, with cracking voice'; *č'in nuk'* 'high, thin, respectful voice' – when congenital such a voice is mocked as effeminate. Combinations with *²o²tan* 'heart' include *mak ²o²tanil* 'having a high, rumbling voice that forces words out with some difficulty' = *ma² ²o²tanil*; *nakal ²o²tanil* 'being reticent, not speaking much'; *šmakmun ²o²tanil* 'speaking with much stumbling on words and stammering'; *slab ²o²tanil* 'being resentful, resentful inner speech'; *muk' ²o²tanil* 'being quiet of nature, not talking much'; *šna²et ²o²tanil* 'being slow and deliberate of speech as well as serious and not talkative – born that way.' Combinations with *²ak'* 'tongue' include *k'ol ²ak'* '(speaking with) folded tongue (a congenital deformation of mouth)'; *lut ²ak'* '(speaking with) the tip of the tongue remaining almost constantly between the teeth'; *sel ²ak'* '(speaking with) the tongue being poked way out of the mouth'; *kac' ²ak'* '(speaking with) the tongue hanging out of the side of the mouth (the mouth being on the side of the face).' Combinations with *²e* 'mouth/teeth' include *pok ²e* 'toothless (speech), or speech that sounds that way'; *tub ²e* '(speaking with) mouth all squinched up and pursed with lips poked out (whether it be while talking or smoking or just natural)'; *ȼ'oy ²e* '(speaking out of side of face because) mouth is on side of face'; *leb ²e* 'big mouth, the edges of which are drawn back in a grimace while speaking'; *šew ²e* '(speaking with) one side of the mouth drooping down'; *noy ²e* 'lower jaw shifting from side to side (during speech – a trait more commonly associated with old people)'; *hamal ²e* 'talking a lot.'

QUOTATIVE

The Tzeltal have another, and very frequently utilized, metalinguistic device: the quotative paradigm. Appearing to be an irregularly inflected intransitive verb, it occurs with no preceding tense or aspect particle, and can refer to past, present, or future events depending upon the context of its use. The paradigm with glosses is as follows: *šon* 'I say, I said'; *šat* 'you say, you said'; *ši* 'he/she says, he/she said'; *šotik* 'we say, we said'; *šiik* 'they say, they said.' Note that the second person plural form is lacking in the paradigm. I cannot explain its absence, but no informant could supply such a form, nor would anyone accept my tentatively proferred *šaeš. The quotative appears in a sentence directly after the word, phrase, sentence, or sentence combination that is being quoted. For example *ya šbanis, ši* can be glossed '"I'm going now," he said'; *wokol ʔaʔwal, šat* is glossed 'you (should) say "Thank you."'

Evaluation of speech and speakers

An important aspect of the Tzeltal metalinguistic system consists of native evaluations of the various types of speech and the speakers thereof. Gossip, especially malicious gossip, envying speech, threats, insults, scolding, and mocking are all disvalued; they are all thought to threaten the social order as well as the individual. Yet these are among the most commonly used genres, and in fact assist in the maintenance of the social order by functioning to control antisocial behavior, to disseminate information (which helps to preserve cultural homogeneity), to create alliances (no matter how temporary), to provide an outlet for hostility (short of blows or murder), and to enculturate children. Songs, prayers, flute music, and other genres of *poko k'op* are highly valued. They are constant in form with little innovation, and are seen as beneficial to the social order, not only because they embody traditions that are to be passed on from generation to generation, but also because they promote harmony among men (in that they involve concerted action) and between man and the supernatural (with the exception of one type of song not considered here).

Elder, respected persons stereotypically speak slowly in measured tones, in a high voice, seriously, profoundly, and with elegant phrasing and choice of words. In a word their speech can be referred to as *rason k'op* (no. 308). Such speech is highly valued and respected, and is rather close to a conceptualization of *poko k'op*, speech of the ancient ancestors. It is not surprising that, in general, fast speech, lacking depth of meaning, not on a serious topic, and with inept phrasing and choice of words is disvalued. However it may be a bit surprising that in some contexts speech having none of the qualities of *rason k'op* can be highly valued. Younger men stereotypically speak more rapidly, less seriously, in a lower and less modulated voice, and employ a variety of forms with multiple and suggestive meanings. Clever *ʔišta k'op* 'playful speech involving plays on words,' a kind of *ʔač' k'op* 'recent speech,' is in fact highly valued, particularly by and in younger men, despite the fact that informants consider it antonymous to *rason k'op*. Spanish words and phrases are in a similarly ambiguous position among the Tzeltal. Although Tzeltal sprinkled with Spanish words is disvalued according to informants, it is obvious that Tzeltal men attempt to display any knowledge that they have of Spanish, particularly younger men, and especially when they are drinking. Women, on the other hand, have a tendency to conceal any understanding of Spanish words and phrases, and very rarely employ them.

Some modes of speaking are of course disvalued independently of context. Ungrammatical speech and incoherent speech are examples. Speech defects of all types, as illustrated above, are all disvalued and are frequently mocked by persons not so afflicted, despite the fact that there is a widely held belief that anyone who mocks a physical or speech defect will be likely to bear or sire children with the defect that was mocked (this belief applies with particular force to pregnant women) (cf. Sapir 1915).

Summing up valued and disvalued speech, it is interesting to note that there are two levels of valued speech. One, corresponding to *rason k'op*, stereotypically applies to older men and is nicely characterized *poko k'op*. The other level, epitomized in clever *ʔištak'op*, stereotypically is used by clever and witty younger men and is seen as a form of *ʔač' k'op*. This neat correspondence of generations of people with generations of speech categories related to contrasting taxonomic categories does not appear to be coincidental (cf. Newman 1955).

Speech event components

The Tenejapa Tzeltal metalinguistic components portrayed in this paper also answer some questions about features pertaining to the various components of the speech event: who or what can serve as a speaker? is an audience necessarily present in the speech situation? is silence believed to be part of the speech event? what topics are common enough to receive labels? what channels are relevant in the speech event? and so on. I will deal with some of these questions explicitly here. Possible speakers include humans of all ages (from birth to death) and in all mental and physical conditions and emotional states, the human heart (as in inner speech from the heart to the person), and musical instruments (including flute, harp, drum, guitar, violin, and cornet), but not supernatural beings or animals except in myths or folktales. No audience is necessary for a speech event as shown by the meanings of *pihtem k'op* (no. 294) and *stukel k'op* (no. 326). Silence is felt to be an important component of the speech event as shown by *č'abal k'op* (no. 61), *č'ayem k'op* (no. 62), and *kehčem k'op* (no. 151) among others. It is perhaps relevant to note in this respect that speech cut off in midstream during a conversation (as with *kehčem k'op*), so that the speaker can go outside to urinate or defecate, is supposed to be resumed when the speaker returns for if this were not done, then it is believed that the speaker's *chamarra* (male outer garment) would surely get burned in the fire soon. The appendix contains many *k'op* combinations that illustrate the variety of topics considered worthy of labeling, and they are too numerous to list here. The question of permissible channels is rather difficult. Although some postural indicators accompanying speech are encoded in the *k'op* inventory, very few gestures are considered. But this corresponds well with the notable lack of elaboration of gesture among the Tzeltal. The difficulty lies in an interpretation of the categories that can serve as speaker. If we could single out the flute player as the speaker when he is playing the flute (cf. *ʔamay k'op*, no. 22), then one could call the flute music the channel with less hesitation. But informants are highly equivocal on this point. Then too, what of the inner speech noted (cf. *naʔnu k'op*, no. 257; *nop'il k'op*, no. 270; *ʔahtal ʔoʔtan k'op*, no. 7)? Perhaps the channel here can be singled out as thoughts.

Conclusion

In conclusion I should state that the Tenejapa metalinguistic inventory shows very clearly a propensity on the part of native speakers to view speech as a crude key to reading the thoughts and characters of others. Speech can sometimes conceal intent, but it is always the intent that the hearer is trying to find out about, except in the highly formalized genres of *poko k'op*, and even here individual performers and performances are evaluated on the basis of formal correctness, voice quality, speed, and so on. Speech is felt to be potentially very powerful, to the extent that a person could fall ill and die from the talk of someone else. Little wonder that the Tzeltal talk about it so much.[3]

APPENDIX

1. *ʔač' k'op* /recent speech, modern speech (i.e., speech of relatively recent times)/
2. *ʔahk'iš k'op* /talk that has taken place just a short time ago (i.e., a matter of minutes or hours)/
3. *ʔahk' naš k'op* /talk occurring for only a short while, a short conversation/
4. *ʔahk'ol k'op* /talk coming from above, or from a high place (e.g., talking from trail above house, etc.)/
5. *ʔahk'ubal k'op* /talk that takes place during the nighttime/
6. *ʔahtal k'op* /counting; talk concerning counting/
7. *ʔahtal ʔoʔtan k'op* /talk within the heart; serious thought on a subject/
8. *ʔahwalil k'op* /talk coming from an *ʔahwalil* (i.e., boss, politico, important person, etc.)/
   /talk concerning an *ʔahwalil*/
9. *ʔainem k'op* /words, talk, or conversation that has already occurred/
10. *ʔaintesbil k'op* /words or talk that has been brought forth/

11. *ʔakil kʼop* /talk occurring in a grassy area/
    /talk concerning grass/
12. *ʔakiltik kʼop* /talk that occurs on a grassy slope or in a meadow/
    /talk concerning a grassy slope or meadow/
13. *ʔakʼol kʼop* /contented, happy speech from contented, happy speaker/
14. *ʔakʼol ničim kʼop* /speech coming from a very contented, happy speaker/
15. *ʔala kʼop* /very soft, low speech, almost whispering/
    /speech in which the word *ʔala* 'little' occurs frequently/
16. *ʔalal kʼop* /speech of a baby/
17. *ʔalan kʼop* /talk occurring or coming from down below (e.g., from down the
    trail, down the valley, etc.)/
18. *ʔalanehem kʼop* /speech brought forth slowly and with considerable effort,
    as a sick person would speak/
19. *ʔalkawéta kʼop* /talk promising things that are never delivered/
20. *ʔaltik kʼop* /wasted words, conversation that is a waste of time/
21. *ʔamakʼ kʼop* /talk occurring in a house clearing/
22. *ʔamay kʼop* /talk (i.e., the sounds) made by a flute being played/
23. *ʔančil kʼop* /women's speech/
24. *ʔaníma kʼop* /speech of a person, now dead, that occurred while he was still
    living/
    /speech concerning dead persons/
25. *ʔanimal kʼop* /rapid speech, speech rapidly delivered/
26. *ʔantíwo kʼop* /ancient speech, speech from the olden days/
27. *ʔantíwo nameh kʼop* /very ancient talk, speech forms coming from the begin-
    ning of the world, speech forms and content from
    the very earliest times/
28. *ʔatimal kʼop* /talk concerning bathing/
29. *ʔaw kʼop* /shouting, yelling/
30. *ʔawunem kʼop* /shouts that have already subsided/
31. *ʔaʔyeh kʼop* /stories, conversation, chatting/
32. *bačʼehem kʼop* /speech brought forth with much difficulty from mouth of a
    very sick person/
33. *bačʼil kʼop* /Tzeltal, the Tzeltal language (LIT 'genuine speech')/
34. *bačʼen kʼop* /talk occurring on top of a rock or rocky cliff/
35. *bahkʼel hohtel kʼop* /grunting and groaning of a sick person who is in pain but
    who keeps trying to get up and walk around/
36. *balamilal kʼop* /much noise, the sound of much talking/
37. *bankilal kʼop* /quarreling, arguing, and fighting a lot, usually while drunk/
38. *bayel kʼop* /much talk, many words/
    /uproar, noise/
39. *bel kʼop* /talk that travels – as with a message or letter that is brought some-
    where/
    /talk that occurs while speaker is walking/
40. *bol kʼop* /rude, crude, or stupid speech/
41. *bolobem kʼop* /drunken talk, drunken babbling/
42. *čaltamba kʼop* /dispute, argument/
43. *čičel kʼop* /advice, counsel/
44. *činčin kʼop* /talk (i.e., the sounds) of a guitar being played/
45. *čobol kʼop* /many words, much talk/
46. *čʼakal kʼop* /the spoken truth, very truthful speech/

47. *ƚʼakbil kʼop* /speech that has been continued; conversation continued after a pause/

48. *ƚʼeʔel kʼop* /speech coming from person who is lying on his side (e.g., in bed)/

49. *ƚʼotol kʼop* /speech that is poor and indistinct (i.e., speaker not speaking well)/
    /talk in which the speaker's head is turned away from the listener/

50. *čahpahem kʼop* /speech of person who has paid his debt to society (i.e., paid for a crime)/
    /argument, quarrel, or fight that has been straightened out/

51. *čapal kʼop* /speech of person who has paid for crimes and has now straightened himself out/

52. *čapʼil kʼop* /agreement, pact, settlement/

53. *čebal kʼop* /bad advice, misadvice, malicious misadvice/

54. *čikan kʼop* /sounds of people talking as heard from a distance; the talk can be heard but not understood (hearer perhaps 200 or more meters from the interaction situation)/

55. *čiknahem kʼop* /an answer given by one person to another that sheds some light on a question or problem that the other had; illuminating speech (e.g., X loses machete and goes around asking people if they know where it might be; then he runs into Y who says 'Oh, yes, I saw Z picking up your machete yesterday when you weren't looking'; in this case, what Y has said is *čiknahem kʼop* for X)/

56. *čol kʼop* /explanation/
    /excuse, alibi/

57. *čolbil kʼop* /advice, sermon, preaching speech/

58. *čonolehel kʼop* /talk in which things are offered for sale/

59. *čopol kʼop* /rude speech, ignorant speech, stupid speech/

60. *čukohom kʼop* /talk concerning and tying up someone (especially a criminal) and bringing them back to jail in Tenejapa center (such talk usually done by president and *regidores* or other authorities)/

61. *čʼabal kʼop* /silence, or near silence (during conversation or visit); pause in a conversation/

62. *čʼayem kʼop* /speech or conversation that was audible, but which has faded out as the speakers have gone out of earshot/
    /lost speech, lost words, forgotten words, speech that has slipped the mind of the speaker/

63. *čʼinčʼin kʼop* /the noise of many voices (e.g., at the market); din hurting the ears (louder than *wočʼwočʼ kʼop*)/

64. *čʼiwič̃ kʼop* /speech taking place in the market place/
    /bargaining and pricing speech peculiar to the market place/
    /talk concerning the market or going to market/

65. *čʼol kʼop* /speech of Tiltecos (i.e., Chol speakers)/
    /any completely alien tongue/

66. *čʼultesel kʼop* /blessing; general prayers for someone's health and well-being/

67. *čʼunbil kʼop* /speech (i.e., orders or suggestions) that has been obeyed/

68. *ečeh kʼop* /exaggeration, lies/

69. *ʔečʼ kʼop* /speech that includes several repetitions of the word *ʔečʼ* (a plant name – bromeliad)/

70. *ʔehkʼečil kʼop* /made-up talk, invented talk/

71. ʔek' k'op /talk concerning the stars, especially when it includes repeating the word ʔek'/
72. ʔelek' k'op /talk concerning thieves (e.g., giving the names of thieves or accusing certain people of being thieves)/
73. ʔep k'op /the sounds of much talk or conversation/
74. ʔermáno k'op /using the word ʔermáno 'brother' Sp.; calling people kermáno 'my brother'/
75. ʔesmahem k'op /made-up talk, invented talk that is not true and that has already been passed on/
76. ʔesmatabil k'op /made-up talk, invented story (e.g., X tells Y that Z wants to kill Y when it's not true)/
77. hačbil k'op /an argument or fight that has been started by someone/
78. hahčem k'op /an argument or fight that has arisen/
79. hakal k'op /talk that is heard from a distance, the specific words of which are unintelligible/
80. hak'bil k'op /response or answer made to someone who has talked first/
81. halah k'op /wordy, verbose speech; talking for a long time/
82. halatesbil k'op /response that is delayed by answerer/
83. hamal k'op /true, sincere speech/
84. haʔmal k'op /talk occurring in the field (i.e., scrub, pasture, woods)/
85. hamala k'op /talk, conversation occurring in a clearing or open space/
86. hambil k'op /the sound of a newly made drum when it is first played (by the woman who breaks it in)/
87. hap'il k'op /talk the content of which involves someone offering something to someone else/
88. hawal k'op /talk coming from speaker who is lying down on his back (e.g., in bed)/
89. hawḷohem k'op /talk coming from speaker who has fallen backwards, face in the air/
90. hawḷ'unbil k'op /talk in which the word hawḷ'unbil 'it has been thrown down face up' is said one or more times/
91. haʔweh k'op /talk concerning the carrying of water/
92. hayal k'op /low-volume buzzing sound of much talking/
93. hayubem k'op /speech that has been lowered in volume; the sound of speech that has been toned down/
94. hčahp k'op /strange, unfamiliar-sounding speech/ /a strange, unfamiliar language (e.g., English)/
95. helambil k'op /speech in which words from other language(s) are mixed, salted, or sprinkled/
96. helawen k'op /speech that has been passed on to someone for another/
97. helawtesbil k'op /word (i.e., a message) that has been sent by someone to someone else/
98. helbil k'op /the speech of someone who has changed from his native tongue to another/
99. helumtabil k'op /orders or suggestions that have been disobeyed/
100. herinka k'op /speech of a vain person; speaking as if not having time for others; brusque speech or bragging speech/
101. hešohel k'op /verbalized envy, envying talk/
102. hešumtawaneh k'op /the occurrence of envying talk while it is happening/
103. hiḷbil k'op /talk that has been butted in on; talk that has been overridden by a third party who wanted to speak to the original addressee(s)/

104. *hič'il k'op* /talk spoken with high, thin voice, as if the speaker has constricted throat/
105. *hihⱡem k'op* /the talk of X who was talking to Y but who has been pushed aside (by Z who wanted to talk to Y himself)/
106. *hik'abehel k'op* /choking sounds made when food goes down the wrong pipe/ /trying to talk while choking on food/
107. *hik'bil k'op* /inhaled talk, talk produced while breathing inwards/
108. *hilem k'op* /word left with someone, message left with someone/
109. *hinesbil k'op* /talk that has messed up a situation which used to be fine/
110. *hk'al k'op* /a language other than Tzeltal, usually partly understood, as e.g., Tzotzil/
111. *hlam k'op* /a familiar language other than Tzeltal/
112. *hobel k'op* /talk or conversation taking place in or around San Cristobal de las Casas/
113. *hoⱡ' k'op* /speech consisting of questions about possible delicts or misdemeanors of addressee or third party, for purpose of curing/ /interrogation (usually by authorities) concerning interrogee's possible crimes or misdemeanors/
114. *hohk'o k'op* /questions; conversation in which many questions are asked/
115. *hop' k'op* /slander, lies about someone else; gossip about someone else/
116. *hop'il k'op* /slander (with emphasis on the slanderer)/
117. *howiel k'op* /crazy talk, rantings and ravings of a crazy person/
118. *howil k'op* /talking in sleep, talking in delirium/
119. *hoybil k'op* /talk among a group of people arranged in a circle; a circular discussion/
120. *hoyob k'op* /speech coming from a person who spends all his time chatting and talking/
121. *hoyp'inbil k'op* /message that has made a round trip (i.e., same message returns to sender)/
122. *hpošil k'op* /any talking done by a curer, but especially his curing prayers/ /speech concerning a curer or curers/
123. *huʔ k'op* /LIT 'talk that has arrived'; arrival of fruition of event about which there has been previous discussion/
124. *huk'ubahel k'op* /hiccoughing, speech accompanied by hiccoughing/
125. *hulem k'op* /message that has arrived at its destination/
126. *hunabe k'op* /talk, conversation that took place a year ago, (i.e., last year)/
127. *hun minuto k'op* /speech, conversation lasting for a very short time (or for one minute)/
128. *huríha k'op* /talk that is very strange-sounding, speech that is poorly modulated/
129. *húrio k'op* /phony talk; speech of vain person who is slow to respond to another's talk because of self-conceit/
130. *hušhuš k'op* /conversation in which speaker is edging closer to hearer while both are seated/
131. *hut k'op* /slander/
132. *hutbil k'op* /talk in which the speaker has spread the blame for something, so that he alone is not blamed/
133. *huʔtesbil k'op* /talk that has arrived (through efforts of an interested party); fruition of event which was topic of earlier discussion and which some person has helped to bring about/
134. *ʔič'el k'op* /talk in which a conversation is passed on, or a message brought/

135. ʔihkitabil k'op /message left with someone, usually to do something/
136. ʔihk' k'inal k'op /speech occurring at night or late evening/
137. ʔik'awal k'op /calling speech; calling someone to come/
138. ʔik'awaneh k'op /speech telling someone to come somewhere with speaker/
139. ʔilinba k'op /the speech of a person who is angry or upset (e.g., waiting a bit before answering, answering loudly, or being brusque with an answer)/
140. ʔilintabil k'op /failure to answer someone (because of anger)/
141. ʔil ʔoʔtan k'op /speech by someone who comes to another's house and spends time talking even though the other is quite ill/
142. ʔinamil k'op /speech employing the form *kinam* 'my wife'/
143. ʔinɬyo k'op /any or all Indian languages/
144. ʔipal k'op /speech characterized by X passing on untrue stories to Y about misdemeanors of Z/
145. ʔišta k'op /joking conversation, plays on words, puns, metaphor, humor/
146. kahal k'op /talk coming from above (e.g., from above house on trial; from the gods in the sky)/
147. kananlum k'op /talk and prayers by authorities during those fiestas and times of the year (e.g., *Quinto Viernes*) when they come and watch over Tenejapa center (to keep order in the social and spiritual world)/
148. kapal k'op /mixed language (e.g., Tzeltal much mixed with Spanish); mixed speech (e.g., Tzeltal much mixed with Spanish words)/
149. kašlan k'op /Spanish; speech of Ladinos/
150. kečel k'op /'quieted speech'; peace following a fight or argument/
151. kehčem k'op /speech cut off (in midstream) by speaker/
152. kohkombil k'op /much talk, incessant noise of talking/
153. koltawaneh k'op /praise, recommendation, speech that is favorable about someone/
154. komol k'op /slow speech, slow talk/
155. kotol k'op /speech coming from person who is on all fours (e.g., children do this)/
156. kučbil k'op /speech involving an accusation by the speaker about a third party, the accusation usually being false/
157. kuhčem k'op /an accusation, usually true, employing the form *kuhčem yuʔun*/
158. kurih k'op /talk about wanting to go somewhere, usually employing the form *kurik* 'let's go'/
159. kurus k'op /nice speech, good speech, speech treating others well/
160. kuybil k'op /false accusation of someone, believed by listener(s)/
161. k'aem k'op /one's native language, one's accustomed language/
162. k'aʔem k'op /ancient speech, speech from or of the olden days/
163. k'ahk' k'op /inciteful talk, fighting words, loud and conceited speech, provoking speech/
164. k'ahk'al k'op /scolding speech/
165. k'ahk'uben k'op /talk that has led to quarreling; quarreling/
166. k'ahk'utesbil k'op /speech of two people quarreling having been instigated by a third party/
167. k'ahk'uteseh k'op /speech inciting to a quarrel or fight/
168. k'ahtahem k'op /speech of person who has forgotten his native tongue and is using another, especially Spanish/
169. k'aleltik k'op /talk that takes place during the day/

170. *k'an k'op* /speech in which the speaker responds to another person very loudly/
171. *k'anheš k'op* /verbalized envy, envying talk/
172. *k'ank'antik k'op* /speech in which one person responds to another's speech somewhat loudly/
173. *k'an tak'in k'op* /speech in which the speaker is asking for money/ /questions about the cost of things/
174. *k'a?pal k'op* /'garbage speech'; speech that is no good (i.e., speech in which the words don't come·out right, as from a drunk)/
175. *k'asesbil k'op* /speech that has been translated or interpreted (and passed on)/
176. *k'aš k'op* /conversation that is passed on (to another or to others)/
177. *k'ašel k'op* /threatening speech employing the form *k'ašel*/
178. *k'ašem k'op* /speech, talk, or conversation that has already taken place (e.g., yesterday's talk)/
179. *k'ašumtabil k'op* /orders or suggestions that have been disobeyed/
180. *k'atal k'op* /speech of a person looking for a fight; quarrelsome words/
181. *k'atp'ohem k'op* /unintended speech (i.e., when one forgets what one was going to say and says something else instead)/
182. *k'atp'unbil k'op* /speech recounting a third party's conversation, but changing it by accident or design/
183. *k'ayob k'op* /the speech (sounds) made by a drum when it is played/
184. *k'ehbil k'op* /unspoken speech (i.e., counsel from heart) to the effect that the person whose heart is speaking (and who has been wronged by another) should evince little or no outward sign of anger and should hold back immediate vengeance for a later opportunity/
185. *k'ehel k'op* /any other language besides Tzeltal – usually Tzotzil/
186. *k'ešlal k'op* /embarrassed talk, shy talk (i.e., not speaking much or well due to embarrassment or shyness of speaker)/
187. *k'intawaneh k'op* /talk predicting ill that could come to pass – often motivated by anger or envy/
188. *k'išin k'op* /talk evincing the beginning of anger in the speaker/
189. *k'išnahem k'op* /talk evincing anger in the speaker/
190. *k'oem k'op* /a message or letter that has arrived at its destination (over there)/
191. *k'ohkol k'op* /speech cut off in midstream, mid-sentence, or mid-word by the speaker/
192. *k'ohoben k'op* /talk that has petered out because speaker or speakers have already talked a lot and are tired of talking/
193. *k'op* /speech, language, word, sound argument, quarrel, fight, war/
194. *k'otem k'op* /message that has arrived at its destination over there/
195. *k'uben k'op* /message that has arrived here from a long distance away (the distance being relative to the situation at hand)/
196. *k'ubul k'op* /speech as heard from a distance (perhaps up to 100 meters) the words of which are not intelligible/
197. *k'un k'op* /speech slowly stated/
198. *k'unehem k'op* /mildly, gently spoken words; blandly spoken speech/
199. *k'unil k'op* /speech slowly and gently stated/
200. *k'unk'un k'op* /slow speech, speech very slowly stated/
201. *k'usuben k'op* /talk that has petered out because speaker has talked a lot and is tired of talking/
202. *k'ušawaneh k'op* /praise, favorable speech about someone/
203. *k'ušutael k'op* /speech involving promises about helping others (e.g., the new governor promising roads and schools)/

204. *labanbil k'op* /speech that has been mocked, imitated, or made fun of/
205. *labaneh k'op* /mocking speech/
206. *labanwaneh k'op* /the occurrence of mocking speech while it is happening/
207. *lab ʔoʔtanil k'op* /talk evincing inner thoughts on part of speaker concerning his hatred or envy of someone else/
208. *laƚal k'op* /much talk, the noisy sound of many loud voices/
209. *lahiš k'op* /the end of a conversation/
      /a person's final unsuccessful attempt to talk someone else into doing something/
210. *lamahem k'op* /the ending of a conversational turn/
      /the ending of a quarrel, argument, or fight/
211. *lehtamba k'op* /slander; malicious slander/
212. *lekil k'op* /friendly talk, praise, eloquent speech/
213. *lihkem k'op* /a quarrel, argument, or fight that has begun/
214. *loʔil k'op* /frivolous talk, humor, jest (particularly applies to interaction during Carnaval)/
215. *loʔloʔel k'op* /deceptive talk, deception, trickery through words/
216. *luben k'op* /tired talk; speech of a tired person/
217. *lubul k'op* /speech of a very weak person, or of a person who feels very weak at the time/
218. *lǔcul k'op* /talk coming from someone who is positioned on the limb of a tree/
219. *lukul k'op* /speech from someone who is lying down/
220. *maestro k'op* /talk by *maestros* (i.e., schoolteachers)/
      /talk by anyone on the subject of *maestros*/
221. *mahkem k'op* /announcement by a woman that she is pregnant/
222. *makal k'op* /a message that has been blocked, that won't arrive at its destination/
223. *mamal k'op* /speech of an old man/
224. *mantohbil k'op* /speech of a mean person or an enemy who deceives his audience by talking nice/
225. *manya k'op* /misleading talk, con-man talk/
226. *martóma k'op* /speech by *mayordomas* (generally serious, no joking)/
      /talk by anyone on the subject of *mayordomos*/
227. *mayal k'op* /speech coming from someone whose head is bowed while speaking/
      /slow respectful talk (low volume, not too wordy)/
228. *mayli k'op* /telling someone to wait (i.e., *maylia* 'wait')/
229. *meʔba k'op* /pouting talk from one with a wounded ego (usually a child); whining talk/
230. *meʔbal k'op* /speech of someone grieving over the memory of a departed one/
231. *meƚel k'op* /talk coming from someone who is lying down/
232. *mečel k'op* /speech in which the words don't come out as the speaker intended (this is congenital rather than temporary)/
233. *meʔel k'op* /speech of an old woman/
234. *meʔinem k'op* /talk that has been augmented; the subject has been added to/
235. *meʔintesbil k'op* /a word or subject that has been taken up and augmented by someone/
236. *melahem k'op* /rumor, talk that is passed on from household to household/
237. *melambil k'op* /one word, having traveled through a group and returned to the initiator of the word/
238. *melbil k'op* /well prepared (and articulated) speech/

239. *melȼahem k'op* /a problem, argument, or quarrel that has been repaired or resolved/
240. *melel k'op* /true words, truth, truthful speech/
241. *mel ʔoʔtan k'op* /sad talk (often about losses); speech evincing sadness in speaker/
242. *milmil k'op* /speech of someone who is threatening to kill/
243. *minúto k'op* /speech whose topic is minutes/
    /talk or conversation lasting for a very short time/
244. *močol k'op* /speech of someone who is lying down/
245. *moem k'op* /speech of someone who has just climbed up something (e.g., a tree)/
246. *mukin k'op* /talk that is done secretly, hidden from others/
247. *muk'ul k'op* /speech occurring in a loud, low, open voice/
248. *mulanbil k'op* /pleasant talk appreciated by others (usually involves a nice voice with pleasant quality)/
249. *mulil k'op* /accusation of a crime/
250. *nahkahtik k'op* /talk among several people sitting down/
251. *nahtil k'op* /a long chat or conversation/
252. *nail k'op* /speech of the *hnail* (counselors for *alférezes*)/
253. *nakal k'op* /speech from someone who is in a sitting position/
254. *nak'bil k'op* /speech not heard by addressee(s) because speaker's head is turned the other way/
    /secretive, hidden talk (subject not secret, but participants are hiding)/
255. *naʔli k'op* /speech concerning the remembrance of an unpleasant experience (e.g., a bad meal at the market the other day)/
256. *nameh k'op* /ancient speech, speech of the olden days/
257. *naʔnu k'op* /silent speech to oneself in which a debt that the person himself owes is recalled and thought about/
258. *naʔnubil k'op* /speech (aloud) concerning the remembering of a debt owed by the speaker/
259. *naʔ ʔoʔtanil k'op* /reminiscing about a pleasant experience/
260. *nelesbil k'op* /talk concerning the replacement in mid-term of one official by someone else (due to the official's not being able to finish out his term)/
261. *nihil k'op* /speech from someone who has his head bent forward and down/
262. *nihkel k'op* /speech from someone who is trembling or shaking while speaking/
263. *nilnil k'op* /low rumbling sound of many indistinguishable voices talking/
264. *nitbil k'op* /talk that involves a third party in a situation involving blame; having been touched by blame through words spoken by another/
265. *niwak k'op* /speech of adults, grown-up speech/
266. *nohel k'op* /talk of a houseful of people/
267. *nohpen k'op* /words or phrases that have (recently) been learned/
268. *nopȼahem k'op* /conversation of people who have moved closer to a nonparticipant audience which can now hear what is being said/
269. *nopol k'op* /speech of people talking close by/
270. *nop'il k'op* /unverbalized thoughts about blaming someone for a crime/
271. *notbil k'op* /speech of a criminal who is tied up while talking/
272. *nuhp'inbil k'op* /an answer or response that has been made by someone/

273. *nuhul k'op* /speech of a person (usually old) standing and talking with head bowed down looking at the ground/
    /speech (i.e., sounds) made by a chicken clucking after it has been placed under an upside-down basket, while waiting to serve in a soul-retrieval ceremony/
274. *nupk'abal k'op* /greetings, salutations/
275. *ʔoʔbol sba k'op* /speaking very little, like a child just learning to speak/
    /faltering speech because speaker is guilty of some delict and is about to cry/
276. *ʔoč k'op* /beginning of an argument or fight/
277. *ʔočem k'op* /an argument or fight that has begun/
278. *ʔok'em k'op* /speech mixed with crying or following a crying bout/
279. *ʔok'es k'op* /speech (i.e., sound) coming from a bugle or cornet when it is played/
280. *pahal k'op* /speech conveying the sentiment that the speaker is in agreement with someone else/
281. *pakal k'op* /speech coming from person whose head is facing the ground (usually occurs when speaker is playing at ventriloquy, trying to make the audience think the sound is coming from nowhere)/
282. *pakbil k'op* /response, answer/
283. *pak'al k'op* /conversation, discussion/
284. *pas k'op* /quarreling, arguing, fighting/
285. *pasbil k'op* /words or speech fashioned by someone already; prepared words or speech
286. *pašyal k'op* /conversation taking place during a walk or trip/
287. *patil k'op* /'afterwards speech'; speech turn preceded by someone else's/
288. *pat ʔoʔtan k'op* /special traditional speech (i.e., prayers) of *alférezes* on ritual occasions/
289. *pawor k'op* /asking a favor/
290. *pay k'op* /asking someone to kill, wound, or cast a spell on a third party/
291. *payal k'op* /speech of someone who is facing away from audience/
    /inciteful speech (cf. *pay k'op*) that has been accepted by the addressee who will do as asked/
292. *peč'el k'op* /much talk/
293. *perton k'op* /apology, begging someone's pardon, asking forgiveness/
294. *pihtem k'op* /speech of person talking to self; speech of someone who has been left alone (in house, in fields, etc.)/
295. *pim k'op* /much talk/
296. *pimil k'op* /drunken talk, talking on and on making little sense/
297. *poko k'op* /'ancient speech,' traditional speech, speech of ancient ancestors of modern Tzeltal speakers/
298. *polbil k'op* /truthful and factual speech/
299. *pore k'op* /speech of poor people/
300. *pošil k'op* /talking (including prayers) done by a curer in order to cure someone/
301. *puhkem k'op* /widely advertised rumor about someone's petty crimes/
302. *pukbil k'op* /announcement, notice, publication of news/
303. *pukuh k'op* /insults, insulting speech/
304. *pus k'op* /speech occurring inside a *temazcal*/
    /talk on the subject of *temazcals*/

305. *p'ih k'op* /intelligent, wise talk/
306. *p'ihil k'op* /intelligent speech, speech that makes sense/
307. *p'olmal k'op* /talk in which things are offered for sale, 'commerce talk'/
308. *rason k'op* /truthful speaking, eloquence, profound speech; sensible, intelligent ideas, slow and deliberate pronunciation; especially the speech of older, cool-headed persons/
309. *restíko k'op* /testifying; speech of a witness/
310. *sab k'op* /talk occurring early in the morning/
311. *sahsah k'op* /whispering/
312. *sayp'ohem k'op* /speech that trails off into nothing as the speaker falls asleep (especially apt for describing drunk person)/
313. *sbabi k'op* /that which is said first, the first thing said/ /initiation of conversation routine, first conversational turn/
314. *senyóra k'op* /talk or speech directed to *senyóra hme?kašail* 'earth-mother' (i.e., praying to her)/
315. *slahíbal k'op* /the last conversational turn; the final portion of a conversation/
316. *sokem k'op* /speech that is no good in that speaker has poor speaking ability/
317. *solahem k'op* /completed prayer or round of prayers/
318. *solem k'op* /speech, message, or word that has been passed on to someone for another/
319. *solesbil k'op* /speech that has been translated, interpreted, and passed on/
320. *son k'op* /singing while accompanying oneself with the guitar; song with guitar accompaniment/
321. *sore k'op* /poor speech or bad-sounding speech (e.g., speech from someone with *čehkel nuk', wohč'ol nuk'*, etc.)/
322. *spisil k'op* /talk on the subject of everything/ /the speech of everyone/
323. *stek'leh k'op* /speech of an adolescent, adolescent speech/
324. *stenleh k'op* /talk or conversation occurring on plain or plateau/
325. *stenoh sba k'op* /conversation with several people talking at once so that the speech of any one individual can't be understood/
326. *stukel k'op* /talking alone with no response from listener(s) who may or may not be present/
327. *suhtem k'op* /broken promise, 'Indian-giver talk,' word that has been gone back on/
328. *suht k'op* /broken promise, 'Indian-giver talk,' word that has been gone back on (*suhtem k'op* is the preferred form)/
329. *suhtib k'op* /response, answer, reply/
330. *sukleh k'op* /talk or conversation coming from or occurring on a small hill/
331. *sutet k'op* /the passing around of one word from person to person in a group (especially in a game that children play)/
332. *ɂ?ahɂun k'op* /moaning and groaning as when sick — saying ʔah ʔah/
333. *šaket k'op* /talk from a distance to someone in house, coming from someone who doesn't want to come in/
334. *ɂ?awet k'op* /speech that comes out very loud, that is shouted/
335. *šcuɂil k'op* /talk in which the topic is the sweethearts (i.e., lovers) of women not present/
336. *šhahun k'op* /the laughing brr-ing, startled sound that we make if someone throws water on us when we are nude/
337. *šhururet k'op* /speech or conversation the sound of which approximates a whirring sound/

338. *šihpawet k'op* /speech of a baby jumping up and down (while seated) trying to say something (but too young to really speak)/
339. *šin k'op* /talking to the left (i.e., going around a circle starting on the left of the speaker – going clockwise addressing each person in turn)/
340. *šʔiwana k'op* /speech consisting of one or more occurrences of the exclamation *kere šʔiwana*/
341. *šiwel k'op* /speech very softly articulated due to fear/
342. *šk'ahk'et k'op* /short speech, speech said as if not having time for anyone; greetings cut short/
343. *šmišmun ʔoʔtan k'op* /talk evincing inner thoughts on part of speaker concerning his desire to hit someone/
344. *šohleh k'op* /speech or conversation occurring in or coming from a ravine, canyon, or valley/
345. *šohol k'op* /incompetent or non-fluent speech; not being able to say what one wants to say/
346. *šot'bil k'op* /conversation that is interrupted or cut short by the speaker/
347. *šuhkehem k'op* /envious talk (i.e., *hešohel k'op*) that has 'fallen to one side' thus not affecting the envied person/
348. *šuhkin k'op* /prayers made by curers to insure that a person who has been envied (i.e., *hešohel k'op*) will not be affected and that the words of envy will 'fall to one side' thereby missing their target/
349. *šʔumet k'op* /speech accompanied by smiling (of speaker); talking with a smile)/
350. *tahimal k'op* /kidding around, kidding speech (e.g., when someone says 'I'm going now' and doesn't mean it)/
351. *takin k'op* /social talk not accompanied by liquor/
352. *tawal k'op* /verbalized envy, envying talk/
353. *tawaltawaneh k'op* /the occurrence of envying talk while it is happening/
354. *tek'el k'op* /speech coming from person who is standing up/
355. *tenel k'op* /conversation with several people talking at once so that the speech of any one individual can't be understood/
356. *tihawal k'op* /talk in which the speaker voices his regret that he has done something for someone/
357. *tihtamba k'op* /argument, quarrel, fight/
358. *tihwaneh k'op* /rousting speech; telling someone to wake up/
359. *tikunbil k'op* /a message that has been sent by someone to another by means of a messenger/
360. *tik'bil k'ahk' k'op* /gossip, tattling/
361. *tinil k'op* /speech coming from someone who has his head bowed/ /slow respectful talk/
362. *tinil mayal k'op* /speech performed with head slightly bowed and rocking from side to side, usually while seated (implies awe, reverence, and embarrassment due to speaker being in presence of superior being)/
363. *tohol k'op* /wasted words, a waste of time/
364. *tohoteswaneh k'op* /speech correcting someone in speech or behavior/
365. *tohtoh k'op* /talk of a hunter saying *tohtohtoh* while pointing out the track of a rabbit to his dog/
366. *tok'tawaneh k'op* /the occurrence of insulting speech while it is happening; speech insulting one's mother/
367. *toyba k'op* /boasting, lies that are boasting/

368. *toyem k'op* /speech that is excessively self-assertive, that is loud and forceful coming out with great self-confidence (negatively-valued)/
369. *tuč'bil k'op* /speech cut off by another person interrupting (to interject something)/
370. *tulank'op* /very loudly articulated speech/
371. *tup'en k'op* /silenced talk, silenced gossip (i.e., gossip about a criminal is silenced by the criminal serving time and paying his debt to society)/
372. *tutin k'op* /speech characterized by thin, high, squeaky voice – like that of a woman (not negatively valued in general)/
373. *t'ihšem k'op* /words that won't come out; words that are blocked by some problem internal to the speaker/
374. *t'isebil k'op* /speech interrupted by someone else speaking/
375. *t'uhbil k'op* /speech that sounds very nice – good articulation, sound, and choice of words/
376. *t'ut' k'op* /speech very reticently articulated, hardly speaking/
377. *ʔubinahem k'op* /speech accompanied by panting, breathing hard (especially from tiredness of the speaker)/
378. *ʔuɬehem k'op* /talk or speech (especially a request to marry daughter) whose import or content has been accepted positively (rather than negatively) by another/
379. *ʔuɬ k'op* /much talk, the sound of much talking/ /nice talk, good talk/
380. *ʔuɬil k'op* /much talk, the sound of much talking/ /nice talk, good speech/
381. *ʔuɬilal k'op* /pleasant talk (e.g., saying nice things the way a man talks to a woman he wants to marry); complimentary talk/
382. *ʔumaʔ k'op* /the sounds made by a mute vainly trying to talk/
383. *ʔuʔnil k'op* /talk about things belonging to people, especially to self; possession talk/
384. *ʔuninahem k'op* /speech accompanied by whimpering (and crying)/
385. *ʔutaw k'op* /scolding, scolding speech/
386. *waʔel k'op* /talking to the right; i.e., going around a circle of people by talking to people starting at the right of the speaker – done at official gatherings/
387. *wahtan k'op* /questions by X about how many ears of corn Y will plant/
388. *walak' pat k'op* /talking (badly) behind one's back/
389. *walk'ombil k'op* /speech to Y denying what one said to X (i.e., saying one thing to a person and then denying it to the person's opposition)/
390. *walk'unbil k'op* /verbal response to someone's speech consisting of saying the same thing right back to him/
391. *wašaneh ta k'ahk' k'op* /inciteful speech; asking someone to harm someone else (LIT 'words put in fire')/
392. *wayal k'op* /talk occurring while speaker is lying down/
393. *wayčil k'op* /speech evincing the desire of speaker(s) to go to bed to sleep/
394. *wehtesbil k'op* /blame that has been invented for something and laid on someone; verbal fabrication/
395. *wekwek k'op* /the sound of children copying ducks quacking/
396. *weweštik k'op* /speech occurring on Thursday/ /speech concerning the day Thursday/

397. *wiʔnal kʼop* /'hungry speech'; speech of a hungry person; speech of a person who is fasting/
398. *winik kʼop* /men's speech/
399. *woč'woč' kʼop* /the sound of many voices, not comprehensible (e.g., at market) (louder than *wošwoš kʼop*)/
400. *wohe kʼop* /talk or conversation that took place yesterday/
    /talk or conversation on the subject of yesterday/
401. *wohe čahe kʼop* /talk or conversation that took place recently/
    /conversation about things that happened recently; recent news/
402. *wokolok kʼop* /saying 'please'/
403. *wošem kʼop* /ready response to scolding talk; defending oneself handily (verbally) when one is being scolded by another; answering right back/
404. *wošwoš kʼop* /subdued sound of many voices (e.g., at market) (softer than *woč'woč' kʼop*)/
405. *wulwul kʼop* /drunken speech; talking and talking while drunk/
406. *yaʔel kʼop* /a short conversation, speaking for a short time/
407. *yakubel kʼop* /speech of person or persons who are drinking rum or chicha (implies frequent shouts)/
408. *yan kʼop* /a language other than Tzeltal, but partly understood/
409. *yanahem kʼop* /speech utilizing non-native language/
    /speech with a very strange, perhaps foreign sound/
410. *yehtal kʼop* /well formed speech accompanied by nice voice/
411. *yihil kʼop* /speech of an old (i.e., matured) person – man or woman/
412. *yipal kʼop* /loud speech/
413. *yočib kʼop* /talk occurring in the market center called *yočib*/
    /talk or conversation about the market center called *yočib*/
414. *yočol kʼop* /subdued murmuring of many voices talking, as in market on a slow day or at a slow hour/
415. *yom kʼop* /discussion involving several people who have assembled to decide something/
416. *yombil kʼop* /decision or conclusion reached by several people who have assembled to discuss some future action (e.g., 'Let's put X in jail')/

11

BLACK TALKING ON THE STREETS

ROGER D. ABRAHAMS

Deny the Negro the culture of the land? O.K. He'll brew his own culture – on the street corner. Lock him out from the seats of higher learning? He pays it no never-mind – he'll dream up his own professional doubletalk, from the professions that *are* available to him . . . These boys I ran with at The Corner, breathing half-comic prayers at the Tree of Hope, they were the new sophisticates of the race, the jivers, the sweettalkers, the jawblockers. They spouted at each other like soldiers sharpening their bayonets – what they were sharpening, in all this verbal horseplay, was their wits, the only weapons they had. Their sophistication didn't come out of moldy books and dicty colleges. It came from opening their eyes wide and gunning the world hard.

. . . They were the genius of the people, always on their toes, never missing a trick, asking no favors and taking no guff, not looking for trouble but solid ready for it. Spawned in a social vacuum and hung up in mid-air, they were beginning to build their own culture. Their language was a declaration of independence. (Mezzrow & Wolfe 1969:193–4)

Black is . . .: Being so nasty and filthy you cook in all the big downtown restaurants . . . Exploited by the news/Tortured by the blues/breaking the rules/and paying your dues . . . Realizing 'they' all look alike too! . . . Playing the 'dozens!'
(From a Black cocktail napkin)

Blacks do indeed speak differently than whites. Here I do not refer to the phonological and morphological differences much discussed in the literature of Black English, but rather to the ways in which Blacks use talk as part of their daily lives. Whether or not it is sufficient basis for an argument of *cultural* differences (as Mezzrow implies above), it seems clear that Afro-Americans in the United States do constitute a separate *speech community*. That is, they differ from other groups in the varieties of speech they employ and in the ways they use these varieties in carrying out the ritual (predictable) dimension of their personal interactions. Or, to put it in Hymes' terms for speech community, they 'share rules for the conduct and interpretation of speech, and rules for the interpretation of at least one linguistic variety' (Hymes 1972:54).

We recognize, then, this sense of community in Black speaking in a great many ways – not least of which is the kind and intensity of talk about talk which one encounters in conversations and the special in-group names given by the speakers to ways of talking. Such Black terms for speech events constitute one important dimension of their system of speaking, and focus on speech use in very different ways from the usages of Euro-American discourse. This is not to say that there are not parallel terms or analogous practices in standard American English. Rather, the range, the intensity, the proliferation of terms, and the importance of such events are, as a whole, quite different from the configuration of communicative systems found elsewhere.

The existence of this distinct speaking community is recognized by Blacks (as well as whites) in their lore about themselves. One hears discussions not only about how *bad* or *country* some Blacks talk, but also how *lame* and uninformed whites are at communicating with each other. The Black ability to use words artfully and playfully is often encountered as an explanation of how and why Blacks outwit whites in certain conflict situations. There is thus a ground-level recognition of speaking differences among Blacks that gives the idea of a distinct speaking community a sense of analytic reality. Furthermore, analysis is carried on by the Black speakers themselves in discussions about the effectiveness or ineffectiveness of someone's abilities at using speech on some level of performance.

Perhaps the clearest indication of the distinctiveness of the Black speech community lies in the use of speech in the pursuit of public *playing*, and a parallel use of silence or other verbal restrictions in the more private sectors of the community. That is, attitudes toward work and play differ in Afro- and Euro-American communities. In Black communities, work is essentially a private matter, something learned in the home as part of the respectable and cooperative ideals of home life. Play, on the other hand, is inappropriate for the most part in the home, but rather is regarded as a public kind of phenomenon. Playing, in fact, is an important way in which one distinguishes oneself in public, and engaging in witty verbal exchanges is one important way of playing. (In the Euro-American system, on the other hand, play tends to be regarded as something appropriate for an adult to do in private – certainly something you don't usually want to get caught at, unless you're a member of a team. Work is the way in which one distinguishes oneself, and is therefore properly a public activity.) Thus, one crucial distinction to be made with regard to defining the Black speaking community is between house talk, especially 'around moms,' and street talk. Because active verbal performance in the street is one of the main means of asserting one's presence and place, there are a greater number of terms for street talk than for house talk. In the house, communications often are defined in terms of a Momma's imposed set of restrictions, especially when the speaking is defined as playful (Abrahams 1973). Here the restrictions may be on the subject of discussion, the vocabulary used, the amount of noise generally permitted to emanate from the residents of the house, and the communication relationships pursued in that ambience. There are, of course, numerous modes of talk, especially in the area of conversation, which are shared in both worlds. But the distinctions between the two are dramatic, for in the street world certain kinds of play are regarded as a norm – and valued as such – which are out of place for the most part in the house.

In general women – and especially female heads of households and older women – speak differently than men. Women are expected to be more restrained in their talk, less loud, less public, and much less abandoned. Parents attempt to instill this in the girls in their family by attempting to get them never to talk loudly or curse, not even when involved in street encounters. As Louise Meriwhether explains it in her autobiography, 'Daddy even didn't want me to say darn. He was always telling me: "It's darn today, damn tomorrow, and next week it'll be goddamn. You're going to grow up to be a lady, and ladies don't curse"' (1970:28). But the problem is more than cursing. Any kind of public talk may not be respectably ladylike. The house is the locus of a woman's sense of respectability, and it is by respectability canons that a woman is judged by her community and especially her peers (Wilson 1969). Communication is regarded as properly restricted there, to the point that silence from children (especially in the presence of Momma) is highly valued.

The major difference between the house and the street worlds, beyond the relative privacy and restriction, lies in the kind of relationships pursued and the varieties of communication used. The house world is populated in the main by members of the family. The home is regarded as the place to keep the family together. Here (and in the church) is therefore where Momma asserts her respectability most fully. In the street world, on the other hand, male friendships are established and kept up, and this is done by maintaining the possibility of *playing* (with all that comes to mean) at all times. This essay deals primarily with the communication events most characteristic of street behaviors, understanding that street includes all areas regarded as public.[1]

Elliot Liebow's study, *Tally's Corner*, describes how one friendship circle operates. His description is characteristic of other such groups.

On the streetcorner, each man has his own network of... personal relationships and each man's network defines for him the members of his personal community. His personal community, then, is not a bounded area but rather a web-like arrangement of man–man and man–woman relationships in which he is selectively attached in a particular way to a definite number of discrete persons ...

At the edges of this network are those persons with whom his relationship is affectively neutral, such as area residents whom he has 'seen around' but does not know except to nod or say 'hi' to as they pass in the street ...

In toward the center are those persons he knows and likes best, those with whom he is 'up tight'; his 'walking buddies,' 'good' or 'best' friends, girl friends, and sometimes real or putative kinsmen. These are the people with whom he is in more or less daily, face-to-face contact, and whom he turns to for emergency aid, comfort or support in time of need or crisis. He gives them and receives from them goods and services in the name of friendship, ostensibly keeping no reckoning. Routinely, he seeks them out and is sought out by them. They serve his need to be with others of his kind, and to be recognized as a discrete, distinctive personality, and he in turn serves them the same way. They are both his audience and his fellow actors. (1967:161–3)

Liebow's use of the metaphor of performance is appropriate here because friendship is not only defined by whom one may call upon for aid, but more important, with whom one may *play*.

In such a person-centered society a man establishes his reputation. A man with a *big rep* is so judged, in part, by the number of people he is able to call friend and therefore call upon for such goods and services as well as joke with. Both are implied in the word *play*. Because a reputation is so person-centered, it needs to be constantly guarded. As Rap Brown put it: 'Once I established my reputation, cats respected it ... If I went out of my neighborhood, though, it was another story. I'd be on someone else's turf and would have to make it or take it over there' (H. R. Brown 1969:15). This is echoed in Piri Thomas' comment, 'In Harlem you always lived on the edge of losing rep. All it takes is a one-time loss of heart' (1967:58).

This personalistic, reputation-centered approach has been noted by numerous ethnographers. Somewhat complicating the matter, Herbert Gans has noted this feature as a general characteristic of lower-class socialization, which he calls an 'action seeking' style of life; but the manner in which Blacks set up the action and the modes of performance differ from that of any other ethnic enclave. (For an indication that these differences are perceived and maximized on the street level, see Suttles' [1968:65ff.] description of lower-class Italian-American reactions to Black performance style.)

In such a street world, one must dramatize oneself constantly, and one is therefore always looking for opportunities to do so. Perhaps the most important means one has to do so in the Black world – and especially in the cities – is through verbal performances. In this expressive life style, performance and especially talk become the major means for establishing friendships – a process Rainwater describes as 'a single adaptation in lower-class Negro society, which has as its primary goal the maintenance of reciprocity between members on the basis of a symbolic exchange of selves, *an entertainment of each by the other*' (1970:378, my italics).

There is ample testimony to the importance of learning to talk well to operate successfully outside the home environment (a move Claude Brown repeatedly calls 'coming out of the house' – 'cutting loose from. . . parents' [1966; see esp. pp. 166ff]). Not only do the ethnographic studies carried out by myself, Kochman, Kernan, Hannerz, Rainwater, the Milners, and others underline this feature of Black life style, but such an in-group commentator as Malcolm X describes how crucial it was to learn to talk right to establish his *rep* wherever he went, especially in Harlem when he was operating as a pimp–waiter (1965). Rap Brown devotes a whole chapter to his street education which emphasizes the relationship between learning to talk well and the development of his reputation:

> I used to hang out in the bars just to hear the old men 'talking shit.' By the time I was nine, I could talk Shine and the Titanic, Signifying Monkey three different ways, and Piss-Pot Peet for two hours without stopping. Sometimes I wonder why I even bothered to go to school. Practically everything I know I learned on the corner . . .
> The street is where young bloods get their education. I learned how to talk on the street, not from reading about Dick and Jane going to school and all that simple shit. The teacher would test our vocabulary every week, but we knew the vocabulary we needed. They'd give us arithmetic to exercise our minds. Hell, we exercised our minds by playing the Dozens . . .
> There'd be sometimes 40 or 50 dudes standing around and the winner was determined by the way they responded to what was said. If you fell all over each other laughing, then you knew you'd scored. It was a bad scene for a dude that was getting humiliated. I seldom was. That's why they called me Rap, cause I could rap. (H. R. Brown 1969:25-7, 30; for similar accounts see Abrahams 1970a, chapter 2)

It would be easy to conclude from such accounts that this attitude and verbal practice characteristic only of Black enclaves in the big cities. To do so would be to be misled by the urban terms that Brown uses. In fact, the focus on using (among other techniques) verbal abilities as a means of establishing and maintaining reputation is a widely observed Afro-American characteristic which extends to Black communities outside the United States (e.g., Wilson 1969; Abrahams & Bauman 1971). But most important for the present argument, verbal *playing* has been reported from a number of non-urban communities (e.g., Ferris 1972; Lewis 1964; Friedland & Nelkin 1971) as part of a complex in which males find meeting places where they can pursue their male expressive behaviors – in spite of it being judged as *bad* by both the respectables and, when pressed to it, themselves.

Although much described in the literature, these behaviors are all too often judged from a Euro-American perspective which sees them as 'idling' or 'killing time' without recognizing the system by which they operate. Street-level terms are *hanging* (Keiser 1969), *hanging out, taking care of business.* [2]

Even those who do not accord much significance to expressive phenomena in their analyses of Black culture acknowledge the importance of a
certain range of talking in these interactive settings. For instance, Hylan
Lewis in his *Blackways of Kent* reports that in the Piedmont community
which he studied there was much 'public idling' which he associated with
male behavior. He noted 'specific idling places, informal idling cliques, a
range of conventional idling behavior, and certain days and periods when
idling is expected' (1964:68).

The importance of talk in such situations is nowhere so clearly reflected
as in the large number of terms describing the varieties of such talk. In
fact, these terms are a good index not only to the importance of talk but to
the range of speech events whereby such public friend-groups celebrate
themselves while getting the action going. The street world is thought of
as the public world and therefore one in which playing is appropriate. This
does not mean that in verbal interactions on the street only play is found,
but rather that it seems to operate as a norm – or at least a constant in-
cipiency – and other events are distinguished from it. This may account
for the great number of ground-level distinctions made with regard to
verbal *playing* or *signifying*.

Play is a difficult phenomenon to describe in any culture. On the one
hand play relies on the distinction between it and the 'real' or the 'serious.'
On the other, for such play to operate successfully, there must be a recognizable relationship between it and the real world. One of these vital
connections is that for play to operate successfully, there must be a sense
of threat arising from the 'real' and 'serious' world of behavior. The threat
of incursions from the real world must be constant. That is, in the most
successful kinds of play, the most constant message must be the deeply
ambivalent one: this is play – this is *not* play. With joking activity (which
accounts for most *playing* in the street world) this paradoxical message is
very commonly carried out by the use of the same aggressive, hostile
formulaic devices found in use in real arguments – i.e., the same curses,
boasts, devices of vilification and degradation, etc. This is precisely what
one finds in the Black street world – so much so that the passer-by often has
a hard time discerning whether joking or a real argument is taking place.
Indeed, it becomes an important part of the show on many occasions to
keep even the other participants wondering whether one is still playing.

This blurring of the line between play and seriousness is often observable
in the terms which are used to describe the communicative event. *Cursing*,
for instance, may be either a device of *playing*, or used very seriously, as
are *mounting, charging, getting on someone's case*, and many others. The very
same words that constitute a *put-down* or a *put-on* in one situation may be
used as playful *woofing* or *talking shit* in another. This is why it is important
to be at home, on your *own turf*, when you begin to use these devices. One

can suddenly find that one has *gone too deep*, and that what one thought to be jokes are being taken very seriously indeed. But it also means that if one wants to test someone on one's own turf, one can use these devices with an outsider without giving clear cues as to whether one is being serious or not. Or in the most extreme circumstances, one can use them to start a real fight. This is why neither the witty, aggressive, traditional devices nor even the generic terms for them can be used as the primary basis of a taxonomy (even though they are the data which originally indicated that a ground-level taxonomy exists).

Only the most extreme forms of play are regarded as appropriate only on the street. The range of joking called (among other things) *talking smart* may occur wherever women and men find themselves in courtship-level conversation – though the smart talk is as often used to fend off a courting move as it is to encourage or continue it. *Talking smart*, however, is primarily regarded as street talk because it involves the kind of display of wit which is most useful and appropriate in public places. Nevertheless, it is a style of talk carried on between the participants without any need for an audience, and is often reported as occurring just between two people who find themselves in some situation of contention. That these *are* reported in anecdotal form, however, indicates the close relationship between such *smart talking* and *talking shit*. A good display of wit is too valuable to waste it only on a two-person conversation. It must be repeated to a larger audience later, one which can admire the witty verbal control.

There are, in this recognition of distinctions within the Black speaking community, three basic kinds of street-talk events: those intended primarily to pass on information, those in which interpersonal manipulation or argumentation involving a display of wit is going on, and those in which play is the primary component of the interaction. This distinction is keyed as much by proxemic and kinesic elements as by verbal means. The more informational, the more private the interaction. The more wit is involved, the more the possibility of onlooker involvement. When men are talking in public and primarily with other men (i.e., *to* them, with messages meant primarily for their ears), the major indication of what range of speaking event is going on is given by how their bodies are stationed. The most casual kind of grouping in which *talking shit* or *woofing* is probably taking place is a group standing or sitting shoulder-to-shoulder, in either a line or semicircle, where the passing action may be observed without disturbing the state of talk. As the discussion gets *deeper* (the more intensively stylized and aggressive or the more personal), the participants get closer to each other, stationing themselves so that you can make eye contact with whoever is talking. The instigators of talk will maintain their mobility, for they will be dramatizing their talk with action. A good talker will somewhat immobilize the others around him. The more one commands attention, the longer his talk is countenanced. He must receive constant verbal and kinesic support from the others. (For interesting pictures, see Keiser 1969:*passim*; Friedland & Nelkin 1971.) This support is indicated in a number of verbal and kinesic ways – one of which is the bending at the waist and knees. The deeper the bending, the greater the supportive intensification, it would seem. In all adult interactions, but especially public ones, participation must be actively indicated constantly. As one commentator noted: 'Unlike a white audience, careful to suppress enthusiasm, the black man and woman were silent [and still] only when they were negative and suspicious' (Keegan 1971:7).

The older the members of the group talking, the less low-level kinesic activity will go on among the non-talking members. But with adolescents who are just perfecting the style of their *pimp walk* (see Johnson 1971:19 and Ellis & Newman 1971:302 for descriptions) there is a need to *style* constantly. As Kenneth R. Johnson describes this grouping technique:

When talking in a group, the participants (say four or five young Black males) will often adopt a kind of stationary 'pimp strut' ... while [they] are talking, they stand with their hands halfway in their pockets, and they move in the rhythmic, fluid dance-type way (without actually walking) to punctuate their remarks. The arm that is free will swing, point, turn and gesture as conversation proceeds ... This kind of behavior always accompanies a light or humorous conversation, or a conversation about masculine exploits. It never accompanies a serious discussion about more general topics (planning something, difficulties with parents, political issues, etc.). (1971:19)

If two (or more) people are seen engaging in close talk, facing each other and maintaining eye contact, the assumption is that something *deep* is going on, either one is *running something down* to the other – passing on valid information on which he is supposed to act – or that one is *running a game* on the other, *hyping* or *shucking* him – passing on invalid information. If two are arguing and engaging in talking smart, they will face each other but be farther apart and more mobile than when getting the *run down* on something.

If two (or more) are in a casual state of talk they will signify this by looking outward. This is even true when two friends meet on the street and shake hands. If they are not *hipping* someone to something that is *happening*, they will gaze away even while still shaking or just holding hands. The more other-person-centered the talk becomes (of the 'have you heard about so-and-so' sort concerning mutual friends or acquaintances), the closer the two will come, and the more their bodies will face each other, especially if the news of the other's *business* is concerned with a life-change (moving, any sort of conflict or confinement).

These kinesic and proxemic observations might be used to describe street behaviors of any age. But, as noted above, there are differences in the amount of movement within a group depending on how recently the young men have learned to *walk their walk* and *talk their talk*, to *style* their actions to make themselves appear *cool* (under control through stylistic moves) and *hip* (informed).

Performing by *styling* is thus one of the means of adapting oneself to the street world, of developing a public persona through which one can begin to establish and maintain one's *rep*. Naturally, as a young man learns how to *style*, he is much more self-conscious of how he is coming over to the others, and he therefore constantly looks for openings in which he can demonstrate his styling abilities. At first he does this almost formularistically – by imitation of those whom he has observed and admired. Later, when he has lived with *styling* devices, he will be less self-conscious and more able to take the styling for granted and thus be more message-oriented in his stylized communications.

Though it is in walking and dressing well that such a young man asserts his style most immediately, it is often in learning to *talk shit*, to effectively play with words by *talking that talk*, that his street image will be most firmly established. (This is especially true of the *pimp* or *cat* approach to the streets. The alternative gorilla approach of using one's strength is explored in Abrahams 1970a:85–96 and in Firestone 1964, and is commented upon in Hannerz 1969:115 and Milner & Milner 1972:319–20. For somewhat different taxonomies of available social roles 'on the street,' see Ellis & Newman 1971 and Strong 1940.) This is what Rap Brown seems to have meant when he stressed the origin of his name in his ability to contest effectively with words, and how central this was to his *high rep*.

Because *styling* is so important during this period of life, the Black community tends to view certain performances as being age-specific to adolescence. That is, there are a number of speech events which continue to be played throughout life when men congregate, but because they are more self-consciously stylized during adolescence, their names and the self-conscious dimension of their performance may be rejected. Thus, among the older members of the community, the names for these practices may become pejorative; certainly, their practice becomes less habitual, more restricted. But the same patterns of interaction may be observed throughout a man's life as long as he identifies with his peer group and engages in congregations on the street or some other equally public place.

Whenever men get together to engage in talk, this may lead to an increasingly stylized set of behaviors which, as they become more stylized, will be progressively more aggressive, more contest-oriented, and more centered on witty style and delivery. This progression, too, is taken note of in Black terms for self-conscious interactions, being referred to in a number of ways like *going deep, getting heavy, really getting into it*, or *getting to it*. The heavier or deeper the performance, the more attention the interchange will attract, and the more responding movement (a kind of dancing with) and answering verbal response (continuatives of the *right on* variety) will arise.

In this realm there seem to be important age-differentials in what speaking events arise most often in such states of talk. Among the younger adolescents, the devices used are not only more formulaic but also shorter. The older the group, the more time is given the performer to develop his point; thus, jokes, toasts (long narrative often heroic verses), and personal experience narrations emerge more often with older performers.

Hannerz describes such differences in regard to these aggressive verbal practices, focussing on the fuzzy semantic boundaries of the in-group descriptive terms *joning* and *joking*.

Verbal contests occur among young males as well as among adult counterparts... This is the phenomenon which has become most known [in the literature] as 'the dozens,' but it is also known as 'sounding' and under some other local names. The term most often used in Washington, D.C., is '*joning*' ...
Joning is an exchange of insults ... The boundaries of the concept are a little fuzzy; there is some tendency to view joning as any exchange of insults of a more or less jocular type in sociable interaction among children and adolescents. Joning is definitely associated with joking. For smaller boys it seems to shade imperceptibly into the category of 'cracking jokes,' and when joning occurs in a peer group sociable session it is often preceded and followed by other kinds of jokes. These are also exchanged in a manner resembling a contest, and some of them have a form and content somewhat similar to jones...
The exchanges can occur between two boys who are alone, and it is even possible for them to jone on some third absent person, usually one of their peers, but the typical situation involves a group of boys: while a series of exchanges may engage one pair of boys after another, most members of the crowd function as audience, inciters, and judges – laughing, commenting upon the 'scoring,' and urging the participants on...
As the boys become men they gradually cease to amuse themselves with joning. Although verbal aggression continues, it becomes less patterned; the insults contain hardly any references to mothers any more, and if a man, often by chance rather than intentionally, should say anything which could be construed as an abuse of another's mother, the latter might simply say, 'I don't play that game no more.' (1969:129–30)

Just what the difference is between this and adult joking behaviors is not quite clear from either the literature or my own observations, except that, as noted, the younger men use more formulaic devices, and are therefore less improvisational in their contest techniques than adults. Ferris's (1972) argument with regard to his Mississippi informants suggests that the older one gets, the less fictional and the more personal stories may get.

There is, however, a tendency to identify all such adolescent *playing* with the specific practice of *playing the dozens*. This leads to a use of the same terms for all aggressive play on a more particular level as synonyms for the dozens. But, as Rap Brown pointed out above, these same groups may want to distinguish between different kinds of *playing*: *cracking* on the other person, on the other person's family, or on yourself. Another important distinction is the use of boasts in the same context.

There are, then, terminological distinctions made by the participants in the public street world of the Black speaking community which suggest the existence of a native taxonomy of ways of speaking. Thus, in my original formulation, I worked out the distinctions on the level of the terms – as they were distinguished by some speakers at some time. But it became clear that these distinctions are acted on even in those Black communities that do not have a contrast-set of terms. Therefore, the taxonomy must be described with regard to the distinctions in speaker-to-speaker relationships and strategies. However, because these terms do provide some sense of the distinction, one ground-level term will be given for each taxonomic slot – and the terms will be surveyed and discussed in an appendix.

I regard this taxonomy as an underlying record of some of the most important distinctions in Black life, felt, acted upon, and judged if not always named by agrarian and post-agrarian Black communities in the United States. Interactions which are named in one community but not in another are nevertheless practiced in both. Further, many of the names for these ways of speaking change constantly from time to time and place to place, but the patterned interactions and the relations between the types of situated speech remain essentially constant (at least as far back as our data will take us).

Fig. 13 presents the relationships between the major ways of speaking on the street, emphasizing the continuities between patterns of interaction and persuasion from casual conversation to stylized playing with words in the aggressive, contest situation characteristic of *playing the dozens* and *woofing*. There are a number of techniques of manipulation used in both serious and playful aggressive contexts, like *mounting*, *bragging*, and others. These will be discussed in the appendix of terms.

The taxonomy is divided in three parts from talk in which information is the focus, to the most stylized, in which more concern is shown for the artful patterning of the utterance than the message. With the former the style is buried in favor of the message; the interaction to be effective must seem relatively spontaneous. With the latter, the message is subordinated or

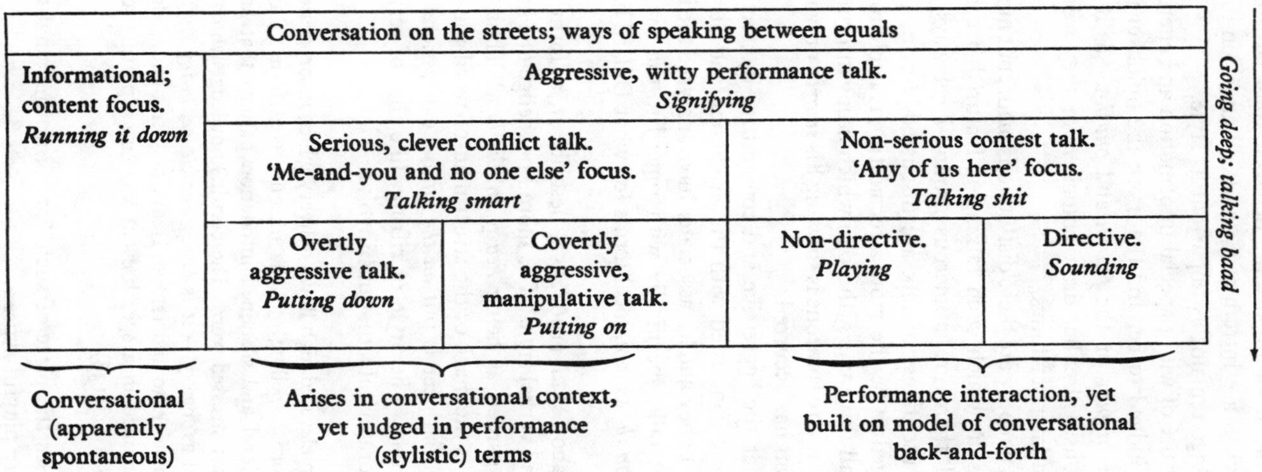

Going deep; talking baad →

Conversation on the streets; ways of speaking between equals

Informational; content focus. *Running it down*	Aggressive, witty performance talk. *Signifying*			
	Serious, clever conflict talk. 'Me-and-you and no one else' focus. *Talking smart*		Non-serious contest talk. 'Any of us here' focus. *Talking shit*	
	Overtly aggressive talk. *Putting down*	Covertly aggressive, manipulative talk. *Putting on*	Non-directive. *Playing*	Directive. *Sounding*
Conversational (apparently spontaneous)	Arises in conversational context, yet judged in performance (stylistic) terms		Performance interaction, yet built on model of conversational back-and-forth	

Fig. 13

disavowed (since it is all just play) while the intensity and effectiveness of presentation become most important. Between these are interactions in which stylized devices are introduced – and call attention to themselves – but in which message remains as important as style.

The greater the use of wit or special information and energy, the *heavier* the interaction is judged to be, and the more the onlooker is entertained. This is as true of *hipping* or the *put-on* and *put-down* as it is in *woofing*, for such interactions will either draw onlookers or they will become performance pieces in later retellings.

In other words, not only are these distinctions made, but more important, exceptional scenes in which such talking is featured become topics for further talk. And there are numerous ground-level ways in which the effectiveness and usefulness of talk are discussed. Again, the *deeper* the interaction is judged to be the more a recounting is liable to occur. These scenes may be of all three types, those in which *heavy* information is being passed on (*rifting*), where someone is showing his *smarts*, or where a remarkable capping session has occurred.

Less noticed that the aggressive and competitive interactions in Black talk have been those concerned with the discussion and dissemination of information. Only Labov and his associates have analyzed the importance of such talk in street talk, specifically with regard to the concept terms of *rifting* and being *on the square*, local terms for what Dillard has referred to as *fancy talk*.

Rifting is, as Labov *et al.* (1968:152) describe it, a 'form of display, of both knowledge and verbal style.' The more knowledge one has of a subject the more he is regarded as being *heavy in the head*. Thus, it is not just verbal style which is the mark of the street man-of-words; in certain situations when a potential peer is put *on the square*, expressions of knowledge are equally important. The style of rifting, like that of sermonizing and other formal and oratorical situations involves

a style of speech – an elevated high flown delivery which incorporates a great many learned Latinate words, spelling out the uncontracted form of function words with characteristic level and sustained intonation pattern that lays extra stress and length on the last stressed word. The occult knowledge which is delivered in this way is described as 'heavy' – it is *heavy knowledge, heavy stuff*, or *heavy shit*; and too heavy for outsiders to understand. Heavy or secret knowledge is learned by rote; adepts are examined in a speech event known as 'putting someone on the square.' (Labov *et al.* 1968:136)

Hannerz discusses the place of such *heavy* informational talking in the range of other more playful types.

All prestige accrued from being a good talker does not have to do with the strictly utilitarian [manipulative] aspect. A man with good stories well told and with a good repartee in arguments is certain to be appreciated for his entertainment value, and those men who can talk about the high and the mighty, people and places, and the state of the world, may stake claims to a reputation of being heavy 'upstairs.' (1969:85)

He later discusses two men from the neighborhood in which he worked who were known for this weightiness of knowledge, causing their friends and neighbors to regard them as 'intellectuals' (p. 106).

That this is a Black role-type is noted by many Black writers. For instance, George Cain in his remarkable *Blueschild Baby* observes:

J.B., the storyteller ... found in all civilizations, preserver of unwritten histories, keeper of legends and oral tradition. Daily he holds forth, as at an African market-place. Surrounded by black faces reflecting the moods of his narrations, he translates what is in the white mind and media into the idiom of his audience. Every corner has its J.B., that funny nigger who makes a crowd dance with laughter at themselves and their shortcomings...
Many dismiss him as bullshit, unable to see his role or contribution, but like all black people, they're respectful of knowledge so don't protest too vehemently...
On the absence of truth-telling media James and those like him evolved. Street-corner philosophers with all the technique of gifted actors, they hold the most difficult audience in the world (1970:29–30)

Often this performance of knowledge is commented upon in a meta-lingual and metacritical way, leading to further routines by the *heavy* talker on his streetcorner training. Typical of such speeches is one reported briefly from a Florida conservative Black politician, Norman E. Jones: 'His education, he once said, consists of "Ph.D.'s" from "the University of Beale Street, the University of Harlem and many other universities throughout the nation – generally called the street where people exist"' (Hooker 1972:4; for a longer routine, see Killens 1972:157).

However, such *heavy* displays are more likely to occur while *playing*, for in the *hanging* situation such *playing* is a constant possibility. It is in this range of situations, also, that there is the greatest number of terms, and they change most frequently. These terms (given in the appendix) sometimes indicate more particularity in distinguishing techniques of wit and argumentation that might have been used to make the taxonomic chart deeper in the realm of playing. For instance, some communities make a distinction between the *clean* and the *dirty dozens*. By this they mean, in the case of the former, that the joke is directly aimed at one of the others in the interacting group, while the latter directs them at some member of the other's family. Further, there are a number of such *clean* techniques, such as *bragging* or *boasting*, in which the main reference is the speaker, or *charging* and *mounting* in which the other is the target; or the general *capping* remark, which may be a witticism which only indirectly downs the other.

Beyond these distinctions, there are terms (and much discussion) which may refer to such intensification of verbal performances – though they may have reference to non-verbal presentational effects. These are terms like *styling*, *having the flash* (Woodley 1972:11), *styling out*, or *showing out*, which point out dramatically foregrounded presentational techniques; but more often they are concerned more with clothing and hair style than verbal display.

Similarly, if an interaction is regarded as a dramatic success, comment will occur with regard to how someone really got *on someone's case* or *charged all over him*. (Sale 1971:90, 104, has the Blackstone Rangers refer to *getting shot through the grease*.) But if such a strategy fails, the instigator is liable to be accused of being *lame, running off at the mouth, or talking off the wall shit* (not knowing what he is talking about). Since this arises in comment on the informational content of a person's argument, he also may be accused of wanting to appear to be serious but being interpreted as *playing*. In such a context, any of the terms for *signifying* may be used negatively, like *talking shit* (now with an emphasis on the last word) or *woofing*. Older terms are *spouting* and *muckty muck* (Major 1970) and *boogerbooing* or *beating your gums* (Hurston 1942).

Similarly, terms like *jiving* and *shucking* may be used to call someone at a *lame* use of speech. Or if someone begins to *go deep* in an inappropriate context (not with close enough friends, or using techniques of a younger age-set), he may be called on it with an 'I don't play that shit' kind of remark, or 'I laugh, joke, and smoke, but I don't play' (see Abrahams 1970b). On the other hand, if the thrust of the remarks does hit home but they are regarded as inappropriate – an attempt to start a fight – the response will be the slightly different 'You better not play that shit with *me*.'

In such situations, there are a number of disavowal techniques, re-classifying the remarks into the category of *playing*, like 'Man, I was only bullshitting.' This strategy of trying to get out of an uneasy verbal situation in certain cases is engineered by the other as part of his strategy of a *put-down*. In such a case, the speaker seeking an out will have to do the more extreme act of verbal subjugation termed *copping a plea*, *gripping* (Kochman 1970; Sale 1971:43), or the most recently encountered *eating cheese* and *cowdown* (Woodley 1972:143). This most often occurs when someone (or a group) has really gotten *on your case*, or more extremely if you are suspected of wrongdoing, being put *on the square* (Labov et al. 1968).

Perhaps the most important dimension of the discussion on the judgment criteria used with regard to these situated ways of speaking is that one of the best things that can be said of the street talker is that he *comes on baad*. This obvious inversion of the term seems certainly to arise in opposition to the household respectability perspective. It is the expression of this opposition between the two 'worlds' of Black life that presents the largest problem in the description and analysis of an Afro-American world order – the problem of accounting for this high valuation of *baadness*. We know that these values are the opposite of the private respectable world and operate then primarily in the public realm. Furthermore, the recent studies of child rearing and language learning carried on by Young and by Ward indicate that a certain amount of this *baadness* is encouraged among the precocious within the home, with even the baby's first movements being positively interpreted as aggression (Young 1970; Ward 1971). The ramifications of this establishment of the contrarieties between these worlds and the accompanying ambivalent attitude toward public display are only now being noticed and analyzed. But in this area of investigation, I am convinced, lies one of the key dimensions of those role and behavior configurations that will enable us to designate not only the patterns of characteristics of the Black speaking community, but the integrity and uniqueness of Black culture in general.

APPENDIX: THE TERMS

Since the existence of this taxonomy, and the importance of verbal wit in understanding the street world, arose because of the use of terms for ways of speaking in some Black communities, it might be useful to review what these terms are and what speaking strategies and relationships they have been used to name. I will do this in sections, by key terms.

There are certain basic semantic problems involved in such a presentation, however. This is not only because of the number of terms involved, but because the same terms are used in different Black communities at different times to designate different types of speech events. Yet it seems important to present what data are available to demonstrate these problems and to indicate that there is an historical dimension to this taxonomy of ways of speaking.

Signifying

An example of how semantically confusing such a presentation can become can be seen in Kernan's discussion and review of the scholarship concerning the term *signifying*. In *Deep Down in the Jungle*, reporting on Black folklore in one Black neighborhood in Philadelphia, I had heard the term used for a wide variety of verbal techniques united by the single strategy of verbal manipulation through indirection. The examples I reported there, which were quoted by Kernan, were

[an] ability to talk with great innuendo, to carp, cajole, wheedle and lie ... in other instances, to talk around a subject ... [or] making fun of a person or situation. Also it can denote speaking with the hands and eyes ... Thus it is signifying to stir up a fight between neighbors by telling stories; it is signifying

to make fun of the police by parodying his motion behind his back; it is signifying to ask for a piece of cake by saying 'my brother needs a piece of that cake.' (Abrahams 1970b:51–2)

Kernan then notes, agreeing that for most of her Oakland informants 'some element of indirection was criterial to *signifying*,' nevertheless 'many would label the parodying of the policeman's motions *marking* and the request for cake *shucking*' (Kernan 1971:88). It is impossible to judge from her data whether these acts might be both *signifying* (as the general term), and *marking* or *shucking* as kinds of *signifying*, or whether contrast existed among these three terms on the same taxonomic level. For my Philadelphia informants, at least, the former was the case (though the most common term at that time for *shucking* was *jiving*, or, among the older people, *jitterbugging* or *bugging*).

But the labelling problem is even more complicated in Kernan's description of *signifying*; she notes that for Thomas Kochman's Chicago informants, *signifying* and *sounding* are used interchangeably, while most of her Oakland informants 'referred to the direct taunts which Kochman suggests are the formal features of signifying, when its function is to arouse emotions in the absence of directive intent [as in a verbal duelling game] as *sounding* or *woofing*' (1971:89). But, she goes on, using herself as an informant: 'As a child in the Chicago area, my age group treated *signifying* and *sounding* as contrasting terms... *Signifying*... was a fairly standard tactic ... employed in *sounding* (as a verbal insult game). That is, the speech event *sounding* could involve either direct insults *sounds* or *signifying*, indirect insults ...' (pp. 89–90). However, with my Philadelphia informants, *sounding* and *woofing* were commonly used to refer just to the game of mother-rapping, *playing the dozens*. On the other hand, Rap Brown seems to insist on a basic distinction between *playing the dozens* and *signifying*, in which it is clear that the latter means, for him and his peers, what my Philadelphia informants called *mounting* and what Blacks in many parts of the country last year were calling *charging*, *cracking*, or *harping*. 'Signifying is more humane [than *playing the dozens*]. Instead of coming down on somebody's mother, you come down on them' (H. R. Brown 1969:27). He further complicates matters by equating signifying with any kind of intensifying verbal activity (exclusive of the *dozens*), and not just putting someone down, by noting:

before you can signify you got to be able to rap ... Signifying allowed you a choice – you could either make a cat feel good or bad. If you had just destroyed someone or if they were down already, signifying was also a way of expressing your own feelings... Signifying at its best can be heard when the brothers are exchanging tales. (pp. 27–30)

Brown here seems to be setting up some kind of range and hierarchy of speaking events running from the most general term, *talking shit*, anyone's talk from the most casual to the most stylized and witty, to *rapping* or semi-public, spontaneously witty talk, to *playing the dozens* and *signifying*, openly competitive, public, witty, hyperbolic, highly stylized talk (including tales). But the place of *signifying* in this speech map would not be validated by Kernan's (1971) or Kochman's (1970) data, nor mine (see also Mezzrow & Wolfe 1969; Anderson 1959; Milner & Milner 1972; Eddington 1967; Hurston 1935 for more specific uses of the term).

These difficulties are more apparent than real, especially to the ethnographer of speaking. Clearly what we have here are terms which are used on more than one level in a taxonomy of ways of speaking, and which are used in different places and times to describe related but different speaking activities. Further, what I hope I have shown in the taxonomy is that with *signifying* we have a term not only for a way of speaking but for a rhetorical strategy that may be characteristic of a number of other designated events.

Rapping

There are numerous terms to be found for casual talk, such as *beating the gums*, *gum beating*, *jawblock* (Mezzrow & Wolfe 1969). But none of these are place-specific to talk in public. With many informants in the last ten years there has been the feeling that the term *rapping* was the appropriate one for this public (street) talking – a perspective seemingly shared by Kochman when he noted that 'Rapping [is] used ... to mean ordinary conversation' (Kochman 1970:146; see also Keiser 1969: 72; Milner & Milner 1972:306; Claerbaut 1972:77; Woodley 1972:144). But when asked whether terms like *sounding* or *shucking* were a kind of *rapping*, informants' responses are usually an initial giggle and then an 'I guess so.' I think that the reason my informants laughed when I asked them whether such terms are kinds of *rapping* was that while on the one hand rapping means 'just talking,' on the other hand in its most common uses it refers to interactions somewhat less public than the larger *playing* contest activities. That is, *rapping* in its more pointed uses is something generally carried on in person-to-person exchanges, ones in which the participants don't know each other well; it is often therefore a kind of *out of the house* talking which is primarily manipulative.

Kochman, in his full study of the semantic field of the term *rap*, indicates that he has observed three common uses:

(1) When *running something down*, providing information to someone.

(2) *Rapping* to a woman – 'a colorful way of asking for some pussy,' used at the beginning of a relationship only, most used by *pimp-talkers*, *jivers*, the most fluent and lively men-of-words. This use I have therefore included under the concept term of *running a game* (a placing recognized or accepted by every one of my informants).

(3) As the verbal dimension of a *con*, when *whupping the game* (Kochman 1970: 147).

To Hip

Running something *down*, as discussed in the body of the paper, refers to *straight*, valid-information–centered conversations, and may be distinguished from ones in which either *game* is being *run* or *played*. That is, *running it down* commonly means giving advice to someone in a situation in which a decision has to be made, or *hipping* someone to *what's happening*, letting him know of some possible activity or of the doings of others. 'Running it down is the term used by ghetto dwellers when they intend to communicate information, either in the form of an explanation, narrative, giving advice, and the like ... running it down has simply an informative function, telling somebody something that he doesn't already know' (Kochman 1970:154–5, with quotations from King 1965, Claude Brown 1966, and Iceberg Slim 1967). 'Run it down: to tell the whole truth of whatever is in question' (Major 1970:98; see also Killens 1972:24, 41; Claerbaut 1972:78; Milner & Milner 1972: 301, *to run down game*). Once one has had it *run down* to him, he is *down, in the know* (cf. Thomas 1967:210, 243; Milner & Milner 1972:299).

The earlier term, and one which is still widely in use, is *to hip* – 'to inform a person of something he should know; to put [someone] wise' or *to be hipped* (to) – 'informed; hep, knowledge; wise to' (Wentworth & Flexner 1960:258; see also Gold 1960:146; Milner & Milner 1972:302; Claerbaut 1972:68).

The basic distinction here is between the contest-focussed message of *running it down*, *hipping* someone to something, or *hitting on* a given subject, and the style-focussed message of *signifying*, styling which is foregrounded by the devices of making a point by indirection and wit. This is not to say that *running it down* has no style, or *signifying* has no content, but that their primary focus differs in this regard. Note that *signifying* here is designated only with regard to its street uses (see Kernan 1971:87ff for a discussion of sex-specific differences).

Talking Shit

Most *signifying* arising in the street world is of a sort in which the participants in the interaction engage in talk to elicit more talk – to get some *action* going. Witty remarks will be made calling for a response in kind. Though such exchanges often sound like arguments to outsiders, there is no rhetorical intent to create a status distinction.

There are many terms which have been employed for this kind of *signifying* play, *talking shit* seeming to be the most common today. Older terms, some of which are still in use, are *woofing* (though in most communities this refers to more particular events like *playing the dozens* or *sounding*), *telling lies*, *shag-lag*, and *bookooing*. Hurston uses all four terms on this level in her works:

> Woofing is a sort of aimless talking. A man half seriously flirts with a girl, half seriously threatens to fight or brags of his prowess in love, battle or financial matters. The term comes from the purposeless barking of dogs at night. (Hurston 1935:305)

She makes it plain, however, in her numerous *woofing* scenes, that 'aimless talking' means an active display of wits.

The term most widely used now is *talking shit*, at least according to students from all over the country. That it is not just a student term is testified by Killens' use of it (Killens 1972:26, 40), by the Milners (1972:309), and by Major's reference to the expression and by Friedland and Nelkin's reporting of the term from a migratory labor camp in connection with a man-of-words and his abilities to joke and rhyme on people effectively (Friedland & Nelkin 1971:152).

On the other hand, there are types of behavior in which the talker does seek to establish dominance or to *signify* to evade a situation in which he is already dominated. A distinction is made between *putting down* or *low-rating* in which witty devices are used to establish dominance, and *copping a plea*, in which an already dominated person attempts to establish equilibrium by admitting his subordinated status. (Kochman 1970 and Rainwater 1970 both report this term, as well as the less extremely deferential *gripping*; see also Major 1970:41.) Thomas, discussing the strategy, notes: 'Mom was asking us to cop a plea to the white man ... A – accept, B – behave, C – care.' The term also means *to rat on*, inform on (Thomas 1967:134, 243). The most recently reported term (from Texas) for this is *eating cheese*. These terms are of recent usage in this sense, but may inhabit the same semantic field as *tomming*, *jeffing* (cf. Kochman 1970; Eddington 1967) or *playing Uncle Tom* – though in present usage the *tomming* of slaves tends to be regarded as closer to *shucking* in that it uses deference as a means of achieving some sense of dominance, and is therefore one type of *putting on* behavior. In the absence of actual reportings of such behavior labeled as *tomming*, however, I would not so categorize it; it should be noted, however, that the Marster-John stories (Abrahams 1970a) represent similar accommodative strategies in narrative form to *tomming* (cf. Kochman 1970:149).

Putting on involves the entire range of strategies for verbal manipulation to establish control. Essentially the term refers to 'play-acting for real,' using any of the devices of playing but in a situation in which eventually a psychological dominance is sought by the speaker, even if the person (or persons) being *put-on* doesn't recognize this. *Putting on* therefore involves a use of any of the strategies in one or another of its manifestations. As *running a game* or *whupping game* (cf. Kochman 1970; Milner & Milner 1972:301; Claerbaut 1972:65, 78, 86) it will actively involve all three – deference, dominance, and parity. With other *put-on* styles, the range is not so wide. *Putting on,* in any case, emphasizes the dominance strategy, and would have been regarded as a special kind of *put-down* except that my informants in both Philadelphia and Austin insist that a *put-on* is not a *put-down* but something quite distinct.

The difference is primarily in regard to where the speaker stands in regard to those he wishes to dominate. With a *put-down*, the dominance is already apparently felt, the speaker ratifying the relationship with each *put-down*. With a *put-on*, the dominance is not yet established; thus the speaker needs a less tendentious mode of asserting control, using a wide number of artful talking techniques. That there is a strong relationship between the two is indicated by the recognition by street talkers that some of the techniques of *putting* someone *on* can also be used to *put* them *down*.

Put Down

There seems to be a basic distinction between the *put-down* style that relies on sharpness of perception and verbal focus and one in which the speaker gets louder and louder. This distinction is noted by communities most commonly when *loud-talking* is regarded as an inappropriate way to achieve a put-down. Hurston (1934) defines *loud talk me* in her glossary as 'making your side appear right by making more noise than the others,' but her use of the term in the novel is pejorative (p. 158). On the other hand, Heard gives us a *loud-talking* scene, using the term in which our response is intended to be ambivalent. In this use of the technique by a pimp, he uses a proverb, 'Talk loud and draw a big crowd' (1968:227; this use of the term differs from its employment in the *put-on*; see below).

Mounting, downing (Abrahams 1970a; Eddington 1967:198), and *ranking* are the same terms as used in one form of *playing the dozens*; the relationship is hardly fortuitous, for the same verbal devices are used in the *put-down* for serious purposes and in the *dozens* for play. In this serious interpersonal context, when the *mounting* is extended and one person is strongly *put down*, that has been called *getting on his case* or *charging* – though *downing* is not the only technique used in such situations.

Put-On

Loud-talking (or *louding*) (in a different meaning than above) and *marking* are two special techniques of achieving a *put-on*. Both involve a performance not overtly directed to the object of the remark. *Louding* is where the speaker is talking to others (or himself) loud enough so that the person referred to can hear – but when that person reacts, the speaker can reply to the effect 'Oh, I wasn't talking to you.' To be pulled off most effectively, the 'overheard' remark must refer to the overhearer in some oblique way. (Kernan 1971 gives an extended description, pp. 129–37, as do Labov *et al.* 1968:*passim*, but esp. pp. 14ff and 27ff) Mezzrow & Wolfe (1969) report the practice, perhaps in a more formal game context, as *snagging*. My informants agree that this is a way of *putting* someone *on*, but many argue that it may be a *put-down* as well. Kernan's examples would seem to argue the same way.

Marking, on the other hand, in its largest sense is simply the Black term for dramatic imitation or aping. It is not always used pejoratively. However, when the imitation is addressed to others than the person imitated, and especially when it is done in his presence but without his recognition, this is regarded as a *put-on* device. (*Marking* in the larger sense of imitation can be found in any verbal interaction as an intensifying device, especially in jokes and *getting on* someone's *case*. Kernan surveys the technique and its uses [1971:137–43]). In the case where *marking* is used as a *put-on* device, it too can turn into a *put-down*.

With *running a game* we are in a domain of street performance in which verbal manipulation is central (see Killens 1972:*passim*, but esp. pp. 22ff; also Milner & Milner 1972:301; Claerbaut 1972:65, 78, 86). Here the speaker uses as many techniques as possible to convince his target audience of the validity of his credentials, so that he may exploit them for sexual favors, money, or simply to enhance his reputation. With professional men of words, the *pimps, jivers, mackmen*, etc., *running* some sort of *game* is a constant preoccupation. Other men share in this to the extent that they have the ability to use their words to assert and maintain their *rep*.

There are many terms for running a game, all more or less synonymous. One term commonly used for this domain is *talking bullshit*. Claude Brown describes his persuasive powers of performance using this term:

> When Dad tried to talk to me, it never work out... It was easier for me [to get hit] than trying to listen to all that stupid shit he was telling me with a serious face. Sometimes I would bullshit him by looking serious and saying something that made him think he was saying something real smart. I had a special way of bullshitting everyone I knew, and that was how I bull-shitted Dad. (1966:45)

Kochman's discussion of *rapping* describes that term as the most casual dimension of the *gaming* complex of terms (see also Suttles 1968:159; Milner & Milner 1972:306; Claerbaut 1972:76). *Jiving* and *shucking* seem to refer to more intensive *rapping*, with an accompanying growth in the amount of purposeful deception involved in such talking. Both of these are complicated terms historically and semantically. *Jive* and *jiving* used to mean simply the argot of the young Blacks on the street (see, e.g., Hurston 1942) and *jive-talk* was still used in this sense until recently. But because of the types who had greatest command over this style of talking, *jive* and *bulljive* came to be used in more and more pejorative contexts, as they are today (Strong 1940; Major 1970; Grange 1968; Rainwater 1970; Gold 1960; Claerbaut 1972; Milner & Milner 1972). The negative features fastened upon are an overstress on *styling* (obviously *styling* which doesn't come off) or too much emphasis on dominance at the expense of the parity strategy implied in *rapping*. Mezzrow and Wolfe make a distinction between *jive* and *high-jive*, the latter involving the use of 'fancy-talk,' a variety more commonly found in the semi-private courtship situation: 'High-jive: intellectual patter, the smoothest and most elaborate line. Highjiver: smooth character with a very fancy and intellectual line of talk' (1969:306).[3]

Shucking and *jiving* are often used as one term. *Shucking* is also used to refer to any kind of name-establishing *bullshit*, though not so strongly focussed on knowledge of the in-group terms as *jiving* (see Abrahams 1970b, though the etymology for *shucking* there is faulty, as it is in Gold – the base reference of the term almost certainly goes back to a corn-shuck, either in regard to the practice of the corn-shucking performance gathering or to the expression 'lighting a shuck,' i.e., using a burning shuck for light for some peer-grouping activity [cf. Hurston 1934:206]; Rainwater 1970:284; Kochman 1970; Cain 1970; Milner & Milner 1972:307; Claerbaut 1972:79; Killens 1972:25, 141).

Shucking, where it is used, refers to the artful means by which one person can get around another by whatever means he can devise. It therefore involves more devious means than *rapping*, especially as Kochman explores the two terms:

> *Shucking, jiving, shucking and jiving* or S-ing and J-ing, when referring to language behavior practiced by blacks when interacting with one another on the peer-group level, is descriptive of the talk and gestures appropriate to 'putting someone on' by creating a false impression, conveying false information, and the like. The terms seem to cover a range from simply telling a lie, to bullshitting, to subtly playing with someone's mind. (1970:154)

This use of *shucking and jiving* differs in white – Black interactions only in the actual techniques used, not in the motives or intensity.

More intense and indicating deceit are terms like *hyping* and *conning*, but these are less often used in reference to in-group street-talking activity, and more in commentary on effective talking by some of their members in interactions outside the group (Mezzrow & Wolfe 1969:306).

Hoorawing

Hoorawing, an active contest of wits in which everyong may join, is the most volatile of all the categories for ways of speaking. It is known by a number of terms even within the same community. *Hoorawing* or *talking hooraw shit* seem to be the oldest terms here according to my older informants in both Philadelphia and Texas. Other names are *signifying* (Kochman 1970; Rainwater 1970), *joning* (Hannerz 1969; Rainwater 1970), *screaming, ranking, cracking, snapping, sounding* (Thomas 1967; Labov *et al.* 1968; Abrahams 1970b), *woofing* (Abrahams 1970b), and *telling lies*. The practice is commonly carried on in trading short formulaic items, but among adults often includes the longer narrative items like *jokes, toasts,* or *stories*. Hurston's books, especially *Mules and Men* (1935), eloquently describe this practice and with many texts. The importance of this kind of verbal play is discussed throughout the literature (see especially Hannerz 1969; Labov *et al.* 1968; Rainwater 1970; Abrahams 1970a,b; Kochman 1970). The larger term for this kind of *play* is *cutting contest* (see, for instance, Mezzrow & Wolfe 1969: 1971) and, by extension, a friend with whom one can *play*, a *cutting buddy, cutting man,* or *cutty* (Abrahams 1970b).

As Rap Brown pointed out, a distinction is often made between verbal contests involving insults to members of the families of the other contestants and those which aggrandize or deprecate in other ways. Explicitly or implicitly, there are further distinctions made in the playing of the clean dozens: to devices which are *lies* about oneself (whether they are aggrandizing of self doesn't seem to matter – if they are exaggerations they may be termed *bragging*, even if the content is about how poor or hungry or thin you are); to devices which wittily discuss the shortcomings of others, sometimes referred to as *mounting*; and simply witty remarks which build upon the word-play of others, *capping*. (Abrahams 1970d; Eddington 1967:198; Claerbaut 1972:60; Mezzrow & Wolfe 1969:304 define it as 'having the last word, go one better, outdo,' but their use of the term indicates a speaking frame of reference primarily.)

Boasting seems to mean intensive talk about oneself in a contest situation, whether one is emphasizing one's strengths or shortcomings. Thus, there may be exchanges based on how quick one is, how strong, or how hungry, lazy, tired, or whatever. (The same witticisms may be used to discuss someone else, in which case they are noncompetitive devices simply used to flavor conversational discussions.) These self-aggrandizing devices are also called *lies*, though that term is generally used for stories, jokes, and tall tales.

Dick Gregory, in his book *Nigger*, shows how important it was in learning how to cope with the realities of street life (and how he developed his comic sense) to learn a repertoire of these self-degrading *boasts*, by which he could capitalize on an underclassed position, building it into a strength (Gregory 1964:40–2). The technique emerges in many other works by Black authors.

More commonly, such *hoorawing* takes the form of *mounting*, attacking the other(s) by denigrating them. This may be done either by boasting at the same time or just *putting* the other *down*.[4]

NAMAKKE, SUNMAKKE, KORMAKKE: THREE TYPES OF CUNA SPEECH EVENT

JOEL SHERZER

Cuna society (in both San Blas and the interior Darien Jungle) is striking for vitality and richness in speech usage.[1] From a formal or ceremonial point of view, there are many genres of speaking – chiefs' chants which deal with history, politics, and religion; formal speeches which are uttered by official and non-official individuals; long *ikar* which are used to cure diseases, hunt animals, make fermented drinks, and direct girls' puberty rites; and secret charms which enable an individual to have power over another individual or an object in nature. There is also a rich variety of non-ceremonial or colloquial genres – animal and plant stories, comical songs, lullabies, riddles, and linguistic games. Speaking ability at any level (from colloquial and conversational to formal and ceremonial) is highly valued and is a source of personal prestige among the Cuna.

It is not the purpose of this paper to deal in detail with all Cuna genres of speaking but rather to describe three basic patterns found in Cuna speech events and to discuss the constellations in speech usage that are associated with each of them. The three patterns are expressed most clearly in

1. the chanting and talking that occurs in the centrally located village congress house;
2. curing and related *ikar*;
3. *kantur ikar* which occurs during girls' puberty rites.

The three patterns will be investigated by means of descriptions of the events, focusing especially on the addressor, addressee, and the linguistic variety. It will be shown that the most important distinction between congress events on the one hand and curing and girls' puberty rites events on the other involves the role of individual creativity and flexibility in speech usage. In congress events, chanters and speakers creatively adapt their speech to fit particular situations. This individual flexibility does not exist in curing and related *ikar* or in *kantur ikar*; performances of each of these are fixed and predetermined.

From the Cuna point of view, in their ceremonial performances, a chief in the congress *namakke* 'chants,' a person who knows curing texts *sunmakke* 'speaks,' and a *kantule* (the central figure at girls' puberty rites) *kormakke* 'shouts.' The Cuna word which refers to a particular text (conceived as known but not as written) in any of these three basic genres is *ikar*. *Ikar* means 'path' or 'road' in both the concrete sense of a path in the jungle or village and the figurative sense of a way of life. But it also refers to particular texts and to verses of these texts. Thus congress chants about God are called *pap ikar* 'god's way'; about the Cuna ancestors, *tatkan ikar* 'the ancestors' way'; etc. Similarly, there are curing *ikar*, such as *kapur ikar* or *kurkin ikar*. Finally, in girls' puberty rites, there is *kantur ikar*.

Since the Cuna themselves use *ikar* to refer to particular texts, I will also use this term here. It avoids the confusing use of English terms such as chant, which from the Cuna point of view is a mode of channel use or a means of performing, or text, which tends to imply something written, either by natives or by outside investigators.

Congress events

The speech event characterized by the chanting of chiefs in the central congress house is called by the Cuna *konkreso* 'congress,' *namakke* 'chanting,' *onmakke* 'performing or publicly gathering,' *sakla namakke* 'chief chanting,' or *omekan pela* 'the women and everybody,' each term referring to a different aspect of the event. It occurs about every other evening; it may, however, occur with greater or lesser frequency, according to circumstances which will be discussed below.

Towards sundown, the men and women of the village begin to gather in the congress house. After the handling of such village business as communal work tasks, public discussion of some wrongdoing, and advice (*uanaet*) to a wrongdoer, the central or major event of the evening – the chanting by a particular chief – begins. This chanting, together with an interpretation by a chief's spokesman (*arkar*), lasts several hours.

The seating arrangements for such evening *konkresos* is significant. There are two chiefs who sit in hammocks, their feet hanging on either side of the hammock and barely touching the ground. In Cuna, this position is called *nai* 'hanging.' One of the chiefs chants (*namakke*) and the other responds (*apinsue*). There must be at least two chiefs present in order for the event to occur at all. A chief cannot chant without an *apinsuet* 'responder.' And the *apinsuet* must be another chief. One or several other chiefs generally *mai* 'lie' in other hammocks strung parallel to those of the chanter and the responder. But the non-participating chiefs might also be seated, along with the *arkars* on the *arkar* benches on either side of the chiefs' hammocks. The *arkars* sit on the *arkar* benches. A few other village officials sit here too. These include the first chief's secretary, policemen, and especially respected medicine men. The women and their young children sit on benches around the central hammocks and *arkar* benches. Very young children soon go to sleep on blankets or mats, which are stretched on the ground in front of the women. If babies cry during the congress proceedings, they are carried outside by their mothers or older female relatives. The men of the village sit on the very outer rows of benches surrounding the women. The individual seating arrangement is not random; everyone always sits in the same place. These seats are not formally assigned by anyone, but have developed over the years.

It is interesting that the congresses in which chanting occurs are thought of as being especially for the women. Women do not attend other congresses. In the chanting congresses they literally surround the chanting and in turn are surrounded and seemingly protected by the men. The arrangement is as in Fig. 14.

The chanting portion of the congress is as follows. When all other business is done, the chanting chief and the responder sit up in the required position. The chanter very softly begins to chant. At the end of each verse (*ikar*) the responder chants a stretched-out *teki* 'thus, it is so.' As the chanting begins, several 'policemen' call out *kapita marye* 'don't sleep,' *nue ittomarye* 'listen well.' These policemen's calls are repeated periodically throughout the chanting, but not during the subsequent *arkar* interpretation. As the chanting continues it becomes progressively louder and ideally the chief is literally booming out his verses once the chant gets into full swing. The chant lasts between one and a half and two hours and termin-

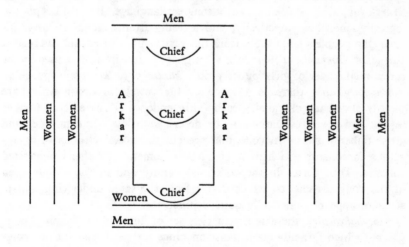

Fig. 14

ates with the chanting chief suddenly lowering his voice. When the chanting is over, the chanting chief and the responder lie back in their hammocks in the *mai* position. Then one *arkar* stands up to interpret the chant that has just been performed. His interpretation lasts about one hour. When he finishes he says *itto markua* 'you have heard,' marking the ending of a formal speech.

The subject matter of the chant and its interpretation is historical, political, and religious – the three woven together to varying degrees. The degree to which history, politics, or religion is stressed depends on the region (section of San Blas or of the interior jungle), the 'intellectual' tradition the chanter belongs to (who his teachers are), and the personal choice of the chanter himself. Thus a chant might deal with the great Cuna seers (*neles*) – their lives and their relationship to Cuna history; or it might recount the history of Bolivar and Columbus in the new world; or again it might discuss something that happened on another island several days before and how it can be interpreted as a signal of events to come.[2] A major function of all of these chants is social control – individuals are encouraged to behave properly and according to Cuna traditions. The chants remind them at length of these traditions. Ancient traditions and history, religion (both Cuna and Christian), recent local events, etc. are all transformed and suitably related to particular immediate social problems and concerns. This feature of congress chanting – the transformation and adaptation of material to fit particular situations – is the defining characteristic of congress speech events in general and will be discussed at greater length below.

The linguistic variety employed in congress chants is called *sakla kaya* 'chief's language' or *konkreso kaya* 'congress language.' It is distinct phonologically, morpho-syntactically, and lexically from colloquial Cuna (*tule kaya* 'the people's language'), from the variety used in curing and related *ikar* (*suar mimmi kaya* '*suar mimmi* language'), and from that used by the ceremonial leader of girls' puberty rites (*kantur kaya* '*kantule* language').

Phonologically, there is a tendency for vowels to occur which are usually elided in colloquial speech. This tendency is carried even further in the two speech situations to be described below – curing rites and girls' puberty rites.[3] In colloquial speech, the vowel elisions bring together consonants which undergo further, sometimes rather complicated changes. Thus forms in the colloquial variety and in the variety used in the congress chants, which derive from the same underlying source, at times appear phonetically quite distinct.

Morphologically, there is first a rich set of 'linking' or 'framing' morphemes which formally mark clause openings and closings. All Cuna ceremonial genres have an elaborate set of such morphemes; there is some overlap across genres but for the most part each genre has its own set. Second, there are a large number of nominal and verbal prefixes and suffixes which are used only in congress chanting or, if they do occur in colloquial speech, have much more limited distribution than in congress chanting. Once again, each genre has its own set of such affixes, with some overlap among genres. These affixes will not be discussed here; to do so would require the presentation of a rather involved analysis of the Cuna linguistic system.

Syntactically, the congress chants make use of very few transformational operations which zero out noun phrases and verb phrases; in fact the verses consist of utterances which are kernel-like in structure.[4] There is considerable repetition of the same noun phrases and verb phrases and in general a system of striking grammatical parallelism operating throughout the chants.[5] One important result of this pattern of repetitions and parallelism is increased length of the chant as a whole. In fact, all of the phonological and morpho-syntactic devices discussed here – retention of underlying vowels, extended use of special affixes, proliferation of 'linking' morphemes, and grammatical parallelism – operate together in maximizing the length of the chant. It is noteworthy then that actual length of performance is one of the esthetic criteria by which the Cuna judge speaking ability in general and individual speakers or performers in particular.[6]

Lexically, there are certain words which are used in congress chants which do not occur in colloquial speech or which have different meanings in colloquial speech. Examples are *tuttu* which means 'flower' in colloquial speech and 'woman' or 'child' in congress chants, and *tulepiiti,* a word not found in colloquial speech and which refers to Panamanians and Colombians in congress chants.

The linguistic characteristics just described are exemplified in the following portion of a congress chant. The chant deals with the ancestors of the present inhabitants of the San Blas village of Mulatuppu and this particular section describes the plants and animals provided by God for these people. It is especially representative of the types of grammatical parallelism caused by the repetition of noun phrases and verb phrases. In the cited forms, vowels which are elided in colloquial speech are placed in parentheses, affixes which are used especially in congress chanting are placed in brackets, and 'linking' words and morphemes are underlined.[7]

Chanting chief:

we yal(a)se   pap(a) [l] anparmial(i)mar[ye] sokel ittole eka   masmu[l]
this world   God   that he sent us   for him banana root
akk ᵂekar[ye]   oparye
in order to care for
'God sent us to this world in order to care for banana roots for him'

Responding chief:
teki   'it is so'

Chanting chief:
eka[l]   inso tark^{w}amu[l] akk^{w}ekar[ye]   *sokel ittolete sunna ipiti oparye*
for him   taro root   in order to care for
'in order to care for taro roots for him'

Responding chief:
teki   'it is so'

Chanting chief:
al inso   eka [l] wakup tula[l] akk^{w}ekar   *sokel ittole al ipiti oparye*
          for him yam living   in order to care for
'in order to care for (living) yams for him'

Responding chief:
teki   'it is so'

Chanting chief:
al inso   eka[l]   moe   tula[l] akk^{w}ekar   *sokel ittole al ipiti oparye*
          for him squash living in order to care for
'in order to care for (living) squash for him'

Responding chief:
teki   'it is so'

Chanting chief:
al inso   eka[l]   osimu[l]   akk^{w}ekar   *soker ittole pap(a) [l]*
          for him pineapple root in order to care for   God
anka[l] yal(a) [l] uksamar[ye]
to us   world   he gave us
'in order to care for pineapple roots for him God gave us this world'

Responding chief:
teki   'it is so'

Chanting chief:
pap(a)   yannu   kalukan(a) urpis(a)[ye] an soke aal akk^{w}ekan
God   wild boar strongholds he left   in order to care for
nonimar an soke
we came
'God left wild boar strongholds; we came in order to care for them'

Responding chief:
teki   'it is so'

Chanting chief:
pap(a)   moli kalukan(a) urpisa takle an soke ka[l]   akk^wekan
God   tapir strongholds he left   for him in order to care for
nonimar [ye] an soke
we came
'God left tapir strongholds; we came in order to care for them for him'

Responding chief:
teki   'it is so'

Chanting chief:
pap(a)   wetar   tula   urpisa takleye an soke al
God   wild boar living he left
akk^weka   nonimar[ye] an soke
in order to care for we came
'God left (living) wild boar; we came in order to care for them'

Responding chief:
teki   'it is so'

Chanting chief:
pap(a)   us(u)   tula[k^wa] urpisa takle an soke al akk^weka
God   agouti living   he left   in order to care for
nonimar[ye] an soke
we came
'God left (living) agouti; we came in order to care for them'

Responding chief:
teki   'it is so'

I have described here some of the more salient features of the linguistic variety used in congress chanting. But the primary or defining characteristic of this genre is the development of metaphors – established themes which are repeated, built on, and elaborated in detail. It is especially this aspect of congress chanting which the audience does not understand and which must be interpreted for it afterward by the chief's spokesman (*arkar*). An example is the use of terms about weapons such as rifles to refer to natural elements such as thunder. Or the comparison of the architectural structure of a Cuna house with the political structure of Cuna society. More elaborate examples and particularly examples which demonstrate the way in which these metaphors are appropriately developed to fit particular situations will be given below as part of the comparison of the three basic types of Cuna speech event.

Congress chanting takes place in most villages every other evening. It also occurs when a chief from one island visits another island for one or more days or when many chiefs from different islands gather together on a particular island for several days ('traditional congresses'). In both of these instances, the visiting chief or chiefs spend all of their time (except for eating, sleeping, and some visiting with friends) in the congress house. Present with the honored visitor(s) are one or more host chiefs, village officials, and other men. Upon the arrival of such a visiting chief the congress is opened and the visitor performs a long greeting – arkan kae – with one of the host chiefs. Arkan kae is chanted and makes use of the same linguistic variety used in congress chanting. It also resembles congress chanting in that while one of the two greeting chiefs namakke 'chants,' the other apinsue 'responds' – teki 'it is so.' However in arkan kae the two chiefs reverse this situation several times. Furthermore, there is no arkar interpretation and no fixed audience. People come and go during the chanting and often the women of the village bring in beverages which the chiefs and others present drink, briefly interrupting the ceremony in order to do so. During their stay on an island visiting chiefs usually chant every night and sometimes in the morning as well. In 'traditional congresses' each of the visiting chiefs has a turn to chant and there is chanting from early morning until noon and then again from early evening until late at night. Such chanting has the structure that has already been described above for ordinary congress chanting.

Another congress speech event, in some ways quite different from chiefs' chanting, is speech-making. Speech-making occurs either in the congresses described above with men and women present and before the chanting begins[8] or in congresses attended by men only and in which there is no chanting. Speeches, which are performed in colloquial Cuna but in a special speech-making style, deal with a range of topics: communal decisions about village political and economic matters; transgressions that have been committed – deciding who did them, what penalty to assign, etc.; advice to a wrongdoer (sometimes as his sole punishment); general advice to an entire village concerning proper behavior or to particular persons about the performance of their roles; and reports by individuals or groups concerning work or duties performed, trips made, or events witnessed. Individual and communal advice is given by chiefs. The advice is then usually interpreted and elaborated on by arkars. Interpretations often involve the creative and flexible adaptation of metaphors described above for congress chanting. Speeches by individuals other than congress officials are directed at the center of the congress, the place in which the chiefs lie and the arkars sit. The village officials are the immediate addressees and the other men and/or women present constitute the audience. All speech-making is characterized by length and individual development and creativity.

I have thus described one type of Cuna speech event, which is most clearly and formally structured in ceremonial congress chanting but aspects of which are also present in congress speech-making. Basically it entails four participant units – addressor, addressee or responder, interpreter, and audience. There is first a performance by the addressor and then an interpretation by another individual. In congress chanting, the addressor and responder are both chiefs. Their roles are each named – *sakla* 'chief' and *apinsuet* 'responder'; as is that of the interpreter – *arkar* 'chief's spokesman.' In congress speech events – chanting and speech-making – texts are not fixed but rather there is a great deal of individual creativity and development, most notably in the form of the adaptation of metaphors to immediate situations and social problems. In a good performer, such as a well known chief, the metaphors are so intricate and involved that most members of the audience do not understand them. This focus on individual creativity in speech use contrasts sharply with the use of speech in the two other speech situations to be discussed – curing rites and girls' puberty rites.

Curing events

Cuna diseases are cured by means of both medicine (*ina*) and language, usually in combination. There is a rich medicinal tradition and in each village there are many specialists in pharmaceutical medicines (*inatulet*). In addition to medicine, curing *ikar* are used for a large variety of diseases and afflictions, such as difficulty in childbirth, madness, great fever, severe headache, shortage of natural ability (*nika*), and epidemics. All of these *ikar*, with the exception of *apsoket ikar* 'the way of the mass or epidemic curer' have the following speech event structure. The sick person lies in his hammock in his house. Under the hammock is a box of wooden dolls called *suar mimmi* 'stick babies' (also called *suar nuchu* 'stick dolls'). It is these dolls which carry out the actual business of the curing. But in order for them to do their work, they must first be told how to do it. This is achieved by means of the appropriate *ikar*, which is performed by an individual who is named for the *ikar* he knows – *muu ikar wisit* 'knower of *muu ikar*' or *muu ikar tule* 'muu ikar man' (named for *muu ikar*, which is used to aid women having difficulty in childbirth); *kurkin ikar wisit* 'knower of *kurkin ikar*' (used in curing severe headaches); etc. The *ikar* knower sits on a stool in front of the *suar mimmi*. The *ikar* is thus not aimed at the sick person but rather at the *suar mimmi*. In terms of the components of speech (see Hymes 1972), the addressor is the *ikar wisit* '*ikar* knower' and the addressees are the *suar mimmi*. The sick person is not an active participant in this event. He is usually asleep or lost in suffering. It is even possible that he is not present.[9] In any case it is rare that the sick person understands the special linguistic variety which is used in these *ikar*.[10] Other individuals who are present in the house may listen but they generally go about their business and talk among themselves. Thus within the single setting, house, there are two speech events taking place − the curing *ikar* and ordinary conversation.

The *ikar* generally lasts about one and a half hours. It deals with the origin of the disease in question and the sorts of things that must be done in order to cure it. Depending on the type of disease and its course, the *ikar* is repeated several days in succession. Each time, the knower enters the house, sits down in front of the *suar mimmi*, performs the *ikar*, and then gets up and leaves.

It is important to point out the major characteristic which differentiates the curing *ikar* from the congress *ikar* which were described above. This is that in the congress, the *ikar* is followed by an interpretation for the audience of men and women. The interpretation stresses the fact that the audience is not a mere audience but the ultimate and crucial addressee of the message of the *ikar*. This audience must not only listen but understand the *ikar*. It is for this reason that the *arkar* explains what the chief has just chanted. In curing *ikar*, there is no audience − just addressor and addressee. The addressor is the knower of the *ikar* and the addressee, the *suar mimmi*. There is no interpretation and there is no need for one according to Cuna theory, since the *ikar* is performed in a linguistic variety which the *suar mimmi* understand − *suar mimmi kaya* 'suar mimmi language.' It is interesting to note, however, that although most persons present during the performance of a curing *ikar* do not understand or even pay attention to the referential aspects of the *ikar*, they are no doubt aware of its social and stylistic properties. In this sense, in their status as 'nonknowing auditors,' they help to validate its medicinal efficacy and social importance.[11]

There are a number of Cuna speech events which, while they are not curing events *per se*, are quite similar to curing events in their structure. Furthermore, the linguistic variety employed in these events is identical to that of the curing *ikar* − that is, *suar mimmi kaya* (with the exception of certain *ikar*-specific lexical items which in fact can be noted for curing *ikar* as well). First there is *ina uanaet* 'advice to medicine,' which is performed by *inatuleti* 'pharmaceutical medicine specialists' to their medicine (the addressee) in order to give it life and to counsel it. *Ina uanaet* describes the origin of the medicine and its purpose. Although there are established objects of medicinal value − plants, tree bark, etc. − it is possible to *uanae* 'advise' any object and thereby give it the power of medicine. Then there is *apsoket ikar*, which is used in mass or epidemic curing and to exorcise unpleasant spirits. Since there is not in this case a single sick person but rather many with more expected, i.e., the disease is all over the village and perhaps several villages, the *ikar* is not performed within a single house. Instead it is performed in the central congress house by one or several mass curers (*apsoketi*). But once again the *suar mimmi*, in this case very large ones, are the addressees. That is, as in the other curing *ikar*, the addressor is the *ikar* knower and the addressee, the *suar mimmi*.

Another *ikar* of this type is *masar ikar* 'the way of the *caña brava* (a type of bamboo)' which is performed after a person's death.[12] The *masar ikar* knower begins his performance in the house of the deceased and continues along with the corpse until it is placed in its mainland grave, all the time performing this extremely long *ikar*. The addressee of *masar ikar* is in this case the *masar* '*caña brava*.' As in curing *ikar* there is no interpretation; the *masar* perfectly well understands the linguistic variety addressed to it.

A similar structure is found in *pisep ikar* 'the way of the *pisep* (a medicinal plant)' which is used to render someone an efficient hunter. A fragrant solution consisting of *pisep* and other ingredients is prepared; in this solution the prospective hunter will bathe. But first *pisep ikar* must be performed by its knower. It is the *pisep* plant which is the addressee; this *ikar*, like *ina uanaet* and *masar ikar*, is in a linguistic variety which is essentially that of the curing *ikar* – *suar mimmi kaya*.

There are other *ikar* which are performed in the *suar mimmi* variety and which have as addressees such objects as snakes, bees, etc. Finally, there is a series of *ikar* whose addressee is *inna* 'chicha' (the fermented drink consumed at girls' puberty rites). These *ikar* are used to make the drink stronger, to sober up the performer, etc. They are performed by the knower either in the presence of the *inna* or else in the knower's home. In either case, the *inna* listens and understands the *ikar*; there is no interpretation.

The curing and related *ikar* sound to my non-Cuna ear as if they are chanted. The Cuna, however, say that they are *sunmakke* 'spoken,' when they are performed for their primary and ceremonial purpose – advising medicine, curing a disease, aiding a deceased person on his path through the other world, rendering a person an effective hunter, etc. They may be performed for other purposes as well, however, in which case they are *namakke* 'chanted.' The principal difference between the *namakke* 'chanting' and *sunmakke* 'speaking' of these *ikar* is that in *namakke* the performer *wai sae*, i.e., tenses his voice by means of pharyngeal tightening. *Wai sae* is not done, however, in the *namakke* of congress *ikar*. (*Sunmakke* and *namakke* are modes of channel use in the Hymes 1972 framework.) The other purposes for which curing and related *ikar* might be performed (and in which they are *namakke*) are teaching (by a knower to a student), practicing (by a knower or a student), or personal pleasure (for example during the festivities associated with girls' puberty rites).[13]

Suar mimmi kaya carries the phonological tendency already noted for *konkreso kaya* to an even more conservative degree, i.e., underlying, abstract vowels are practically always retained in those linguistic environments in which such retention is possible.[14] Morphologically, there is a set of affixes characteristic of this variety, some but not all of which are also found in the *konkreso kaya*.

Syntactically, and similar to *konkreso kaya*, there are few transformational operations which zero out noun and verb phrases. Each 'verse' of an *ikar* is short and kernel-like in structure. As in *kongreso kaya*, repetition of noun phrases and verb phrases is used in systems of grammatical parallelism throughout each *ikar*.[15] It is in the lexical realm, however, that curing and related *ikar* are most distinctive. There are many lexical items that are used only in curing and related *ikar*; i.e., not in *konkreso ikar* or *kantur ikar* or in colloquial speech. These tend to fall into certain semantic fields – kin terms, body parts, celestial bodies, natural elements, animals and plants, disease terms, and movements of persons and things. There are also lexical items which are specific to individual *ikar* or even to a particular tradition (version) of a single *ikar*.

A portion of *kurkin ikar* (used in curing severe headaches and in improving brain power) illustrates the characteristics of *suar mimmi kaya*. This *ikar* calls on particular trees (by addressing itself to *suar mimmi* made of these trees) to use their strength to aid the ailing individual. The cited section describes the roots of these trees. Vowels which are elided in colloquial speech are placed in parentheses, affixes which are used especially in curing and related *ikar* are placed in brackets, and lexical items particular to *kurkin ikar* are underlined.

<u>kurkin</u> ipekan[ti][ye]   [olo]pillise   <u>pupawal(a)</u>kan akku(e)k^wic(i)[ye]
trees   to the level of gold roots   reach
'trees, your roots reach the level of gold'

<u>kurkin</u> ipekan[ti][ye]   [olo]pillise   pe   maliwaskakan upo(e)k^wic(i)[ye]
trees   to the level of gold your small roots   are placed
'trees, your small roots are placed into the level of gold'

<u>kurkin</u> ipekan[ti][na][ye]   [olo]pillise   pe   maliwaskakan(a)
trees   to the level of gold your small roots
piokle[ke]k^wic(i)[ye]
are nailed
'trees, your small roots are nailed into the level of gold'

<u>kurkin</u> ipekan[ti][na][ye]   [olo]pillipi[ye]   ap(i)ka(e)k^wic(i)[ye]
trees   the very level of gold are resisting
'trees, within the very level of gold you are resisting'

kurkin ipekan[ti][na][ye] [olo]pilli   aktikkimakk(e)kʷici
trees   the level of gold weigh a lot
'trees, you weigh a lot in the level of gold'

kurkin ipekan[ti][na][ye] [olo]pilli   kʷamakk(e)kʷici
trees   the level of gold are firmly placed
'trees, you are firmly placed in the level of gold'

kurkin ipekan[ti][na][ye] [olo]pilli   aktitimakk(e)[kʷa]kʷic(i)[ye]
trees   the level of gold are moving
'trees, you are moving in the level of gold'

kurkin ipekan[ti][na][ye] [olo]pillipi[ye]   kin(a)ka(e)kʷic(i)[ye]
trees   the very level of gold are accumulating
'trees, you are accumulating within the very level of gold'

As in the congress events described above, metaphors are also prominent in curing and related *ikar*. Thus in *kurkin ikar*, hat is used to represent the head or the brain; women's beads, a tree's fruit; and the level of gold, great depth in the ground. In *pisep ikar* the movement of the *pisep plant* in a box and its exit from the box symbolize the birth and thus the origin of this plant. However, in sharp contrast to congress events, the metaphors employed in curing and related *ikar* are not elaborated and developed by the *ikar* knower. Rather, they are fixed in each *ikar* and are repeated identically in each performance of the *ikar*. In fact, the entire *ikar* is fixed and pre-determined.[16] In this respect, of course, curing *ikar* are strikingly different from congress chanting and speaking which are characterized by individual creativity and development. I will discuss this contrast in greater detail below after describing a third Cuna speech event type – that associated with girls' puberty rites.

Girls' puberty rites

When a Cuna girl reaches puberty, her hair is ceremonially cut. It is worn short for the rest of her life. If he chooses to and if he can afford to, the girl's father provides food for village-wide puberty rites.

The puberty rites are the only occasions during which Cuna individuals are permitted to drink alcoholic beverages. When it is announced that the time for these rites has arrived, the men of the village go to the mainland and gather sugar cane, each man being required to return with a required amount. Then the cane is squeezed into juice and, under the direction of an expert in such matters, the fermented drink *inna* 'chicha' is prepared. When it is decided that the *inna* is strong enough, the rites begin. They may last one, two, or three days, according to the particular type of *inna* 'chicha festival' that is being held.[17] A special house (*surpa*) is built for the young girl in question and she is placed within this enclosure, only her head above ground. Her hair is cut according to prescribed techniques by the ceremonial cutter (*iet*), who is a woman, and her assistants, who are also women. The *surpa* is located outside the large chicha house (*inna neka*) in which the festivities occur. These festivities include various games and dances which are performed only on these occasions.[18]

Central to the whole affair is the performance of the *kantules* and their assistants, who alternate lying in a centrally placed hammock, two at a time, and shout (*kormakke*) the very long *kantur ikar* 'the way of the *kantule*,' which describes in detail the entire ceremonial proceeding – preparing *inna*, hair cutting, etc. While the *kantules* and their assistants shout, they shake rattles and play a long flute (*kammu*). (The *kantule*'s name derives from this flute – *kammu* 'flute' + *tule* 'man' > *kantule*.) The simultaneous shouting, rattle-shaking, and flute-playing; the required inebriated state of the performers; and the general noise level of the surrounding festivities within the *inna neka* render it extremely difficult to listen to and understand the words of the *kantur ikar*. But it turns out that no persons are trying to listen to this *ikar* nor is it intended for them. It is rather the *kammu* 'flute' which is the addressee of the messages 'shouted' by the *kantule* and his assistants. *Kantur kaya* 'kantule language,' the linguistic variety used in this event, is shared by the *kantule* and the *kammu*. Apart from the *kantule* and his assistants (the addressors) and the *kammu* (the addressee), there are no other participants in this event. There is no audience (the persons present are involved in other activities) and there is no interpretation – none is needed for the sole addressee, the *kammu*. As in the curing *ikar* discussed above, however, the persons present can be viewed as 'non-knowing auditors,' aware of the social and stylistic significance of the *kantule*'s *ikar*, but not its referential details.

As stated above, the *kantur ikar* is *kormakke* 'shouted' during the chicha festival proceedings. Like the curing *ikar*, however, it is *namakke* 'chanted' during teaching and practicing sessions. In these sessions, the *kammu* 'flute' is not involved.

Phonologically, *kantur kaya* resembles *suar mimmi kaya* in the retention of underlying, abstract vowels. Morphologically, it makes use of a set of affixes, some but not all of which are also found in other varieties. Syntactically this variety resembles the other ceremonial varieties in its short, kernel-like sentences and overall grammatical parallelism. Once again, it is particularly in the area of lexicon that *kantur kaya* distinguishes itself from the other varieties. It contains a large number of lexical items which occur only in it, i.e. not in colloquial speech, congress *ikar*, or curing *ikar*. The lexical items specific to *kantur kaya* are for the most part related to the puberty rites – participants, the drink, places, time of day, etc. Most important from the perspective of the theme which I am presenting in this paper, *kantur ikar*, like the curing *ikar* and distinct from congress events, involves an absolutely fixed text; there is no individual alteration or creative development of themes and metaphors. *Kantur ikar* is ideally performed identically each time.

I have discussed the general characteristics of three types of Cuna speech event:[19]

1. the chanting and speaking which occurs in the central *onmakket neka* 'congress house';
2. medicinal and related *ikar*;
3. kantur *ikar*, which occurs at girls' puberty rites.

The defining components of these events are outlined in Table 9.

From the Cuna point of view, congress chanting and speaking, curing *ikar*, and *kantur ikar* constitute three distinct ceremonial traditions. The linguistic varieties used in each share some characteristics, namely phonological conservatism (from the perspective of a set of ordered rules from underlying, abstract forms) and syntactic or grammatical parallelism caused by the retention and repetition of noun and verb phrases (rather than their disappearance through transformational operations).[20] The three varieties are distinguishable primarily on the basis of the lexical items which are specific to each. From the lexical point of view, it is also possible to subdivide each of these traditions or speech event types – according to both individual *ikar* and particular subtraditions (geographic and personal).

In addition to lexical specialization, the major difference between congress events on the one hand and curing and puberty rites events on the other is the kind of linguistic ability and competence required. In curing and puberty rites events, no individual linguistic creativity is permitted. Each *ikar* is required to be performed identically each time.[21] Individuals who want to learn *ikar* study with knowers (*wisit*), the knower chanting a section and then the student repeating. This student–teacher relationship continues until the student is able to perform an exact replica of his teacher's *ikar*. At this point the teacher announces to an evening congress that his student has 'graduated', i.e., that he is now a knower of the particular *ikar*. Similarly with regard to *kantur ikar*. It must be learned exactly as performed by the *kantule*. And when the *kantule* feels that his student can perform the *ikar* word for word, exactly as he himself does, he announces this fact in an evening congress and declares that his student is now also a *kantule*. These 'graduations' are formal affairs; they involve a long speech in the congress describing the learning process and, often, a written letter of graduation, which is read and shown in the congress. Congress events

TABLE 9

Setting	Linguistic variety	Modes of channel use	Addressor	Addressee
1. Congress events Congress house				
a. chief chanting or speaking	konkreso kaya	namakke, sunmakke	Chief	Responding chief and audience
b. arkar interpreting	Colloquial (arkar speech-making style)	sunmakke	arkar	Audience
c. speech-making	Colloquial (speech-making style)	sunmakke	Speech-maker	Village officials and audience
2. Curing and related ikar Private house	suar mimmi kaya	sunmakke/ceremonial performing; namakke (wai sae)/teaching, learning, practicing, performing for pleasure	ikar visit	suar mimmi, medicine, caña brava, snake, etc.
3. kantur ikar inna neka 'chicha house'	kantur kaya	kormakke/ceremonial performing; namakke/teaching, learning	kantule and assistants	kammu

are quite different. Each *ikar* and each speech in the congress is new and different; it is not intended to be an exact replica of previous performances. In each performance the chief or speech-maker draws on established Cuna themes and metaphors and develops them to fit the particular situation at hand. For example a common theme in congress chants and speeches is the comparison of women and children with flowers. A chief who is a good speaker develops this theme in his performance. He may for example chant at length about all the different types of flowers in the Cuna environment, how they grow, how they smell, what they look like, how they are cared for, etc. In all of this he will never explicitly state that the flowers represent women and children. It is the task of the *arkar* who interprets the chief to explain to the audience the subtleties of the chant; for example, that each flower represents a type of woman or child and that the entire chant was about the details of women's duties and proper behavior in the raising of children. It is important to stress that such chants are aimed at the audience and intended to instruct them. Since the more involved the development of metaphors, the more difficult it is for the audience to follow, the *arkar*'s role of interpretation is a crucial one.

Another example of the development and especially of the creative adaptation of established themes and metaphors occurs in the advice (*uanaet*) given to a new chief. This is performed by an incumbent chief and is either spoken or chanted. Some of the metaphors which occur here are the representation of different individuals in Cuna political structure by the various poles in a Cuna house, of chiefs by powerful trees in the jungle, of criticism of chiefs by members of the community by the throwing of mud balls and darts, and of a chief's needed ability to hold his temper by a large trunk in which he can store things.[22] Each new performer of this *uanaet* then has a range of possibilities at his disposal; these involve which metaphors he selects, the order in which he develops them, and the detailed ways in which he develops them.

Especially characteristic of the individual creativity involved in congress events is not only the selection of appropriate metaphors and themes, but their adaptation to particular situations. This occurs in chiefs' chanting and speaking, in *uanaet*, and in arguments and speeches. My first example is from a speech given by a chief as an *uanaet* to a newly selected chief.[23] The context is as follows. It is the opening evening of a 'traditional congress' on the island of Tuppak. The island has chosen a new chief and it is the task of the chief who has been selected first chief of the 'traditional congress' to advise him. The newly selected chief had been a chief once before but was removed from office for misbehavior.[24] Thus he is being reinstated. The spoken *uanaet* is as follows. The chief discusses the building of a house. He says that sometimes, after you have built a house, the *puar* 'central post,' although it appeared to be strong, turns out to be rotten and does not support the house. So it must be removed and not used for a while. The rotten part must be cut away and the pole must be watched to make sure that all of the rotten part has been eliminated. When it is certain that the pole is free from rot, it can once again be used as the central post of a house. This discussion of the central post of a house derives from the political structure metaphor mentioned above. But here it is creatively developed by the speaker in order to render it perfectly appropriate to the situation at hand — the reinstatement of a chief who is basically good (i.e., he knows the required Cuna traditions) but who had made some mistakes and therefore had to be removed from office for a while.

My next example involves a case of social control in the San Blas mainland village of Karetto.[25] During the day most of the men of the village had been off working in the jungle. One of the men who stayed behind took advantage of the situation and played around with a wife of one of the absent men. He was caught and, as is typical in such cases, the matter became the subject of a lengthy discussion in the evening's congress. The man in question defends himself as follows. He gives a long, involved, and expressive speech in which he says that he had been off in the jungle working as usual and became very hungry. He came across a ripe pineapple which belonged to another man. Since he was hungry and since the pineapple was ripe, he ate it. The speech, with its highly developed metaphor, suspensefully and expressively presented and elaborated, is greatly appreciated, and the man is pardoned.[26]

Speaking and Cuna roles

There are many Cuna roles which are specifically and explicitly defined with reference to speech. A chief (sakla) is a man who knows Cuna traditions well, can speak and chant them at great length, and can develop them appropriately to fit situations. A chief's spokesman (arkar) also knows traditions and furthermore is able to listen to a chant or speech and, without knowing its content in advance, interpret it on the spot for an audience. Arkars study with chiefs and good ones eventually become chiefs. The various curing and related ikar knowers achieve their role through the perfect memorization of a particular ikar. Similarly, the kantule knows perfectly the long kantur ikar. Each such role is conceived of as discrete. Thus a man may be a sakla and a kapur ikar wisit or an arkar and a kantule, etc.[27] A chief is not a better chief because he happens also to be a kapur ikar wisit. Rather he is a chief and a kapur ikar wisit — two distinct roles. This concept of discrete roles is made explicit in the Cuna notion of kurkin, which can be translated roughly as 'ability.'[28] Each ability is a separate *kurkin.* Thus a man who is a chief and a *kapur ikar wisit* has two *kurkin.* A man who is an *arkar,* a *muu ikar wisit,* and a *kantule* has three *kurkin.* Of course it is prestigious to have many *kurkin* but it must be stressed that these *kurkin* do not accumulate into a single multifaceted role; they are always kept quite distinct.[29]

The ideal representative of a particular role is quite a different person depending on the type of speech event he is an expert at. A *kantule* or a knower of a curing *ikar* is an individual who has great powers of memorization. He is able to repeat word for word long *ikar* each time the *ikar* is performed. The Cuna recognize this ability and refer to such individuals as people with great memories. On the other hand, a chief is an individual who, although he must also have good memory in order to remember Cuna history and traditions, must be able especially to apply appropriately, creatively, and flexibly these traditions to particular social and political problems that arise in the village. Individuals who hold several roles may have both sets of abilities. Often, however, they are particularly good at one but only average at another. Thus a well known Mulatuppu ceremonialist knows more than ten different curing *ikar*; he is also a respected *inatulet* 'specialist in pharmaceutical medicine.' And he is an *arkar*, having been chosen for this role because of his knowledge of Cuna traditions. However, he is not a particularly effective *arkar*. He does not speak very loudly or forcefully, desired characteristics in congress events but not in curing and related *ikar*. Nor does he often stand up in the congress and make long speeches appropriate to particular situations, as do good chiefs and *arkars*. But he does have an extraordinarily good memory and has a busy schedule of cases in which he is called upon to perform for sick individuals.

In conclusion I have shown that speaking is central to the definition of the major roles in Cuna society – chief, chief's spokesman, various curing and related *ikar wisit*, and *kantule*. But the definition or conception of speaking is different for the different roles. There are basically two constellations:

1. Knowledge of Cuna traditions and ability to apply these traditions (as well as other material – experiences, anecdotes, stories, etc.) creatively to specific situations in appropriate ways. This constellation of speaking is associated with the two primary roles in the Cuna congress – *sakla* 'chief' and *arkar* 'chief's spokesman.' It is also associated with speeches by any individual in the congress.

2. Absolute, complete, perfect, word-for-word memorization of particular *ikar*. This constellation of speaking is associated with two different Cuna traditions – curing and related *ikar* and *kantur ikar* – and their respective specialists.[30]

It is interesting to relate the two constellations of Cuna speaking and three speaking traditions to the three main aspects of Cuna social life.

1. Politics. For the Cuna, politics is an ever-changing dynamic area involving the complications of relations with a nearby government (Panama), economic relations with Panamanian and Colombian traders, comings and goings of Cuna men (to and from Panama City, the Canal Zone, and United Fruit plantations in the province of Bocas del Toro), intimate interisland relations, intraisland problems (cooperative economic ventures, stealing, etc.), and so forth. All of these political questions are handled in the evening congresses – spoken and chanted. They require individuals who are flexible and good at quickly maneuvering in order to meet new demands and situations. The creative flexibility–adaptation associated with the speaking constellation used in congresses thus matches Cuna political requirements.[31]

2. Curing and 3. Girls' puberty rites and consummation of chicha (*inna*). The interwoven medicinal and religious aspects of curing rites and the ancient ceremony of girls' puberty rites do not allow for any flexibility whatsoever but rather demand absolute adherence to fixed forms, which have been passed down through generations. In these events there is power in the word as long as it is in no way altered.

Thus, although it is correct to say that speaking is important to the Cuna and central to their social life, it is essential to point out that there are two basic and contrasting constellations of speaking, each associated with different types of speech event, with different ceremonial traditions, and with different roles in Cuna society. The Cuna themselves are aware of this richness and complexity of their speech usage and are extremely proud of it.[32]

13

THE CONCEPT AND VARIETIES OF
NARRATIVE PERFORMANCE IN EAST
EUROPEAN JEWISH CULTURE

BARBARA KIRSHENBLATT-GIMBLETT

Oyf a mayse fregt men kayn kashe nit
(Yiddish proverb)

Informants' statements, memoirs, previous studies, and collectors' comments in the introductions to their published materials show a remarkable consistency in their insistence that narration is a cultural focus in east European Jewish society (Gross 1955:10, 11; Olsvanger 1965:xxii–xxiii; B. Weinreich 1957:145, 151; Ravnitsky 1922:iii–iv; Schwarzbaum 1968:88; Holdes 1960:4–5; Bialostotski 1962:158). From the statements examined, the following emerges:

1. Stories are important and storytelling is frequent in this culture.
2. This has been the case from time immemorial. The Aggadah, the stories (and other non-legalistic materials) in the Talmudic-Midrashic literature, and the fame of ancient saints and sages as narrators are often cited as evidence of the antiquity of the Jewish penchant for narration.
3. Everyone can tell stories.
4. There are no professional storytellers who are hired for the sole purpose of telling stories.
5. Stories may be told at almost any time.
6. There are no 'public performances' for the sake of storytelling alone.
7. Jewish narrators are specialists in parables and jokes.

These notions are prevalent in both academic and non-academic circles and are accepted here as representing this society's own view of its narrational habits.

Yiddish terms are available for distinguishing types of storytelling acts (following Hymes' [1967] terminology): *dertseyln a mayse* (tell a story); [1] *zogn a vits* (say a joke); *gebn* or *brengen a moshl* (present a parable), and other formulations. But when talking about the larger unit of discourse of which the storytelling act is a part, one does not usually refer to stories or narration. Stories are told during *shmuesn* (conversing, chatting), *lernen* (teaching, studying), a *droshe* (sermon), *batkhones* (improvisation of the pro-

283

fessional wedding jester). Nor is a story told in conversation distinguished terminologically from the same story told in a sermon even though the two performances will differ. The terms for story-telling acts and those for speech events appear to be autonomous, that is, speech events that contain stories are not distinguished terminologically from those that do not and story-telling acts are not distinguished terminologically on the basis of the speech event in which they appear. Most important, the discriminations which *are* made by the terminology are consistent with the fact that storytelling is not scheduled as an activity in its own right but always seems to occur as part of another activity. This would suggest that *conceptually* storytelling is subordinated to these other activities even though in *practice* narration is known to dominate encounters, in cases where people spend more time telling stories than doing anything else.

Consistent with this pattern of subordination is the absence of professional storytellers. Although there are certainly individuals who are expert and respected raconteurs, no one gets paid specifically for telling stories, that is, there are people who are narrative specialists without being professional narrators. Preachers and wedding jesters are paid for preaching and merrymaking respectively and in performing their services they tell stories. But they are not hired as storytellers. Furthermore, preachers such as the Dubner *maged* and *rebes* or religious leaders such as the Bal-shem-tov, who are famous as brilliant storytellers, as heroes of cycles of tales, and as the originators of many tales, are preachers and *rebes* first and great storytellers second. Similarly, their stories are a means which they use to serve their goals as religious leaders, teachers, and upholders of the righteous life. Their stories are not usually ends in themselves.

Furthermore, the telling of stories for their own sake runs counter to the professed speech ideals of the community and is therefore inappropriate for the *lamdn* (scholar, learned man, Talmudist), who is expected to express these ideals. In contrast, indulging in narration for its own sake is anticipated from people of lower status such as women, lower-class men, and deviants, for example, pranksters. Women are expected to gossip, to engage in idle talk, to talk all at once, to talk excessively, and to tell stories both to make a point and for their own sake. This pattern is more clearly realized among the lower-class women, especially, for example, among the fishwives in the markets who are famous for their curses and rude speech. Bialostotski's memory of the narrational habits of his grandparents is instructive here.

I never heard a single anecdote or fairytale (*maysele*) from my grandfather. I also never heard a single Yiddish song from him, of course. He was totally immersed in Halakah (the legislative part of the Talmud or rabbinical literature, as opposed to Aggadah), Shulhan Aruk (the collection of laws and prescriptions governing the life of an Orthodox Jew), restrained piety, praying, prayers, Torah (Pentateuch). But my grandmother, she implanted the Yiddish folk tune in me; she told me a fairytale; she asked a riddle, and while speaking to people, freely uttered proverbs and witticisms.

Was my grandmother an exception then? Many grandmothers and mothers were like this. (1962:164, my translation)

Like Bialostotski's grandmother, lower-class men, who are not very learned, and pranksters, who are considered deviants, are expected to indulge in narration for its own sake. Various regions have their favorite pranksters, the most famous of whom are Hershele Ostropoler, Shmerl Snitkever, Yosl Marshelik, Shloyme Loydmirer, Motke Khabad, Froyim Greydiger, Shayke Fayfer, and Leybele Gotsvunder (Holdes 1960:6–7). Many of these pranksters actually lived even though a lot of tales told about them are apocryphal. They are the heroes of cycles of anecdotes concerning the jokes they actually played and clever things they said. They are also famous as witty anecdote tellers in their own right (Ravnitsky 1922:vi) and some of them were professional wedding jesters (*batkhonim*) (see Bialostotski 1962:224).

Therefore, with the exception of the Hasidim who encouraged the telling of rounds of saints' legends and pious tales as an activity in its own right (see Mintz 1968:4), indulging in narration for its own sake ostensibly runs counter to the speech ideals of the community as exemplified by the very learned men, who, when they do narrate, prefer to tell a story to make a point. Prayer and learning are supposed to occupy them, especially in the *besmedresh* (prayer and study house), and they are expected to give the study of Halakah, the legal part of the Talmud, precedence over Aggadah, the stories and other non-legalistic material in the Talmud. Ideally, then, taletelling is subordinated to other kinds of discourse rather than indulged in for its own sake. In practice, however, people do engage in storytelling sessions to a greater or lesser degree, depending on subculture, social class, sex, and individual preference or inclination.

Descriptions of actual storytelling performances, both from informants and from published sources, indicate that narration is not an undifferentiated domain. My observations of Jewish immigrant narrators in Toronto at present are consistent with these descriptions. It emerges that there are various types of speech events in which stories play an important role and though not defined by the society in terms of storytelling, these events may require that stories be told, may be dominated by narration, will be structured so as to accommodate taletelling, and will influence the form of the narrative performance.

My aim, then, will be to characterize storytelling in east European Jewish culture of the late nineteenth and early twentieth centuries, particularly in tradition-oriented circles. An examination of descriptions of actual performances will help to clarify the relationships between ideal and real behavior, between terminology and the ways in which people talk about narration on the one hand and the forms storytelling events take, on the other. The discussion will proceed from the least to the most formal types of narration and will conclude with a comparison of formal and informal storytelling with special reference to the parable. The aim of comparing a parable told in a formal sermon with one used in informal conversation will be to show how the speech event affects the structure of the narrative performance. The data are of necessity drawn from a variety of sources: previously published ethnographies of traditional Jewish life in eastern Europe at the turn of the century, memoirs and autobiographies, the observations of Yiddish folktale collectors and scholars, and my own fieldwork in 1968–71 among Jewish immigrants in Toronto who were asked to describe narration in the Old World and who were also observed in spontaneous performances. Biographical data on the informants are provided in the appendix to this chapter.

Social settings for narration

The major settings for storytelling are the same as those for daily activities: the home, the schools, the synagogue and the *besmedresh*, the Hasidic court, the places of work and business, especially workshops, stores, and the market. Other settings which are associated with storytelling are travel (both walking and riding in a wagon) and involuntary communities (hospitals, army). Life in tradition-oriented circles entails a strict separation of the sexes and a clear definition of the domains appropriate to each. Appropriately, whereas women do much of their storytelling at home to other women and to children, men do much of their narrating to other men in the *besmedresh* where they gather several times a day for prayer. Most important for storytelling is the time at twilight between the afternoon and evening prayers (*tsvishn minkhe un mayrev*) when the men are waiting for the sun to set so that they can say the evening prayers. Both sexes have occasion to narrate in the course of their daily business activities in shops, markets, and on the streets.

Life in all settings is qualified by the distinction between 'everyday' and 'special day.' The Sabbath and holidays associated with the calendar year and life cycle constitute 'special days.' The normal proceedings of everyday life are suspended and other activities take their place, among them storytelling. These are occasions when sustained narration may occur because of the leisure time created by the suspension of work, school, and other everyday preoccupations.

Informal storytelling in dialogue

The most informal and most common type of speech event, one in which stories are a regular and expected part, is *shmuesn* (chat, converse). This may explain why, in answer to my question, 'When do people tell stories?' an informant said, 'There is no set time for telling a story. It just happens when it occurs to someone' (Informant 1; my translation). As Beatrice Weinreich notes in her pioneering discussion of the occasions for narrating Yiddish folktales about the prophet Elijah, 'Since in this culture, stories are so frequently made use of as illustrations to conversational subjects, stories are employed by adults at any time' (1957:151).

Despite its pervasiveness in social interaction, informal storytelling may be differentiated on the basis of whether or not stories are told for their own sake or to make a point, whether or not stories told for their own sake dominate the encounter, and whether or not the participants take turns at narrating. Four types of informal storytelling emerge: story as gloss, single story as topic, storytelling round, and storytelling solo. After describing each type as it is realized in east European Jewish culture, I will compare the four types in order to clarify the distribution of the distinguishing features and discuss why it is that more combinations of these features are theoretically possible than are actually realized.

TYPE A: STORY AS GLOSS

Several narrators whom I questioned expressed the view that although stories can be told outright, they are much more effective if they are used as a gloss on the immediate conversation or social interaction; 'A story is fine, but one that is used at the right moment is even better' (see also Gross 1955:7). Since a full discussion of the structure of parable narration in conversation will figure in the comparison of informal and formal storytelling below, the account here will be confined to the markers which are used to signal that a narrative example will be told and the standards of excellence for this type of narration.

If a tale is being used as a gloss, it is characteristically prefaced with a formula on the model of *dos folk zogt a moshl* (the folk says a parable), *faran a moshl bay yidn* (there is a parable among Jews), *der besht git oyf dem a moshl* (the Bal-shem-tov tells a parable about that). Such formulas as *mayn mame flegt zogn* (my mother used to say) and *mayn tate hot lib gehat tsu zogn* (my father liked to say) do not include the word *moshl* but are other options for introducing a proverb or a parable or a performance which includes both (see Gross 1955:11). Variations on these opening formulas are consistent in citing a prestigious source for the parable, be it the Bal-shem-tov or some other famous sage, or in establishing the traditionality of the parable by attributing it to Jews in general or one's parents in particular.

Traditional tales, both those told for their own sake and those used as illustration, typically begin with *a mol iz geven* (once there was), *in a shtetl iz geven* (in a *shtetl* there was), *iz a mol gekumen* (once [someone] came), and similar formulas, usually followed by an enumeration of the characters in the tale (see also B. Weinreich 1957:115–18). *Mesoyres* (legends) can also appear in conversation as topic or gloss and are generally marked in some way as true, *un dos is a mayse-shehoye* (and this is an actual occurrence).

Norms of interpretation and standards of excellence specifically for stories used as a gloss are recognized both by traditional Jewish narrators and by writers on the Yiddish folktale:

I remember how in a conversation Shmarye Levin narrated a folk witticism which was wonderfully fitted to the matter with which we were dealing. When everyone had finished laughing and wondering at his astuteness, one person remained cold and untouched. 'I have already heard this story,' he exclaimed with disappointment. Only when the crowd had left, did Shmarye Levin become furious in front of me. 'What does he mean? Am I a storyteller (*mayse-dertseyler*), a joker (*vitsnmakher*), who entertains the audience? How can a person not understand that the most important thing is the "application" (*'aplikatsye'*), the application (*onvendung*), the fitting [of the story] to the matter being discussed?' (Elzet 1937:11–12, my translation)

Although Levin is stating as a general principle that the art is in the application of the story and not in the story itself, a view often expressed by my informants as well, the listener who infuriated him was at fault for evaluating this particular performance as a 'story in itself' type and requiring that the tale be novel rather than as a 'story as gloss' type which should have been appreciated for its appropriateness. That the proper standard by which to evaluate a parable performance is appropriateness is further indicated by the currency of such traditional retorts as *der moshl past zikh vi a patsh tsu a gut shabes* (that parable is as appropriate as a smack [in reply to] 'good Sabbath') or *a moshl kegn di nekhtike varenikes* (a parable appropriate to yesterday's stuffed dumplings).

The story as gloss is important in the context of learning dialogues as well. As Schauss points out, 'The rebe, as the melamed was called, was not content with translating the Bible. The literal meaning of the words was not the major importance. The rebe had to amplify and interpret the words according to the explanations of the Aggadah of the Talmud and Midrashim' (Schauss 1950:106). The Aggadah is composed in large measure of stories. Shtern believes that 'there existed a kind of tradition of pedagogy orally transmitted which passes from generation to generation in the families of teachers and the sons of teachers as a collection of textual readings in the form of short aphorisms and tales' (Shtern 1950:84, my translation).

TYPE B: SINGLE STORY AS TOPIC

Informants, while valuing parables more highly and mentioning them more often when asked about storytelling, do recognize that a story also figures in conversation as topic in itself: 'When people get together, they have to talk about something. One person tells a story' (Informant 1, my translation). Although 'It just happens when it occurs to someone' (*ibid.*), stories which are preformulated and relatively self-contained must be integrated into the non-narrative discourse of which they are part. There are several options for accomplishing this. Glossing, as discussed above, is one. Another is for the story to serve as a continuation of a line of thought already established by the preceding discourse: 'I have seen your phonograph machine, this one here, and I am reminded of a true story (*mayse-shehoye*) from several decades ago ...' (Rechtman 1958:250, my translation). Similarly jokes may be introduced in connection with an ongoing topic: *dos dermont mikh in a vits* (that reminds me of a joke). Or the story can serve to initiate a new conversational topic. When there is no clear connection between the story and the ongoing conversation, the narrator can avoid being accused of a *non sequitur* by framing his narration with comments which indicate that he is aware that his story is 'off subject' and which tell his listeners that they should *not* look for any connections between his story and the topic of the immediate conversation: *nekhtn hob ikh gehert a sheynem vits* (I heard a good joke yesterday). If it is not clear that the story is being told as a topic in its own right and without connection to what was being discussed, the speaker may be reprimanded: *tsu vos iz dos shayekh* (what is the connection)? Such comments indicate that a speaker respects the logical organization and thematic unity of discourse and either tells a story which is on subject, waits until people exhaust a subject and then initiates a new topic by telling a story, or pardons himself for disrupting the focus of conversation. Interestingly, once one person has taken the liberty to tell a story for its own sake, the chances are good that a round of stories will ensue, although the participants have the option of returning to the topic of conversation which the story may have interrupted or continuing the subject introduced by the story or starting a new topic altogether.

The story told for its own sake also figures in the *rebe's* and *melamed's* discourse in *kheyder* where it serves to refresh the interest of the children they are teaching. Shtern explains that 'when the *rebe* was in a good mood, he used to tell a story from time to time' (Shtern 1950:48, my translation), usually stories about Jewish wise men and heroes. Informant 1 remembers his Hasidic *melamed* using stories in a similar fashion to break up long stretches of concentrated learning: 'He rests a little and he tells the children a story and all the children listen to the story. They are interested. And after the story the children feel like fresh people. These stories make the children want to learn, make them want to run to school' (my translation). One of Shtern's teachers was in the habit of beginning teaching by drawing a deep pinch of snuff, telling a joke or funny tale, taking another pinch of snuff and only then beginning the lesson (Shtern 1950:80). Schauss also notes that the *rebe* occasionally told the children stories which were not directly connected with the Bible and Talmud (1950:106). Nonetheless, the consensus is that these teachers were far more likely to use stories as examples to illustrate points in the lesson.

TYPE C: STORYTELLING ROUND

In addition to the sporadic appearance of stories in conversation, many reports attest to the prevalence of storytelling rounds, even though the very learned, who in point of fact are in the minority, would tend to dissociate themselves from them. By far the most frequent time for telling stories in the round form is the hour of twilight each day. In the *besmedresh* storytelling is a favorite daily pastime before and after prayers, but especially at twilight after the afternoon prayers have been said during the hour the men wait for the evening prayers to begin (*tsvishn minkhe un mayrev*). The *besmedresh* is the center of male activity in the *shtetl*. Any time of the day or evening a quorom can be found there and by late afternoon the place is full of men who come to say the afternoon and evening prayers. While the men wait for the sun to set, they discuss community matters, study, chat, and tell stories (see Shtern 1950:98). Young boys who are not in *kheyder* at the time might play around and behind the oven and are constant listeners to the various stories told there (see Shtern 1950:114). Many of the tales narrated by one of my male informants, particularly the saints' legends, were heard at these times. When travelling, he would come to a strange town and in order to make himself known, he would immediately go to the *besmedresh* where he would participate in the prayers and engage in the storytelling. Being a stranger, he brought fresh tales which were well appreciated.

Virtually everyone I asked about storytelling mentioned the time *tsvishn minkhe un mayrev* as an important occasion specifically for storytelling rounds:

[The men] sat in the synagogue, and ... finished praying *minkhe*. As they waited for *mayrev*, they gathered themselves around a table there, people gathered around. People started to tell tales. Stories were told. This one tells such a story and that one tells such a kind of story. (Informant 1, my translation)

During this time, children in *kheyder* were left alone, and while waiting for their teacher to return after the evening prayers, they told stories for their own sake and took turns at narrating:

There are pleasant hours at the kheyder also, especially the hour of twilight. Each afternoon the *melamed* goes to *shul* for afternoon and evening prayers, lingering between the two short services to chat with the men he meets there, so that in all he is away about an hour. In winter, the school is dark by this time and candles are too expensive to waste during the melamed's absence. The children sit in darkness, close together on the benches at the table where they study, or huddle near the oven for warmth . . .

Above all, this is the hour for stories. Crowding together against the winter cold and the fear of the wonders they are describing, they tell each other tales in which themes carried over from pagan myths jostle with folklore rooted in the Talmud. In the melamed's absence the strict program of Hebrew erudition is broken into by a medley that mingles biblical miracles with the spirits and demons shared by all the folk, Jews and peasants alike. The boys tell each other in turn about the spirits who throng the shul after midnight, and the tricks they play on anyone who has to sleep there – so that a beggar would rather sleep on the floor of the humblest house than enjoy the honor of a bench in shul (Zborowski & Herzog 1962:91)

This description of the setting in which children customarily exchange stories is corroborated by several of my informants as well.

In these story-dominated events, there is a preoccupation with narratives as things in themselves. For this reason and because the narratives are pre-formulated and relatively self-contained (they can be understood without reference to any preceding conversation or narration), there is a tendency for story-dominated events to be organized like beads on a string. Free association, one story triggering the recall of another, is an important organizing feature of these events. In addition, there are two other principles at work. First, there is the tendency for a series of stories belonging to a genre or cycle or pertaining to a particular theme or hero, to be told in succession until no more can be recalled or interest flags. Second, there is sometimes a building of intensity to climactic points, as competitive narrators vie with each other and try to top each other's jokes or as the tellers of saints' legends and their audience become caught up in the spirit of the tales they are narrating.

When examining the ways in which informants talk about these story-telling rounds, it is important to note that firstly, despite the fact that tales become the dominant mode of discourse, they still talk about what they are doing as *shmuesn*, as *farbrengen* (have a good time), as *tsuzamen kumen* (get together), and even refer to narration as *zikh durkhshmisn mayses* (to have a chat consisting of stories). The fact that a round of stories occurs apparently does not change the definition of the speech event. It is still *shmuesn*. The only difference is that instead of one story being told, several are told: *me dertseylt a mayse* (a story is told) or *me dertseylt mayses* (stories are told). There are no superordinate narrative performance categories. To indicate the dominance of narration one simply uses the plural to indicate that more than one story was told. Although it is possible to inventory the times when storytelling rounds are likely to occur (see B. Weinreich 1957:145ff), it is sufficient here to note that anywhere and any time people spend enough time together to feel they need to pass the time, to be sociable, to talk about something, stories are likely to be told one after the other with people taking turns at narrating. Typically, these occasions occur during social visits, holidays, especially the Sabbath afternoon, rites of passage, during tedious or repetitive work, while travelling, or while confined, for example, in a hospital. When asked about occasions for narration, my informants specified these settings and indicated specifically that *rounds of tales were told by the various participants*: 'After bar mitzvahs. People make weddings. People get together. People chat a little. One tells this story. One tells that story. And so it goes' (Informant 1, my translation). Conceptually then, storytelling rounds are an extension of the telling of a single tale in conversation rather than a special kind of speech event.

In the cases discussed so far, 'leisure' and 'sociability' appear to be the prerequisites for storytelling rounds. As Ravnitsky put it, 'when ... Jews meet each other for no particular purpose ...' (1922:iii). However, in Hasidic circles, this type of storytelling event – storytelling is the dominant mode of discourse and people take turns at narrating – is institutionalized and has acquired a sacred character. For the Hasidim, storytelling is very closely associated with the Sabbath ritual and with anniversaries celebrating the day upon which a famous *rebe* died:

> Storytelling won an established place in the life of the earliest hasidim and it became part of the Shabbes ritual. On the Shabbes, the men met three times to pray and to share communal meals. At those times, particularly at the third meal when the Shabbes was waning, the Rebbes often wove their teachings into an extended metaphor or parable or told an illustrative tale. The hasidim added a fourth communal meal, the melaveh malkeh, at which it became customary to gather at the Rebbe's table to hear stories of hasidic saints and sages...
>
> ... Tales are exchanged casually at the besmedresh or in any social situation, but storytelling has also maintained its unique ritual significance, and so the hasidim 'in the New World' continue to gather to tell stories on the yohrtsait 'anniversary of the day of death' of the Rebbes and at the melaveh malkeh at the close of the Shabbes. These gatherings may be held in the besmedresh or shtible or in someone's house. As in the past hasidim partake of a simple meal of rye bread, herring and onions, salt, fruit, potatoes, and tea. Brandy, often homemade, is offered, and blessings are exchanged; the singing is strong. The association with the Shabbes strengthens the sacred character of the storytelling, as in the tales themselves the mere mention of the Shabbes renews a chain of associations – the fellowship, the special dishes, and the meetings with the Rebbe.
>
> ... The Rebbe also leads the storytelling. If the Rebbe is not present, an honored elder or a learned visitor may be called on to begin the evening with a tale. The

storytellers usually vary. One story recalls another and the tales range from miracles to humorous anecdotes.

... During and after the telling of tales there is conversational byplay, with the Rebbe sometimes commenting on the deeper or the more obscure meaning of the tales. Questions are raised and alternatives are discussed. (Mintz 1968:4–5)

This description of the Hasidic Sabbath storytelling session makes it clear that storytelling is the *dominant* but not the only mode of discourse. In the case of this institutionalized storytelling occasion, there are a greater number of restrictions than in other instances of this type. The time is set – the *melave malke* or the anniversary of the death of a *rebe*. The preferred genres are pious, didactic tales, especially parables and tales about great sages and saints. The order in which people narrate is specified – the *rebe*, an honored elder, or learned visitor begins the narrating though the narrators vary.

The dominance of the storytelling notwithstanding, however, even the *melaveh malkeh* storytelling sessions among the Hasidim are not defined in terms of storytelling but rather are still defined in terms of *shmuesn, lernen, farbrengen*, although much narrating is not only expected, but required.

TYPE D: STORYTELLING SOLO

Just as storytelling rounds are an extension of the telling of one tale in conversation so too are solo narrative performances. Instead of people taking turns at narrating one person does it all. But rather than having the character of the formal monologues performed by the *batkhn* and *bal-darshn*, who get paid, who only perform under very special conditions at a pre-established time and place and for a very limited range of occasions, the solo narrations are considerably more casual and depend upon the availability and willingness of a gifted storyteller who can sustain a whole encounter with his recounting. If such an individual is present then his solo performance simply constitutes yet another option for accomplishing *shmuesn*. Were he not to narrate solo fashion, others might take turns or people might spend most of their time talking with only the odd story thrown in here and there. Furthermore, even if one person does all the narrating, the others do take turns at talking and there tends to be the considerable conversational byplay typical of *shmuesn*. We should note here that except for the solos of parents, grandparents, teachers, or other adults, when they narrate to children, storytelling solos are not mentioned by informants and collectors as often as the other kinds of narrative performance, if at all.

Nonetheless, coachmen, tailors, cobblers, and wandering students are especially famous as raconteurs and are known even as early as the eighteenth century to be excellent narrators who often dominate a whole session with their storytelling:

They [the Jews] are fond of staying up late in the night, particularly in the winter, and whiling away the time with endless series of stories. The stranger who is a good raconteur is sure of a kind reception wherever he may chance to stay; but his nights will be curtailed by the extent of his fund of stories, for his audience will not budge as long as they suspect that the stranger has not spent all the arrows from his quiver. The wandering beggar-students and tailors have the reputation for storytelling; it was by one of the latter that a large number of fairy tales were related to me. (Weiner 1899:44–5).

Bialostotski describes a tailor who told stories and sang songs constantly while sewing. As a child, Bialostotski remembers that if he could snatch a minute when his grandfather was not watching over him at the *besmedresh*, he would run over to the tailor's place to hear the carrying on. The tailor would already be surrounded with others like him, tailors and shoemakers, and he would tell funny stories some of which were traditional and some which were true happenings in the *shtetl* (1962:166–7). And from the late eighteenth and early nineteenth century we have evidence that Jewish waggoners and coachmen were fine storytellers who entertained their passengers on long journeys:

the greatest of the Romantic poets of Poland, Adam Mickiewicz (1788–1856), told his friend Chodvko of a certain Jewish 'balagole' or coachman with whom he had travelled for two days, and who had proved to be an exquisite story-teller. The stories narrated by that 'balagole' made a powerful impression upon Mickiewicz (Schwarzbaum 1968:2)

The other time when one person dominates as narrator is when adults tell stories to children. In this case, adults are naturally more skilled narrators than children and this is sufficient to justify their monopolizing the floor even though they may not be exceptional narrators by adult standards. These same people may never dominate an adult storytelling session. The favored times for adults to tell stories to children are Friday evening and Saturday afternoon because these are times when work is tabooed and children need to be occupied. Bialostotski describes how in the early evening of the Sabbath his grandmother sat him down near the warm oven and commenced telling him stories about *tsadikim* (saints). Consistent with Bialostotski's observation, Informant 1 notes that it is in the home that the mother is most important as a storyteller. She is often the one who tells stories to the children when they are very young and later to the daughters in particular, since as soon as the boys are old enough they go to the synagogue with their father.

Children were also told stories in *kheyder* by various adults who on occasion dominated an encounter with their tales. Shtern quotes one teacher he knew as saying, '"A teacher needs to know how to tell a lot of stories, because Jewish children are delighted with a story"' (1950:85, my translation). But the *rebe* and *melamed* were not the only narrators:

Sometimes during hours when the children were at leisure the *rebetsin* [*rebe*'s wife] also told them stories of ghosts and goblins which she had heard from her mother, who had heard them from her grandmother, and so on. Some of the children of the higher grades were proficient in telling wonderful stories which they had heard from their fathers and older brothers, stories of the prophet Elijah, of Solomon and the Queen of Sheva, of Alexander the Great, of Napoleon, and others. (Schauss 1950:106)

None of the tales which my informants reported were intended specifically for children, although children often listened to them. In fact, of the more than seven hundred stories which I recorded from Toronto Jewish narrators, not one was a 'children's story,' although people remembered stories that they had heard when they were children. But despite the insistance that there were no stories specifically for children, informants and collectors indicate, first, that for the very young child there were special 'narratives,' some in the form of short, formulaic or semi-formulaic, semi-nonsense parodies of adult folktales (see Vanvild 1923 for examples of tales which appear to have been tailored for children), and second, that children in *kheyder* had their own tales which they transmitted to each other, some of which were strikingly different from adult stories with reference to their use of dramatization and prescribed body gestures (see Shtern 1950:58, 61). It appears then that when children are together, have leisure time and are being supervised, an older person will monopolize the floor and tell stories to the children. If the children are unsupervised they will tell stories to each other.

Four types of informal storytelling compared

Most highly valued, then, is the use of stories as an illustration to conversational or situational topics (Type A). But stories in conversation may also be told for their own sake. When this is the case, one option is for the odd tale, especially in the case of jokes and humorous anecdotes, to be embedded in conversation as a topic in and of itself (Type B). Another option is for several stories to be told in succession either in the form of a round, the participants taking turns at narrating (Type C), or in the form of a solo, one person doing all the narrating (Type D). In all four cases (Types A, B, C, D), the participants do take turns at speaking even when they do not exchange the narrator role. The four types of informal storytelling identified here involve choices from among the following alternatives:

1. Either stories are told toward some other end (Type A) or they are told as ends in themselves (Types B, C, D).

2. If stories are told as ends in themselves, they may either be subordinated to other kinds of discourse (Type B) or they may dominate the encounter (Types C, D).

3. If stories are allowed to dominate the encounter, the participants may either take turns at narrating (Type C) or allow one person to do all the storytelling (Type D).

TABLE 10.   *Distribution of choices in informal storytelling events*

	Speaker roles alternate	Story is end in itself	Storytelling dominates	Narrator roles alternate
Type A (story as gloss)	+	−	−	
Type B (single story as topic)	+	+	−	
Type C (story round)	+	+	+	+
Type D (story solo)	+	+	+	−

The distribution of these choices in each type of informal storytelling event is presented in chart form in Table 10.

Although theoretically it should be possible to have storytelling rounds and solos consisting mainly or exclusively of parables, this does not occur in practice. We do find that in the course of the special storytelling sessions among the Hasidic males on the Sabbath and on the anniversary of the death of a Hasidic saint, it is common for some clarification and discussion to follow a tale. Sometimes this conversational byplay is supplemented by another story told to illuminate a point made in the tale preceding. But it is highly unlikely for a chain of several parables to be told either as a round or as a solo. Theoretically, a round or solo of parables would have to consist of a succession of (1) framed tales recounting previous parable performances, (2) parables which are subordinated one to the other, (3) parables told as a gloss to the conversational byplay between parables, or (4) some combination of the above. Any of these alternatives would be extremely difficult to sustain. It is much more demanding to use a tale to gloss something than to tell it for its own sake. When tales are told for themselves, it is often the case that there are many other narratives that could serve as functional equivalents for the tale actually told. The opposite is true of a tale used as a gloss. But difficulty is not the only or even the most important factor. There also appears to be a contradiction involved in dominating a speech event with a series of parables since parables in this culture are intended as means to an end to which they are usually subordinated rather than as an end in themselves. I have neither witnessed nor encountered in the Yiddish folktale literature of the last century a storytelling round or solo composed primarily of parables. In contrast, examples can be brought forward from the literature (see, for example, Buber 1961:16; 1962:44) to support the contention that parables typically figure in story-subordinated speech events rather than in story-dominated ones, notwithstanding the range of ways a parable performance may be realized and the tendency of famous parable users to use one option more than or to the exclusion of others.[2]

Therefore, when a story is told as a gloss it is more likely to be followed by conversation or by story as topic than by another parable. A typical pattern is observed by Ravnitsky:

when a group of Jews gathers at some celebration or several Jews meet each other for no particular purpose, their favorite recreation is to narrate merrily or to listen very attentively to a true Jewish saying, a genuine Jewish folk joke: one proceeds to say an appropriate joke, tailored to what is being discussed in conversation, and sometimes indeed right after that yet another . . . And it is always just like that: when two Jews meet, a sequence of jokes ensues. (1922:iii–iv, my translation)

Ravnitsky's observation presents three possibilities – (1) the story as gloss, (2) story for its own sake, and (3) storytelling round – not only as frequently realized options within conversation but also as all being likely to occur in one encounter, one leading into the other, in the order he indicates.

Formal storytelling in monologues

The two types of monologues most common in tradition-oriented circles are the *droshe* (sermon) and *batkhones* (rhymed improvisations of the professional wedding jester). More modern and worldly is the term *rede* (speech). As one informant humorously explained: '*a droshe iz a rede mit a yarmulke*' (a sermon is a speech with a skull cap). In addition there is the *hesped* (funeral oration) said for a great man. These are among the most formal types of speech events in which stories figure. A detailed ethnography of speaking in the context of religious learning is needed and may provide evidence for discussing the sermon as an extension, elaboration, and formalization of ways of speaking developed in the learning context, for example, the copious use of *psukim* (verses of a sacred book) in Hebrew-Aramaic, Yiddish translations and paraphrases, and the unfolding of meaning in Yiddish through the method of *drash* (non-literal [esp. scholastic] interpretation of a text), which is one of two major tactics taken in learning, the other being *pshat* (literal interpretation). Similarly, in both sermons and learning, parables play an important role in the explication and artistic elaboration of meaning, and when a professional preacher is performing, in chastising and moralizing.

There are sermon specialists, the *bal-darshn* (preacher) and *maged* (preacher), who are often itinerants. Larger communities might have a resident preacher. However, others are also expected to preach. The *rov* holds sermons, especially on *shabes-tshuve* (the Sabbath between Rosh Hashonah and Yom Kippur) and *shabes-hagodl* (the Sabbath before Passover). In addition, the groom is expected to speak, *zogn a pshetl* (present a hair-splitting argument on some point in the sacred text) or *haltn a droshe* (preach a sermon), at his wedding to show his learning. Even the *bar-mitsve bokher* (boy commemorating his thirteenth birthday) may be expected to *zogn a pshetl* or *haltn a droshe* as best he can. Therefore, virtually every adult male is expected to be able to control this kind of discourse to some extent as a way of showing his learnedness.

Occasions appropriate for holding a sermon range from the most common – after the reading of the Torah or between *minkhe* and *mayrev* any day of the week in the *besmedresh* or synagogue, and at weddings – to the least common, for example, possibly at *barmitsves, khanukse bes-hakneses* (dedication of a new synagogue), *kheskes-hatoyre* (to commemorate the acquisition of a new Torah).

The sermons of the *bal-darshn* and *maged*, if on a weekday, might last an hour, and if on a Sabbath, might extend to two hours. A continuous flow of speech and the unfolding of meaning are primary since the whole sermon is essentially the interpretation and clarification of the meanings of a clearly quoted biblical verse which serves as the 'essential and obligatory opening *(petihta* proem) of the public sermon preached in the synagogue' (Noy 1971:174). This scriptural verse is from the weekly portion of the Torah readings. 'As teachers of the folk, ... they liked to clothe their thoughts and teachings in folk parables or put them into the form of folk legends' (Bergmann 1919:88, quoted by B. Weinreich 1957:48). Preachers are more likely to realize the fullest form of the *moshl* performance in sermons where explicitness, elaboration, and extended discourse are highly valued and where *shtrofn* (chastising) and *musern* (moralizing) are expected.

Informant 1 explains that in Silmeric in the 1920s and 1930s, itinerant preachers would arrive in summer, for the most part, because it was too difficult to travel in winter and too cold to sit and listen to them. Upon arriving the preacher hung a large placard on the synagogue door. Beautifully lettered, the sign announced that he would preach on a given theme.

At dusk during the week, when people had finished with the day's business, he would preach for about an hour, from the place in the synagogue or *bes-medresh* where the rabbi usually stands. He had no fee and was not invited. The better he spoke the more he was paid. After he finished his sermon, the beadle or warden collected money from the congregation and gave it to the preacher. If a *bal-darshn* was very good, everyone would flock to hear him and to offer him room and board. Although in the course of his sermon the preacher told stories, he did not generally narrate as a soloist in private homes, according to Informant 1, who also notes that in contrast with the preacher, the *batkhn* is invited to perform and he fixes his fee ahead of time.

Shtern's recollection of the various itinerant preachers that visited his town of Tyszowce is consistent with Informant 1's account and is instructive here for the distinctions he makes between a proficient and an incompetent preacher, for the description of the responses appropriate to each, and for the account of how storytelling figures as one of the criteria of excellence in sermon performance:

In the time between the afternoon and evening prayers one often heard here [in the *besmedresh*] a *maged* [preacher] who was passing through deliver a sermon and ... [someone] would stand at the door with a plate to gather money ... for the preacher from those leaving the synagogue after the evening prayers.

If the preacher was one of the respectable preachers the audience used to listen with mouth and ears and the preacher used to rock the audience with his heartfelt tune and beautiful parables and tales. For long weeks afterwards, the people from the *besmedresh* used to repeat the preacher's tune and retell his parables and tales. Such a preacher also used to stay for the Sabbath and deliver his sermon Saturday afternoon, in winter in the *besmedresh* and in summer in the large synagogue. Then even women used to come hear the sermons. In summer they used to fill the women's section and in winter they used to stand around the walls of the *besmedresh* wrapped in many shawls. Other women used to fill the anteroom of the *besmedresh*, and older women – pious ladies – used to enter the *besmedresh* with boldness and stand by the oven and listen to the sermon from there. But if the preacher was one of the pedestrian preachers (who circulated from town to town on foot with his bundle on his shoulders), or as we used to call them, 'common preachers,' there was a noise in the *besmedresh*, an uproar. Everyone did what he pleased: talked, chatted, argued, and *kheyder* boys played. And so the preacher preached to himself. If this preacher ... had a habit of stuttering or mumbling and at the same time used to bring forth examples which were not coherent, then *besmedresh* boys, jokers used to listen to this preacher ... Then they really had something to mock and imitate. (Shtern 1950:95–6, my translation)

Since women and men are supposed to be separated and the *besmedresh* was a male preserve and had no women's section, women who came to hear the preacher had to stand around the walls of the *besmedresh*.

The *batkhn* (entertainer at a wedding, specializing in humorous and sentimental semi-improvised rhymes) can in part be characterized as a symbolic inversion of the *bal-darshn*. Sometimes called a *marshelik* (jester) or *lets* (buffoon), the word *batkhn* derives from the Aramaic *badah, beduha* (merrymaker), according to Jastrow (quoted by Lifschutz 1952:50). The *batkhn* functions in the capacity of 'master of ceremonies, speaker, improvisator, singer, comedian, juggler and performer of similar arts' (Lifschutz 1952:68) and his principal concern is to make the wedding guests happy. His performance at weddings falls into two parts: before the wedding ceremony his task is to make the guests weep, the appropriate mood for approaching the marriage ritual; after the ceremony he is obliged to make them laugh. When being serious, he uses some of the *bal-darshn's* techniques but when making merry, he may invert those very strategies and indulge in parody, the result of which is a striking affinity to the famous pranksters discussed above. In both halves, the *batkhn* has recourse to stories; anecdotes and jokes being of special importance in his merrymaking.

There were different types of *batkhonim*. Some resembled the preachers, 'playing the pious role of chaste humorist reciting rhymes or Talmudic parables' (Lifschutz 1952:49) and preaching seriously on Talmudic and biblical texts. Therefore, the *batkhn* had to be familiar with the rabbinic literature and had to be somewhat learned. The Rabbi Eliezer Sislevitch was a *batkhn* of this type in Poland in the mid-nineteenth century:

> He was an eminent scholar, an ordained rabbi whose discourse was interspersed with sayings of the sages, quotations from the midrash, and homiletic interpretations based on numerical values of the letters of given words and mnemonic devices. He deftly interpolated the names of the parents of the bride and groom in a Biblical passage. Moreover, he was a God-fearing man, who always carried with him a volume of the Talmud. He refused to participate in the ceremony known as *bazetsns* of the bride, for that would require his presence in the midst of women. He also never announced donations of wedding gifts because he said:
> How would it look if I just got through a Torah discourse – and if it is in rhyme is it not Torah? – and then followed this with shouting out the wedding gifts like an auctioneer on the mart? It would be a desecration of the honor of the Torah. (Lifschutz 1952:49)

Many *batkhonim*, however, indulged in humorous *parodies* of learned religious discourse and satirical rhymes, asked riddles, especially catch riddles, did magic tricks, performed as clowns, and told stories. This type of *batkhn* was severely criticized by the Talmudic scholars for taking liberties with biblical and Talmudic passages and for interpreting them sacrilegiously. In fact, a great deal of our information on the *batkhn* comes from regulations governing wedding entertainers, especially condemnations of their 'lasciviousness' and attempts to suppress them. Nonetheless, they were tolerated much more than actors who, along with the theatre, received maximum resistance. Though not a prestigious, nor even a particularly respectable social position, the *batkhn* did have some power because he was feared. People knew he could and did use his rhymes to cause social embarrassment and therefore took care to cultivate his friendship: 'they were amused by his apt parables, paraphrases and merry songs and then proceeded to censure him as a sinner. As a rule he was considered a man who wasted his time on foolishness . . .' (Lifschutz 1952:51). Repeatedly in the accounts of the *batkhn's* performances, the *batkhn* is likened to the preacher with respect to some serious preaching on religious texts which he may do, and as noted above, some of the tales which he may tell. The following account is from Posen in the mid-nineteenth century:

> The *marshalik* took care of the entertainment, by telling all kinds of anecdotes, which he presumably heard from the preachers of Dubnow and Karnitz, two itinerant preachers then known for their witticisms. If the *marshalik* repeated known jests too frequently, the guests would not refrain from sarcastic remarks. This added point to the table talk and maintained the gay atmosphere. As soon as the *marshalik* opened his mouth to announce the wedding gifts, a penetrating '*sha!*' was heard, which was aimed at silencing the chatter at the tables. In announcing the wedding gifts, making thorough use of the art of recitation, the *marshalik* celebrated his greatest triumph. By means of various remarks, he characterized each donor and his gift, which called forth outbursts of laughter, sometimes to a dangerous degree. (Lifschutz 1952:72)

The preacher did influence many traditional narrators in the towns where he performed, not least of which were the *batkhonim*. Similarly, the *batkhn's* stories and jests were repeated by other raconteurs.

Important for the effectiveness of a *batkhn's* performance is that his materials be fresh. Informant 1 explained that in his town the *rebe*, whose job forced him to attend many weddings, once criticized the *batkhn* for using the same spiel at every wedding, to which the *batkhn* replied, 'If you didn't go to all the weddings, you would never know it was the same one.' The telling of old jokes will make the *batkhn* the target of sarcastic remarks.

Although novelty per se is not emphasized, the preacher must be able to sermonize on a variety of topics because he is expected to address himself to the particular text in the Torah which is being read at the time he arrives in a town to give his sermon. The preacher who only knew one sermon was a great source of amusement in Informant 1's town as people watched him tax his ingenuity in finding some way to relate his one sermon to the passage of the week.

The sermon and *batkhn's* spiel are among the most formal types of contexts in which storytelling occurs. Formality is achieved however by virtue of what happens not to narration but to the non-narrative discourse in which the stories are embedded. It is noteworthy that restricting the narrator role in storytelling solos did not produce a formal speech event but that restricting the speaker roles, which automatically precludes the exchange of narrator roles, does make for a formal speech event. This is yet another indication that speech events are defined in terms of the features of non-narrative discourse even when they are dominated by storytelling. Although there is very little alternating of speaker roles, if the audience is bored with an inept preacher or *batkhn*, there may be speaker overlap, as members of the audience ignore the performer's presence and proceed to converse with each other as if he were not there. In cases where the audience is attending to the preacher or *batkhn*, its participation tends to be limited to signals of approval and disapproval in the form of murmurs, laughter, and other forms of phatic communication. In the case of the *batkhn's* performance, the audience may make sarcastic remarks, urge the *batkhn* to perform something in particular and generally be more vocal, perhaps because more merry, than when listening to a preacher. The time and place are strictly set and these performers only operate in a very limited range of specified settings for clearly defined occasions. They are specialists and in contrast with non-specialists, they get paid for their labors. The preacher, whose services are highly valued, is not paid directly because officially, as is the case with the Rabbi, he is not allowed to use the Torah or other sacred duties to make a living. Religious learning and observance are activities which one engages in for intrinsic reasons. In contrast, the *batkhn* is paid directly and his performance is bought as one would buy a service. The genres appropriate to the preacher's performance are pious, moralizing tales. The *batkhn* has recourse to these genres, especially in the preceremony phase of his performance and to humorous anecdotes after the wedding ceremony.

Informal and formal storytelling compared

A major distinction between informal and formal storytelling involves the exchange or lack of exchange of speaker roles respectively. And, while informal speech events may be dominated by storytelling (Types C and D), there are no formal speech events in which narration is the focus. In addition, narration is conditioned by the speech event in which it appears. A comparison of how parables are told in conversation as opposed to sermons will reveal some of the forms this conditioning takes.

The fullest form of parable-telling is seldom realized in conversation, where conciseness, indirectness, and closure may be desired, but is expected in sermons, which last from one to two hours and in which elaboration and explicitness are highly valued. A parable performance, at its fullest, consists of the following components:

1. Stimulus – a topic in the conversation, a question, or something about the ongoing discourse or social interaction precipitates the need for a parable.

2. Announcement – formula indicating that a *moshl* is about to ensue and therefore that what follows should be interpreted analogically.

3. *Moshl* – example or illustration in the form typically of a traditional tale but also can be a description or statement (proverb or aphorism).

4. *Nimshl* – explanation of that to which the *moshl* refers and possible elaboration of the relation of the *moshl* to its object.

5. *Muser-haskl* – an epigrammatic formulation of the general principle or moral of the tale often in the form of a proverb or aphorism.

At its very briefest, typically in conversation, a parable performance may consist of only a reference to a story the listeners know well. They need only be reminded of it for it to have its impact. At its fullest, typically in a sermon, a parable performance will exhibit all five components and the *nimshl* may be expanded to a size sometimes even greater than the *moshl* itself.

Generally, a parable is used in conversation precisely because it is metaphoric and therefore indirect. Being a neat, closed formulation, often clinched by an epigrammatic punchline or moral, followed sometimes by an explosive burst of laughter, it is usually unanswerable and can be used to silence the other party or to terminate discussion. The *nimshl* works in the opposite direction. It is a way of opening the parable up, of unfolding meaning, of achieving explicitness, and of expanding the performance. Being more open in form than the neatly formulated parable, the *nimshl* is also a way of making a transition from the *moshl* to ordinary discourse. As such it invites discussion and rejoinder, actions which the telling of the parable in conversation may have been designed to curtail. Therefore the *nimshl* is likely to appear in a very brief form in conversation if at all whereas it tends to be an essential feature of sermon performance.

The elaborating of the *nimshl* outside of the sermon context is likely to be considered excessive although respected males who are learned and older do take this liberty. Sholem Aleichem's recollection of his grandfather's narrational habits is instructive here:

> Breathtaking stories of ancient Jews and noblemen Grandfather knew by the dozen, and the children would have listened to all of them with delight if Grandfather had not had the unpleasant habit of squeezing a moral (*muser-haskl*) out of each tale: one had to be a pious Jew and have faith in God ... The moral would be followed by a lecture, and then he would start upbraiding the children for heeding the Spirit of Evil, for having no desire to pray, study, and serve God, and for wanting only to fish night and day, pick pears, and get into mischief with worthless, emptyheaded Boguslav boys ... (Rabinovich 1955:184)

Indeed, the grandfather, who is taking advantage of his status as an older, pious male, is behaving here in a manner more appropriate to a sermon than a *shmues*. Like a preacher, he follows his tale with a *muser-haskl* and *'funem muser-haskl [hot er] lib [gehat] araynfaln glat in muser arayn un nemen shtrofn di kinder . . .'* (and from the moral, he loved to fall directly into moralizing and to chastise the children . . .) (Rabinovich 1944:246). The preachers were expected to vehemently moralize and chastise, to urge their listeners to be righteous.

There are however times in conversation when it is considered appropriate, indeed essential, to provide the *nimshl*, namely, when one reports on how someone used a parable in the past. The result is a framed tale, the frame being the *nimshl*. In the following example, recorded during a storytelling round devoted to stories for their own sake, a woman, who prefers parables to stories, tells such a framed tale about how she had previously used a parable to make a point:

Informant 2
Listen, this I have to tell you, an instance, that actually I used this and it was appropriate. Just a few days ago I was at my brother's and my sister-in-law was telling me how at her *balmitsve* [sic] [a boy's coming of age and assumption of religious responsibilities when he reaches thirteen], her brother was there with his son and they talked to each other, it was really disgraceful. The son said something to the father which wasn't very nice and the father in return answered.

I said, 'Well, it looks like they both speak the same language.' So I remembered a story my mother used to tell me.

She says once on *yonkiper* [Day of Atonement], the mother usually stays in the synagogue all day long, and she left cooking on the stove a *tsimes* [a vegetable or fruit stew], which is a carrot pudding and it cooks all day and at the end of the *tones* [fast] when they come home to eat, it'll be just right. The daughter came to visit the mother in *shul* [synagogue] and she sits for a while and she *davns* [prays], prays with her and spends the afternoon. So the mother reminds herself about that *tsimes* so she says to her, 'Tokhter [daughter], daughter,' she says, 'Did you look in on the pot to see if that *tsimes* isn't going to be burnt, if it's cooking?'

She says, 'Mother, before I left I looked and the *tsimes iz tsekokht vi drek* [the stew is cooked like shit]' which means . . .

Audience
Never mind.

Informant 2
However, so the mother was so embarrassed and she says, 'In a synagogue, in a holy place, this is how you talk? *Ikh gib dir a patsh bakakste zikh shoyn* [I'll give you a smack that will make you shit yourself at once].
And this is the way that son and the father . . .

In this case, the sequence is *nimshl, muser-haskl, moshl* announcement, *moshl,* and brief reference to the *nimshl* again. The *nimshl,* which appears first, functions here both to indicate the stimulus for the narration, to explain how the parable applies to the reported conversation, and to highlight the aesthetic excellence of the performance by highlighting the appropriateness of the tale. Then comes the *muser-haskl* – 'I said, "Well, it looks like they both speak the same language"' – which is drawn from the report of the life situation and which points to the direction the parable will take. There follows the *moshl* announcement – 'So I remembered a story my mother used to tell me' and then the *moshl* itself. In the case of reports of parable performances, the expected sequence is commonly reversed as a way of making the stimulus for the parable intelligible. Indeed, the *nimshl* and stimulus may actually be combined, a procedure which makes sense when one realizes that in a normal parable performance the *nimshl* really functions to define the stimulus and its connection to the parable.

Similarly the *muser-haskl* is perhaps more likely to appear in sermons than in conversation. In sermons, the *muser-haskl* is typically used to create closure after a drawn-out *nimshl* has diffused the impact of the *moshl.* Should the *muser-haskl* appear in conversation, there are several options. In her analysis of Hasidic tales recorded from oral tradition by Jerome Mintz, Margaret Woodruff distinguished

first, whether the proverb or saying was uttered by the narrator as his comment on the story, or by a character in the story; and second, whether the proverb or saying was an integral part of the story, necessary to its point, a punch-line; or simply a succinct formulation of a point already made by the action related in the story. (1972:4)

As noted by Gross (1955:11) some performers have the habit of introducing their parables with the *muser-haskl,* usually in the form of a proverb. It is probably more customary, however, to conclude with it.

The options discussed so far depend on the speech event in which the *moshl* figures and upon the predilections of individual narrators. Commentators on great Jewish preachers have noted, for example, the *Dubner maged's* preferred pattern was the sequence: stimulus, *moshl* announcement, *moshl, nimshl, muser-haskl* (optional), but that on occasion he was known to narrate in a more 'Aesopic' or 'La Fontainean' fashion according to Bialostotski (1962:66), that is, stimulus, *moshl* announcement, *moshl, muser-haskl.*

Although narration is indeed highly valued in east European Jewish culture, the presence, absence, or dominance of storytelling is not what defines a speech event. Narration is conceptualized as an act rather than as an event (following Hymes' [1967] terminology) and as subordinate to various kinds of non-narrative discourse even when it dominates an encounter. The speech event does however condition the storytelling performance, the genres used, and the fullness of their performance. But neither the speech events nor the narrations are distinguished terminologically in terms of one another.

A basic distinction does inhere between informal speech, or speech involving conversational give and take, and formal speech, such as we find in *droshe* and *batkhones*, or speech in the form of a monologue where there is no exchange of speaker roles. Narration figures in all of them. The formal events entail the performance of a specialist, often one who is paid for speaking; a prearranged time, place, and occasion; restrictions on audience participation; limitations on the genres of narrative that may be drawn upon; the use of marked prosodic, paralinguistic, and kinesic features (rhyme, intoning, stylized gestures); increased code-switching between Yiddish and Hebrew-Aramaic; and fullness of elaboration of the forms used. A summary of the distribution of these features is presented in chart form in Table 11.

The cultural focus on narration, rather than elaboration in specialized storytelling events and by professional narrators, works in the opposite direction to take the form of pervasiveness. Almost anyone can narrate at almost any time or place despite the fact that males, older people, and individuals of higher status have more prerogatives and that sociable occasions lend themselves best to extended storytelling for its own sake.[3]

> *A hun mit a hon,*
> *Di mayse heybt zikh on.*
> *A kats mit a moyz,*
> *Di mayse lost zikh oys.*

> A rooster and a hen,
> The story begins.
> A cat and a mouse,
> The story is over.
> (Traditional closing formula for the Yiddish Märchen)

APPENDIX: BIOGRAPHIES OF INFORMANTS

Informant 1: Male; born around 1914 in Varta, near Lodz; father was a Hasidic *rebe*; attended *yeshiva* until age of nineteen; lived in Siradz 1933–9; was incarcerated during World War II; lived in Israel 1949–52; arrived in Toronto, Canada, 1952; used to earn living as *shoykhet* (ritual slaughterer); now works as *mazhgiekh* (supervisor of Jewish dietary laws in an institutional kitchen) at Baycrest Home for the Aged; is a practicing Hasid today; resides in Downsview, a suburb of Toronto; speaks Yiddish, English, German, Polish, Hebrew; married with children.

TABLE 11. *Distribution of features*

Feature	Informal				Formal	
	TYPE A Story as gloss	TYPE B Story as topic	TYPE C Story round	TYPE D Story solo	Story in *batkhones*	Story in *droshe*
Stories dominate	−	−	+	+	−	−
Novelty primary	−	+	+	+	+	+
Text-context fit primary	+	−	−	−	−	+
Increased restrictions on narrative genres	−	−	−	−	+	+
Location restricted	−	−	−	−	+	+
Occasion restricted	−	−	−	−	+	+
Performance scheduled	−	−	−	−	+	+
Special prosodic and paralinguistic features required	−	−	−	−	+	+
Performer is paid	−	−	−	−	+	+
One person does all speaking	−	−	−	−	+	+
One person does all narrating	−	−	−	+	+	+
Performer must have special qualifications	−	−	−	+	+	+
Increased explicitness and/or fullness of form	−	−	−	+	+	+

Informant 2: Female; born 1915 in Brest-Litovsk; father ultra-Orthodox tailor from Kobryn; finished public school; arrived in Toronto, Canada, 1929; husband owns and operates paint store; now resides in Downsview, suburb of Toronto; is now a Conservative Jew; speaks Yiddish, English, Polish, some Hebrew; married with children.

V

THE SHAPING OF ARTISTIC STRUCTURES IN PERFORMANCE

INTRODUCTION

That verbal art and artistic verbal performance should figure prominently among the concerns of the ethnography of speaking is not surprising, since to participant and analyst alike the verbal art forms of a culture and the situations in which they are employed represent the most conspicuous, attractive, or powerful sectors of the speech activity of any society. Yet a truly ethnographic approach to verbal art, in the sense of a focus upon the situated use of verbal art forms conceived of as communicative process, is, like the ethnography of speaking itself, a relatively recent development. Anthropologists, linguists, and folklorists alike have tended overwhelmingly to view verbal art, like language, as abstracted from social use. In all three disciplines, the unit of analysis in the study of verbal art has been the textual item, the myth, legend, song, or ritual speech, treated as a self-contained entity. To be sure, anthropologists at least have recognized and acknowledged the association of these items with events, but the principal frame of reference against which they have been studied – when such factors have been studied at all – is the culture or society as a whole. That is, the item is conceptualized as collective representation, shaped primarily by the shared culture, history, language, or character (in the collective psychological sense) of the members of the society in which it is current, and secondarily perhaps – more among folklorists than anthropologists – by the cumulative effects of long-term transmission through time and space. This is a highly normative conception, in that it is founded upon an implicityly posited normal form of the traditional item which persists through time, underlies all the various empirical versions that may be collected, and represents the standard by which they are identified and evaluated.

The ethnography of speaking, however, provides a very different perspective on verbal art. Taking the social situation as the unit of analysis, examined in terms of the functional interrelationships which obtain among all its components (of which the textual item is only one), makes it possible to view the resultant text as an emergent, uniquely shaped in the process of performance. Regna Darnell's paper on the correlates of Cree narrative performance analyzes this process on one level, in terms of the complex interrelationships which obtain in the performance situation among the identities and linguistic capabilities of the participants, their social relationships, the demands of the Cree narrative tradition, the physical setting, and the stories themselves. The old man's story, as well as those of Father, discussed earlier in the paper, are in every sense the unique products of these interrelationships, and far more is to be lost than gained by viewing them simply as

311

additional versions of traditional Cree tale types, for this would be to homogenize out of consideration the uniqueness of the performance. What is especially striking about this situation is that Darnell's narrator could neither have experienced its like before nor anticipated its configuration – this is far from the predictable, repetitive event structure that anthropologists have tended to see at work in social life. Nevertheless, the old man was able to use his competence creatively to adapt to the situation and carry off a performance. If we consider that every situation must be in some way unique for its particpants, the general import of Darnell's analysis becomes apparent: the creative and adaptive use of competence becomes a crucial subject for investigation.

Harvey Sacks' analysis of the telling of a dirty joke in conversation demonstrates the process by which the emergent form is shaped on another level. Sacks has come to the analysis of this verbal art form through an interest in conversation, and is thus able to take for granted what folklorists and anthropologists have not seemed to consider, that narrative may be a conversational genre (cf. the paper by Kirshenblatt-Gimblett, section IV). By a process of painstakingly microscopic analysis, applied to an unedited transcript of the conversation in which the joke is told, Sacks is able to elucidate in fine terms the interactional dynamics which shape the traditional narrative into a unique product of this specific situation. This story, like the story of the old man discussed by Darnell, is a collective product in a sense of the term very different from collective representation; it is collective in the sense that it is the joint production of all the participants in the situation within which it is performed.

Michael Foster's analysis of Iroquois ritual speech is of a somewhat different order than the other two papers, but develops a crucial point which must be articulated with the insights they provide. Foster points out that the ritual speeches he discusses are highly variable in content and length. The object of his analysis, however, is not to uncover the factors which generate the variable forms, but rather to establish those elements of the form which are minimally obligatory, which must be present for a speech to count as a valid instance of the genre, namely the performative elements of thanking or beseeching, and the statements which validate the performatives from the point of view of the native Iroquois theory of speech acts. These, in a sense, are the primary contribution of the form itself to the rendition which emerges; the tradition also provides formal materials which may contribute to the expansion of the speeches, conditioned by other situational factors of the kind discussed by Darnell.

In addition to helping to reshape our notion of the materials of verbal art, these papers develop certain ideas which are particularly suggestive as contributions toward a theory of performance which goes beyond the sense of performance simply as action. The performative nature of the Iroquois speeches discussed in Foster's paper points up most clearly that speech performance is not simply the doing of speech, but the doing of speech for some purpose. Foster presents us with a functional analysis of the minimal speech which operates on two levels – the performative utterances establish what the speech as a whole is to accomplish, while the other minimal components work within the speech to validate the performatives. Sacks carries his functional analysis to a more detailed internal level, concerned not with the overall function of the entire joke transaction, but with the function within the conversation of individual utterances (as well as laughs and silences), in the shaping of the situation.

Sacks' analysis also uncovers a phenomenon that would appear to have important implications for a theory of the performance specifically of verbal art, and which is also attested to by Darnell's findings. Perhaps the easiest way to conceptualize performance in the artful sense (a more limited sense of the term 'performance') is to view it as occurring whenever an item of traditional verbal art is used, i.e., taking the item (identified as artful on purely formal grounds) as a key to performance. Both Darnell's and Sacks' papers make clear the inadequacy of such an undifferentiated notion of artistic verbal performance. Darnell's interpreter, because of her role in the situation, was called upon to translate the words of the Cree stories for the ethnographer, yet she realized quite clearly the difference between rendering the story in this stripped-down way, and telling it with appropriate paralinguistic, prosodic, and kinesic features, which marked it as artful to the Cree. In other words, she was called upon to tell the story, in a certain fashion, but not to perform it. The distinction was highlighted for her by her anomalous position in the situation – by traditional Cree standards, she should not have been rendering the story at all in the presence of an old man – and by the fact that the formal strength of the tale was sufficient to make her shift into a performance mode despite herself. The suggestion here seems to be that certain verbal art forms, though presentable in a variety of modes, contain or carry with them, because of cultural expectations, an impulse toward the performance mode, in which they are framed as art.

Sacks finds a similar phenomenon at work in the situation which he analyzes, with the added factor that in his material the distinction between performing a verbal art form and rendering it in another mode (e.g., reporting it), becomes part of the strategic resources of the participants in the conversation. Both of the participants who tell jokes in the situation analyzed by Sacks are able to frame them in such a way that if the response is negative they can disclaim having told the jokes as performance, and fall back on a claim to having presented them simply as information concerning the knowledge and behavior of an absent party, or a guess concerning the intentionality of one of the participants in the interaction. It is clear that Darnell's and Sacks' informants maintain at least an implicit distinction between the performance of verbal art and the rendering of verbal art forms in some other mode, and our analytical theories of artistic verbal performance must be consistent with ethnographic truths of this kind (cf. Hymes, section VI, and Hymes 1974).

The papers by Victoria Bricker and Gary Gossen, dealing with similar materials from two adjacent Mayan groups, introduce several additional factors to be taken into account in the ethnographic study of verbal art. They are particularly concerned with the ways in which stylistic preferences within cultures and the culture-specific esthetic principles associated with them contribute to the shaping of artistic structures.

Bricker analyzes the syntactically and semantically parallel metaphorical couplets which constitute the essential stylistic feature of formal speech in Zinacantan, though not overtly identified as such by the Indians themselves. However, the implicit recognition of the couplet form as essential to formal speech, for which Bricker provides several kinds of evidence, represents both the wherewithal for marking an utterance as formal, and, together with the valuation of formal speech as good speech, the formative impulse to cast in couplet form speech which occurs in a formal context.

The Zinacanteco couplets discussed by Bricker represent an instance of canonical parallelism, the pervasive repetition with systematic variation of phonic, grammatical, and semantic structures, identified by Jakobson as central to much of the world's oral poetry (1960, 1966, 1968). Bricker suggests that the dyadic nature of the couplet is consistent with the pervasive dualism of Zinacanteco culture, as is the basic division of the domain of speaking into two segments, formal (good) speech and informal (bad) speech. It is interesting in this regard that, for the neighboring Chamula, discussed by Gossen, parallelism represents a more continuous function, consistent there with their more diversified conception of the domain of speaking, and the pervasive metaphor of cosmic (solar) heat with which parallelism is linked.

Gossen, in contrast with Jakobson and Bricker, reserves the term parallelism for syntactically parallel lines, excluding pairs of lines which are semantically but not syntactically repetitive. For the Chamula, to use Gossen's term, the stacking of increasing numbers of dyadic sets (including syntactic, semantic, or verbatim repetitions) on the same theme, going beyond the individual couplet, becomes for the speaker a means of expressing increasing amounts of metaphorical heat, and thus marking a more finely graded scale of formality and symbolic significance. The emergent structures may thus be made consistent with the speaker's feelings, the symbolic significance of his message, and the demands of the context, through the relative proliferation of parallel lines. This use of parallelistic forms contributes to the shaping of structures in Chamula performance in a diachronic as well as synchronic sense, in that competence in the use of stacking is acquired developmentally, with mastery of limited parallelism and stacking in the genres of Speech for People Whose Hearts are Heated contributing to the development of ability to use the more complex and extensive forms of Pure Speech.

Perhaps the most important contribution of Gossen's paper is that it presents us with an analysis of a structured esthetic of spoken language in culture-specific terms. By showing how the domain of Chamula verbal art is defined and organized from the native point of view, he demonstrates an important potential contribution of the ethnography of speaking to the anthropological study of verbal art, namely, the means of circumventing the a priori analytical definition of verbal art in favor of the esthetic principles by which the people themselves define artistic verbal performance and shape artistic structures.

Taken together, Bricker's paper on Zinacantan, including historical and comparative data from Yucatan, Gossen's on Chamula, and Fox's on Roti (see section II), add significantly to the growing literature on parallelism in oral poetry. By going beyond strictly formal features into the ethnographic context and cultural dynamics of parallelism, these authors have marked out a significant line of research in the study of this widespread poetic phenomenon.

CORRELATES OF CREE NARRATIVE
PERFORMANCE

REGNA DARNELL

Folklore as a discipline has all too often existed in a vacuum from which texts are abstracted for the edification of outsiders about the cultural context of their performance. Recent collaboration between folklorists and anthropologists, much of which comes under the general rubric of sociolinguistics, has taken an important step toward correcting the limitations of such a perspective. Many students of traditional material have learned to expect and value different versions of the same story told by different individuals or by the same individual at different times depending on the nature of the social occasion. It has become clear that a living folk tradition has a potential for creativity and modification such that the most interesting text may be one which is adapted on the spot to a new audience or a new situation. The feedback between audience and performer may be crucial to the organization of a performance. The folklorist, as a result, can no longer rely solely on a tape recorder in front of an isolated informant, although that individual may be, in other contexts, an authentic performer of his folk tradition. Narrative performance is in essence *social* activity.

This paper will discuss in detail a single instance of creative performance by an old Cree man recognized by his community as a carrier and performer of traditional Cree cultural material. It will be shown that the old man organized the event in a traditional manner, was responded to as an authentic performer in his narration and accompanying conversation, and freely adapted his traditional material to the presence in the audience of outsiders (investigator and spouse, plus tape recorder). The old man was successful in this situation in maintaining the performance to the secondary audience – his Cree hosts and part of his own family – as a validation of his own status of traditional performer. This itself was enhanced, for the Indian portion of the audience, by the fact that he was performing in front of outsiders who wanted to know 'what it was really like' in the old days.

The tapes were recorded in Wabasca, Alberta,[1] in March 1971. The occasion came about almost by accident at the insistence of our hosts, a seventy-year-old Cree man (henceforth Father) and his daughter Marie-Louise who had served as a Cree instructor with the investigator at the

University of Alberta that year. An extremely casual atmosphere was maintained throughout the visit and many traditional stories and anecdotes were recorded from the father. However, our host did not feel that he was the best person in the community to tell us these things, and preferred that we meet an old man who was nearly a hundred years old and knew much more about traditional Cree ways. We would have to pay him to sing and tell stories for us but it would be well worth our while. We agreed, primarily out of curiosity about the relationship of the two men, representing different generations, but to the outsider both 'old' and therefore both appropriate teachers and performers of traditional Cree materials.

Before turning to the old man's performance[2] it will be necessary to sketch the background in terms of our hosts and their relationship to traditional materials. Marie-Louise served as interpreter throughout.[3] Because of her experiences in teaching Cree she was aware of my interests in Cree and partially aware of the grammar of the language and how to explain it to a non-native audience. She was, moreover, multilingual, speaking some German and Chinese because she had lived in Germany and Hong Kong with her husband. She was interested both in linguistic differences and in the preservation of traditional Cree materials, although she had not herself lived on the reserve for many years.

Marie-Louise had never attempted to become a performer of traditional Cree materials but had considered the possibility that she might be able to do so. Certainly she was interested in hearing the stories again, which is the way most new performers declare their intent. She had sent her youngest child, a boy of six, to spend the winter on the reserve and go to school there so he would learn about his Indian heritage. His grandfather was somewhat discouraged by the boy's progress in the Cree language but enjoyed his company and taught him whatever he could. Father thought that the boy had difficulty speaking Cree because he spent most of his time with his aunt (Marie-Louise's sister) and her children. Most of the Cree he learned was in this context. Since these children also spoke English (they owned one of the dozen or so television sets in the community) he did not have to depend on Cree to communicate. Father believes that although all of the children in Wabasca speak English, a few have not learned Cree. Some children on the reserve actually do understand Cree but refuse to respond to it. Father noted that this is 'something very nasty that the Indian has, he is ashamed of himself.'

Thus, Father has a profound and self-conscious pessimism about the future of the Cree language and culture which may not actually be borne out in fact. There are many young people in Wabasca and other northern Alberta communities who are eager to learn traditional materials; some will even perform them in the absence of a better-qualified individual to do so.

They must, however, always defer to an established performer. Clearly, then, there will be *at least* one more generation of traditional performers. Although the effects of culture change have been great, particularly in the areas of education, material culture, and religion (Wabasca has been a major center for Catholic missionaries for some time), individuals still have the option of moving through the traditional Cree life cycle, at least with regard to performance of oral material.

Our host, however, felt isolated from the younger portion of the Cree community because he lived alone and did not understand many of the new influences. He felt that the young people did not want to speak Cree and would be offended if they were expected to do so. He realized that this reflected the inferior position of Indians in the larger society, but did not himself understand why Indian people should have to communicate among themselves in a 'foreign language.' He recalled that when he was a young man, Indians all spoke Cree except if a white man was present who would not understand Cree. He agreed that many young Indians were now trying to learn Cree but thought that grownups would never be able to learn the way 'a person who grows up with' the language learns it. He agreed that such people might learn to speak Cree for purposes of everyday interactions, but did not see how they would be able to learn traditional Cree or maintain the old ways without having been taught from childhood.

Father was, in many ways, reluctant to talk about traditional Cree ways because he believed that people now did not respect them. At the age of seventy, he has watched Cree people turn away from the teachings of their elders and does not believe they share his values. He explained that in the old days, sons respected their fathers because the old men had 'special powers' and could protect their children. Today the powers have been lost and this sanction to authority no longer exists.

Father himself remains with the old ways and does not feel that he has a right to force his beliefs on others. He understands English because he studied it in school many years ago, but is very reluctant to use it. He understood his daughter's translations and our comments, often correcting or adding to her rendition of his remarks. For example, he frequently began his reply before the translation was completed. Our conversational Cree is at approximately the level of his English, a fact which increased his confidence in talking to us. Minimal communication could be sustained easily when his daughter was not present to translate, each speaking his own language and understanding the other. This situation did not seem to embarrass him.

Informally during our visit, Father told us a number of traditional Cree stories, frequently reminding Marie-Louise that he had told these same stories to her as a child. Marie-Louise was apparently quite concerned that we might be bored by the stories and commented that 'they are all quite similar.' She noted that she remembers them as being much more exciting when she was a child. She remembered the stories well enough to jump ahead in her translation on several occasions.

Her major difficulty as a translator in this informal context was whether or not to *perform* the stories. She was able to articulate this difficulty quite clearly, explaining that we could see Father's gestures and hear his tone of voice. She felt 'silly' both performing them and simply translating. Performance was inappropriate because she was a young woman and etiquette required that she simply listen to an old man. But the stories are meant to be performed and they lose their effect if told in a monotone. In practice, conversation was usually translated in the form: 'He says . . .'; for example, 'He thinks Cree will die out.' Marie-Louise was not herself responsible for this opinion and was trying to clarify her father's views. However, in a long narrative she frequently translated in the first person: 'I have seen it happen.'[4] At many points she began to tell a story formally and lapsed into a style with gestures and voice qualities which were not imitations of her father's but her own way of rendering the story as performance. Father seemed pleased by this.

Father's stories were extremely well told and organized. Many of these were stories about Wisahkitchak, the culture hero, and how he made the world into what it is now. For example:

> Wisahkitchak was walking around a lake.
> He came upon a large boulder.
> 'It seems you have been here a long time,' he said.
> 'I'll make you a present of his fur robe.'
> He went on walking.
> It looked like rain. He became chilly.
> He had been foolish to leave his robe, he thought.
> He went back.
> He took it off the stone and teased the stone.
> 'What will you do?' he said.
> The rock chased him.
> He ran through the brush. The boulder just went
> faster.
> He ran up a large hill. Still it came.
> At the top he ran fast downhill. He tripped.
> The rock came and sat on him. It almost killed
> him.
> A night-hawk came along.
> Wisahkitchak begged for help. He promised the
> bird he would make it beautiful if it got the
> rock off.

The night-hawk flew very high.
It made a strange sort of noise.
When the bird made that rude noise, the rock
flipped over.
Wisahkitchak got up and stretched.
The bird sat there and waited [for Wisah-
kitchak].
Wisahkitchak took dirt and made stripes on its
wings. It is a very attractive bird now.
Then Wisahkitchak did something extra. He
stretched the bird's mouth and added yellow
marks to it.
Wisahkitchak always does things this way.
He does something to undo the good he has
done.

Such stories are traditionally called *atayohgewin* or sacred stories. Under
the influence of the missionaries, many native people refuse to consider
them religious in content. Secularization facilitates continued performance
without cultural conflict. Father believes that the stories about Wisahkitchak are fables which no one considers to be true. Wisahkitchak is a kind
of prankster, with the religious context of the Algonkian culture hero
having been lost. Another narrator on a different occasion insisted that the
term *atayohgewin* be translated 'fictitious stories.' He believed it was important to transmit these stories to the younger generation, but they had become
completely secular for him. The attitude is commonly expressed in this area
that 'we didn't have any religion before the white man came.'

Most individuals are quite articulate about the philosophical tightrope
necessary to reconcile cultural pride and religious teaching. Stories are often
followed by long discussions which fall outside any formal literary genre,
being classified as 'just talk,' but interpreting themes of the stories in terms
of present times. This is particularly common with another class of Cree
traditional materials, *achimowan*. *Achimowana* are stories about the past;
they include tales of the old days, in which the speaker disavows personal
knowledge of what he tells through frequent use of the particle *-esa*. They
also include stories about an individual's past experiences which are told
first-hand, and recent events. They are, however, more formal than mere
conversation and the audience is expected to defer to the performer until
he concludes.

An example of this genre is the story Father told as the only one he had
ever heard about a real *wihtigo* (a man who becomes a cannibal). Belief in
wihtigo spirits is still quite strong in this area. *Wihtigo* is used to threaten
children. Individuals who eat too much may be rebuked or teased by calling

them *wihtigo*; this usage is not serious. On the other hand, an individual who is extreme in behavior may be seen as a potential *wihtigo* and assiduously avoided. [5] Most native people do not like to talk about *wihtigo* spirits to white men because they know they are disbelieved. The stories about the *wihtigo* are considered to be true. Father pointed out that they 'do exist in people's minds and beliefs.' Besides, he did not think that people had the imagination to invent stories like these.

People in the old days did not tell lies. It was not done. There was no reason to kill a man unless he had done something or unless there was something terribly wrong with him really. It's quite true that nowadays that it seems unbelievable, but these things did take place, years ago.

Therefore, Father thought that even if an outsider does not believe in *wihtigo* spirits, they are more real than the *atayohgewin* which occurred before the world was as it is now. [6]

After Father had concluded his story, we asked about the morality of killing the *wihtigo*. This provoked a long discussion between Marie-Louise and her father. Father explained that before Christianity came to North America the land was under an evil influence 'and that is why things happened as they did.' The person who became a *wihtigo* was a reincarnation of something evil. But today people have different beliefs and that is no longer possible. Today the Indians have lost the powers they used to have. People were fooled by the evils that existed then. What they took to be good was not actually good, it was evil in origin. Many people lived very good lives at that time, although, of course, many people did not. Father believed that things had changed very little.

The question which bothered both Marie-Louise and her father was whether or not the killing of a *wihtigo* was justifiable according to Christian morality. Father pointed out that the man in the story who had killed his uncle to protect the rest of the community had been very upset. Then one night he had a dream and heard someone say to him, 'All right, that's enough now; you have paid for your sins. You have saved a lot of lives.' Father continued: 'Then he stopped crying, but he didn't live very long after that.' The ambivalence of Marie-Louise was greater:

I suppose, if you look at it that you are committing murder, it is a sin, isn't it? Even though you are saving a lot of lives, it's still . . . particularly if it's your uncle. But there's a lot at stake. If someone's going to kill you, you must defend yourself, right? That's only a natural law.

Father agrees with Christianized rationalization but doesn't think a man could possibly kill his own children, though Indian custom prescribed this as the only possible remedy for a *wihtigo*. Father's personal view is that he would rather let himself be killed by a child who became a *wihtigo*. Both Father and daughter explain the matter in white terms, although they still understand the reasons for the killing in traditional terms.

One difficulty in obtaining traditional Cree texts from Father was the existence of obscene elements in many of the Wisahkitchak stories. Marie-Louise told us that her father had never told her any dirty stories and insisted these stories were traditionally told only in all-male company. Neither was willing to comment on whether these stories were traditionally told to children. The definition of obscenity, like the morality of the *wihtigo*'s punishment, comes from the Catholic missionaries. Marie-Louise, who had refused, during the past year, to discuss obscenity in Cree with university students learning the language, in this situation was embarrassed even to discuss the stories. At one point, after some discussion in Cree, Father asked her if she wanted to hear a story which she knew contained obscene elements. She said 'no thanks' and provoked much laughter. When translating, she broke out of the semi-performance entirely when asked to say that someone burned his ass-hole. Her response was 'I can't say that' with much embarrassment and an unsually loud, nervous voice. Father agreed, after this, to take a shortcut in telling us these stories (which he obviously enjoyed but did not feel his daughter should hear); he decided to omit the parts that were 'not nice,' although he pointed out that this would make the stories quite brief.

Marie-Louise was so upset by the obscene references in the stories before Father agreed to cut them out, that she omitted a whole section of one Wisahkitchak story. After completing the initial translation, she decided to backtrack and tell us what she had left out.

Once Wisahkitchak was walking and lamenting about his loneliness. 'Nothing ever happens. I never even make any rude noises at people.' That's where the accident happened. [Apparently Wisahkitchak made rude noises at a fox who later paid him back when he had lost his eyes.] One time when Wisahkitchak was crawling around looking for his eyes, the fox saw him, you see, he was spying on him. The fox took a piece of wood and would poke him in the eye with it, in the socket he would stick it. And Wisahkitchak would cry out 'Twigs in my eyes.' [After this episode Wisahkitchak finds the spruce tree, fashions himself new eyes, and proceeds on his travels.] [7]

With this background, it is now possible to return to the formal setting in which the community's oldest man was invited to come and tell a set of honored but outside visitors about the old days and traditional Cree way of life. Although the context of visiting anthropologist was not an entirely natural one in native terms, it was treated as such to a great extent by all participants. The narration and song performance became an excuse for various observers to hear the old man's performance and to reaffirm both their pride in what he said and their recognition of his position as revered elder. The positioning of participants in Father's cabin illustrates the observance of traditional Cree canons of performance demeanor (see Fig. 15).

When the old man and his wife (hereafter old woman) arrived, my husband and I were sitting at the kitchen table talking to Marie-Louise and her father. Father got up, found the largest and most comfortable chair in the room, and escorted the old man to it. This chair was placed at the center of the room. There were no general introductions, although the old man was told who we were. At no time did the old man turn his body to face Father or Marie-Louise although he turned his head toward them occasionally. His wife was then seated next to him, between him and the table where we were sitting. The old woman aligned herself facing her

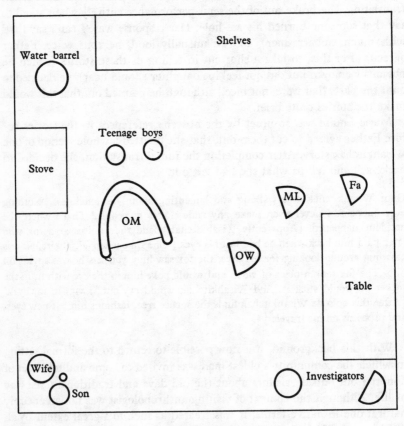

Fig. 15

husband with her back turned toward Marie-Louise and Father; she sat very close to him but not touching. The two old people thus formed a closed circle, reflecting both the self-effacing public behavior expected of a married Indian woman and the closeness of these two individuals.[8] The circle was further reinforced by both spouses crossing their legs toward each othet, thereby closing out the other participants. The old woman remained silent during most of the afternoon; her husband frequently spoke for her. Her only contribution to her husband's performance was to dance while he played the drum, at his instruction.

Father remained at his original seat, which left him very much in the background. As host and a younger man, he was obliged to defer to the greater cultural knowledge of the old man. He listened carefully and attempted to help Marie-Louise in her translations. He seemed to feel that he too was one of the listeners and therefore was learning more about his own culture. Marie-Louise, because she was a much younger woman, felt that she should be as unobtrusive as possible. She made a few polite remarks to the old woman but avoided direct conversation with the old man. This was reflected in her change of position to a point behind the old man's line of vision. Because of her role as translator, Marie-Louise could not retire into the background as a Cree woman of her age would normally do. Her role was reflected by her position between the old man and the white visitors. By turning her head, she could also consult her father behind her. Thus in terms of the group initially present, my husband and I constituted the primary audience and Marie-Louise and her father were observers from backstage. Their presence in a subsidiary position validated the old man's role of traditional performer in that they listened and accepted his right to speak for them and Cree people generally.

During the conversation (which continued for several hours) a number of other observers arrived. The old man's son and his wife came in, accompanied by a small child. They moved into the room, the husband first, positioning themselves squatting in the corner just inside the door.[9] They aligned their bodies facing the old man and listened carefully to him. The son greeted Father but did not otherwise speak to anyone in the room. His presence there was explained somewhat later by his father: this is the one child who remained at home with his parents. The old man referred to him as 'babysis' (the Cree diminutive suffix plus the English word baby), although telling us that he was fifty-three years old. During the old man's lifetime, this son could not become a household head in his own right and was socially subordinate in many contexts.

The last arrivals were two teenage boys. They stood for some time in the doorway, apparently hoping for an invitation to enter. Finally they moved into the room and positioned themselves behind the old man. Neither of them moved further into the room than the center of the old man's back. Both stood quietly without fidgeting and did not speak to anyone in the room. They were accepted by all native participants as appropriate listeners and learners as long as they did not interrupt the old man's speech. These young men were of the age where interest in old Cree traditions begins to manifest itself to identify potential future performers.

Before the old man could sing a traditional song or tell a story, a number of preliminaries had to be performed. These preliminaries had the function of making a gradual transition from the everyday world of Wabasca in 1971 to the mythological time framework in which traditional stories are situated. The old man could not simply plunge into his narratives. First he had to lead the audience through a progression of reference points.

1. He began by emphasizing the importance of his stories and the need to treat them seriously.

2. Then he presented personal biographical validation of his status as an old-fashioned or bush Indian.

3. Then he moved to a discussion of how Indian life was in the old days, many years ago.

4. From the Indian past in which things were much different than they are now, it was appropriate to move to mythological time. The traditional song, dealing with human powers in an old-style Indian world, made the transition complete; the song was formal traditional performance but still in real or everyday time.

5. With the story, the old man at last broke through from the normal world to the supernatural one.

Because he was speaking to virtual strangers, the old man first had to establish his relationship to the event. He did this by speaking of his relationship to Father, whom he spoke of as a younger brother: 'I will tell stories for his sake. I love him just like a younger brother, just the same as if he was breast-fed by my mother.' Father accepted this fictive kin designation by occasionally speaking directly to the old man, for example, urging him to continue a narrative by calling him 'older brother' (a term of respect frequently used among unrelated or distantly related adult men). The old man then explained to Marie-Louise that her father thought a great deal of him, although he and his wife didn't know her well at all. Because we were introduced by Father and he wanted the old man to speak to us, it was acceptable for him to tell us seriously of the old Cree ways.

The old man was extremely concerned that his words be believed and that his audience respect the matters of which he spoke. Before any narrative event could proceed, he found it necessary to specify this. The old man wanted the stories written down and was not entirely confident that an accurate record of his important words would be made by the tape recorder. Marie-Louise was embarrassed by his insistence on this point, apparently not realizing that her father had said virtually the same things earlier the same day in speaking to us alone. As a result, she did not translate the old man's remarks literally:

OM: I'm going to tell them these sacred stories. I don't want them to repeat them wherever they go because maybe I'm lying [i.e., maybe they think I'm lying]. They should keep to themselves that story.
ML: He's telling it to you for your enjoyment.
OM: People get jealous for nothing [i.e., other Indians resent it when stories are told to white men]. I don't want every person to know what I'm telling.
ML: Some of the people have been cheated somehow; however he would like to tell you his story that he experienced in a dream.
OM: Many people ask me to tell stories but I don't do it often. I tell you because you are going to preserve our language.
ML: There are only certain people he would gladly tell stories to.
OM: These I'm telling stories to, I feel sorry for them. I feel sorry for your Dad, he sent you [Marie-Louise] here. I'll sing anyway, for sure I'm lying.
ML: [no translation]

This interchange reflects the traditional denial of competence which begins Cree narrative events. The speaker is not an individual but a performer of traditional material which is independent of his personal identity. Even if he speaks of his own dream visions, he is speaking of something outside himself. This is part of the formality of storytelling etiquette, and Marie-Louise is unsuccessful in shortening it by her failure to translate.

Father's version of concern for the integrity of the stories was equally intense although expressed less formally in a conversation about many topics, i.e., not as part of a recognized performance. He had always wanted to tell old Cree stories on tape, but some (Indian) man once accused him of being a liar and it hurt him. In spite of this, he would tell stories to us because we had come to hear about the Cree way of life from him. He had been approached by the Metis Association and by Indian Affairs and had refused: 'To make a man tell a story or to recount legends of the past that are discredited as lies later on or made like fairy tales, really does something to a man's pride.' Because many people find the old stories so unbelievable, many Indians have refused to tell them. Father believes that it is useless to talk about the kinds of powers that Indians used to have because no one believes it any more. He knows people who still have such powers; one of his uncles could make a fox fur stand up and dance. But mostly he is reluctant to tell such stories because people laugh.

Having established that the stories were to be taken seriously, the old man then told about his own life, situating himself in the world of the traditional Cree Indian. He mentioned his age – ninety-seven years and six months – several times. Marie-Louise became impatient and translated it saying, 'He said that before.' His wife was ninety-one years old. They had been married for seventy-three years. The old man stressed that he and his wife used to be very good-looking. He insisted that Marie-Louise translate his statement that they were now ugly. Marie-Louise apparently considered this boasting and attempted to ignore it (unsuccessfully). Twice the old woman had almost died. She was very stooped because she had been sick. The old man continued discussing his advanced age:

> Now *she* can only lie on one side.
> So can *I*.
> *We* are getting too old.

The parallelism which expresses the unity of the two old people and the old man's solicitousness for his wife (especially in referring to her before himself) was ignored by Marie-Louise in her translation. She seemed to feel that if the old man was to interpret Cree culture he should not insert personal biographical details. Father, however, appeared to accept the validating role of these statements.

In his lifetime, the old man explained that he had killed 403 moose. He retired from hunting in the bush more than thirty years ago when he was sixty-five, because he was too old. Father and Marie-Louise laughed politely at this, a way of affirming the old man's special status. His age and continued agi'ity, both mental and physical, reinforced his performing role as an interpreter of old Cree ways. Frequently the old man commented that he was getting old, expecting a denial from the audience, both native and white. He noted that his weight was now less than two hundred pounds, that of course being a great weight for a Cree man. (The old man is an extremely impressive-looking individual because of his great height and heavy build, both accentuated by a bushy beard.)

The old man was much concerned to explain how strong he had been as a younger man. He used to be able to pack seven hundred pounds for a short distance. In his youth he was a wrestler and he had never been beaten. Father confirmed that he had seen the old man wrestle when he was about ten years old. Once he was all black and blue because a man grabbed him across the waist; that man was very strong. The old man then noted, in a formulaic apology, that the visitors would think he was a big liar: 'I'm getting carried away with my stories.'

The old man was also eager to establish that he did not drink. He used to many years ago but had not for the past eleven years. Drunkenness is, of course, a frequent criticism of Indians by white people, and most Cree people are sensitive about it. The old man expressed the matter in terms of its effect on his ability to control himself and behave in a respectable manner. Again, Marie-Louise's translations reflect her view of the matter (she definitely drinks) but follow the Cree rather closely:

OM: Because maybe I make a mistake in my speech or maybe I will not talk right or I'll get mad or maybe I'll fall. That's the thing I'm scared of. I'd like to have my right mind as long as I live.

ML: He's talking about alcohol and that business ... and he feels that he wants to keep his sanity and walk, you know, instead of staggering around. He might fall down and break his neck.

After placing his own life in the context of traditional Cree culture, the old man then felt obliged to discuss how different things were today than they had been in the past. Again, this is a theme elaborated on by almost all narrators as a preamble to their presentations of traditional materials. The audience is expected to respond with an affirmation of eagerness to listen and learn. The old man began with a formal narrative of his early experiences: [10]

The first time I saw Wabasca, there were only eight houses.
My father was alive then.
He passed away eighty years ago.
My mother passed away sixty-five years ago.
She lies close by at the church.
Of religion there was nothing.
Of the church [building] there was nothing.
They lived in tipis.
They were very poor, these people.

The old man continued more conversationally, telling us that now there were almost three hundred houses but they were all scattered around in the Indian style, not like a town.

As a young man, he worked hard. Again the narrative became stylized:

In the bush I walked to get food to eat.
There wasn't much food around.
Long ago there wasn't anything around to make a living with.
I used a piece of wood to keep my clothing together
 [there were no buttons then].
The people were very poor.
Many times people died by freezing because they couldn't keep warm.
They used straw or rabbit fur to keep their feet warm.
It's a wonder how people continued to live.
I was very poor.
Many times I didn't have a blanket to use.

When I went hunting, I'd go to sleep watching the campfire.
I believe all this because I have seen it.
Anyone that didn't see it wouldn't believe what I am telling.
I am old.
I'm telling stories now.
Right now I'm in that thing [tape recorder] speaking.

All of this may be taken as affirmation of his right to speak of these things. Without the experiences, he would not have been in a position to speak of the traditional Cree way of life.

An earlier conversation with Father had brought out many of the same points, although not in the context of validating his own role as an authentic performer. He believed that young people should be made aware of what had gone on in the past. They have no idea how difficult life was then. He went trapping one spring with his uncle and they found only sixteen muskrats between them. They raised cattle and they survived by their wits. Whatever they had was handmade. Marie-Louise interrupted at this point to say that she didn't think young people would be interested in these things. Father agreed that young Indians today took everything for granted. This began a long digression on how Indians were ashamed of their own people and customs.

Father remembered that when he was ten years old he lived in Athabasca. They had a fairly good life. There was enough money and there were jobs to be had. People didn't have to rely on welfare. But the jobs that were available for Indians were backbreaking. He used to pull freight boats on the Athabasca River for the Hudson's Bay Company from daybreak to dusk. It was five hundred miles with a lot of falls; they had to unload the boats and carry the cargo around the falls. 'Those people were crazy.' They became useless slaves. A man was laughed at for carrying only a hundred pounds and there was great rivalry among the men. A trapper had an easier life because at least he had dogs. Very few people had horses. They hunted little animals and received maybe ten dollars for a muskrat pelt. Today, very few people still trap. The muskrats have almost disappeared because flooding has destroyed their food. It is now harder for an Indian to make a living in the traditional Cree way.

The old man's first formal acting was to sing a traditional song. His ritual opening was a statement that this was his own song. 'Someday I will be dead and you won't be able to listen to my songs. The night is long when I start singing my songs.' This is very much in the traditional context of teaching only those who wish to learn and understand the importance of what is being taught. After the introduction, the old man backtracked and explained that his drum had to be heated so that it would have the proper tone. Father eventually heated the drum over his stove and returned it to the old man, who remained sitting at the center of the room throughout. Then the old man explained that he was trying to think of a song. This too was a formulaic apology. The old man, like most Cree elders, had only a few songs which were his by virtue of dreams or other supernatural validation.

The explanation of the special status of this song was Christian, though in line with the traditional Cree manner of learning and performing songs:

OM: I never used any lies. Right now I'm thanking God. I'm going to sing now.
ML: It's a religious song.
OM: Now, I want to respect what God left on this earth. Now, this song I'm going to sing respected Indians. They knew God existed. Also the priests knew God existed. So we go along with them.
ML: He's talking about religion now. He feels the song, uh, ceremonial chant, he's going to sing you about – Before the priests came, it wasn't . . . you know, Indians believed in God.
OM: There is lots on my mind. God is so good. I like some people better than others. But I love God more than I do man. Could be I'm not worth much, not very good [religious meaning].

The song he sang was an Indian one relating his own dream experience. In accordance with the secrecy usually accorded visions, he did not explain the meaning of his song.

After completing his song, the old man put down his drum and signalled by clapping his hands that the song was over. After some casual conversation he decided to tell a traditional Cree story, again from one of his dreams. Although the elements are found in many traditional stories, the old man did not tie his tale to any of the traditional cycles or heroes. The story was translated in segments decided for the most part by the old man, although Marie-Louise often misunderstood or interrupted because she could not translate. Her father in such cases attempted to clarify the meaning in Cree and occasionally in English. The old man listened carefully but did not understand more than a few words of English and never contributed to the discussion unless asked by Father in Cree. Marie-Louise did not speak directly to the old man when she had problems.

The difficulties in translation were multiple in cause. Marie-Louise was extremely nervous because she did not feel that she could translate adequately. Earlier the same day her father had told her that her translations of his stories were not good enough. In fact he didn't think her English was good enough to translate either.[11] Father felt that formal education was necessary to translate. He had been away to school but it was mainly religious, and he thought that was no education whatsoever. His total English repertoire had been 'yes,' 'no,' 'I don't know,' 'sure.' Later he learned more English but had not used it for many years. Marie-Louise had managed fairly well, however, as long as she was translating for her father.

The old man presented an entirely different situation. Marie-Louise's performance as translator was expected to measure up to his as storyteller. She was a young woman and therefore not anywhere near the same status as the man whose ideas she presumed to translate. She was very nervous about making a mistake, especially in light of her father's great deference toward the old man. Moreover, traditional Cree stories contain a great deal of archaic lexicon with which she was not familiar. She did not know the old man's style of speaking at all well and was often confused by him. His Cree was very terse in style and many times Marie-Louise failed to understand the logic behind his sequential statements. The old man assumed that anyone would know these things and did not elaborate. Although traditionally questions are appropriate at narrative segments and pauses, Marie-Louise was too nervous as translator to take advantage of this chance.

The narrative itself was somewhat rambling, partially because the old man grew tired of interruptions and consultations about translation. However, the narrative as interpreted for us by Marie-Louise and her father illustrates quite clearly the generational hierarchy of appropriate performance and of ritual knowledge. Only the old man, of the three, was an authentic performer in this context. Marie-Louise's father did not yet have the self-confidence to perform independently, particularly since his own children had shown little interest in traditional Cree culture. Our conversations with him showed clearly that he had the competence to perform traditional materials but did not feel comfortable doing so. His daughter showed even less knowledge of these stories and no desire to attempt performance. However, she knew much of the material and could easily step into such a role later in life if she found herself in an appropriate situation to do so (in practice, only if she returned to the reserve with her children).

The narrative itself will be presented in segments, with comments on its organization and segmentation:

> Once there was a person who was said to be strong.
> He was called Bear.
> He was about four feet tall, this much maybe [gesture] .[12]
> He saw three men, who were very strong.
> He knew them from sleep [he saw them in a dream].
> He took them just like friends ... his boys ... his slaves.

Father began translating, with the statement about seeing the men in sleep, his practice of repeating for emphasis the main points made by the old man. He validated the claim that Indians used to have strange powers 'just like in the dream' described. A translation problem arose over the status of the main character's companions. Three different Cree words were suggested. The old man said 'boys.' Father said 'slaves' or 'boys.' Marie-Louise translated the narrative version as 'friends, companions.' She finally settled for 'They became his servants, more or less.' The Cree meaning of 'they recognized his superior status and therefore decided to follow and serve him' is not easily translated and none of the participants could solve this difficulty in English. The old man appeared not to understand what was causing the difficulty.

> The first time he [Bear] met people, he was walking.
> And he had only enough meat for lunch.
> All of a sudden, he came upon a wooded hillock.
> He was eating that meat.
> He thought he saw it [the hillock] coming
> toward him.
> He took a stick. At first he stuck it on
> the ground.
> Then he took a stick over there and he
> stuck it further toward the hillock.
> He saw this hillock; he thought it moved.

Marie-Louise at first translated the word glossed 'wooded hillock' as 'island.' Father initially accepted this as an adequate translation. But as the old man made it clear that there were bushes on the island, he tried to clarify. He told Marie-Louise somewhat impatiently that it was not *nimistihk*, 'island' but *mistagwakeyaw*. The problem was obviously that Marie-Louise did not know the meaning of this word. The old man explained to Father that it meant 'woods' or 'prairie.'[13] Marie-Louise finally decided that it was indeed an island but that it wasn't on water:

It was, uh, what it means is that there was a group of trees, you see, and the person was pulling on this piece of land. Otherwise it was all plain, you know, without any trees.

Note here also that Marie-Louise has jumped ahead of the story. She refers to a man pulling on the 'island' although the old man has not yet mentioned this. This demonstrates that she knows the story motif and can therefore make sense out of the unfamiliar word by knowing what will come next. This too is a way in which young people learn traditional materials, particularly given the correction in use of the word which Father forced her into considering.

Marie-Louise became somewhat confused with the reasons that the little but strong man marked the ground with a stick. The old man simply repeated that the man put a stake in the ground. Father added that he marked it because he didn't believe that the ground was moving and wanted to be certain. Marie-Louise then explained to us that he thought it moved. Father continued in Cree:

He thought that it [the hillock] was as if it moved. He marked it but he only continued to eat meat [i.e., he did not go on to investigate]. Next time he looked at it, he said, 'It's true, behold.'

With the direct quotation in his explanation, Father had broken into narrative performance himself. Although this reflected his enthusiasm to clarify, it was culturally inappropriate because the old man was the authentic performer and should have been deferred to. After his performance in Cree, Father attempted to explain in English, apparently feeling uncomfortable since he had been so aggressive.

> He left that place.
> He came upon a person who was sitting like this.
> There was so much bush around there.
> There was a man ten feet tall pulling on the
>   hillock.
> 'Could you come with me?' that small, four-
>   foot-high one said to the man.
> 'Yes, if you want, I will go with you,'
>   he said to that strong man.
> 'Over here are two of my brothers that you
>   will have to make friends with before
>   I will go with you.
> 'You know, they are stronger than you are,'
>   the tall man said this to him.

Marie-Louise's translation was much more explicit as to the attributes of the two men and the reason for their responses. This information would not, of course, have been necessary for an all-Cree audience. She explained that the tall man decided he might come because he knew that the man was 'only very small but that he was very strong.' That is, the man who was pulling the hillock had the power of choice and made his decision on the basis of strength (with its implication of courage) rather than taking account only of the man's small stature. Marie-Louise at several points confuses the attributes of the major character, referring to him as 'young' rather than 'small.' In both cases, of course, a potentially negative attribute must be overcome by the man before his adventures can proceed satisfactorily.

The decision which must be made by the tall man is reinforced by his statement that the small man must also persuade his brothers to join him. (Cree keeps these 'he's' straight by the use of proximate and obviative third person forms.) These are the three men whose appearance was previewed by the first segment of the narrative. Again, by recognition of the powers of the small man these men will choose to accompany him on his adventures.

> So the tall man let go of the land he was pulling and went
>   with the short man.
> Then the short man heard a noise as if
>   someone was breaking trees.
> It was a very loud noise.
> Finally they saw a man.
> 'What are you making?' that little one said.
> 'I came here with my brother, he asked me
>   along,' this strong one said.
> 'Now will you come with me?' that little
>   one asked him.
> The man was making a rope by peeling logs and
>   winding trees together.
> The short man came and he made a rope out
>   of them, more or less.
> And he asked the man who was doing this
>   [before] if he would come with him.
> And this man agreed that he would.

There was great difficulty over explaining how the trees were made into rope. More interesting, however, is the manner in which the second brother was persuaded to join the expedition. The man who was pulling the hillock, the first brother, told the man who was winding trees, the second brother, that the small man with him had requested that he come. His positive feeling toward the small man was conveyed by his use of the term '(little) brother.' This honorific form made it clear that he had accepted the man in whose company he travelled, although he was very small. The second brother was given additional evidence of the little man's strength and courage when he performed the same task, that of winding trees into a rope. On this basis, he agreed to join them.

> And they left, the three of them.
> And then they looked for someone [else].
>   They still looked for one.
> That one they were going to find.
> The man they had just picked up, the one
>   that was making the rope, was twelve feet
>   tall.
>
> Next then they came upon that other man
>   standing up.

> The man picked up a piece of stone, a rocky
> mountain.
> He took it and moved it, always in the
> same direction.
> Now the short man said to him, 'If you're
> not strong, why do you do that?'
> 'Rocky mountain people are living in the
> mountains they said I made,' the man said.
> This man said, 'I have been sent by the spirit
> who is named God to build these mountains
> because people in the future will be
> numerous and they will speak different
> tongues.
> 'The Frenchmen will speak French.
> 'The Englishmen will speak English.
> 'The Chipewy will speak Chipewyan.
> 'The Ukrainians will speak Ukrainian.
> 'And the Crees will speak their own language.
> 'And in the end a lot of hardship and bad luck
> will come upon all these different races.'

Father reinforced the conclusion by reiterating that the mountains were made so that people would be there. He also said that all the different peoples should use the land, just like they do now. Marie-Louise noted that people would survive in the future because of the mountains being there. She invented a closing line: 'And this is one of the stories that tells about how mountains were formed.' The old man's closing was quite different:

Now it's down in the book [tape recorder] as it was said when I was a child in Crane Lake area.

Marie-Louise ignored this. The old man continued:

Now there's something else I was going to tell them. The man [who made the mountains] predicted that in the future people would start growing their beards again. Their beards would grow as they had done originally. In that time all men had whiskers and all women didn't. All the first people used to wear long gowns. If a couple were walking with their backs covered, with their backs to you, you would think they were the same. But if you were to call to them, they would turn around and one would have a beard. Then you could tell the difference.

I know that they [the investigators] will live happily together for the rest of their lives and I might meet them in the next world.

The old man then clapped his hands to show that his story was finished.

This double ending is not unique in Cree narrations. The formal story ended with the third brother's predictions for the future. But the old man telling the story wanted to make some comment which was intended for his particular audience. In this sense it might be called the moral or epilogue. He was responding to the fact that my husband had a beard (as did he) and that another white man he knew well had a beard. This was a way for the old man to include these outsiders in his rendition of traditional Cree material. It also served as a gradual transition back to the everyday conversational world. The style of the Cree changed radically, with the dignity and solemnity of the sacred story broken. This made it possible for all the participants to talk about the story.

The old man's attempt to return gradually to the spatiotemporal framework of everyday life was not entirely successful. Both Marie-Louise and Father were thinking in terms of the performance of traditional material and did not easily switch into a lighter vein. Apparently sensing the disapproval, the old man and his wife went home soon afterwards.[14] Marie-Louise and Father were silent for some time afterwards, lost in meditation about the old Cree world. Later, Father commented that the old man had changed the ending, perhaps because he was nervous about telling a sacred story to a white man. He then agreed that the story had been finished but did not understand why there had been more after that.

Both Marie-Louise and her father failed to perceive the skill with which the old man had concluded his narrative. For him, the formal narrative device paralleled the one he had used in beginning his story. He completed his narrative in mythological time with a formal ending. He then used a character from the sacred story to bridge the gap between the supernatural and everyday worlds. As at the start of his story, the progression was gradual.

1. First he spoke of old Indians with beards, who had been very close to mythological times in the Indian past.

2. Then he referred to more recent Indians who did not have beards.

3. Next, the old man followed his own progression into the future, saying that Indians would have beards again.

4. Finally he tied his nattrative to the present and future activities of the individuals present in the particular interaction. He used the theme of the beard from his prediction of the future by a mythological character to comment about the visitors to whom he had been speaking. He gave his approval to the individuals (perhaps in the manner of a priest blessing his congregation) and referred to the (Christian) future in which he would see these people again.

Although the Cree of northern Alberta have been considerably influenced by missionaries, ethnic diversity, and depreciation of Indian culture and language by Indian and white alike, traditional Cree genres of formal speaking persist and adapt. The Cree language is still spoken in its traditional functional complexity. The performance situation described here makes it clear that Cree narrative is still changing and adapting. Although the old man of this performance is not the same performer his grandfather would have been, his cultural tradition has been sufficiently strong to remain viable under a very different way of life. The Cree narrative tradition is not a static thing; its strength lies in the ability to adapt to whatever lives its performers may come to live. There is, therefore, a continuous interaction between context of performance, individual performer, and culture change. [15]

AN ANALYSIS OF THE COURSE OF A JOKE'S TELLING IN CONVERSATION

HARVEY SACKS

0.0   In this paper we examine the sequential organization of the telling of a dirty joke in conversation.[1] For the organization of the joke and also of its telling we find that there is a single most decisive feature: the joke is built in the form of a story. The decisiveness of that feature involves the fact that, there being means for sequentially organizing the telling of a story in conversation, the sequential organization of the telling of this joke's being built in the form of a story is largely given by those means. This telling is composed, as for stories, of three serially ordered and adjacently placed types of sequences which we call the preface, the telling, and the response sequences. We shall proceed by considering each of them in turn, intending that the adequacy of such a characterization as is developed in terms of these types for these materials will provide support to our proposal that the joke's construction in the form of a story is indeed its decisive feature.

0.1   In what follows we shall largely be concerned to subject the utterances of the fragment, of which we present a transcription at the close of this section, to analysis in terms of how they figure in the three types of sequences we have proposed to constitute organizational parts of the telling. In this endeavor one recurrent theme may be extracted for introductory comment. While the three types, as types, are serially ordered and adjacently placed, it obviously is incorrect to propose that given the initiation of some particular preface, a telling and a response sequence are sure to occur, or to occur without other materials intervening. There are built-in conditions for terminating a telling before the completion of a response sequence; at the preface, for example, if the joke can be recognized as known, by recipients, from the characterization of it that occurs in the preface. But potential conditions for a termination do not always result in that happening, as is illustrated a variety of times in the ensuing discussion, for example, at sections 1.2–1.4.

Supposing that each sequence type can be put together to contain such a set of components as will make a subsequent type appropriate, and can also take a course which makes that type's completion or the occurrence of its subsequent problematic, the fragment we are here concerned with is of particular interest because in it the telling is brought to completion though each part contains materials which could inhibit that happening. If no materials inconsistent with continuation occur, a characterization of the course of the telling can be readily developed. Here what we shall be trying to do is to characterize a telling course that goes to completion across the recurrent presence of materials that could yield termination. Our focus then is with determining how and where potentially terminative materials are introduced, how they can be incorporated within a telling's course, and the sorts of effects other than terminative they can have.

Here then is the fragment of conversation within which the joke is told.[2] Its teller, whom we pseudonymize as 'Ken,' is, like 'Roger' and 'Al,' a teenager around sixteen–seventeen years old. 'Dan' is an adult and the therapist in what is a group therapy session which the others attend, a fact which never again figures in our discussion.

1.	Ken:	You wanna hear muh-eh my sister told me a story
2.		last night.
3.	Roger:	I don't wanna hear it. But if you must,
		(1.0)
4.	Al:	What's purple an' an island. Grape– Britain.
5.		That's what iz sis//ter –
6.	Ken:	No. To stun me she says uh there was these three
7.		girls an' they just got married?
8.	Roger:	Ehhh//hehh hhh hhh
9.	Ken:	An' uh –
10.	Roger:	⌈Hey waita se(h)cond.
11.	Ken:	⌊( ) –
12.	Al:	Heh!
13.	Roger:	Drag tha(h)t by agai(h)n hehh//hehh
14.	Ken:	There – There was these three *girls*. And they
15.		were all *sis*ters. An' they'd just got married
16.		to three *bro*thers.
17.	Roger:	You better have a long talk with you sis//ter.
18.	Ken:	Waita – waita min//ute.
19.	Roger:	Oh. // Three brothers.
20.	Al:	Eheh
21.	Al:	eh//heh!
22.	Ken:	And uh – // so–
23.	Al:	The brothers of these sisters.
24.	Ken:	No they're different – mhh/hh
25.	Al:	heh
26.	Ken:	You know different families. // (no link-up.)

27. Roger: 'S closer thn be*fore,* // hhh
28. Ken: So –
29. Al: Heh! hh hh
30. Ken: *Quiet.*
31. Al: hh hh // hhhh
32. Ken: So, first of all, that night, they're – on their
33.   honeymoon the – uh mother-in-law, says – (to 'em) well
34.   why don'tcha all spend the night here an' then you
35.   cn go on yer honeymoon in the *mor*ning. First night,
36.   th'mother waiks up t'the first door an' she hears
37.   this *uuuuuuuuuuhh!* hh Second door is *HHOOOOHHH!*
38.   Third door there's nothing. She stands there fer about
39.   *twun*ny-five minutes waiting fer sumpna happen, –
40.   nuthin.
                (1.0)
41. Ken: Next morning she talks t'the first daughter, and she
42.   sz – uh how come ya – how com y'went YEEEEEAAAAGGGHH
43.   last night, 'n daughter sez well, it *tic*kled mommy,
44.   'n second girl, how come ya screamed. Oh mommy it
45.   *hurts.* hh Third girl, walks up t'her – why didn'
46.   ya *say* anything last night. W'*you* told me it was
47.   always impolite t'talk with my mouth full,
                (2.0)
48. Ken: hh hyok hyok,
                (1.0)
49. Ken: Hyok.
                (3.0)
50. Al: *HA-HA-HA-HA,*
51. Ken: ehh heh heh // hehhh
52. (Al):   hehhhehhheh hhh
53. Roger: Delayed reactio(h)n
54. Al: hehh I hadtuh think // about it awhile you know?
55. Roger: hhh heh
                (1.0)
56. Roger: hehh hh hehh hhh You mean the deep hidden meaning
57.   there doesn't hitcha right awa(hh)y heh heh //
58.   hehhhhhh hehhhhhh
59. Al: hh hhh // hhh
60. (Dan):   (yeh. I // guess so.)
61. Al: What he meant to say is that – that uhm
                (1.0)
62. Roger: Ki//nda got psychological over//tones (   )
63. Al: (   )
64. Ken: Little sister's gittin // *ol*der.
65. (Roger): hehh hh hehh

66.	Ken:	ehheh heh that's what I *mea(h)n* tuh // say,
67.	Dan:	*Sounds* like it,
68.	Ken:	Fer twelve years old tellin me – I didn't even // know –
69.	Roger:	How d'ya know she's just not repeating what she heard
70.		an' doesn't know what // it means.
71.	Al:	She have to explain it to ya Ken?
72.	Ken:	Yeah, she had to explain me to detail to me,
		(0.7)
73.	Al:	Okay, good. Gladju gotta sister that knows //
74.		something,
75.	Ken:	hh hhh
76.	Ken:	She told me she was eating a hot dog,
		(4.0)
77.	Ken:	hh
78.	Roger:	Wha' does that mean,
79.	Ken:	hh hh
80.	Al:	Yeah c'mon // explain it // to us,
81.	Ken:	heh
82.	Ken:	heh
83.	Al:	Explain // us – explain everything you know Ken,
84.	Ken:	hhh! Nuh *I (hh) du(h)nno* I just said that
85.	Al:	Explain everything.

1.0   Stories and jokes built in the form of stories, told in conversation, properly have their telling begun, as this one does (see lines 1–6), with what we call a preface sequence. In one common sort which does involve the appropriateness of initiation of its subsequent, the telling sequence, the preface can take a minimal length of two turns, the first involving talk by the intending teller and the second by an intended recipient. We shall develop a characterization of the preface sequence of our fragment by first considering such features as it has in common with minimals like it that do make the telling sequence appropriate, thereafter proceeding to examine its variant course in some detail. This procedure will be repeated when, subsequently, we consider the telling and response sequences.

Prefaces with two utterance minimal courses, whose courses make initiation of a telling appropriate, can involve, first, a party, the intending teller, producing an utterance that combinedly contains such sequentially relevant components as: an offer to tell or a request for a chance to tell the joke or story; an initial characterization of it; some reference to the time of the story events' occurrence or of the joke's reception; and, for jokes particularly, a reference to whom it was received from if its prior teller is known or known of by recipients. Such a group of components should be packed into an utterance whose first possible completion, which will usually coincide with its first sentence's first possible completion, is supposably the point of transition from intending teller's talk to recipient reply.[3] If such a first utterance is followed by another, done by an intended recipient of the story or joke, which accepts or requests the telling, then the preface sequence can take a minimal length, be two turns long, and thereafter the telling sequence can be undertaken, intending teller re-acquiring the floor for that project.

If an intending teller's first utterance contains such components each of them can be sequentially operative, and in different ways. The 'offer' component is concerned with the turn-to-turn organization of the preface sequence, operating to provide that a next turn should be occupied with one of the methodic responses to an offer, e.g., an acceptance. The mentioning of the source provides information which recipients can use to determine whether they might know the joke. A telling being contingent on a joke's supposed supposable unknownness to recipients, the mentioning of the source gives recipients material with which they might initially consider the possibility that the joke is known to them, and exhibits to them that teller is oriented to that contingency of the telling. If recipients have heard one recently from the same source they can proceed to check out whether it is the intended joke that they know. The initial characterization (which can involve, e.g., 'a real dirty joke,' 'something wonderful,' 'a really odd thing,' and the like) can serve to motivate a positive reply, can be used in developing a negative one ('this is no time for jokes'), and seems to have as a distinctive structural job informing recipients about the sort of response teller seeks after his telling, thereby aiding recipients in listening throughout to find, from the telling, such materials as are relevant to the production of such a response and to its positioning. For example, indicating that 'a real dirty joke' is being projected informs that laughter is desired in the response sequence and that it should be done on the recognition of a punchline. Mentioning the time of occurrence or reception deals with the placing of the story in some conversation, as, when the time can be seen to be between last interaction and this one the story is then warranted for telling via its status as possibly news, a status that can also be relevant to where the tellable is placed within a conversation, e.g., early in it. We say that each of these components 'can' be consequential in order to note that some might not be on any given telling occasion. For example, information with regard to the desired response may not get shown to have been attended to because information like that is not exhibited until the response sequence and that is not in a particular telling actually got to. Or, the feature having a value which is consistent with the telling, as a 'last night' reception can be, that facet is subsequently unmentioned or alluded to and the telling is allowed without our being able to see that it is allowed in part by virtue of the mentioned reception time in particular.

Given the foregoing discussion it is easy to see how a preface sequence can come to be longer than its minimal version, the sources for its expansion initially involving uses recipients can make of the particularities of the features of the first utterance to either initially reject or otherwise delay the telling. Expanded prefaces which result in a telling are what we are here interested in developing characterizations of.

1.1   In his preface first utterance Ken combines an offer to tell, 'You wanna hear ... ,' an indication of his source, '... my sister told me ... ,' that a 'story' is forthcoming, and such a reference to the time of its reception, '... last night ... ,' as will make the currently intended telling be seen as having been done on the first occasion he could use to tell it to these recipients. He does pack these components into an utterance whose transition occasion is indeed its first possible completion point. This latter feature of it is not however achieved in its most characteristic way, via single-sentence construction, the transition point occurring at the first possible completion of its first sentence, though it is nonetheless achieved. In part because such a construction as he does use is consistent with the proposed rule, and also because the way he proceeds recurs at preface and preface-like positions, we raise for consideration the possibility that his use of what is begun as a sentence internal correction, '... muh-eh my ... ,' and is turned into a way to start a second sentence in the preface without having the first go to completion, does indeed constitute a method for satisfying the first possible completion transition use rule while building an utterance in which that does not coincide with its first sentence's first possible completion. I am suggesting that his construction can be viewed as a device whereby transition points are avoided, but not overrun, their occurrence being here and elsewhere rather delicately attended matters. While he does not use the word 'joke,' or propose that it is a dirty joke that he will be relating, that it is at least a joke that he intends to tell seems appreciated at least by Al (see line 4), and probably by Roger too (see the discussion in section 2.3). Since these appreciations might be mystifying, we note that the telling of dirty jokes has occupied a good part of the approximately twenty minutes the participants have been talking together.

1.2   Ken then stops and Roger, an intended recipient, produces an utterance that orients to the offer and permits the telling. He does this by first producing what on its own would be a rejection ('I don't wanna hear it . . .'), then adding a counter-offer ('. . . but if you must'). A rejection alone would both register a disappreciation and have that serve, sequentially, to at least initially inhibit the telling. An acceptance alone would serve sequentially to occasion the telling while also registering an initial appreciation. With the combination he employs he can use means for registering his at least initial disappreciation without having its vehicle do its characteristic sequential job. That combination, of a rejection and a counter offer, is furthermore available, a matter indicatively suggested by recalling its use in other sorts of offer responses, as when to an invitation someone replies, 'No. I can't come over. Why don't you come here?' As each of the main sequential options to an offer carries affiliated interactional and emotional information, the rejection–counter offer combination constitutes one technique-class for separating sequential and other information. At least one technical sort of interest of the possibility may be developed. An intending teller, who can use an offer form in his prefacing utterance, can alternatively use a request form. Acceptance of a request involves a similar sequential import for the telling as acceptance of an offer, but a different interactional import; it can, for example, constitute a favor. Such a combination as Roger had done permits recipient to pick his interactional response and his sequentially consequential response separately, and thereby prevents intending teller from fully controlling both, given that both are involved in any response, by his control over the choice between using an offer or a request form. Note, in that regard, to a request, an acceptance may be done which registers more approval than the sequential job requires. To 'Would you mind . . . ?' someone can reply, 'Go ahead . . .' or 'Mind? I'd love it.'

1.3　Al can take a turn specifically before Ken resumes. As an intended recipient he too may accept or reject the offer. As Roger has given permission, Al needn't talk unless inhibiting the telling is what he is interested in doing. One condition for a telling being that the intended joke or story is not already known to current recipients, an intended recipient can conditionally reject by guessing the joke or story that is to be told. Among the interests of that possibility are: if the guess is correct, it is not that the, e.g., joke goes untold, but that an intended recipient has told it, and to the intending teller who, for sure, knows it. If alternatively the guess is incorrect, its teller has nonetheless used a space another has made for a joke's telling to tell one first. Doing a guess has a basis in its use as a conditional rejection and involves the guesser in using the mentioned source to find a joke that might be the joke. But Al, while knowing of the sister – she has been mentioned in previous sessions – has never met her and couldn't tell the joke he does tell because it has been received by him from her. Apparently he uses the mentioning of the source to employ what he knows about the sister, that she is twelve years old, to occasion telling a joke which can be delivered as a guess by being the sort of joke such persons tell. That involves his treating the mentioned source as a possible characterizer of the joke and that, as we noted, is one common component of the preface first utterance. Al then uses a place for doing rejection to produce a candidate rejection, where even if he was right about the sort of joke, that might inhibit its telling or occasion his self-congratulation after it, and also he gets a chance to deliver a joke himself, to deliver one, furthermore, that he can treat as 'not his' and if not treated as funny, not his failure. On its completion it gets no laughter, and he does indeed disaffiliate from it.

1.4 With his 'No. To stun me she says ... ,' Ken closes the preface sequence and starts the telling. By setting the telling up via 'No,' he treats Al's joke under its sequentially legitimizing guise – as a guess, that status having been its basis for being told, whose failure reoccasions the originally intended telling, and now, furthermore, as a correction to Al's guess. With '... to stun me ...' Ken promises that the joke to come is of a different sort than the distinctly childish one that Al delivered as what the sister might have told. Ken has found a way to use the course of the preface sequence to strengthen his basis for the telling. What was previously deliverable by permission is now deliverable as a correction on what another has said.

2.0   The telling sequence

A joke's or a story's telling having been appropriately prefaced, its teller should proceed directly to tell it to its completion. In contrast with the organization of the preface sequence, place for the talk of recipients within the course of the telling sequence need not be provided by the teller and the telling can then take a minimal length of one teller turn.

2.1 If recipients choose to talk within the telling sequence, they may have to do their talking interruptively. For, as teller need not provide them with places, they cannot await their occurrence, and seeing no use to await such an occurrence, a basis for interrupting is given. And though they will get a chance, on its completion, by virtue of the organization of the response sequence that expectable place is not projectably usable for various of what the telling's course might involve them in being concerned to say, and in fact they do talk, and do talk interruptively, within the telling sequence. While sanctionable interruptions are located via utterance units in process there are at least several bases for recipient talk, in stories or jokes, without occasioning the sanctioning that interruptions can otherwise legitimate. For example, a recipient can note a failure to hear some just-produced fragment or can assert the occurrence of an understandability problem. Given just the foregoing we are prepared for noticing and appreciating the orderliness of some rather fine, and not obviously related, co-occurrent features of recipient talk within the telling sequence here. The two sequences that recipients initiate in the course of the telling, i.e., lines 10ff, and lines 23ff, are both begun interruptively and both involve understanding problems. But also involve interruptions placed at points of possible transition, in constructional terms, for utterances outside of stories. We are proposing that an observable conjunction in these particular materials which does not involve obviously related matters is *un*coincidental. The conjunction is between that the talk is interruptive, that it is placed very close to points of possible transition in non-story constructional terms, and that the talk's business concerns understanding problems. That conjunction has a basis which is, again, that provision for the talk of recipients need not be provided by the teller, and, alternatively, that recipients are allowed to find things to say within the telling sequence (one group of those things to say involving understanding problems). Having been thus provided with basis for talking which will need to be done interruptively, positioning it with a formal attention to generally usable transition points, makes its intended lawfulness as visible as is consistent with its interruptive status. Note that the foregoing account required no reference to the fact that a joke, or a dirty joke, was being told. It used only that something built in the form of a story was being told.

2.2   By introducing some considerations specific to the telling sequence for jokes (built in the form of a story) we can further extend the observable orderlinesses of the materials we are examining.

Since responses to stories require an understanding of them and can reveal the failure thereof, a recipient who feels a failure in the story's course and can intrude to seek clarification is motivated to do so because he can thereby be aided in avoiding a misresponse. No special motive for raising a failure beyond its occurrence need be had where stories are concerned, for failures to hear or understand have such a potential consequentiality. For jokes, however, one needn't remedy failures of understanding in order to respond appropriately since there is available a general way to appropriately respond which can be used whether one understands or not, i.e., laughter produced at the recognized completion. One's failures of understanding are concealable. Furthermore, for jokes and dirty jokes in particular, but not for stories generally, there are grounds for avoiding the assertion of occurred understanding failures. Jokes, and dirty jokes in particular, are constructed as 'understanding tests.' Not everyone supposably 'gets' each joke, the getting involving achievement of its understanding, a failure to get being supposable as involving a failure to understand. Asserting understanding failures can then reveal, e.g., recipients' lack of sophistication, a matter that an appropriately placed laugh can otherwise conceal. For jokes, and dirty jokes in particular then, the assertion of understanding failures, while legitimate, is expectably more restricted than for stories otherwise, and the assertion is distinctly of interest beyond being an index of the presence of non-understandings.

The foregoing locates a particular class of understanding failures as eligible for use where jokes or dirty jokes are being told. They are such as claim that a located failure implicates some defect of the joke or its telling. If such a claim can be developed by a recipient the talking that understanding failures allow within the course of a telling can be done; can be done without the failure implicating recipients' supposable sophistication in a negative way; can indeed be used, by requiring teller to venture a clarification of what he may only know by rote, to cause teller to himself become the subject of the understanding test he seemed to be administering, and can thereby constitute one best way of both legitimizing a disappreciation of the joke and lawfully heckling the telling. We are suggesting that the failures of understanding asserted, interruptively, by these recipients of the joke's telling are of just that sort, and we shall now attempt to explicate their sources in the joke telling, hoping thereby to locate the defects which recipients grasped.

2.3　Before doing that, however, let us attend to some ways in which the fact that the joke is dirty figures in the recipient talk. Both sequences, the first involving the possible implication that the girls got married to each other and the second that the sisters married their own brothers, involve drawing specifically obscene implications, ones which happen to be unintended by the teller, where: attending to obscene implications of not necessarily obscene matters constitutes one specifically appropriate procedure for listening to get a dirty joke in its course of presentation. These understandings then are consistent with such a sort of search for obscenity as recipients of a dirty joke are properly occupied with.

2.4　By treating 'just got married' in a usual sense, as involving that the subjects of that predicate married each other, Roger makes available for notice what he can then, by virtue of that being at least illegal, make cause for wonder. While Roger's 'understanding' is surely feigned, it does involve the sort of option that jokes are made with, as the following quote (in which the option, though intended, is not taken up) evidences:

'My friend's 90 years old widower father is still pretty spry and also a fast thinker in a crisis. He proved this recently to a slightly younger widow who was a matrimonial activist. Striking suddenly one evening, she said to him, "Don't you think we should get married?"

'"Why, yes," the old man parried, as his head ducked the noose, "but who would have us?"'[4]

Turning then to lines 23ff, Al appears also to have ignored a restriction on the application of a possible interpretation. We consider this one a bit more fully because, in another publication (Sacks 1972), we developed rules which apply to just such materials and which make the method of Al's inference technically available. We proposed there that there is a class of category collections, of which the collection 'family,' which includes such categories as 'mother,' 'father,' 'sister,' 'brother,' etc., is a prototype. If categories from such a collection are being used to refer to some group of more than one person, the basic interpretational rule is: treat the set of persons so referred to as co-incumbents of one unit *if one can*. Having applied the rule, and ignored the latter restriction, Al can propose to have heard the 'brothers' and 'sisters' to be in one family, and thereby to have located a possible obscenity the joke did not intend or a failure of knowledge of its designer, the failure involving, of course, not knowing that brothers can't marry their own sisters, though that fact could perfectly well have served him as grounds for seeing the relevance of the restriction the rule contains.

We have now come to some ways in which the fact that this is a joke that is being told figures in the course of its telling and that it is a dirty joke also figures. We have also come to see that the interruptive utterances of recipients are methodic, and that quite fine-feature co-occurrences can be made observable and subject to structural explication. We have further come to see that there are quite different ways that the statuses 'built in the form of a story,' 'joke,' 'dirty joke' figure. All of the foregoing has been done, finally, with attention being directed almost exclusively to the organization of the telling in conversation, not (yet) to that of the joke itself.

3.0 The response sequence

A joke-telling sequence's completion, intendedly accomplished by its punchline, occasions its response sequence. In minimal courses that consists wholly of laughings. As each recipient may laugh, and as laughings are a prime exception to the 'no more than one at a time' speaker turn-taking rule for conversation, the laughings can overlap. In minimal courses the joke response sequence consists wholly of laughings that partially overlap.

Laughings, which for conversation generally are competitive with talking at the points where the former might be done, have a priority claim on a joke's completion. But each recipient is not obliged to laugh. Each who chooses not to can orient to its priority status by being silent in favor of those who might choose to. Consequently, delayed laughings and silence too are systematic possibilities on joke completions. But the conversation system is designed to minimize gaps and silences. Consequently, where they are systematically possible the system contains techniques which encourage gap minimization and which provide remedies for silences. There is a group of such techniques available for use at the joke response sequence position in particular. Their use organizes the talk that composes expanded response sequences for jokes. That being so, an at least initial technical interest in expanded response sequences for jokes is in their evidencing that facet of what we can intend by 'organized' which involves that even for 'second order' structural problems there are structural solutions. That is, the possible use of less than minimal responses leaves a potential gap; the existence of that potential gap poses a turn organizational problem for whose reduction there are solutions; those solutions inhibit the use of one apparent alternative to a minimal response, i.e., no response and encourage another alternative, i.e., an expanded response sequence. That turns out to be the alternative to a minimal response sequence by virtue of the intrusion of relevance of turn organizational considerations which the possibility of no responses poses because it yields a silence.

3.1   In order to set up the sorts of expansions joke response sequences can take we proceed first to show how delayed recipient laughter and silence are distinctively systematic possibilities on joke completions.

For conversation generally, at the points at which laughing might be done by current non-speakers it is competitive with the possibility of talk by them or others. Since laughings are responsive, potential laughers will be concerned to have their laugh locate what it is responsive to. And since laughings are very locally responsive – if done on the completion of some utterance they affiliate to last utterance and if done within some utterance they affiliate to its current state of development – the concern to have one's potential laugh locate what it is intendedly responsive to requires that it be done as rapidly as possible. For delay, allowing other talk to intervene between a laugh and its target talk, can have the result that the laugh will be heard as aimed at other than what it is intended to respond to, and not as a response that happens to be more or less delayed to some locatable prior event. It is in that sense that for conversation generally, i.e., without specification of the particular sorts of loci involved, delayed laughing is not a systematic projectable possibility.

Jokes are special occasions for laughings in that laughings have a priority claim on a joke's completion. Though each recipient is not obliged to, any recipient may laugh. Each who chooses not to can orient to its priority claim by not taking a first opportunity to talk (the joke completion, being a point of transition, is such an opportunity), by being silent in favor of those who might choose to laugh. Since each recipient is not obliged to laugh, any can choose not to without causing no laughter to be a consequence, except of course in two-party conversation. That makes two-party conversation joke telling a very different situation than where more than two are involved. For reasons such as this we are specifically not considering joke telling in two-party conversation in this paper.

Each and therefore all recipients declining to laugh on its first possibility, on the joke's intended completion, and all who decline to laugh also declining to talk, a second chance for laughings that are delayed occurs before talk breaches a developing silence. Alternatively, any who decline to laugh can have a chance for laughing delayedly, and before talk, if any choose to laugh. For, as one's laughing does not exclude others', any who have not taken a first opportunity to laugh can, another having started a laugh, produce a delayed laugh that joins, overlaps the latter's.

Whereas then for conversation generally potential laughers are motivated to laugh as soon as possible, the situation of jokes making provision for a chance to laugh with delay, potential laughers can wait, to see, for example, whether others do, before starting or choosing not to. Delayed laughs can both precede talk and locate that it is the joke they follow that they are responsive to. Delayed laughing being possible, each might also choose not to laugh delayedly and there is then a systematic possibility of gaps or silences, the orientation to laughing's priority claim being satisfied by not talking if not laughing.

3.2   If gaps or silences are systematically possible, that structural fact is itself significant. For, to repeat, this conversation system is designed to minimize gaps and silences. It is then expectable that where those possibilities are structural, there will be means for discouraging their happening, for encouraging laughings when they are priority items, and for encouraging their non-delayed production. We shall consider those means now, develop some limits to their operation, and then proceed to consider the import of another mechanism which operates at those limits.

The means for encouraging laughing, and for encouraging its non-delayed production, while surely familiar, seem unnamed and not functionally appreciated. Our name for them is 'the recipient comparative wit assessment device.' The device's operation has its base in the following: given a potential gap between a punchline's completion and the start of recipient laughings, and given that recipient laughings may overlap, recipient laughs are potentially differentiable in terms of their relative starts. If relative starts are then oriented to, they can provide materials with which to comparatively assess recipients. And recipients themselves orienting to this potential use of their relative laugh starts, are then encouraged to laugh as soon as possible, to try to be first, and therefore to attempt to laugh before it can be seen whether others will laugh at all. (Recall: jokes and dirty jokes in particular are used as 'understanding tests.') The power of this device is that it encourages recipients to try to laugh before they have seen whether others will, and once any recipient has laughed whether on those grounds or others, each other recipient is thereby also encouraged to laugh as soon as he can.

There is then a mechanism which encourages non-delay of laughings on joke completions, and, laughings occurring, encourages other recipients to laugh as soon as any have begun. However, the mechanism not being readily applicable if none laugh allows each to delay to see if others will, where it is at all possible that none might. And such an initial delay being usable, an encouragement for its use resides in that not only does none laughing undercut the recipient wit comparative assessment device, it also permits the non-laughing's concertedness to be used to negatively grade the joke or its telling.

The success of a decision not to laugh in setting up its use to negatively grade a joke telling turns then on that decision being arrived at by the set of recipients, where each is subject to individual pressure to laugh before that possibility can be checked out, and thereby to undercut the possibility. The choice to laugh or not to laugh is not free, nor consequential independently of what others do, which can be inaccessible when the choice is at hand. But if all do not laugh then a different assessment is possible from the one that can be made if various recipients laugh with differentiated starts. If the set of recipients laugh rapidly and overlappingly their responses will not be graded negatively, nor will the joke be. If, however, the set of recipients do achieve non-laughing then the silence that ensues arms them with materials of talk with which to either respond to the telling or to a critique that the teller might develop, responding to their non-response. This situation for jokes seems a specification of what is a general technique for dealing with silence's occurrence in conversation. That is, generally, silence can be handled by turning the silence into a topic or by turning into a topic the preceding utterance or sequence by way of that feature of it that it produced a silence.

In summary then, the comparative wit device can serve, via its potential use to encourage laughings quickly, blindly, or on some laugh start, or, delay having occurred for laugh starts or for some laugh's start relative to others, to occasion talk about the relative wit of recipients. The joke grading device can serve, via its potential use to encourage delay, or, delay by each yielding the observability of the fact that none may laugh, and none then choosing to laugh, to occasion talk directed to grading the joke and teller's wit negatively.

The foregoing locates and leaves us with a range of potential problems that response sequences can engender for participants, and we turn our attention to the instant response sequence for its bearing on these matters, for what it can teach us.

3.3 While the instant response sequence does contain laughs, there are sufficient aberrancies to those laughs to make the fact that it contains talk assessing the laughs and the telling altogether expectable. Such aberrancies as the following may be noted: the first two laughs do not overlap, are separated by a gap; the teller and not a recipient laughs first, and not on completion but after a gap; both teller's first laugh and recipient's subsequent first laugh are mirthless, and brief.

Section 3.2 left us with no alternative first move to laughter in the response sequence, though it suggested that a concerted absence of recipient laughter was possible via each recipient's use of a potential delay to check whether others would laugh. While this choice would expectably yield talk directed to its assessment, it was left unexamined how that talk might get started, in the face of the priority to laughter yielding silence if not laughter. Here we consider materials which bear on that issue. Mirthless laughter, which here constitutes the first production, by both teller and a recipient, seems a particularly interesting object. Why, if laughter be mirthless, is it done at all? And how does it shape the course of talk which succeeds its occurrence?

In pursuit of accounting for the occurrence of mirthless laughter, the argument of section 1.2 seems relevant. A mirthless laugh perhaps constitutes a way to produce a sequentially appropriate object, where that object is laughter, while stripping it of much of the rest of what laughter otherwise carries, emotionally and interactionally. While it is certainly of interest that such stripped-down laughing is done, our concern now is with some problems its use solves, and with some its delayed, teller-begun, nonoverlapped mirthlessness pose.

Ignoring the teller's laugh for the moment, a delayed recipient laugh that is mirthless, or, as here, specifically mocking (as our transcript attempts to indicate that Al's is), can serve to occasion transition to talk that assesses the telling, without having the fact that some recipient laughed served to make that laugh's delay or the non-laughing of others set up the use of the comparative wit assessment device. Al's delayed and mocking laughter as an only recipient laugh can then constitute means for arriving at response sequence talk without giving materials which could be used to have that laugh serve to aid a possible defense of the joke and critique of the recipients' wit.

Recipient use of such a laugh has a further safety to it in that besides being a first and delayed recipient laugh, it follows teller's mirthless laugh, teller's mirthlessness suggesting that teller might well be not intending to defend the joke's funniness. If then Al's laugh's mirthlessness gains some assurance of its safety from Ken's laugh's mirthlessness, what might be sources for Ken's laugh having gone first and been mirthless?

Recalling, again, that the conversation system is designed to minimize gaps, we may note: whenever a party's utterance is such as to have particular sorts of nexts appropriate on its completion there are means available to such a party for post-indicating completion's occurrence, it having occurred to teller's satisfaction and both no such subsequent and silence having ensued. He can repeat the utterance or its completion or he may offer a candidate response himself, as in the case of questions the questioner may follow a pause after his intended completion with a candidate, guessed answer ('Why did you do it?' [pause] 'Because of her?'). Were such a possibility to apply to jokes too, there is then a basis for Ken laughing first if, as here, his laugh succeeds not his completion but a gap after his completion. Having got an understanding of why Al's – a recipient's – laughing can be done while being done mirthlessly, we turn to consider why Ken, the teller, might produce a mirthless laugh, it being unpuzzling for him to laugh mirthfully.

A mirthful laugh would claim the joke's funniness, propose an intention to defend its funniness. If recipients expectably feel otherwise, such a defense will involve an argument ensuing. For such an argument's strength, from teller's perspective, recipient laughing is surely relevant. For such an argument's strength then, teller's best position would involve his being second laugher, joining any first recipient laughter. Here, not only has that not occurred, but Ken has been throughout apprised of recipient dis-appreciation of the joke's telling. A mirthless laugh on his part can then suggest that he is prepared to leave the joke's funniness unargued, whereas we shall, shortly, see that a defense of the telling can nonetheless be ventured by him. His laugh, occasioned by the gap on his completion, can then launch the response sequence without committing him to a defense of the joke's funniness, as Al's does not weaken recipient's potential critique of its funniness.

The question we are now faced with, consideration of which will close our consideration of the joke's telling, is: does a teller have means for defending a joke's telling if he concedes its unfunniness, if, that is, he does not attempt to attack the absence of (mirthful, undelayed, overlapping) recipient laughter? Our materials are again useful on this score.

If Ken or any teller concedes his joke's unfunniness, allows the appropriateness of no or mocking laughter by recipients, how can the telling, which in the first instance is warranted by the joke's supposable funniness, be defended? One such procedure has already appeared and been briefly noted in section 1.3. Al's joke, lines 4–5, having been delivered in a position which would involve it being legitimately done if as a guess, and having been, subsequent to its telling, proposed by him to be Ken's sister's joke, was delivered in a way that contained defenses against having its unfunniness to this audience serve as a negative reflection of Al's wit though he was indeed the local teller. Thus, a joke inserted into a preface sequence by an intended recipient can be warranted for its telling apart from claims to its funniness. While such a procedure, which involves attributing a bad joke to someone else, will not suffice for a joke told by the intending teller within the telling sequence, attribution is potentially usable, given that jokes and this joke are commonly accompanied by an indication of whom the current teller received them from, that feature providing the makings of an attributive transformation of the telling, by the teller.

Recalling our early observation that jokes built in the form of stories are told with the use of the organizational techniques used for stories, that fact, in combination with the fact that the sister has been mentioned as a source, provides the basic resources for developing a legitimation of the telling. A story can have its telling warranted by virtue of the surprise its events involved or the surprising news its teller learned from them that he can figure his recipients do not yet know. While such a story point can be introduced in its preface, means for introducing it after the story's apparent completion are available. (Note that while Ken did not provide such materials in his preface, his preface revision, line 6, did include a possible such characterization, '...To stun me...') And a perfectly usual instance is indeed used here on Ken's behalf by Al. 'What he meant to say is...,' line 61, which Ken agrees to the use of, line 66, and then uses to attach a story point to his telling, line 68, turning it, or claiming that its import all along was as a report of something surprising about his sister which he learned and which the joke's telling to him by her teaches.[5]

16

WHEN WORDS BECOME DEEDS: AN ANALYSIS OF THREE IROQUOIS LONGHOUSE SPEECH EVENTS

MICHAEL K. FOSTER

Among the modern Longhouse Iroquois, whose eastern population is spread over twelve reserves in Quebec, Ontario, and New York state, there has survived an ancient oratorical tradition which enters into almost every phase of traditional religious and political life. This is the thread that runs through the diverse institutions of the Handsome Lake religion, the Confederate Council of the Iroquois League, the individual rites surrounding death and curing, and the ceremonies of the agricultural cycle. The sight of speaker after speaker representing a family, a clan, a 'side of the fire' (moiety), or a whole nation, and taking his turn at formal talk, is familiar to all those who have worked with the conservative Iroquois. I have summarized elsewhere the different categories of speakers who carry this tradition, and have discussed their training and standards for successful performance (Foster 1971). In this paper I want to narrow the concern to a set of three closely related speeches. Except as specific qualifications will be made, all of these are associated with the agricultural ceremonies.

The speeches can be separated into two sets of one and two speeches respectively, depending upon their ritual purposes as conceived by the Longhouse people. In a set by itself is the *kanõhõnyõk* 'let there be thanks' which is usually referred to in English as the Thanksgiving Address.[1] Its purpose is to give thanks to the Creator for the many benefits of the natural world. In long versions (on the order of forty-five minutes) these benefits are elaborated in considerable detail; in brief versions (two minutes) they are treated under a few summary headings. In the other set are the two speeches *hayẽˀkõthwas* 'he burns tobacco,' referred to as the Tobacco Invocation or the Tobacco Burning, and *konéhõ:ˀ*, whose etymology is uncertain, but which goes by the English name Skin Dance at Six Nations Reserve.[2] The purpose of these speeches is to 'beg' the Creator (the more formal term 'beseech' will be used in this paper) for the return of the same items mentioned in the Thanksgiving Address. The Tobacco Invocation and Skin Dance, both of which last from fifty minutes to well over an hour, cannot be abridged in the same way as the Address.

354

All three speeches are based upon a hierarchy of spirit forces that inhabit various 'stations' along the 'path' from the earth to the Sky World,[3] but they vary in the manner of delivery (phrasing, voice intonation), use of extra-linguistic aids, and staging. A study of some thirty versions of the speeches has shown that it is more fruitful to consider them not as separate and wholly contrastive types, but as complementary expressions of a single underlying pattern. What primarily motivates the choice of a form is whether a speech is to count as a thanking event or as a beseeching event. And, as this paper will attempt to show, these two concepts are themselves complementary in Iroquois culture.[4] For the Six Nations Iroquois there is little functional difference between the Tobacco Invocation and the Skin Dance, and there is a strong suggestion that one derives from the other historically.

The feature which serves most explicitly to differentiate between a thanking and a beseeching event is a key utterance which occurs at the end of sections of speeches and which has the form and meaning designated by J. L. Austin (1963, 1965) as performative.[5] Such utterances are called key for three reasons: (1) in their capacity as words that are also acts they serve to define what a speech as a whole is to count as, i.e., whether it is to be a thanking or beseeching event; (2) they come at the end of sections and are the climax of a sequence of other statements; and (3) they are, in brief versions of the speeches, the main thing left after a great deal else has been excised. The second point raises one of the central concerns of this paper: what is the relationship between the performative utterances and the other statements in the speeches? For this we turn to Austin, who has suggested that while the uttering of certain words may often be the crucial part of an act, this is seldom the only requirement: 'speaking generally, it is always necessary that the *circumstances* in which the words are uttered should be in some way, or ways, *appropriate*, and it is very commonly necessary that either the speaker himself or other persons should *also* perform certain *other* actions...' (1965:8, italics his). To deal with the problem of appropriate circumstances and accompanying actions – what John Searle (1969) calls the 'preparatory conditions' for the act – is to build a theory of the total speech act (Austin 1965:52). In Iroquois speeches, the other statements, which actually constitute most of what is said, are concerned precisely with specifying the conditions for valid performance. If Austin, Searle, and other ordinary language philosophers can be said to expound a philosophical theory of speech acts, the Iroquois speeches can be said to expound a native theory of speech acts. This notion will occupy us in the final section of this paper, following a review of the general form of Iroquois ceremonial and discussion of the nature of performatives in Iroquois oratory.

The agricultural cycle and how it works

A clue that helped me in an early stage of fieldwork to understand the complex agricultural cycle was furnished by Enos Williams, a speaker in the Seneca Longhouse at Six Nations Reserve: 'At the Midwinter Festival we beg the Creator for everything; most of the rest of the time we are thanking him for what he gave us.' This is something of an oversimplification (nonetheless appreciated by the green anthropologist for whom it was intended) of a process that could be elaborated as follows: there are fifteen ceremonies 'passed' at the Six Nations longhouses[6] (see Table 12). Most of these are one-day affairs, but two of them, which may be considered the hubs of the ceremonial year, last from three to eight days. These are the Midwinter Festival and the Green Corn Festival.

TABLE 12.   *The agricultural cycle of ceremonies*

a.	Bush Dance	[a]i. Raspberry Festival
[a]b.	Drying Log Dance	j. Bean Dance
c.	Maple Dance	k. Thunder Ceremony
d.	False Face Ceremony	l. Corn Testing Ceremony
e.	Seed Planting Dance	m. GREEN CORN FESTIVAL
[a]f.	Sun and Moon Dance	n. Harvest Festival
g.	Corn Sprouting Dance	o. MIDWINTER FESTIVAL
h.	Strawberry Festival	

[a]Performed infrequently or now extinct, but still remembered by living informants. The term 'dance' refers to a whole day's events.

During Midwinter and Green Corn the Tobacco Invocation and Skin Dance are performed.[7] The pervading mood, particularly at Midwinter, is one of hopeful expectation. The pervading mood at the one-day ceremonies is one of gratitude. Most of the short ceremonies occur after the appearance of some item in the course of the year (the flowing of maple sap in the early spring, the appearance of berries in June and the cultivated food plants during the summer and fall), and their main purpose is to return thanks for the items that were 'begged for' at the two big festivals.[8] What provides the unifying principle throughout the flurry of ceremonial activity is the notion the Iroquois have of their compact with the Creator. Man asks the Creator for the benefits of the natural world, addressing words to him in the Tobacco Invocation and Skin Dance. The Creator responds by furnishing the things requested. (Their appearance is proof of the viability of ritual acts.) It is then man's turn to honor a commitment, and a thanksgiving ceremony is planned. The whole process is an extension of a basic Iroquois theme, that of reciprocity to the supernatural.

The speeches

All three speeches are based upon the same hierarchy of items beginning with those that are 'lower, younger, and less important' and rising sequentially through those that are 'higher, older, and more important.' It is possible to interpret this in a quite literal sense of relative closeness to the earth. Each of the items in the list forms a separate section or 'word' in the speeches, following an ancient Iroquois practice of segmenting long discourses. The breaks between the three major groups (I, II, and III) represent conceptual cleavages made by the Iroquois themselves. The prologue and epilogue serve to frame the rest of the speech. In them the speaker mentions his appointment by the Longhouse officials and asks forbearance on the assembly's part for shortcomings of the performance. The wording in these sections, as in others, is quite stereotyped.

TABLE 13. *Outline of a whole speech*[9]

	a.	Prologue: the Assembly
	b.	Our Mother, the Earth, that which supports our feet
	c.	Bodies of water
I	d.	Grasses
Earthly	e.	Berries and other fruit
Spirit	f.	Trees
Forces	g.	Animals
	h.	Birds
	i.	The Sisters, Our Sustenance [corn, beans and squash]
II	j.	Our Grandfathers, the Thunderers, whose voices come from the west
Lower	k.	Our Elder Brother, the Sun, the daytime luminary
Pantheon	l.	Our Grandmother, the Moon, the nighttime luminary
	m.	Our Grandparents, the Stars
III	n.	The Four Messengers, Our Guardians
Upper	o.	The Wind
Pantheon	p.	Handsome Lake, Our Great Leader
	q.	The Creator
	r.	Epilogue

If Tables 12 and 13 are compared it will be seen that there is a rough equivalence between the list of ceremonies and the list of items in the hierarchy. The fit is close but by no means perfect, and some of the discrepancies could only be resolved by bringing additional data to bear and seeking a deeper analysis, and even then there are loose ends. However, we will have to be content here with the general congruity of the two orders, a congruity that may be formulated as follows: what the speeches represent as 'lower to higher' the ceremonies represent as 'earlier to later' in the annual round.[10] More thoughtful interpreters see this relationship, and it is appropriate for a speaker to mention in a relevant section of a speech that a particular ceremony was performed (e.g., in the section on the strawberry that the Strawberry Festival was passed; in the section on Our Sustenance that Seed Planting, Corn Sprouting, Corn Testing, and the Harvest Festival were passed, and so on).

The commonest expression of the hierarchy is the Thanksgiving Address itself. It is the most variable form in terms of length, and the least marked in terms of intonation, line structure, and the use of extralinguistic aids.[11] Each section of the Address, except the prologue and epilogue, begins with a formula such as 'And now we direct our words to this' or 'And now we'll speak again.' The item is mentioned as having been 'left' on earth for mankind, and its uses are detailed. (The latter aspect is one of the first things to be omitted in a shorter version, however.) The speaker then raises the question of the compact between man and the Creator: the Creator determined that there should be ceremonies of thanksgiving, and he decided upon the manner in which they should be given. This is phrased as a direct quotation of the Creator's will, the term *hawé ̓ö:* 'he decided, ordained, thought, willed' being used again and again. The section begins at a point in distant past time when the Creator foresaw the great events of the creation. Verbs are preponderantly future tense continuative forms ending in *-ak* or *-hak*. In the middle of the section there is a shift to the present or immediate past – the time period encompassed by the most recent ceremonial cycle. The whole sequence culminates in the performative segment ('we now give thanks for the item') whose indicative modality signifies both semantically and morphologically a moment in present time at which words are transformed into actions.

We can strip the section down to its essential elements to show this movement (A, B, and C in Table 14) if we let X stand for one of the Earthly Spirit Forces and Y stand for one of the non-terrestrial 'helpers.' This is not the way a section would actually be spoken, and a sample section is attached as an appendix to this chapter to give some idea of the richness of the speeches. The section closes with a standard formula which for most speakers is 'And thus it will be in our [or your] minds,' meaning that the state of thankfulness should prevail – a kind of declaration of sincere intentions for the whole assembly (on sincerity conditions, see p. 365 below). We might note that the section contains an elemental summary of the ceremonial process of the agricultural cycle – the compact between man and the Creator; indeed it might be said to embody that process.

Grammatically, thanking performatives are built upon the same verb root *-nöhönyö-* that appears in the name of the Address, *kanöhönyök*. In the

TABLE 14. *Speech section*

A1. The Creator decided, 'There will continue to
be X on earth and it will have certain uses' *or* 'Y will
have a certain duty to fulfill.'
A2. He also decided, 'People will always give
thanks when they see X again' *or* 'People will always be
grateful that Y is fulfilling its duties' *and* 'People
will always gather to express their gratitude.'
B1. Truly we have seen X again, *or* We believe Y
has been carrying out the duties assigned.
B2. The appropriate ceremony was carried out.
C. So now we give thanks for X *or* Now we give
thanks to Y.[12]

---

typical form used for the Earthly Spirit Forces, *atetwanóhõnyõ^ɔ* 'we give
thanks for it,' the performative is indicated by the use of the indicative (or
aorist) prefix *a-* and the punctual suffix *-ɔ*. This is as close as the Iroquoian
languages come to Austin's formula for performatives, namely that they are
first-person present indicative active forms. Two variants occur in the
sections above the Earthly Spirit Forces: *atshetwanóhõnyõ^ɔ* 'we thank him'
for male recipients (the Sun, Handsome Lake, and the Creator), and
atyethinóhõnyõ^ɔ 'we thank her/them' for female or any plurality or recipients (the Moon, the Thunderers, the Four Messengers). These words are
identical to the first form except in the use of different pronominal prefixes,
-shetwa- (we to him) and *-yethi-* (we to her/them), which are transitive forms
including reference to an animate object. The items on earth, however, are
believed to have been made by the Creator, and when the form *atetwan-
óhõnyõ^ɔ* 'we give thanks for it' is used the Creator is the *implied* recipient
although no animate object is specified. At any rate, the Earthly Spirit
Forces themselves do not seem to be the direct recipients. We translate
these forms as 'we give thanks *for* the earth, bodies of water, grasses, berries,
etc.' The beings of the Lower and Upper pantheons, on the other hand, are
regarded as being somewhat independent of the Creator, not so much part
of his 'handiwork' (*howayẽnátẽHta^ɔ*) as his cadre of 'Helpers' (*shakoi-
hótõnyõ^ɔ*). The use of transitive pronominal forms indicates that it is the
Helpers rather than the Creator who are the recipients of the people's
gratitude in the Lower and Upper pantheons. We therefore translate the
thanking performatives in these sections as 'we give thanks *to* the Thunderers, the Sun, the Moon, the Stars, etc.' These data when combined with
those from informant interviews and mythology (see Hewitt 1928) support
the notion of pantheons in Iroquois religious belief.

There is one other important variation in thanking performatives, the form *atetwatatnõHõnyõ*ˀ which occurs in the prologue. This could be translated as 'we are thankful for one another.' The reflexive meaning 'for one another' is achieved by inserting the prefix -[*a*] *tat-* just before the verb root. However, speakers generally prefer to translate this word as 'we greet one another.' While the reflexive prefix is partly responsible for this, it becomes clear from an examination of many forms that the root -*nõhõnyõ*- embraces the senses of both greeting and thanking, concepts that in English, at any rate, are semantically quite different if we are to accept Searle's analysis (1969:62ff).[13]

Before we compare the Thanksgiving Address with the Tobacco Invocation and the Skin Dance, we should try to account for the great variation in length of different versions of the Address. Closing versions generally are brief, and neophyte speakers often give short openings also. The purpose of a closing Address is still to express the assembly's gratitude. The following closing was made by the late Howard Sky at Six Nations Reserve:

I. We assembled and went this far this
    evening,
   We will now give thanks again.
   We will speak about that which he created:
    Our Mother as we call her.
   We roll into one that which she holds,
   Our Mother the Earth, as we call her.
   And thus it will be in our minds.

II. And now we will speak about his Helpers,
    Those he himself appointed, Our Creator.
    They are Our Guardians, and give us
     health and happiness.
    So again we give thanks to them this
     evening.
    And thus it will be in our minds.

III. Now we come to Our Creator, he who dwells
     in the true world beyond the sky.
     Reverently we thank him again this
      evening
     For the health and happiness he gives us.
     And thus it will be in our minds.

Referring to Table 13 above, we can see at once that the items relegated to separate sections in the long opening by Enos Williams have been compressed by Howard Sky into three brief and quite generalized groupings. The status of the groupings as sections, even though these are much shorter than sections of the long opening, is attested to by the generally similar pattern of repeated elements in each, by the presence of thanking performatives in each, and by the use of the standard closing formula 'And thus it will be in our minds' at the end of each one. The structural rules governing reduction involve the cutting down and remodeling of the material of the hierarchy. Among other things, specific item names are replaced by larger category names. The Earthly Spirit Forces are subsumed under 'the Earth, Our Mother,' and the items of the Lower and Upper pantheons are subsumed under 'His Helpers, Our Guardians.' The Creator is given a separate section as in long versions. The Cayuga word that effects the structural change, *aethihwe³nõ:ni³* 'we roll/bundle them together,' is itself a performative.

We have given examples of the two extremes in length in order to show the importance of the performative segment of thanking. Versions of intermediate length also involve principles of reduction although less drastic ones. Whatever the length, the performative remains intact. For this reason and reasons which will become clearer in the next section of this paper, performatives are taken as being constitutive of the speeches as wholes.[14]

While much of what has been said about the Thanksgiving Address could also be said about the Tobacco Invocation and Skin Dance, the latter two may not be cut down to brief versions. In the Tobacco Invocation the appointed speaker stands near a fire built in the cookhouse, which adjoins the longhouse, chanting into the smoke which 'carries the words skywards' and placing a pinch of Indian tobacco in the flames as he 'begs' for the return of items of the hierarchy. Except in minor ways that need not concern us here, the first part of each section is the same as that of sections of the Address. There is the mention of the Creator's plans, the people's ceremonial duties, the uses of the items; and there is mention of the people's having seen the item and having held the appropriate ceremony. The important differences occur toward the end of sections in the performative slot. We give just this part from a version by Enos Williams:

> ....
> The people are beseeching you again,
> those living on earth,
> That it [some item] remain here
> As it was when the earth was young.
> And now from the Indian tobacco
> The smoke will rise
> Carrying the message up
> [*Tobacco here placed on fire*]
> It is from those living on the earth,
> It is what they are asking for.

The performative utterances are *setwaihwá'nek* 'we beseech again' and *ōtēnitēhtha'* 'people are asking for it' (the latter being an 'implicit' performative [Austin 1965:53ff] since it is not indicative-punctual but serial tense).[15] The Skin Dance follows the Tobacco Invocation very closely in wording and speaking style. Both are kinds of chants. The setting, however, is different. In the Skin Dance the speaker takes his place beside the singers' bench which has been put in the center of the longhouse. Following a long introductory dance set done by the assembly in a large oval formation about the bench the speaker starts in with the first section of the speech. While he is chanting the assembly continues around, but in a slow walk. When he finishes a section the dancing starts again, and this pattern of alternation continues until the end. The performative segment is similar to that of the Tobacco Invocation, except that there is no reference to tobacco. Instead, having said what the people are beseeching and asking for the speaker says *tshē swanéhōh, kwá:híh,* which some interpreters translate as 'Now dance the Skin Dance, do it!'[16] The dancing starts immediately following this.

A native theory of speech acts

We have treated the speeches so far only structurally. We have hardly done justice to their rich thematic content. While much of this must be omitted from consideration here, there is a set of propositions, contained mainly in the prologue and epilogue though present elsewhere, that are linked to the performative segment as preparatory conditions. To recall what is at issue we may cite a passage from Austin (1965:14–15) which, incidentally, makes clear the relevance of performative analysis to the ethnography of speaking. For a performative to carry through as a valid and happy act,

there must exist an accepted conventional procedure having a certain conventional effect, that procedure to include the uttering of certain words by certain persons in certain circumstances... Where, as often, the procedure is designed for use by persons having certain thoughts or feelings ... then a person participating in and so invoking the procedure must in fact have those thoughts or feelings...

The first half of the statement refers to all performative utterances, the second half particularly to the ones we have been discussing. The uttering of the prescribed words does not itself constitute an act: the setting, participants, and motives must be appropriate. Failure to meet the requirements may result in complete failure, or limited success with 'unhappiness.' We said before that a rigorous statement of preparatory conditions (Searle 1968, 1969) would constitute a theory of the 'total speech act' (Austin 1965:52), and that therefore a similar statement in the Longhouse speeches would constitute a native theory of the speech act. In the latter case we use the term 'theory' somewhat loosely since the conditions are not presented systematically. Because of this we must extract them from numerous statements in the speeches and give them in summary form.

1. *The ultimate sanction and/or requirement for ritual acts comes from the Creator.* Everywhere in the speeches the Creator's wishes are expressed as his 'thoughts' or 'decisions.' The very Thanksgiving Address itself is sanctioned by the Creator. Enos Williams says in the prologue, 'And the Creator decided, "This is how it will always begin: people will thank me... They will have the *kanŏhŏnyŏk.*"' Corbett Sundown of Tonawanda Reservation, New York, says: 'And this is what Our Creator did: he decided, "The people moving about on the earth will simply come to express their gratitude"' (Chafe 1961:17, sentence 6). The authority behind these commandments is further elaborated in Iroquoian mythology (Hewitt 1928:568) and the Code of Handsome Lake (Parker 1913:51, and cf. Chafe 1961:2).

2. *There is a conventional way of ordering items mentioned in the speeches.* Speakers instruct themselves to begin by mentioning 'lower' items and then to take up 'higher' items. Corbett Sundown says, quoting the Creator, '"They will begin on earth, giving thanks for all they see. They will carry it upward, ending where I dwell"' (Chafe 1961:43, sentences 180-1). While there is a disagreement among speakers over the precise sequence, they all agree upon the hierarchic principle and follow the same general pattern, except during those ceremonies when it is purposely reversed. Even here, the order, though inverted, obeys the hierarchic principle.[17] It is hard to say whether the event would still be valid and happy if the items were, in the words of one interpreter, 'jumbled up.' This has not been observed, and the interpreter's remark refers to this man's own training by his father in which he was given scrambled versions of the Address and told to give them back in the correct order.

3. *Setting is NOT a necessary condition for valid performance, because of the Creator's omnipresence.* The Address is most frequently heard in the longhouse on ceremonial days, but it is not restricted to this situation. In the prologue Enos Williams says that it should be given 'wherever, whatever the occasion,' and in the epilogue he concludes by saying that people should feel gratitude 'day and night' because the Creator is always 'looking on intently and listening intently to them.' Since the Creator always is, and is everywhere, no place would be inappropriate to render thanksgiving, except the setting of one of the death rites. There remains the question of why the speaker bothers to mention setting since it is a purely negative condition. The answer to this may be that setting is *usually* a determining factor in performative acts, and the speaker may thus feel the need to deal with it even if only to dismiss it.

4. *The speaker must be appointed.* A literal translation from Enos Williams is: 'To me was delegated the task of this speech; from me all our voices will issue forth.' It would be unthinkable that a speaker should simply rise and start in. He should first be approached by a Longhouse official (called in English 'faithkeeper'), and it is even proper, in line with strong norms of modesty, to allow himself to be 'coaxed' while stressing his inadequacy for the task. It is always an honor to be appointed to a ritual role. And even if there is no faithkeeper present on a particular occasion, the speaker should be asked by someone on his side of the fire. A violation of the appointment principle would undoubtedly invalidate the act, although such a thing was never observed. There is, however, a penumbral region that speakers sometimes wander into when they get carried away by their own words. The whispered comments are 'That is too personal,' 'He's got too much "I" in there,' etc., all of which suggest that at times the speaker's personal identity is beginning to interfere with his appointed role as spokesman for a group. The criticism can be very harsh.

5. *The speaker prescribes certain terms to be used when addressing the spirit forces.* There is a general principle that underlies the use of all names (for persons as well as for deities) in the longhouse: the proper native term should be used.[18] Referring to Table 13, we can see that each item has an appropriate descriptive term, and many have kinship terms. The earth is 'that which supports our feet' and 'Our Mother'; the cultivated foods are 'Our Sustenance' and the 'Sisters'; the Thunderers are 'those whose voices come from the west' and 'Our Grandfathers'; the sun and moon are respectively 'Our Elder Brother, the daytime luminary' and 'Our Grandmother, the nighttime luminary'; the Four Messengers are 'Our Guardians'; and Handsome Lake is 'Our Great Leader.' For each item there is the metalingual instruction *tetwanõHõkwaʔ* 'we call it' or 'we are related to it.' The designations themselves are quite standard across language and reserve lines. The function of these appositive-like formulae remains to be fully studied in future research. The Iroquois notoriously extend kin terms and other forms of address in a figurative way in all sorts of directions.[19] Here we will mention only two general points that tie in with the present analysis. First, so far as the use of kin terms is concerned, it will readily be seen that a sampling of lineal (mothers and grandmothers) and collateral (brothers and sisters) kinsmen is made, and this sampling forms the nucleus of the Iroquois matrilineage. What is the point of singling out this little piece of social structure in the speeches? It might be said that just as the individual finds his place in the society and relates to it through his matrilineage, so the society as a whole finds its place in and relates to the cosmological order, represented by the hierarchy, by extending the same system of terms to it. Secondly, except for the 'Sisters,' whose precise relationship to man is

not grammatically specified in the term used, all the terms designate senior kinsmen, and these categories are traditionally accorded special respect. Here again there is a kind of proportionality between the attitude that an individual should have towards important kinsmen (respect) and the attitude the whole assembly should have towards the supernatural (reverence).

6. *The speaker should be sincere.* To follow through on the fifth point, we find that the attitude of reverence is made explicit in a word which functions adverbially and which usually immediately precedes thanking performatives: *etwatewayẽ:nõ:niˀ* 'we do it carefully, properly, reverently.' Chafe (1961) translates a recurrent line in the version by Corbett Sundown as 'And give it your thought, that we may do it properly: we now give thanks for [some item].' It is a call for a unity of motive before the act.

Sincerity counts more than correctness of procedure. There is a certain laxness in longhouse procedures generally (field observations, and cf. Shimony 1961:141). People are told that they should participate in rituals even if health or some other factor such as not being properly dressed in Indian clothing makes them feel inhibited. The speaker explains ahead of time that a lame person may sit on the singers' bench during the Great Feather Dance and 'pass' the dance just as effectively as the most enthusiastic young warrior. Or, when a pail of strawberry or sap juice is passed at the Strawberry and Maple festivals, it is sufficient merely to say *nya:wẽh* 'thank you' or *athenõHõnyõˀ shõkwayaˀtihsˀõ* 'I thank him, Our Creator'; and it is not really necessary to say anything at all. The important thing is to have one's mind on the Creator. This may explain, at least in part, why people do not seem especially interested in variations in the content and length of speeches. 'It doesn't matter; it's all the same.'

However, this is based upon the assumption that a speaker has made the proper ritual apology in the prologue and/or epilogue. Corbett Sundown says, 'And now I simply ask forgiveness if it should perhaps happen that we inadvertently drop some of the ritual as it proceeds; do not think, "He does it intentionally"' (Chafe 1961:89). Enos Williams says, 'I ask for your patience in the matter of this speech.' I have heard speakers criticized for not properly humbling themselves, but provided the apology is made there is considerable tolerance of lapses of memory, stage fright, misstarts, and so on – all of which occur fairly regularly, especially among younger speakers.

To summarize these points, we may say that in the Iroquois view, for a performative of thanking or beseeching to carry through, the act must originally have been ordained by the Creator; specific items should be mentioned in a definite order; there is no restriction as to setting (except for death rituals); the speaker must have been duly appointed; proper terms of address should be used; and, most important, the act should be carried out in a sincere spirit.

Conclusion

The purpose of this paper has been twofold. On the one hand it has been argued that a particular kind of utterance with a distinct grammatical form serves as the organizing principle for a class of speech events. Here a relatively simple underlying unit of meaning and form is found to set the guidelines for a whole emergent event. On the other hand, this small unit has been found to be intimately bound up with a native theory of speech acts. A clear conclusion is that the speeches have an overriding 'meta-lingual' concern; for while words of thanking and beseeching may be spoken in but the briefest instant, their effectiveness in reaching and placing a claim upon the Creator depends upon very careful preparation.[20]

APPENDIX

[Translation of Section f (see Table 13, p. 357) on 'Trees' from a long opening version of the Thanksgiving Address by Enos Williams]

And now we will speak again.
He decided, 'There will be trees growing here and there on the earth,
'And there will be whole forests of standing trees,
'Forests that have been set upon the earth.'
And indeed there are trees here and there,
There are whole forests of standing trees.
He decided this also, 'It will be important to them,
'For medicines can be made from them.'
Surely they are still growing.
And they grow in different ways.
He decided, 'All of them will have names, each one:
'That is how people will know them, those living on the earth.
'And this will be a source of happiness in the families.
'People will depend upon them
'When there is a change in the wind.
'When the wind turns cold,
'People will be able to keep warm.'
And surely they are cooperating with us,
The live coals he left on the earth.
He decided, 'They will work to bring happiness to the families on the earth.'
And we think that it is still coming to pass.
He carefully decided this: 'There will be a leader among the trees,
'And they will say, those living on the earth,
"It is that one, the Maple, a special tree."'
And he decided, 'When the wind turns warm,

'The sap will flow.
'The trees will be tapped,
'And the sap will be collected.
'It will be boiled down by the people,
'And it will be possible for them to swallow it.
'And then they will gather to thank me.'
Now when the wind turned warm we did indeed see new sap
    flowing,
And it happened that we swallowed it again.
It was possible for us to gather
At what has been called the 'Maple Festival.'
We thanked him in the way he prescribed for us at ceremonies.
We think that the ceremony did go through.
It will be our thought: we are grateful that he is still sending
    them, the trees standing upon the earth.
He meant them for our use, those of us still moving about
    on the earth.
So now reverently we thank him, he who in the sky dwells,
Our Creator, and so it will be in our minds.

THE ETHNOGRAPHIC CONTEXT OF SOME TRADITIONAL MAYAN SPEECH GENRES

VICTORIA R. BRICKER

It is a well documented fact that during the Colonial period, the Indians of Middle America often expressed their thoughts in semantic couplets (and occasionally, triplets). The largest corpus of such materials is in the Nahuatl language, but other languages such as Otomí, Quiché and Yucatec Maya are also represented. Garibay (1953) has documented the use of couplets by the Nahuas and Otomís of central Mexico. Edmonson (1971) has shown that the *Popol Vuh*, the sacred book of the Quiché Maya of highland Guatemala, is written in semantic couplets; so too are the *Chilam Balam of Chumayel* and the *Ritual of the Bacabs*, both of which are written in Yucatec Maya (Edmonson 1968).

The essence of such couplet poetry is that ideas are expressed in parallel form.

Sometimes a thought will be complemented or emphasized through the use of different metaphors which arouse the same intuitive feeling, or two phrases will present the same idea in opposite form ... Another device used in lyric poetry, as well as in discourses and other forms of composition, consists of uniting two words which also complement each other, either because they are synonyms or because they evoke a third idea, usually a metaphor ... Examples of this are the following: flower-and-song which metaphorically means poetry, art, and symbolism; skirt-and-blouse which implies woman in her sexual aspect; seat-and-mat which suggests the idea of authority and power; face-and-heart which means personality. (León Portilla 1969: 76–7)

Whereas the semantic structure of the metaphorical couplet has been analyzed in some detail (Edmonson 1968, 1973; León Portilla 1969), its ethnographic context has not. Indeed, a contextual analysis is impossible for the sixteenth-century documents written in couplets. But fortunately this verse form still survives in many parts of Mesoamerica, including the area of highland Chiapas where I have conducted most of my research and the peninsula of Yucatan where I have recently begun some investigations. From the Yucatan peninsula I have obtained some data from the nineteenth century which link the couplet tradition of the sixteenth century with the ethnographic use of couplets today. But my most complete information comes from Zinacantan in highland Chiapas, where the couplet structure is identified exclusively with ritual or ritualized speech. Structure, context, content, and use are the salient variables of Zinacanteco speech.

The couplet genres of Zinacantan

STRUCTURAL FEATURES

The Zinacanteco taxonomy of speech neatly distinguishes between those genres which are characterized by the couplet structure and those which have no structural properties in common. On the most general level the speech genres are classified as *k'op* 'formal speech' and *lo\?il* 'informal speech.'[1] The noun *k'op* means 'word, language, argument, war, curing ceremony,' while the noun *lo\?il* means 'hearsay, news, conversation, discussion, joke' (Laughlin n.d.a). Expressions derived from the root *-k'op* refer to contemplation (*k'opoh \?o\?on*), planning (*k'oplal*), praying (*k'opon, k'op rio\š*), myth or legend (*\?antivo k'op*), and frivolous talk or joking (*\?i\štol k'op*) (Laughlin n.d.a). Song (*k'evuh*) and prayer-greeting (*krasya*) are the only formal genres labelled by terms not based on the root *-k'op*. The names of the principal genres of 'informal discourse' – gossip (*lo\?iltabe*), discussion (*lo\?iltael*), and humorous talk or joking (*¢e\?eh lo\?il, \?i\štol lo\?il, loko lo\?il*) – are derived from the root *-lo\?il* (Fig. 16). All the formal genres are structurally alike: they are expressed as semantic couplets. The informal genres have no common structure, and the semantic couplet structure is characteristic of none of them.

The six verses of the prayer that follow illustrate the structural principles quoted from León Portilla (1969:76–7) above.

1. *\?ana yaya tot,*
     \?ahvetik:
   Well grandfather,
   Lord:

2. *k'u yepal mi li\? čamala hlumale?*
     mi li\? čamala kač'elale?
   How long have you been waiting here for my earth?
       How long have you been waiting here for my mud?

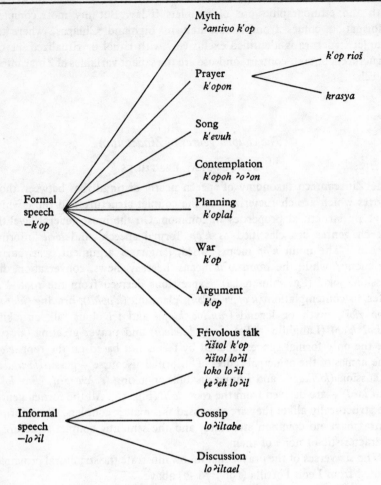

Fig. 16.   Zinacanteco speech genres

3. *ʧobolon tal;*
     lotolon tal.
   I am gathering together here;
   I am meeting here.

4. *tal kilbe smeʔanal na;*
     tal kilbe smeʔanal k'uleb
   I see the house of poverty;
   I see the house of wealth

5. *li yah⁷abtele,*
　li yahpatane.
Of His laborer,
Of His tribute-payer.

6. *li č'ul ⁷iskipulae, htotot;*
　hme⁷ot.
Holy Esquipulas, thou art my father;
Thou art my mother.

The second couplet employs synonyms: 'earth' and 'mud.' The fourth couplet uses antonyms: 'house of poverty' and 'house of wealth.' Each set of parallel terms in the first, second, fifth, and sixth couplets evokes a third idea: 'grandfather' and 'Lord' together connote elder; 'earth' and 'mud' together connote arrival (because the traveller's feet are stained with earth and mud); 'laborer' and 'tribute-payer' together connote vassal; 'father' and 'mother' together connote parents.

Verses 2–6 are not only semantically parallel, they are also *syntactically* parallel. Syntactic parallelism is characteristic of many, but not all, Zinacanteco couplets. Each of the five verses in question is composed of (1) a frame, part or all of which appears in both lines of the verse, and (2) one or more slots which are filled by pairs of variable elements that complement each other. In the second verse, the frame is:

k'u yepal li⁷ čamala h-/k-_____?
How long have you been waiting here for my _____?

and the variable elements are the noun stems *-lumal* 'earth' and *-ač'elal* 'mud,' which occur as the terminal words of the couplet. The allomorphs of the first person subject pronoun, *h-* and *k-*, serve as the syntactic environment of *-lumal* and *-ač'elal*. However, the variable elements are not always noun stems, nor do they necessarily occur at the end of frames. In the third verse, the variable elements are the verb roots *ɫob-* and *lot-* and the slots which they fill occur in initial position:

_____-olon tal.
I am _____here.

Zinacanteco couplets utilize most of the grammatical categories listed by Jakobson (1968:604) for parallelism and contrast: parts of speech, numbers, cases, aspects, moods, voices, classes of abstract and concrete words, animates and inanimates, appellatives and proper names, affirmatives and negatives, and 'diverse syntactic elements and constructions.'

The pairs of terms that fill the slots in syntactic frames form meaning sets. Each pair of terms, even if they are antonyms, shares at least one meaning component that defines the set. Thus although, in the sixth verse, the noun roots *-tot* 'father' and *-me*ʔ 'mother' are antonyms, they share the meaning component 'parent' which is the 'sense' of their use in the couplet. The two terms exhaust the possibilities of the set 'parent' by accounting for the two sexual alternatives (which are the only alternatives). Moreover, a pair of terms 'fixes' the meaning of both terms when there might be ambiguity if only one term were used. The pairing of 'mother' with 'father' in the sixth verse indicates that the meaning component 'parent' is the one intended, not the other possible meaning component 'male.' This disambiguating function of pairing is even more effective when one of the terms in question has several homonyms (see Edmonson 1971:xi-xii for further discussion of this point).

Another interesting structural feature of Zinacanteco couplets is the frequent use of Spanish loan words as complements for Tzotzil terms in syntactic frames:

7. *yuʔun i smuk'ta k'ine,*
   yuʔun i smuk'ta paskuae.
   For his great festival,
     For his great celebration.

8. *čiʔuk ʔoʔlol č'ul vinahel,*
   čiʔuk ʔoʔlol č'ul lorya.
   With the center of divine Heaven,
     With the center of divine Glory.

9. *ti čanib yo stoh,*
   ti čanib yo skantela.
   Of his four lowly torches,
     His four lowly candles.

In each example the first slot is filled by a Tzotzil word (*k'in, vinahel, toh*) and the second slot is filled by a Spanish loan word (*paskua, lorya, kantela*). The loan words function as synonymic complements for Tzotzil words that may not have Tzotzil synonyms.

In other examples, both slots are filled with Spanish loan words:

10. *ʔak'o noš č'ul pertonal;*
    ʔak'o noš č'ul lesensya.
    Only grant holy pardon;
      Only grant holy forgiveness.

11. *skotol č'ul rioš,*
skotol č'ul santo.
All the holy gods,
All the holy saints.

The loan words *pertonal* (Sp. *perdonar*), *lesensya* (Sp. *licencia*), and *santo* (Sp. *santo*) refer to concepts that may have been foreign to the aboriginal Zinancanteco religion, for there are no Tzotzil synonyms for these terms. Sixteenth-century Tzotzil did, however, have a word for 'God,' *ču* (Calnek 1962:58), but it has been completely replaced by the loan word *rioš* (Sp. *Dios*), perhaps because of its original association with idolatry.

CONTEXT, CONTENT, AND USE

Verses 1–6 introduce a type of prayer that Zinancantecos call *krasya* (literally 'grace,' from Sp. *gracia*), which Cancian (1965:56–7) glosses as a 'prayer-greeting.' Cancian uses this term

to refer to a whole class of formalized conversations between persons in ritual contexts. Both speak at the same time, with a prayer-like intonation. The speeches are almost always interval-markers in a ritual, and are most often greetings at the beginning and end of important segments. The wording of the speeches is not absolutely set, but the general content seems to be fairly generally known, though younger people and women often mumble their way through them. The person in the senior role (usually the older person) sets the pace, and the junior person responds, usually following a few words behind. (Cancian 1965:57n)

The interrogative form of the second verse marks the prayer as a greeting, that is, as a prayer that requires a complementary couplet response from a social inferior:

12. *lok' tal lalumal;*
lok' tal lavač'elal.
Your earth has ended here;
Your mud has ended here.

In general, prayers describe what is going on in rituals. Songs (*k'evuh*) closely resemble prayers in their context, content, and function (Haviland 1967:50). The principal difference between prayers and songs is that prayers are simply recited, while songs are sung to a musical accompaniment of stringed instruments (violin, harp, guitar) or a wind–percussion trio composed of one flute and two drums. A song is identified by the couplets which compose it, not by the music which accompanies it. Different groups of verses that are sung to the same tune are called different songs.

Prayers and songs are similar in content when they both refer to the same ritual event. During the fiesta of San Lorenzo, the patron saint of Zinacantan, homage is paid both to San Lorenzo and to another saint called Esquipulas. The cult objects associated with Esquipulas include two necklaces of coins wrapped in layers of cloth bags and stored in a wooden chest. In the course of the ritual in honor of the saint the bags are taken out of the chest, the necklaces are removed from the bags, and the coins are counted. The order of ritual events is determined by musicians, informally in conversation, and formally in song. In the following verses of a song the musicians order the cult leaders to unwrap the coin necklaces:

13. *lok'es bo sč'a sničim ba;*
    lok'es bo šč'a sničim sat;
    Now take out the flowery [divine] face;
    Now take out the flowery [divine] visage;

14. *ʔiskipula č'ul kahvaltik,*
    ʔiskipula č'ul yaya tot.
    Of Esquipulas our holy Lord,
    Of Esquipulas our holy grandfather.

And the cult leaders respond in prayer (without music):

15. *člok' ʔo sničim ba;*
    člok' ʔo sničim sat li sinyor ʔiskipulae.
    His flowery [divine] face will be taken out;
    His flowery [divine] visage will be taken
    out, Señor Esquipulas.

The content of argument (*k'op*), like prayer and song, is thematically related to associated non-verbal behavior. In the following example, a woman scolds her drunken husband whose belongings were stolen from him:

16. *ba saʔo tal ti k'usi ʔač'ayohe,*
    ti k'utik ʔahip ʔeč'el.
    Go look for what you lost,
    For what you threw away.

17. *skoh ʔačopolal;*
    skoh ʔapentehoal.
    It was because of your evilness;
    It was because of your waywardness.

18. *ʾa ʾičʾay hpokʾ,ʾ šači;*
ʾa ʾičʾay hpišol,ʾ šači ʾun.
'Ah my kerchief lost itself,' you say;
'Ah my hat lost itself,' you say then.

19. *kʾusi šahbalinbe ʾun leʾe?*
kʾusi šahkʾelbe ʾun leʾe?
Why should I be worthy of you like that?
Why should I look after you like that?

The woman's complaint has some ethnographic validity; either because they later cannot remember where they left their clothes or because other men take advantage of their helplessness and steal them, Zinacanteco men do customarily lose their hats and kerchiefs when they pass out from excessive drinking.

Prayers, songs, and arguments are expressed wholly and consistently in couplets which are usually both syntactically and semantically parallel. The couplet structure of myth, or the other hand, is looser and less consistent:

20. *ʾa ti voʾne,*
ʾital nohel.
Once upon a time,
A flood came.

21. *ʾičam ti končaveetike,*
ti baʾyi kriščanoe čam hʾoʾlol;
The dwarfs died,
The first people, half died;

22. *ʾisbah sbaik tak kahon hʾoʾlol,*
ʾimuyik ta teʾ hʾoʾlol;
Half shut themselves up in coffins,
Half climbed trees;

23. *ʾiskušik sat teʾ,*
ʾiyipanik čočob;
They crunched nuts,
They lived on acorns;
(Laughlin n.d.b, Tale 7)

Only two verses in this example (nos. 22 and 23) are both syntactically and semantically parallel; one verse (no. 21) is semantically, but not syntactically parallel; and one verse (no. 20) should probably not be considered a couplet at all.

Joking is referred to by several terms in Zinacantan: *ʔištol k'op, ʔištol loʔil, loko loʔil,* and *ȼeʔeh loʔil.* The first three terms are synonyms for 'frivolous talk'; the last term refers to any kind of informal speech that evokes laughter. Most joking is informal (*loʔil* rather than *k'op*) and is not expressed in couplets. Some joking interactions, however, begin with proverb-like utterances (see Gossen 1973) which have a two-part construction and are semantically, but not syntactically parallel:

> 24. *buȼ²u tol šk'opohe,*
> *yuʔun šʔilin.*
> He who talks too much,
> Is quarrelsome.

> 25. *k'unk'un šatih lavobe;*
> *k'an me štuč' yak'il.*
> Slowly you play your instrument;
> Maybe its string will break.

A joking interaction is composed of two or more insulting verbal utterances from at least two speakers. An insulting remark is one which claims that the person in question has personal qualities or behavior patterns which members of his community judge to be undesirable for someone of his age, sex, or role. Such remarks are critical or disapproving and therefore are related in content and function to scolding speech.

The opening gambit of a joking interaction is usually an *implied insult.* Its denotative or literal meaning is innocuous as far as the person at whom the remark is directed is concerned, but its connotative meaning is insulting to him. The person who initiates a joking interaction expresses his opening insult implicitly in order to protect himself should his words be taken as he had not intended them to be (as criticism or defamation rather than joking). If his opening remark is received as an insult and the response to it is an accusation of defamation, he will ask that his remark be taken literally and claim that the implied meaning was accidental. The distinction between explicit and implied insults is upheld in legal contexts. In determining whether an offending utterance is a joking insult or a defamatory insult, the magistrate of Zinacantan considers whether the denotative meaning of the remark is insulting before deciding who, if anyone, is guilty of defamation (see Bricker 1973a and n.d.a for additional information on Zinacanteco joking behavior).

The cryptic examples cited above are implied insults. The first couplet (no. 24) implies that the joking partner talks so much that he appears quarrelsome. The second couplet (no. 25) is said to the musician who falls asleep over his instrument to encourage him to play faster.

Having made my case for the association of formal speech with couplets, it is only fair to add that Zinacantecos do not themselves talk about structure as a criterion for differentiating between formal and informal speech even though all Zinacantecos use couplets when they sing, pray, or scold. Instead, what serves as the criterion for classification at this level is the value judgment in terms of good (*lekil*) and bad (*čopol*). The formal speech genres are 'good' and the informal speech genres are 'bad.' But even if Zinacantecos do not talk about structure, they do give it implicit recognition in parodies of formal speech. I quote, first, some verses from a bonesetter's prayer:

26. *yašal bak,*
    yašal č'ušuv;
   Green bone,
       Green muscle;

27. *likanik ʾun;*
    hulavanik.
   Rise then;
       Get up.

28. *k'elavil č'ul bak!*
    k'elavil č'ul č'ušuv!
   Look, holy bone!
       Look, holy muscle!

29. *vaʾlanik ʾun!*
    tek'lanik ʾun!
   Stand erect then!
       Stand firm then!

30. *hulavanik ʾun, bak!*
    kušanik ʾun, č'ušuv!
   Get up then, bone!
       Recover then, muscle!

31. *ʾunenal yol bak,*
    ʾunenal yol č'ušuv.
   Tender little bone,
       Tender little muscle.

which should be compared with a parody of it:

32. *yašbil ton,*
    yašbil ʔak';
    Green stone,
    Green vine;

33. *ʔunenal bak,*
    ʔunenal č'ušuv.
    Tender bone,
    Tender muscle.

34. *šač'an bak!*
    šač'an č'ušuv!
    Stretch out, bone!
    Stretch out, muscle!

35. *naʔo lavave, bak!*
    naʔo lavave, č'ušuv!
    Remember your place, bone!
    Remember your place, muscle!

36. *mu šakomłan ʔač'en č'ušuv!*
    mu šakomłan ʔač'en bak!
    Don't leave your cave, muscle!
    Don't leave your cave, bone!

These verses are the linguistic part of a mock curing ceremony that is performed every Christmas and New Year's Day. The curer-impersonator pretends to cure a female-impersonator and her 'husband' of imaginary wounds which were supposedly inflicted on them by a bull-impersonator. The 'curer' strikes their genitals whenever he speaks of healing their broken bones and torn muscles. The non-linguistic behavior provides a context in which 'bone' and 'muscle' together connote penis and 'cave' and 'place' together connote vagina (Bricker 1973b). The fact that the parody of the prayer is expressed in couplets suggests that the couplet structure is intrinsic to prayer.

Finally, couplets are the verbal expression of a dualistic principle that is pervasive in Zinacanteco culture. This principle is usually expressed as a contrast between the terms *bankilal* (older, senior, superior, male, right, larger, upper) and *ʔic'inal* (younger, junior, inferior, female, left, smaller, lower) and it is applied to the domains of kinship, religious and political roles, physical objects, and natural features of the landscape (Bricker n.d.b; Vogt 1969:238–45).

Whenever a ritual is performed by a *bankilal–ʔiȼ'inal* pair of religious practitioners, this fact is noted in prayer and song in parallel form:

37. *martomorey bankilal,*
    martomorey ʔiȼ'inal;
    Senior Mayordomo Rey,
    Junior Mayordomo Rey;

But although couplets express pairs of ideas and sometimes refer to pairs of individuals, the *actions* or *behavior* to which they refer are not paired. Instead, each couplet refers to a pair of attributes that characterize a particular action. In other words, the dualistic structure of formal speech is not a characteristic of the behavior which that speech describes.

TEMPORAL IMPLICATIONS

Gossen (1970) has found that in the neighboring Tzotzil-speaking community of Chamula the speech genres are most generally classified in terms of whether they are 'ancient' (*ʔantivo*) or 'recent' (*ʔač'*). Zinacantecos do not explicitly classify their speech genres in those terms, but when asked, in the case of each speech genre, which of the two terms best applies, the responses invariably place the formal (or couplet) genres in the 'ancient' category and the informal genres in the 'recent' category. By 'ancient,' Zinacantecos mean that the formal genres are traditional in contrast with informal speech which is spontaneous or 'new.'

The fact that the formal genres are considered 'ancient' in contrast with the informal 'recent' genres suggests some antiquity for the couplet genres. There is some evidence, albeit slight, that the association of formal speech with the couplet structure has some time depth. First of all, some of the vocabulary in the couplets seems to be archaic in the sense that those who recite them can neither gloss them nor interpret them, yet they were common enough in the sixteenth century to have been listed in Tzotzil dictionaries of the time. For example, the word *ʔahvetik* in the first couplet cited in this paper was spelled *aghauetic* in a sixteenth-century dictionary and was glossed as 'nobleman' (Sp. *hidalgo*) (Calnek 1962:82), but Zinacantecos do not know what the word means.

Second, a nineteenth-century Tzotzil document has recently come to light at the Smithsonian Institution,[2] which gives some additional time perspective to my Tzotzil data. The document is a proclamation, dated August 7, 1812, from the King of Spain in Cádiz to the Indians of Chiapas, ordering them to beware of the lies of Napoleon. In that year Cádiz was the only Spanish city that had not fallen to Napoleon. The text obviously was not the work of a Tzotzil Indian, but was probably composed by a priest who had returned to Spain after spending many years in highland Chiapas among Tzotzil speakers. According to Robert M. Laughlin (personal communication), an expert on the Tzotzil language, the text is written in excellent and idiomatic Tzotzil, but is probably not an example of the Zinacanteco dialect. More important, Laughlin pointed out to me that parts of the text are expressed in couplets (transcription as in the original):

> 38. *ytal ta yan,*
> > *slecóg osil*
> > There came from another,
> > A different land
>
> 39. *jun coló huinic,*
> > *hun mu ibeiluc tzameshuaneg.*
> > An evil man,
> > A treacherous killer.
>
> 40. *Napoleon*
> > *sbiil.*
> > Napoleon
> > Is his name.
>
> 41. *spasog sbá lolo huaneg;*
> > *spasog sbá gnoxol.*
> > He has become a deceiver;
> > He has become our neighbor.

This implies that the person who wrote the text, although probably not an Indian, was familiar with the structural characteristics of Tzotzil formal speech.

On the other hand, the occurrence of Spanish loan words and Christian themes in couplets suggests that the content, if not the structure, of the formal genres has been subject to change since 1524, when Spaniards first penetrated the highlands of Chiapas. In verses 7–9, a Tzotzil word in one phrase is complemented by a Spanish synonym in the other. In verses 10 and 11, both slots in the couplet frame are occupied by Spanish loan words.

But if the Zinacantecos were willing to alter the content of their prayers and songs in the interest of conversion to Catholicism, the same cannot be said for structure. All Zinacanteco prayers are expressed in couplets, including those addressed to Catholic saints. If a Zinacanteco prays to one saint, he does so in terms of two of its attributes, but if he calls upon more than one saint, the number of saints is usually two or a multiple of two:

42. *šci²uk li santorenso,*
    či²uk li santorominko,
    With San Lorenzo,
    With Santo Domingo,

43. *či²uk li č'ul mariya rosaryo, vinahelal ²ant̸,*
    vinahelal sinyora.
    With holy Mary of the Rosary, Heavenly Woman,
    Heavenly Lady.

Both lines in the first couplet refer to male saints. The second couplet refers to one female saint, who is described first in terms of a Tzotzil attribute (*²ant̸*), and then in terms of a Spanish synonym for that attribute (*sinyora*). The couplet structure seems to have been so basic to the Zinacanteco conception of prayer that Catholic worship was cast in the same mold.

Comparative data from Yucatan

The metaphorical couplet as a formal device in Mayan speech has a longer known history in the Yucatan peninsula than in highland Chiapas. Edmonson (1968) has demonstrated that passages from the *Ritual of the Bacabs* and the *Chilam Balam of Chumayel* can be scanned in terms of semantic couplets. Although both manuscripts date from the eighteenth century, Roys (1933:6, 1965:vii) believes that they were copied from much older manuscripts written during the seventeenth century or even earlier. The *Ritual of the Bacabs* 'consists largely of medical incantations' (Roys 1965:vii). The more heterogeneous *Chilam Balam of Chumayel* includes examples of song, history, ritual, prophecy, incantation, and riddles.

The couplet genres of modern Yucatec speech are proverbs (*p'is k'ìin*), prayers (*š payal či²*), riddles (*ná²at*), and history (*²úučben t'àan*).

Some proverbs interpret events in terms of their significance for the future. This class of proverbs is called prophecy (*tomoh či²*). The following is an example of a prophetic proverb:

44. *t u yàak'il š mehen k'úume²,*
    ma² t u č'úuyul š nuh k'úumi².
    The vine of an unripe squash,
    Will not support a mature squash.

It implies that an immature child cannot be expected to support his father.

Prayers include blessings (*pul kili²ič t'àan*) and incantations (*k'aš ²ik' t'àan* and *wač ²ik' t'àan*). Incantations may be used to cast spells (*k'aš*

ʔik' t'àan) or to lift them (wač ʔik' t'àan). A priest protects a newly planted
cornfield by casting a spell on it; he cures a bewitched patient by reciting an
incantation to lift the spell that made him ill. The following incantation
invokes the services of the four winds, God, and San Miguel to protect a
cornfield:

45. *k u yantal;*
     *in k'ubik saka*ʔ
   Here it is;
     I offer this gruel

46. *ti*ʔ *nohol* ʔ*ik',*
     *y éetel ti*ʔ *k'ak'al moson k'amik;*
   To the south wind,
     And to the tumbling whirlwind to receive;

47. *bey šan ti*ʔ *noh lak'in* ʔ*ik';*
     *bey ti*ʔ *túun ti*ʔ *kan ti*ʔ*iƚ in kòol šan.*
   So also to the great east wind;
     So then to the four corners of my cornfield
     also.

48. *k u yantal;*
     in k'ubik
   Here it is;
     I offer it

49. *ti*ʔ *yùum báalamó*ʔ*ob,*
     *ti*ʔ *šaman* ʔ*ik',*
   To the Lord Jaguars,
     To the north wind,

50. *ti*ʔ *čikin* ʔ*ik',*
     *ti*ʔ *nohol* ʔ*ik',*
   To the west wind,
     To the south wind,

51. *ti*ʔ *nohoč dios yùumbil,*
     yùum san migel arkanhel.
   To the great God the Father,
     Lord San Miguel Archangel.
           (after Redfield and Villa Rojas 1934:339)

Riddles are popular in Mayan communities. A typical riddle is:

52. *wi^ʔih t u bin;*
    ná^ʔah t u sùut. bá^ʔasi^ʔ?
  It goes thirsty;
    It returns full. What is it?

The answer is 'a water bucket' *(č'òoy)*.

The couplet structure is also evident in the following excerpt from a folk historical account of the Caste War of Yucatan (1847–53):

53. *bwenoh ti^ʔ yá^ʔabač sufrimientoh*
    u páadesert:
  Well a great suffering
    They suffered:

54. *t u láakal nohǒč,*
    čičan;
  All the old,
    (And) the young;

55. *t u mèen t u tàal u huntartik,*
    čuká^ʔan henteh ti^ʔ kàahalkàah.
  Because they came to round them up,
    The people trapped in all the towns.

56. *k u taal má^ʔ čéen ti^ʔ hun p'éel kàah;*
    má^ʔ čéen hun túul henteh k u čí^ʔiki^ʔ;
  They came not just to one town;
    Nor did they recruit only one person;

57. *sinoh keh t u láakal,*
    le henteh k u molko^ʔ.
  But it was all of them,
    Those people whom they recruited.

58. *wáah k u lah kíinsik*
    wáah má^ʔ t yantal y éetel.
  For they killed everyone
    Who would not be with them.

It seems clear that, with the exception of song *(k'àay)*, which seems to have been heavily influenced by Spanish rhyming conventions, the traditional couplet genres of Yucatec Maya speech survive today.

The examples suggest that Yucatec Maya couplets are not as 'tight' in structure as Tzotzil couplets. In Zinacantan, prayers are invariably both semantically and syntactically parallel in structure. Yucatec Maya prayers are always semantically, but only rarely syntactically parallel. The same is true of other Yucatec Maya formal genres. Of the fifteen Yucatec Maya examples I have cited, only four of them (nos. 44, 50, 52, and 54) are obviously syntactically parallel. It can be argued that four other couplets (nos. 46, 47, 49, and 56) exemplify *partial* syntactic parallelism on the grounds that they contain some framing elements such as *ti²-* in nos. 46 and 49, *bey-* and *ti²-* in no. 47, and *má² čéen-* and *hun* + numerical classifier- in no. 56. The other seven examples are semantically parallel in terms of synonymy (nos. 45, 48, 51, and 53) or apposition (nos. 55, 57, and 58).

All Yucatec Maya speech genres are classified as *t'àan* 'word, language, speech.' Although each of the couplet genres has its own label, they are not grouped together into any one category that might be defined as formal speech. Their classification is strictly functional. Thus here, too, we can ask: what role does structure play in the definition of speech genres?

An answer to this question may be provided by some documents I discovered in the State Archives of Yucatan in Mérida during the summer of 1971. The relevant documents date from the early years of the Caste War of Yucatan, the conflict which is described in the example of folk history cited above (couplets 53–8). In 1850, some of the Indian leaders of that rebellion founded a new religious cult based on the concept of a Talking Cross. The Cross supposedly dictated the sermon and five letters which I found in Mérida.

The sermon was delivered to the inhabitants of Chan Santa Cruz, the cult center, on 15 October 1850. The contents are largely prophetic in nature. For example, the people of Chan Santa Cruz were told on that day:

> 59. *bíin a w ohelté²ešeʔ,*
> *kristianoh kàahé²eš,*
> It is going to be made known to you,
> You Christians who live here,

> 60. *tèen in w éet máané²eš t u láakal ʔòorah;*
> *tèen k u máan in w áalkab táanil tiʔ té²eš*
> *t u táan enemigóʔob*
> That it is I who am always at your side;
> That it is I who go before you confronting
> the enemy

61. *t y óʔolal máʔ y úučul téʔeš,*
    miš hun p'éelóʔob in sihsàh máasewaliléʔeš.
    So that nothing will befall you,
    Not one thing, oh you Indians whom I
    engendered.

This passage seems to be expressed in semantic couplets as are other
portions of the text. But not all passages can be scanned so easily in terms
of parallel couplets. In fact a later copyist, perhaps feeling that a prophetic
text should be expressed in couplets, rewrote some passages in that form.
The later version of the Sermon of the Cross which I consulted is today the
sacred book of the Indians of X-Cacal, who are descendants of the rebels
who established Chan Santa Cruz as their cult center (Villa Rojas 1945).[3]
The manuscript was copied in 1903 from another manuscript first written
down in 1887, which was in turn copied from the 1850 manuscript or
from a copy of it.

What in the 1850 manuscript appears as:

t u mèen t u k'uč t u ʔòorahil
because the hour has come

has been edited in the later version to read:

t u mèen k'uč t u ʔòorahil t u háʔabil
because the hour and the year have come

which can be scanned as the couplet:

62. *t u mèen k'uč t u ʔòorahil,*
    t u háʔabil.
    Because it has arrived in the hour,
    In the year.

In another example, the 1850 manuscript gives:

miš hun p'éel hustisiah bíin mèentáʔak tèen
not a single judgment will be made for me
máʔ t u bèeliʔ.
that is not right.

This was later rewritten as:

> *máʔ u yantal u mèentáʔal tèen miš hun p'éel*
> it has never been that there was made for me,
> *hustisiah máʔ t u bèeliʔ wáah š máʔ t u tòohil.*
> not a single judgment that was not just, nor one
> that was not right.

which can be scanned as the couplets:

> 63. *máʔ u yantal*
>   *u mèentáʔal tèen*
> It has never been
> That there was made for me

> 64. *miš hun p'éel hustisiah máʔ t u bèeliʔ,*
>   *wáah š máʔ t u tòohil.*
> Not a single judgment that was not just,
> Nor one that was not right.

In the next example, the copyist made two phrases which were originally only semantically parallel, also syntactically parallel, changing:

> 65. *u tiáʔal káʔa h y úʔub čičan,*
>   *y éetel nohòč*
> In order that the young may hear,
> And the old

to:

> 66. *u tiáʔal káʔa h y úʔub čičan;*
>   *y éetel káʔa h y úʔub nohòč;*
> So that the young may hear;
> And the old may hear;

The five letters supposedly dictated by the Cross were written during 1851. Four were sent to Miguel Barbachano, the Governor of Yucatan; the fifth was sent to the Commander General of Valladolid. They, too, contain prophecies and they are partly expressed in couplets. They differ from other letters of the time both in content and structure.

Even dates are expressed in couplets in the letters:

67. *bayhelela⁷ t u šòokol 28*
   u mèesil agosto
   Here today in the twenty-eighth count
   Of the month of August

as are other passages, such as:

68. *y ó⁷olal a mèentik u šòokol,*
   y ú⁷ub:
   So that you make them read,
   (And) understand:

69. *čičan,*
   y éetel nohoč,
   Young,
   And old,

70. *ká⁷a h yanak a w ohetké⁷eše⁷ in w éet máané⁷eš;*
   ti⁷á⁷anen t a w ičilé⁷eše⁷;
   That I accompany you;
   That I am among you;

71. *táan in máan*
   in šíimbat yukatane⁷.
   As I travel through
   (And) visit Yucatan.

These data suggest that Yucatec Maya speakers, like Tzotzil speakers, implicitly differentiate speech genres in terms of structure. This may be clearly seen by comparing the prophetic letters dictated by the Cross with other letters written by Indians during the Caste War. Ordinary letters began with the standard flowery salutation:

in yamahil noh talan ʈikbé⁷enil yùume⁷,
My beloved and most excellent Sir,

and closed with:

halilih u šùul in t'àan ti⁷ a ʈikbé⁷enilo⁷.
Verily my words to Your Excellency have ended.
ká⁷a h yùumil ti⁷ dios u kanáant a santoh pišan
May the Lord God care for your holy soul
t u yá⁷abal há⁷ab.
for many years.

But they were not written in couplets.

The fact that the Sermon of the Cross, which is a non-traditional instance of prophecy, was expressed at least partially in terms of semantic couplets implies that the couplet structure is essential to prophecy. This argument is reinforced by the fact that the later copyist(s) rewrote parts of the text, making some of the phrases more parallel in structure. In fact, it may be that the more traditional examples of couplet verse are not just more consistent in their structure, but are the culmination of generations of editing and reediting. One might argue further, by analogy, that the traditional genres of Zinacanteco speech evolved through similar stages before becoming enshrined as perfect couplets, or 'good' speech.

Conclusions

In this paper I have considered the structure and function of Mayan couplet speech, using data from Zinacantan in highland Chiapas and from several communities in the Yucatan peninsula. I began by showing that couplets may be either syntactically or semantically parallel, or both, and that syntactic parallelism is very common in Zinacanteco couplet speech, but relatively rare in Yucatec Maya couplets. I then discussed the ethnographic context of Zinacanteco couplet speech, arguing that Zincantecos use syntactic and/or semantic parallelism to mark formal speech. My data from the Yucatan peninsula were not as complete as for Zinacantan, but they did suggest that those Yucatec Maya speech genres which correspond in name and function to the Zinacanteco formal genres (and have not been influenced by Spanish rhyming conventions), are likewise marked by semantic, and sometimes also syntactic, parallelism.

I noted that neither the Zinacantecos nor the Yucatecan Maya refer to structure when they classify speech genres. Rather, their classifications are made strictly in terms of function, moral value, or provenience (traditional or recent). However, analysis of two versions of a nineteenth-century Yucatecan document suggested that even though the couplet structure of formal speech is not as cognitively salient, the Maya will rephrase unstructured speech which has a ritual functional in terms of both semantic and syntactic couplets. I therefore conclude that it is possible that whenever informal recent unstructured speech begins to serve ritual functions, then it is gradually rephrased in terms of couplets, perhaps according to the model provided by the two versions of the nineteenth-century Yucatec Maya document. By this argument the genres of Zinacanteco formal speech which employ the couplet structure loosely and inconsistently, would be in the transitional stage exemplified by the 1850 and 1887 (or 1903) versions of the Sermon of the Cross.[4]

18

TO SPEAK WITH A HEATED HEART: CHAMULA CANONS OF STYLE AND GOOD PERFORMANCE

GARY H. GOSSEN

This paper explores a central metaphor which Chamulas use to talk about and evaluate speaking. I shall attempt to show how this metaphor – heat – functions as a basic canon of native criticism of nearly all kinds of speech performances which Chamulas recognize, from ordinary language to formal ritual speech and song. Heat possesses great religious significance because its primary referent is the sun deity (*htotik k'ak'al* 'Our Father Sun'), who created and now maintains the basic temporal, spatial, and social categories of the Chamula cosmos. Controlled heat, therefore, symbolizes order in both a diachronic and synchronic sense. Language is but one of several symbolic domains which Chamulas think and talk about in terms of heat metaphors. Ritual action, the life cycle, the agricultural cycle, the day, the year, individual festivals, political power, economic status – all are measured or evaluated in units which derive ultimately from 'Our Father Sun,' the giver of order. Canons of verbal style and performance will therefore be described as ideal patterns which extend, in homologous fashion, into the whole fabric of Chamula social life and expressive behavior. I hope, thereby, to show how certain Chamula ethical and esthetic values behave as a unitary normative code.

After describing the community and the categories of cosmology which give symbolic power to the heat metaphor, I shall briefly outline the categories of verbal behavior which Chamulas recognize. Within this folk taxonomy, which can be seen as a continuum of style in which the individual genres are expressed, I shall discuss patterns of formalism, style, redundancy, and dyadic construction which are part of adult linguistic competence. Nearly all criteria which Chamulas use to evaluate these esthetic patterns are also moral criteria which apply to other aspects of their society. Controlled cycles of heat provide the metalanguage of native criticism for evaluating what is well spoken and beautiful. The same cycles of metaphorical heat provide the criteria for the good and the desirable in the life cycle, social relations, and cosmology. This equivalence leads me in the final section to some speculation about a dimension of Chamula thought which might be called philosophy of language.

The community: heat and cosmos

Chamula is one of the eleven municipios in the state of Chiapas, Mexico, which speak Tzotzil, which belongs to the Tzeltalan group of Maya languages. Genuine bilingualism is minimal; perhaps 5% of the population, mostly men, speak Spanish well as a second language. More than forty one-room primary schools (first four grades), built in the last twenty years, have so far failed in their goal of teaching Spanish to significant numbers of Chamula children.

Some 40 000 Chamulas live patrilocally in over a hundred scattered hamlets near the top of the Chiapas Highlands, at an average elevation of 7600 feet. All Chamulas engage to a greater or lesser extent in swidden agriculture. The subsistence base consists of maize, beans, squash, and cabbage, in approximately that order of importance. In the many cases in which their own land is insufficient to produce enough food, Chamulas engage in cottage industries, such as the manufacturing of charcoal, pottery, backstrap looms, or furniture. Chamulas are governed by a political hierarchy which is partly traditional (*Ayuntamiento Regional*, consisting of sixty-two positions or *cargos*) and partly prescribed by Mexican law (*Ayuntamiento Constitucional*, consisting of six positions, including that of the chief magistrate, or *Presidente*). A religious hierarchy consisting of sixty-one major positions supervises ceremonial activities and cults to the saints and also coordinates its ritual activities with those of the political hierarchy. Political authority on the local level lies in the hands of past cargoholders and heads of segments of patrilineages. Religious authority in the hamlets is exercised by shamans, past religious cargoholders, and again by elder males in the patrilineages.

Chamula religion and cosmology form a complex syncretistic system which is the product of sixteenth-century Spanish Catholicism and pre-Columbian Maya cults to nature deities, particularly to the sun (now identified with Christ), the moon (now the same as the Virgin Mary), water spirits, and earth lords. The other saints, including the patron saint of Chamula, San Juan, are kinsmen of the sun (the son of the moon). Chamulas also believe in individual animal soul companions which share certain aspects of people's spiritual and physical destinies.

Basic to Chamula cosmological belief is that they live in the center of the universe. They view their home municipio as the only truly safe and virtuous place on the earth. As physical distance increases, and as linguistic and social groups become ever more unlike Chamula, danger lurks more threateningly. The edges of the earth are populated by demons, strange human beings, and huge wild animals. From there one can see the terrifying spectacle of the sun and moon deities plunging into and emerging from the seas every day on their respective vertical circuits around the island universe. Not only does the sun deity delimit the spatial limits of the universe, but he also determines the temporal units (days and solar years) by the duration and position of his path. It was the sun who established order on the earth. He did this in progressive stages, separately creating the first three worlds and then destroying them, for people behaved improperly. Chamulas say that behavior equivalent to that of the people in the first three creations may still be found at the edges of the universe and, occasionally, among bad Chamulas. It is only the Fourth Creation which has been successful. This is a moral world which Chamulas must constantly strive to defend from bad behavior and evil people. Language, particularly the oral tradition, is a crucial tool for the defense, continuity, and ritual maintenance of the Fourth Creation. Perhaps the most important trait of language which provides power in Chamula social life is its capacity to express metaphorical heat in controlled, predictable cycles. Competent language use, like the sun, is characterized by measured, controlled patterns of intensity. This is expressed in various forms of redundancy which come from the 'heated heart.' According to Chamula exegesis, language shares the quality of cyclical heat with other ritual substances such as rum, incense, candles, and tobacco. It is therefore necessary to report in some detail the meaning of heat in Chamula cosmology. [1]

'Our Father,' the sun, is a primary and irreducible symbol of Chamula thinking and symbolism. At once in the concept of the sun, most units of lineal, cyclical, and generational time are implied, as well as the spatial limits and subdivisions of the universe, vertical and horizontal. Most of the other deities and all men are related lineally or spiritually to the sun creator. Day and night, the yearly agricultural and religious cycles, the seasons, the divisions of the day, most plants and animals, the stars, the constellations, as well as language, are the gifts of the sun, the life-force itself. Only the demons, monkeys, and other negative supernaturals were logically prior to and hostile to the coming of order. These forces killed the sun early in the First Creation and forced him to ascend in the heavens, thus providing heat, light, life, and order. Hence, the Tzotzil words for 'day' (*k'ak' al*) and 'fiesta' (*k'in*), which provide fundamental temporal references for Chamulas, are directly related to the Tzotzil word for fire (*k'ok'*) and the proto-maya word for sun, heat, and divinity (*k'inh*), respectively. It is also relevant that one of the several names for the sun creator is *htotik k'ak'al* or 'Our Father Heat (day).'

The fundamental spatial divisions of the universe, the cardinal directions, are derived from the relative positions of the sun on its east—west path across the heavens:

east: emergent heat (or day)
west: waning heat (or day)
north: side of heaven on the right hand (of the sun)
south: side of heaven on the left hand (of the sun)

The principal temporal divisions of each day are also described in relation to the position of the sun on its path across the sky. For example, 'in the afternoon' is generally expressed in Tzotzil as 'in the waning heat (or day).' 'In the mid-morning' is expressed as 'the heat (day) is rising now.' The fiestas, which are perhaps the most commonly used temporal markers within the annual cycle, are considered to be mini-cycles of heat. Their name (*k'in*, related to sun, heat, and divinity) implies the presence of the heat metaphor. Furthermore, one is able to specify almost any day in the year by referring to stages of, or days before or after, one of the more than thirty fiestas which are celebrated annually in Chamula. In referring to a certain day in relation to the fiesta cycle, one says, for example, *sk'an to ʔošib k'ak'al ta k'in san huan*, which means 'It is three days before (until) the fiesta of San Juan.' This is usually understood as I have translated it, yet the relationship of the words for fiesta to the words for heat and deity is such that it is possible to understand this as 'three daily cycles of heat before a major (religious) cycle of heat.'

In all of these temporal references, two themes emerge which are significant in understanding the heat metaphor in relation to language. First, heat is divine and primordial; its primary referent is the sun creator, giver of temporal, spatial, and social order. Second, heat, like its primary sun referent, is cyclical. Each day finished is both a cycle of heat completed and an affirmation of the holy integrity of the sun deity. The same can be said of each year, each agricultural season, each festival, each human life. Indeed it can even be said of the largest temporal units which Chamulas recognize: the four creations of man, of which we are now in the most successful, the Fourth. In all of these, cycles of heat express and confirm the most basic principles of patrifocal order. For example, male religious officials constantly partake of the heat metaphor in properly carrying out their duties. They are said to be 'helping the sun (or the saints, the sun's kinsmen) to bear the burden of the year.' This burden implies heavy financial responsibility, as well as sponsorship of highly redundant ritual actions throughout the year. These invariably involve ritual substances such as rum, tobacco, tropical flowers, incense, fireworks, candles, which express actual and metaphorical heat. Furthermore, the counter-clockwise direction which religious officials invariably follow through ritual circuits is, according to Chamula premises, the horizontal equivalent of the sun deity's vertical orbit. Officials thus move as the sun moves in their microcosm of ritual space (see Gossen 1972a). Another critically important aspect of ritual action which relates to the sun is of course the language used to conduct it. Ritual language, prayer, and song are all laced with metaphors for heat, as expressing homage, praise, and petition to the sun deity and his kinsmen. The highly redundant style of the ritual genres expresses the sacred and cyclical heat of religious transaction.

Heat expresses order in everyday life as well as in ritual life. The daily round of domestic life centers on the hearth, which lies near the center of the dirt floor of nearly all Chamula houses. The working day usually begins and ends around the fire, men and boys sitting and eating to the right of the hearth (from the point of view of one who faces the interior from the front door), women and girls to the left of the hearth. Furthermore, men in this patrifocal society always sit on tiny chairs, thus raising them above the cold, feminine ground, and wear sandals, which separate them from the ground and complement their masculine heat. Women, on the other hand, customarily sit on the ground, which is symbolically cold, and always go barefoot, which, symbolically, does not separate them but rather gives them direct contact with the cold, feminine earth. Coldness, femininity, and lowness are logically prior to heat, masculinity, and height. This follows from the mythological account of the coming of order. The male sun was born from the womb of the female moon and was then killed by the forces of evil and darkness. This in turn allowed him to ascend into the sky to create the cosmos, cyclical time, and patrifocal order.

The individual life cycle is also conceived of as a cycle of increasing heart from a cold beginning. A baby has a dangerously cold aspect. The individual acquires steadily increasing heat with baptism and sexual maturity. The heat of the life cycle reaches a fairly high level with social maturity, which is expressed by marriage and reproduction. The acquisition of heat may be carried further through a cargo or shamanistic career. Death plunges one into the cold from whence one came. Thus, life and death are also elementary expressions of the hot–cold syndrome of Chamula values. Life-crisis rituals and cargo initiations include symbols of life (hot and integrative) and death (cold and disjunctive). Hot and cold are also fundamental categories in the bewildering complexity which characterizes Chamula theories of illness. In sum, in nearly all aspects of Chamula life, mundane and sacred, increasing heat expresses the divine and order-giving will of the sun himself. We shall see below that language is no exception to this rule.

Kinds of verbal behavior

A bewildering number of processes, abstractions, and things can be glossed as k'op, which refers to nearly all forms of verbal behavior, including oral tradition. The term k'op can mean the following: word, language, argument, war, subject, topic, problem, dispute, court case, or traditional verbal lore. Chamulas recognize that correct use of language (that is, the Chamula dialect of Tzotzil) distinguishes them not only from non-humans, but also from their distant ancestors and from other contemporary Indian- and Spanish-speaking groups. According to Chamula narrative accounts, no one could speak in the distant past. That was one of the reasons why the sun creator destroyed the experimental people of the First and Second creations. The more recent people learned to speak Spanish and then everyone understood one another. Later, the nations and municipios were divided because they began quarreling. The sun deity changed languages so that people would learn to live together peacefully in small groups. Chamulas came out well in the long run, for their language was the best of them all (they refer to Tzotzil as baƚ'i k'op or 'true language'). Language, then, came to be the distinguishing trait of social groups.

The taxonomy of k'op, which appears in Figs. 17 and 18, was elicited several separate times from six male informants ranging in age from eighteen to sixty-five over the period of one year. It should be noted that no data from female informants are considered. This gives a definite but unavoidable male bias to this study. I used both formal question frames and informal discussion to discover the kinds of verbal behavior which Chamulas recognize.[2] The two figures should be more or less self-explanatory. The reader will probably note that I have not made an effort to describe the taxonomy as a grid of uniform or symmetrical criteria and distinctive features. Such a scheme would be a distortion of the way in which Chamulas view the taxonomy. For example: time is a relevant criterial attribute for distinguishing level-3 categories of 'new words' and 'recent words'; for other categories at the same level (3) of the taxonomy, place of performance is a defining feature ('court speech'); for still others at the same level (3) performer of the words is the relevant feature ('children's improvised games'). Similarly, heat appears as a stated defining attribute in the name of only one level-2 category ('speech for people whose hearts are heated'). We know, however, that genres of 'pure speech' have greater metaphorical heat value than the intermediate category which bears its name. Therefore, although I use the term 'level' in referring to the scheme, I do not attach any uniform 'deep structure' information to it. Levels are used only as descriptive conventions. Although I frequently recorded taxa at level 5 in the field, I have not recorded them in this abbreviated version

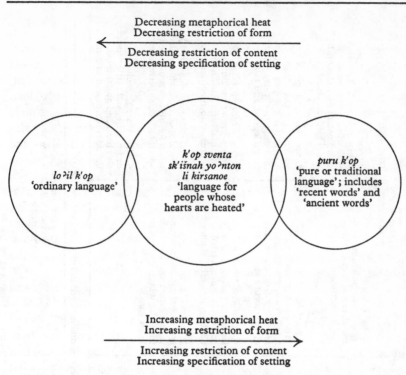

Fig. 17. A brief scheme of a Chamula folk taxonomy of verbal behavior

of the classification because responses at this level were far from consistent from informant to informant. I include level-5 items in a few of the brief genre descriptions below, but only when the majority of my informants recognized them. Much more useful than any abstract explanatory grid one might impose on the taxonomy are the Chamula explanations of the super-categories. These are included in Fig. 18.

'Ordinary language' (*lo ʔil k'op*) is restricted in use only by the dictates of the social situation and grammaticality or intelligibility of the utterance. It is believed to be totally idiosyncratic and without noteworthiness in style, form, or content; it is everyday speech. As one moves from left to right in Figs. 17 and 18, progressively more constraints of various sorts apply to what a person says (content) and how he says it (form). The intermediate category ('language for people whose hearts are heated') contains kinds of verbal behavior that are neither 'ordinary language' nor 'pure words.' They are restricted with regard to form (that is, how people will speak), but they are unpredictable as far as content is concerned. A common Chamula explanation for this kind of emotional speech emphasizes the

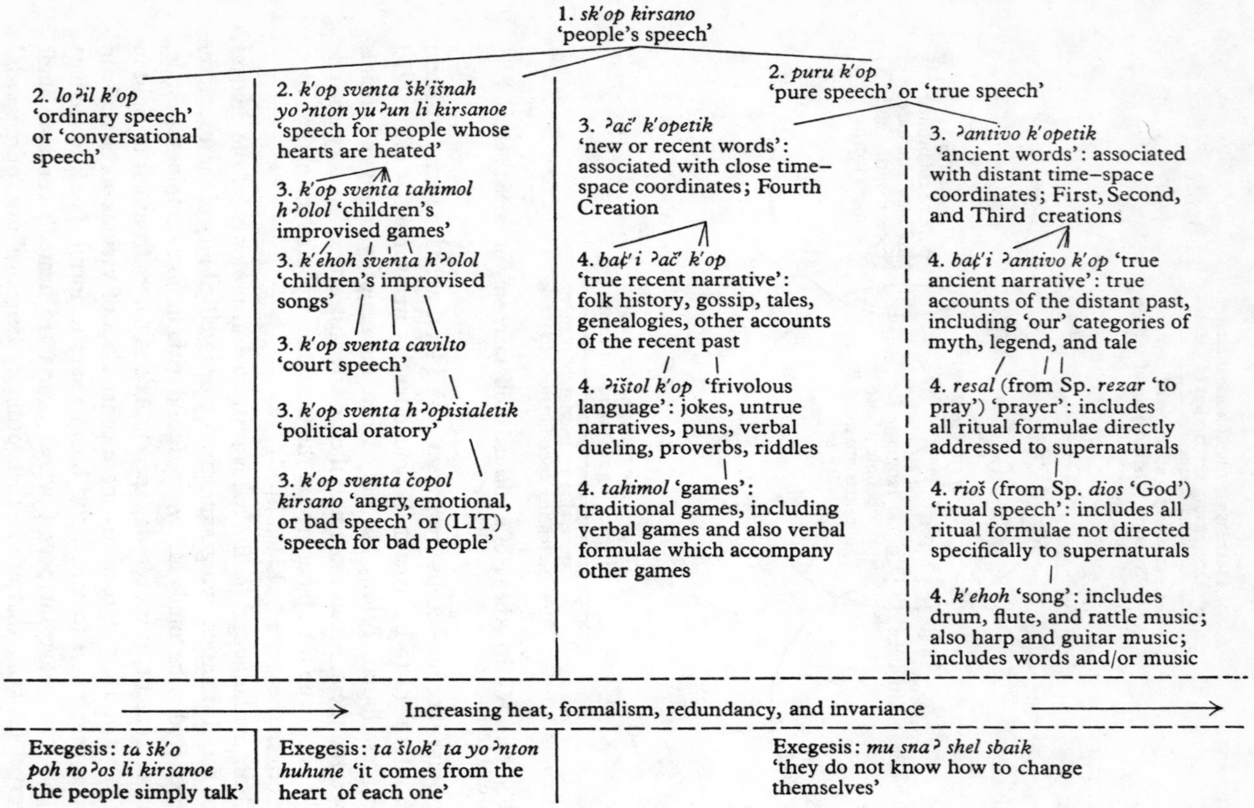

Fig. 18. A folk taxonomy of Chamula verbal behavior

1. sk'op kirsano 'people's speech'

2. lo?il k'op 'ordinary speech' or 'conversational speech'

2. puru k'op 'pure speech' or 'true speech'

2. k'op sventa ?k'išnah yo?mton yu?un li kirsanoe 'speech for people whose hearts are heated'

3. k'op sventa tahimol h?olol 'children's improvised games'

3. k'ehoh sventa h?olol 'children's improvised songs'

3. k'op sventa cavilto 'court speech'

3. k'op sventa h?opisialetik 'political oratory'

3. k'op sventa čopol kirsano 'angry, emotional, or bad speech' or (LIT) 'speech for bad people'

3. ?ač k'opetik 'new or recent words': associated with close time–space coordinates; Fourth Creation

4. bat'i ?ač k'op 'true recent narrative': folk history, gossip, tales, genealogies, other accounts of the recent past

4. ?istol k'op 'frivolous language': jokes, untrue narratives, puns, verbal dueling, proverbs, riddles

4. tahimol 'games': traditional games, including verbal games and also verbal formulae which accompany other games

3. ?antivo k'opetik 'ancient words': associated with distant time–space coordinates; First, Second, and Third creations

4. bat'i ?antivo k'op 'true ancient narrative': true accounts of the distant past, including 'our' categories of myth, legend, and tale

4. resal (from Sp. rezar 'to pray') 'prayer': includes all ritual formulae directly addressed to supernaturals

4. rioš (from Sp. dios 'God') 'ritual speech': includes all ritual formulae not directed specifically to supernaturals

4. k'ehoh 'song': includes drum, flute, and rattle music; also harp and guitar music; includes words and/or music

Increasing heat, formalism, redundancy, and invariance

Exegesis: ta šk'o poh no?os li kirsanoe 'the people simply talk'

Exegesis: ta šlok' ta yo?mton huhune 'it comes from the heart of each one'

Exegesis: ta šlok' ta yo?mton 'it comes from the heart of each one'

Exegesis: mu sna? shel sbaik 'they do not know how to change themselves' individual, idiosyncratic qualities of the performance: 'It comes from the heart of each person.' The term referring to all of these intermediate forms, 'language for people whose hearts are heated,' implies an elevated, excited, but not necessarily religious attitude on the part of the speaker. The state of excitement produces a style of verbal behavior in the intermediate forms that also occurs in the genres of 'pure words.' Yet, because content in the former depends on the individual whim of the speaker, these forms are not included by Chamula as a part of 'pure words.' It is only with the joint presence of prescribed content and form in genres to which all people ideally have equal access that we reach 'pure words,' on the right-hand side of the continuum shown in Figs. 17 and 18. As Chamulas told me, 'Pure words' do not know how to change.' The heat metaphor implies a transition into a more stylized form of speech, and continues from the intermediate category into the domain of 'pure words,' which contains the 'genuine' Chamula genres of oral tradition. The implication is an obvious, but, I believe, important one: Chamula oral tradition ('pure words') is only a part of a continuum of styles of verbal behavior occurring in other, less standardized contexts. The classes of verbal behavior that are transitional carry vital information for making sense of what is 'pure words.' Furthermore, Chamula children begin to learn some of the transitional forms (particularly improvised games, songs, and emotional speech) long before they begin to experiment with 'pure words.' It therefore seems crucial to consider the whole of verbal behavior rather than just those genres having constant form and content. This will be discussed in greater detail below.

Within 'pure words,' the criterion of time association is the most important one in distinguishing the secular forms ('recent words,' associated with the present Fourth Creation) from those having greater ritual and etiological significance ('ancient words,' associated with the First, Second, and Third creations). 'Recent words' are colder for they do not refer to the full four-cycle creation period. 'Ancient words' are hotter, for they were given and refer to events from the very beginning of order. Several apparent discrepancies in the scheme strike the non-Chamula observer. For example, certain stylistic features of 'ancient words' may also be found in verbal aspects of 'children's improvised games,' which are thought to be idiosyncratic expressions of individual whims in the present. This does not constitute an internal inconsistency in the taxonomy, but rather illustrates an important aspect of Chamula language learning: children probably would not be able to recognize, understand, or learn the formal genres of 'ancient words' if they did not experiment with the content, styles, rhythms, and syntax in their informal play behavior. Another example of apparent inconsistency is also instructive. Gossip might seem to the American or European observer to be excluded from anyone's oral tradition, for it cannot become truly 'traditional' overnight. Tradition is, however, a relative thing. In Chamula, gossip does belong to 'pure words' most of the time. Gossip, as the Chamulas see it, is not idiosyncratic or original in the way that intermediate types of verbal behavior are. Gossip is part of 'true recent narrative' because it is a statement of fact, a segment of information known by several people in a single form, which ideally will be passed on as a whole. All, theoretically, have equal access to it. To illustrate: the gossip among women at a waterhole about the chief magistrate's oration to the Chamulas at a past festival is 'true recent narrative,' whereas the oration itself is not. The oration ('political oratory') belongs to the transitional category of 'speech for people whose hearts are heated' because no one knew what he was going to say, only how he would say it. Another illustration may help to clarify the taxonomic criteria. Emotional speech ('speech for bad people') uses devices of cadence, repetition, syntax, and metaphor that are also found in 'pure words'; however, if a murder or some other noteworthy event followed the quarrel, an account of the entire event, including the language used in the quarrel, would probably be worthy of retelling as 'true recent narrative.'

A continuum of style as expressed in individual genres

In this section I should like to discuss a continuum of style as it is expressed in individual genres of the taxonomy. The following are examples of good (*lek*) speech performances by Chamula standards (cf. the taxonomy presented in Figs. 17 and 18). Space does not allow inclusion of examples of bad performance. Furthermore, I do not have such examples, labelled 'bad' by Chamulas, for all of the genres. In most cases, an error in pattern of repetition (i.e., syntax, couplet sets, or sequence of dyadic sets) would render a given performance weaker as an example of its class. In presenting the 'good' stylistic examples which follow I shall proceed from a cue suggested by the taxonomy itself: that increasing formalism, redundancy, and invariance are expressions of the order-giving metaphor of heat, and that 'to speak with a hearted heart' according to proper stylistic rules is the linguistic equivalent of doing the sun deity's will. In this way esthetics of language become subject to some of the same rules that apply to ethical social behavior.

There is, of course, much stylistic overlap between the genres, yet part and parcel of the genre's information and function is the way it is stated and performed. One of the main canons of good performance in all genres is proper cyclical patterning according to their respective rules; stylized, patterned speech is a symbol for the order-giving heat which is desirable in other classificatory domains as well. As the genres acquire greater ritual importance, they require greater heat of performance. This is expressed in greater metaphorical stacking and greater density of the semantic load. Hence, for a cargoholder to speak a formal genre well is to partake of the cyclical nature of the sun deity. Similarly for a child to speak verbatim lines well in a game is also to participate in the heat metaphor. In sum, 'to speak with a heated heart' means using prescribed redundant style competently.

Throughout, I shall emphasize that redundancy and invariance of syntax, information, and cadence are ways of saying, 'These symbols matter.' 'Ordinary language' is typically cold in that it is believed to be idiosyncratic and non-redundant. Specialized genres are increasingly hotter as their time–space associations become greater. That is, 'language for people whose hearts are heated' (emotional but idiosyncratic speech) marks the beginning of rising heat; 'recent words' (genres associated with the Fourth Creation) are intermediate in kind and invariance of heat redundancy; 'ancient words' (genres associated with the first three creations and distant time–space coordinates) form an extreme statement of metaphorical heat. Thus, greater time–space depth carries with it redundant stylistic associations which are themselves symbols for cyclical heat, the stuff of the cosmic order. In particular, dyadic constructions or couplets enter into these patterns of redundancy. These have been recognized cross-culturally as important stylistic devices (cf. Jakobson 1966; Fox 1971 and this volume; Edmonson 1971:90–1, 104–5; Kramer 1970; and Bricker this volume). These dual or parallel constructions behave as elementary structures of Chamula formalism. A term which I have coined for the purposes of discussing Chamula style is 'metaphorical stacking.' By this I mean the tendency to repeat lines and themes for emphasis, in slightly different form; the greater the repetition, the more crucial the information. It is most typical of the more formal genres ('ancient words'), in which consecutive dyadic constructions restate important configurations of religious symbols time and time again, according to their importance for the maintenance of the social order. Elementary forms of metaphorical stacking occur in the less formal genres as well.[3]

'ORDINARY SPEECH'

This has been discussed above. Here let me repeat simply that this is conventional speech. No one thinks about it as a special form, except to contrast the 'correct' Chamula dialect with the 'incorrect' neighboring Tzotzil dialects. It has no restrictions as to form and content except that it be intelligible, grammatical, and appropriate.

THE MARGINAL GENRES: 'SPEECH FOR PEOPLE
WHOSE HEARTS ARE HEATED'

'Language for people whose hearts are heated' represents the beginning of
a continuum of restriction as to form, content, and setting in Chamula
verbal behavior. It is more stylized than 'ordinary language,' yet it is not
'pure words.' This type of verbal behavior is distinguished from regular
speech (*lo ʾil k'op*) in that 'people's hearts are becoming heated' (*šk išnah
yo ʾnton yu ʾun li kirsanoe*). I have discussed above the significance of heat
in the Chamula value system. It has great positive value, for that which
is 'hot' is strong, mature, and life-giving. Yet heat is also dangerous when
abused or uncontrolled, as drunken behavior demonstrates. The symbolic
essence of heat is of course the sun deity, which is also the marker of
cyclical time and order *par excellence*. It is therefore not surprising that
repetition of phrases, metaphors, words, and ideas characterizes nearly
all normative statements about the social order. It might be said that human
social order depends upon repetition of rule-governed behavior as communicated and understood through language. Repetition and mastery of
the use of language, furthermore, signal a child's successful socialization
as well as adult mastery or cultural specialties. Repetition stands out as a
distinctive feature of marginal genres. Speakers are excited, their hearts
are hot, yet one does not know beforehand just what the speakers will say.
And herein lies the critical difference which, according to Chamulas,
excludes these genres from the stable genres which compose 'pure words.'
The marginal genres show the redundant features of form and style which
characterize the whole oral tradition, yet their content still comes from
'within each one' (*šlok' ta huhune*); it is original and has not come intact
from another source of another person. That explains why, from the
Chamula point of view, the kinds of speech described in this section are
neither 'ordinary language' nor 'pure words' but something in between.
It should also be noted that the kinds of situations dealt with by these
genres are either learning processes (as in children's games), challenges
to the social order, or efforts to rectify it (as in court cases, scolding speech,
and oration). Thus, the less formal part of the style continuum may be
characterized by some variation in content and structure.

'Children's improvised games'

These games, including verbal and non-verbal components alike, tend
usually to be imperfect children's imitations of adult behavior. The most
typical verbal component of these games is related to language learning.
It is verbatim repetition of words and phrases, often three or four times.
(This style may also occur in emotional speech, court speech, and political
oratory, the other less formal genres).

lok' an me! lok' an me! lok' an me!
Get out! Get out! Get out!

(From a 'children's improvised game')

This form of repetition is related not only to the other forms of 'speech for people whose hearts are heated,' but also to the genres of 'pure words,' as we shall see below.

'Children's improvised songs'

These songs are imperfect children's imitations of 'song,' a genre that occurs in 'pure words.' An important linguistic component of 'children's improvised songs' is experimentation with metaphorical couplets, which are the most important stylistic building blocks of the formal genres of 'ancient words.' For example, the following song line came from a child's song of speculation about what animal soul he had. The small boy (four years old) sang it as he struck a cat with a stick:

> pinto čon un bi.
> Spotted animal (you are).
>
> pinto bolom un bi.
> Spotted jaguar (you are).

As an adult 'song' the performance was imperfect on several counts. However, the couplet which the child used has a structure like hundreds which exist in more formal genres: same syntax in two lines, with a one-word synonym substitution in the second line.

'Court speech'

'Court speech' refers to the language used by political officials, defendants, plaintiffs, and witnesses at court hearings that occur every day of the year except fiesta days. Verbal competence is absolutely crucial to anyone's success in court. Emotions, of course, play a vital part in all court happenings. The stylistic canons for 'heated hearts' are nearly always apparent in 'court speech.' However, because each case is theoretically unique, one does not know beforehand what people will say, only how they will say it. The outstanding stylistic trait of 'court speech' is parallel syntax. (This style occurs in emotional speech, political oratory, and narratives.)

> ʔoy ša shayibuk velta ʔelk'anik.
> Many times already you have stolen.
>
> šavelk'an čihe.
> You steal sheep.

šavelk'an ti ʔalak'e.
You steal chickens.

šavelk'an ti ʔisak'e.
You steal potatoes.

savelk'an ti maʔil e.
You steal squash.

šavelk'an ti k'uʔil e.
You steal clothing.

šavelk'an ti ʔitah e.
You steal cabbage.

šavelk'an ti tuluk'e.
You steal turkeys.

skotol k'usi šavelk'an.
You steal anything.

ʔaʔ ša noʔoš muyuk bu šavelk'an
   be sbek' yat li kirsanoetik;
The only things you don't steal
   from people are their testicles;

ʔaʔ ša noʔoš čaloʔ.
And those you only eat.

('Court speech,' from a court session in which
the Presidente was chastising a female sheep thief)

Note that the repeated syntax, with one-word substitutions, is related to the
metaphorical couplet and serves as an intensifier of the message. We will
see below that, although this form of speech is idiosyncratic in content,
its style of redundancy and parallelism is repeated throughout the oral
tradition.

'Political oratory'

'Political oratory' includes all public announcements made by religious
and political officials outside ritual settings. Like 'court speech,' 'political
oratory' has highly predictable stylistic components; yet each performance
is theoretically different, which is why it does not qualify as 'pure speech.'
The stylistic devices that characterize it have already been discussed –
parallel syntax, metaphorical couplets, redundancy of message, and verbatim repetition.

'Speech for bad people'

The Chamula term for this genre is somewhat misleading, for this category
of speech refers to any heated, emotional, drunken, or angry discussion.

Heat is ideally desirable, for it represents the sun creator himself. Yet uncontrolled heat, that is, heat without measured cycles, is threatening. For example 'speech for bad people' is so named for it sometimes leads to machete fights and killings if it is not handled with care. Therefore, emotional and excited speech is desirable if controlled and used in defense of the norm; it is undesirable if uncontrolled and use offensively against the norm. 'Speech for bad people' thus refers to the excited language of those whose hearts 'heat up,' *possibly* to the point of no control.

The characteristic linguistic forms of this uncontrolled speech are as follows: multiple metaphorical restatements that may be in couplet form, but also in the form of longer restatements of sentence length, parallel syntax with one- and two-word substitutions, and simple verbatim repetition. Like other forms of the intermediate class, individual performances are unique and theoretically cannot be repeated. In this less formal style a repetition of ideas is expressed in non-parallel repetition. This style also occurs frequently in court speech, political oratory, and narratives. It is a form of metaphorical stacking.

> mi mu vinikukot, šaman ti ʔanȼ'e, penteho.
> If you were a man, you would buy a woman, you
> damned coward.

> čak'an ʔavahnil, pere moton šak'an.
> You want a wife, but as a gift you want (her).

> mu šak'an, kabron, mu šak'an šaman.
> You refuse to, you bastard, you refuse to buy (her).

> ('Speech for bad people,' from an angry exchange
> between a man and his future son-in-law)

'PURE WORDS'

'Pure words' include those genres having constraints of three types: form, content, and social setting. Although less variation in form and content is permitted, generally the 'semantic load' of words and phrases is greater in this more formal part of the style continuum than in the less formal styles discussed above. 'Pure words' include the stable genres of Chamula oral tradition. As a unit, 'pure words' carry a linguistic arsenal of defense for the Chamula way of life. Part of the strength of these genres seems to relate to the fact that the cyclical view of time, the very underpinning of the Chamula view of cosmic order, serves as an attribute that both unifies 'pure words' and subdivides into two major classes, 'recent words' and 'ancient words.' 'Recent words' were learned or acquired in the present, Fourth Creation; 'ancient words' relate to the coming and formal maintenance of the Chamula social order.

'Recent words: true recent narrative'

'True recent narrative' includes 'true' narrative accounts of Fourth Creation events that are worth repeating as a unit and to which all persons ideally have equal access. Stylistic traits of 'true recent narrative' are familiar continuities from 'speech for people whose hearts are heated.' However, the joint presence of these traits with fixed content that is supposedly true qualifies these narratives as a genre of 'pure words.' Individuals may add emphasis in the telling of the event, but they should stick to the facts. Emphasis is given by greater or lesser density of stacking of metaphorical couplets. This serves speakers and listeners as a measure of what in the narrative is judged to be important and what is trivial. Greater redundancy of an idea, in the form of metaphorical couplets, parallel syntax, or longer semantic restatement, underlines the importance of the idea. The example which follows illustrates typical composition and a point of emphasis in a single couplet based on parallel syntax. The following fragment, from a text entitled 'The Time of the Fever,' tells of the influenza epidemic of 1918, which followed the Mexican Revolution. This is a particularly well performed passage, for it leaves little doubt in the listener's mind that the most important fact in the passage is that the epidemic was sent as a punishment from the sun.

> veno,
> Well, then,
>
> k'alal ʔital ti k'ak'al čamel ti voʔne e
> When the fever came long ago
> pero veno haʔ la smul ti hkaransa
> It was because of the crimes of the *carrancistas.*
>
> ʔiliktal tahmek ta ʔolon ʔosil.
> It came from Hot Country.

Parallel metaphorical couplet
> { la la sčik'ik tal ti htotik e,
>   Our Father, the Sun, brought it upon them,
>
>   la la sčik'ik tal ti santoetik e
>   The saints called it down upon them. }

> pere ʔora tana ʔun.
> But then something else happened.

'Recent words: frivolous language'

What 'true recent narrative' accomplishes with prose accounts of true breaches of the social order, 'frivolous language' accomplishes with laughter. The genre actually consists of five subgenres (which might be called fifth level taxa in the context of Fig. 18). All of these express or refer to ambiguous or deviant behavior, and all elicit laughter from participants and onlookers. Laughter appears to underline the norm by placing the deviant or ambiguous item of behavior in sharp relief against the norm. Using this technique, they effect social control in informal settings and also in formal settings, when other means are not applicable. In all of the subgenres of 'frivolous language' stylistic constraints are rigid, and great emphasis is given to multiple meanings. Form, content, social setting, and range of alternative meanings are more or less constant, thus qualifying them for inclusion in 'pure words.' Brief descriptions of the genres are given below.

'Lies'

'Lies' are prose jokes which tell of admittedly untrue events. The subgenre might be glossed as a 'tall tale.' Nearly always there is a superficial theme which makes the 'lie' sound like 'true recent narrative,' but there is always a second, usually sexual, theme which lies beneath the apparent surface theme. The laughter which 'lies' elicit emphasizes by contrast what the norm is and should be. 'Lies' share almost all stylistic traits with 'true recent narrative.' The difference is in the verity of the events reported and in the semantic dimension.

'Genuine frivolous talk'

This most widely used subgenre of 'frivolous language' consists of hundreds of sets of suggestive words and phrases that have minimal sound shifts from one to the next. Words or phrases are spoken alternately by two players as a form of verbal dueling. The player who cannot respond to a challenge loses. As in 'lies' there is a surface meaning and a second meaning or more. It is a characteristic form of boys' and men's joking behavior and frequently accompanies bantering about sexuality and sexual fantasies in this rather strait-laced society. It is a very popular form in which boys and young men strive to achieve excellence, for skill with language is highly prized and respected. There are few better indicators of adult political and ritual potential than virtuosity in this genre as an adolescent. The following is a typical exchange of 'genuine frivolous talk' and is characterized by prescribed minimal sound shifts from one word or phrase to the next.

Boy I (challenging)	ʔak'bun ʔaviš.
	Give me your sister.
Boy II (replying)	ʔak'bo ʔaviš.
	Give it to your sister.
(From a verbal duel,	'truly frivolous talk')

'Obscure words'

Although glossed as 'proverb,' this subgenre of 'frivolous language' has a different nature and apparently more complex role than proverbs have in western societies. Ultimately, Chamula 'obscure words' make normative statements, but they do this by suggestion, never by actual explicit statement. In fact, they will often state the opposite of the norm. The reason for this is that their social setting demands circumlocution. They imply normative deviation by metaphor and try indirectly to correct it, and because the referent situation is usually obvious to offender, speaker, and others, they are remarkably funny. Both linguistic form and range of possible referent situations are more or less constant. Prescribed dyadic syntax, but not necessarily couplets, and dyadic semantic domains characterize the genre's style. (See Gossen 1973 for further examples.)

> ta štal li Hoʾ e,
> It is going to rain,
>
> pere ta štakih ta ʾora.
> But it will dry up right away.
>
> (An 'obscure word' or proverb)

'Riddles'

Chamula riddles behave as jokes and nearly always involve double meanings, usually emphasizing sexual or ambivalent topics which are points of stress in Chamula society. They are generally of two types, classified by linguistic form: fixed formulas and prose. In both cases, the form and content are more or less fixed, although the ambiguous referents (that is, 'possible answers') may fluctuate within a given range of alternatives. Following is an example of the formula type. Like most of the other genres of 'pure words,' this type of riddle is characterized by dyadic syntax and corresponding meanings.

> hmeʾ kumagre haval,
> My comadre is face up,
>
> kumpagre nuhul. k'usi ʾun?
> My compadre is face down. What is it?
>
> Answer: teša.
>   A roof tile.
> (A 'question word' or riddle)

'Buried words'

This subgenre behaves as a prose riddle, but is usually used to refer to specific situations, to describe and control specific cases of normative deviation. It uses the familiar parallel structures, discussed above, but the key words are nearly always sexual or scatological puns. Like 'obscure words,' 'buried words' frequently call attention to some error in personal appearance or behavior. In a sense they tell an offender what is 'wrong' by involving him in a suggestive guessing game. The humor underlies the norm but also mitigates potential hard feelings and quarrels.

'Recent words: games'

This genre includes verbal and non-verbal aspects of those games having definite rules and names. It is sometimes divided further into children's games, which are combined verbal and non-verbal performances, and adults' games, which are mostly verbal. The latter overlap with the subgenre of 'frivolous language.' In reference to children's games, it is important to note that they include rule-governed action of both a verbal and non-verbal nature. This implies that the verbal-non-verbal distinction is not particularly significant to Chamulas. It is rather the rule-governed aspect, the moral dimension, the predictability, which matter as criteria for inclusion of the genre in 'pure words.'

The verbal component is usually a combination of fixed lines of emotional speech and set formulae. The emotional lines accompanying the action are verbatim repetitions (usually in twos and threes) of key words and phrases. Frequently there are also set, redundant formulae, which must be said to make the game 'correct.' One such line comes from a kind of hide-and-go-seek game called Peter Lizard (*petul ʔokoč'*) in which the child playing Peter Lizard hides, while the other children try to find him, shouting:

> buyot?   buyot?
> Where are you?   Where are you?
>
> buyot, petul ʔokoč?
> Where are you, Peter Lizard?

When they find him (he helps by giving whistle signals), they pursue him and eventually trap him by piling on top of him. Thus, both actions and speech have constraints of form and content in true Chamula 'games.'

'Ancient words: true ancient narrative'

This narrative genre shares many stylistic traits and performance aspects with 'true recent narrative' (see above). The important difference between the two is content, this being related to the temporal dimension. Like all genres of 'ancient words,' 'true ancient narrative' reports or refers to events of the first three creations. As such, most of the narrations are etiological and explanatory. Related to the role of 'true ancient narrative' in stating the coming of the present order is a greater message redundancy than one finds in 'true recent narrative.' Items of assumed knowledge about the nature and establishment of order require more metaphorical stacking, for emphasis, than the threats to order which are reported in 'true recent narrative.' An example of this pattern follows. It is a fragment from a narrative about the Second Creation relating the origin of Ladinos[4] from the offspring of a Second Creation Ladino woman and her dog. Note the symmetry of this fragment, built of couplets.

Parallel couplet	šinulan ʔanȼ, The Ladino woman,
	šinulan ȼeb; The Ladino girl;
Interrogative couplet	k'uyepal ʔoy? How many were there?
	čib sbi. Two of them.
Parallel couplet	ȼ'akal ta šanav, Behind her it walked,
	ȼ'akal ta sbeʔin: Behind her it travelled:
Semantic couplet	sčiʔuk sȼiʔ, She and the dog,
	muyuk bu ta šanav stuk. She did not walk alone.

Not all texts are as symmetrical and redundant as this one, nor is symmetry necessarily present throughout a text. The fragment, however, illustrates a general tendency for all genres of 'ancient words' to utilize greater stylistic redundancy than 'recent words.' This relates to the kind of information carried; it is crucial, basic knowledge that must be understood by all and formally maintained. Hence, still greater metaphorical heat is implied here than in genres previously discussed. Furthermore, 'true ancient narrative' (and less frequently 'true recent narrative') often is characterized by the more formal style of metaphorical restatement of an idea in couplets and multiples thereof. This metaphorical stacking for emphasis is present in the example below. Not accidentally, the heat of redundancy in three related couplets refers to none other than the sun deity himself.

Non-parallel metaphorical couplet	sakub lek ti banamil e. The earth brightened.
	lok' la talel ti htotik e. The sun came out.

Non-parallel metaphorical couplet	sakhaman ša la talel ti šohobale. Its rays came forth in soft white radiance. heč la ti htotik ta vinahel e yal la talel ta banamil So it was that the sun in heaven came down to earth
Non-parallel metaphorical couplet	ta la spas yan ti kirsanoetik e, To make some other people, melʒah ti kirsanoetik e. To prepare mankind once again.

(From a text of 'true ancient narrative')

'Ancient words: prayer'

'Prayer' is ritual language addressed to supernaturals. It consists wholly of formal, bound couplets. I have never heard a 'prayer' composed of smaller elements. Its use implies a ritual setting. Hence, still greater metaphorical heat is implied here than in genres previously discussed. All adult Chamulas know some 'prayers'; religious specialists know hundreds. In all cases the components remain the same; highly redundant, metaphorical couplets with prescribed content and a more or less fixed order, the content and order of the couplets being determined by the specific ritual setting. This form also occurs constantly in 'language for rendering holy' and in 'song.' Metaphorical stacking is used to emphasize religious symbols.

Parallel metaphorical couplet	lital ta yolon ʔavok, I have come before your feet, lital ta yolon ʔak'ob. I have come before your hands.
Parallel metaphorical couplet	šciʔuk hnup, With my wife, šciʔuk hčiʔil, with my companion,
Parallel metaphorical couplet	šciʔuk kol, With my children šciʔuk hnič'nab. with my offspring.
Parallel metaphorical couplet	hbeh yoh kantila, But a feeble candle (I bring), lah yoh ničim, But a withered flower (I bring),

<table>
<tr><td>Parallel
metaphorical
couplet</td><td>{</td><td>muk'ta san huan,
Great San Juan,

muk'ta patron.
Great Patron.</td></tr>
</table>

Parallel
metaphorical
couplet
{
muk'ta san huan,
Great San Juan,

muk'ta patron.
Great Patron.
(From a 'prayer of salutation' for San Juan)

The text illustrates a pattern of 'ancient words': the greater the symbolic significance of a transaction, the more condensed and redundant will be the heated language used to conduct it.

'Ancient words: ritual speech'

'Ritual speech' includes all ritual language not directed to supernaturals. Like 'prayer,' some kinds of 'ritual speech' must be known by all adult Chamulas; religious and political specialists know the dozens of kinds required for their respective tasks. 'Ritual speech' is used by ritual officials and laymen to talk among themselves on the elevated plane of the ritual setting. It is constantly present in Chamula life, from drinking ceremonies to installation of new ritual officials to bride-petitioning rites. Since it always accompanies ritual transactions, its content is as varied as these settings. The style (with some exceptions, such as drinking toasts) is very much like that of 'prayer,' and it is remarkably constant from one setting to the next. Like 'prayer,' it is built almost entirely of bound formal couplets, which are theoretically irreducible components for the composition of 'ritual speech.' The relationship of redundancy of style and content to the high symbolic significance of the transaction applies to 'ritual speech' as it does to 'prayer.'

'Ancient words: song'

'Song' may be seen as the opposite end of a continuum of formalism and redundancy beginning with 'ordinary language' (*loʔil k'op*). Again, the truly heated heart is speaking. 'Song' has all of the formal stylistic attributes of 'prayer' and 'ritual speech,' plus musical form and instrumental accompaniment (harp, guitar, and rattle). It is language so hot that it becomes, as it were, an essence, like the smoke of tobacco or incense. 'Song' is present together with these other hot sacred substances at nearly all Chamula public rituals and at most private ones. No major Chamula ritual performance takes place without musicians. (Holy Week festivities are a near exception to this rule.) 'Song' may be said to be the highest form of language addressed to supernaturals. The instruments are said to sing with heated hearts just as people do. 'Song' is thus an extreme statement of metaphorical heat, for the musical form and heavily 'stacked' couplet structure together make it possible to repeat them *ad infinitum* until the ritual events they accompany have concluded. Directed to the sun deity and his kinsmen (the saints), they are the pure essence of linguistic heat.

Parallel metaphorical couplet	sk'ak'alil la ʔak'inal e, It is the day of your fiesta, sk'ak'alil la ʔapaškual e, It is the day of your joy,
Parallel metaphorical couplet	muk'ulil san huan e, Great San Juan, muk'ulil patron e. Great Patron.
Parallel metaphorical couplet	k'uyepal čihšanavotik ʔo ta hlikel bi! How soon we are to be walking! k'uyepal čihšanavotik ʔo ta htabel bi! How soon we are to be commencing the procession!
Parallel metaphorical couplet	sk'ak'alil ʔaničim ba, It is the day of your flowery face, sk'ak'alil ʔaničim sat. It is the day of your flowery countenance.
Nonsense syllables as parallel metaphorical couplet	la la li la lai la ʔo la la li la lai la a la la li la lai la a la la li la lai la ʔo

(A section from the first of the four 'songs of praise for San Juan.' San Juan is the patron saint of Chamula.)

Language, style, and cosmos

Throughout I have suggested that metaphorical heat gives some conceptual unity to the range of redundant style which Chamulas recognize as necessary and proper for good performance of the respective genres of their oral tradition. I also have suggested that the same metaphor operates as a fundamental organizational concept in Chamula thought, ethics, religion, and cosmology. This should hardly come as a surprise, for oral tradition, like any expressive domain, is a 'social fact' which shares organizational principles with the society in which it lives.

In language itself, words and strict rules for combining them can generate infinite numbers of sentences. Chamula oral tradition is more invariant than the Tzotzil language in which it is expressed, for the traditional genres involve stylistic patterns which, by Chamula explanation, 'do not know how to change' (*mu sna? shel sbaik*). Their traditional genres which 'do not know how to change' also deal with assumptions and rules which themselves should not vary beyond given alternatives. This brings us to the fact, stated many times above, that oral tradition is primarily concerned with norms and limits of permitted variation within them. In this sense, Chamula oral tradition is a more or less invariant expressive system that provides information which helps people to deal with more or less invariant aspects of the social system. It therefore is fitting and consistent that the primary invariable aspect of Chamula cosmos – the sun deity – should provide a native metalanguage for talking about some of the invariable canons of language use.

These canons are expressed in a clear continuum from lesser to greater stylistic formality, invariance, and redundancy as one moves from ordinary discourse to 'ancient words.' The complexity of semantic reference also changes from one-word–one-referent relationships in ordinary discourse, through punning and verbal play with multiple ambiguous referents in the marginal genres and in 'recent words,' to highly complex ritual and religious symbolism in 'ancient words.' In every case the style of a genre of *k'op* has metaphorical value of its own, enabling a speaker to establish the mood and symbolic significance of his utterance by the way he speaks. The continuum of style is an approximation of the language-learning process itself. Children begin their mastery of *k'op* by learning to repeat single words correctly and relate them to the correct referents. Greater linguistic sophistication is required for using metaphoric restatement, parallel syntax, punning, and other forms of linguistic play. Mastery of formal dyadic couplets and other parallel structures, and the hundreds of alternative ways they can combine, plus the technique of 'metaphorical stacking,' are even more sophisticated techniques which Chamulas master only in the 'mature heat' of adulthood.

Thus, the life cycle, language learning, stylistic complexity of language genre, context of performance, and metaphorical heat are all intimately related to sun primacy in Chamula thought. This characterizes the whole of *k'op* and not just formal genres. A piece of gossip in 'true recent narrative' does not require great stylistic embellishment and redundancy because its message is not crucial to the formal maintenance of order. It usually deals only with a breach in the present social order. It corrects informally. In contrast, redundancy and formal dyadic style are required in order to give the proper emphasis to words which refer to ritual symbols, those objects and concepts which are highly imbued with multiple meanings. The diffuseness of the semantic referents of ritual symbols seems to require verbal representations which are analogous to the concepts themselves. For example, the sun is omnipotent and omnipresent. This makes intelligible the dozens of metaphors, sometimes stated consecutively and in dyadic structures, which are used to talk about him and to him. The sun deity's multiple aspects and the cycles of time which he represents make a kind of cyclically patterned style of speech appropriate for talking to him and of him. Like meets like. Similarly, 'to speak with a heated heart' is to do justice to any specialized language use, for Tzotzil ('the true language') itself was a gift of the sun.[5]

VI

TOWARD AN ETHNOLOGY OF SPEAKING

INTRODUCTION

The papers in the four preceding sections represent detailed analyses of particular problems relevant to the ethnography of speaking. Although the papers are closely focused and deal with specific societies, they also raise general methodological and theoretical questions, with wider implications. By contrast, the papers in this final section address themselves primarily to broader issues of method and theory.

The first paper, by Allen Grimshaw, discusses a range of relationships between method and theory in the ethnography of speaking, with particular reference to some of the papers in this volume. Consistent with contemporary linguistics, sociology, and anthropology, Grimshaw stresses the importance of accounting for native intuitions in an ethnography of speaking. But he also warns that the notion of native intuitions cannot be used uncritically; in fact the ethnography of speaking, by its insistence on the interrelation of language and social life, provides new ways of investigating intuitions which avoid the circularity of arbitrarily dealing with linguistic, social, or cultural intuitions as separate systems. Grimshaw also notes the necessary progression from descriptions of particular aspects of speaking to coherent ethnographies of speaking to theory.

During the past decade and even at times in this volume, 'the ethnography of speaking' and 'the ethnography of communication' have been used almost interchangeably.[1] One of the contributions of this field has been the understanding that various communicative modes (verbal, proxemic, kinesic) are not absolutely independent of one another but are rather interrelated in various ways in various societies. Nevertheless, the papers in this volume do focus on speech as a central concern. None of the authors purposely avoids dealing with other communicative modes; indeed, such factors as paralinguistics, kinesics, proxemics, silence, and music are dealt with in many of the papers, in their interrelationship with speaking (see papers by Abrahams, Bauman, Darnell, Gossen, Irvine, Philips, Reisman, Sacks, Salmond, Sherzer, and Stross).

Similarly, although the contributors clearly recognize that there are various communicative channels in use in the societies with which they deal, they tend to focus on the spoken. In this regard, Keith Basso, in a programmatic essay which develops from his very meticulous work with the Western Apache, reminds ethnographers of speaking of the importance of writing as a mode of language use. The point he makes is basic to the ethnography of speaking. It is theoretically and methodologically incorrect to arbitrarily exclude writing from a description, since its functions and uses are not universally predictable, but vary from society to

417

society. What some people do by means of spoken language, others do by means of writing, and still others by means of silence. It is the total system which must ultimately be described.

Dell Hymes has been the most energetic and productive advocate of the ethnography of speaking since he first called the field into being in 1962. Largely through his contribution, the ethnography of speaking has influenced anthropology, linguistics, folklore, sociology, education, and literary criticism, though in various ways and to varying degrees.

The breadth of scope that has characterized his work is evident once again in his contribution to this section. In 'Ways of Speaking,' Hymes argues, ultimately, that grammar is but one way of looking at language. It is only by recognizing the multiplicity of potential ways of speaking and the ways these are selected and organized in particular societies that we can ever hope to account adequately for linguistic creativity or to develop a truly universal theory of language. It is from the perspective that Hymes develops here that we can best see that language and speech, from the everyday colloquial to the most verbally artistic, are not deviations from grammar but creative exploitations of the incredible diversity of linguistic resources available for speaking.

DATA AND DATA USE IN AN ANALYSIS
OF COMMUNICATIVE EVENTS

ALLEN D. GRIMSHAW

The papers in this volume present a wide range and impressive quantity of new empirical data on how people talk and on the rules which govern that talk and its interpretation. Authors have used their data in several different ways, variously (1) organizing descriptive frames from which testable propositions can be derived; (2) creating theoretical frames which facilitate the search for new data sets; (3) actually testing theories. In this connection I would like to elaborate somewhat on the theme of the interaction of data and theory – or more specifically, the uses of societally or culturally specific social behaviors in moving toward identification of behaviors (and structural features constraining those behaviors) characteristic of men in all societies. I will do this by remarking on: (1) sources of data (and their dangers); (2) some modes of organizing data in our search for descriptive adequacy, and (3) reasons for formalization and possibilities for theory which has explanatory adequacy. While I will not always make it explicit, all of what I say should be seen against a comparative backdrop – the 'theys' of specific ethnographic reports and the 'us' of our own society combined into a global 'us' – social man wherever he is found.

Data

Concern about the validity of informant reports is central to the ethnographic enterprise. Labov (1972b) recently chastised a group of linguists about the dangers of circularity and reflexivity in the theory-informed intuition-theory confirmation cycle. He cited a study by Spencer (1972) to demonstrate that while linguists' intuitions about the acceptability of utterances may be acclaimed by other linguists, people in the 'real' world may have quite different intuitions about acceptability – and talk quite differently.[1] Ethnographers working in cultures other than their own are characteristically careful to distrust their *own* intuitions – but may be quite willing to trust the intuitions which their informants have about *their* languages – and to accept uncritically questions and answers about their informants' behaviors from the informants themselves. Surely we should be at least as skeptical of the reports of unsophisticated native informants as we are of those of trained linguists.[2]

At least four types of data have been used in papers published in this volume – each of the types of data *may* imply different perspectives on theoretical interpretation. I would like to suggest the possibility that the different types of data are more or less critical at varying points in the process of theoretical development – in the movement from observational to descriptive to explanatory adequacies.

While Chomsky in *Aspects of the Theory of Syntax* (1965) refers only to descriptive and explanatory levels of adequacy, he earlier included a level of observational adequacy and wrote:

we can sketch various levels of success that might be attained by a grammatical description associated with a particular linguistic theory. The lowest level of success is achieved if the grammar presents the observed data correctly. A second and higher level of success is achieved when the grammar gives a correct account of the linguistic intuition of the native speaker, and specifies the observed data (in particular) in terms of significant generalizations that express underlying regularities in the language. A third and still higher level of success is achieved when the associated linguistic theory provides a general basis for selecting a grammar that achieves the second level of success over other grammars consistent with the relevant observed data that do not achieve this level of success. In this case, we can say that the linguistic theory in question suggests an explanation for the linguistic intuition of the native speaker, and specifies the observed data Hymes for directing me to this discussion.)

My conception of levels of adequacy differs somewhat from that of Chomsky; reflecting differences in the methodological and theoretical problems confronting sociolinguistics and 'autonomous linguistics.'[3] I intend the concept of observational adequacy to reflect the great richness of social interaction and of the contexts in which it occurs and I mean to imply that this level of adequacy may be harder to attain for grammars of strategies of verbal interaction than for grammars of languages (see note 3). Observational adequacy implies that all relevant data needed for adequate structural descriptions and for the discovery of rules are collected, whether those data be speech utterances, kinesic accompaniment to speech, knowledge of social relationships, intended ends of speech events, or whatever (Hymes 1967, 1972). In my view this appears to be a task of greater magnitude than 'enumeration of the class ... of possible sentences' (Chomsky 1965:31),[4] particularly since ethnographers of communication must select from a behaviorally rich universe of social interaction with only minimally developed theoretical cues as to what data are most needed.[5]

In summary, to Chomsky's criterion that data be reported accurately I want to add the criterion that all *relevant* data be collected if observational adequacy is to be achieved. Chomsky would not, I believe, disagree. It is simply that a smaller corpus will serve for linguistic analysis than for adequate ethnographies of speaking.

I find Chomsky's specification of requirements for a linguistic theory heuristically useful in suggesting necessary dimensions for descriptive adequacy of grammars of social interaction, *viz.*, the enumeration of possible behaviors (*viz.*, observational adequacy); of possible structural descriptions of those behaviors; of possible generative grammars of interpretive procedures (Cicourel 1969, 1970); and specification of functions relating the behaviors to the structural descriptions and the latter to grammars (Chomsky 1965:31). Also following Chomsky, I would suggest that the next step is one of specifying evaluative procedures for the determination of explanatory adequacy. The procedure for evaluation I want to invoke at this time, however, is simply that of the introduction of experimental variables and controls to test the power of different grammars – the search for universals and *their* explanation must wait until we have specified intrasystemic invariance and variability through an examination of categorical, semi-categorical, and variable rules and violations within societies (or cultures). At some point, however, we must attend directly to universals in communicative acts.[6]

While acknowledging that reality is actually considerably more complex, it can be argued for my purposes here that four types of data are used in the papers above. They include:

1. 'natural' speech (and other communicative behavior) observed in natural settings;

2. 'natural' speech (and other communicative behavior) observed in contrived settings (which *can* become natural), *viz.*, in gatherings convened by the ethnographer or in experimental groups, etc.;

3. elicited speech (and/or other communicative behavior) and/or rules about that speech or other behavior reported by informants to ethnographers in response to direct inquiry;

4. historical and/or literary materials.[7]

There is obviously considerable overlap amongst these categories as they appear in the papers in this volume; nonetheless I think it can be claimed that different criteria of adequacy particularly apply to the several types of data as outlined. Criteria of observational adequacy (as defined above) are clearly most relevant in natural settings. However, the other types of data are also produced in contexted situations and researchers should not ignore, for example, the purposes for which historical materials were originally produced (Gottschalk 1945), or the presence of audiences when elicitation is being done.

Following the definition of descriptive adequacy I am using here, *viz.*, the enumeration of all possible behaviors and grammars, it would seem that criteria might best be approximated with data observed in constructed settings and in straight elicitation; in both such instances the investigator has greater control over the information which may be available. (The necessary *caveats* about imposition of the investigator's own etic frames are assumed.) Finally, using explanatory adequacy as I have, it would seem that constructed settings, which permit the introduction of experimental variables and controls, would be most likely to meet criteria. There will also be instances, however, where direct elicitation procedures can be used to *identify* critical variables and there will be other fortunate happenstances in which natural settings provide the full range of occasions needed for testing theories (or the relative power of specific grammatical formulations). I find it difficult to assign the data obtained from examination of historical and literary materials to any of the three levels of adequacy; I simply don't know enough about such materials.

The papers above also presented data on different varieties of speech (or other communicative acts) in a range of different speech communities. A partial listing of types of speech acts would include: greetings, insults, requests, gossip, story-telling, silence, speech-making, and discussing. These and other types of communicative behavior simultaneously vary along two dimensions: (1) conscious awareness (by participants) of engaging in a special kind of behavior and concomitant awareness of rules; and (2) amenability to experimental manipulation and/or accessibility to elicitation.[8]

Analysis: Formal and otherwise

While I do not mean to imply a hierarchy of virtue – some kinds of analyses do seem logically to precede others – and as analyses become more formalized and complex different kinds of questions come to be implied. Generally, it seems to me that fine-grained anecdotal description may be a first step (and a very critical one) in which identification of *pattern and variation* are undertaken. In brief, an interesting phenomenon is identified. Once pattern and variation begin to emerge, taxonomies seem naturally to follow – at least if you will accept my claim that an ordered universe is axiomatic for social scientists. Such taxonomies have been generated through use of distinctive feature analysis (or perhaps validated in that manner); through componential analysis; or simply by the sorting of data into sets or classes of events.

It seems to me that a next analytic step for many ethnographers of communication will be in the direction of the adoption (or adaptation) of notation systems and the writing of grammars or proto-grammars. I have observed elsewhere that Goffman may be moving in precisely such a direction as he gets deeper and deeper into the analysis of microinteraction – that I would not be surprised at all if he would soon need a formal notation and rule-discovery procedures for social interactional transformations (Grimshaw 1973b). I find a number of the papers in this volume convincing and exciting precisely because they have moved toward the writing of grammars or proto-grammars without the loss of the 'juice,' or 'drama' of real-life interaction.

Once we have grammars, of course, it is imperative that we move back to the real world in which there are (for each linguistic, sociological, or sociolinguistic system) semi-categorical and variable rules as well as categorical rules (on these rules see the discussion of Labov's work, including citations, in Grimshaw 1973a) and extrasystemic universals. It is particularly important, it seems to me, to pay attention to rule violations and to variable rules (which are *not* the same as optional rules). Most contributors who based their papers on the analysis of contemporary speech acts and events (as well as those who used historical or literary materials) attended to violations. Sankoff's paper is particularly valuable in this regard because she has taken the next step and moved to the systematic analysis of violation ... what seems to me to be a critically important and still largely neglected area of sociolinguistic inquiry.

In defense of formalism

It will be evident from what I have already said that I favor movement in the direction of rule-specification and what has been labeled, frequently negatively, formalism. In closing my remarks I would like to suggest some reasons for my aesthetic inclination towards formalism (which I think is not incompatible with the richness of ethnographic description which none of us wants to lose). I have reviewed some of them elsewhere in an attempt to explain our collective tropism for universals (Grimshaw 1973a).

Briefly, the reasons for formalizing statements on speech – whether that formalization is essayed through taxonomies, feature analysis, statement of grammars, heuristic paradigms such as Hymes' SPEAKING (1967, 1972), or whatever – are as follows (this is not an exhaustive catalogue; those I list here seem particularly germane to the current discussion):

1. Patterned uniformities are 'there' (in the same sense that mountain peaks are 'there' for climbers). We axiomatically hold that there is order in the universe – and we want to know what that order is.

2. Research is facilitated through the narrowing of problems (we know what and what not to look for).

3. Codification highlights parallels with other domains (as in Gary

Gossen's identification of the mutually implicative metaphor of heat in the speaking and cosmological systems of the Chamula).

4. Formalization reveals parallels across systems, *viz.*, the possibility that similar types of rules operate in linguistic, sociological, and sociolinguistic systems. There are possibilities for a unified theory of human behavior.

I might add, though it will for some readers overlap with the first reason given, *viz.*, that they're there, that it's simply fun to look for patterns and to try to capture them in formal statements.

Unasked — and unanswered — questions

I have left unasked many questions about conceptual frames used in the collection and analysis of those data by ethnographers of speaking. In particular, I am concerned about the precise nature of the impact of our etic presuppositions on research design and elicitation procedures. I have also left unresolved the implicit questions I have raised about reliability and validity of data, the usefulness of informants' intuitions, different modes of analysis, the usefulness of formalization (and its possible costs), and so on.

I submit that progression from 'ethnographies of speaking' to an 'ethnology of speaking' is both scientifically and aesthetically desirable. If contributors to this volume and other 'ethnographers of speaking' share that goal they will have to attend to both my unasked and my unanswered questions.

20

THE ETHNOGRAPHY OF WRITING

KEITH H. BASSO

The study of writing systems has had a long history within the discipline of anthropology and opinions concerning its importance, as well as the kinds of theoretical problems to which it should properly address itself, have exhibited considerable diversity. Nineteenth-century evolutionists seized upon the presence or absence of writing as typological criteria which, when used to define different levels of cultural development, served handily to distinguish 'civilization' from its antecedent stages (cf. Bastian 1860; Maine 1873; McClennan 1876; Tylor 1865). Shortly before 1900, interest shifted to the history of writing itself, and in the years that followed a number of unilinear schemes were propounded which purported to trace the evolution of graphic communication from its simplest forms to the appearance of full-blown alphabets (e.g., Cohen 1958; Diringer 1949, 1962; Fevrier 1948; Gelb 1963; Mallory 1886, 1893; Moorhouse 1953). In the 1930s and 40s, by which time American anthropologists had turned their attention to other issues, writing systems figured prominently in discussions of stimulus diffusion, independent invention, internal patterning, and the acceptance, rejection, and modification of diffused cultural traits (cf. Kroeber 1948). During the same period, however, the study of writing began to suffer at the hands of linguists. Depicted by members of the emergent structural school as a pale and impoverished reflection of language, writing was consigned to a position of decidedly minor importance. Textbooks continued to include brief chapters on the subject, but this was to emphasize that writing and language were entirely distinct and that the former had no place within the domain of modern linguistics (cf. Bloomfield 1933; Bolinger 1968; Gleason 1961; Hockett 1958; Langacker 1968; Lyons 1968). As a consequence of these views, and the uncompromising way in which they were expressed, interest in writing systems declined abruptly. It has continued at a low ebb ever since, neither transformational linguistics nor fresh approaches to cultural evolution having had salutary effects, and it is my impression that with some notable exceptions (e.g., Chao 1968; Conklin 1949a, 1949b, 1953; Ferguson 1971; Goody 1968; Goody & Watt 1962; Gelb 1963; Greenberg 1957; Hymes 1961,

425

1962, 1964b) contemporary anthropologists and linguists are of the opinion that the study of writing, though certainly not without intrinsic value, has little relevance to broader problems in either field.

In this paper I want to suggest that the study of writing systems can be profitably aroused from its current slumber by placing it squarely in the context of the ethnography of communication. In contrast to earlier approaches, which have dealt almost exclusively with the internal structure of written codes, the one proposed here focuses upon writing as a form of communicative *activity* and takes as a major objective the analysis of the structure and function of this activity in a broad range of human societies. Such a perspective does not obviate the need for adequate code descriptions – on the contrary, studies of this kind remain essential – but it intentionally goes beyond them to place primary emphasis upon an understanding of the social and cultural factors that influence the ways written codes are actually used. In this way, attention is directed to the construction of models of performance as well as to models of competence, to the external variables that shape the activity of writing as well as to the conceptual grammars that make this activity possible.

Above all, the present approach takes into full account the fact that writing, wherever it exists, is always only one of several communication channels available to the members of a society. Consequently, the conditions under which it is selected and the purposes to which it is put must be described in relation to those of other channels. This requirement suggests that the ethnographic study of writing should not be conceived of as an autonomous enterprise, divorced and separate from linguistics, kinesics, proxemics, and the like, but as one element in a more encompassing field of inquiry which embraces the totality of human communication skills and seeks to generalize about their operation *vis-à-vis* one another in different sociocultural settings. Viewed in this light, the study of writing takes on new life, added substance, and broader scope. Simultaneously, I believe, it finds a comfortable but non-trivial place in modern linguistic anthropology.

The ethnography of a writing system necessarily begins with a description of the code itself. The adequacy of such a description should be judged by its ability to permit someone who is unfamiliar with the code – but who is competent in the spoken language of which it is an isomorph and familiar with the process of reading in general – to produce and decipher legible written messages. In other words, it should provide him with the knowledge necessary to become literate in this language. This means, of course, that the phonetic, prosodic, and (in some cases) kinesic values of graphic symbols must be identified and defined in strict accordance with distinctions persons already literate in the language recognize as valid, necessary, and appropriate. If these distinctions are not disclosed, or if they are arbitrarily replaced with distinctions derived from some other system of writing, the knowledge necessary to use the code correctly will almost certainly remain hidden.[1]

In addition, an adequate description of a written code should include a formulation of rules governing the following kinds of phenomena:

1. The forms and meanings of alternate representations. Capitalization and italicization in contemporary alphabetic scripts such as English serve as useful illustrations.

2. The combination of discrete symbols into larger constructions that are functionally equivalent to words. Here, of course, one confronts the rules of spelling, certainly the most critical component in any system of writing.

3. The combination of words into still larger units such as sentences, as well as the arrangement of these units into rows, columns, circles, or whatever other models may be appropriate. Although rules determining these arrangements are usually quite simple, they cannot be ignored because besides specifying the order in which messages are inscribed they indicate the order in which they are read – right to left, top to bottom in Chinese; left to right, top to bottom in French; boustrophedon in certain ancient scripts, etc.

4. All graphic devices implied by the term punctuation. To take some familiar examples from written English, 'spaces' separate words, 'question marks' and 'exclamation points' may signal the completion of sentences, and 'indented lines' mark the beginning of paragraphs.

It should be obvious that just as cultures may contain lexically labelled categories denoting units of language so may they include categories denoting units of writing. In our own culture, for example, every written symbol is named (e.g., 'a,' 'b,' 'one,' 'two,' 'period,' 'comma,' 'semicolon,' etc.), and a number of lexemes are available to classify higher-level constructions as well (e.g., 'number,' 'line,' 'stanza,' 'page,' etc.). In a native American Indian script still in use among Western Apaches living in east central Arizona, none of the symbols have specific names, but each is classified according to whether it 'tells what to say' (i.e., denotes some unit of speech) or 'tells what to do' (i.e., denotes some set of ritual gestures) (Basso and Anderson 1973). Other folk taxonomies of writing need to be studied because, surprising though it may seem, we do not yet possess an exhaustive inventory of the dimensions of contrast used by the world's peoples to partition graphic symbols into functionally significant classes. This kind of information is basic to the modification and improvement of existing comparative typologies which, though apparently adequate for alphabetic and syllabic scripts (Voegelin & Voegelin 1961), are deficient with respect to systems composed of logographic, phraseographic, and mnemonic signs (Basso and Anderson 1973).

Armed with an adequate code description, the ethnographer of writing may turn his attention to a more complex set of problems involving the code's manipulation in concrete situations. What is called for, essentially, is a grammar of rules for code use together with a description of the types of social contexts in which particular rules (or rule subsets) are selected and deemed appropriate. As Hymes (1962, 1964b, 1972) has suggested, a useful way to begin such a task is to discover the classes of communication acts – in our case, acts of writing or writing events – which are recognized as distinct by members of the society under study. Having determined the dimensions on which these classes are conceived to contrast, instances of each class may be analyzed in terms of relationships that obtain among a set of heuristically isolable components which compose the act itself. As identified by Jakobson (1960) and Hymes (1962, 1964a, 1964b, 1972), these components include the status and role attributes of participants, the form of the message, the code in which it is communicated, a channel of transmission, and the physical setting in which the message is encoded and decoded. The aim of analyses framed in these terms is to demonstrate covariation among components, thus revealing structure in the performance of communication events and paving the way for an examination of their functions.

By way of illustration, I would now like to consider selected aspects of 'letter writing' as this activity is conceptualized and performed by faculty members and graduate students at an American university. I shall assume that the code in use is a written version of standard American English, that transmission is accomplished through services provided by the United States Postal Service, and that a portion of the messages identified as 'letters' may be classified more specifically in accordance with categories presented in the folk taxonomy which appears in Table 15. I shall concentrate on the distinction between 'formal' and 'personal' letters and, holding constant the variable of setting, focus on the interrelationships that exist between participants, form, topic, and function. Although my discussion is intentionally brief and by no means thorough, it should serve to demonstrate the applicability of Hymes' strategy to the study of writing, and, in addition, convey some idea of the kinds of questions such a strategy requires us to ask.

Participants. Every act of 'letter writing' involves at least one sender and one receiver, and it is only to remark upon the obvious that the nature of their social relationship exerts a powerful influence on the decision to exchange 'formal' or 'personal' letters. My informants receive 'personal

TABLE 15. *Partial taxonomy of 'personal' and 'formal' letters*

1.0 letters	1.1 personal letters	1.1.1	thank-you letters
		1.1.2	bread-and-butter letters
		1.1.3	gag letters
		1.1.4	letters from home
		1.1.5	love letters
		1.1.6	Dear John letters
		1.1.7	Dear Jane letters
		1.1.8	poison pen letters
		1.1.9	pen pal letters
	1.2 formal letters	1.2.1	business letters
		1.2.2	credit letters
		1.2.3	letters of application
		1.2.4	letters of introduction
		1.2.5	letters of recommendation
		1.2.6	letters of transmittal
		1.2.7	letters of resignation
		1.2.8	letters to the editor
		1.2.9	letters to the manager/ management
2.0 notes			
3.0 cards			

letters' from 'parents,' 'relatives,' and 'friends,' the latter being described as persons with whom one has engaged in sustained face-to-face interaction and shared feelings of 'closeness,' 'affection,' 'sorrow,' 'trust,' 'sympathy,' 'anger,' 'love,' and 'generosity.' 'Formal letters,' on the other hand, are exchanged by parties whose relationship is characterized by the absence of social proximity. On some occasions, the sender and receiver are completely unknown to each other, but even in those instances where some prior relationship exists it is by definition less affective, less intense, and less firmly grounded in bonds of genuine mutual concern. As one informant put it, 'You send personal letters to people who count as *people*. Formal letters go to people – sure – but not because you care about them as individuals.'

Form. According to my informants, 'formal letters' should be typewritten on 'good quality paper,' which is 'white' or 'off-white' in color and of a 'standard size'; they are composed with an eye to neatness, proper grammar and punctuation, well constructed sentences, and the careful avoidance of words or lengthier constructions that are 'obscene.' 'Formal letters' also begin with 'headings' giving the name and address of the receiver, regularly contain honorifics and stock phrases (e.g., 'Dear Sir'; 'Please let me know if I may be of further assistance'), and should not be decorated with 'doodles,' 'designs,' or 'cartoons.' In contrast, 'personal letters,' though sometimes typed, are usually handwritten, and may be penned or pencilled on paper of any quality, any color, and any size, including 'notebook paper,' 'paper napkins,' or 'anything you can write on, fold, and put in an envelope.' Letters in the 'personal' category lack 'headings,' and may incorporate 'sloppy grammar,' 'weird punctuation' (e.g., omission of all commas and periods), 'obscenities,' and a variety of non-orthographic representations depicting objects such as flowers, animals, landscapes, people, or 'anything you feel like drawing.'

Topic. As indicated by the various subtypes of 'formal' and 'personal' letters, these two classes of message pertain to distinct spheres of social experience. 'Formal letters' deal primarily with topics that arise in the course of relationships with public institutions (or persons representing such institutions), particularly those which provide goods and services in exchange for money or which figure prominently in one's occupation or profession. Only 'letters to the editor' and 'letters to the manager,' which my informants claim can address themselves to a wide variety of topics, do not have a direct bearing on commercial activities, professional matters, or employment. 'Personal letters,' on the other hand, focus on more 'intimate' topics which are related to aspects of the exclusive relationship that exists between sender and receiver. 'Personal letters' may contain discussions of the sender's innermost wishes and desires, his emotional ups and downs, his attitudes toward other people (including the receiver), or simply – and very frequently – his own reactions to recent events. Letters of this kind convey more of the sender's 'inner self' and 'private world,' and therefore can be expected to include topics of immediate relevance to his need for self-expression which may appear 'trivial' or 'insignificant' to anyone except the receiver.

Function. Althouth some of the subtypes of 'personal' and 'formal' letters are categorized according to topic (e.g., 'love letters,' 'business letters') and the social identities of sender and/or receiver (e.g., 'letters from home,' 'pen pal letters,' 'letters to the editor'), the majority are classified on the basis of their intended purpose or function. Thus, 'gag letters' are meant to provoke humor, 'Dear John' and 'Dear Jane' letters to terminate a relationship based on heterosexual love, and 'thank-you letters' to express gratitude for the receipt of a gift or service. 'Letters of resignation' sever an occupational relationship, 'letters of application' request the establishment of one, and 'letters of introduction' clear the way for an encounter between some person known to the sender but unknown to the receiver. With respect to the general distinction between 'formal' and 'personal' letters, my informants agreed that the former are more likely to be directive or pragmatic in function ('aimed at getting things done,' as one individual put it), while the latter can be expected to be more expressive. The greatest area of overlap, it was noted, occurs with respect to referential functions, since there is an equal probability that both 'formal' and 'personal' letters will contain requests for information on particular topics (e.g., 'When does Jones intend to sell the Amco stock?' 'How long has Pam been preggers?').

Obviously, much more could be said about 'letter writing' in America, but the material presented to this point should be sufficient to suggest that the distinction between 'formal' and 'personal' letters is matched by variation in the form and content of these types of messages, their immediate functions, and the kinds of social relationships that obtain among individuals who exchange them. 'Formal letters' are commensurate with social distance, conform to a number of stylistic requirements, dwell upon topics of an impersonal nature, and serve primarily pragmatic functions. In comparison, 'personal letters' reinforce social solidarity, permit a greater degree of stylistic freedom, focus on more individualized topics, and function expressively. Unremarkable though these findings may seem to persons already familiar with American culture they illustrate the premise that the components of writing events can be described and analyzed in systemic terms. Simultaneously, and even more important, they demonstrate the feasibility of investigating the activity of writing as a dynamic component in the conduct and organization of social relations.

As I have implied earlier, the most conspicuous shortcoming of traditional studies of writing is that they reveal very little about the social patterning of this activity or the contributions it makes to the maintenance of social systems. Fully aware that the past cannot be held responsible for what the present deems important, I have also implied that these topics should be of vital concern to the ethnography of writing.

How, for example, is the ability to write distributed among the members of a community, and how does the incidence of this ability vary with factors such as age, sex, socioeconomic class and the like? With what types of activities is writing associated, and in what types of settings do these activities customarily take place? What kinds of information are considered appropriate for transmission through written channels, and how, if at all, does this information differ from that which is passed through alternate channels such as speech? Who sends written messages to whom, when, and for what reasons? Is the ability to write a prerequisite for achieving certain social statuses, and, if so, how are these statuses evaluated by other members of the community? How do individuals acquire written codes in the first place – from whom, at what age, under what circumstances, and, again, for what reasons? What are the accepted methods of instruction and of learning? And what kinds of cognitive operations are involved? Is writing considered a source of pleasure and fulfillment? Is excellence in writing valued as a form of graphic and literary art? In short, what position does writing occupy in the total communicative economy of the society under study and what is the range of its cultural meanings?

These and a host of related questions are rarely asked by ethnographers and linguists, but answers to them are essential if we are to gain a full appreciation of the varied roles played by graphic communication systems in human societies. As stated previously, the realization of this aim depends upon our willingness to augment analyses of the structure of written codes with analyses of their manifest and latent functions in particular sociocultural settings. For it is only on the basis of a comparative study of writing that we can begin to generalize about its effects on the development and organization of cultural systems (and vice versa) as well as its influence upon the lives of individuals.

By now I hope it is evident that studies of the kind proposed here have relevance beyond the subject of writing per se to broader issues of theoretical and applied interest in linguistics and anthropology. For example, grammars of cultural rules that guide the use of written codes can contribute directly to a more general definition of communicative competence and a fuller understanding of the conceptual skills it may entail. On the other hand, rigorous functional analyses are indispensable to modern evolutionary studies that attempt to explain the emergence, survival, or disappearance of cultural forms in terms of their role in promoting or inhibiting adaptation to particular cultural environments. Finally, it is easy to see how a knowledge of the values and attitudes that illiterate peoples bring to graphic communication would be of significant value in the formulation and implementation of effective literacy programs.

Adequate ethnographies of writing do not yet exist because linguists and anthropologists alike have grown accustomed to investigating written codes with only passing reference to the social systems in which they are embedded. In this essay, I have suggested that the time has come for this strategy to be reversed. When all is said and done, we shall find that the activity of writing, like the activity of speaking, is a supremely social act. Simultaneously, I believe, we shall find that it is far more complex – and therefore more intriguing – than we have suspected heretofore.

WAYS OF SPEAKING

DELL HYMES

We start from the speech community conceived as an 'organization of diversity'; we require concepts and methods that enable us to deal with that diversity, that organization. The great stumbling block is that the kinds of organization most developed by linguists presuppose the grammar as their frame of reference. (By grammar is meant here the genre of grammars.) Since its invention in classical antiquity, the grammar has been dominated by association with analysis of a single, more or less homogeneous, norm. In earlier periods the choice of norm was determined by social constraints. Linguistics, as grammar, came into existence to dissect and teach just that language, or language-variety, that embodied valued cultural tradition (Homeric Greek, the Sanskrit of the Vedas, the Chinese of the Confucian classics), not just any language; indeed, not any other language at all. The grammar, like the language, was an instrument of hegemony. In recent times the choice of norm has been determined often enough by factors intrinsic to the linguistic task. Although the class background of linguists favors the 'standard' of the schools, considerations of simplicity, clarity, fullness, of whatever is advantageous to the linguistic task itself, have also entered. Linguists have often been as decisive as schoolmasters in excluding things. With the schoolmaster, exclusion may have been for reasons of prestige and pedantry; with the linguist, it may most often have been for the sake of a model or an elegant result; but the consequence in relation to the speech patterns of a community as a whole has not been too different. Much of those patterns, when not ignored, can be accommodated only in terms of deviations from the privileged account. It is not revealed in its own right.

Now, if members of a community themselves class certain patterns of speech as deviant, mixtures, marginal, or the like, that is a significant fact; but we do not want to be trapped into having to treat phenomena that way, merely because of the limitations of the model with which we start. Where community members find patterns natural, we do not want to have to make them out to be unnatural.

The available term for an alternative starting point is style. We propose to consider a speech community initially as comprising a set of *styles*. By 'style,' we do not in the first instance mean one or another of the specific uses to which this protean term has been put, but just the root sense of a way or mode of doing something. We need to use the term neutrally, generally, for any way or mode, all ways and modes.

Recently a way of dealing with speech styles has been made explicit by Ervin-Tripp (1972), building on work of Gumperz (cf. Gumperz 1972:21). Their achievement fits into the history of achievements with descriptive concepts in linguistics. That history can be seen as one of the successive discovery of concrete universals, such that language could be described in terms relevant to a specific system, yet applicable to all; terms, that is, free of bias due to a particular context, and mediating between given systems and general theory, doing justice to both. In phonology, the concepts of the phoneme, and then of distinctive features, have been such. In morphology, the generalizations of the morpheme as a concept for all formatives of a language, and of terms for grammatical categories, processes, and types, were also such. Much of this work was accomplished by Boas, Sapir, Bloomfield, and their students, and depended upon universalizing the range of languages to be described. Recent efforts in syntactic and semantic analysis have had a related aim, pushing the search for universal aspects of grammar to new depths, although sometimes at the expense of specific systems. We have reached a point at which the concept of grammar itself is that which needs to be transcended.

In recent years a number of linguists have recognized this possibility (e.g., Whorf, Firth, Harris, Joos), but their insights have not been systematically followed up. (On this point, and others in this section, cf. Hymes 1970.) Styles have been noted with regard to a variety of bases (authors, settings, groups), but not style itself as the general basis of description. Often enough the notion of style has been invoked ad hoc, simply to save the ordinary grammatical analysis (as often with role and status differences (see Hymes 1970)). Ervin-Tripp has now generalized two principles of modern linguistics, the syntagmatic and the paradigmatic relations, and freed them from dependence on a particular sector of grammar, or on a formal grammatical model. She develops two notions, *rules of co-occurrence*, and *rules of alternation*. The point, obvious after the event, yet novel and liberating, is that one can characterize whatever features go together to identify a style of speech in terms of rules of co-occurrence among them, and can characterize choice among styles in terms of rules of alternation. The first concept gives systematic status to the ways of selecting and grouping together of linguistic means that actually obtain in a community. The second concept frees the resulting styles from mechanical connection with a particular defining situation. Persons are recognized to choose among styles themselves, and the choices to have social meaning. (This is the vantage point from which a variety of phenomena treated separately under headings such as bilingualism, diglossia, standard and non-standard speech, and the like, can be integrated.)

These notions are well exemplified in Ervin-Tripp's study (1972). Here I want to build upon them in the three sections that follow, by considering further their relationship to the description of a speech community: (a) more enters into speech styles than is usually identified linguistically, and (b) the concept of speech styles requires specification and supplementation in an ethnography of speaking. Finally, (c) the notion of style is not just an alternative to the notion of grammar, but has application to grammar itself, as something socially constituted.

The two elementary functions

For nearly half a century American linguists have taken as fundamental to their science the assumption that in a speech community some utterances are the same in form and meaning (Bloomfield 1933:144; Swadesh 1948:257 note 11; Postal 1968:7, 12, 217). The assumption has enabled them to identify relevant differences, as opposed to irrelevant differences, and thus to identify the elementary units in terms of whose relationships a grammar is defined. Built into the assumption has been the corollary that relevant differences were of just one kind. As Bloomfield once put it, when a beggar says 'I'm hungry' and a child says 'I'm hungry,' to avoid going to bed, the linguist is interested just in what is the same in the two utterances, not in what is different. From his standpoint, the utterances count as repetitions. 'You're hungry,' 'he's hungry,' 'she's hungry,' 'it's hungry,' etc., would count as structurally revealing contrasts, as to grammatical forms. 'It's dungaree' (pronounced to rhyme with 'hungry') would be a revealing contrast, as to features of sound. 'I'm hungary' (pronounced to rhyme with 'hungry'), said perhaps by a representative of an east European country, would be an instance of homophony between distinct forms (as in 'pair,' 'pear') and perhaps open up consideration of contextual differentiation, differences between written and spoken forms of the language, and the like. None of this would broach the possibility that utterances of the same forms, in the same order, might be, not repetition, but contrast. Yet there are two standpoints from which utterances may be the same or different in form and meaning.

The second kind of repetition and contrast in language has been demonstrated especially well in the work of Labov in New York City (1966). One line of evidence for his study consisted precisely of the respect in which successive utterances of the same forms, in the same order (from the one point of view) were not repetitions, but in contrast. The presence or absence of *r*-constriction after a vowel in a word, indeed, the degree of *r*-constriction, is variable in New York City speech. The variation is associated with social status, on the one hand, and with context, on the other. In situations of the same degree of self-consciousness persons of different social status will differ in the proportion of *r*-constriction in their speech. Persons of the same social status, indeed, the same person, will differ as between situations of less self-consciousness and more (as between situations of lesser and greater formality in a sense). Labov went to the third floors of department stores, chosen for differences in the social status of their customers and employees, and asked the location of something that he knew was located on the floor above. The clerk would respond with an utterance including 'on the fourth floor.' Labov would say, 'Huh?' or the equivalent, and the clerk would repeat. The proportions of *r*-constriction differed among stores, as anticipated, and also as between first utterance and repetition. There was more *r*-constriction in the second, presumably somewhat more self-conscious, utterance.

There is an import, a meaningfulness, to the differences in *r*-constriction. Persons are judged, and judge themselves, in terms of this among other features of speech. It is not, of course, that such a feature is simply an automatic manifestation of identity. As indicated above, one and the same person will vary. The feature does have a social meaning, such that presence of *r*-constriction is positively valued, and its absence disvalued, in assigning social standing. But the 'creative' aspect of language use enters here as well. The *r*-ness of an utterance may spontaneously express the identity of the speaker; and it may express the speaker's attitude toward topic, hearer, or situation. The more *r*-less style may be consciously adopted by a politician to convey solidarity with voters as a 'regular' guy.

This is a general fact about such features. Not all babytalk is used by, or to, babies. We have to do with features in terms of which utterances may contrast, features subject to meaningful choice as much as the kinds of features usually described in grammars.

In short, the speech styles of communities are not composed only of the features and elements of ordinary grammar, differently related. Speech styles are composed of another kind of feature and element as well. The competence of members of a community has to do with both kinds.

The two kinds of repetition and contrast, the two kinds of features, could be distinguished as 'referential' and 'stylistic,' and I shall frequently make use of these two terms as shorthand labels. We must be careful not to overinterpret these terms, or any other pair of terms. Both kinds of features are to be understood as elementary *diacritic* features, and as based on two complementary elementary diacritic functions, constitutive of linguistic means.

The relevant 'referential' difference that makes syllabically identical pronunciations of 'hungry' and 'dung(a)ree' initially different does no more than differentiate; it does not express any part of the meaning of a state of the stomach (or soul), or of the material of a pair of trousers. Just so the relevant 'stylistic' difference between 'I'm hungry' with light aspiration, and 'I'm hungry' with heavy aspiration of the *h*-, does not of itself express the particular meaning of the contrast. Difference in aspiration is available as a stylistic feature in English, just because it is not employed as a referential feature. (Unlike Hindi, in which /pil/ and /phil/ would be different forms in the lexicon, they are the same form in the English lexicon, differently expressed.) But difference in aspiration, like vowel length, and other elementary English stylistic features, is just that: elementary. It is available for use, just as the differences between /h/ : /d/, /p/ : /b/, etc., are available for use, diacritically. In one instance its use may be metalinguistic, to clarify a meaning: 'I said "phill," not "bill."' In other instance, it may be used to express attitude – emphasis being employed for the sake of insistence, hostility, admiration, etc. In yet another kind of case, it may be used to qualify the attributes of something talked about, as to just how big, or intense, or the like, something was; such uses verge on the referential meanings of utterances ('It was big, I mean, bi:::g').

This last kind of case should be paired with another. The kinds of meaning we often think of as stylistic, expressive, attitudinal, and the like, are of course frequently encoded in languages in lexicon and grammar. There are words for emotions and tones of voice, and 'expressive' elaborations in morphology and morphophonemics proper (cf. Ullman 1953; Stankiewicz 1954, 1964; Van Holk 1962). When one considers linguistic means from the standpoint of the communication of a given kind of meaning, one finds features of both the 'referential' and 'stylistic' kind involved. To a very great extent, features of the type here called 'referential' are involved in what may be said to be *designative* and *predicative* roles: naming things talked about and stating things about them. Yet what is talked about may be conveyed with aid of stylistic features ('No, not that one, the bi:::g one'), and the logical standing and truth value of sentences may depend crucially on stylistic features (e.g., features which define the sentence as mocking rather than sincere). To a very great extent, features of the type here called 'stylistic' are involved in what may be said to be *characterizing* and *qualifying* roles: modifying things talked about and saying how what is said about them is to be taken. Yet, as observed just above, lexical and grammatical ways of accomplishing these purposes exist.

The situation is parallel to that of lexicon in relation to grammar. De Saussure observed that a general theory of language could not be confined to either, because what was done in one language by lexical means was done in another grammatically and conversely. It is the same at a deeper level with the 'referential' and 'stylistic' vectors of language. Within a given system the features and structures of the two are intertwined, *imbricated*, one might say. From the standpoint of a comparison of systems in terms of functions served by them, both must be considered, or part of the verbal means of a community will be missed, and with it, essential aspects of a general theory.

Consider aspiration, for example. On a referential basis alone, it is not a phonological universal: some languages have it, some do not. On a referential and stylistic basis, quite possibly all languages employ it as a conventional means of expression. Indeed, I venture to speculate that a number of features, not now recognized as universal, will prove to be so, when the stylistic vector of language is taken into account. The initial question about features, then, is whether or not they are conventional means in all communities. It is a *second* question to ask if they serve referential function (as distinct from stylistic). Just because the referential and stylistic use of features is interdependent within individual systems, and because stylistic function is itself universal, the number of features that have stylistic use, when they do not have referential, and that hence are truly universal, is likely to be substantial.

Other candidates for status as linguistic universals include vowel length, reduplication, pitch accent, syllabification, word order, and properties such as a minimal vowel system. In Wasco, for example, a purely phonological analysis, seeking to eliminate redundancy, might arrive at a system of three vowels (i, u, a). Yet one can hardly use Wasco appropriately without employing a vowel primarily serving rhetorical emphasis, low front *ae* (as in English 'hat'). Generally phonological analysis, seeking to eliminate redundancy, and to find in languages only systems of differences, discard essential features of communication. A phonological feature, redundant from the standpoint of economically distinguishing words, may yet identify normal or native speech, and contrast with its absence. (Try speaking English without the redundant voicing of nasals [m, n, ng]; a telling case is analyzed in Hymes 1970.) The loan-words with phonological particularities set aside in some 'economical' analyses are still in use in the community. The fewer 'phonemic' (referentially based) vowels a language has, the more likely it is to make use of other vowels for stylistic purposes. In sum, the phonological analyses we need, that will be adequate to the actual phonological competence of persons, will include more than the phonology we usually get.

Notice that the more general approach enables us to reach deeper generalizations in particular cases as well as universally. Linguists have debated for some time as to whether the syllable was necessary, or useful, in the analysis of particular languages. I would suggest that syllabification is an ability that is part of the competence of normal members of every speech community, that it is a universal. Communities will be found to differ, not as to the presence or absence of syllabification, but as to the location of its role. In some communities the syllable will appear fundamental to the usual phonemic analysis; in others it will be found essential to the analysis of certain styles (styles of emphasis and metalinguistic clarity, for example, or of speech play, or verbal art). The debates as to the status of the syllable have been possible only because conceptions of structure, and competence, have been too narrow.

Again, once it is accepted that 'headline style' is part of English competence (e.g., 'Man bites dog'), it will be found artificial to postulate the presence of articles in underlying English syntax (e.g., 'A man bites a dog') as in current approaches derived from Chomsky. The elementary relations will be seen to be between 'man', 'bite,' and 'dog,' and the presence or absence of article to be a second matter, a matter of the style of the discourse in question. A good deal of trouble has been needlessly wasted, trying to account for the article in English on too narrow a basis.

It is thus in the interest of ordinary linguistics, as well as of sociolinguistics, to recognize the dual nature of the elementary diacritic functions in language.

Structures and uses

Speech styles, we have said, comprise features and constructions of both kinds (referential and stylistic). Let us now say more about the place of speech styles in the ethnography of speaking. Let us first make a further distinction among kinds of functions in speech. The two elementary diacritic functions are part of what may be generally called *structural functions*, as distinct from *use functions* (following here for convenience the common distinction between language structure and language use). 'Structural' functions have to do with the bases of verbal features and their organization, the relations among them, in short, with the verbal means of speech, and their conventional meanings, insofar as those are given by such relationships. 'Use' functions have to do with the organization and meaning of verbal features in terms of nonlinguistic contexts. The two are interdependent, but it is useful to discriminate them. It seems likely that rules of co-occurrence can be considered to have to do with structural functions, and rules of alternation with use functions. The analysis of rules of alternation, in other words, entails the analysis of components of use in context, such as the relevant features of the participants in a speech event, of the setting, the channel, and so forth. (See Hymes 1972 for a heuristic analysis of components of speech events.) The principle of contrast for identification of relevant features, as opposed to repetitions, applies here as well, but the features of the situation are not verbal.

RELATIONS AMONG STRUCTURES

Notice that rules of co-occurrence define speech styles in an entirely general, open fashion. The relevant speech styles of a community cannot be arrived at mechanically, for one could note an infinite number of differences and putative co-occurrences. One must discover relevant differences in relation to analysis of context. Doubtless communities differ in the relative importance, or 'functional load,' of particular contexts, and components of contexts, in the determination of styles. Persons, or personal roles, may be a predominant basis for such determination in one community, not so much in another. So also for contexts of activity, group membership, and institutional settings. There is a parallel here, of course, with the differences among languages in the relative significance of semantic categories as bases for grammatical organization (tense, aspect, mode, person, shape, etc. – cf. Hymes 1961b for a tentative scheme for comparison). Just as with referential, so with social meanings: one must start with a general framework, and expect that certain kinds of meaning will be expressed in every community, even if in different ways or to different degrees of elaboration. Men's and women's roles may be intrusive in ordinary grammar in one case, a dimension of consistently organised styles encompassing a variety of features in another, and but marginally visible in verbal means in yet another. Likewise, the functions of deixis, and of textual cohesion, may differentially involve referential and stylistic features in different communities, and even become the chief principle or dimension of one or another style.

In sum, communities differ in the number and variety of significant speech styles, and in the principal bases of their delimitation. This is one of the important and interesting things about communities, needing to be described and to be connected with its causes in their other characteristics and their histories.

Major speech styles associated with social groups can be termed *varieties*, and major speech styles associated with recurrent types of situations can be termed *registers*. Speech styles associated with persons, particular situations, and genres could be termed simply *personal*, *situational*, and *genre* styles. An adequate set of terms cannot be imposed in advance of case studies, however, but will grow interdependently with them. We can, however, and need to, say something more about the relations among kinds of style and stylistic features.

Let me reiterate that speech styles are not mechanical correlations of features of speech with each other and with contexts. The criterion of a *significant speech style* is that it can be recognized, and used, outside its defining context, that is, by persons or in places other than those with which its typical meaning is associated, or contrasted with relation to the persons and places with one or more other styles. Thus one may determine styles associated with castes, classes, ethnic groups, regions, formality, oratory, sermons, and the like, but one must also notice the use of these styles, or of quotations or selections, or stereotypes of them, to convey meanings by, to, and about other persons and situations. Likewise, one must not confine one's attention in church, say, to the style of the sermon, but also notice the style of the speech before, after, and perhaps during it. There probably are customary linkages in these respects, and they need to be determined. A style defined first of all in terms of a group may be also the style for certain situations, or the style, in fact or aspiration, of certain other persons, certain genres or parts of genres, and so on. Within its defining setting a style may be prominent or obscured in relation to what else goes on. There may be clashes within communities as to the admissibility of certain linkages, or as to prominence or lack of it. (The histories of religion, literature, and the stage have many examples.)

Let me say a little about the scale along which stylistic features must be considered, especially with regard to genres, since the disciplines that study verbal genres — folklore, literature, rhetoric, and stylistics — are major sources of insight for the general linguistics that will incorporate stylistic function. First, stylistic features may simply be present in discourse without defining a significant style. Their presence may simply convey a certain tinge or character, perhaps quite locally. We are likely to consider speech with a great many such effects 'colorful' (perhaps too colorful, distractingly or seemingly aimlessly so); relative richness of harmony, as it were, can distinguish verbal as well as musical styles, but it may be an incidental flavoring rather than an organizing principle.

Beyond the fact of the presence of stylistic features are kinds of groupings of such features that do constitute organized use, or define a conventional use of verbal means. Two principal kinds of grouping come to mind. There are the kinds which can be said to color or accompany the rest of what is done, and the kinds which can be said to define recurrent forms. For the first, one can speak of *stylistic modes*, and for the second, of *stylistic structures*.

A principal aspect of *stylistic modes* is a set of modifications entailed in consistent use of the voice in a certain way, as in singing, intoning, chanting, declaiming, etc. Modifications of the visual form of speech, in writing and printing, go here as well. Note well that what count as instances of these things are culturally defined. The modifications that are the basis for considering speech to be in a certain mode are on a continuum with the incidental use of features that has been called coloring just above. A basic problem is to discover the relation of such continua, or variables, to qualitative judgments, such that members of a community categorize speech as the presence of a mode or structure. A lilt in the voice may or may not count as singing; a pleonasm, pronunciation, or technical term may or may not count as formal or learned discourse. Sometimes a single instance is enough to define or frame the rest of what is said. Sometimes the definition is negotiated, and shifting frequencies of features manifest the negotiation, as in a proffered move from formal to informal relationship; sometimes the ranging of features between stylistic poles manifests temporary appeals to the presuppositions of one or another of them.

The importance of these kinds of features, not usually included in grammars or well studied by most linguists, is patent when one confronts masterful oral narrative style, so rich in its use of such features. Until now the printed pages from which most of us know such styles have left such mastery in oblivion, but the experiments of Tedlock in the presentation of Zuni narrative (1972) open a new era. Such features may be essential ingredients of the 'levels' of speech central to the structure of a society. Among the Wolof of Senegal, there is a fundamental, pervasive contrast between 'restrained' and 'unrestrained' speech. It saliently distinguishes the caste of professional speakers, *griots* and nobles, as two poles, but applies as well to other contrasts of status, as between men and women, adults and children, and even applies to contrast in the conduct of the same person, as between a low and high, petitioner and patron, role. All aspects of verbal means enter into the contrast of modes, but the most striking involve use of the voice. Irvine (MS.) summarizes these dimensions in the accompanying table.

	High	Low
Pitch	Low	High
Quality	Breathy	Clear
Volume	Soft	Loud
Contour	Pitch nucleus last	Nucleus first
Tempo	Slow	Fast

Any aspect of verbal means may be the ingredient of a mode including aspects which a conception of competence as perfection would not lead one to notice at all. In the Senegal community of Kayor the pinnacle of the nobility, the Damel, must make mistakes in minor points of grammar. Correctness would be considered an emphasis on fluency of performance, or on performance for its own sake, that is not appropriate to the highest of nobles (Irvine MS.).

Stylistic structures comprise verbal forms organized in terms of one or more defining principles of recurrence and/or development. They have, so to speak, a beginning and an end, and a pattern to what comes between. What are often called 'minor genres' belong here: riddles, proverbs, prayers, but also minimal verse forms, such as the couplet, and such things as greetings and farewells, where those have conventional organization. It seems best to designate such things as *elementary, or minimal, genres*. (They need not be minor in their importance.)

We must bear in mind that one may sing something that is not a song, and present a song without singing it; that is, *modes* and *structures* are indeed distinct, and their connections problematic, to be discovered in the given case. Moreover, it would be a mistake to assume that the essential principle of a form of speech is always structure, never mode. Most often it is structure, but to generalize would be equivalent to recognizing form in music only insofar as one can identify sonata pattern, rondo, twelve-tone scale, or the like. Delius is a case in point. He did turn to sonata-form works in consequences of the First World War (unfortunately, we never hear recitals or recordings to judge them ourselves), but the works of his in the standard performance repertoire are those in which the secret of organization is his own, and the development inextricable from the handling of harmony and orchestration, i.e., of 'color.' (Musical terminology will prove a great resource for exploration of speech styles, as a matter of fact.)

Both kinds of groupings of features, modes and structures, enter into more complex groupings, which may be designated *complex genres*. Thus Zuni *telapnanne* 'tale' can comprise formal speaking delivery, a mode of delivery called 'raised up speech,' a monotone chant with one auxiliary tone, and passages of conversational looseness (Tedlock, personal communication).

Genres, whether minimal or complex, are not in themselves the 'doing' of a genre, that is, are not in themselves acts, events, performances. They can occur as whole events, or in various relationships to whole events. The structure of an event may encompass preliminaries and aftermaths, may allow only for partial use of a genre, or even just allusion to it, and so forth. And I want to consider performances as relationships to genres, such that one can say of a performance that its materials (genres) were reported, described, run through, illustrated, quoted, enacted. Full performance I want to consider as involving the acceptance of responsibility to perform, to do the thing with acceptance of being evaluated.

Obviously genres may vary, from simple to complex, and from looseness to tightness in what they accommodate, incorporate, permit, as to modes and other genres. The 'novel' is an easy example; it may take the form of letters (Richardson's *Pamela*), verse (Pushkin's *Eugen Onegin*), and simulated journalism, among others.

It is tempting to generalize the categories of genre and performance, so that all verbal material is assignable to some genre, and all verbal conduct to some kind of performance. My own hunch is that communities differ in the extent to which this is true, at least in the sense of the prevalence of tightly organized genres, and of evaluated performance (of 'being on stage' in speech). If the categories are needed as general descriptive concepts, then the differences can be registered by an additional distinction within each, perhaps *fixed genres*, and *full performance*.

RELATIONS AMONG USES

The connection between genres and performances is one aspect of the general connection between styles defined in terms of rules of co-occurrence and their uses in contexts in a community. First, recall the proposal that significant speech styles be considered those that can be contrasted in or beyond their initial defining context. The proposal has two complications. The degree to which this is possible may itself be a dimension on which communities differ. Just as speech communities, historical periods, and persons differ in the degree to which they consider appropriate use of words and phrases to be context-specific, so also with stylistic features and structures. A tightly context-bound style may be highly valued. On the other hand, unique structures, stylistic relationships, may emerge in a single event, and be remembered and valued for their qualities. Nevertheless, it would seem that evaluation of the emergent qualities of a single event, and recognition of the appropriateness of a context-specific style, would both presuppose comparison. The comparison may be implicit, rather than observable in the immediate situation, but it would be discoverable by inquiry outside the situation. (From such considerations we see the failure inherent in a conception of sociolinguistics as a method of obtaining 'real' data. Realistic, observational data are essential, if styles, many of whose features are unconscious or not producible on demand, are to be studied; but styles involve kinds of underlying competence and judgments based on competence as well.) We need to consider both context-bound styles and emergent properties, in order to deal with stylistic change. One aspect of stylistic change is narrowing or expansion of contextual constraints (rather like spread or contraction of the range of distribution of a phonological or grammatical feature), and another is the imitation or emulation, and consequent conventionalization, of emergent properties. But the central considerations here are that speech styles are not merely observed co-occurrences and correlations, but subject to contrast and choice, and that they are not merely appropriate or inappropriate, but meaningful.

The notion of rules of alternation carries us into the analysis of the contexts of speech styles, but, as noted before, such analysis is ethnographic and sociological as well as linguistic. When the meanings of speech styles are analyzed, we realize that they entail dimensions of participant, setting, channel, and the like, which partly govern their meanings. And analysis of the relevant features of these dimensions is found to implicate more than alternation of speech styles. It subtends norms of verbal conduct, or inter-action, in general – things such as rights to turns at talking, acceptable ways of getting the floor, whether more than one voice can be speaking at a time, and so on. (Here again musical terminology is a resource: *ripieno*, *concertante*, and *ritornello* catch features of some speech events.) And both speech styles and norms of verbal conduct have underlying meanings in common, mean-ings which involve community attitudes and beliefs with regard to language and speech. The Wolof styles cited above, for example, embody a notion and values fundamental to Wolof society, having to do with 'honor' (*kerse*), and with 'one of the most fundamental Wolof cultural assumptions [namely] that speech, especially in quantity, is dangerous and demeaning' (Irvine MS.).

I cannot go into the analysis of norms of verbal conduct, attitudes, and beliefs here, but have sketched some of their dimensions, and some of the evidence of types of speech community in this regard elsewhere (Hymes 1972). Here I can only sketch the place of this part of the ethnography of speaking in relation to the whole, with reference to terminology for the parts.

If one accepts 'ethnography of speaking' as name for the enterprise, still the name refers to the approach, or the field, not to the subject matter itself. One can engage in an ethnography of speaking among the Zuni, but what one studies is not in any usual sense 'Zuni ethnography of speaking.' (What the Zuni consciously make of speaking is important, but part of the whole.) An ethnography of law among the Zuni studies Zuni law, and an ethno-graphy of speaking studies Zuni speaking. I myself would say: Zuni *ways of speaking*. There are two reasons for this. First, terms derived from 'speak' and 'speech' in English suffer from a history of association with something marginal or redundant. While linguists have commonly distinguished 'speech' from 'language' in a way that might seem to serve our purpose, they have commonly taken back with the hand of usage what the hand of defini-tion has offered. In practice, 'speech' has been treated as either elegant variation for 'language' (thus, Sapir's book *Language* was subtitled 'An introduction to the study of speech' and 'interaction by means of speech' has been equated with knowledge of a single language by Bloomfield, Bloch, Chomsky, and others), or as a second-class citizen, external to language, mere behavior. (Thus for many writers 'act of speech' does not mean a complex social act based on underlying competence extending beyond grammar, but mere physical manifestation.) Indeed, 'speech' has been used so much as interchangeable with 'language' that Sherzer and Darnell (1972) felt constrained to add 'use,' and to talk of the analysis of 'speech use.' I do not myself like 'speech use,' because I am disturbed by what should be a redundancy, that is, 'speech' should indicate use in a positive sense. Nevertheless, it does not, and adequate terms seem to require some joining of the key term that English provides with complements that make it free of the redundant or reductive connotations.

My second reason for favoring *ways of speaking* is that it has analogy with 'ways of life,' on the one hand, and Whorf's term 'fashions of speaking,' on the other. The first analogy helps remind anthropologists that the ways of mankind do include ways of speaking, and helps remind linguists that speaking does come in ways, that is, shows cultural patterning. And since Whorf was the first in the American linguistic and anthropological tradition, so far as I know, to name a mode of organization of linguistic means cutting across the compartments of grammar, it is good to honor his precedence, while letting the difference in terms reflect the difference in scope of reference. (Whorf had in mind the usual features of grammars, considered from the standpoint of active life as cognitive styles.)

Our analysis so far would point to ways of speaking as comprising two parts, speech styles and their contexts, or means of speech and their meanings. The limitation of these terms is that they do not readily suggest part of what enters into ways of speaking, namely, the norms of interaction that go beyond choice of style, and the attitudes and beliefs that underlie both. 'Contexts' and 'meanings' also both leave the focus on 'styles' and 'means,' and seem to deprive the second part of the equality, and relative autonomy, that must be recognized in it. The Ngoni of southern Africa, for example, have maintained their distinctive norms of verbal conduct, while losing their original, Ngoni language; they still consider maintenance of the norms of verbal conduct definitive of being a proper Ngoni. (I owe this example to Sheila Seitel.) It does not seem happy to talk of the maintenance of Ngoni 'contexts' or 'meanings of means of speech' in this connection. A positive term is wanted. Of the possibilities that have occurred to me, all but one have the defect that they might be taken to imply more than is intended. 'Ways of speaking' would serve on this level as well; but contexts are not always sure to differentiate the two senses, especially in the case of a novel terminology, and we need to be clear if we can be. 'Patterns of speech/ speaking,' 'forms,' 'modes' seem to say too much or too little, or to conflict with other uses of the differentiating word. The expression that does not is: *speech economy* (cf. Hymes 1961a). We can then readily distinguish *means of speech* (comprising the features that enter into styles, as well as the styles themselves), and *speech economy*. The pair are parallel in utilizing 'speech,' which may be a mnemonic advantage. The two concepts are of course interrelated, even interdependent (as said, meanings lie in the relationships), and from a thoroughgoing standpoint, the speech economy of a community includes its means of speech as one of the components that enter into its pattern of relationships. The historical autonomy of the two, and the major division of labor in our society between those who study verbal means and those who study conduct, makes the division appropriate.

Consideration of the stylistic component of language, then, has led us to a conception of the ethnography of speaking that can be expressed in the following form:

WAYS OF SPEAKING

Means of speech   *Speech economy*

The direction of our discussion so far has been consistently away from grammar toward other things, but grammar itself is not exempt from becoming what those who use it make of it, and hence in some respects a style.

Languages as styles

It is not only in situations of heterogeneity that a constitutive role of social factors can be glimpsed. If we abstract from heterogeneity, and consider only a single language, indeed, only a single grammar, a radically social component still appears. Consider the California Indian language Yokuts, as described by Stanley Newman.[1]

Newman reports that the words he recorded were short, composed of a stem and mostly but one or two suffixes, almost never more than that. Newman noticed, however, that the underlying patterning of the suffixes implied the formal possibility of longer sequences. He reports (1964 (1940): 374):

An instructive exercise ... was to construct words having four or five suffixes and ask the informant for a translation. Although such words complied with the grammatical rules and could be translated by my informant without any difficulty, they seldom failed to provoke his amusement. It was obvious that these words were impossibly heavy and elaborate. To the Yokuts feeling for simplicity they were grammatical monstrosities.

From Newman's account it appears that the longer words were not deviant (not derivatively generated in the sense of Chomsky (1965:227 note 2). Their interpretation posed no problem at all. They were of the same degree of grammaticalness in a formal sense as shorter sequences, but they were not acceptable. At best they were marginally marked for humor or pomposity, but Newman notes no examples of such use, besides, inadvertently, his own. He goes on to report:

Although Yokuts words, with the notable exception of the 'do' verbs (regarded as the linguistic property of children), tend to sketch only the bare and generalized outlines of a reference, the language possesses syntactic resources for combining words in such a way that its sentences could attain any degree of notional intricacy and richness. A passage of Macaulay's prose, with its long and involved periods, could be translated into grammatically correct Yokuts. But the result would be a grammarian's idle fancy, a distortion of the syntactic idiom of Yokuts. The language is as diffident in applying its means of elaboration in syntax as in suffixation. (p. 376)

The basis of the restraint is a general Yokuts demand for severe simplicity, a value that a colleague finds to underlie Yokuts narrative style as well. Newman contrasts the Yokuts value with an expressive value he finds implicit in English, arguing for the equal validity of each. To the English imagination the Yokuts style appears drab, 'but, by the same token, the stylistic features of English cannot appeal to the intuitions of a Yokuts native' (p. 377). He follows Sapir in regarding each language as 'like a particular art form in that it works with a limited range of materials and pursues the stylistic goals that have been and are constantly being discovered in a collective quest' (p. 377).

One can object to wording that personifies a language; it is the Yokuts-speaking community that works with a range of materials and pursues stylistic goals. Nevertheless, an important point is clear. If grammar is identified with what is structurally possible (as Newman identifies it in a paragraph summed up by the remark that 'It [grammar] tells what a language can do but not what it considers worthwhile doing' [p. 372]), or even with what is possible and transparent (as were Newman's four- and five-suffix words), then the community has drawn a line within the grammatical. On the basis of shared values, common to language and its uses in narrative, the community judges utterances that are formally possible as impossible in speech. This is a creative aspect of language use not taken into account in linguistic discussion, or overridden, the judgments of speakers being sacrificed to the requirements of formal statement. But notice that to get a native speaker to agree to the naturalness of one of Newman's monstrous words would not be to get him to see something he had not previously realized. He realized the grammatical possibility when Newman presented the forms to him. It would be to get him to change his native intuition. In a crucial sense, grammatical Yokuts is not what is possible to the grammar, as a device, but what is possible according to Yokuts norms. Here without intrusion of schools or pedants, we have a normative definition of possible Yokuts that is best described as aesthetic or stylistic in nature. For the Yokuts community, Yokuts is after all in that sense what they make of it.

Notice that the same grammar, as a formal device, is consistent with a drawing of the stylistic line in different places. The place might change over time within the same community. Yokuts judgments of Yokuts utterances would change, but formal grammar would not record it. By the same token, different communities of Yokuts speakers might draw the line in different places. Judgments of utterances would contrast, and again formal grammar not register the difference.

It would seem then that what Yokuts speakers know, their underlying competence, includes a dimension of style in the most essential way. Nothing about special speech styles and specific components of situations is involved; just plain Yokuts, showing that grammar is a matter of community 'should' as well as 'could,' is inherently normative.

The Yokuts case involves relations among given elements (although one can imagine that such restraint inhibits elaboration of affixes and other machinery, and favors its opposite, as Newman at one point suggests). The content of languages can itself be regarded from the standpoint of style, and again in terms of the exercise of an ability, a creative aspect of language use. Style is not only a matter of features other than referential, or of the selective use of features of both kinds; it also has to do with the selective creation of new materials and letting go of old. As languages change, they do not change wholly randomly, or lose structure in accordance with the second law of thermodynamics. They remain one relatively consistent set of realizations of the possibilities of language, rather than another. And they have the character they do in this regard partly because of choices by their users. It is possible to consider some kinds of change, including sound change, coming about in part because of social meaning associated with features, more prestigeful variants replacing less prestigeful ones. It is possible to consider some changes as coming about in response to internal imbalances and pressures, and to cumulative drifts which make some avenues of change far more tractable than others. But some changes cannot be understood except as changes over time in what users of the language find it most desirable or essential to say. Changes in the obligatory grammatical categories of a language, or in the relative elaboration of these, are such. Sometimes one can find a consistency (a 'conspiracy') in the semantic character of a variety of seemingly unrelated changes and trends. I have tried to show this to be the case for Wasco (Hymes 1961b, section 5), presenting evidence that in recently coined words, in recent changes in affixes marking tense-aspect and post-positions marking case relations, and in trends in the derivation of verb themes, there is common a certain cognitive orientation.

It is important to avoid two misunderstandings. First, to recognize the orientation, or style, is not to project an interpretation upon defenseless material. Not just any trait of the language is entered in evidence, but traits that have recently been brought into being, that represent choices, creative activity, on the part of the community. Second, no inference can be directly made to the minds of speakers. One's evidence is of the result of changes that must have had some psychological reality for those that introduced and accepted them; but evidence independent of the language is needed to demonstrate their psychological reality for a later speaker. In point of fact, it is unlikely that surviving Wasco speakers, all multilingual, and using the language only rarely, would show much evidence. Linguistic relativity in Whorf's sense is dependent on a more fundamental type of relativity, that of the function of linguistic means. Speakers of different generations may provide evidence of a common grammar, but for one the grammar may be only something remembered, for the other the central verbal instrument for handling experience.

It is worth noting that linguistic inference of underlying grammatical knowledge is in the same boat as Whorf's inference of underlying cognitive outlook. Both argue to a capacity or characteristic of users of language from linguistic data alone. The linguistic data are both source and evidence for the claimed characteristics. The criticism of circularity lodged against Whorf attaches to work in grammar which identifies a formal analysis with psychological reality without independent test. (Newman's presentation of constructed words to speakers was informally such a test.)

I am saying that the import of cognitive styles in languages is problematic, needing to be established, not that there is no import (cf. Hymes 1966). The same holds for all speech styles, and means of speech in general. In other aspects of life we recognize that the means available condition what can be done with them. We recognize that the tools available affect what is made without reducing outcomes to tools alone. Somehow there has been a schizophrenic consciousness in our civilization with regard to verbal tools. Some have taken them as determinants of almost everything, others have denied that they determine anything. One suspects a reflection of a long-standing conflict between 'idealist' and 'materialist' assumptions, language being identified with the 'idealist' side, so that to argue for its determinative role was to seem to argue for one philosophical outlook and against another. (Something of this interpretation of matters seems current in the Soviet Union.) For others, it is all right to speak of the great role of language in general, but never of languages in particular. One suspects a resistance to a long-standing tendency to treat some linguistic particularities as inferior, or a reflection of a climate of opinion in which any explicit limitation on mental freedom is resented. Here a statement of position must suffice.

First, it seems inescapably true to me that the means available to persons do condition what they can verbally do, and that these means are in important part historically shaped. Second, such a view is not derogation of differences; what can be done may be admirable.

In this connection, it should be noted that fluent members of communities often enough themselves evaluate their languages as not equivalent. It is not only that one language, or variety, often is preferred for some uses, another for others, but also that there is experience with what can in fact be best done with one or the other. This sort of differential ability has nothing to do with disadvantage or deficiency of some members of a community relative to others. All of them may find, say, Kurdish the medium in which most things can best be expressed, but Arabic the better medium for religious truth. Users of Berber may find Arabic superior to Berber for all purposes except intimate domestic conversation (Ferguson 1966).[2]

But, third, differences in available means and related abilities do exist in ways that pose problems. In some respects the problems are inherent in the human condition, insofar as each of us must be a definite person in a world changing unpredictably and without our consent or control. In other respects problems are inherent only in certain social orders and circumstances, and could in principle be solved. It is my conviction that the requisite social change requires knowledge of actual abilities and activities, and that a linguistics of the sort sketched above can contribute to such knowledge.[3]

NOTES

PREFACE

1. The 1962 essay was anticipated by the last section of Hymes 1961a; see also Hymes 1961b.

2. For the historical antecedents of the ethnography of speaking, its place within contemporary anthropology, and its relationships with other disciplines (including other subdisciplines and approaches concerned with the relationship between language on the one hand and culture, society, and the individual on the other) the reader should consult Hymes (1962, 1964a, 1966, 1970, 1971), Grimshaw (1973), and Gumperz (1972).

INTRODUCTION

1. Any effort of this kind must acknowledge the stimulus and influence of Hymes' productive formulations; see Hymes 1962, 1964, 1967, 1972.

2. The notion of competence owes its principal currency to the work of Chomsky (1965:3–9), but has been implicit in ethnographic theory at least since Goodenough 1957 (Hymes 1970b). See also Frake 1964:132. Hymes' critique of Chomsky on competence and performance has been especially important in our own thinking on this matter (see Hymes 1971a).

3. The term and concept 'organization of diversity' is from Wallace (1970), but see also Hymes, this volume, section VI.

4. On means of speaking, see Hymes' paper in this volume, section VI.

5. Emergence, as a philosophical concept, is associated with the work of Alexander (1920 (II):45–6). For an application of the concept to sociological theory see McHugh 1968.

6. Ervin-Tripp, Gumperz, Hymes, Labov, and others have systematically criticized the narrow limitations of most abstract linguistic theory from a social and anthropological perspective since the early 1960s (see references in Preface and Labov 1966, 1970). To be sure, such figures as Sapir and Jakobson have always operated in terms of a far broader conception of linguistics than much current work would imply.

7. A useful introduction to this line of linguistic analysis and its philosophical antecedents is Rosenberg & Travis 1971. See also Jacobs & Rosenbaum 1970; Fillmore & Langendoen 1971; Lakoff 1972. For a discussion of the relationship between recent trends in linguistic theory and the ethnography of speaking, see Sherzer 1973.

8. Folklorists have been represented in both major collections on the ethnography of communication; see Dundes & Arewa 1964 and Dundes, Leach & Özkök 1972. Two recent collections which exemplify the developing importance of the ethnography of artistic verbal performance in contemporary folkloristics are Paredes & Bauman 1972 and Ben-Amos & Goldstein 1973.

9. The work of Goffman (see, e.g., 1961, 1964, 1971) and Garfinkel (1967) has been particularly influential in this line of sociological analysis. See also Cicourel 1970, the recent collection by Sudnow (1972), Sacks 1972, and Schegloff 1972.

10. The beginnings of a base for close local comparison are available for at least two areas: highland Chiapas (see the papers by Bricker, Gossen, and Stross in this volume), and the Caribbean (see Abrahams & Bauman 1971, Reisman 1970, and Reisman's paper in this volume).

CHAPTER 1. A QUANTITATIVE PARADIGM FOR THE STUDY OF COMMUNICATIVE COMPETENCE

1. The / / notation is not meant to represent phonemic brackets, but simply an abstract phonological representation.

2. This and other symbols are explained in the appendix to this chapter.

3. A statistical analysis of the one-environment variability hypothesis has been developed by D. Sankoff and P. Rousseau (in press).

4. I wish to thank the Canada Council and the Ministère de l'Education, Québec, for their support for the Montreal French project. I am grateful to the following people who contributed to the analysis of examples discussed in this paper: Suzanne Laberge, for her work on the collection and analysis of the Tok Pisin material; Eleanor Herasimchuk, for further help with the Tok Pisin data; Dorothée Bertrand-Mineau, Henrietta J. Cedergren, Michèle Chiasson-Lavoie, Suzanne Laberge, Monique Dumont, Jean-Jacques Gagné, Robert Sarrasin, and Marjorie Topham for their work on the Montreal French project. I wish to thank Henrietta Cedergren, John Gumperz, Eugene Hammel, Dell Hymes, Paul Kay, William Labov, Marc Leduc, Clair Lefebvre, Paul Pupier, and Madeleine St-Pierre for helpful discussion of some of the specific issues discussed in the paper, though the opinions expressed are my own.

CHAPTER 2. LANGUAGE IDENTITY OF THE COLOMBIAN VAUPÉS INDIANS

1. Data for this paper were gathered in the *Comisaría del Vaupés*, the eastern part of which forms the Colombian sector of the central Northwest Amazon. This region, half in Colombia and half in Brazil (see Fig. 4), is characterized by multilingualism and by the use of Tukano as a lingua franca. The central Northwest Amazon is about the size of New England, and has a population of about 10 000 (Sorensen 1967:670). The *Comisaría del Vaupés* has a territory of 90 625 sq. km, and the most recent census (Rodríguez 1962) gives a figure of approximately 14 000 for the total population. Although the multilingual region this paper is concerned with includes adjacent Brazilian territory, my field work was carried out mainly in Colombia, specifically in the Papurí drainage to the south of the Vaupés River. Therefore, my conclusions mainly apply to the Colombian Vaupés.

2. See Helm 1968, particularly the paper by Hymes, pp. 23–48.

3. For further ethnographic information on the Vaupés, see Goldman (1948, 1963), Sorensen (1967), Reichel-Dolmatoff (1971), and Jackson (1972).

4. For example, see Basso (1973), Owen (1965), and Sankoff (1968).

5. Ph.D. research was carried out in Colombia from October 1968 to November 1970, with support from the Danforth Foundation and the Stanford Committee for Research in International Studies. Eighteen months of this time was spent with a group of Bará Indians on the Inambú River in the Vaupés. I am grateful to the following people who read earlier drafts of this paper: James Fox, Charles Frake, Joseph Greenberg, Christine Hugh-Jones, Dell Hymes, Theodore Johnson, Michelle Rosaldo, Renato Rosaldo, Gillian Sankoff, Joel Sherzer, and Bernard Siegel.

CHAPTER 3. 'OUR ANCESTORS SPOKE IN PAIRS'

1. 'Beliefs and consequences' are an extraordinarily interesting genre. They are all injunctions with the following form: 'Don't do X; if you do X, then Y.' For example: 'Don't sweep the house during the middle of the day. If you sweep the house during the middle of the day, the chicken will disappear.' 'Dream interpretations' resemble 'beliefs and consequences' but many of these are based on a principle of inversion. Dreaming of something often – though not always – implies its opposite.

2. There can be no denying that I initially affected Rotinese speech events. As long as I was regarded as a rank outsider, somehow associated with the government and the world at large, Rotinese tended to interlard their speaking, in my presence, with a great deal more Malay than I believe they would have ordinarily. The Rotinese attitude toward 'mixing speech' comes down to not using Malay where some Rotinese form of speaking is expected. The converse is also true; Malay has its expected usage.

3. I have analyzed some of the formal properties of Rotinese ritual language in Fox (1971a) and traced certain pervasive idioms in Rotinese rituals in Fox (1971b). I am presently at work on a lengthy study of this language and on a dictionary of its dyadic sets. I feel it necessary to point out that in writing Rotinese my seemingly peculiar orthography (*laö* for *la'o* or *la:o*, for example) is based, with only minor modification, on the previous orthography established by the Dutch linguist J. C. G. Jonker (1915:1–5). Listings in the dictionary I am preparing on ritual language will be cross-referenced to Jonker's equivalent listings for ordinary language (Jonker 1908). This dictionary, when completed, should be a useful complement to Jonker's dictionary; anyone interested in Rotinese may be able to compare the use of a word in ordinary language with its special use in ritual language.

4. As in the Mayan traditions of canonical parallelism discussed in this volume (see Bricker; Gossen), the pairing of words in Rotinese can be shown to be the identifying element of all that is considered 'ancestral speaking.' Thus whereas 'proverbs,' 'songs,' and 'chants' are based on a strictly defined parallelism, 'riddles,' 'beliefs and consequences,' 'dream interpretations,' and 'mockery' evidence a somewhat looser pairing.

5. One of the most astute observations on this idea of stereoscopy, rather than redundancy, was made by the Chinese scholar Peter Boodberg (1954:Cedule 017–541210): 'Indeed parallelism is not merely a stylistic device of formularistic syntactical duplication; it is intended to achieve a result reminiscent of binocular vision, the superimposition of two syntactical images in order to endow them with

solidity and depth, the repetition of the pattern having the effect of binding together syntagms that appear at first rather loosely aligned.'

6. My own knowledge of Rotinese dialects is probably only slightly better than that of some Rotinese. My advantage is that I can rely on the previous dialect research of the linguist Jonker, have done my fieldwork in four separate areas of the island, and have gathered at least one long text in nearly all the domains. I feel certain the role of the dialects in ritual language is more complex and subtle than I can indicate at present. In what follows, I, too, must take the view of a specific dialect, that of Termanu, where I concentrated my research. The few examples I cite here ought to be considered as aspects of a more comprehensive phenomenon.

7. The research on which this paper is based was supported by a Public Health Service fellowship (MH023, 148) and grant (MH-10, 161) from the National Institute of Mental Health and was conducted, in Indonesia (1965–6), under the auspices of what has now become the Lembaga Ilmu Pengetahuan Indonesia. Further research has continued under an NIMH grant (MH-20659-01), through Harvard University, for the Comparative Study of Formal Dyadic Languages in Eastern Indonesia. This paper was written during the tenure of a fellowship at the Center for Advanced Study in the Behavioral Sciences, Stanford, California. I am particularly indebted to Professor Roman Jakobson for his continuing encouragement of this research on parallelism.

CHAPTER 4. WARM SPRINGS 'INDIAN TIME'

1. It is relevant here to make it clear that there are a variety of ways in which activities can be interpreted as being conceptually related to one another at Warm Springs. Early in the paper the point was made that war dancing and worship dance activities differ in that one is social or secular and the other sacred. Yet at the same time, both kinds of activities have many of the same organizational features. Similarly, in the present context, one might mention: (a) a funeral, which is being treated here as a large-scale event, also has all of the features of these so-called subevents that mark changes in social status, except that it must occur just after a person has died; (b) the naming and coming out of mourning do not have to take place at a communitywide memorial dinner; gatherings of kinsmen and friends at a home for these purposes also occur; (c) there are other activities besides those which take place at these communitywide events that are involved in both the initiation and termination of mourning, especially for the spouse of the deceased.

Katherine French's dissertation on Warm Springs social ceremonialism (1955) deals with the considerable variation in the ways in which 'ritual segments' are combined at Warm Springs.

CHAPTER 5. CONTRAPUNTAL CONVERSATIONS IN AN ANTIGUAN VILLAGE

1. Roman Jakobson has said, 'Rules which remain only rules are insupportable for poetry. Every rule is at the same time a source of deviation. The rules themselves take on meaning.' (Lecture, Massachusetts Institute of Technology, 1969; see Jakobson 1966 and Levin 1950).

2. My thanks to Dr Nils Hansegård and his wife for their stimulating hospitality and for so generously making their house in Rensjoen available to us.

3. Robert Hunt (personal communication) suggests also a relation between inter-

ruption and the length of a 'scene' – subject, speaker, or whatever. Different people and cultures have different tolerances for scene length, at which point there will be interruptions.

4. Fundamental historical work on social structure in Antigua has been done by Goveia (1965). On connections between creole language and the history and structure of West Indian societies, see Alleyne (1963) and Mintz (1971).

5. See also Fuad Khuri (1968: note 5, p. 705: 'Abusive language to Africans is a serious assault often tried before a court. They do not consider it as a joke, therefore, when a Lebanese husband scolds his wife by using abusive language, but as a serious fight') and Marc Swartz (1969).

6. There is evidence also of the persistence of these conventions through time. Oscillation between noise and order is reported from Africa without its attendant Caribbean ambiguities. George Herzog and C. G. Blooah (1936) tell us about a Jabo drum signal that gives the command: 'Stop ye the noise, speak ye one by one,' and Laura Bohannan writes the following about the Tiv in *Return to Laughter*: ... 'In this case, however, it was quite clear that the two men had brought a dispute for arbitration. At Kako's sign, one began his story, interrupted by questions from all the notables and punctuated by sarcastic comment and injured denial from the other. Soon everyone was saying so much, and so loudly, that no one could hear. Then someone screamed, "Shut up! Shut up!" until all had taken up the cry. Then a silence, and the case slowly warmed up to a shouting point again' (1954:51–2). Thus I would argue that these conventions represent part of the *underlying culture* of Antiguan *villages*.

Other formal patterns of African speaking that are relevant to the West Indies have been described by Geneviève Calame-Griaule (1963) and James W. Fernandez (1967) among others.

7. I conducted the research on which this paper is based as a Research Fellow of the Institute of Caribbean Studies, University of Puerto Rico. My thanks to Richard Morse, then its director; and also to Dell Hymes, John Murra, and Sidney Mintz, who in many ways have helped me to understand whatever I do about speech in the Caribbean. J. Oliver Davis and his family were and are a constant source of encouragement and support. Sue Finan suggested some helpful changes. An earlier version of this paper was presented to the Anthropological Society of Washington in 1968, and I should like to thank them for their hospitality on that occasion.

CHAPTER 6. NORM–MAKERS, NORM–BREAKERS

1. Native terms and transcriptions from the native language follow the established conventions for written Malagasy.

CHAPTER 7. SPEAKING IN THE LIGHT

1. The scope of the paper comprehends the period between the beginnings of Quakerism, in the early 1650s, and the advent of Toleration in 1689. Occasional points are supported by quotes from the immediately subsequent period of Quakerism where they refer or pertain to the period under consideration.

2. An anti-Quaker pamphlet of 1672 says of the Quakers' profession, 'his *Religion* is nothing but *Phrases*, being a superstitious observer of *new Minted Modes* of speaking' (R. H. 1672:3, italics his).

3. The discussion which follows quotes extensively from primary sources, in order to give the reader as full a sense as possible of the data on which the paper is based. All quotations are from the period 1650–89, except as indicated in note 1 above; later editions of certain works have been used for reasons of availability or convenience.

4. 'Do not your teachers joyn with the world in feastings, in idle speeches, and in foolish jeastings [sic] that do administer no grace to the hearers, telling tales and stories which are pleasing to the flesh?' (Payne 1655:28, misnumbered p. 36).

5. Friends referred to their own Quaker doctrine as the *Truth*. For a discussion of the various senses in which the term was used, see Bauman 1970.

6. A systematic comparison between 'true' (Quaker) and 'false' ministers was a common theme in seventeenth-century Quaker polemical tracts (e.g., Burrough 1657; Caton 1671; Fox 1657c:99; Knight 1675).

7. The term *opening* was also used for personal, internal experiences of God's word; see, e.g., Banks 1798:47.

8. This text, from I Peter 4.11, was a basic and often-quoted charter for the Quaker ministry. See also, e.g., Adamson 1656:5 and Aynsloe 1672:13.

9. 'Guard against superfluous words, impertinently brought in, such as, "I may say; As it were; All and every one; Dear friends; and friendly people," with sundry others of the like kind, which add nothing to thy matter, spoiling its coherence and beauty of expression' (Bownas 1847:58–9). Compare the discussion of 'stall formulas' in Bruce Rosenberg's *The art of the American folk preacher* (1970:66–8).

10. Concerning these and related testimonies, see D. Barclay 1831:512–71.

11. William Caton was thus typical of Quaker ministers: 'And after that the *Lord* had fitted me for his *Work* as aforesaid, I was much exercised in going to *Steeple-Houses*, insomuch, that there seldom passed *a first day* of the *week*, but I was at one, or another, and I was also often in *Markets*, where I was moved to declare *Gods* [sic] *eternal Truth*, which through his Infinite Mercy I was become a *Witness* of' (Caton 1689:10, italics his). It was part of Quaker doctrine that the true church was in God, not in mere buildings, thus the term *steeple house* in place of 'church.'

12. Crook's statement is noteworthy in connection with the Quaker conviction that the minister's words were not his own, but God's; thus it was to be expected that when Crook held back from speaking the words he was given, someone else should speak the same words to the meeting.

13. The research on which this paper is based was supported by a grant from the American Philosophical Society, which is hereby gratefully acknowledged. I would also like to thank the staffs of the Quaker Collection, Haverford (Pa.) College Library, and Friends House (London) for their unfailing courtesy and cooperation in the conduct of this research.

CHAPTER 8. STRATEGIES OF STATUS MANIPULATION IN THE
WOLOF GREETING

1. Field observation among the Wolof was carried out from September 1970 to September 1971, largely in the village of Kïr Matar (name fictionalized). Kïr

Matar is in Senegal, in a region formerly known as the kingdom of Kayor.

2. Even if verbal interaction is interspersed with relatively long silences, it is still a state of talk which must be verbally initiated and terminated.

3. Goffman's examples, however, refer to sequential omissions of greetings (that is, not greeting someone whom one has recently greeted), rather than spatial omissions.

4. Wolof society is divided into a number of ranked status groups, or castes. Some two-thirds of the village population in Kïr Matar belong to the noble caste; the rest belong to various lower castes, of which the most numerous and most conspicuous are the griots, or praise-singers (*gewel* in Wolof).

5. It is important to note that this dyad emerges from the data – that it is not a theoretical model imposed upon a communicative situation. Hymes (1967) has pointed out that the dyadic sender–receiver model of communicative action is inadequate as a universal descriptive tool.

6. The Wolof orthography used in this paper is based on the system suggested by Stewart (1966). Because the speech of Kïr Matar shows cetrtain differences in pronunciation from the speech of Dakar as described by Stewart, my spelling of particular words sometimes differs from his, though his orthography as a whole is adequate to both regions. Some common Wolof names (e.g., Ndiaye, Diop) have not been altered from the way they are normally spelled in Senegal.

7. These rules are, of course, only a more precise way of formulating what has already been stated in Table 7 and the discussion of Table 7. One major benefit of formulating them in this way – as a phrase-structure grammar – is to show that the greeting, as a structured stretch of discourse, may be analyzed in a framework which includes both the structure of the event and the internal structure of its own constituents.

It will be noted that the linguistic model I have used is not the 'extended standard theory' based on Chomsky (1965 and later writings), but an earlier model based on Chomsky (1957). I have used the earlier model because I felt that for the material I am dealing with, certain notions developed in the early theory but dropped in the later one are useful and appropriate. What I wish to retain is the notion of kernel and derived forms, and the possibility of optional transformations. I prefer to view one form of the greeting, the one I have presented through phrase-structure rules, as more basic in that the status roles assigned to speakers at the beginning of the discourse are held constant throughout; other greeting forms (those arrived at by performing my transformational rules) must start out with this 'kernel' role assignment and may only alter the roles later in the greeting. The operations I present as transformations are strategies to change the nature of the event which are attempted *after* the event has already begun, and which may very well fail. Moreover, the place of 'meaning' in the analysis of a linguistic event – which was a major consideration in the development of the 1965 theory, and is the main issue in the admissibility of optional transformations – may be different in an event involving two persons from what it is in utterance of a single speaker.

8. Note that the flow chart represents the same material as the phrase-structure rules do; it differs from them only in making the options open to particular speakers more visually striking. Like the phrase-structure rules, the flow chart cannot in itself show the kinds of operations which I have represented in the transformational rules.

9. The text of the proverb runs as follows:

sawaa	dyi,	sawaa	dyi,	gaty-	angga	. tya,	ndam-
greeter/	the/	greeter/	the/	shame/	Pres./	at,in/	glory,victory/

angga	ca.
Pres./	at, in.

The greeter, the (other) greeter, there is shame at (one), there is glory at (the other.)

10. Ultimately the local chief, Songo Aminata, manages to avoid a battle by convincing Lat Dior that the king was himself at fault for abandoning Kayor – and those who took advantage of the king's absence should not be blamed for doing so. The historical narrative from which this text is drawn was told to me by M. Malik Mbengue.

11. Cf. Goffman (1967:82–3): 'Demeanor images ... pertain more ... to the way in which the individual handles his position than to the rank and place of that position relative to those possessed by others.'

12. Cf. Trager's 'voice qualities' or 'vocal qualifiers' (1964:276–7); also Crystal's 'non-segmental phonetic and phonological characteristics of utterance' (1971:185).

13. Although I present only two 'features' of paralinguistic phenomena for the purposes of this discussion, I believe that these two are in fact subdivided into four independently varying features, whose independent variation arises largely in non-greeting contexts. These four variables are pitch, volume, rapidity, and verbosity. For instance, a combination of + high pitch and – loud seems to be used in baby talk, when an adult is speaking to an infant (an infant too young to take a part in the greeting).

14. The work on which this paper is based was made possible by PHS Training Grant No. 1 – F01 MH47638–01 (CUAN) from the National Institute of Mental Health. I am also particularly grateful to Dell Hymes for his suggestions and criticism.

CHAPTER 9. RITUALS OF ENCOUNTER AMONG THE MAORI

1. Maori terms in parentheses refer to stages or categories of the ritual, discussed in more detail on pp. 202ff.

2. The following system of formal notation is used in the rules:

( )	optional
{ }	choose one
[ ]	features
R	repeat
<	increases
→	rewrite as
/	in the context of
:	instruction follows

Following the formal statement of each rule, when appropriate, is a prose re-statement of the same rule, enclosed in single quotation marks.

CHAPTER 10. SPEAKING OF SPEAKING

1. These factors do not correspond directly to the factors discussed in Hymes (1962), although they are clearly related.

2. *bankilal k'op* could mean either of these two things, but a third gloss, the only one given in the appendix, is the primary meaning of the form combination, making it an obvious monolexemic term. Although the exact lexemic status of many of the terms given in the appendix is certainly debatable, I believe that a case could be made for viewing them all as monolexemic, the most questionable of them being composite lexemes in accordance with Conklin's (1962) formulation.

3. Research relevant to this paper was carried out in Chiapas, Mexico, January–May 1971, and was supported by National Science Foundation Grant GU-1598 to the University of Texas. The paper has benefited from comments and criticism by Penny Brown and Fadwa El Guindi.

CHAPTER 11. BLACK TALKING ON THE STREETS

1. I do this recognizing that I am continuing to commit an error of my past studies of Black communication styles, justly pointed out by Valentine (1972), by treating primarily Black male behavior patterns. I have done this because there are more data on this street dimension of Black culture. But I hope to redress this lack in future studies in which the more private and less performance-centered dimensions of talking Black will be discussed. (For preliminary attempts in the United States and the British West Indies, see Abrahams 1970a,b,c.)

2. The term *business* in the sense of personal concerns is a focal term in Afro-American communities. Though this is not the appropriate place to fully explore the semantic field of the Black uses of the term, there are some features which are important to point out. *Business* essentially means 'name' maintenance. Thus, if a woman uses the term, it is liable to be in protection of her sense of respectability, warning others that her doings are 'nobody's business but my own.' On the other hand, when a man says 'I'ma *t.c.b.* [take care of business]' he is generally referring to leaving to see others, to maintain his connections, his friendship (or loveship) networks. *T.c.b.* generally is taken to mean 'I'm going to see a man about something which (I want you to think) is important'; but it also can refer to pursuing a sexual conquest or to the sexual act itself. For an important early commentary on the special Afro-American use of the term see F. L. Olmsted, *A Journey in the Seaboard States* (1856:206).

3. Puckett and Dillard discuss the uses of these traditions of eloquence (Puckett 1926:38ff; Dillard 1972:245–59), and I survey the West Indian literature and the possible African backgrounds (Abrahams 1970c). Hannerz discusses the uses of such talk on the streets, as do Mezzrow and Wolfe, though the latters' interpretation seems wrong-headed (Hannerz 1969:85; Mezzrow & Wolfe 1969:195).

4. I want to thank John Szwed and Robert Farris Thompson, Tony Terry and Robert Wilson, for talking some of the matters out. To the editors I am even further indebted – and far beyond matters editorial – for they both helped in the conceptualization and rendering of the paper at times when despair had settled in. Beverly Stoeltje's discussion of women *talking smart* clarified my ideas in this area. Marilyn Sandlin, too, bore up under the despair and the frenzy, typing the (too) many drafts. Barbara Babcock-Abrahams not only drew the chart many times, but helped with many other finishing touches.

CHAPTER 12. 'NAMAKKE,' 'SUNMAKKE,' 'KORMAKKE'

1. The Cuna Indians live today principally in two areas: (1) on islands and mainland communities in the Comarca de San Blas, off the northeastern coast of Panama, and (2) on the other side of the Cordillera de San Blas in the Darien Jungle, along

the Bayano and Chucunaque rivers. The research on which this paper is based was carried out in 1970 and 1971 in San Blas, Panama, mainly on the island of Sasartii-Mulatuppu. Although what I report here holds in general for all Cuna, there exists considerable regional variation with regard to matters of detail.

2. Various sections of San Blas stress different subjects in their chants and islands in these sections group themselves together for 'traditional congresses.' Thus one section tends to chant about the great Cuna *neles*; another about Christ, Columbus, and Bolivar; etc. There are rivalries among these sections concerning who chants about the proper subjects. For an excellent discussion of these and related matters see Howe 1974.

3. The elidible vowels occur at the ends of morphemes so that many morphemes can be said to have long and short forms. These vowels are *variables* in the sense of Labov (1970). However, as distinct from Labov's variables, they are not conditioned by participant (location in social organization) and context (casual to careful), but rather by genre – ordinary conversation, chief's chant, curing *ikar*, etc.

4. In the sense of Chomsky (1957) which, of the various models of generative-transformational grammar currently in use, seems to be the best suited to a syntactic analysis of Cuna ceremonial genres.

5. For a discussion of grammatical parallelism in general see Jakobson (1968); for its occurrence in Cuna texts see Kramer (1970) and Sherzer & Sherzer (1972).

6. The only Cuna genre of speaking which is supposed to be short is the *sekreto*, a charm-like utterance used to control objects and persons.

7. The transcriptions used in this paper are more 'phonological' than 'phonetic.' 'Single' stop consonants (p, t, k^w) are pronounced voiced and 'double' stop consonants (pp, tt, kk, kk^w) are pronounced voiceless.

8. There are also occasions on which chiefs speak rather than chant either because they prefer to, because there is no other chief to respond (*apinsue*), or because of an interdiction on chanting, such as when someone has just died on the island.

9. I owe this observation to Larry Blount, for whom *kurkin ikar* was once performed, in his absence and without his knowing it.

10. This fact is not mentioned in Lévi-Strauss' interesting analysis of *muu ikar* (1963). Lévi-Strauss argues that the suffering woman goes through the same analysis that he the analyst has and is thereby cured.

11. I am grateful to both James Howe and Dell Hymes for stressing this point, the former from the perspective of Cuna ethnography and the latter from the point of view of the ethnography of speaking in general.

12. That is, if the relatives of the deceased are willing to pay for it. There is no requirement that it be performed.

13. During puberty rites festivities *ikar* knowers often perform either for themselves or for an audience. In the latter case, the audience usually provides a bottle of rum. That individuals enjoy listening to curing *ikar* during these festivities and that they are even willing to pay for it (in the form of a bottle of rum) shows that these *ikar* are appreciated and valued as verbal art as well as instruments of curing.

14. See note 3.

15. It is interesting that from a generative-transformational point of view the linguistic varieties used in all three ceremonial events described in this paper (congress chanting, curing *ikar*, and *kantur ikar*) are phonologically and syntactically

more basic, abstract, or underlying than colloquial speech. This matches nicely the traditional nature ascribed by the Cuna to these varieties.

16. The only permissible variation has to do with the specific purpose of an *ikar* within its general purpose. This is not at the will of the individual *ikar* knower but is rather determined by the particular nature of the disease (as communicated by a *nele* 'seer') or the particular object of the *ikar*. Thus although *pisep ikar* can be used in the hunting of various animals, the ones mentioned in the *ikar* are those that the hunter has said he is interested in. Notice that the principle at work here is quite different from that described above for congress events in which chanters and speakers draw on well known themes and metaphors but develop them and elaborate on them in very individual ways.

17. There are several types of chicha festivals, each with a different name as well as different sets of *ikar* and festivities associated with it. In addition, there is a great deal of regional variation in what occurs in these rites.

18. There is a different set of games and dances for each type of chicha festival.

19. There are many speech events and types of speaking which I have not discussed – *sekretos* (charm-like utterances), linguistic games, riddles, lullabies, etc.

20. See note 15.

21. See note 16.

22. For an excellent discussion of Cuna metaphors of political structure, see Howe MS.

23. I personally attended this *uanaet* in April 1971.

24. It is fairly common for this to happen. Cuna chiefs are chosen on the basis of their knowledge of traditions. Once in office, they are not always suited for the political realities of governing a village; they might, for example, be tempted to misuse their authority. So they are removed from office. But, once again, because of their knowledge of traditions, they are available for reinstatement.

25. I am grateful to Mac Chapin for this example.

26. *Osi* 'pineapple' can be used as a metaphor for 'woman' in *konkreso kaya*. (See Chapin 1970:9.) Its meaning in the speech described here can be understood in terms of a semantic classification of fruit in San Blas. (See Sherzer 1972.) All edible plants are grouped into various classes according to a number of socioeconomic features. The features are such factors as whether the plant has an owner, whether a non-owner can take some of the fruit if he tells the owner, whether the fruit is ripe, etc. Pineapples belong to that class of fruit which have an owner and which one has the right to eat on the spot if one is hungry and the fruit is ripe. Thus the metaphor fits perfectly the case under discussion. That it succeeded in getting its speaker off the hook demonstrates the degree to which verbal ability is appreciated among the Cuna.

This example is a striking illustration of the 'creative aspect of language use.' It is unfortunate that Chomsky, who dwells at such length on this aspect of language (see, for example, Chomsky 1968), limits it to the ability to utter and understand a novel sentence. Investigation of actual speech usages provides much richer and more exciting data.

27. One cannot, however, be both a chief and an *arkar*, since these are two participants within a single speech event.

28. It also means 'hat,' 'head,' and 'brain,' as in *kurkin ikar* (see above.).

29. To this, James Howe (personal communication) adds that 'though each role is discrete, and though each person keeps his various roles separate, his general position in his village and in the region is in part the sum of his roles, and the fact that each man can build up a total configuration of roles that is unique, even if the separate roles are not, is important to status competition.'

30. The two constellations can also be viewed as two sets of esthetic criteria, from the perspective of the Cuna view of verbal art.

31. I am grateful to Olga Linares de Sapir for pointing out how well the type of speaking ability expected of chiefs matches the realities of the Cuna political situation.

32. The research for this paper was supported by NSF Grant GU-1598 to the University of Texas. My understanding of Cuna ethnography of speaking has benefited greatly from long discussions with Mac Chapin, James Howe, June Howe, and Dina Sherzer. They all commented on an earlier draft of this paper, as did Dell Hymes.

CHAPTER 13. CONCEPT AND VARIETIES OF EAST EUROPEAN JEWISH
NARRATIVE PERFORMANCE

1. The transcription of Yiddish words reflects the basic features of the speaker's dialect pronunciation. The Hebrew-Aramaic components of Yiddish and Hebrew-Aramaic words used by Yiddish speakers are rendered according to their east European pronunciation rather than the modern Israeli way. The transliteration system used here is consistent with that used by the Yivo Institue for Jewish Research, the Library of Congress, and Uriel Weinreich, *Modern English–Yiddish Yiddish–English Dictionary* (1968). Translations and glosses are in parentheses and are based on the Weinreich dictionary. I have not altered the way that Yiddish words are transliterated in passages quoted from other published works. Yiddish words commonly used in English follow the conventional English spelling.

2. It is not uncommon to be told of a Hasidic saint or great *magid* (preacher), for example, that 'It was always some outward occasion that brought him to narrating' (Buber 1962:44), that is, a topic in the conversation or something about the immediate context. In the case of a narrator such as the *magid* of Mezritsh, we are told that 'When he spoke, he did not supply systematic connections, but threw out a single suggestion, or a single parable without spinning it out and tying together the threads. His disciples had the task . . . of working over what had been said and suppling the missing links' (Buber 1961:16), a style suited to the mystical tendencies of Hasidism. We also find that the parable user was known to get so carried away that his didactic purpose might become obscured by the intrinisic interest of the tale and what started out as a gloss (Type A) might end up as a topic (Type B) (see Buber 1962:44).

3. This paper has benefited from the helpful suggestions of Richard Bauman, Dan Ben-Amos, Dell Hymes, Yekhiel Lifschutz, Shlomo Noble, Mordkhe Schaechter, Isaiah Trunk, Beatrice Weinreich, and Wolf Younin. The data for this study were gathered with the help of grants from the Canada Council and the Folklore Division, National Museum of Canada.

CHAPTER 14. CORRELATES OF CREE NARRATIVE PERFORMANCE

1. The dialect spoken in Wabasca, the home reserve of the Big Stone Band, is Plains Cree. This area is close to the boundary between Plains and Woods Cree, marked by a switch from /y/ to /th/ in certain phonological environments.

2. The old man is referred to in this manner throughout because it is his age which determines his role as an authentic carrier of the tradition. In the eyes of native people his personal identity is subordinate.

3. Father's comments were made in Cree and translated loosely by Marie-Louise at this time. The tapes were later transcribed with more detailed translations. Quotations of Father's remarks are from Marie-Louise's translation.

4. This is the style of the narrator in traditional Cree stories. Actors in the stories are quoted directly with 'he said' or 'he thought' as in introduction.

5. For example, when a man accused of beating his wife fled into the bush with his family last year, my Cree hostess, a woman of about sixty, refused to let her husband go trapping until he was caught, 'because he might be a *wihtigo* now.'

6. However, this does not account for the traditional Cree stories in which a *wihtigo* and Wisahkitchak appear in the same narrative. Many performers deny the existence of these stories when asked to reconcile the two different time frameworks. Analytically we may assume that *wihtigo* is not an individual but a psychological state personified. This state could exist in mythological time and simultaneously in present time, just as the animal actors in the sacred stories do. Each individual manifestation is representative of the category but does not exhaust it – *wihtigo*, bear, etc. (The only exception is that children may be called Wisahkitchak if they are very cunning or play a practical joke; this is a simile based on common behavioral attributes, as is the reference to *wihtigo* for someone who eats too much.)

7. Only one narrator has ever attempted to explain to me why all the stories begin: 'Wisahkitchak was walking.' This narrator explained that because they were growing up, he would tell his child audience the beginning of the story. In the beginning, Wisahkitchak was sitting. Where he was sitting, there was nothing. There was only a piece of dirt. Wisahkitchak blew on it and it grew bigger. He wondered how big to make it. This piece of dirt was the world itself. Then Wisahkitchak made a coyote, Wisahkitchak told the coyote to run around the edge of the world and come back. He came back and told Wisahkitchak how big the world had become. This happened many times. Wisahkitchak kept blowing. He didn't have enough. While the coyote was gone, Wisahkitchak made more animals, mostly game animals and birds. Then he sent the coyote for what might be the last time. Wisahkitchak got tired of waiting for this little coyote. Then Wisahkitchak got up for the first time. He got up and went off walking to look for the coyote. This is the beginning of the story and the end. The rest of the stories about Wisahkitchak branch off on his travels; this story is the roots. Nobody has ever heard that Wisahkitchak stopped walking so he must still be looking for that coyote.

8. Father explained at some length that many Indians used to beat their wives or ran from one woman to another. These two old people had been married for seventy-three years and had been particularly close throughout their lives. On occasion they can be seen holding hands, a gesture very rare for Cree adults and unashamedly symbolic of their relationship.

9. The positioning of the old man's son and his wife raises some interesting questions as to the ability of a non-native to acquire culturally appropriate intuitions for behavior. My husband, who has had limited contact with Indian people, drew an initial diagram of positioning in this interaction in which he reversed the positions of the man and woman. The intuition he applied was a European one, in which a man would always permit his wife to enter a room before him and to sit closer to the center of the interaction. In this case, the son would then be in direct alignment with his father and the wife closer to the audience and other participants.

I objected to this positioning as factually inaccurate as well as subjectively inappropriate to Cree culture. A woman is always considered secondary to her husband and her positioning will reflect this. Thus, the son entered the room and squatted unobtrusively on the floor to listen to his father. His wife followed him and stayed in the space remaining between him and the door. Their small child remained very close to her between the two parents. We tested our understanding of the role relationships involved by asking an unrelated native person working on the tape transcriptions to tell us where the two individuals would position themselves. She said without hesitation that the woman would follow her husband and remain behind him. The moral is that the anthropologist or other outsider can indeed learn to approximate the standards of the culture; there is no inherent reason why he cannot, given sufficient time and exposure to the culture, do so in a way which approximates that of the native member of the society.

10. Prose is used to record normal casual conversation. Formal or stylized speech is given in poetic lines to approximate the tone of the original.

11. This judgment was confirmed by other native speakers listening to the tapes. Marie-Louise had not used Cree regularly for some time, and although she frequently had heard formal narratives, she had probably never tried to translate them before.

12. The use of the proximate forms for the small but strong man throughout the narrative indicates the identification of the old man with this character. Although he himself was a large man by Cree standards, his feeling of inferiority toward the special powers Indians used to have (in mythological times as well as in the recent past) was unmistakable. The smallness, however, was balanced by strength which the old man felt he had, although he was otherwise a man of no special powers. The obviative forms used for the people met by the small but strong man show that the main character observes the events of the narrative as an outside observer. He is, so to speak, an eyewitness to great things which are part of the Cree heritage. The proximate–obviative distinction organizes the narrative in the sense that it eliminates confusion: the main hero who provides the plot line in his physical movement from one situation to another, is always the focus of the narrator's attention. The other people and events are further away and seen only in relation to the journey of the main character. The only exceptions come when the main character is not participating at all.

13. This part of the story reflects the recent migration of the Cree from the woodlands to the prairies. Many story motifs assume a wooded environment which is no longer familiar. This wooded hillock would, indeed, constitute an anomaly in the western Canadian prairies, perhaps the reason Marie-Louise does not know the word.

14. The old man was extremely concerned about the quality of his performance. In fact, he phoned about an hour later to ask how he sounded on the tape. By then we were expected to have discussed his performance and settled on an evaluation.

15. I would like to thank Marie-Louise Kortuem, Samuel Auger, and Noel Boscius for their patience and hospitality to a student of their traditional ways and of their language. Frances Thompson and Roy Cardinal aided in translation of the Cree text and Carl Urion in the transcription. I am also grateful to A. L. Vanek, who has served as aid and sounding board in many ways.

Field research was sponsored by the Boreal Institute of the University of Alberta. Transcription and analysis were supported by the Department of Indian Affairs and Northern Development (in conjunction with a course in Cree language) and the General Fund of the University of Alberta.

CHAPTER 15. ANALYSIS OF THE COURSE OF A JOKE'S TELLING

1. The examination of the joke itself will be reserved for a later report.
2. The transcript was produced by Gail Jefferson. The notational conventions which follow are hers.

/	indicates upward intonation
//	indicates point at which following line interrupts
(n.o.)	indicates pause of n.o. seconds
[	indicates simultaneous utterances when bridging two lines
( )	indicates something said but not transcribable
(word)	indicates probably what said, but not clear
but	indicates accent
emPLOYee	indicates heavy accent.

3. The descriptive sections offered to provide a general background for the discussion of our particular fragment could have a good deal of supporting data, which are available, presented with them. Both to put in such data and to make the general discussion, which they support, responsive to them in a detailed way, would far exceed the space and time available. That will be done, subject to the same constraints, subsequently, as has been done throughout the course of our research reports.

4. From a section in *True* magazine entitled 'This Funny Life,' June 1970, p. 68.

5. Independent and convergent critiques of an earlier draft by Erving Goffman, Mel Pollner, and Manny Schegloff occasioned very extensive revisions. Schegloff provided very considerable assistance during the course of the revisions but has not seen the final draft. The reader owes to them an absence of much error, and to me the errors that remain.

CHAPTER 16. WHEN WORDS BECOME DEEDS

1. The oratorical tradition is carried in all five of the northern Iroquoian languages (Mohawk, Oneida, Onondaga, Cayuga, and Seneca), although principally the last three. Forms are given in Cayuga unless otherwise indicated. The method of transcription used here is based on that developed for other Iroquoian languages (Lounsbury 1953; Chafe 1967), but modified to fit Cayuga. There are four oral vowel phonemes a, e, i, o and two nasal vowel phonemes ẽ, õ. Consonant phonemes consist of the stops t, k, the spirant s, the resonants r, n, and the laryngeals h and ?. There are two semivowels y, w. In brief, the stops are voiced and lenis before vowels and semivowels, voiceless, fortis, and released before consonants except r and ?. s is lenis and voiced before vowels and palatalized before y and r. In odd, unstressed syllables the laryngeals h and ? metathesize with the preceding vowel (written in these instances with upper case letters H and ?). Compare *kanóhõnyók*, the name of the Address, with *atetwatátnõHõnyõ?* 'we greet one another' (p. 360). The second syllable of *kanóhõnyók*, *nõh*, which is stressed and even, has changed position in the second word based on the same verb root. In that word it is in an odd and unstressed position and written *nõH*. This is a visual cue to remind the reader of the laryngeal metathesis, which in this case would yield a phonetic output of

[adedwadatnhŏŏnyŏʔ], where the doubling of the nasal ends up as lengthened ŏ:. However, when h is followed by a consonant or semivowel in an odd unstressed position only partial metathesis takes place, the preceding vowel becoming unvoiced and merging with features of the h as in *howayěnátěHtaʔ* 'his handiwork' (p. 359). Sequences such as *sh*, *tsh*, and *th* represent clusters and not digraphs. Length is indicated by a colon and stress by an acute accent. The spellings in note 18 are different from those used here and come from Speck (1949).

2. Some informants say that the English gloss derives from the Cayuga word for animal hide, *kanéhwaʔ*, and refers to the head of the water drum used in this ritual (cf. Speck 1949:138 and Chafe 1961:2, note 1). For reasons that will soon become apparent I reject the name 'Thanksgiving Dance' for this speech.

3. I owe the terms to W. N. Fenton (personal communication). The hierarchy is outlined in Table 13.

4. Cf. Speck 1949:34. I do not wish to give the impression that these are the only rituals concerned with beseeching and thanking. These notions are pervasive in Iroquois culture. In a longer analysis we should have to include at least the Great Feather Dance (cf. Shimony 1961:143) and some versions of the Men's Personal Chant (*atǒ:wěh*).

5. I use this term despite the uneven course that this concept has followed since Austin's initial formulation. Austin's distinction between constatives (sentences with truth values) and performatives (sentences without truth values but capable of being 'happy' or 'unhappy') did not survive the further development of his own analysis (see Austin 1965:Ch. 5ff), let alone the extended critiques by Searle (1968, 1969) and Q. Skinner (1970). Searle began with a notion raised by Austin that probably *all* utterances, even constatives, have some force as acts; and probably all utterances, even performatives, have 'propositional content.'

The problems raised by performative analysis have generated much interest in the field of philosophy itself. See, for instance, the articles adjoining Skinner's by J. R. Cameron and J. Houston in the same issue of *Philosophical Quarterly* (vol. 20, no. 79). There have also been linguistic treatments (Ross 1970; Richards 1971).

It was probably Hymes who first pointed out the relevance of Austin to an ethnographic approach to speaking in two brief references (1964a:37, 1964b:27) and a review (1965) of Austin's *How to do things with words*. Helen Hogan (1971) made use of the concept of performative verbs in her ethnography of communication among the Ashanti of West Africa, seemingly unaware of Austin, and there is another paper by Finnegan (1969) on the same geographic region. No one has gone further than Philip Ravenhill (1972) in exploring the strengths and weaknesses of Austin–Searle for cross-cultural comparison. Using data from Malinowski's *Coral gardens and their magic* (1935, vol. 2; see also Malinowski 1923), Ravenhill has effectively argued against an uncritical application of performative analysis, based on English, to other languages (and cultures).

6. The number of ceremonies varies from longhouse to longhouse. The author has collected extensive notes on the Seneca and Sour Springs longhouses at Six Nations Reserve. For other treatments see Morgan (1901:175ff), Parker (1913:81ff), Speck (1949), Fenton (1936, 1941), Shimony (1961:140ff), Blau (1969), Tooker (1970), Wallace (1970:50–8). This has been an area of major interest in Iroquois studies.

7. This holds true at least for the Sour Springs Longhouse. At the Seneca and Onondaga longhouses the Skin Dance is performed at both festivals, but the Tobacco Invocation is performed only at Midwinter.

8. Cf. generalizations by Morgan (1901:175) and Speck (1949:34). All of these statements are oversimplifications of a highly complex pattern which would be impossible to explain fully here.

9. This is a table of contents for an opening version of the Thanksgiving Address by Enos Williams. The precise order in which items are mentioned varies from speaker to speaker, although the overall inventory is the same and all speakers say they follow the principle of hierarchy. The problem in some cases is to determine relative age, height, and importance of items. A translation of section f on the trees is appended at the end of this chapter.

10. Given the Iroquois penchant for mnemonic devices reflected in their use of the Condolence Cane and the Handsome Lake Code sticks (see Fenton 1950 and a reconsideration of the problem in Fenton 1971), we might go so far as to suggest that the speeches serve as oral mnemonics for the complex ceremonial round.

11. By intonation I refer to the suprasegmental (or what Crystal [n.d.] prefers to call *non*-segmental) phenomena of stress, pitch, sonority, and rhythm. There is greater regularity of these phenomena in the Tobacco Invocation and the Skin Dance to the extent of creating an almost monotonous effect. The intonation of the Address is closer to that of ordinary conversation, i.e., it shows a greater variation in pitch range and rhythm. Intonation is more closely tied to syntax in the Address, to line structure in the Tobacco Invocation and Skin Dance. Line here refers to a unit which may be a phrase or clause, but is seldom a complete sentence and which has a distinct onset and termination (both marked by heavy stress). It is a unit of performance rather than grammar. In this paper lines are indicated in passages from speeches as they would be in poetry. For a discussion of this subject see Tedlock 1972.

12. The reason for saying *for* and *to* will become clear shortly.

13. This should serve as a warning when applying Austin–Searle cross-linguistically and cross-culturally. Actually, the *grammatical* form of Iroquoian and English performatives is quite similar, but the terms are semantically somewhat different, as are some of the 'preparatory conditions.' Chafe (1967:72, item 1261), who gives the meaning of the corresponding Seneca root *-noõnyõ-* as including 'rejoice in, express gratitude, greet, thank,' translates the word differently in different parts of Corbett Sundown's Thanksgiving Address (cf. Chafe 1961:17, sentence 11, vs. p. 157, item 73). The ambiguity is further attested to by the purely vocative forms based upon the same particle: *nya:wĕh* 'thank you/thanks' and *nya:wĕh skĕnõʔ*, the formal greeting.

14. Evidently Parker (1910:27) grasped the key role of performatives – without, of course, venturing into the problem theoretically – when he characterized an entire speech concerned with the cultivated foods as follows: 'In the Green Corn Thanksgiving the leader rises and says, "Diettinónnio' diohé'kon, *we give thanks to our sustainers.*"' The Seneca word 'Diettinónnio'' is equivalent to the Cayuga word *atyethinóhônyöʔ* we have been discussing.

There remains, at least logically, the problem of accounting for the validity of short versions, since the 'preparatory conditions' are omitted from mention. The speaker may feel justified in giving a short version at the end of a ceremonial day because the events of the day should by then have established a context in which the preparatory conditions are obvious. A long version would be rather redundant, whereas a long opening version partly helps to create the context in which ritual acts may validly take place.

15. The serial is used to express habitual activity and is indicated in *õtĕnitĕhthaʔ*

by the lack of a tense prefix marker and the suffix -*ha*ʾ. Indicative forms designate a single *act* in time, and we might say that serials, used as implicit performatives, designate an *activity* in time. Requests are made through the agency of extra-linguistic aids (smoke and dancing) and are, in a sense, processes rather than single events.

16. The translation is uncertain. It is possible that the form *swanéhŏh* is based on the same root as the word for the Skin Dance, *konéhŏ:*ʾ. We would then say that the segment *swa-* was the second-person plural pronomial prefix, the root was -*néhŏ-*, and the imperative was -*h*. But this cannot be stated definitively until the meaning of the name *konéhŏ:*ʾ is itself cleared up (cf. note 2).

17. This happens at least at two longhouses, Sour Springs at Six Nations and Tonawanda in New York state, during the Tobacco Invocation and Skin Dance. At Sour Springs the order of the Middle and Upper pantheons is reversed (although the order of items within the pantheons is the same). At Tonawanda, according to Chafe (1961:11 and personal communication) the whole 'sequence is recited first in reverse order and then repeated in the normal order.'

18. Use of the wrong name risks having the message go to the wrong recipient. It is said, for example, that Handsome Lake insisted on the change from *hawéni:yu* 'Controller' to *sŏgweadì:sŏ* 'Maker-of-our-bodies' – the Creator – because the anti-Creator, the Evil Minded Twin, could also be designated as 'Controller' (Speck 1949:29; spellings Speck's). Indian personal names present something of a problem since people usually address each other by their English names even when not speaking English, so there are often embarrassing pauses in formal longhouse announcements of rituals while the speaker tries to remember a performer's name.

19. This has frequently been pointed out for procedures of the Confederate Council where terms such as 'uncle' and 'nephew' are used to designate whole tribes, but many other examples could be adduced. The term *naʾtekĕnataHnŏ:te*ʾ 'they [zoic] are siblings' is used in the speeches to refer to classes of animate, non-human spirit forces (trees, animals, food plants, etc.). The speaker talks of classes of items rather than attempting to list them separately.

20. I am indebted to Mr Enos Williams, the late Howard Sky, Mrs Alta Doxtador, Mrs Greta Wright, and the whole Longhouse community at Six Nations Reserve in Ontario for helping me to understand a remarkable religious tradition. I am also grateful to Floyd G. Lounsbury, William N. Fenton, Wallace Chafe, Dell Hymes, Gordon Day, Barbara K. Foster, Joel Sherzer, and Regna Darnell, who in various ways have stimulated the thinking that went into this paper. Chafe's *Seneca Thanksgiving Rituals* (1961) provides meticulous Seneca data which parallel the Cayuga data I have collected. My research, which has been spread out over the last two and a half years, was initially sponsored by the National Science Foundation (GS 2909) and later by the National Museum of Man, National Museums of Canada (Ottawa).

CHAPTER 17. THE ETHNOGRAPHIC CONTEXT OF SOME
TRADITIONAL MAYAN SPEECH GENRES

1. The distinction between *k'op* and *loʾil* is equivalent to Voegelin's (1960) contrast between casual and non-casual speech.

2. The document was brought to my attention by James Hulse Rauh and Munro S. Edmonson.

3. This manuscript was photographed by Milt Machlin and Bob Marx during a visit to X-Cacal described in the May 1971 issue of *Argosy* magazine, in which they published the first two pages of the manuscript (Machlin & Marx 1971). I obtained a photocopy of the manuscript with the help of Marshall E. Durbin and Nelson A. Reed.

4. The fieldwork for this paper was supported by NIMH Predoctoral Fellowship MH-20, 345, Wenner-Gren Foundation Grant no. 2807, the Harvard Chiapas Project directed by Evon Z. Vogt, and grants from the Harvard Graduate Society and the Tulane University Council on Research. I am deeply grateful to those institutions for making the research possible.

To Munro S. Edmonson go my special thanks for his advice in translating the Yucatecan documents. I am grateful also to Eleuterio Póot Yah, who spent many hours helping me elicit, transcribe, and translate the Yucatecan data. The Tzotzil data are based on interviews with six informants; three of them, Domingo Pérez Hacienda, Domingo de la Torre Pérez, and José Hernández Gerónimo, deserve special mention for their immeasurable assistance with my research. Finally, I would like to express my appreciation to Dell Hymes, Robert M. Laughlin, and Michelle Zimbalist Rosaldo for their valuable suggestions for improving the paper.

CHAPTER 18. TO SPEAK WITH A HEATED HEART

1. More detail on Chamula world view and cosmology can be found in Gossen (1972a, 1974a). More extensive ethnographic data on Chamula appear in Pozas (1959) and Gossen (1974b).

2. See Gossen (1972b) for methodology and complete descriptions of all the genres. See papers by Victoria R. Bricker on Tzotzil-speaking Zinacantan and Brian Stross on Tzeltal-speaking Tenejapa, both in this volume, for comparative data on speech genres recognized in Maya Indian communities which are contiguous with Chamula.

3. *Grammatical parallelism* as I use it in this paper is one of the stylistic devices used to build *metaphorical couplets*. In particular it is the principal structural trait – same syntax in two consecutive lines, with one- and two-word substitutions in the second line – which characterizes what I call the *parallel metaphorical couplet*. Both this form and the *non-parallel metaphorical couplet* have dyadic semantic construction – same idea repeated with slightly different images in the second line. The two couplets differ in that the latter form does not have parallel syntax. There are other *dyadic constructions*, of which verbatim repetition, question and answer sets, verbal duel exchanges, and contrastive semantic sets (as in proverbs) are examples. Information in all of these dyadic constructions may be emphasized by means of the device which I call *metaphorical stacking*. Stacking is a form of message redundancy in which the speaker repeats critical information, usually in consecutive dyadic increments, until he achieves the desired emphasis. Metaphorical stacking is most typical of 'ancient words,' in which phrases referring to multivocal sacred symbols are the ones most commonly stacked for emphasis. However, stacking may also occur as an emphatic device in 'recent words' and in the marginal genres. Stacks composed of consecutive dual constructions which 'say' the same thing – or give different aspects of the same thing – may have as many as twenty lines (or ten couplets), the number depending upon the relative importance of the symbols being discussed.

4. Term used in Chiapas for people who are non-Indians from a cultural point of view.

5. My fieldwork in Chamula, state of Chiapas, Mexico, was undertaken at the suggestion of Professor Evon Z. Vogt, whose Harvard Chiapas Project is now approaching its fifteenth continuous year. I am grateful to him and numerous fieldworkers in this project for providing background linguistic knowledge and field facilities, as well as intellectual stimulation and encouragement while I was in the field. In the summer of 1965, I was supported by a National Science Foundation Cooperative Fellowship; in 1968–9 – the major portion of my fieldwork – I was supported by a predoctoral fellowship and an attached research grant from N.I.M.H. This financial support is gratefully acknowledged.

SECTION VI. INTRODUCTION

1. Thus Hymes' 1962 article is called 'The ethnography of speaking,' while the Gumperz and Hymes collection (1964) is entitled *The ethnography of communication*. For further discussion of the relationship between the ethnography of speaking and the ethnography of communication, see the preface to 'Toward linguistic competence' (Hymes 1973).

CHAPTER 19. DATA AND DATA USE IN AN ANALYSIS OF COMMUNICATIVE EVENTS

1. Spencer (1972, reported by Labov in 1972b) found that twenty graduate students in linguistics accepted exemplary sentences from 'classic' articles in linguistics which were not accepted by twenty graduate students in another field or by twenty non-academics. It may be that the injunction I suggest is redundant.

2. '... the rules of codification by which the deep structure of interpersonal relations is transformed into speech performances are independent of expressed attitudes and similar in nature to the grammatical rules operating on the level of intelligibility ... By accepting the native's view of what is and what is not properly part of a dialect or language, linguists have tended to assume these co-occurrences rather than investigate them empirically.' (Gumperz 1971:305–6).

3. There is no place, in this brief note, to expand these differences in a satisfactory manner. It can be noted, however, that sentences usually function as statements, questions, or imperatives and that a relatively parsimonious set of elements is involved in (syntactic) characterization of sentences in a language. There are in the case of, e.g., verbal strategies, an as yet unknown number of functions (though that number may turn out to be smaller than now appears to be the case). An equally ill-specified set of elements (which hopefully will also turn out to be parsimonious) will be involved in as yet unwritten grammars of verbal strategies. It may be that native members learn a grammar for performing verbal strategies that permits them to produce an infinite number of such strategies from a small set of elements in a manner analogous to that in which competent native speakers can produce infinitely varied sentences. An ethnology of speaking, like a universal grammar, will require attention to a competence–performance distinction and to issues paralleling those involved in the current controversy over generative *vs.* interpretive semantics. The precise nature of the problems to be confronted is only dimly sensed at this time.

4. This is again no place for a detailed argument. If, however, it is true that

sentences have primarily three functions, *viz.*, as statements, questions, or imperatives; it will be seen that even those twelve minimum functional categories used in Bales' (1950) 'interaction process analysis' constrain us to augur major problems on the level of observational adequacy.

5. It is true that there are now available a fairly substantial number of theoretical frames for analyzing strategies of verbal interaction and that these frames provide some selectional criteria. Each of these perspectives has illuminated some aspect of this behavior; each of the several scholars doing this work has used available data and has evolved his/her theoretical frame by getting 'immersed' in those data. None, however, has specified what kinds of data would provide critical tests of his own perspective. Since many months can be spent in analysis of a single strategy (e.g., doing reprimands – or requests) or just one speech event (e.g., a ritual greeting) with only one frame of analysis – this is not surprising. We are a very long way from 'enumeration of the class . . . of possible verbal strategies or speech events.'

Some linguists are now increasingly attending to social contexts of speech performance. It is likely that they will also find themselves using wider ranges of data – and that they will also have to undertake their activity with only minimal theoretical cues as to what data are most relevant.

6. For a brief review of Labov's discussion of intrasystemic (categorical, semi-categorical, and variable) rules and a comment on universals, see Grimshaw 1973a.

7. After writing this I read Labov (1972a), which contains an excellent discussion of types of data used by linguists (and sociolinguists) and their advantages and disadvantages.

8. Limitations of space make impossible the elaboration of these dimensions.

CHAPTER 20. THE ETHNOGRAPHY OF WRITING

1. As a general methodological premise for modern ethnography, this point has been made repeatedly in recent years. However, its relevance to the study of writing systems has not been explicitly noted. I am inclined to attribute this oversight to two major factors. On the one hand, cultural anthropologists have not been accustomed to view the description of writing systems as an exercise in ethnographic theory construction. On the other, students of writing only rarely look to modern anthropology for theories and methods that might enhance their own investigations. For further discussion of this point see Basso & Anderson 1973.

CHAPTER 21. WAYS OF SPEAKING

1. Newman's fine grammar, which exemplifies the mature methods of Sapir, has become the material of a virtual industry since the Second World War, having been restated and restructured in a number of papers and at least one book. The information considered here, however, has not been treated as relevant to linguistic theory, so far as I know – commentary enough on the loss of richness to linguistics with the eclipse of the Sapir tradition, which we must seek to restore.

2. Cf. a European case representative of many: 'L'accession rapide de l'élite de la société polonaise à l'humanisme, dans la seconde moitié du 16e siècle, posa de façon aiguë le problème des moyens d'expression. Pour les nouvelles aspirations artisitiques, seul le latin convenait avec ses ressources de vocabulaire, de syntaxe, de métrique et ses qualités d'abondance et de précision, tandis que le polonais

demeurait l'apanage d'un univers spirituel médiéval qui n'avait trouvé jusqu'alors qu'une expression fragmentaire et qui commençait tardivement a prendre un essor encore timide. L'auteur analyse les aspects de ce bilinguisme et son évolution jusqu'à la fin du 16e siècle, évolution au cours de laquelle un humanisme créateur a présidé à l'élaboration de la langue littéraire en Pologne' (Backvis 1958). Cf. Jones 1953 on English in the same period.

3. This paper forms the basis of a section in a book on the concept of language which I am preparing for the 'Key concepts in the social sciences' series published by Harper and Row.

REFERENCES

PREFACE

Bright, W. (1966). *Sociolinguistics*. The Hague.

Ervin-Tripp, S. (1969). Sociolinguistics. In L. Berkowitz (ed.), *Advances in experimental social psychology*, vol. 4. New York. 91–165.

Grimshaw, A. (1973). Sociolinguistics. In W. Schramm, I. Pool, N. Maccoby, E. Park, F. Frey and L. Fein (eds.), *Handbook of communication*. Chicago, 49–92.

Gumperz, J. J. (1962). Types of linguistic communities. *Anthropological Linguistics* 4:28–40.

  (1964). Linguistic and social interaction in two communities. In Gumperz and Hymes 1964:137–54.

  (1972). Introduction. In Gumperz and Hymes 1972:1–25.

Gumperz, J. J. and Hymes, D. (eds.). (1964). *The ethnography of communication*. *American Anthropologist* 66(6), part 2.

  (eds.) (1972). *Directions in sociolinguistics: the ethnography of communication*. New York.

Hymes, D. (1961a). Linguistic aspects of cross-cultural personality study. In B. Kaplan (ed.), *Studying personality cross-culturally*. New York. 313–59.

  (1961b). Functions of speech: an evolutionary approach. In F. C. Gruber (ed.), *Anthropology and education*. Philadelphia. 55–83.

  (1962). The ethnography of speaking. In T. Gladwin and W. C. Sturtevant (eds.), *Anthropology and human behavior*. Washington, D.C. 13–53.

  (1964a). Directions in (ethno-) linguistic theory. In A. K. Romney and R. G. D'Andrade (eds.), *Transcultural studies in cognition*. *American Anthropologist* 66(3), part 2:6–56.

  (1964b). Introduction: toward ethnographies of communication. In Gumperz and Hymes 1964:1–34.

  (1966). On 'anthropological linguistics' and congeners. *American Anthropologist* 68:143–53.

  (1967). Models of the interaction of language and social setting. *Journal of Social Issues* 23(2):8–28.

  (1970). Linguistic method in ethnography: its development in the United States. In P. L. Garvin (ed.), *Method and theory in linguistics*. The Hague. 249–325.

  (1971). Sociolinguistics and the ethnography of speaking. In E. Ardener (ed.), *Social anthropology and linguistics*. London. 47–93.

  (1972). Models of the interaction of language and social life. In Gumperz and Hymes 1972:35–71.

Sherzer, J. and Darnell, R. (1972). Outline guide for the ethnographic study of speech use. In Gumperz and Hymes 1972:548–54.

475

Slobin, D. I. (ed.) (1967). *A field manual for cross-cultural study of the acquisition of communicative competence*. Berkeley, Calif.

INTRODUCTION

Abrahams, R. D. (1967). The shaping of folkloric traditions in the British West Indies. *Journal of Inter-American Studies* 9:456–80.
  (1972). Talking my talk: Black English and social segmentation in Black communities. *Florida F/L Reporter* 10:29–38.
Abrahams, R. D. and Bauman, R. (1971). Sense and nonsense in St. Vincent: speech behavior and decorum in a Caribbean community. *American Anthropologist* 73:762–72.
Alexander, S. (1920). *Space, time and deity*. 2 vols. New York.
Bauman, R. (1971). An ethnographic framework for the investigation of communicative behaviors. *Asha* 13:334–40.
  (1974). Quaker folk linguistics and folklore. In Ben-Amos and Goldstein 1974. 255–63.
Ben-Amos, D. and Goldstein, K. (eds.) (1974). *Folklore: performance and communication*. The Hague.
Cazden, C. B., John, V. P. and Hymes, D. (eds.) (1972). *Functions of language in the classroom*. New York.
Chomsky, N. (1965). *Aspects of the theory of syntax*. Cambridge, Mass.
Cicourel, A. (1970). The acquisition of social structure: toward a developmental sociology of language and meaning. In J. R. Douglas (ed.), *Understanding everyday life*. Chicago. 136–68.
Dundes, A. and Arewa, E. O. (1964). Proverbs and the ethnography of speaking. In Gumperz and Hymes 1964:70–85.
Dundes, A., Leach, J. W. and Özkök, B. (1972). The strategy of Turkish boys' verbal dueling rhymes. In Gumperz and Hymes 1972:130–60.
Fillmore, C. J. and Langendoen, D. T. (eds.) (1971). *Studies in linguistic semantics*. New York.
Frake, C. (1964). Notes on queries in ethnography. In A. K. Romney and R. G. D'Andrade (eds.), *Transcultural studies in cognition. American Anthropologist* 66(3), part 2:132–45.
Garfinkel, H. (1967). *Studies in ethnomethodology*. Englewood Cliffs, N.J.
Goffman, E. (1961). *Encounters*. Indianapolis.
  (1964). The neglected situation. In Gumperz and Hymes 1964:133–36.
  (1971). *Relations in public*. New York.
Goodenough, W. H. (1957). Cultural anthropology and linguistics. In P. L. Garvin (ed.), *Report of the Seventh Annual Round Table Meeting on Linguistics and Language Study* (Georgetown University Monograph Series on Languages and Linguistics 9). Washington, D.C. 167–73.
Gumperz, J. J. (1964). Linguistic and social interaction in two communities. In Gumperz and Hymes 1964:137–53.
  (1967). On the linguistic markers of bilingual communication. *Journal of Social Issues* 23(2):48–57.
Gumperz, J. J. and Herasimchuk, E. (1973). The conversational analysis of social meaning: a study of classroom interaction. In R. Shuy (ed.), *Sociolinguistics: current trends and prospects* (Georgetown University Monograph Series on Languages and Linguistics 25). Washington, D.C. 99–134.
Gumperz, J. J. and Hymes, D. (eds.) (1964). *The ethnography of communication. American Anthropologist* 66(6), part 2.

References 477

(eds.) (1972). *Directions in sociolinguistics: the ethnography of communication.* New York.

Hymes, D. (1961). Linguistic aspects of cross-cultural personality study. In B. Kaplan (ed.), *Studying personality cross-culturally.* New York. 313–59.

(1962). The ethnography of speaking. In T. Gladwin and W. C. Sturtevant (eds.), *Anthropology and human behavior.* Washington, D.C. 13–53.

(1964). Introduction: toward ethnographies of communication. In Gumperz and Hymes 1964:1–34.

(1966). Two types of linguistic relativity. In W. Bright (ed.), *Sociolinguistics.* The Hague. 114–65.

(1967). Models of the interaction of language and social setting. *Journal of Social Issues* 23(2):8–28.

(1970a). Bilingual education: linguistic vs. sociolinguistic bases. In J. E. Alatis (ed.), *Bilingualism and language contact* (Georgetown University Monograph Series on Languages and Linguistics 23). Washington, D.C. 69–76.

(1970b). Linguistic method in ethnography: its development in the United States. In P. L. Garvin (ed.), *Method and theory in linguistics.* The Hague. 249–325.

(1971a). Competence and performance in linguistic theory. In R. Huxley and E. Ingram (eds.), *Language acquisition: models and methods.* New York. 3–24.

(ed.). (1971b). *Pidginization and creolization of languages.* Cambridge and New York.

(1972). Models of the interaction of language and social life. In Gumperz and Hymes 1972:35–71.

(1973). The scope of sociolinguistics. In R. Shuy (ed.), *Sociolinguistics: current trends and prospects* (Georgetown University Monograph Series on Languages and Linguistics 25). Washington, D.C. 313–33.

Jacobs, R. A. and Rosenbaum, P. S. (eds.) (1970). *Readings in English transformational grammar.* Waltham, Mass.

Kochman, T. (1969). Social factors in the consideration of teaching Standard English. *Florida F/L Reporter* 7:87–8 and continued.

Labov, W. (1966). *The social stratification of English in New York City.* Washington, D.C.

(1970). The study of language in its social context. *Studium Generale* 23:30–87.

Lakoff, R. (1972). Language in context. *Language* 48:907–27.

McHugh, P. (1968). *Defining the situation.* Indianapolis.

Paredes, A. and Bauman, R. (eds.) (1972). *Toward new perspectives in folklore.* Austin, Texas.

Philips, S. U. (1970). Acquisition of rules for appropriate speech usage. In J. E. Alatis (ed.), *Bilingualism and language contact* (Georgetown University Monograph Series on Languages and Linguistics 23). Washington, D.C. 77–101.

Reisman, K. (1970). Cultural and linguistic ambiguity in a West Indian village. In N. Whitten and J. Szwed (eds.), *Afro-American anthropology.* New York.

Rosaldo, M. Z. (1973). I have nothing to hide: the language of Ilongot oratory. *Language in Society* 2:193–223.

Rosenberg, J. F. and Travis, C. (eds.) (1971). *Readings in the philosophy of language.* Englewood Cliffs, N.J.

Sacks, H. (1972). On the analyzability of stories by children. In Gumperz and Hymes 1972:325–45.

Schegloff, E. A. (1972). Sequencing in conversational openings. In Gumperz and Hymes 1972:346–80.

Sherzer, J. (1973). On linguistic semantics and linguistic subdisciplines: a review article. *Language in Society* 2:269–89.

Sherzer, J. and Bauman, R. (1972). Areal studies and culture history: language as a key to the historical study of culture contact. *Southwest Journal of Anthropology* 28:131–52.

Shuy, R. (MS.). Sociolinguistics and medical history. Presented at the Third International Conference on Applied Linguistics, Copenhagen. To appear in *Proceedings*.

Sudnow, D. (ed.). (1972). *Studies in social interaction*. New York.

Vološinov, V. N. (1973). *Marxism and the philosophy of language*. New York.

Wallace, A. F. C. (1970). *Culture and personality*, 2nd ed. New York.

Weinreich, U., Labov, W. and Herzog, M. (1968). Empirical foundations for a theory of language change. In W. P. Lehmann and Y. Malkiel (eds.), *Directions for historical linguistics*. Austin, Texas. 95–188.

SECTION II INTRODUCTION

Labov, W. (1966). *The social stratification of English in New York City*. Washington, D.C.

Wallace, A. F. C. (1970). *Culture and personality*, 2nd ed. New York.

CHAPTER 1. A QUANTITATIVE PARADIGM FOR THE STUDY OF COMMUNICATIVE COMPETENCE

Bailey, B. L. (1971). Jamaican creole: can dialect boundaries be defined? In D. Hymes (ed.), *Pidginization and creolization of languages*. Cambridge. 341–8.

Bailey, C.-J. N. (1969–70). Studies in three-dimensional linguistic theory: (1) Some implicational phenomena in dialectology. (2) Implicational scales in diachronic linguistics and dialectology. (3) Lectal groupings in matrices generated with waves defined along the temporal parameter. (4) Mesomodels of linguistic change. *University of Hawaii Working Papers in Linguistics* 1/8:105–38; 1/10: 245–9; 2/4:109–24; 2/6:149–56; 2/8:1–4.

(1970). Building rate into a dynamic theory of linguistic description. *University of Hawaii Working Papers in Linguistics* 2/9:161–233.

(1971). Trying to talk in the new paradigm. *University of Hawaii Working Papers in Linguistics* 1/5:111–37.

(1972). The patterning of language variation. To appear in R. W. Bailey and J. L. Robinson (eds.), *Varieties of present-day American English*. New York.

Bickerton, D. (1971). Inherent variability and variable rules. *Foundations of Language* 7:457–92.

Bloch, B. (1948). A set of postulates for phonemic analysis. *Language* 24:3–46.

Brunel, G. (1970). Le français radiophonique à Montréal. M.A. thesis, Université de Montréal.

Cedergren, H. (1972). Interplay of social and linguistic factors in Panama. Ph.D. thesis, Cornell University.

(1973). On the nature of variable constraints. In C.-J. N. Bailey and R. W. Shuy (eds.), *New ways of analyzing variation in English*. Washington, D.C. 13–22.

Cedergren, H. and Sankoff, D. (1974). Variable rules: performance as a statistical reflection of competence. *Language* 50:333–55.

Day, R. (1971). A study in syntactic variation: the copula in Hawaii. Paper read at American Anthropological Association Annual Meeting.

DeCamp, D. (1971). Toward a generative analysis of a post-creole speech continuum. In D. Hymes (ed.), *Pidginization and creolization of languages*. Cambridge. 349–70.

(1973). What do implicational scales imply? In C.-J. N. Bailey and R. W. Shuy (eds.), *New ways of analyzing variation in English*. Washington, D.C. 141–8.

Elliot, D., Legum, S. and Thompson, S. A. (1969). Syntactic variation as linguistic data. In R. Binnick *et al.* (eds.), *Papers from the fifth regional meeting, Chicago Linguistic Society*. Chicago. 52–9.

Ervin-Tripp, S. (1972). On sociolinguistic rules: alternation and co-occurrence. In J. J. Gumperz and D. Hymes (eds.), *Directions in sociolinguistics*. New York. 213–50.

Fischer, J. L. (1958). Social influence in the choice of a linguistic variant. *Word* 14:47–56.

Gumperz, J. J. (1962). Types of linguistic communities. *Anthropological Linguistics* 4:28–40.

(1964). Linguistic and social interaction in two communities. *American Anthropologist* 66(6), pt. 2:137–53.

(1965). Linguistic repertoires, grammars, and second language instruction. In C. W. Kreidler (ed.), *Report of the Sixteenth Annual Round Table Meeting on Linguistics and Language Study* (Georgetown University Monograph Series on Languages and Linguistics 18). Washington, D.C. 81–90.

(1968). The speech community. *International Encyclopedia of Social Sciences*. New York. Vol. 9: 381–6.

Halliday, M. A. K. (1964). The users and uses of language. In M. A. K. Halliday, A. McIntosh and P. Strevens (eds.), *The linguistic sciences and language teaching*. London.

Hockett, C. F. (1950). Age-grading and linguistic continuity. *Language* 26:449–57.

Hymes, D. (1962). The ethnography of speaking. In T. Gladwin and W. C. Sturtevant (eds.), *Anthropology and human behavior*. Washington, D.C. 13–53.

(1967). Models of the interaction of language and social setting. *Journal of Social Issues* 23(2):8–28.

(1968). Linguistic problems in defining the concept of 'tribe.' In J. Helm (ed.), *Essays on the problem of tribe*. Seattle. 23–48.

(1969). Functions of speech and linguistic theory. In *International days of sociolinguistics*. Rome. 111–44.

(1972a). Models of the interaction of language and social life. In J. J. Gumperz and D. Hymes (eds.), *Directions in sociolinguistics*. New York. 35–71.

(1972b). Towards communicative competence. MS.

Jakobson, R. (1960). Concluding statement: linguistics and poetics. In T. A. Sebeok (ed.), *Style in language*. New York. 350–73.

Laberge, S. and Chiasson-Lavoie, M. (1971). Attitudes face au français parlé à Montréal et degrés de conscience de variables linguistiques. In R. Darnell (ed.), *Linguistic diversity in Canadian society*. Edmonton. 89–126.

Labov, W. (1965). On the mechanism of linguistic change. In C. W. Kreidler (ed.), *Report of the Sixteenth Annual Round Table Meeting on Linguistics and Language Study* (Georgetown University Monograph Series on Languages and Linguistics 18). Washington, D.C. 91–114.

(1966). *The social stratification of English in New York City*. Washington, D.C.

(1969). Contraction, deletion, and inherent variability of the English copula. *Language* 45:715–62.

(1970). The study of language in its social context. *Studium Generale* 23:30–87.

(1971). Methodology. In W. O. Dingwall (ed.), *A survey of linguistic science.* College Park, Md.: University of Maryland, Linguistics Program. 412–97.

(1973). Where do grammars stop? In R. Shuy (ed.), *Sociolinguistics: current trends and prospects* (Georgetown University Monograph Series on Languages and Linguistics 25). Washington, D.C. 43–88.

Labov, W., Cohen, P., Robins, C., and Lewis, J. (1968). A study of the nonstandard English of Negro and Puerto Rican speakers in New York City. New York: Columbia University, Department of Linguistics, Cooperative Research Report 3288.

Lefebvre, C. (1971). La sélection des codes linguistiques à la Martinique: un modèle de communication. M.A. thesis, Université de Montréal.

Ma, R. and Herasimchuk, E. (1968). The linguistic dimensions of a bilingual neighborhood. In J. Fishman, R. L. Cooper, R. Ma *et al.* (eds.), *Bilingualism in the barrio.* New York.

Mitchell-Kernan, C. (1971). *Language behavior in a Black urban community.* Berkeley: Monographs of the Language Behavior Research Laboratory, University of California, Berkeley, no. 2.

Picard, M. (1972). Schwa deletion in function words in Canadian French. Paper read at the Annual Meeting of the Canadian Linguistic Association.

Ross, J. R. (1972). The category squish: endstation Hauptwort. In P. M. Peranteau, J. N. Levi and G. C. Phares (eds.), *Papers from the eighth regional meeting, Chicago Linguistic Society.* Chicago. 316–28.

(1973). The fake NP squish. In C.-J. N. Bailey and R. W. Shuy (eds.), *New ways of analyzing variation in English.* Washington, D.C. 96–140.

Sag, I. A. (1973). On the state of progress on progressives and statives. In C.-J. N. Bailey and R. W. Shuy (eds.), *New ways of analyzing variation in English.* Washington, D.C. 83–95.

Saint-Pierre, M. (1969). Problèmes de diglossie dans un bourg martiniquais. M.A. thesis, Université de Montréal.

Sankoff, D. and Rousseau, P. (in press). A method for assessing variable rule and implicational scale analyses of linguistic variation. To appear in L. Mitchell (ed.), *Computers in the Humanities.* Edinburgh.

Sankoff, D. and Sankoff, G. (1973). Sample survey methods and computer assisted analysis in the study of grammatical variation. In R. Darnell (ed.), *Canadian languages in their social context.* Edmonton. 7–63.

Sankoff, G. (1968). Social aspects of multilingualism in New Guinea. Ph.D. thesis, McGill University.

(1969). Mutual intelligibility, bilingualism, and linguistic boundaries. In *International days of sociolinguistics.* Rome. 839–48.

(1971). Quantitative analysis of sharing and variability in a cognitive model. *Ethnology* 10:389–408.

(1972a). Cognitive variability and New Guinea social organization: the Buang *dgwa. American Anthropologist* 74:555–66.

(1972b). Language use in multilingual societies: some alternative approaches. In J. Pride and J. Holmes (eds.), *Sociolinguistics.* London. 33–51.

(1973). Above and beyond phonology in variable rules. In C.-J. N. Bailey and R. W. Shuy (eds.), *New ways of analyzing variation in English.* Washington, D.C. 44–66.

Sankoff, G. and Cedergren, H. (1971). Some results of a sociolinguistic study of Montreal French. In R. Darnell (ed.), *Linguistic diversity in Canadian society.* Edmonton. 61–87.

Sankoff, G. and Laberge, S. (1973). On the acquisition of native speakers by a language. *Kivung* (Journal of Linguistic Society in Papuan New Guinea) 6:32–47.

Sankoff, G., Sarrasin, R. and Cedergren, H. (1971). Quelques considérations sur la distribution de la variable QUE dans le français de Montréal. Paper read at the Congrès de l'Association canadienne-française pour l'Avancement des Sciences.

Shuy, R., Wolfram, W. A. and Riley, W. K. (1968). *Field techniques in an urban language study.* Washington, D.C.

Weinreich, U., Labov, W. and Herzog. M. (1968). Empirical foundations for a theory of language change. In W. P. Lehmann and Y. Malkiel (eds.), *Directions for historical linguistics.* Austin, Tex. 97–195.

Wolfram, A. (1969). *Detroit Negro speech.* Washington, D.C.

CHAPTER 2. IDENTITY OF THE COLOMBIAN VAUPÉS INDIANS

Atlas de Colombia (1969). Instituto geográfico 'Agustín Codazzi.' Bogotá.

Barth, F. (1964). Ethnic processes on the Pathan-Baluch boundary. In G. Redard (ed.), *Indo-Iranica.* Wiesbaden.

(1969). Introduction. In F. Barth (ed.), *Ethnic groups and boundaries.* New York.

Basso, E. (1973). The use of Portuguese relationship terms in Kalapalo (Xingu Carib) encounters: changes in a central Brazilian communications network. *Language in Society* 2:1–21.

Blom, J.-P. (1969). Ethnic and cultural differentiation. In F. Barth (ed.), *Ethnic groups and boundaries.* New York.

Blom, J.-P. and Gumperz, J. J. (1972). Social meaning in linguistic structures: Code-switching in Norway. In J. J. Gumperz and D. Hymes (eds.), *Directions in sociolinguistics: the ethnography of communication.* New York.

Brüzzi Alves da Silva, A. (1962). *A civilização indígena do Uaupes.* Saõ Paulo.

Chomsky, N. (1965). *Aspects of the theory of syntax.* Cambridge, Mass.

Ervin-Tripp, S. (1972). On sociolinguistic rules: alternation and co-occurrence. In J. J. Gumperz and D. Hymes (eds.), *Directions in sociolinguistics: the ethnography of communication.* New York.

Ferguson, C. (1959). Diglossia. *Word* 15:325–40.

Giacone, A. (1965). *Gramática, dicionario e fraseologia da lingua Dahceie ou Tucano.* Belem-Para.

Goldman, I. (1948). Tribes of the Uaupés-Caquetá region. *BAE Bull.* 143(3):763–98.

(1963). *The Cubeo: Indians of the Northwest Amazon.* Illinois Studies in Anthropology 2. Urbana.

Goodenough, W. H. (1971). *Culture, language and society.* A McCaleb Module. Reading, Mass.

Greenberg, J. (1960). The general classification of Central and South American languages. In A. Wallace (ed.), *Selected papers, International Congress of Anthropological and Ethnological Sciences.* Philadelphia. 791–4.

Gumperz, J. (1962). Types of linguistic communities. *Anthropological Linguistics* 4:28–40. Reprinted 1970 in J. Fishman (ed.), *Readings in the sociology of language.* The Hague. 460–72.

(1964). Hindi-Punjabi code-switching in Delhi. In H. Lunt (ed.), *Proceedings of the Ninth International Congress of Linguists*. The Hague. 1115–24.

(1968). The speech community. *International Encyclopedia of the Social Sciences* 9:381–6. Reprinted 1971 in *Language in social groups: essays by John J. Gumperz*. Stanford.

(1969). Communication in multilingual societies. In S. Tyler (ed.), *Cognitive anthropology*. New York. 435–48.

Gumperz, J. and Wilson, R. (1971). Convergence and creolization: a case from the Indo-Aryan/Dravidian border in India. In D. Hymes (ed.), *Pidginization and creolization*. Cambridge. 151–67.

Helm, J. (ed.) (1968). *Essays on the problem of tribe. Proceedings of the 1967 Annual Spring Meeting of the American Ethnological Society*. Seattle.

Hymes, D. (1962). The ethnography of speaking. In T. Gladwin and W. C. Sturtevant (eds.), *Anthropology and human behavior*. Washington, D.C. Reprinted 1968 in J. Fishman (ed.), *Readings in the sociology of language*. The Hague. 99–138.

(1967). Models of the interaction of language and social setting. In John Macnamara (ed.), *Problems of bilingualism. Journal of Social Issues* 23(2):8–28.

(1968). Linguistic problems in defining the concept of 'tribe.' In J. Helm (ed.), *Essays on the problem of tribe*. Seattle. 23–48.

Jackson, J. (1972). Marriage and linguistic identity among the Bará Indians of the Vaupés, Colombia. Ph.D. dissertation, Stanford University.

Koch-Grünberg, T. (1909–10). *Zwei Jahre unter den Indianern Reisen in Nordwest Brasilien*. Berlin.

Kök, P. (1921–2). Ensayo de gramática Dagseye o Tokano. *Anthropos*, vols. 16–17.

Labov, W. (1966). *The social stratification of English in New York City*. Washington, D.C.

Lambert, W. (1967). A psychology of bilingualism. *Journal of Social Issues* 23(2): 91–109.

Owen, R. (1965). Patrilocal band: a linguistic and cultural heterogeneous unit. *American Anthropologist* 67:675–90.

Reichel-Dolmatoff, G. (1971). *Amazonian cosmos: the sexual and religious symbolism of the Tukano Indians*. Chicago.

Rodríguez Bermudez, J. (1962). Informe de la división de asuntos Indígenas, *Memoria del Ministro de Gobierno al Congreso de 1962*:76–7. Bogotá.

Rubin, J. (1968). *National bilingualism in Paraguay*. The Hague.

Sankoff, G. (1968). Social aspects of multilingualism in New Guinea. Unpublished . Ph.D. dissertation, McGill University.

Sorensen, A. (1967). Multilingualism in the Northwest Amazon. *American Anthropologist* 69(6):670–82.

(1969). The morphology of Tukano. Ph.D. dissertation, Columbia University. University Microfilms, Inc., Ann Arbor, Mich. 1970.

(1970). Multilingualism in the Northwest Amazon: Papurí and Piraparaná regions. Paper given at the Thirty-ninth International Congress of Americanists, Lima.

CHAPTER 3. 'OUR ANCESTORS SPOKE IN PAIRS'

Boodberg, P. (1954). Syntactical metaplasia in stereoscopic parallelism. *Cedules from a Berkeley Workshop in Asiatic Philology*. 017–541210.

Coolhaas, W. P. (1971). *Generale Missiven van Gouverneurs-Generaalen Raden aan*

Heren XVII der Verenigde Oostindische Compagnie, vol. IV, 1675–1685. The Hague.

Edmonson, M. S. (1970). Notes on a new translation of the Popul Vuh. *Alcheringa* 1:14–23.

Evans, I. H. N. (1953). *Religion of the Tempasuk Dusun of North Borneo.* Cambridge.

Fox, J. J. (1971a). Semantic parallelism in Rotinese ritual language. *Bijdragen tot de Taal-, Land- en Volkenkunde* 127:215–55.

  (1971b). Sister's child as plant: metaphors in an idiom of consanguinity. In R. Needham (ed.), *Rethinking kinship and marriage.* London. 219–52.

  (1971c). A Rotinese dynastic genealogy: structure and event. In T. Beidelman (ed.), *The translation of culture.* London. 37–77.

  (1972a). The Ndaonese. In F. Le Bar (ed.), *Ethnic groups of insular Southeast Asia.* New Haven, Conn.

  (1972b). The Helong. In F. Le Bar (ed.), *Ethnic groups of insular Southeast Asia.* New Haven, Conn.

  (MS.). Dictionary of Rotinese formal dyadic language.

Hardeland, A. (1858). *Versuch einer Grammatik der Dajackschen Sprache.* Amsterdam.

Heijmering, G. (1843–4). Zeden en gewoonten op het eiland Roti. *Tijdschrift voor Nederlandsch-Indië* V(ii): 531–49, 623–39; VI(i): 81–98, 353–67.

Jakobson, R. (1966). Grammatical parallelism and its Russian facet. *Language* 42:398–429.

Jonker, J. C. G. (1908). *Rotineesch-Hollandsch Woordenboek.* Leiden.

  (1913). Bijdrage tot de Kennis der Rottineesche Tongvallen. *Bijdragen tot de Taal-, Land- en Volkenkunde* 68:521–622.

  (1915). *Rottineesche Spraakkunst.* Leiden.

Kate, H. F. C. ten (1894). *Verslag eener Reis in de Timorgroep en Polynesië.* Leiden.

Kramer, F. W. (1970). *Literature among the Cuna Indians* (Etnologiska Studier 30). Göteborg.

Lowth, R. (1753). *De sacra poesia hebraeorum.* Oxford.

  (1779). *Isaiah X-XI.* London.

Manafe, D. P. (1889). Akan Bahasa Rotti. *Bijdragen tot de Taal-, Land- en Volkenkunde* 38:634–48.

Pollen, D. A., Lee, J. R. and Taylor, J. (1971). How does the striate cortex begin the reconstruction of the visual world? *Science* 173:74–7.

Sherzer, D. and Sherzer, J. (1972). Literature in San Blas: discovering Cuna Ikala. *Semiotica* 6:182–99.

CHAPTER 4. WARM SPRING 'INDIAN TIME'

Ervin-Tripp, S. (1972). On sociolinguistic rules: alternation and co-occurrence. In J. Gumperz and D. Hymes (eds.), *Directions in sociolinguistics.* New York. 213–50.

Frake, C. (1964). How to ask for a drink in Subanun. In J. J. Gumperz and D. Hymes (eds.), *The ethnography of communication. American Anthropologist* 66(6), part 2:127–32.

French, K. (1955). Culture segments and variation in contemporary social ceremonialism on the Warm Springs Reservation, Oregon. Ph.D. dissertation, Columbia University.

Goffman, E. (1963). *Behavior in public places.* New York.

Hall, E. T. (1959). *The silent language.* New York.

Hallowell, A. I. (1937). Temporal orientation in western civilization and a preliterate society. *American Anthropologist* 39:647–70.

Hymes, D. (1971). Competence and performance in linguistic theory. In R. Huxley and E. Ingram (eds.), *Language acquisition: models and methods*. London and New York. 3–24.

Philips, S. U. (1972). Participant structures and communicative competence; Warm Springs children in community and classroom. In C. B. Cazden, V. P. John and D. Hymes (eds.), *Functions of language in the classroom*. New York. 370–94.

Schegloff, E. A. (1972). Sequencing in conversational openings. In J. J. Gumperz and D. Hymes (eds.), *Directions in sociolinguistics*. New York. 346–80.

Spier, L. (1935). *The prophet dance of the Northwest and its derivates*. General Series in Anthropology, no. 1. Menasha, Wisc.

Steiner, S. (1968). *The new Indians*. New York.

Whorf, B. L. (1950). An American Indian model of the universe. *International Journal of American Linguistics* 16:67–72.

CHAPTER 5. CONTRAPUNTAL CONVERSATIONS IN AN ANTIGUAN VILLAGE

Abrahams, R. (1962). Playing the dozens. *Journal of American Folklore* 75:209–20.

Alleyne, M. (1963). Communication and politics in Jamaica. *Caribbean Studies* 3(2):22–61.

Basso, K. (1970). 'To give up on words': silence in Western Apache culture. *Southwestern Journal of Anthropology* 26:213–30.

Bohannan, L. (1954). *Return to laughter*. New York.

Calame-Griaule, G. (1963). L'art de la parole dans la culture africaine. *Présence Africaine* 47 (3 trimestre):73–91.

Cassidy, F. G. and LePage, R. G. (1967). *Dictionary of Jamaican English*. Cambridge.

Fernandez, J. (1967). Revitalized words from 'The Parrot's Egg' and 'The Bull that Crashes in the Kraal': African cult sermons. In J. Helm (ed.), *Essays on the verbal and visual arts*. Seattle, Wash. 45–63.

Goodman, P. (1963). *Making do*. New York.

Goveia, E. (1965). *Slave society in the British Leeward Islands*. New Haven, Conn.

Herzog, G. and Blooah, C. G. (1936). *Jabo proverbs from Liberia*. London.

Hymes, D. (1967). Models of the interaction of language and social setting. *Journal of Social Issues* 23(2):8–28.

(MS.). On communicative competence.

Jakobson, R. (1966). Grammatical parallelism and its Russian facet. *Language* 42:399–429.

Khuri, F. (1968). The etiquette of bargaining in the Middle East. *American Anthropologist* 70(4):698–706.

Lamming, G. (1960). *The pleasures of exile*. London.

Lauria, A. (1964). 'Respeto,' 'Relajo' and interpersonal relations in Puerto Rico. *Anthropological Quarterly* 37:53–67.

Levin, H. (1950). Notes on convention. In H. Levin (ed.), *Perspectives of criticism*. Cambridge, Mass.

Mintz, S. (1971). The socio-historical background to pidginization and creolization. In D. Hymes (ed.), *Pidginization and creolization of languages*. Cambridge. 481–96.

Reisman, K. (1970). Cultural and linguistic ambiguity in a West Indian village. In N. Whitten and J. Szwed (eds.), *Afro-American anthropology*. New York. 129–44.

Smith, R. T. (1956). *The Negro family in British Guiana.* London.
Swartz, M. J. (1969). The cultural dynamics of blows and abuse among the Bena of southern Tanzania: a study of dominant symbols in everyday life. In R. Spencer (ed.), *Forms of symbolic action.* Seattle. 126–33.
Wilson, P. (1969). Reputation and respectability: a suggestion for Caribbean ethnology. *Man* 4:70–84.

CHAPTER 6. NORM-MAKERS, NORM-BREAKERS

Block, M. (MS.). *Why do Malagasy cows speak French?*
Goffman, E. (1971). *Relations in public.* New York.

CHAPTER 7. SPEAKING IN THE LIGHT

Adamson, W. (1656). *An answer to a book, titled Quakers principles quaking.* London.
Aynsloe, J. (1672). *A short description of the true ministers and the false.* [N.p.].
Banks, J. (1798). *A journal of the life . . . of . . . John Banks.* London.
Barclay, D. (1831). *An apology for the true Christian divinity.* New York.
Barclay, J. (1833). *Select anecdotes . . . of the Society of Friends.* New York.
Basso, K. (1970). 'To give up on words': silence in Western Apache culture. *Southwestern Journal of Anthropology* 26:213–30.
Bauman, R. (1970). Aspects of Quaker rhetoric. *Quarterly Journal of Speech* 56:67–74.
   (1972). Quakers, seventeenth century. In R. Darnell (ed.), *Prolegomena to typologies of speech use.* Texas Working Papers in Sociolinguistics, Special Number, March 1972.
   (1974). Quaker folk-linguistics and folklore. In D. Ben-Amos and K. Goldstein (eds.), *Folklore: performance and communication.* The Hague. 255–63.
Bownas, S. (1847). *A description of the qualifications necessary to a gospel minister.* Philadelphia.
Braithwaite, W. C. (1961). *The beginnings of Quakerism.* 2nd ed. Cambridge.
Brinton, H. H. (1952). *Friends for 300 years.* New York.
Burke, K. (1961). *A rhetoric of religion.* Boston.
Burrough, E. (1657). *A just and lawful trial of the teachers and professed ministers of England.* London.
   (1672). *The memorable works of a son of thunder and consolation.* London.
   (1831). Epistle to the reader. In G. Fox, *The mystery of the great whore unfolded.* Philadelphia.
   (1939). A vindication of the people of God, called Quakers. In E. Burrough, *Three early Quaker writings by Edward Burrough.* San Francisco (California State Library Occasional Papers, Reprint Series, no. 6).
Caton, W. (1671). *The moderate enquirer resolved.* [N.p.].
   (1689). *A journal of the life of Will. Caton.* London.
Crook, J. (1791). *The design of Christianity, with other books, epistles and manuscripts of . . . John Crook.* London.
Dickinson, J. (1847). Journal. In T. Wilson and J. Dickinson, *Journals of . . . Thomas Wilson and James Dickinson.* London.
Farnsworth, R. (1663). *The spirit of God speaking in the temple of God.* London.
Fell, M. (1710). *A brief collection of remarkable passages.* London.
Fox, G. (1657a). Something farther concerning silent meetings. In G. Fox, *Gospel truth demonstrated.* London, 1706.
   (1657b). The second covenant. In G. Fox, *Gospel truth demonstrated.* London, 1706.

(1657c). Who are to be silent and who to speak. In G. Fox, *Gospel truth demonstrated*. London, 1706.

(1684). Concerning exhortation, and admonition, from several plain truths manifested and declared from the spirit of God. In G. Fox, *Gospel truth demonstrated*. London, 1706.

(1765). *A journal or historical account . . . of George Fox.* London.

Fox, G., Stubbs, J. and Furley, B. (1660). *A battle-door for teachers & professors to learn singular & plural.* London.

Gratton, J. (1720). *Journal of the life of . . . John Gratton.* London.

Higginson, F. (1653). *A brief relation of the irreligion of the northern Quakers.* London.

Knight, N. (1675). *A comparison between the true and false ministers.* [N.p.].

Marshall, C. (1844). *The journal . . . of Charles Marshall.* London.

Nuttall, G. F. (1952). *Early Quaker letters from the Swarthmore MSS. to 1660.* London.

Parnel, J. (1675). *A collection of the several writings [of] . . . James Parnel.* [N.p.].

Payne, J. (1655). *A discovery of the priests.* London.

Penington, I. (1863). A brief account concerning silent meetings. In I. Penington, *The works of Isaac Penington.* Philadelphia.

Penney, N. (ed.) (1907). *First publishers of truth.* London.

R. H. (1672). *Plus ultra or the second part of the character of a Quaker.* London.

Richardson, J. (1867). *Life of John Richardson.* Philadelphia.

Rosenberg, B. (1970). *The art of the American folk preacher.* New York.

Samarin, W. (1971). *The language of religion.* Working paper prepared for the session on language and religion at the Annual Meeting of the Society for the Scientific Study of Religion, Chicago, October 1971.

Smith, J. (1873). *Bibliotheca anti-Quakeriana.* London.

Stafford, R. (1689). *The truth which God hath shewed unto his servant.* London.

Story, C. (1829). *A brief account of the life . . . of . . . Christopher Story.* London.

Symonds, T. (1656). *The voyage of the just.* London.

Turford, H. (1807). *The grounds of a holy life.* Philadelphia.

Walker, H. E. (1952). *The conception of a ministry in the Quaker movement and a survey of its development.* Thesis, University of Edinburgh.

Wright, L. (1932). *The literary life of the early Friends, 1650–1725.* New York.

CHAPTER 8. STRATEGIES OF STATUS MANIPULATION IN THE WOLOF GREETING

Chomsky, N. (1957). *Syntactic structures.* The Hague.

(1965). *Aspects of the theory of syntax.* Cambridge, Mass.

Crystal, D. (1971). Prosodic and paralinguistic correlates of social categories. In E. Ardener (ed.), *Social anthropology and language* (ASA Monograph #10). London. 185–206.

Frake, C. (1964). Notes on queries in ethnography. In Romney & D'Andrade (eds.), Transcultural studies in cognition. *American Anthropologist* 66(3), pt. 2:132–45.

Goffman, E. (1961). *Encounters: two studies in the sociology of interaction.* Indianapolis, Ind.

(1967). *Interaction ritual: essays on face-to face behavior.* New York.

(1971). *Relations in public.* New York.

Hymes, D. (1967). Models of the interaction of language and social life. *Journal of Social Issues* 23(2):8–28.

Labouret, H. (1934). *Les Manding et leur langue*. Paris.

Stewart, W., Babou, C., Pedtke, D. *et al.* (1966). *Introductory course in Dakar Wolof.* Washington, D.C.

Trager, G. (1964). Paralanguage: a first approximation. In D. Hymes (ed.), *Language in culture and society*. New York. 274–9.

CHAPTER 9. RITUALS OF ENCOUNTER AMONG THE MAORI

Banks, *Sir* J. (1896). *Journal*, ed. Sir J. Hooker. London.

Metge, J. (1967). *The Maoris of New Zealand*. London.

Ngata, *Sir* A. T. (1959). *Nga moteatea*. Wellington, N.Z.

CHAPTER 10. SPEAKING OF SPEAKING

Berlin, B. (1968). *Tzeltal numeral classifiers*. The Hague.

Bricker, V. (1973). Three genres of Tzotzil insult. In M. S. Edmonson (ed.), *Meaning in Mayan languages*. The Hague. 183–203.

Conklin, H. (1962). Lexicographical treatment of folk taxonomies. In F. W. Householder and S. Saporta (eds.), *Problems in lexicography*. Bloomington, Ind. 119–41.

El Guindi, F. (1972). The nature of belief systems. Doctoral dissertation, University of Texas at Austin.

Gossen, G. (1972). Chamula genres of verbal behavior. In A. Paredes and R. Bauman (eds.), *Toward new perspectives in folklore*. Austin, Tex. 145–67.

Hymes, D. (1962). The ethnography of speaking. In T. Gladwin and W. C. Sturtevant (eds.), *Anthropology and human behavior*. Washington, D.C. 15–53.

Newman, S. (1955). Vocabulary levels: Zuni sacred and slang usage. *Southwest Journal of Anthropology* 11:345–54.

Sapir, E. (1915). *Abnormal types of speech in Nootka*. Ottawa.

Stross, B. (1967). The Mexican cantina as a setting for interaction. *The Kroeber Anthropological Society Papers* 37:58–89.

(1973). Reconstructed humor in a Tzeltal ritual formula. *International Journal of American Linguistics* 39:32–43.

CHAPTER 11. BLACK TALKING ON THE STREETS

Abrahams, R. D. (1970a). *Positively Black*. Englewood Cliffs, N.J.

(1970b). *Deep down in the jungle* ..., revised edition. Chicago.

(1970c). Traditions of eloquence in the West Indies. *Journal of Inter-American Studies and World Affairs* 12:505–27.

(1970d). Rapping and capping: Black talk as art. In J. Szwed (ed.), *Black Americans*. New York, 143–53.

(1973). *Toward a Black rhetoric: being a survey of Afro-American communication styles and role-relationships*. Texas Working Papers in Sociolinguistics no. 15.

Abrahams, R. D. and Bauman, R. (1971). Sense and nonsense in St. Vincent: speech behavior and decorum in a Caribbean community. *American Anthropologist* 73(3):262–72.

Anderson, A. (1959). *Lover man*. New York.

Brown, C. (1966). *Manchild in the promised land*. New York.

Brown, H. R. (1969). *Die Nigger die!* New York.

Cain, G. (1970). *Blueschild baby.* New York.

Claerbaut, D. (1972). *Black jargon in White America.* Grand Rapids, Mich.

Dillard, J. (1972). *Black English.* New York.

Eddington, N. (1967). The urban plantation: the ethnography of oral tradition in a Negro community. Ph.D. dissertation, University of California at Berkeley.

Ellis, H. and Newman, S. (1971). 'Gowster,' 'Ivy-Leaguer,' 'Hustler,' 'Conservative,' 'Mackman,' and 'Continental': a functional analysis of six ghetto roles. In E. G. Leacock (ed.), *The culture of poverty: a critique.* New York. 299–314.

Ferris, W. (1972). Black prose narrative in the Mississippi Delta: an overview. *Journal of American Folklore* 85:140–51.

Firestone, H. (1964). Cats, kicks and color. In H. S. Becker (ed.), *The other side.* New York. 281–97.

Friedland, W. and Nelkin, D. (1971). *Migrant.* New York.

Gold, R. (1960). *A jazz lexicon.* New York.

Grange, K. (1968). Black slang. *Current Slang* III(2).

Gregory, D. with Lipsyte, R. (1964). *Nigger.* New York.

Hannerz, U. (1969). *Soulside.* New York.

Heard, N. (1968). *Howard street.* New York.

Hooker, R. (1972). Florida Black supports Wallace. *Race Relations Reporter* (December): 4.

Hurston, Z. (1934). *Jonah's gourd vine.* Philadelphia.

(1935). *Mules and men.* Philadelphia.

(1942). Story in Harlem slang. *American Mercury* (July):84–96.

Hymes, D. (1972). Models of the interaction of language and social life. In J. J. Gumperz and D. Hymes (eds.), *Directions in sociolinguistics.* New York. 35–71.

Iceberg Slim (1967). *Pimp: the story of my life.* Los Angeles.

Johnson, K. R. (1971). Black kinesics – some non-verbal patterns in Black culture. *Florida F/L Reporter* 9:17–21, 57.

Keegan, F. (1971). *Blacktown, U.S.A.* Boston.

Keiser, R. (1969). *The vice-lords: warriors of the streets.* New York.

Kernan, C. (1971). *Language behavior in a Black urban community.* Berkeley, Calif.

Killens, J. (1972). *Cotillion.* New York.

King, W., jr (1965). The game. *Liberator* 5:20–5.

Kochman, T. (1970). Toward an ethnography of Black American speech behavior. In J. Szwed and N. Whitten (eds.), *Afro-American anthropology: contemporary perspectives.* New York. 145–62.

Labov, W., Cohen, P., Robins, C. and Lewis, J. (1968). *A study of the non-standard English of Negro and Puerto Rican speakers in New York City,* vol. II. New York.

Lewis, H. (1964). *Blackways of Kent.* New Haven, Conn.

Liebow, E. (1967). *Tally's corner.* Boston.

Major, C. (1970). *Dictionary of Afro-American slang.* New York.

Malcolm X with Haley, A. (1965). *The autobiography of Malcolm X.* New York.

Meriwhether, L. (1970). *Daddy was a numbers runner.* New York.

Mezzrow, M. and Wolfe, B. (1969). *Really the blues.* New York.

Milner, C. and Milner, R. (1972). *Black players.* Boston.

Olmsted, F. L. (1856). *A journey in the seaboard states.* New York.

Puckett, N. (1926). *Folk beliefs of the Southern Negro.* Chapel Hill, N.C.

Rainwater, L. (1970). *Behind ghetto walls.* Chicago.

Sale, R. T. (1971). *The Blackstone rangers.* New York.
Strong, S. (1940). Social types in the Negro community of Chicago. Ph.D. dissertation, University of Chicago.
Suttles, G. (1968). *The social order of the slums.* Chicago.
Thomas, P. (1967). *Down these mean streets.* New York.
Valentine, C. (1972). *Black studies and anthropology: scholarly and political interests in Afro-American culture.* Reading, Mass.
Ward, M. (1971). *Them children: a study in language learning.* New York.
Wentworth, H. and Flexner, S. (1960). *Dictionary of American slang.* New York.
Whitten, N. and Szwed, J. (1970). *Afro-American anthropology: contemporary perspectives.* New York.
Wilson, P. (1969). Reputation and respectability: suggestions for Caribbean ethnology. *Man* 4:70–84.
Woodley, R. (1972). *Dealer: portrait of a cocaine merchant.* New York.
Young, V. (1970). Family and childhood in a Southern Negro community. *American Anthropologist* 72:269–88.

CHAPTER 12. 'NAMAKKE,' 'SUNMAKKE,' 'KORMAKKE'

Chapin, M. (1970). *Pab igala: historias de la tradición kuna.* Panama.
Chomsky, N. (1957). *Syntactic structures.* The Hague.
——— (1968). *Language and mind.* New York.
Howe, J. (1974). The political organization of a Cuna island village. University of Pennsylvania Ph.D. dissertation.
——— (MS.) *Carrying the villages: Cuna political metaphors.* In C. Crocker and J. D. Sapir (eds.), *The social use of metaphor.* Ithaca, N.Y.
Hymes, D. (1972). Models of the interaction of language and social life. In J. J. Gumperz and D. Hymes (eds.), *Directions in sociolinguistics.* New York. 35–71.
Jakobson, R. (1968). Poetry of grammar and grammar of poetry. *Lingua* 21:597–609.
Kramer, F. W. (1970). *Literature among the Cuna Indians. (Etnologiska Studier 30).* Göteborg.
Labov, W. (1970). The study of language in its social context. *Studium Generale* 23:30–87.
Lévi-Strauss, C. (1963). The effectiveness of symbols. In C. Lévi-Strauss, *Structural anthropology.* New York. 186–205.
Sherzer, D. and Sherzer, J. (1972). Literature in San Blas: discovering the Cuna *Ikala. Semiotica* 6(2):182–99.
Sherzer, J. (1972). Análisis semántico de *sappi turpa* en Mulatupo (San Blas). *Actas del II Simposium Nacional de Antropologia, Arqueologia y Etnohistoria de Panama.* Panama. 501–12.

CHAPTER 13. CONCEPT AND VARIETIES OF EAST EUROPEAN
JEWISH NARRATIVE PERFORMANCE

Bergmann, J. (1919). *Legenden der Jüden.* Berlin.
Bialostotski, B. J. (1962). *Di mesholim fun dubner magid un andere eseyen.* New York.
Buber, M. (1961). *Tales of the Hasidim: the early masters,* trans. O. Marx. New York.
——— (1962). *The tales of Rabbi Nachman,* trans. Maurice Friedman, Bloomington, Ind.

Elzet, Y. (1937). Vits un humor. In S. Miler, *Funem yidishn kval*. Winnipeg. 3–14.

Gross, N. (1955). *Mayselekh un mesholim*. New York.

Holdes, A. (1960). *Mayses, vitsn un shpitslekh fun Hershl Ostropoler*. Warsaw.

Hymes, D. (1967). Models of the interaction of language and social setting. *Journal of Social Issues* 23:8–28.

Lifschutz, E. (1952). Merrymakers and jesters among Jews (materials for a lexicon). *Yivo Annual of Jewish Social Sciences* 7:43–83.

Mintz, J. (1968). *The legends of the Hasidim: an introduction to Hasidic culture and oral tradition in the New World*. Chicago.

Noy, D. (1971). The Jewish versions of the 'animal languages' folktale (AT670) – a typological structural study. *Scripta Hierosolymitana* 22:171–208.

Olsvanger, I. (1965). *Royte pomerantsen*. New York.

Rabinovich, S. [Sholem Aleichem] (1944). *Funem yarid: lebnsbashraybungen. Ale verk fun Sholem Aleykhem*, vol. 3. New York.

——— (1955). *The great fair: scenes from my childhood*, trans. T. Kahana. New York.

Ravnitsky, Y. Kh. (1922). *Yidishe vitsn*. Berlin.

Rechtman, A. (1958). *Yidishe etnografye un folklor: zikhroynes vegn der etnografisher ekspeditsye ongefirt fun Sh. Anski*. Buenos Aires.

Schauss, H. (1950). *The lifetime of a Jew throughout the ages of history*. Cincinnati, Ohio.

Schwarzbaum, H. (1968). *Studies in Jewish and world folklore*. Berlin.

Shtern, Y. (1950). *Kheyder un bes-medresh*. New York.

Vanvild, M. (ed.) (1923). *Bay undz yidn*. Warsaw.

Weiner, L. (1899). *The history of Yiddish literature in the nineteenth century*. New York.

Weinreich, B. (1957). The Prophet Elijah in modern Yiddish folktales. M.A. thesis, Columbia University.

Weinreich, U. (1968). *Modern English–Yiddish Yiddish–English dictionary*. New York.

Woodruff, M. (1972). Hasidic tales containing proverbs or proverb-like formulations. MS.

Zborowski, M. and Herzog, E. (1962). *Life is with people*. New York.

INTRODUCTION TO SECTION V

Hymes, D. (1974). Breakthrough into performance. In, D. Ben-Amos and K. Goldstein (eds.), *Folklore: performance and communication*. The Hague. 11–74.

Jakobson, R. (1960). Linguistics and poetics. In T. Sebeok (ed.), *Style in language*. Cambridge, Mass. 350–77.

——— (1966). Grammatical parallelism and its Russian facet. *Language* 42:399–429.

——— (1968). Poetry of grammar and grammar of poetry. *Lingua* 21:597–609.

CHAPTER 15. ANALYSIS OF THE COURSE OF A JOKE'S TELLING

Sacks, H. (1972). On the analyzability of stories by children. In J. J. Gumperz and D. Hymes (eds.), *Directions in sociolinguistics: the ethnography of communication*. New York. 325–45.

CHAPTER 16. WHEN WORDS BECOME DEEDS

Austin, J. L. (1963). Performative-constative. In C. E. Caton (ed.), *Philosophy and ordinary language*. Urbana, Ill. 22–54.

——— (1965). *How to do things with words*. New York.

Blau, H. (1969). Calendric ceremonies of the New York Onondaga. Ph.D. dissertation, New School for Social Research, New York.

Chafe, W. L. (1961). *Seneca thanksgiving rituals* (Bureau of American Ethnology bulletin 183). Washington, D.C.

(1967). *Seneca morphology and dictionary* (Smithsonian contributions to anthropology 4). Washington, D.C.

Crystal, D. (1969). *Prosodic systems and intonation in English.* Cambridge.

[n.d.] . Intonation and metrical theory. Mimeographed.

Fenton, W. N. (1936). An outline of Seneca ceremonies at Coldspring Longhouse (Yale University Publications in Anthropology 9). New Haven, Conn. 3–23.

(1941). *Tonawanda longhouse ceremonies: ninety years after Lewis Henry Morgan.* (Bureau of American Ethnology bulletin 128). Washington, D.C.

(1950). *The roll call of the Iroquois chiefs; a study of a mnemonic cane from the Six Nations Reserve* (Smithsonian miscellaneous collections, III(15)). Washington, D.C.

(1971). The New York State wampum collection: the case for the integrity of cultural treasures. *Proceedings of the American Philosophical Society* 115:437–61.

Finnegan, R. (1969). How to do things with words: performative utterances among the Limba of Sierra Leone. *Man* 4:537–52.

Foster, M. K. (1971). Speaking in the longhouse at Six Nations Reserve. In R. Darnell (ed.), *Linguistic diversity in Canadian society.* Edmonton, Alta. & Champaign, Ill. 129–54.

Hewitt, J. N. B. (1928). *Iroquoian cosmology, second part* (Bureau of American Ethnology, annual report 1925–26, 43:449–819). Washington, D.C.

Hogan, H. M. (1971). An ethnography of communication among the Ashanti. (Penn–Texas working papers in sociolinguistics, no. 1). Austin, Tex.

Hymes, D. (1964a). Directions in (ethno-) linguistic theory. *American Anthropologist* 66(3):6–56.

(1964b). Introduction: toward ethnographies of communication. *American Anthropologist* 66(6):1–34.

(1965). Review of Austin's *How to do things with words.* *American Anthropologist* 67:587–8.

(1972). Models of the interaction of language and social life. In J. J. Gumperz and D. Hymes (eds.), *Directions in sociolinguistics.* New York. 38–71.

Lounsbury, F. G. (1953). *Oneida verb morphology* (Yale University publications in anthropology 48). New Haven, Conn.

Malinowski, B. (1923). The problem of meaning in primitive languages. Supplement 1 in C. K. Ogden and I. A. Richards, *The meaning of meaning.* New York (8th ed., 1946).

(1935). *The language of magic and gardening.* Vol. 2 of *Coral gardens and their magic.* New York. Reprinted Bloomington, Ind., 1965.

Morgan, L. H. (1901). *League of the Ho-Dé-No-Sau-Nee or Iroquois,* ed. H. M. Lloyd. New York.

Parker, A. C. (1910). *Iroquois uses of maize and other food plants* (New York State Museum bulletin 144). Albany, N.Y.

(1913). *The code of Handsome Lake, the Seneca prophet* (New York State Museum bulletin 163). Albany, N.Y.

Ravenhill, P. L. (1972). Religious utterances and the theory of speech acts (paper read at the Round Table Meeting on linguistics and language studies, Georgetown University, March 1972). Mimeographed.

Richards, B. (1971). Searle on meaning and speech acts. *Foundations of Language* 7:519–38.

Ross, J. R. (1970). On declarative sentences. In R. A. Jacobs and P. S. Rosenbaum (eds.), *Readings in English transformational grammar*. Waltham, Mass. 222–72.

Searle, J. R. (1968). Austin on locutionary and illocutionary acts. *Philosophical Review* 77:405–24.

(1969). *Speech acts; an essay in the philosophy of language*. Cambridge.

Shimony, A. A. (1961). *Conservatism among the Iroquois at the Six Nations Reserve* (Yale University publications in anthropology 65). New Haven, Conn.

Skinner, Q. (1970). Conventions and the understanding of speech acts. *Philosophical Quarterly* 20:118–38.

Speck, F. G. (1949). *Midwinter rites of the Cayuga long house*. Philadelphia.

Tedlock, D. (1972). On the translation of style in oral narrative. In Américo Paredes and Richard Bauman (eds.), *Toward new perspectives in folklore*. Austin, Tex. 114–33.

Tooker, E. (1970). *The Iroquois ceremonial of midwinter*. Syracuse, N.Y.

Wallace, A. F. C. (1970). *The death and rebirth of the Seneca*. New York.

CHAPTER 17. THE ETHNOGRAPHIC CONTEXT OF SOME TRADITIONAL

MAYAN SPEECH GENRES

Bricker, V. R. (1973a). Three genres of Tzotzil insult. In Munro S. Edmonson (ed.), *Meaning in Mayan languages*. The Hague. 182–203.

(1973b). *Ritual humor in Highland Chiapas*. Austin, Tex.

(n.d.a). Some Zinacanteco joking strategies. In B. Kirshenblatt-Gimblett (ed.), *Speech play on display*. The Hague.

(n.d.b). The structure of classification and ranking in three highland Mayan communities. *Estudios de Cultura Maya* IX.

Calnek, E. E. (1962). Highland Chiapas before the Spanish conquest. Ph.D. dissertation, University of Chicago.

Cancian, F. (1965). *Economics and prestige in a Maya community*. Stanford, Calif.

Edmonson, M. S. (1968). Metáfora maya en literatura y en arte. *Verhandlungen des XXXVIII. Internationalen Amerikanistenkongresses Stuttgart-München 12. bis 18. August 1968*, II:37–50.

(1971). *The book of counsel: The Popol Vuh of the Quiche Maya of Guatemala*. Middle American Research Institute Publication 35. New Orleans, La.

(1973). Semantic universals and particulars in Quiche. In Munro S. Edmonson (ed.), *Meaning in Mayan languages*. The Hague. 235–46.

Garibay K., A. M. (1953). *Historia de literatura nahuatl*. Mexico, D.F.

Gossen, G. H. (1970). Time and space in Chamula oral tradition. Ph.D. dissertation, Harvard University.

(1973). Chamula (Tzotzil) proverbs: neither fish nor fowl. In Munro S. Edmonson (ed.), *Meaning in Mayan languages*. The Hague. 205–33.

Haviland, J. B. (1967). /Vob/ *Traditional music in Zinacantan*. MS.

Jakobson, R. (1968). Poetry of grammar and grammar of poetry. *Lingua* 21:597–609.

Laughlin, R. M. (n.d.a). *The great Tzotzil dictionary of San Lorenzo Zinacantan*. Smithsonian Contributions to Anthropology. Washington, D.C.

(n.d.b). *Zinacanteco folktale texts*.

León Portilla, M. (1969). *Pre-Columbian literatures of Mexico*. Norman, Okla.

Machlin, M. and Marx, B. (1971). First visit to three forbidden cities. *Argosy* 372(5):18–29.

Redfield, R. and Villa Rojas, A. (1934). *Chan Kom: a Maya village.* Carnegie Institution of Washington Publication 448. Washington, D.C.

Roys, R. L. (1933). *The book of Chilam Balam of Chumayel.* Carnegie Institution of Washington Publication 438. Washington, D.C.

(1965). *Ritual of the Bacabs.* Norman, Okla.

Villa Rojas, A. (1945). *The Maya of east central Quintana Roo.* Carnegie Institution of Washington Publication 559. Washington, D.C.

Voegelin, C. F. (1960). Casual and noncasual utterances within unified structure. In T. A. Sebeok (ed.), *Style in language.* Cambridge. 57–68.

Vogt, E. Z. (1969). *Zinacantan: a Maya community in the Highlands of Chiapas.* Cambridge, Mass.

CHAPTER 18. TO SPEAK WITH A HEATED HEART

Edmonson, M. S. (1971). *Lore: an introduction to the science of folklore and literature.* New York.

Fox, J. J. (1971). Semantic parallelism in Rotinese ritual language. *Bijdragen tot de taal-, Land- en Volkenkunde* 127:212–55.

Gossen, G. H. (1972a). Temporal and spatial equivalents in Chamula ritual symbolism. In W. Lessa and E. Z. Vogt (eds.), *Reader in comparative religion,* 3rd ed. New York.

(1972b). Chamula genres of verbal behavior. In A. Paredes and R. Bauman (eds.), *Toward new perspectives in folklore.* Austin, Tex. 145–67.

(1973). Chamula (Tzotzil) proverbs: neither fish nor fowl. In M. S. Edmonson (ed.), *Meaning in Mayan languages.* The Hague. 205–31.

(1974a). Another look at world view: aerial photography and Chamula cosmology. In E. Z. Vogt (ed.), *Aerial photography in anthropological field research.* Cambridge, Mass.

(1974b). *Chamulas in the world of the sun: time and space in a Maya oral tradition.* Cambridge, Mass.

Jakobson, R. (1966). Grammatical parallelism and its Russian facet. *Language* 42:398–429.

Kramer, F. (1970). *Literature among the Cuna Indians.* Ethnologiska Studier 30. Goteborg, Sweden.

Pozas, R. (1959). Chamula: un pueblo indio de Los Altos de Chiapas. *Memorias del Instituto Nacional Indigenista* VIII. Mexico, D.F.

SECTION VI INTRODUCTION

Gumperz, J. J. and Hymes, D. (eds.) ·(1964). *The ethnography of communication.* *American Anthropologist* 66(6), pt. 2.

Hymes, D. (1962). The ethnography of speaking. In T. Gladwin and W. C. Sturtevant (eds.), *Anthropology and human behavior.* Washington, D.C. 13–53.

(1973). Toward linguistic competence. Texas Working Papers in Sociolinguistics 16.

CHAPTER 19. DATA AND DATA USE IN AN ANALYSIS OF
COMMUNICATIVE EVENTS

Bales, R. F. (1950). *Interaction process analysis: A method for the study of small groups*. Cambridge, Mass.

Chomsky, N. (1964). The logical basis of linguistic theory. In H. Lunt (ed.), *Proceedings of the Ninth International Congress of Linguists* (Cambridge, Mass., 1962). The Hague. 914–1008.

(1965). *Aspects of the theory of syntax*. Cambridge, Mass.

Cicourel, A. V. (1969). Generative semantics and the structure of social interaction. In *International days of sociolinguistics* (Proceedings of the Second International Congress of the Luigi Sterzo Institute):173–202.

(1970). The acquisition of social structure: toward a developmental sociology of language and meanings. In J. D. Douglas (ed.), *Understanding everyday life*. Chicago. 136–168.

Gottschalk, L. (1945). The historian and the historical document. In L. Gottschalk, C. Kluckhohn and R. Angell, *The use of personal documents in history, anthropology and sociology*. Bulletin 53. New York. 1–75.

Grimshaw, A. (1973a). Rules in linguistic, social, and sociolinguistic systems and possibilities for a unified theory. In R. W. Shuy (ed.), *Sociolinguistics: current trends and prospects* (Georgetown University Monograph Series on Languages and Linguistics 25). Washington, D.C. 289–312.

(1973b). Rules, social interaction and language behavior. *Tesol Quarterly* F(1): 99–115.

Gumperz, J. (1971). *Language in social groups*. Selected essays with an introduction by Anwar S. Dil. Stanford, Calif.

Hymes, D. (1967). Models of the interaction of language and social setting. *Journal of Social Issues* 23(2):8–28.

(1972). Models of the interaction of language and social life. In J. Gumperz and D. Hymes (eds.), *Directions in sociolinguistics: the ethnography of communication*. New York. 35–71.

Labov, W. (1972a). Some principles of linguistic methodology. *Language in Society* 1(1):97–120.

(1972b). How non-existent grammars are generated. Lecture at Indiana University, April.

Spencer, N. (1972). Differences between linguists and non-linguists in intuitions of grammaticality–acceptability. Paper presented at the winter meeting of the Linguistic Society of America, Atlanta, Ga., December.

CHAPTER 20. THE ETHNOGRAPHY OF WRITING

Basso, K. H. and Anderson, N. (1973). A Western Apache writing system: the symbols of Silas John. *Science* 180:1013–22.

Bastian, A. (1860). *Der Mensch in der Geschichte*. Leipzig.

Bloomfield, L. (1933). *Language*. New York.

Bolinger, D. (1968). *Aspects of language*. New York.

Chao, Y. R. (1968). *Language and symbolic systems*. London.

Cohen, M. (1958). *La grande invention de l'écriture et son évolution*. Paris.

Conklin, H. C. (1949a). Preliminary report on field work on the Islands of Mindoro and Palawan, Philippines. *American Anthropologist* 51(2):268–73.

(1949b). Bamboo literacy on Mindoro. *Pacific Discovery* 2(4):4–11.

(1953). *Hanunóo–English vocabulary.* University of California Publications in Linguistics 9. Berkeley.

Diringer, D. (1949). *The alphabet: a key to the history of mankind.* London.

(1962). *Writing.* New York.

Ferguson, C. A. (1971). Contrasting patterns of literacy acquisition in a multilingual nation. In W. H. Whiteley (ed.), *Language use and social change.* London. 234–53.

Fevrier, J. (1948). *Histoire de l'écriture.* Paris.

Gelb, I. J. (1963). *A study of writing.* Chicago.

Gleason, H. A. (1961). *An introduction to descriptive linguistics,* rev. ed. New York.

Goody, J. (1968). *Literacy in traditional societies.* Cambridge.

Goody, J. and Watt, I. (1962). The consequences of literacy. *Comparative Studies in Society and History* 5:304–45.

Greenberg, J. (1957). Language and evolutionary theory. In his *Essays in linguistics.* Chicago. 56–65.

Hockett, C. F. (1958). *A course in modern linguistics.* New York.

Hymes, D. (1961). Functions of speech: an evolutionary approach. In F. C. Gruber (ed.), *Anthropology and education.* Philadelphia. 55–83.

(1962). The ethnography of speaking. In T. Gladwin and W. C. Sturtevant (eds.), *Anthropology and human behavior.* Washington, D. C. 15–53.

(1964a). Directions in (ethno-)linguistic theory. *American Anthropologist* 66(3), pt. 2:6–56.

(1964b). The ethnography of communication. *American Anthropologist* 66(6), pt. 2:1–34.

(1972). Models of the interaction of language and social life. In J. J. Gumperz and D. Hymes (eds.), *Directions in sociolinguistics.* New York. 35–71.

Jakobson, R. (1960). Concluding statement. Linguistics and poetics. In T. A. Sebeok (ed.), *Style in language.* Cambridge, Mass. and New York. 350–73.

Kroeber, A. L. (1948). Story of the alphabet. In *Anthropology,* rev. ed. New York.

Langacker, R. W. (1968). *Language and its structure: some fundamental linguistic concepts.* New York.

Lyons, J. (1968). *Introduction to theoretical linguistics.* London.

Maine, H. S. (1873). *Ancient law: its connection with the early history of society and its relation to modern ideas.* New York.

Mallory, G. (1886). *Pictographs of North American Indians. Fourth Annual Report of the Bureau of American Ethnology* (1882–3). Washington, D.C.

(1893). *Picture-writing of the American Indians. Tenth Annual Report of the Bureau of American Ethnology* (1888–9). Washington, D.C.

McClennan, J. F. (1876). *Studies in ancient history.* London.

Moorhouse, A. C. (1953). *The triumph of the alphabet: a history of writing.* New York.

Tylor, E. B. (1865). *Researches into the early history of mankind and the development of civilization.* London.

Voegelin, C. F. and Voegelin, F. M. (1961). Typological classification of systems with included, excluded and self-sufficient alphabets. *Anthropological Linguistics* 3(1):55–96.

CHAPTER 21. WAYS OF SPEAKING

Backvis, C. (1958). *Quelques rémarques sur le bilinguisme latino–polonais dans la Pologne du XVIᵉ siècle.* Brussels.

Bloomfield, L. (1933). *Language.* New York.

Chomsky, N. (1965). *Aspects of the theory of syntax*. Cambridge, Mass.

Ervin-Tripp, S. (1972). On sociolinguistic rules: alternation and co-occurrence. In Gumperz and Hymes 1972:213–50.

Ferguson, C. A. (1966). On sociolinguistically oriented surveys. *The Linguistic Reporter* 8(4):1–3.

Gumperz, J. J. (1972). Introduction. In Gumperz and Hymes 1972:1–25.

Gumperz, J. J. and Hymes, D. (eds.) (1972). *Directions in sociolinguistics: the ethnography of communication*. New York.

Hymes, D. (1961a). Functions of speech: an evolutionary approach. In F. Gruber (ed.), *Anthropology and education*. Philadelphia. 55–83.

(1961b). On typology of cognitive style in languages (with examples from Chinookan). *Anthropological Linguistics* 3(1):22–54.

(1966). Two types of linguistic relativity. In W. Bright (ed.), *Sociolinguistics*. The Hague. 114–65.

(1970). Linguistic theory and the functions of speech. *International days of sociolinguistics*. Rome. 111–44.

(1972). Models of the interaction of language and social life. In Gumperz and Hymes 1972:35–71.

Irvine, J. T. (MS.). Caste stereotypes: the basis for interaction. For a University of Pennsylvania dissertation in anthropology.

Jones, R. F. (1953). *The triumph of the English language*. Stanford, Calif.

Labov, W. (1966). *The social stratification of English in New York City*. Washington, D.C.

Newman, S. S. (1964)(1940). Linguistic aspects of Yokuts style. In D. Hymes (ed.), *Language in culture and society*. New York. 372–7.

Postal, P. (1968). *Aspects of phonological theory*. New York.

Sapir, E. (1921). *Language*. New York.

Sherzer, J. and Darnell, R. (1972). Outline guide for the ethnographic study of speech use. In Gumperz and Hymes 1972:548–54.

Stankiewicz, E. (1954). Expressive derivation of substantives in contemporary Russian and Polish. *Word* 10:457–68.

(1964). Problems of emotive language. In T. A. Sebeok, A. S. Hayes and M. C. Bateson (eds.), *Aspects of semiotics*. The Hague. 239–64.

Swadesh, M. (1948). On linguistic mechanism. *Science and Society* 12:254–9.

Tedlock, D. (trans.) (1972). *Finding the center: narrative poetry of the Zuni Indians*. From performances by Andrew Peynetsa and Walter Sanchez. New York.

Ullman, S. (1953). Descriptive semantics and linguistic typology. *Word* 9:225–40.

Van Holk, A. (1962). Referential and attitudinal constructions. *Lingua* 11:165–81.

INDEX OF NAMES

Figures in italics indicate an article by the person named.

497